Microsoft® Office 365

A SKILLS APPROACH

2019 Edition

Cheri Manning

Catherine Manning Swinson

MICROSOFT OFFICE 365/2019: A SKILLS APPROACH

1 2 3 4 5 6 7 8 9 RMN/RMN 1 0 9 8 7 6

ISBN 9781260079449
MHID 1260079449

Managing Director: Terry Schiesl

Director: Wyatt Morris

Senior Product Developer: Alan Palmer

Executive Marketing Managers: Tiffany Russell & Corban Quigg

Content Project Manager: Harvey Yep

Buyer: Susan K. Culbertson

Designer: Matt Backhaus & Egzon Shaqiri

Cover Image: TBD

www.mhhe.com

Contents

brief contents

contents

word 365

chapter **3**

Formatting Documents

chapter **4**

Working with Pictures, Tables, and Charts

chapter **5**

Working with Reports and Collaborating with Others

Addendum

excel 365

chapter 1

chapter 2

chapter 3

chapter **4**

Formatting Worksheets and Managing the Workbook

chapter 5

Adding Charts and Analyzing Data

preface

How well do you know Microsoft Office? Many students can follow specific step-bystep directions to re-create a document, spreadsheet, presentation, or database, but do they truly understand the skills it takes to create these on their own? Just as simply following a recipe does not make you a professional chef, re-creating a project step by step does not make you an Office expert.

The purpose of this book is to teach you the skills to master Microsoft Office 365 in a straightforward and easy-to-follow manner. But Microsoft® Office 365: A Skills Approach goes beyond the how and equips you with a deeper understanding of the what and the why. Too many times books have little value beyond the classroom. The Skills Approach series has been designed to be not only a complete textbook but also a reference tool for you to use as you move beyond academics and into the workplace.

WHAT'S NEW IN THIS EDITION

With Office 365, Microsoft changed the delivery method for new features for users who have an Office 365 subscription. Rather than waiting for the next version of Office to be released, users with a 365 subscription will now receive new features through automatic updates to their account. Why does this matter to you? Because while we feel this book is still a solid reference for you to use, it could mean that certain content in this book may be out of date. But there is hope! If you signed up for a SIMnet account along with purchasing this book, the electronic version of this textbook (the SIMbook) will be updated along with Microsoft's updates. This means the text in the SIMbook, along with the simulated environment used for the exercises, will reflect any changes made to Office 365. In addition, your SIMbook may include additional content that could not be accommodated in the printed version of the textbook.

ABOUT TRIAD INTERACTIVE

Triad Interactive specializes in online education and training products. Our flagship program is SIMnet—a simulated Microsoft Office learning and assessment application developed for McGraw-Hill Education. Triad has been writing, programming, and managing the SIMnet system since 1999.

Triad is also actively involved in online health education and in research projects to assess the usefulness of technology for helping high-risk populations make decisions about managing their cancer risk and treatment.

about the authors

CHERI MANNING

Cheri Manning is the president and co-owner of Triad Interactive. She is the author of the Microsoft Excel and Access content for the Skills Approach series and SIMnet. She has been authoring instructional content for these applications for more than 20 years.

Cheri began her career as an Aerospace Education Specialist with the Education Division of the National Aeronautics and Space Administration (NASA), where she produced materials for K–12 instructors and students. Prior to founding Triad, Cheri was a project manager with Compact Publishing, where she managed the development of McGraw-Hill's Multimedia MBA CD-ROM series.

CATHERINE MANNING SWINSON

Catherine Manning Swinson is the vice president and co-owner of Triad Interactive. She is the author of the Microsoft Word and PowerPoint content for the Skills Approach series and SIMnet. She also authors SIMnet content for Computer Concepts, Microsoft Outlook, Windows, and Web browsers. She has been authoring instructional content for these applications for more than 20 years.

Catherine began her career at Compact Publishing, one of the pioneers in educational CD-ROM-based software. She was the lead designer at Compact and designed every edition of the TIME Magazine Compact Almanac from 1992 through 1996. In addition, she designed a number of other products with Compact, including the TIME Man of the Year program and the TIME 20th Century Almanac.

CONTRIBUTORS

> **Kelly Morber,** *Saints Philip and James School, English Teacher and Malone University, M.A.Ed.*

> **Timothy T. Morber,** *MEd, LPCC-S, Malone University*

Office 365

Essential Skills for Office Chapter Overview

chapter **1**

introduction

This chapter introduces you to Microsoft Office. You will learn about the versions of Microsoft Office and how they differ. You will learn about the shared features across the Office apps and how to navigate common interface elements such as the Ribbon and Quick Access Toolbar. You will learn how to open and close files as well as how to create new blank files. You will search for help, use the *Tell Me* feature, and work with messages that appear when you first open files. You will learn the different ways to save and share files, including through your OneDrive account. You will become familiar with the Office account and learn how to modify the account as well as the look of Office.

Skill 1.1 Introduction to Microsoft Office

Microsoft Office is a collection of business "productivity" apps (computer programs designed to make you more productive at work, school, and home). The most popular Office apps are:

Microsoft Word—A word processing program. Word processing software includes powerful formatting and design tools that allow you to go beyond simple text files and create complex documents such as reports, résumés, brochures, and newsletters.

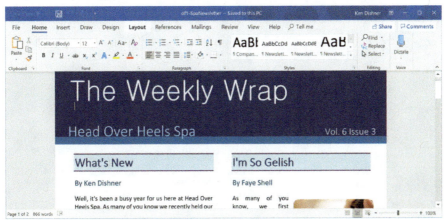

FIGURE OF 1.1

Microsoft Excel—A spreadsheet program. Originally, spreadsheet apps were viewed as electronic versions of an accountant's ledger. Today's spreadsheet apps can do much more than just calculate numbers—they include powerful charting and data analysis features. Spreadsheet programs can be used for everything from managing personal budgets to calculating loan payments.

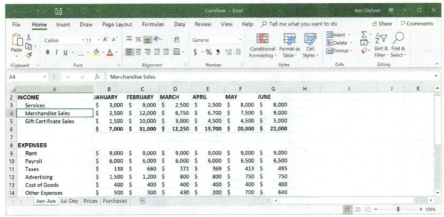

FIGURE OF 1.2

Microsoft Access—A database program. Database apps allow you to organize and manipulate large amounts of data. Databases that allow you to relate tables and databases to one another are referred to as *relational* databases. As a database user, you usually see only one aspect of the database—a *form*. Database forms use a graphical interface to allow a user to enter record data. For example, when you fill out an order form online, you are probably interacting with a database. The information you enter becomes a record in a database *table*. Your order is matched with information in an inventory table (keeping track of which items are in stock) through a *query*. When your order is filled, a database *report* can be generated for use as an invoice or a bill of lading.

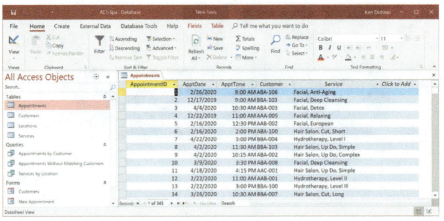

FIGURE OF 1.3

Microsoft PowerPoint—A presentation program. Presentation apps are used to create robust multimedia presentations. A presentation consists of a series of electronic slides. Each slide contains content, including text, images, charts, and other objects. You can add multimedia elements to slides, including animations, audio, and video.

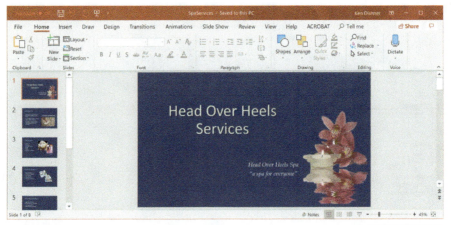

FIGURE OF 1.4

To open one of the Office apps in Windows 10:

1. Click the Windows **Start** button (located in the lower left corner of your computer screen).
2. Scroll the list of apps on the Start menu.
3. Find the app in this list and click the app you want to open.

There are two main ways to license and pay for the installed version of Microsoft Office:

Office 365—This version allows you to download and install Office and pay for it on a yearly or monthly subscription basis. Office 365 includes full versions of the Office apps along with online storage services for your files. Microsoft is continually updating Office 365 with security and bug fixes. In addition, the apps are updated with new features twice a year. If you have an Office 365 subscription, Office will prompt you when an update is available.

Office 2019 (on-premises)—The on-premises version of Office allows you to install Office and pay for it once. The on-premises version of Office receives security and bug fixes, but does not receive new feature updates. In addition, certain features available in Office 365 are not available in Office 2019 on-premises, including the Editor in Word and PowerPoint's Designer feature.

Because this book is written for Office 365 which is continually being updated, your version of the software may look different than the screenshots shown here. For example, after the Office 2019 on-premises version of the software was released, Microsoft updated the look of the Ribbon and Backstage in the apps.

If you have the 2019 on-premises version of Office, the Ribbon will look like this:

FIGURE OF 1.5

If you have the updated Office 365 version, the Ribbon looks more like this:

FIGURE OF 1.6

Be aware that although the interface has changed, the steps to complete the skills are the same. SIMnet (the software that accompanies this textbook) is updated with the new feature and interface changes twice a year.

tell me more

Office apps are available to you on a variety of platforms. The features available depend on which version of the apps you are using:

> **Desktop apps**—Full-featured version of the Office apps that you download and install on your computer. If you are creating complex documents or presentations or performing complicated calculations on large amounts of data, you will most likely need the desktop version of the app. If you purchase an Office 365 subscription or the Office 2019 on-premises version, you will be downloading and installing the Desktop app version of the software.

> **Online apps**—Available at https://office.com. These apps are accessed through a Web browser (no installation required) and allow you to create and save files online using your OneDrive account (Microsoft's cloud storage service). The online apps have a limited set of features, but depending on your needs that may be enough.

> **Mobile apps**—Free apps available for your tablet device. Similar in features and functionality to the online apps, these apps are designed to run on the iOS and Android operating systems. They offer limited functionality compared to the installed desktop apps.

let me try Live!

Try this skill on your own:

1. Display the Start menu.
2. Open the **Word** app.
3. Keep the app open to work on the next skill.

Skill 1.2 Opening Files

Opening a file retrieves it from storage and displays it on your computer screen. Files can be stored online, such as in your OneDrive, or on the hard drive of your computer. The steps for opening a file are the same for Word documents, Excel spreadsheets, PowerPoint presentations, and Access databases.

To open a recently opened file:

1. Click the **File** tab to open Backstage view.
2. Click **Open**.
3. The *Open* page displays listing the recently opened files.
4. Click a file in the list to open it.

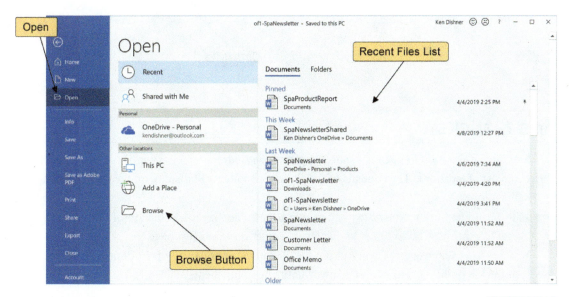

FIGURE OF 1.7

If you do not see the file you want to open in the *Recent Files* list, you can navigate to find the file you want to open:

1. Click the **Browse** button to open the *Open* dialog.
2. Navigate to the folder containing the file you want to open.
3. Select the file name you want to open and click the **Open** button.

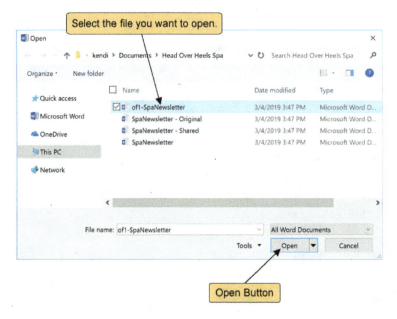

FIGURE OF 1.8

tips & tricks

> If the file you want to open is located in your *Documents* folder, click the **This PC** option in the list of locations. The contents of the *Documents* folder will display on the right. Click a file to open it.

> To open files from recently used folders, click the **Folders** option at the top of the *Recent* page. Click a folder to display its contents in the *Open* page.

> If you use a file frequently, you can pin the file to the list of files to open. Pinned files appear at the top of the list and do not go away until you unpin them.

tell me more

OneDrive is Microsoft's free cloud storage where you can save files and access those files from any computer or device or share the files with others. When you save files to your OneDrive, they are stored locally on your computer and "synched" with your OneDrive account and stored online where you can then access the files from another computer or device that has OneDrive capability.

another method

> To display the *Open* page in Backstage view, you can also press Ctrl + O on the keyboard.
> To open the *Open* dialog from the *Open* page in Backstage view, you can also double-click **This PC** at the left side of the *Open* page under *Other locations*.
> You can also click **Home** in Backstage view to display a list of recently opened files.

let me try Live!

1. Open the student data file **of1-SpaNewsletter** .
   NOTE: You may see a yellow security message at the top of the window. See the skill *Working in Protected View* to learn more about security warning messages.
2. Keep the file open to work on the next skill.

Skill 1.3 Closing Files

Closing a file removes it from your computer screen and stores the last saved version for future use. If you have not saved your latest changes, most apps will prevent you from losing work by asking if you want to save the changes you made before closing.

To close a file and save your latest changes:

1. Click the **File** tab to open Backstage view.
2. Click **Close**.
3. If you have made no changes since the last time you saved the file, it will close immediately. If changes have been made, the app displays a message box asking if you want to save the changes you made before closing.

> Click **Save** to save the changes.
> Click **Don't Save** to close the file without saving your latest changes.
> Click **Cancel** to keep the file open.

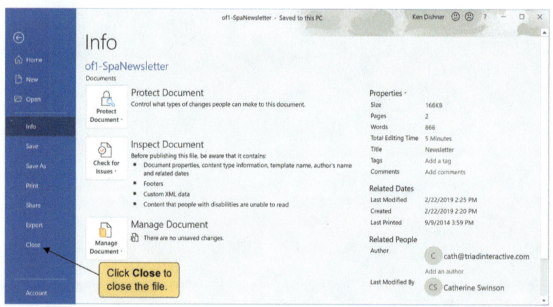

FIGURE OF 1.9

another method

To close a file, you can also press ⎡Ctrl⎤ + ⎡W⎤ on the keyboard.

let me try Live!

If you do not have the data file from the previous skill open, open the student data file **of1-SpaNewsletter** and try this skill on your own:

1. Close the file
2. Keep the app open to work on the next skill.

Skill 1.4 Closing the App

When you close a file, the app stays open so you can open another file to edit or begin a new file. Often, when you are finished working on a file, you want to close the file and exit the app at the same time. In this case, you will want to close the app.

To close an app:

1. Click the **Close** button in the upper right corner of the app.
2. If you have made no changes since the last time you saved the file, it will close immediately. If changes have been made, the app displays a message box asking if you want to save the changes you made before closing.

> Click **Save** to save the changes.
> Click **Don't Save** to close the file without saving your latest changes.
> Click **Cancel** to keep the file open.

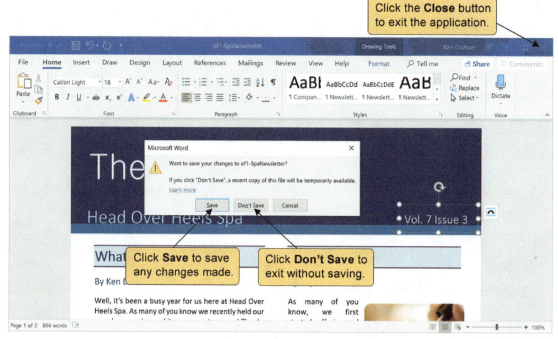

FIGURE OF 1.10

tell me more

Next to the **Close** button in the upper right corner of the app you will see two other buttons:

Minimize —hides the window from view, but does not close the app. The app button is still active on the Windows taskbar. Click the button on the taskbar to display the window again.

Maximize —resizes the app window so it fills the screen. When the window is maximized, the window cannot be moved around the screen and the *Maximize* button is replaced with the *Restore* button . Click the **Restore** button to reduce the size of the window and move it around on the screen.

another method

To close the app, you can also right-click the title bar and select **Close**.

let me try Live!

Open the student data file **of1-SpaNewsletter** and try this skill on your own:

1. Make a change to the document.
2. Close the app.
3. Do not save the change you made.

Skill 1.5 Using the Start Page

Before you can begin working in an app, you must have a file to work on. This can be a file you have worked on in the past, a new blank file, or a new file based on a template. When you launch an Office app you are first taken to the **Start page**. By default, the *Start* page opens to the to the **Home page** which displays a list of recently opened files along with templates for creating new files.

To open a recent file from the *Home* page:

1. Launch the app.
2. The *Start* page opens with the *Home* page displayed.
3. On the right side of the screen, click a template to create a new file or select a file in the list of recent files to open it.

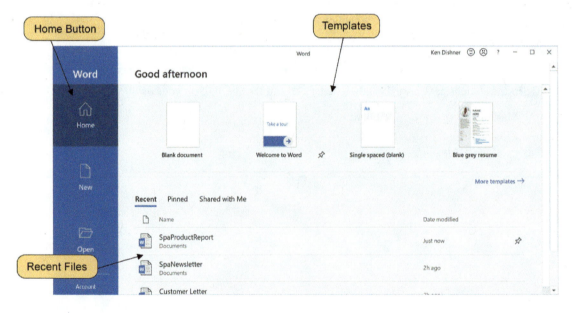

FIGURE OF 1.11

tips & tricks

If you do not see the file you want to open on the *Home* page, click the **Open** option in the left pane. This will display the *Open* page that includes buttons for finding and opening files from other locations such as your computer or your OneDrive.

If you do not see a template you want to use on the *Home* page, click the **More templates** link or the **New** option in the left pane. Either of these will display the *New* page that includes more templates to choose from and the ability to search for templates online.

tell me more

In previous versions of Office when you launched an app, a blank file opened ready for you to begin working. If you want to start a new blank file, click the blank file template in the list of templates. It is always listed as the first option on the *Home* page and the *New* page.

let me try Live!

To try this skill on your own:

1. Launch **Microsoft Word**.
2. Click the **of1-SpaNewsletter** file in the list of recently opened files. If you do not see this file, open a file of your choice.
3. If you will be moving on to the next skill in this chapter, leave the document open to continue working. If not, close the file.

Skill 1.6 Getting to Know the Office User Interface

THE RIBBON

Beginning with Office 2007, Microsoft redesigned the user experience for the Office apps—replacing the old menu bar/toolbar interface with a Ribbon interface that makes it easier to find app functions and commands.

The **Ribbon** is located across the top of the app window and organizes common features and commands into tabs. Each **tab** organizes commands further into related **groups**. The **dialog launcher** appears in the lower right corner of some groups. Clicking this button opens the primary dialog for working with commands in the group. For example, clicking the dialog launcher in the *Font* group will open the *Font* dialog.

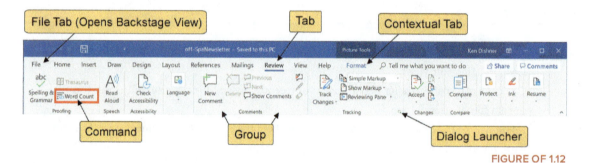

FIGURE OF 1.12

Figure OF 1.12 represents the 2019 version of the Office 365 Ribbon. If you have the Office 2019 on-premises version, your Ribbon may look more like Figure OF 1.13. Although the look of the Ribbon is different, the steps to complete the skills covered in this textbook are the same.

FIGURE OF 1.13

When a specific type of object is selected (such as a picture, table, or chart), a contextual tab will appear. **Contextual tabs** contain commands specific to the type of object selected and are visible only when the commands might be useful.

Each app includes a **Home tab** that contains the most commonly used commands for that app. For example, in Word, the *Home* tab includes the following groups: *Clipboard*, *Font*, *Paragraph*, *Styles*, and

Editing, while the Excel *Home* tab includes groups more appropriate for a spreadsheet program: *Clipboard*, *Font*, *Alignment*, *Number*, *Styles*, *Cells*, and *Editing*.

tips & tricks

If you need more space for your file, you can minimize the Ribbon by clicking the **Collapse the Ribbon** button in the lower right corner of the Ribbon (or press Ctrl + F1). When the Ribbon is minimized, the tab names appear along the top of the window (similar to a menu bar). When you click a tab name, the Ribbon appears. After you select a command or click away from the Ribbon, the Ribbon hides again. To redisplay the Ribbon permanently, click the **Pin the Ribbon** button in the lower right corner of the Ribbon. You can also double-click the active tab to hide or display the Ribbon.

BACKSTAGE

Notice that each app also includes a **File tab** at the far-left side of the Ribbon. Clicking the File tab opens **Backstage view**, where you can access the commands for managing and protecting your files, including *Save*, *Open*, *Close*, *New*, *Print,* and *Share*.

To return to your file from Backstage view, click the **Back** button located in the upper left corner of the window.

KEYBOARD SHORTCUTS

Many commands available through the Ribbon and Backstage view are also accessible through keyboard shortcuts and shortcut menus.

Keyboard shortcuts are keys or combinations of keys that you press to execute a command. Some keyboard shortcuts refer to **F** keys or function keys. These are the keys that run across the top of the keyboard. Pressing these keys will execute specific commands. For example, pressing the F1 key will open Help in any of the Microsoft Office apps. Keyboard shortcuts

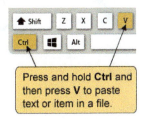

Press and hold **Ctrl** and then press **V** to paste text or item in a file.

FIGURE 1.14

typically use a combination of two keys, although some commands use a combination of three keys and others only one key. When a keyboard shortcut calls for a combination of key presses, such as Ctrl + V to paste an item from the *Clipboard*, you must first press the modifier key Ctrl holding it down while you press the V key on the keyboard.

tell me more

Many of the keyboard shortcuts are universal across all apps—not just Microsoft Office apps. Some examples of universal shortcut keys include:

⌈Ctrl⌋ + ⌈C⌋ = Copy

⌈Ctrl⌋ + ⌈X⌋ = Cut

⌈Ctrl⌋ + ⌈V⌋ = Paste

⌈Ctrl⌋ + ⌈Z⌋ = Undo

⌈Ctrl⌋ + ⌈O⌋ = Open

⌈Ctrl⌋ + ⌈S⌋ = Save

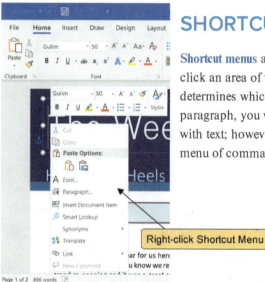

FIGURE 1.15

SHORTCUT MENUS

Shortcut menus are menus of commands that display when you right-click an area of the app window. The area or object you right-click determines which menu appears. For example, if you right-click in a paragraph, you will see a shortcut menu of commands for working with text; however, if you right-click an image, you will see a shortcut menu of commands for working with images.

THE MINI TOOLBAR

The **Mini toolbar** gives you access to common tools for working with text. When you select text and then rest your mouse over the text, the Mini toolbar fades in. You can then click a button to change the selected text just as you would on the Ribbon.

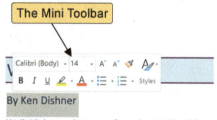

FIGURE OF 1.16

another method

To display the Mini toolbar, you can also right-click the text. The Mini toolbar appears above the shortcut menu. The Mini toolbar that appears at the top of the right-click shortcut menu includes buttons for the features most commonly used in the app, not just text options.

QUICK ACCESS TOOLBAR

The **Quick Access Toolbar** is located at the top of the app window above the *File* tab. The Quick Access Toolbar, as its name implies, gives you quick one-click access to common commands. Some of the commands include *Save*, *Undo*, and *Redo*.

FIGURE OF 1.17

ENHANCED SCREENTIP

A **ScreenTip** is a small information box that displays the name of the command when you rest your mouse over a button on the Ribbon. An **Enhanced ScreenTip** displays not only the name of the command, but also the keyboard shortcut (if there is one) and a short description of what the button does and when it is used. Certain Enhanced ScreenTips also include an image along with a description of the command.

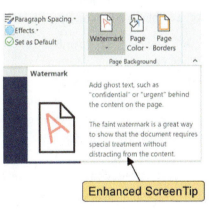

FIGURE OF 1.18

THE OPTIONS DIALOG

The **Options dialog** is where you can control settings for the Office app. When you make a change in the *Options* dialog, the setting applies to the app, not the current active file. This means when you exit the app and open it again, any changes you made in the *Options* dialog will remain.

Although each app has a slightly different set of controls, the *Options* dialog includes areas for controlling proofing options, save options, language, the Ribbon, and Quick Access Toolbar, as well as a general section where you can control some of the user interface features.

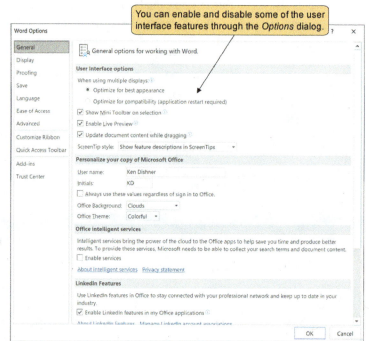

You can enable and disable some of the user interface features through the *Options* dialog.

FIGURE OF 1.19

You can enable and disable some of the user interface features through the *Options* dialog:

1. Click the **File** tab to open Backstage view.
2. Click **Options**.
3. Make the changes you want, and then click **OK** to save your changes
   - Check or uncheck **Show Mini toolbar on selection** to control whether or not the Mini toolbar appears when you hover over selected text. (This does not affect the appearance of the Mini toolbar when you right-click.)
   - Check or uncheck **Enable Live Preview** to turn the live preview feature on or off.
   - Make a selection from the *ScreenTip style* list:
     - **Show feature descriptions in ScreenTips** displays Enhanced ScreenTips when they are available.
     - **Don't show feature descriptions in ScreenTips** hides Enhanced ScreenTips. The ScreenTip will still include the keyboard shortcut if there is one available.
     - **Don't show ScreenTips** hides ScreenTips altogether, so if you hold your mouse over a button on the Ribbon, nothing will appear.

LIVE PREVIEW

The **Live Preview** feature in Microsoft Office allows you to see formatting changes in your file before committing to the change. When Live Preview is active, rolling over a command on the Ribbon will temporarily apply the formatting to the currently active text or object. To apply the formatting, click the formatting option.

Use Live Preview to preview the following:

Font Formatting—Including the font, font size, text effects, and font color

Paragraph Formatting—Including numbering, bullets, line spacing, and shading

Styles and Themes Table Formatting—Including table styles and shading

Picture Formatting—Including correction and color options, picture styles, borders, effects, positioning, brightness, and contrast

SmartArt—Including layouts, styles, and colors

FIGURE OF 1.20

let me try Live!

If you do not have the data file from the previous skill open, open the student data file **of1-SpaNewsletter** and try this skill on your own:

1. Explore the Ribbon. Click on different tabs and observe how commands are arranged together in groups.
2. Click the picture to display the *Picture Tools* contextual tab.
3. Right-click an area of the file to display the shortcut menu.
4. Explore the Mini Toolbar at the top of the shortcut menu. Click away from the menu to hide it.
5. Click the **Insert** tab. In the *Pages* group, roll your mouse over the **Cover Page** button to display the Enhanced ScreenTip.
6. Display **Backstage** view.
7. Click **Options** to open the *Options* dialog.
8. Disable **Live Preview** and change the **ScreenTips** so they don't show feature descriptions. Close the *Options* dialog and save your changes.
9. Click the **Back** button to return to the document.
10. If you will be moving on to the next skill in this chapter, leave the document open to continue working. If not, close the file.

Skill 1.7 Getting Help

The **Tell Me** feature offers a quick way to access commands that you do not know how to find in the Office interface or that take several clicks to get to. By using the *Tell Me* box to access commands, you can save time and frustration by quickly getting to the features you need.

To use *Tell Me* to access a command:

1. Type the word or phrase you want to look up in the **Tell me what you want to do...** box at the top of the window.
2. Office displays a list of commands that match your search.
3. Options with a triangle have a gallery or menu of options associated with it. Point to the option to display more commands from which to choose.
4. Click an option on the list to access that command.

Type the command you are looking for in the *Tell Me* box.

FIGURE OF 1.21

If you want to learn more about a command, you can look it up using the **Help task pane**. Each app comes with its own Help topics specifically tailored for working with that app.

To look up a topic using the Help task pane:

1. Type the word or phrase you want help on in the *Tell Me* box.
2. At the bottom of the menu, point to the *Get Help on [topic]* option.
3. A list of Help topics appears.

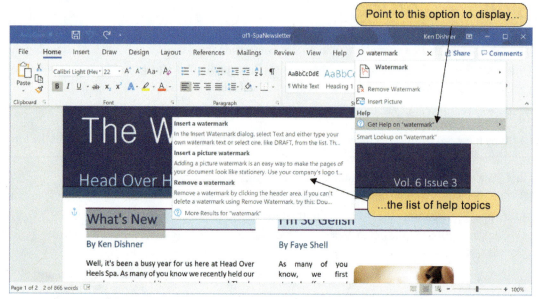

FIGURE OF 1.22

4. Click a topic to display it in the *Help* task pane.

FIGURE OF 1.23

tips & tricks

At the bottom of the list of options, you will see options for **Smart Lookup**. Click the **Smart Lookup** link to search for information on the Internet on the word or phrase you typed.

another method

To open the *Help* window, you can also:

> Press F1 on the keyboard.
> Click the **Help** tab and then click the **Help** button.

let me try Live!

If you do not have the data file from the previous skill open, open the student data file **of1-SpaNewsletter** ⬇ and try this skill on your own:

1. Type **Clipboard** in the *Tell Me* box and display the *Clipboard* task pane.
2. Click the **X** in the upper right corner of the task pane to close it.
3. Type **Watermark** in the *Tell Me* box and display the topic for inserting a watermark in Word in the *Help* task pane.
4. Close the file.

Skill 1.8 Using Smart Lookup

The **Smart Lookup** tool allows you to quickly search the Internet for information about any word or phrase in a document, spreadsheet, or presentation. When you look up a word or phrase, the *Smart Lookup* task pane displays. This task pane has two tabs—*Explore* and *Define*. The *Explore* tab displays search results powered by Microsoft's Bing search engine and returns results from Wikipedia, Bing image search, and other sources on the Web. The *Define* tab displays a definition of the word or phrase from the Oxford Dictionaries.

To look up information about a word or phrase using the *Smart Lookup* tool:

1. Select the word or phrase.
2. Click the **References** tab.
3. In the *Research* group, click the **Smart Lookup** button.
4. The *Smart Lookup* task pane opens displaying information about the word or phrase.

FIGURE OF 1.24

tips & tricks

You can also display the *Smart Lookup* task pane from the *Tell Me* box. First, type the word or phrase you want more information on in the *Tell Me* box at the top of the screen. Click the **Smart Lookup on** link on the menu. The *Smart Lookup* task pane opens with the information displayed.

tell me more

Smart Lookup relies on Microsoft Office's **intelligent services** to retrieve the most up to date search results. You may need to turn on intelligent services in order to use the *Smart Lookup* feature. You can turn on intelligent services by clicking **Options** in Backstage view and then checking the **Enable services** checkbox in *Office intelligent services* section the *Options* dialog.

another method

To look up a word or phrase using Smart Lookup, you can also right-click the word or phrase and select **Smart Lookup** from the shortcut menu.

let me try Live!

If you do not have the data file from the previous skill open, open the student data file **of1-SpaNewsletter** and try this skill on your own:

1. Select the words **Dead Sea** in the middle of the first paragraph of the newsletter.
2. Display the **Smart Lookup** task pane.
3. Review the information on the *Explore* tab.
4. Click the **X** in the upper right corner of the task pane to close it.
5. Close the file.

Skill 1.9 Working in Protected View

When you download a file from a location that Office considers potentially unsafe, it opens automatically in **Protected View**. Protected View provides a read-only format that protects your computer from becoming infected by a virus or other malware. Potentially unsafe locations include the Internet, email messages, or a network location. Files that are opened in Protected View display a warning in the Message Bar at the top of the window, below the Ribbon.

To disable Protected View, click the **Enable Editing** button in the Message Bar.

FIGURE OF 1.25

You can also enable editing from the *Info* page in Backstage view.

1. Click the **File** tab to open Backstage view.
2. Click **Info**.
3. The *Info* page provides more information about the file. If you are sure you want to remove it from Protected View, click the **Enable Editing** button.

tips & tricks

To learn more about the security settings in Office, open the Trust Center and review the options. To open the Trust Center, click the **File** tab and select **Options**. In the *Options* dialog, click **Trust Center** on the left side of the dialog. We do not recommend changing any of the default Trust Center settings.

let me try Live!

Open the student data file **of1-SpaNewsletter** ⤓ and try this skill on your own:

1. If you downloaded the file from the Internet, the file will open in Protected View.
2. Click the **Enable Editing** button to begin working with the file.
3. Navigate to the second page of the document.
4. Close the file.

Skill 1.10 Picking Up Where You Left Off

When you are working in a long document or a presentation and reopen it to work on it, you may not remember where you were last working. The **Pick up where you left off** feature automatically bookmarks the last location that was worked on when the file was closed.

To pick up where you left off in a document or presentation:

1. Open the document or presentation.
2. A message displays on the right side of the screen welcoming you back and asking if you want to pick up where you left off. The message then minimizes to a bookmark tag.
3. Click the **bookmark tag** to navigate to the location.

FIGURE OF 1.26

tips & tricks

The bookmark tag displays only until you navigate to another part of the document. If you scroll the document, the bookmark tag disappears.

tell me more

The bookmark tag is available only in Word and PowerPoint. This feature is not necessary in Excel, since Excel automatically opens to the last active cell position when the workbook was last closed.

let me try Live!

Open the student data file **of1-SpaNewsletter** and try this skill on your own:

1. Navigate to the last location of the file when it was last closed.
2. If you will be moving on to the next skill in this chapter, leave the document open to continue working. If not, close the file.

Skill 1.11 Working with File Properties

File Properties provide information about a file such as the location of the file, the size of file, when the file was created and when it was last modified, the title, and the author. Properties also include keywords, referred to as **tags**, that are useful for grouping common files together or for searching. All this information about a file is referred to as **metadata**.

To view a file's properties:

1. Click the **File** tab to open Backstage view.
2. Properties are listed at the far right of the *Info* page.
3. To add keywords to a file, click the text box next to *Tags* and type keywords that describe the file, separating each word with a comma.

The Author property is added automatically using the account name entered when you installed and registered Office. You can change the author name or add more names by editing the Author property.

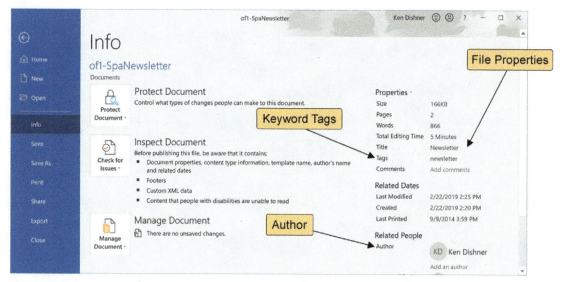

FIGURE OF 1.27

tips & tricks

Some file properties are generated automatically by Windows and cannot be edited by the user, such as the date the file was created and the size of the file.

let me try Live!

If you do not have the data file from the previous skill open, open the student data file **of1-SpaNewsletter** and try this skill on your own:

1. Add a tag to the document that reads **newsletter**.
2. If you will be moving on to the next skill in this chapter, leave the document open to continue working. If not, close the file.

Skill 1.12 Creating a New Blank File

When you first open an Office app, the *Start* page displays giving you the opportunity to open an existing file, create a new blank file, or create a new file based on a template. But what if you have a file open and want to create another new file? Will you need to close the app and then launch it again? The **New command** allows you to create new files without exiting and reopening the program.

To create a new blank file:

1. Click the **File** tab to open Backstage view.
2. Click **New**.
3. The first option on the *New* page is a blank file. Click the **Blank document** thumbnail to create the new blank file.

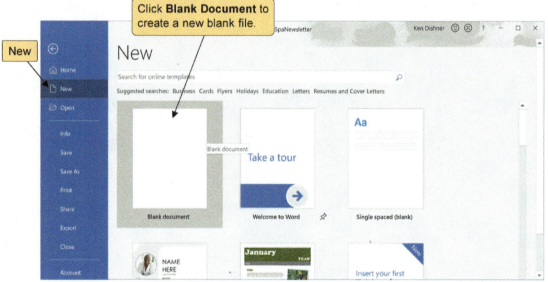

FIGURE 1.28

tell me **more**

In addition to a blank file, you can create new files from templates from the *New* page.

another method

> To bypass the Backstage view and create a new blank file, press insert $\boxed{\text{Ctrl}}$ + $\boxed{\text{N}}$ on the keyboard.
> You can also create a new blank file by clicking the **File** tab to display Backstage view, clicking **Home**, and then clicking the **Blank document** template at the top of the page.

let me try Live!

If you do not have the data file from the previous skill open, open the student data file **of1-SpaNewsletter** and try this skill on your own:

1. Create a new blank file.
2. If you will be moving on to the next skill in this chapter, leave the document open to continue working. If not, close the file.

Skill 1.13 Saving Files to Your PC

As you work on a new file, it is displayed onscreen and stored in your computer's memory. However, it is not permanently stored until you save it as a file to a specific location. The first time you save a file, the *Save As* page in Backstage view will display. Here you can choose to save the file to your OneDrive, your local computer, or another location.

You can also choose to save the file in different formats, including templates and macro-enabled files. This table lists the default and template file formats for Word, Excel, and PowerPoint:

App	Default Format	Template
Word	Word Document (*.docx)	Word Template (*.dotx)
Excel	Excel Workbook (*.xlsx)	Excel Template (*.xltx)
PowerPoint	PowerPoint Presentation (*.pptx)	PowerPoint Template (*.potx)

To save a file to your PC:

1. Click the **Save** button on the Quick Access Toolbar.
2. The *Save As* page in Backstage view appears.
3. On the left side of the page, click **This PC** to save the file to a local drive.
4. At the top of the right side of the page, you will see the name of the folder the file will be saved in. If you want to save the file in this location, type the name of the file in the *Enter file name here* box.
5. If you want to change the file type, click the box below the filename and select an option.
6. Click the **Save** button to save the file.

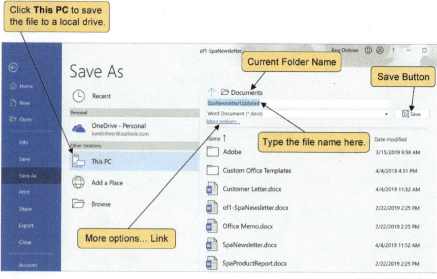

FIGURE OF 1.29

To save the file to a new folder:

1. On the *Save As* page, click the **More options...** link under the *Enter file name here* box.
2. The *Save As* dialog opens.
3. If you want to create a new folder, click the **New Folder** button near the top of the file list. The new folder is created with the temporary name *New Folder*. Type the new name for the folder and press Enter.
4. Double-click the folder to open it.
5. Click in the **File name** box and type a file name.
6. Click the **Save** button.

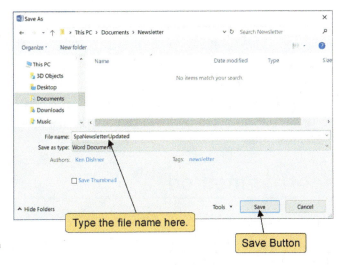

FIGURE 1.30

If you are working on a file that has already been saved, click the **Save** button on the Quick Access Toolbar or press Ctrl + S on the keyboard to quickly save the file as you make changes. The file will be saved to the same location with the same name.

FIGURE 1.31

tips & tricks

> ❯ If the location where you want to save the file is not listed on the right side of the *Save As* page, click the **Browse** button to open the *Save As* dialog. Navigate to the location where you want to save the file.
>
> ❯ If you are working on a file that you want to save but not overwrite the original file, you should save the file with a new name. When you save a file with a new name, the original file still exists in its last saved state and the new file you save will include all the changes you made.

another method

To save a file, you can also:

> ❯ Press ⌷Ctrl + ⌷S on the keyboard.
> ❯ Click the **File** tab, and then select **Save**.
> ❯ Click the **File** tab, and then select **Save As**.

let me try Live!

If you do not have the data file from the previous skill open, create a new blank document and try this skill on your own:

1. Save the file to a new folder inside the **Documents** folder. Name the new folder **Newsletters**.
2. Name the file: **SpaNewsletterUpdated**
3. Close the file.

from the perspective of . . .

A BUSY PARENT

Learning Microsoft Office was one of the best things I did to help manage my family's busy lifestyle. I use Word to write up and print a calendar of everyone's activities for the week. I keep a handle on the family finances with a budget of all expenses in an Excel spreadsheet. I used PowerPoint to create a presentation for my family of our summer vacation pictures. Once I became more familiar with Access, I used it to help organize my family's busy schedule. I created a database with one table for activities, another for parent contact information, another one for carpooling, and another one for the schedule. Being able to organize all the information in a database has been invaluable. And the best part is now I can share and view these files with everyone, even on my tablet. I always thought Office was only for businesses, but now I can't imagine running my household without it!

Skill 1.14 Saving Files to OneDrive

OneDrive is Microsoft's free **cloud storage** where you can save documents, workbooks, presentations, videos, pictures, and other files and access those files from any computer or share the files with others. When you save files to your OneDrive, they are stored locally on your computer and then "synched" with your OneDrive account and stored in the "cloud" where you can then access the files from another computer or device that has OneDrive capability.

To save a file to your OneDrive:

1. Click the **File** tab.
2. Click **Save As**.
3. Verify the OneDrive account is selected on the left side of the page.
4. A list of OneDrive folders appears on the right. Click the **folder** you want to save to.
5. Type the name of the file in the *Enter file name here* box and click the **Save** button.

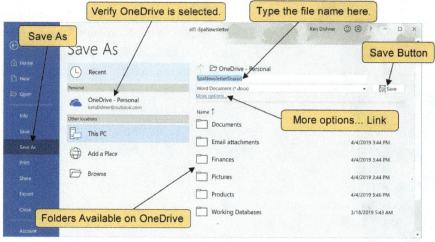

FIGURE OF 1.32

You can also save the file through the *Save As* dialog:

1. On the *Save As* page, click the **More options...** link under the *Enter file name here* box.
2. The *Save As* dialog opens to your OneDrive folder location on your computer.
3. Click in the **File name** box and type a file name.
4. Click the **Save** button.

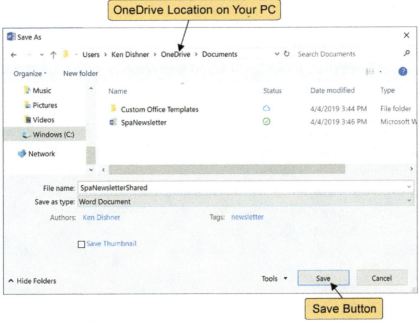

FIGURE OF 1.33

tips & tricks

By default, your OneDrive includes folders for documents, pictures, and files you want to make public. You can save your files in any of these folders or create your own. To create a new folder in your OneDrive, click the **New Folder** button near the top of the file list in the *Save As* dialog. The new folder is created with the temporary name *New Folder*. Type the new name for the folder and press Enter.

tell me more

When you are working on a file that has been saved to your OneDrive, others can work on the file at the same time as you. The app will mark the area being worked on as read only so others cannot modify the same information you are working on.

let me try Live!

Open the student data file **of1-SpaNewsletter** ⬇ and try this skill on your own:

NOTE: You will need a OneDrive account to complete this exercise. In addition, if you are using this in class or in your school's computer lab, check with your instructor before completing this exercise.

1. Save the file to the **Documents** folder on your OneDrive.
2. Name the file: `SpaNewsletterShared`
3. If you will be moving on to the next skill in this chapter, leave the document open to continue working. If not, close the file.

Skill 1.15 Using AutoSave

When a file is saved to your OneDrive, the **AutoSave** toggle is on by default. This means you no longer need to continually save your files in order to not lose your work. Each time your file is saved on your OneDrive, a version of the file is saved in that state. The title bar displays the last saved date and time next to the file name.

To turn the *AutoSave* feature off, click the toggle so it appears in the "Off" state. Click the toggle again to return it to the "On" state and have the files automatically save to your OneDrive.

FIGURE OF 1.34

You can access previous saved **versions** of files from the *Version History* task pane. You can then open those versions and copy and paste content you need or save the version with a new name to create a new file from that version.

To open a previously saved version of a file:

1. Click the click the arrow next to the title in the title bar and select **Version History**.
2. The *Version History* task pane opens displaying the saved versions of the file.
3. In the list of files, click the saved version of the file you want to open.
4. The file will open as read-only. Save the file with a new name to remove the read-only status.

Office 2019 Note: If you have the Office 2019 on-premises version of Office, you will not have the AutoSave toggle in the title bar. In addition, you will not be able to restore versions of files using the method described here.

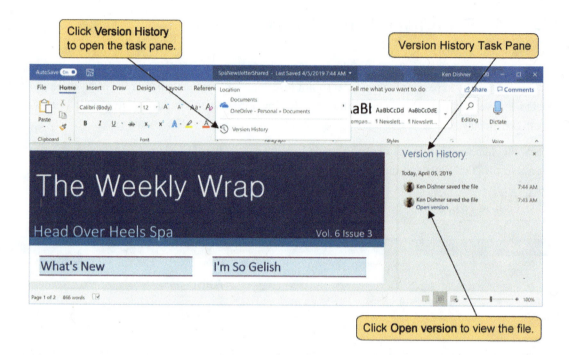

FIGURE OF 1.35

tell me more

Files that are saved locally to a computer and not to a OneDrive or SharePoint account will not display the last saved date and time next to the file name. Instead, you will see *Saved to my PC*.

another method

To display the *Version History* task pane, you can also:

1. Click the **File** tab.
2. Verify you are on the *Info* page.
3. Click **View and restore previous versions** under *Version History*.

let me try Live!

If you do not have the data file from the previous skill open, open a file you have saved to your OneDrive account and try this skill on your own:

NOTE: You will need a OneDrive account to complete this exercise. In addition, if you are using this in class or in your school's computer lab, check with your instructor before completing this exercise.

1. Turn the **AutoSave** feature off.
2. Turn the **AutoSave** feature back on.
3. Make a change to the file and save the file.
4. Open the **Version History** task pane.
5. Open a previously saved version of the file.
6. Close the version you opened.
7. If you will be moving on to the next skill in this chapter, leave the document open to continue working. If not, close the file.

Skill 1.16 Sharing Files using OneDrive

One of the benefits of saving files to your OneDrive is the ability to share files with others. The first step in sharing a file using OneDrive is to save the file to your OneDrive folder. To learn how to save a file to a OneDrive account, see *Saving Files to OneDrive.* Once the file is saved to your OneDrive, you can share it with others from the Ribbon.

To share a file using OneDrive:

1. Click the **Share** button at the far-right side of the Ribbon.
2. The *Share* task pane displays.
3. Type the email address of the person you want to share the file with in the *Invite people* box.
4. Click the drop-down arrow under the box and select whether the recipient(s) can edit or only view the file.
5. If you want to include a note to the recipient(s), click in the message box and a type a message.
6. Click the **Share** button.

FIGURE OF 1.36

REAL-TIME COLLABORATION

When you share files through OneDrive, you can take advantage of Office's **online collaboration** tools. This means multiple people can work on a file at the same time and all the changes are made to one file. When a person works on a shared file, their user account icon appears to the left of the *Share* button for anyone else who also has the file open. Office locks any section of the file currently being worked on. This prevents overlapping changes when multiple people are working on the same file. Office also marks the area being worked on by others and displays a flag at the site of the change with the user's name.

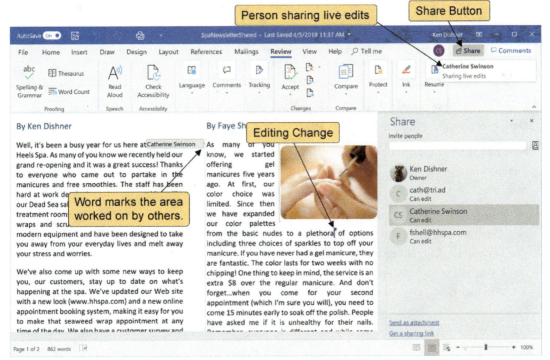

FIGURE OF 1.37

tips & tricks

> To share the file with more than one person, enter the email addresses for each recipient separated by a comma.
> If the file has not been shared, you will be prompted to share the file to your OneDrive or to send the file as an attachment.

tell me more

You can also share a file through a **sharing link**. A sharing link creates a link to your OneDrive that others can access to either view or edit the file. Click the **Get a sharing link** option at the bottom of the *Share* task pane to create a sharing link you can send to others.

another method

To open the *Share* task pane, you can also:

1. Click the **File** tab.
2. Click **Share**.
3. Verify *Share with People* is selected on the left side of the page. Click the **Share with People** button on the right side of the page.

let me try Live!

If you do not have the data file from the previous skill open, open a file you have saved to your OneDrive account and try this skill on your own:

NOTE: You will need a OneDrive account to complete this exercise. In addition, if you are using this in class or in your school's computer lab, check with your instructor before completing this exercise.

1. Display the **Share** task pane.
2. Share the document with **fshell@hhspa.com** and include the message **Please review and edit.** The recipient should be able to edit the document.
3. If you will be moving on to the next skill in this chapter, leave the document open to continue working. If not, close the file

Skill 1.17 Using the Account Page

In the upper right corner of any Office app, you will see the name of the person who is currently logged into Office. The **Account page** lists more information for that user. This account information comes from the Microsoft account you used when installing Office. From the *Account* page, you can view your Microsoft user profile, switch between user accounts, view your product information, and connect to online services.

To view user information:

1. Click the **File** tab.
2. Click **Account**.
3. The current user profile is listed under *User Information*.

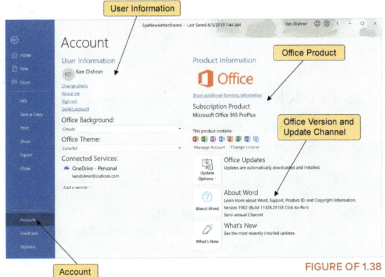

FIGURE OF 1.38

On the right side of the Account page, you will see product information, including the product you have installed (Office 365 or Office 2109). If you have an Office 365 subscription, you or the account administrator (if you are using a school or work account) can choose how often Office is updated (the update channel):

> **Semi-annual channel**—updates in January and July with new features from the Semi-annual (targeted) release. At this point, all users have the new features.

> **Semi-annual (targeted) channel**—updates in September and March with what is expected to be the feature set that will be rolled out to everyone in the semi-annual release.

> **Monthly channel**—updates once a month with new features. These features have not been thoroughly tested and are released to Monthly channel users for feedback.

Office will alert you when a new update is available for Office. You can also check to see if your version is up to date from the Account page.

To check for Office updates:

1. Go to the *Account* page.
2. Click the **Update Options** button and select **Update Now**.
3. If there are new updates, follow the prompts to install the updates. If there are no new updates, close the message box that appears.

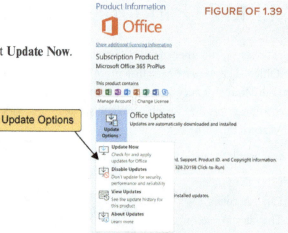

FIGURE OF 1.39

tips & tricks

Click **Change photo** or **About me** under user information to navigate to *live.com* where you can change the image that appears with the user profile and change information for that user as well.

tell me more

Depending on the version of Office you have, multiple accounts can use the same installation of Office. When you switch accounts, any personalization that person has done to Office will be applied. The account will also have access to that person's OneDrive account and all files that have been saved there.

another method

To display the *Account* page, you can also click the user name in the upper right corner of the window and select the **Account Settings** link.

let me try Live!

If you do not have the data file from the previous skill open, open the student data file **of1-SpaNewsletter** and try this skill on your own:

1. Open the **Account** page in Backstage view.

   NOTE: If you are using this in class or in your school's computer lab, check with your instructor about permissions before completing the following steps.

2. Check for new updates to Office.
3. If you will be moving on to the next skill in this chapter, leave the document open to continue working. If not, close the file.

Skill 1.18 Changing the Look of Office

In addition to managing the Office account, you can also control the look of Office from the *Account* page. Changing the **Office background** changes the background image that displays in the upper right corner of the window near the user profile. Changing the **Office theme** changes the color scheme for Office, affecting the look of the Ribbon, task panes, and main working areas.

To change the look of Office:

1. Click the **File** tab to open Backstage view.
2. Click **Account**.
3. Click the **Office Background** drop-down list and select an option to display as the background.
4. Click the **Office Theme** drop-down list and select a color option for your apps.

FIGURE OF 1.40

tell me **more**

In Office 2016, Microsoft added new backgrounds and themes for Office. The new default theme is the *Colorful* theme. This theme recolors parts of the user interface to match the color of the app. For example, in Word the area above the Ribbon appears blue when the *Colorful* theme is applied.

another method

To display the *Account* page, you can also click the user name in the upper right corner of the window and select the **Account Settings** link.

let me try Live!

If you do not have the data file from the previous skill open, open the student data file **of1-SpaNewsletter** and try this skill on your own:

1. Open the **Account** page in Backstage view.

   NOTE: If you are using this in class or in your school's computer lab, check with your instructor about permissions before completing the following steps.

2. Change the Office background to the **Spring** background.
3. Change the Office theme to **Colorful**.
4. If you will be moving on to the next skill in this chapter, leave the document open to continue working. If not, close the file.

Skill 1.19 Customizing the Quick Access Toolbar

The Quick Access Toolbar gives you a fast way to access commands that you use often. By default, the Quick Access Toolbar displays the *Save*, *Undo*, and *Redo* commands. If you use different commands often, you can add commands to and remove commands from the Quick Access Toolbar.

To modify the Quick Access Toolbar:

1. Click the **Customize Quick Access Toolbar** button located on the right side of the Quick Access Toolbar.
2. Options with checkmarks next to them are already displayed on the toolbar. Options with no checkmarks are not currently displayed.
3. Click an option to add it to or remove it from the Quick Access Toolbar.

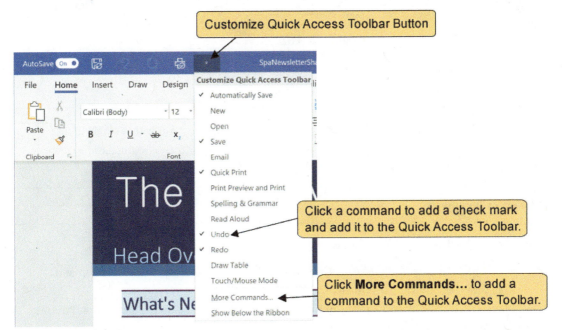

FIGURE OF 1.41

If a command does not appear on the *Quick Access Toolbar* list, you can still add it to the Quick Access Toolbar:

1. Click the **Customize Quick Access Toolbar** button and select **More Commands...**
2. The *Options* dialog opens to the *Customize the Quick Access Toolbar* page.
3. Scroll the list of popular commands or expand the **Choose commands from** list and select an option.

4. Select the command you want to appear on the Quick Access Toolbar and click the **Add** button.

5. You can reorder commands by selecting a command in the list and using the **Move Up** and **Move Down** buttons.

6. When you are finished customizing the Quick Access Toolbar, click **OK**.

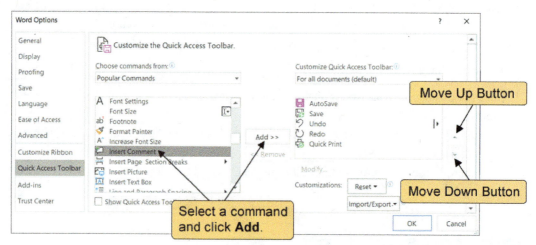

FIGURE OF 1.42

tips & tricks

The **Quick Print** option on the Quick Access Toolbar allows you to print with a single mouse click. If you do not need to change any print settings, this is by far the easiest method to print a file because it doesn't require opening Backstage view first.

tell me more

To reset the Quick Access Toolbar to its original state:

1. In the *Options* dialog, *Customize the Quick Access Toolbar* page, click the **Reset** button and select **Reset only Quick Access Toolbar**.

2. A message displays to verify that you want to reset the Quick Access Toolbar customizations. Click **Yes**.

another method

To open the *Customize Quick Access Toolbar* page:

> Click the **File** tab and click **Options** to open the *Options* dialog. Click **Quick Access Toolbar**.

> Right-click the **Quick Access Toolbar** and select **Customize Quick Access Toolbar...**

let me try Live!

If you do not have the data file from the previous skill open, open the student data file **of1-SpaNewsletter** 📥 and try this skill on your own:

NOTE: If you are using this in class or in your school's computer lab, check with your instructor about permissions before completing the following steps.

1. Add the **Quick Print** command to the Quick Access Toolbar.
2. Open the **Word Options** dialog to the *Quick Access Toolbar* page.
3. Add the **Insert Comment** command to the Quick Access Toolbar.
4. Close the file.

key terms

Microsoft Word

Microsoft Excel

Microsoft Access

Microsoft PowerPoint

Office 365

Office 2019 (on-premises)

Desktop apps

Online apps

Mobile apps

Start page

Home page

Ribbon

Tab

Groups

Dialog launcher

Contextual tabs

Home tab

File tab

Backstage view

Keyboard shortcuts

Shortcut menus

Mini toolbar

Quick Access Toolbar

ScreenTip

Enhanced ScreenTip

Options dialog

Live Preview

Tell Me

Help task pane

Smart Lookup

Intelligent services

Protected View

File Properties

Tags

Metadata

New command

OneDrive

Cloud storage

AutoSave

Versions

Online collaboration

Sharing link

Account page

Office background

Office theme

concept review

1. Which Microsoft Office application is a spreadsheet program?
    a. Word
    b. Excel
    c. Access
    d. PowerPoint

2. Which tab do you click to display Backstage view?
    a. File
    b. Home
    c. View
    d. Contextual

3. To display a shortcut menu _____ an area of the file.
    a. left-click
    b. right-click
    c. double-click
    d. drag over

4. If you have downloaded a file from the Internet and it opens in Protected View, you should never open the file.
    a. true
    b. false

5. Which part of the Office interface is located across the top of the application window and organizes common features and commands into tabs.
    a. Menu bar
    b. Toolbar
    c. Title bar
    d. Ribbon

6. The _____ provide(s) information about a file such as the location of the file, the size of file, when the file was created and when it was last modified, the title, and the author.
    a. file properties
    b. user profile
    c. account information
    d. Options dialog

7. When you save files to your OneDrive, they are available to access from other computers that have OneDrive capability. If you are working on an Excel or Word file, others can be working on the same file at the same time you are working on the file.
    a. true
    b. false

8. You can change user information from which page in Backstage view?

    a. Account

    b. Options

    c. Share

    d. Info

9. Which keyboard shortcut allows you to paste an item from the Clipboard?

    a. Ctrl + C

    b. Ctrl + X

    c. Ctrl + V

    d. Ctrl + P

10. Which part of the Office interface gives you quick one-click access to common commands and is located at the top of the application window above the File tab?

    a. Ribbon

    b. Quick Access Toolbar

    c. Options dialog

    d. Backstage view

Word 365

chapter **1**

Getting Started with Word

introduction

This introductory chapter will teach you some of the basic editing features of Microsoft Word, such as entering, selecting, and deleting text. You will also learn how to correct spelling and grammar errors; find and replace text; and use the cut, copy, and paste commands. In addition, you will look up document statistics, change the magnification of a document by using the Zoom feature, and change the document view. Finally, you will print a document using the typical print settings.

Skill 1.1 Introduction to Word

Microsoft Office Word is a word processing program that enables you to create many types of documents including letters, résumés, reports, proposals, flyers, personal cards, and more. Word's advanced editing capabilities allow you to quickly and easily perform tasks such as checking your spelling and finding text in a long document. Robust formatting allows you to produce professional documents with stylized fonts, layouts, and graphics. Printing and sharing can be managed directly from the Word window. In short, everything you need to create polished professional and personal documents is available in Microsoft Word.

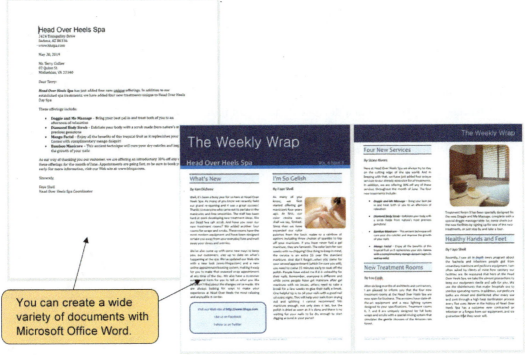

You can create a wide variety of documents with Microsoft Office Word.

FIGURE WD 1.1

Here are some basic elements of a Word document:

> **Font**—also called the typeface, refers to a set of characters of a certain design. You can choose from several preinstalled fonts available.

> **Paragraph**—groups of sentences separated by a hard return. A hard return refers to pressing the Enter key to create a new paragraph. You can assign a paragraph its own style to help it stand out from the rest of the document.

> **Styles**—complex formatting, including font, color, size, and spacing, that can be applied to text. Use consistent styles for headings, body text, notes, and captions throughout your document. Styles also can be applied to tables and graphics.

> **Theme**—a group of formatting options that is applied to an entire Word document. Themes include font, color, and effect styles that are applied to text, tables, graphics, and other elements in the document.

> **Table**—used to organize data into columns and rows.

> **Chart**—transforms numerical data into a visual representation.

> **Graphics**—photographs, SmartArt, or line drawings that can be added to documents.

> **Header**—text that appears at the top of every page in a document.

> **Footer**—text that appears at the bottom of every page in a document.

> **Page Break**—marker in a document that identifies where one page ends and another page begins.

> **Margin**—the blank areas at the top, bottom, left, and right of a page.

> **Citations**—automatically insert references to external sources in the proper format for use in a bibliography.

> **Comment**—a note you add to a document that is not meant to be a part of the document.

> **Track Changes**—feature that marks any changes made to a document by reviewers. Such changes include deletions, insertions, and formatting.

tips & tricks

Microsoft Office includes many other features that can further enhance your documents. If you would like to learn more about these features, begin typing in the **Tell Me** box to the right of the Ribbon tabs. Click the **Get Help on** link at the bottom of the menu to open the *Word Help* task pane.

tell me **more**

Some basic features of a word processing application include:

> **Word Wrap**—places text on the next line when the right margin of the page has been reached.

> **Find and Replace**—searches for any word or phrase in the document. Also, allows all instances of a word to be replaced by another word.

> **Editor**—checks for spelling and grammar errors, as well as writing style issues, and offers solutions to the problem.

> **Document Formatting**—allows the enhancement of the appearance of the document.

> **Draw Tools**—on touch devices, allows for drawing on documents using a pen or your finger.

> **Intelligent Services**—cloud-enhanced features in Office that can offer recommendations to help you work more efficiently. In Word, the *Editor* and *Smart Lookup* features rely on intelligent services.

> **Mail Merge**—creates several documents based on a main document, specified fields, and a list of recipients.

let me **try** Live!

1. From the Start menu, open the **Word** app.
2. Open the student data file **wd1-01-FourNewServices** to review the formatting of a simple letter.
3. Open the student data file **wd1-01-SpaNewsletter** to review the formatting of a more complex document. Close this file when you are finished.
4. If you will be moving on to the next skill in this chapter, leave the **wd1-01-FourNewServices** document open to continue working. if not, close the file.

Skill 1.2 Entering and Deleting Text

The basic function of a word processing application like Microsoft Word is to create written documents. Whether the documents are simple, such as a letter, or complex, such as a newsletter, one of the basic tasks you will perform in Word is entering text. **Word wrap** is a feature in Microsoft Word that automatically places text on the next line when the right margin of the document has been reached. There is no need to press Enter to begin a new line in the same paragraph. Press Enter only when you want to create a break and start a new paragraph.

To enter text in a document:

1. Place the cursor where you want the new text to appear.
2. Begin typing.
3. When the cursor reaches the end of the line, do not press Enter. Keep typing and allow word wrap to move the text to the next line.

If you make a mistake when entering text, you can press the Backspace key to remove text to the left of the cursor, or press the Delete key to remove text to the right of the cursor.

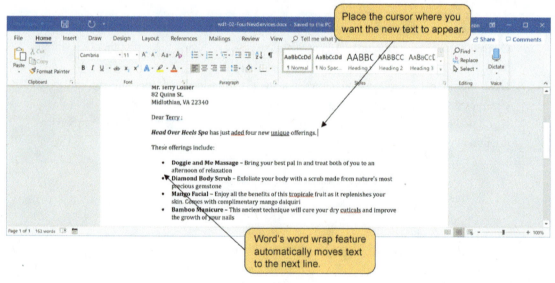

FIGURE WD 1.2

tips & tricks

If you want to force text on to a new line, but do not want to start a new paragraph, press Shift + Enter. This will insert a soft return where the text is moved to a new line without creating a new paragraph.

tell me more

The cursor indicates the place on the page where text will appear when you begin typing, indicated by a blinking vertical line. If you want to edit text you have typed, click in the text to place the cursor anywhere in the document. When you begin typing, the new text will be entered at the cursor point, pushing out any existing text to the right. You can also use the arrow keys to move the cursor around in the document and then begin typing.

let me try Live!

If you do not have the data file from the previous skill open, open the student data file **wd1-02-FourNewServices** and try this skill on your own:

1. Place your cursor at the end of the first paragraph and type the following text:
   `In addition to our longstanding spa services, we have added four new offerings truly unique to Head Over Heels Spa.`
2. Delete the word **truly** from the sentence you typed.
3. If you will be moving on to the next skill in this chapter, leave the document open to continue working. If not, save the file as directed by your instructor and close it.

Skill 1.3 Selecting Text

When you select text in a document, a shaded background appears behind the selected text. You can then apply commands to the text as a group you've selected, such as changing the font or applying the bold effect.

There are several methods for selecting text in a document:

> Click and drag the cursor across the text.
> **To select a single word**: double-click the word.
> **To select a paragraph**: triple-click a word in the paragraph you want to select.
> **To select a line of text**: point to the left margin next to the line you want to select. When the cursor changes to an arrow, click once to select the line of text.

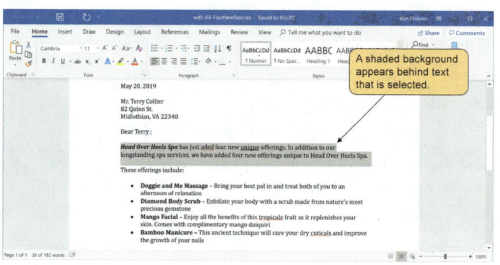

FIGURE WD 1.3

tips & tricks

To select all the text in the document, you can press [Ctrl]+[A] on the keyboard or triple-click the left margin of the document.

another method

To select a paragraph of text, you can also double-click in the left margin next to the paragraph you want to select.

let me try Live!

If you do not have the data file from the previous skill open, open the student data file
wd1-03-FourNewServices ⬇ and try this skill on your own:

1. Select the word **Tranquility**.
2. Select the line **Mr. Terry Collier**.
3. Select the paragraph beginning with **Head Over Heels Spa has just**.
4. If you will be moving on to the next skill in this chapter, leave the document open to continue working. If not, close the file.

Skill 1.4 Checking for Writing Errors as You Type

Microsoft Word can automatically check your document for writing errors as you type. Writing errors include misspellings and grammatical errors. Word can also check for clarity and conciseness and make suggestions to improve your writing. Misspelled words, words that are not part of Word's dictionary, are indicated by a wavy red underline. Grammatical errors appear double-underlined in blue and are based on the grammatical rules that are part of Word's grammar checking feature. Writing suggestions are underlined with a dotted purple line and rely on Office's intelligent services to obtain ever-changing options to improve the writing in your document. When you right-click any type of error, a shortcut menu appears with suggestions for correcting the error and other options.

To correct a writing error:

1. Right-click the red, blue, or purple underlined word.
2. Choose a suggested correction from the shortcut menu.

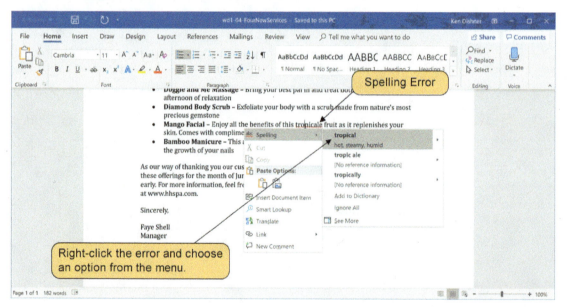

FIGURE WD 1.4

tips & tricks

Although having Word check for writing errors as you type is useful when creating documents, there are times when you may find it distracting. You can choose to turn off the tools for checking for spelling errors or grammar errors. To turn the *Check spelling as you type* and *Mark grammar as you type* features on and off:

1. Click the **File** tab.
2. Click the **Options** button.
3. In the *Word Options* dialog, click the **Proofing** button.
4. In the *When correcting spelling and grammar in Word* section, deselect the **Check spelling as you type** option for spelling errors or the **Mark grammar errors as you type** option for grammatical errors.

tell me more

> Word will not suggest spelling corrections if its dictionary does not contain a word with similar spelling, and Word will not always be able to display grammatical suggestions. In these cases, you must edit the error manually. If the word is spelled correctly, you can choose the **Add to Dictionary** command on the shortcut menu. When you add a word to the dictionary, it will no longer be marked as a spelling error.

> Word's intelligent services rely on communicating with the cloud to provide ever changing options for improving your documents. A number of Office features rely on intelligent services, including Word's *Editor* feature. When intelligent services are enabled, Word provides spelling and writing suggestions based on the surrounding content of the document and provides additional information beyond the spelling suggestion. You can enable and disable the intelligent services through the Word options dialog.

let me try Live!

If you do not have the data file from the previous skill open, open the student data file **wd1-04-FourNewServices** ⬇ and try this skill on your own:

1. Using the right-click method, replace the misspelled word **tropicale** with the correction **tropical**.
2. If you will be moving on to the next skill in this chapter, leave the document open to continue working. If not, save the file as directed by your instructor and close it.

from the perspective of . . .

ADMINISTRATIVE ASSISTANT

It seems like every time I write a memo or a letter, I use all the basic Word skills I learned when I first started using Word. Shortcuts like triple-clicking to select a paragraph of text and cutting and pasting to move text around in a document are tricks I use over and over every day. My boss has terrible eyesight, so every time I review a document with him I am sure to take the zoom up to 150% so he is able to read it better. And trust me, I don't know where I would be without Word's spelling and grammar checker, but no matter what, I always give my documents another read before sending them out to clients.

Skill 1.5 Using the Editor

Regardless of the amount of work you put into a document, a **spelling error** or typo or **grammar error** can make the entire document appear sloppy and unprofessional. All the Office applications include a built-in spelling checker, but Word also includes a grammar checker and writing style checker. In Word, the **Editor** analyzes your entire document for spelling, grammar, clarity, and conciseness errors and displays any potential errors for you to decide how to handle.

To check a document using the *Editor*:

1. Click the **Review** tab.
2. In the *Proofing* group, click the **Spelling & Grammar** button.
3. The first error appears in the *Editor* pane:
   - Potential spelling errors appear with the *Spelling* label near the top of the pane. Review the spelling suggestions and then select an action:
     - Click the correct spelling in the list of suggestions to replace the misspelled word.
     - Point to the correct spelling in the list of suggestions, click the arrow that appears, and select **Change All** to correct all instances of the misspelling in your document.
     - Click **Ignore Once** to make no changes to this instance of the word.
     - Click **Ignore All** to make no changes to all instances of the word.
     - Click **Add to Dictionary** to make no changes to this instance of the word and add it to the main dictionary, so future uses of this word will not show up as misspellings. When you add a word to the main dictionary, it is available for all of the Office applications.

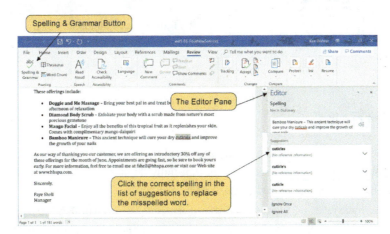

FIGURE WD 1.5

   - Potential grammar errors appear with the *Grammar* label near the top of the pane. Review the grammar suggestions and then select an action:
     - Click a suggestion to make the correction.

- ○ Click **Ignore Once** to skip the grammar error.
- Potential writing errors appear with the *Clarity and Conciseness* label near the top of the pane. Review the suggestions and then select an action:
  - ○ Click a suggestion to make the correction.
  - ○ Click **Ignore Once** to skip the grammar error.

4. After you select an action, the next suspected error is displayed.
5. When the checker finds no more errors, Word displays a message telling you the check is complete. Click **OK** to close the message box and return to your file.

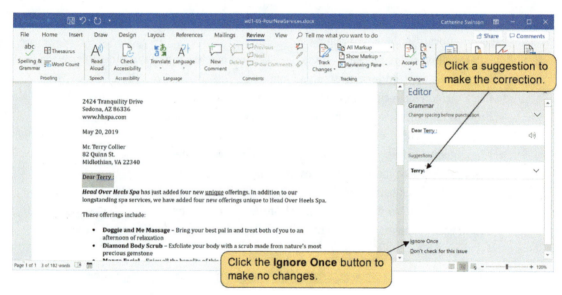

FIGURE WD 1.6

tips & tricks

> Whether or not you use the *Editor*, you should always proofread your files. Spelling and grammar checkers are not foolproof, especially if you misuse a word, yet spell it correctly—for instance, writing "bored" instead of "board."

> If you have repeated the same word in a sentence, Word will flag the second instance of the word as a possible error. In the *Editor* pane, the *Change* button will switch to a *Delete* button. Click the **Delete** button to remove the duplicate word.

another method

To check for spelling and grammar errors in a document, you can also:

> Press the [F7] key
> Click the **Proofing** icon on the status bar.

let me try Live!

If you do not have the data file from the previous skill open, open the student data file
wd1-05-FourNewServices and try this skill on your own:

1. Click at the beginning of the first paragraph in the document.
2. Open the *Editor* to review misspelling and grammar errors in the document.
3. Change the misspelled word **aded** to **added**.
4. Change the misspelled word **cuticals** to **cuticles**.
5. Fix the grammar error, so there is no space before the colon in the greeting line of the letter.
6. If you will be moving on to the next skill in this chapter, leave the document open to continue working. If not, save the file as directed by your instructor and close it.

Skill 1.6 Using Undo and Redo

If you make a mistake when working, the **Undo** command allows you to reverse the last action you performed. The **Redo** command allows you to reverse the *Undo* command and restore the file to its previous state. The Quick Access Toolbar gives you immediate access to both commands.

> To undo the last action taken, click the **Undo** button on the Quick Access Toolbar.
> To redo the last action taken, click the **Redo** button on the Quick Access Toolbar.

To undo multiple actions at the same time:

1. Click the arrow next to the *Undo* button to expand the list of your most recent actions.
2. Click an action in the list.
3. The action you click will be undone, along with all the actions completed after that. In other words, your document will revert to the state it was in before that action.

FIGURE WD 1.7

another method

> To undo an action, you can also press Ctrl + Z on the keyboard.
> To redo an action, you can also press Ctrl + Y on the keyboard.

let me try Live!

If you do not have the data file from the previous skill open, open the student data file **wd1-06-FourNewServices** and try this skill on your own:

1. In the first sentence of the first paragraph, select the word **unique**. Press the **Delete** key to delete the word.
2. Click the **Undo** button to restore the word to the document.
3. Click the **Redo** button to remove the word again.
4. If you will be moving on to the next skill in this chapter, leave the document open to continue working. If not, save the file as directed by your instructor and close it.

Skill 1.7 Finding Text

The **Find** command opens the *Navigation* pane and allows you to search a document for a word or phrase. When you search for a word or phrase in a document using the *Navigation* pane, Word highlights all instances of the word or phrase in the document and displays each instance as a separate result in the pane.

To find a word or phrase in a document:

1. On the *Home* tab, in the *Editing* group, click the **Find** button.
2. The *Navigation* pane appears.
3. Type the word or phrase you want to find in the *Search document* box at the top of the *Navigation* pane.
4. As you type, Word automatically highlights all instances of the word or phrase in the document and displays any results in the task pane.
5. Click a result to navigate to that instance of the word or phrase in the document.

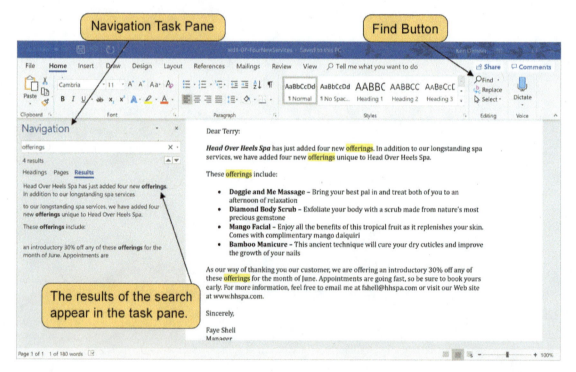

FIGURE WD 1.8

tips & tricks

> The magnifying glass in the Search document box gives you access to more search options. You can choose to search only specific elements in your document, such as tables, graphics, footnotes, or comments. From this menu, you can also open the Find Options dialog. From the Find Options dialog you can set the preferences for searching the document, including matching capitalization, ignoring punctuation, and using wildcard characters in the search.

> Clicking the **X** next to a search word or phrase will clear the search, allowing you to perform a new search.

> To perform more complex searches in your documents, you can use the *Find and Replace* dialog. To open the *Find and Replace* dialog, start on the *Home* tab. In the *Editing* group, click the **Find** button arrow and select **Advanced Find…** The *Find and Replace* dialog opens with the *Find* tab displayed. Click the **More >>** button to expand the *Find and Replace* dialog and view more search options. Here you can choose to find exact matches of words or phrases (including capitalization), search for whole words only, search for special characters, or find formatting in your document. Click the **<< Less** button to collapse the dialog and hide these options.

tell me **more**

In older versions of Microsoft Word, searching for text was performed through the Find and Replace dialog. In Word 2010, Microsoft introduced the Navigation pane as the default method for searching for text in a document.

another method

To display the *Navigation* pane with the *Results* section displayed, you can also:

> Click the **Find** button and select **Find** on the menu.

> Press ⎡Ctrl⎤ + ⎡F⎤ on the keyboard.

let me **try Live!**

If you do not have the data file from the previous skill open, open the student data file **wd1-07-FourNewServices** 📥 and try this skill on your own:

1. Use the *Find* command to search the document for instances of the word **offerings**. You should see four results.
2. If you will be moving on to the next skill in this chapter, leave the document open to continue working. If not, close the file.

Skill 1.8 Replacing Text

The **Replace** command in Word allows you to locate specific instances of text in your document and replace them with different text. With the **Replace All** command, you can replace words or phrases all at once throughout the document.

To replace instances of a word in a document:

1. On the *Home* tab, in the *Editing* group, click the **Replace** button.
2. Type the word or phrase you want to change in the *Find what* box.
3. Type the new text you want in the *Replace with* box.
4. Click **Replace** to replace just that one instance of the text.
5. Click **Replace All** to replace all instances of the word or phrase.
6. Word displays a message telling you how many replacements it made. Click **OK** in the message that appears.
7. To close the *Find and Replace* dialog, click the **Cancel** button.

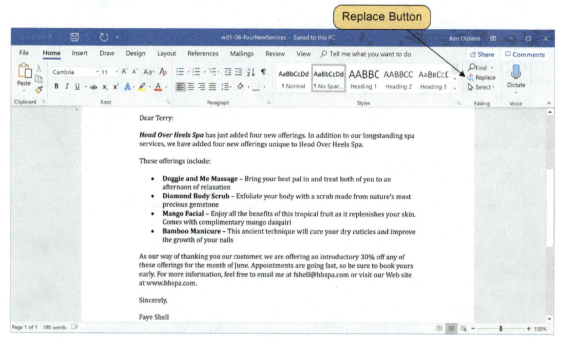

FIGURE WD 1.9

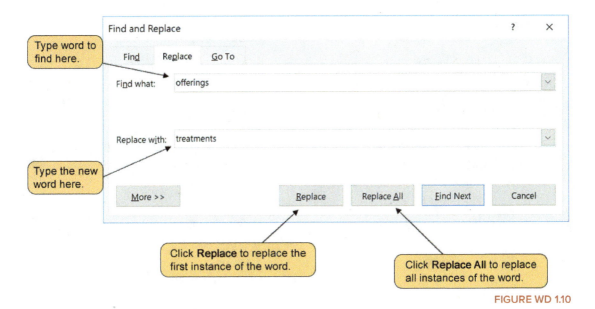

Type word to find here.

Type the new word here.

Click **Replace** to replace the first instance of the word.

Click **Replace All** to replace all instances of the word.

FIGURE WD 1.10

tips & tricks

In addition to text, the *Replace* command can also operate on formatting characters such as italicized text and paragraph marks. The *More >>* button in the *Find and Replace* dialog displays additional options, including buttons that allow you to select formatting and other special characters in the document.

tell me more

The *Go To* tab in the *Find and Replace* dialog allows you to quickly jump to any page, line, section, comment, or other object in your document.

another method

To open the *Find and Replace* dialog with the *Replace* tab displayed, you can also press Ctrl + H on the keyboard.

let me try Live!

If you do not have the data file from the previous skill open, open the student data file **wd1-08-FourNewServices** ⬇ and try this skill on your own:

1. If necessary, place the cursor at the beginning of the document.
2. Open the **Find and Replace** dialog with the *Replace* tab displayed.
3. Replace all instances of **offerings** with **treatments**. There will be four replacements.
4. Click **OK** to close the message box.
5. Click the **Close** button to close the *Find and Replace* dialog.
6. If you will be moving on to the next skill in this chapter, leave the document open to continue working. If not, save the file as directed by your instructor and close it.

Skill **1.9** Using Copy and Paste

The **Copy** command places a duplicate of the selected text or object on the **Clipboard** but does not remove it from your document. You can then use the **Paste** command to insert the text or object into the same document, another document, or another Microsoft Office file, such as an Excel workbook or a PowerPoint presentation.

To copy text and paste it into the same document:

1. Select the text to be copied.
2. On the *Home* tab, in the *Clipboard* group, click the **Copy** button.
3. Place the cursor where you want to insert the text from the *Clipboard*.
4. On the *Home* tab, in the *Clipboard* group, click the **Paste** button.

These same steps apply whether you are copying and pasting text, pictures, shapes, video files, or any type of object in a Word file.

FIGURE WD 1.11

another method

> To apply the *Copy* or *Paste* command, you can also use the following shortcuts:
>
> › *Copy* = Press $\boxed{\text{Ctrl}}$ + $\boxed{\text{C}}$ on the keyboard, or right-click and select **Copy**.
> › *Paste* = Press $\boxed{\text{Ctrl}}$ + $\boxed{\text{V}}$ on the keyboard, or right-click and select **Paste**.

let me try Live!

> If you do not have the data file from the previous skill open, open the student data file **wd1-09-FourNewServices** 🔽 and try this skill on your own:
>
> 1. In the last sentence of the last paragraph, select the text **fshell@hhspa.com**.
> 2. Copy the text to the *Clipboard*.
> 3. Place the cursor in the blank line at the end of the document (under the word *Manager*). Paste the copied text.
> 4. If you will be moving on to the next skill in this chapter, leave the document open to continue working. If not, save the file as directed by your instructor and close it.

Skill 1.10 Using Cut and Paste

The *Copy* command is great if you want to duplicate content in your document, but what if you want to move content from one place to another? The **Cut** command is used to move text and other objects within a file and from one file to another. Text, or an object that is cut, is *removed* from the file and placed on the *Clipboard* for later use. You can then use the *Paste* command to insert the text or object into the same document, another document, or another Microsoft Office file.

To cut text and paste it into the same document:

1. Select the text to be cut.
2. On the *Home* tab, in the *Clipboard* group, click the **Cut** button.
3. Place the cursor where you want to insert the text from the *Clipboard*.
4. On the *Home* tab, in the *Clipboard* group, click the **Paste** button.

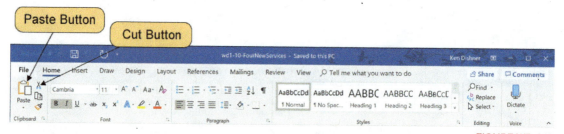

FIGURE WD 1.12

another method

To apply the *Cut* or *Paste* command, you can also use the following shortcuts:

> *Cut* = Press [Ctrl] + [X] on the keyboard, or right-click and select **Cut**.
> *Paste* = Press [Ctrl] + [V] on the keyboard, or right-click and select **Paste**.

let me try Live!

If you do not have the data file from the previous skill open, open the student data file **wd1-10-FourNewServices** and try this skill on your own:

1. Select the last bullet point in the bulleted list in the document. It is the *Bamboo Manicure* bullet point.
2. Cut the selected text. If necessary, delete the extra empty bullet point at the end of the list.
3. Place the cursor at the beginning of the **Mango Facial** bullet point.
4. Paste the cut bullet point. If necessary, press [Enter] to create two bullet points in the list.
5. If you will be moving on to the next skill in this chapter, leave the document open to continue working. If not, save the file as directed by your instructor and close it.

Skill **1.11** Using Paste Options

When you cut or copy an item, whether it be a piece of text, a chart, or an image, Word gives you a variety of ways to paste the item into your document. If you click the bottom part of the *Paste* button (the *Paste* button arrow), you can control how the item is pasted. Each type of object has different paste options. The four **paste options** for pasting text include:

> **Keep Source Formatting** – pastes the text and any formatting that was applied to the copied text.
> **Merge Formatting** – pastes the text to match the formatting of the surrounding text.
> **Picture** – pastes the text as a single picture object rather than individual characters.
> **Keep Text Only** – pastes the text without any formatting that was applied to the copied text.

To paste text using paste options:

1. Place your cursor where you want to paste the text.
2. On the *Home* tab, in the *Clipboard* group, click the **Paste** button arrow.
3. Roll your mouse over each of the paste options to see how the text will appear when pasted. Click an option to paste the text.

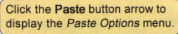
Click the **Paste** button arrow to display the *Paste Options* menu.

FIGURE WD 1.13

tips & tricks

When you paste text using the *Paste* button, Word pastes the text using the keep source formatting option.

tell me **more**

Different object types have different paste options to choose from. Pictures, shapes, SmartArt diagrams, and charts can all be pasted using the same formatting as the original source object or can be pasted as a picture. If the object is pasted as a picture, any formatting or customization applied becomes part of the pasted object and cannot be removed. So, if you want to be able to modify the pasted object, you should use the *Keep Source Formatting* paste option.

another method

To paste text using paste options, you can also right-click and select an option under *Paste Options* on the menu.

let me **try** Live!

If you do not have the data file from the previous skill open, open the student data file **wd1-11-FourNewServices** ⬇ and try this skill on your own:

1. Select the text **Head Over Heels Spa** at the beginning of the first paragraph and copy the text to the *Clipboard*.
2. Place the cursor before **Manager** in the second to last line of the document.
3. Paste the text using the **Keep Text Only** paste command.
4. If you will be moving on to the next skill in this chapter, leave the document open to continue working. If not, save the file as directed by your instructor and close it.

Skill 1.12 Using the Clipboard

When you cut or copy items, they are placed on the *Clipboard*. The *Clipboard* can store up to 24 items for use in the current document or any other Office application. The most recently copied items appear at the top of the pane while the oldest items appear at the bottom of the pane. The *Clipboard* is common across all Office applications—so you can cut text from a Word document and then paste that text into a PowerPoint presentation or copy a chart from Excel into a Word document.

To copy and paste an item from the *Clipboard* into a document:

1. On the *Home* tab, in the *Clipboard* group, click the **Clipboard** dialog launcher to display the *Clipboard* pane.
2. Select the item you want to copy. This can be in the current Word document or in a file open in another application.
3. Click the Copy button to copy the item.
4. Place your cursor where you want to paste the item in the Word document.
5. Click the item in the *Clipboard* you want to paste in the document.

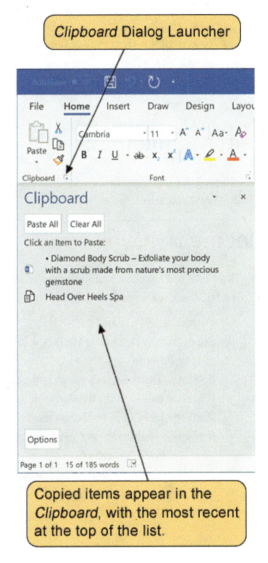

Clipboard Dialog Launcher

Copied items appear in the *Clipboard*, with the most recent at the top of the list.

FIGURE WD 1.14

tips & tricks

> To remove an item from the *Clipboard*, point to the item, click the arrow that appears, and select **Delete**.
> To add all the items in the *Clipboard* at once, click the **Paste All** button at the top of the pane.
> To remove all items from the *Clipboard* at once, click the **Clear All** button at the top of the pane.

another method

To paste an item, you can also point to the item in the *Clipboard* task pane, click the arrow that appears, and select **Paste**.

let me try Live!

If you do not have the data file from the previous skill open, open the student data file **wd1-12-FourNewServices** and try this skill on your own:

1. Display the **Clipboard**.
2. Select the text **Head Over Heels Spa** in the signature line (before the word *Manager*) and copy it to the *Clipboard*.
3. Select the **Diamond Body Scrub** bullet point and copy it to the *Clipboard*.
4. Place the cursor in the blank line at the top of the document.
5. Paste the **Head Over Heels Spa** text from the *Clipboard*.
6. If you will be moving on to the next skill in this chapter, leave the document open to continue working. If not, save the file as directed by your instructor and close it.

Skill 1.13 Zooming a Document

When you first open a document, you may find that the text is too small to read, or that you cannot see the full layout of a page. Use the **zoom slider** in the lower-right corner of the window to zoom in and out of a document, changing the size of text and images onscreen. **Zooming** a document affects only how the document appears on-screen. It does not affect how the document will print.

To zoom in on a document, making the text and graphics appear larger:

> ❯ Click and drag the **zoom slider** to the right.
> ❯ Click the **Zoom In** button (the button with the plus sign on it) on the slider.

To zoom out of a document, making the text and graphics appear smaller:

> ❯ Click and drag the **zoom slider** to the left.
> ❯ Click the **Zoom Out** button (the button with the minus sign on it) on the slider.

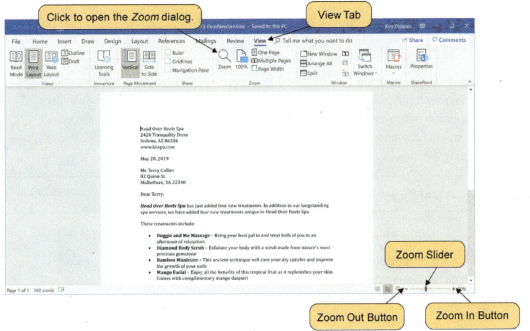

FIGURE WD 1.15

You can use the *Zoom* dialog to apply a number of display presets:

> **Page width**—changes the zoom so the width of the page including margins fills the screen.
> **Text width**—changes the zoom so the width of the page not including margins fills the screen.
> **Whole page**—changes the zoom so the entire page, both vertically and horizontally, displays on the screen. This is a helpful view when working with a page's layout.
> **Many pages**—changes the zoom to display anywhere from one to six pages on the screen at once.

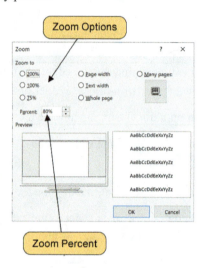

FIGURE WD 1.16

tips & tricks

As you move the slider, the zoom level displays the percentage the document has been zoomed in or out. When zooming a document, 100% is the default zoom level. If you work on a large monitor at a high resolution and need to display your document at a higher zoom percentage, Word will retain the zoom level you set as the new default when opening documents. You won't need to increase the zoom level every time you open a document.

another method

You also can change the zoom level through the *Zoom* dialog. To open the *Zoom* dialog:

1. Click the **zoom level number** next to the zoom slider OR click the **View** tab. In the *Zoom* group, click the **Zoom** button.
2. Click a **zoom preset** or type the **zoom percentage** in the *Percent* box.
3. Click **OK**.

let me try Live!

If you do not have the data file from the previous skill open, open the student data file **wd1-13-FourNewServices** and try this skill on your own:

1. Change the zoom level of the document to **80%**.
2. Change the zoom level of the document back to **100%**.
3. If you will be moving on to the next skill in this chapter, leave the document open to continue working. If not, close the file.

Skill 1.14 Using Word Count

Have you ever had to write a 250-word essay or submit a 3,000-word article? You don't need to guess whether your Word document is long enough (or too long). Word's **Word Count** feature provides the current statistics of the document you are working on, including the number of pages, number of words, number of characters (with and without spaces), number of paragraphs, and number of lines.

To view document statistics:

1. From the *Review* tab, in the *Proofing* group, click the **Word Count** button.
2. The *Word Count* dialog opens and displays the statistics for the document.
3. By default, the document statistics include the text in text boxes, footnotes, and endnotes. To exclude text in these areas, click the **Include textboxes, footnotes, and endnotes** check box to remove the checkmark.
4. Click **Close** to close the dialog.

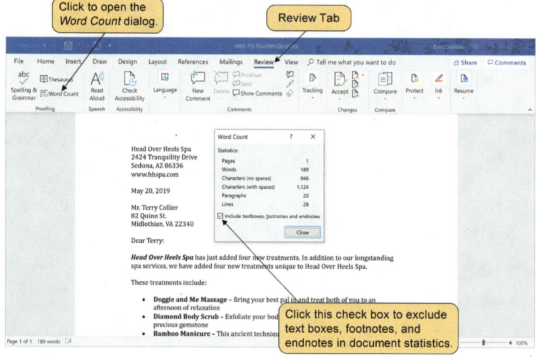

FIGURE WD 1.17

tips & tricks

The number of words and the number of pages in the document are also displayed on the status bar at the bottom of the Word window and as part of the document properties available from the *Info* tab in Backstage view.

another method

To open the *Word Count* dialog, you can also click **Words** on the status bar at the bottom of the Word window.

let me try Live!

If you do not have the data file from the previous skill open, open the student data file **wd1-14-FourNewServices** and try this skill on your own:

1. Open the **Word Count** dialog.
2. Note the number of words in the letter along with other document statistics.
3. Close the **Word Count** dialog.
4. If you will be moving on to the next skill in this chapter, leave the document open to continue working. If not, close the file.

Skill 1.15 Using Views

By default, Microsoft Word displays documents in Print Layout view, but you can display your documents in a number of other ways. Each view has its own purpose, and considering what you want to do with your document will help determine which view is most appropriate to use.

To switch between different views, click the appropriate icon located in the lower-right corner of the status bar next to the zoom slider.

> **Read Mode**—Use this view when you want to review a document. Read Mode presents the document in an easy-to-read format. In this view, the Ribbon is no longer visible. To navigate between screens, use the navigation buttons on the left and right side of the window.

> **Print Layout view**—Use this view to see how document elements will appear on a printed page. This view will help you edit headers and footers, and adjust margins and layouts.

> **Web Layout view**—Use this view when designing documents that will be viewed on-screen, such as a Web page. Web Layout view displays all backgrounds, drawing objects, and graphics as they will appear on-screen. Unlike Print Layout view, Web Layout view does not show page edges, margins, or headers and footers.

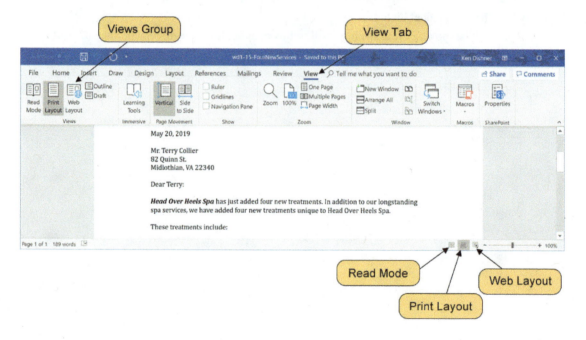

FIGURE WD 1.18

tell me **more**

In previous versions of Word, *Outline* view and *Draft* view were accessible from the status bar. In Word, you access these views only from the *View* tab:

> **Outline view**—Use this view to check the structure of your document. In Outline view, you can collapse the document's structure to view just the top-level headings or expand the structure to see the document's framework. Outline view is most helpful when you use a different style for each type of heading in your document.

> **Draft view**—Use this simplified layout view when typing and formatting text. Draft view does not display headers and footers, page edges, backgrounds, or drawing objects.

another method

To switch views, you also can click the **View** tab and select a view from the *Views* group.

let me **try** Live!

If you do not have the data file from the previous skill open, open the student data file **wd1-15-FourNewServices** ⬇ and try this skill on your own:

1. Switch to **Read Mode**.
2. Switch to **Web Layout** view.
3. Switch back to **Print Layout** view.
4. If you will be moving on to the next skill in this chapter, leave the document open to continue working. If not, close the file.

Skill 1.16 Previewing and Printing a Document

In Word, all the print settings are combined in a single page along with a preview of how the printed document will look. From the **Print page** in Backstage view, you can preview and print all the pages in your document.

To preview and print a document:

1. Click the **File** tab to open Backstage view.
2. Click **Print**.
3. At the right side of the page is a preview of how the printed document will look. Beneath the preview there is a page count. If there are multiple pages, click the next and previous arrows to preview all the pages in the document.
4. Verify that the correct printer name is displayed in the *Printer* section.
5. Click the **Print** button to print.

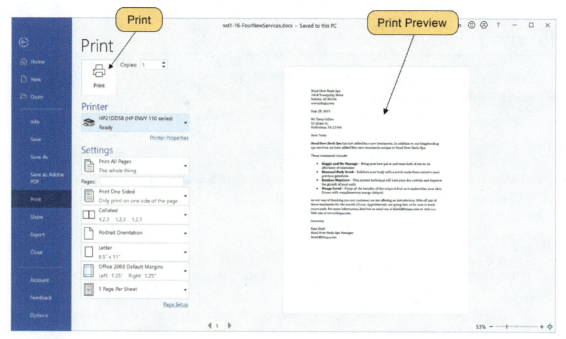

FIGURE WD 1.19

another method

To display the *Print* page, you can also press Ctrl + P.

let me try Live!

If you do not have the data file from the previous skill open, open the student data file **wd1-16-FourNewServices** and try this skill on your own:

1. Display the **Print** page in Backstage view.
2. Print the document. **NOTE:** If you are using this in class or in your school's computer lab, check with your instructor about printing permissions before completing this step.
3. Save the file as directed by your instructor and close it.

key terms

Font	Undo
Paragraph	Redo
Styles	Find
Theme	Replace
Table	Replace All
Chart	Copy
Graphics	Clipboard
Header	Paste
Footer	Cut
Page Break	Paste options
Margin	Zoom slider
Citations	Zooming
Comment	Word Count
Track Changes	Read Mode
Intelligent Services	Print Layout view
Word wrap	Web Layout view
Spelling error	Outline view
Grammar error	Draft view
Editor	Print page

concept review

1. Which of the following actions is used to select a paragraph of text?
    a. single-click the paragraph
    b. double-click the paragraph
    c. triple-click the paragraph
    d. click in the left margin next to the paragraph

2. Grammatical errors in a document are represented by a .
    a. red double underline
    b. blue double underline
    c. red wavy underline
    d. blue wavy underline

3. Which feature in Word automatically places text on the next line when the right margin of the document has been reached?
    a. styles
    b. zoom slider
    c. word wrap
    d. status bar

4. Which command would you use to copy text to the Clipboard and remove it from the document?
    a. Copy
    b. Cut
    c. Undo
    d. Redo

5. Which paste option pastes the text with the original formatting of the copied text?
    a. Keep Source Formatting
    b. Merge Formatting
    c. Keep Text Only
    d. Picture

6. Which command would you use to replace all instances of a word with another word?
    a. Find
    b. Replace
    c. Replace All
    d. Paste All

7. The primary method for finding text in a document is to use the .
    a. Find and Replace dialog
    b. Navigation pane
    c. Clipboard pane
    d. Go To dialog

8. In the *Editor* pane, which command will prevent the word from being marked as a misspelling in all the Office applications, not just Word?

    a. Ignore

    b. Ignore All

    c. Change All button

    d. Add to Dictionary

9. Which would you use to magnify the text on-screen, making the text appear larger?

    a. Zoom Out button

    b. Zoom In button

    c. Page Width command

    d. 100% command

10. In addition to the number of words in a document, the *Word Count* dialog also displays .

    a. the number of tables

    b. the number of charts

    c. the number of pages

    d. the number of images

projects
skill review **1.1**

Data files for projects can be found by logging into your SIMnet account and going to the Library section.

In this project you will be editing the text of a brochure for the Suarez Agency. First, you will reset the magnification of the document. You will then enter, select, and delete text. You will fix spelling and grammar errors in the document. You will edit the document using the *Find* and *Replace* commands as well as the *Cut* and *Paste* commands. Finally, you will review the document statistics using the *Word Count* dialog.

Skills needed to complete this project:

- Zooming a Document (Skill 1.13)
- Entering and Deleting Text (Skill 1.2)
- Selecting Text (Skill 1.3)
- Checking Writing Errors as You Type (Skill 1.4)
- Using the Editor (Skill 1.5)
- Finding Text (Skill 1.7)
- Replacing Text (Skill 1.8)
- Using Cut and Paste (Skill 1.10)
- Using Word Count (Skill 1.14)

Alternate This image appears when a project instruction has changed to accommodate an update to **Microsoft Office 365**. If the instruction does not match your version of Office, try using the alternate instruction instead.

1. Open the start file **WD2019-SkillReview-1-1** and resave the file as:
   `[your initials] WD-SkillReview-1-1`
2. If the document opens in Protected view, click the **Enable Editing** button in the Message Bar at the top of the document so you can modify the document.
3. Change how the document is displayed on your computer by clicking the **Zoom Out** button next to the *Zoom slider* one time so the magnification is **decreased by 10%**.
4. Add text to the document.
   a. Place the cursor on the empty line following the phone number.
   b. Type the following heading: `Our Goal`
   c. Press **Enter**.
   d. Type the following text: `We are dedicated to listening to your needs and working with you to develop a strategic plan to grow your business.`

5. Select and delete text from the document.

    a. In the paragraph under the *Experience* heading, select the text **small** by double-clicking the word.

    b. Press the **Delete** key to remove the text.

6. Check spelling and grammar as you type. Notice how words that Word does not recognize are underlined in red and potential grammar errors are underlined in blue.

    a. Right-click the word **mesage** in the *Experience* section. A list of suggested changes is shown.

    b. Click **message**. Word corrects the spelling of this word.

    c. Right-click the word **is** in the *Client Quotes* section.

    d. Click **are**.

7. Correct spelling and grammar errors using the *Editor* pane.

    a. Press <kbd>Ctrl</kbd> + <kbd>Home</kbd> to move to the top of the document.

    b. Click the **Review** tab.

    c. In the *Proofing* group, click the **Spelling & Grammar** button. The *Editor* pane will open.

    d. For the first error, the text should be **Communication** not **Comunication**. Click **Communication** in the *Suggestions* list to fix the misspelling.

    e. Next, Word finds a grammar error. Click the suggestion in the *Editor* pane to fix the error.

    f. **Alternate** **Morriss** is spelled correctly. Click the *Ignore Once* option in the *Editor* pane.

    g. For the next error, the text is supposed to be **goal** not **gol**. Click **goal** in the *Suggestions* list to fix the misspelling.

    h. A message box appears letting you know the spelling and grammar check is complete. Click **OK** in the message box to close it.

8. Find and replace text in a document.

    a. On the *Home* tab, in the *Editing* group, click the **Find** button.

    b. Type **savvy** in the *Search document* box. You will see two results.

    c. On the *Home* tab, in the *Editing* group, click the **Replace** button.

    d. Notice **savvy** appears in the *Find what* box. If you do not see this, delete any text in the *Find what* box and type the word **savvy** in the box.

    e. Type **know-how** in the *Replace with* box.

    f. Click **Replace All** to replace both instances of the word.

    g. Word displays a message box, indicating that two replacements have been made. Click **OK** in the message box to close it.

    h. Click the **Close** button in the *Find and Replace* dialog.

9. Cut and paste text from one part of the document to another.

   a. Select all the text **in the Suarez Marketing Belief System** at the end of the document (from *The Suarez Marketing Belief System* through *results with integrity*).

   b. On the *Home* tab, in the *Clipboard* group, click the **Cut** button to remove the text and copy it to the *Clipboard*.

   c. Navigate back to the first page and place the cursor at the beginning of **Client Quotes**.

   d. On the *Home* tab, in the *Clipboard* group, click the **Paste** button to paste the text. If necessary, press **Enter** to place **Client Quotes** on its own line.

10. View the statistics for the document.

    a. Click the **Review** tab.

    b. In the *Proofing* group, click the **Word Count** button.

    c. Review the number of pages, words, and paragraphs in the document. Click the **Close** button to close the *Word Count* dialog.

11. Save and close the document.

projects

skill review 1.2

Data files for projects can be found by logging into your SIMnet account and going to the Library section.

In this project, you will be editing the agenda for the Tri-State Book Festival. First, you will change views and adjust the zoom level for the document. You will add and remove text from the document, move text around using the cut and paste commands, and find and replace snippets of text. Finally, you will ensure there are no spelling and grammar errors in the document and then print the document.

Skills needed to complete this project:

- Using Views (Skill 1.15)
- Zooming a Document (Skill 1.13)
- Entering and Deleting Text (Skill 1.2)
- Selecting Text (Skill 1.3)
- Finding Text (Skill 1.7)
- Replacing Text (Skill 1.8)
- Using Copy and Paste (Skill 1.9)
- Using Cut and Paste (Skill 1.10)
- Checking Writing Errors as You Type (Skill 1.4)
- Using the Editor (Skill 1.5)
- Previewing and Printing a Document (Skill 1.16)

1. Open the start file **WD2019-SkillReview-1-2** and resave the file as:
   `[your initials] WD-SkillReview-1-2`
2. If the document opens in Protected view, click the **Enable Editing** button in the Message Bar at the top of the document so you can modify the document.
3. Click the **Read Mode** button on the status bar to view the document in *Read Mode*. Click the **Print Layout** button on the status bar to switch back to Print Layout view.
4. Change how the document is displayed on your computer by clicking the **Zoom In** button next to the *Zoom slider* one time so the magnification is **increased by 10%**.
5. Add text to the document.
   a. Place the cursor on the empty line between *Authors* and *Fiction*.
   b. Type the following text: `The following is a list of authors who will be attending the festival and will be participating in moderated panels. Check the festival agenda for times and locations.`

6. Select and delete text from the document.

   a. In the list of authors, there are two entries for **David Chase**. Select one of the instances of the name.

   b. Press the **Delete** key to remove the text. If there is an extra blank line, press the **Delete** key again to remove it.

7. Find and replace text in a document.

   a. Press $\boxed{\text{Ctrl}}$ + $\boxed{\text{Home}}$ on the keyboard to navigate to the beginning of the document.

   b. On the *Home* tab, in the *Editing* group, click the **Find** button.

   c. Type **event** in the *Search document* box. You will see three results.

   d. On the *Home* tab, in the *Editing* group, click the **Replace** button.

   e. Notice **event** appears in the *Find what* box. If you do not see this, delete any text in the *Find what* box and type the word **event** in the box.

   f. Type **festival** in the *Replace with* box.

   g. Click **Replace All** to replace all instances of the word.

   h. Word displays a message box, indicating that three replacements have been made. Click **OK** in the message box to close it.

   i. Click the **Close** button in the *Find and Replace* dialog.

8. Copy and paste text in a document.

   a. Select the text **Showcased work:** in the *Authors* section of the document. Be sure to select the space after the colon as well.

   b. On the *Home* tab, in the *Clipboard* group, click the **Copy** button to copy the text to the *Clipboard*.

   c. Place the cursor before the text **Living with Big Foot**.

   d. On the *Home* tab, in the *Clipboard* group, click the **Paste** button to paste the text.

9. Cut and paste text from one part of the document to another.

   a. On the second page of the document, select the text **Catherine Cartwright**.

   b. On the *Home* tab, in the *Clipboard* group, click the **Cut** button to remove the text and copy it to the *Clipboard*.

   c. Place the cursor before *Showcased work: A Guide to Eating Out and Eating Well*.

   d. On the *Home* tab, in the *Clipboard* group, click the **Paste** button to paste the text. If *Showcased work: A Guide to Eating Out and Eating Well* appears on the same line as the pasted text, press **Enter** to move the text to a new line.

10. Check spelling and grammar as you type. Notice how words that Word does not recognize are underlined in red and potential grammar errors are underlined in blue.
    a. Press [Ctrl] + [Home] on the keyboard to navigate to the beginning of the document.
    b. Right-click the word **attende** in the second paragraph on the first page of the document. A list of suggested changes is shown.
    c. Click **attendee**. Word corrects the spelling of this word.
    d. Right-click the word **non fiction** in the first paragraph.
    e. Click **nonfiction**.
11. Correct spelling and grammar errors using the *Editor* pane.
    a. Click the **Review** tab. In the *Proofing* group, click the **Spelling & Grammar** button. The *Editor* pane will open.
    b. The first error in the document is a grammar error the text should be **an**, not **a**. Click the correct option in the list of suggestions.
    c. Next, Word finds a spelling error. Correct the misspelling to **available**.
    d. Next, Word thinks there is a repeated word in the title *Drawing in Real Real Life*. There is no error. Click the **Ignore Once** button to move on and not make any changes.
    e. If Word flags the name *Swinson* as a misspelling, click the **Ignore Once** button.
    f. Word finds another spelling error. Correct the misspelling to **Better**.
    g. A message box appears letting you know the spelling and grammar check is complete. Click **OK** in the message box to close it.
12. Print the document.
    a. Click the **File** tab and click **Print**.
    b. Click the **Print** button. **NOTE**: If you are using this in class or in your school's computer lab, check with your instructor about printing permissions before completing this step.
13. Save and close the document.

projects

Data files for projects can be found by logging into your SIMnet account and going to the Library section.

challenge yourself **1.3**

In this project you will be editing a cover letter for a marketing manager position. You will edit the content of the letter by adding and deleting text and replacing text within the document. You will move text around using the *Cut* and *Paste* commands. You will use the spelling and grammar checker to find and fix spelling and grammar errors.

Skills needed to complete this project:

- Zooming a Document (Skill 1.13)
- Selecting Text (Skill 1.3)
- Using Copy and Paste (Skill 1.9)
- Using Paste Options (Skill 1.11)
- Entering and Deleting Text (Skill 1.2)
- Finding Text (Skill 1.7)
- Replacing Text (Skill 1.8)
- Using Cut and Paste (Skill 1.10)
- Using the Editor (Skill 1.5)
- Using Word Count (Skill 1.14)

1. Open the start file **WD2019-ChallengeYourself-1-3** and resave the file as:
   `[your initials] WD-ChallengeYourself-1-3`
2. If the document opens in Protected view, click the **Enable Editing** button in the Message Bar at the top of the document so you can modify the document.
3. If necessary, change the zoom level to view the document at 100% magnification.
4. Select the name **Suarez** from the address block and copy it to the Clipboard.
5. Place the cursor after *Dear Ms.* in the salutation. Paste the copied text using the *Keep Text Only* paste option. Add a colon after the name.
6. Place the cursor at the end of the first paragraph (after the text *marketing manager position.*) Press the **Spacebar** one time and type the following text:
   `After reviewing the job description, I am certain that my marketing expertise is a perfect match for this position with your organization.`
7. Add `, including:` at the end of the second paragraph, beginning with *I am certain.*
8. Remove the typing using the *Undo* command.
9. Re-apply the typing using the *Redo* command.
10. Select the word **urgently** in the last paragraph of the document and delete it.
11. Use the *Find* command to locate all instances of the word **skills** in the document.
12. Use the *Replace* command to replace the third instance of the word **skills** with the word **experience**.

13. Use the *Cut* and *Paste* commands to move the first bullet point in the list, the one beginning with *Extensive proficiency*, so it appears below the bullet point beginning with *Ability to think*.

14. Copy the last name **Smith** from the address block.

15. Place the cursor after the name Jessica at the bottom of the document. Paste the copied text using the *Keep Text Only* paste option.

16. Check spelling and grammar in the letter.

    a. Ignore the misspelling of the word **Streecker** in the address block.

    b. Correct the misspelling of the word **dicuss** in the first sentence of the last paragraph.

    c. Correct the grammar mistake **you're** in the third sentence of the last paragraph.

17. Use the Word Count dialog to review the number of words, paragraphs, and pages in the document.

18. Save and close the document.

projects

Data files for projects can be found by logging into your SIMnet account and going to the Library section.

challenge yourself **1.4**

In this project, you will be editing a safety strategies report for the Spring Hills Community. You will change the view and adjust the zoom level to make working in the document easier. You will fill in information and correct errors in the document. You will practice copying and pasting text. You will check the document for spelling and grammar errors and use the *Find* and *Replace* commands to substitute one word for another. Finally, you will check the document's statistics and print the document.

Skills needed to complete this project:

- Using Views (Skill 1.15)
- Zooming a Document (Skill 1.13)
- Selecting Text (Skill 1.3)
- Using Copy and Paste (Skill 1.9)
- Entering and Deleting Text (Skill 1.2)
- Checking Writing Errors as You Type (Skill 1.4)
- Using the Editor (Skill 1.5)
- Finding Text (Skill 1.7)
- Replacing Text (Skill 1.8)
- Using Word Count (Skill 1.14)
- Previewing and Printing a Document (Skill 1.16)

1. Open the start file **WD2019-ChallengeYourself-1-4** and resave the file as:
   `[your initials] WD-ChallengeYourself-1-4`
2. If the document opens in Protected view, click the **Enable Editing** button in the Message Bar at the top of the document so you can modify the document.
3. Switch to **Read Mode**, and then switch back to **Print Layout** view.
4. Adjust the zoom level so it is set to **110%**.
5. Navigate to the list of full-time officers on the second page of the document.
6. Select **(5 years)** next to *Tyler Fuller* and copy the text to the *Clipboard*.
7. Place the cursor after *Emile Berry* and paste the text you copied. Be sure there is a space between the name and the opening parenthesis.
8. Navigate to the beginning of the document and select the text **simple and easy** in the first sentence of the first paragraph. Delete the text.
9. Place the cursor at the end of the first paragraph. Type the following text:
   `The following are basic safety tips provided by our security team to help you stay safe when going out into the community.`

10. Check for and fix all spelling and grammar errors in the document.
11. Find all instances of the word **Manager**.
12. Replace all instances of the word **Manager** with **Supervisor**.
13. Use the *Word Count* dialog to review the number of words, paragraphs, and pages in the document.
14. Print the document. **NOTE**: If you are using this in class or in your school's computer lab, check with your instructor about printing permissions before completing this step.
15. Save and close the document.

projects

on your own 1.5

Data files for projects can be found by logging into your SIMnet account and going to the Library section.

In this project, you will be working on a marketing sheet for a landscape company. You will change the view and adjust the zoom level to make working in the document easier. You will fill in information and correct errors in the document. You will practice using copying text and using the *Clipboard*. You will use the *Find* and *Replace* commands to substitute one word for another.

Skills needed to complete this project:

- Using Views (Skill 1.15)
- Zooming a Document (Skill 1.13)
- Entering and Deleting Text (Skill 1.2)
- Selecting Text (Skill 1.3)
- Using Copy and Paste (Skill 1.9)
- Using the Clipboard (Skill 1.12)
- Using Undo and Redo (Skill 1.6)
- Using Cut and Paste (Skill 1.10)
- Finding Text (Skill 1.7)
- Replacing Text (Skill 1.8)
- Checking Writing Errors as You Type (Skill 1.4)
- Using the Editor (Skill 1.5)
- Using Word Count (Skill 1.14)
- Previewing and Printing a Document (Skill 1.16)

1. Open the start file **WD2019-OnYourOwn-1-5** and resave the file as:
   `[your initials] WD-OnYourOwn-1-5`
2. If the document opens in Protected view, click the **Enable Editing** button in the Message Bar at the top of the document so you can modify the document.
3. If the document opens in *Read Mode*, switch to **Print Layout** view.
4. Adjust the zoom level to one of your choice.
5. On the second page of the document, type the following on the blank line between *Pricing* and *Greenscapes' Service and Pricing*: `Our prices are competitive with other companies in the area. Each of our technicians is trained to provide the highest quality of service in his or her area of specialty.`
6. Practice selecting text by dragging and clicking. Select a word, paragraph, and line in the document.
7. On the second page, change the text **$89.00 per treatment** to read **$119.00 per visit**.

8. Copy several pieces of text to the *Clipboard*. Paste a text piece into the document and then undo the action.

9. Use the *Cut* and *Paste* commands to rearrange the items in the bulleted list in the *Lawn Maintenance* section.

10. Find all instances of the word **unprocessed** and replace each instance with a word of your choice.

11. Fix all the grammar and spelling errors in the document. *Hint*: *Greenscapes* is not misspelled in the document.

12. Check the number of words and pages in the document.

13. Print the document. **NOTE**: If you are using this in class or in your school's computer lab, check with your instructor about printing permissions before completing this step.

14. Save and close the document.

projects

fix it **1.6**

Data files for projects can be found by logging into your SIMnet account and going to the Library section.

In this project, you will be fixing the résumé of an applicant for a marketing assistant position. There are a number of issues with the document that need correcting. First, you will need to adjust the view and zoom level to be able to work comfortably in the document. Next, you will add missing content and correct incorrect content in the résumé. You will move text using the *Cut* and *Paste* commands and find and replace words to help with readability. Finally, you will correct all grammar and spelling errors in the document.

Skills needed to complete this project:

- Using Views (Skill 1.15)
- Zooming a Document (Skill 1.13)
- Entering and Deleting Text (Skill 1.2)
- Selecting Text (Skill 1.3)
- Using Copy and Paste (Skill 1.9)
- Using Cut and Paste (Skill 1.10)
- Finding Text (Skill 1.7)
- Replacing Text (Skill 1.8)
- Checking Writing Errors as You Type (Skill 1.4)
- Using the Editor (Skill 1.5)

1. Open the start file **WD2019-FixIt-1-6** and resave the file as:
   `[your initials] WD-FixIt-1-6`
2. If the document opens in Protected view, click the **Enable Editing** button in the Message Bar at the top of the document so you can modify the document.
3. Switch to **Read Mode**, and then switch back to **Print Layout** view.
4. Adjust the zoom level to **110%**.
5. The summary section is missing. Type the following paragraph under *Summary*:
   `I am an accomplished professional offering a solid history of top performance in the field of marketing with a focus on the health care and publishing industries. I am skilled in managing multiple projects, meeting deadlines, and resolving issues prior to escalation. I am also detail-oriented, well organized and an effective communicator; I enjoy working on a team, but I also work well independently.`
6. Copy the text: **Expert-level knowledge** and paste it after **Microsoft Excel:** and **Microsoft PowerPoint:**.
7. Copy the text **Experienced-level knowledge** and paste it after **Microsoft Project:**.

8. Cut the text **WordPress: Content management**. If there is a blank bullet after cutting the text, delete the extra line.

9. Place the cursor at the beginning of the bulleted item *Microsoft Word: Expert-level knowledge* and paste the text you cut. If necessary, press **Enter** to move *Microsoft Word: Expert-level knowledge* to a new line.

10. At the end of the document, the GPA for Templeton University should be **3.6**. Fix the error.

11. Use the *Find* command to find all instances of **Microsoft**.

12. All five instances of **Microsoft** should read **Microsoft Office 365**. Use the *Replace* command to fix this error.

13. Cut the line **Trained fellow employees in how to use accounting system** and paste it above **Created and maintained a database of customer information**. If necessary, delete any extra blank lines.

14. Right-click the spelling error **Digetal** and fix it using a suggestion on the shortcut menu.

15. Use the *Editor pane* to correct the remaining misspellings and grammar errors in the document. *Hint*: Both *ETech* and *UniHealth* are the names of corporations and are not misspelled.

16. Save and close the document.

chapter **2**

Formatting Text and Paragraphs

In this chapter, you will learn the following skills:

> Apply fonts and style text
> Copy and paste formatting using the Format Painter
> Use bulleted and numbered list to organize information
> Use styles to format text
> Change paragraph alignment and spacing to effectively use white space
> Format the look of paragraphs by adding shading and borders
> Set and use tabs and indents to improve document layout

introduction

This chapter will cover character and paragraph formatting and alignment to enhance the presentation, professionalism, and readability of documents. You will change the look of text by changing the font, font size, and font color. You will use styles and the *Format Painter* tool to copy formatting and apply it to text. You will convert text into numbered and bulleted lists. You will format paragraphs including changing alignment and spacing. Finally, you will indent text both from default commands on the Ribbon as well as from custom tabs that you set.

Skill 2.1 Using Bold, Italic, and Underline

You can call attention to text in your document by using the **bold**, *italic*, or <u>underline</u> effects. These effects are called **character effects** because they are applied to individual characters or words rather than paragraphs. Remember that these effects are used to emphasize important text and should be used sparingly—they lose their effect if overused. You can apply these effects using similar steps:

1. Select the text you want to emphasize.
2. On the *Home* tab, in the *Font* group, click the button of the effect you want to apply:
   - **Bold**—gives the text a heavier, thicker appearance.
   - **Italic**—makes text slant to the right.
   - **Underline**—draws a single line under the text.

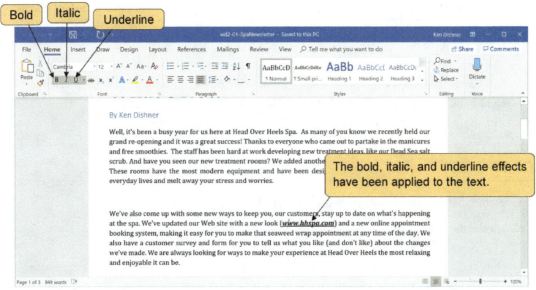

FIGURE WD 2.1

tips & tricks

When text is bolded, italicized, or underlined, the button appears highlighted on the Ribbon. To remove the effect, click the highlighted button, or press the appropriate keyboard shortcut.

tell me **more**

> Some of the other character effects available from the Ribbon include:
>   - **Strikethrough**—draws a horizontal line through the text.
>   - **Subscript**—draws a small character below the bottom of the text.
>   - **Superscript**—draws a small character above the top of the text
> The *Font* dialog contains other character formatting options not available from the Ribbon. These effects include **Double strikethrough**, **Small caps**, and **All caps** among others. To open the *Font* dialog, on the *Home* tab, in the *Font* group, click the dialog launcher. Select an option in the *Effects* section and click **OK** to apply the character effect to the text.

another method

> The following keyboard shortcuts can be used to apply the bold, italic, and underline effects:
>   - Bold = `Ctrl` + `B`
>   - Italic = `Ctrl` + `I`
>   - Underline = `Ctrl` + `U`
> To access the bold, italic, or underline commands, you can also right-click the selected text and click the **Bold**, **Italic**, or **Underline** button on the Mini toolbar.
> To apply an underline style, click the **Underline** button arrow and select a style.

let me **try** Live!

Open the student data file **wd2-01-SpaNewsletter** and try this skill on your own:

1. Select the text **free smoothies** in the first paragraph of the newsletter.
2. Apply the **bold** character formatting to the text.
3. Select the text **online appointment booking system** in the second paragraph of the newsletter.
4. Apply the **italic** and **underline** character formatting to the text.
5. If you will be moving on to the next skill in this chapter, leave the document open to continue working. If not, save the file as directed by your instructor and close it.

Skill 2.2 Changing Fonts

A **font**, or typeface, refers to a set of characters of a certain design. The font is the shape of a character or number as it appears onscreen or in a printed document.

To change the font:

1. Select the text to be changed.
2. On the *Home* tab, click the arrow next to the *Font* box.
3. As you roll over the list of fonts, the Live Preview feature in Word changes the look of the text in your document, giving you a preview of how the text will look with the new font applied.
4. Click a font name from the menu to apply it to the text.

> Cambria is a serif font.
>
> Calibri is a sans serif font.

FIGURE WD 2.2

Word offers many fonts. **Serif fonts**, such as Cambria and Times New Roman, have an embellishment at the end of each stroke. **Sans serif fonts**, such as Calibri and Arial, do not have an embellishment at the end of each stroke. Sans serif fonts are easier to read on-screen and should be used for the main body text for documents that will be delivered and read electronically, such as a blog. Serif fonts are easier to read on the printed page and should be used for documents that will be printed, such as a report.

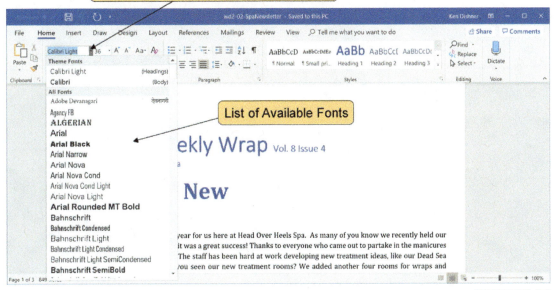

Click the arrow to display the list of fonts.

List of Available Fonts

FIGURE WD 2.3

tips & tricks

If you want to change the font of an individual word, you can place your cursor in the word you want to modify, then select the new font.

another method

To change the font you can also right-click the text, click the arrow next to the *Font* box on the Mini toolbar, and select a font from the list.

let me try Live!

If you do not have the data file from the previous skill open, open the student data file **wd2-02-SpaNewsletter** and try this skill on your own:

1. Select the article title **What's New** on the first page of the newsletter.
2. Change the font to **Calibri Light (Headings)**.
3. If you will be moving on to the next skill in this chapter, leave the document open to continue working. If not, save the file as directed by your instructor and close it.

Skill 2.3 Changing Font Sizes

When creating a document, it is important not only to choose the correct or best font, but also to use the appropriate font size. Fonts are measured in **points**, abbreviated "pt." On the printed page, 72 points equal one inch. Different font sizes are used for the words in the paragraphs and for the headers in a document. The paragraphs of text typically use 10 pt., 11 pt., and 12 pt. fonts. Headers often use 14 pt., 16 pt., and 18 pt. fonts.

To change the size of the font:

1. Select the text to be changed.
2. On the *Home* tab, in the *Font* group, click the arrow next to the *Font Size* box.
3. Scroll the list to find the new font size.
4. Click the size you want.

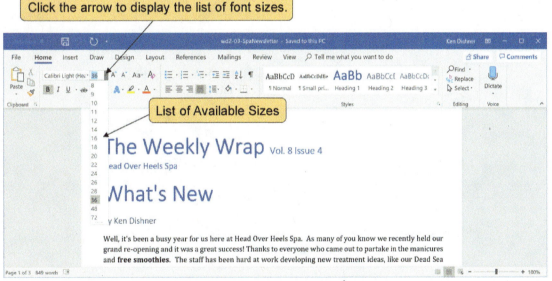

FIGURE WD 2.4

tips & tricks

Sometimes when you are formatting text, you may not be sure of the exact size you want your text to be. You can experiment with the look of text in your document by incrementally increasing and decreasing the size of the font. Use the *Grow Font* or *Shrink Font* button, available in the *Font* group, to change the font size by one increment.

another method

To change the font you can also right-click the text, click the arrow next to the **Font Size** box on the Mini toolbar, and select a font size from the list.

let me try Live!

If you do not have the data file from the previous skill open, open the student data file **wd2-03-SpaNewsletter** and try this skill on your own:

1. If necessary, select the article title **What's New** on the first page of the newsletter.
2. Change the font size to **22 pt**.
3. If you will be moving on to the next skill in this chapter, leave the document open to continue working. If not, save the file as directed by your instructor and close it.

Skill 2.4 Changing Text Case

When you type on a keyboard you use the ⌷Shift⌷ key to capitalize individual letters and the ⌷Caps Lock⌷ key to type in all capital letters. Another way to change letters from lowercase to uppercase, and vice versa, is to use the **Change Case** command. When you use the *Change Case* command in Word, you are manipulating the characters that were typed, changing how the letters are displayed. There are five types of text case formats you can apply to text:

> **Sentence case**–formats text as a sentence with the first word being capitalized and all remaining words beginning with a lowercase letter.
> **lowercase**–changes all letters to lowercase.
> **UPPERCASE**–changes all letters to uppercase, or capital letters.
> **Capitalize Each Word**–formats text so each word begins with a capital letter.
> **tOGGLE cASE**–formats text in the reverse of the typed format, converting uppercase letters to lowercase and lowercase letters to uppercase.

To apply text case formatting to text:

1. Select the text you want to change.
2. On the *Home* tab, in the *Font* group, click the **Change Case** button.
3. Select a text case option from the menu to apply it to the text.

FIGURE WD 2.5

tips & tricks

Headers and titles often use the *Capitalize Each Word* format. One way to ensure that your headers and titles are consistent in text case is to use the *Change Case* command.

tell me more

From the *Font* dialog, you can apply the *All caps* or *Small caps* character formatting to text. Although the *All caps* command produces the same visual results as the *UPPERCASE* command, the core text is different. *All caps* applies character formatting keeping the underlying text the same, while *UPPERCASE* changes the underlying text that was typed to capital letters.

let me try Live!

If you do not have the data file from the previous skill open, open the student data file **wd2-04-SpaNewsletter** and try this skill on your own:

1. Select the text **Vol. 8 Issue 4** in the first line of the document.
2. Use the **Change Case** command to change the letters to all uppercase letters.
3. If you will be moving on to the next skill in this chapter, leave the document open to continue working. If not, save the file as directed by your instructor and close it.

Skill 2.5 Changing Font Colors

Unless you are creating a basic business letter, most documents include graphics, illustrations, and color text. Adding color to text in your document adds emphasis to certain words and helps design elements, such as headers, stand out for your reader.

To change the color of the text:

1. Select the text to be changed.
2. On the *Home* tab, in the *Font* group, click the arrow next to the *Font Color* button.
3. Click the color you want from the color palette.

> Click the arrow to display the font color palette.

FIGURE WD 2.6

tips & tricks

When you change the color of text, the *Font Color* button changes to the color you selected. Click the **Font Color** button to quickly apply the same color to other text in the document.

tell me more

A color theme is a group of predefined colors that works well together in a document. You can apply a color theme to change the color of a number of elements at once. When you change the color theme, the color palette changes and displays only colors that are part of the color theme.

another method

You can change the font color from the Mini toolbar. To display the Mini toolbar, right-click in the text you want to change. Click the arrow next to the *Font Color* button and select the color you want.

let me try Live!

If you do not have the data file from the previous skill open, open the student data file **wd2-05-SpaNewsletter** 🔽 and try this skill on your own:

1. Select the text **I'm So Gelish** on the first page of the document.
2. Change the text to the **Blue, Accent 1, Darker 25%** color. It is the fifth option in the fifth row under *Theme Colors*.
3. If you will be moving on to the next skill in this chapter, leave the document open to continue working. If not, save the file as directed by your instructor and close it.

Skill 2.6 Applying Highlights

Text in a Word document can be highlighted to emphasize or call attention to it. The effect is similar to that of a highlighting marker. When text is highlighted, the background color of the selected area is changed to make it stand out on the page.

Highlighting is very useful when you are sharing a document with coworkers or reviewers. It calls the other person's attention to elements that most need his or her attention. However, highlighting can sometimes be distracting as well. Be careful when using the highlighter in Word; use it only for small amounts of text.

To highlight text in a document:

1. Select the text to be highlighted.
2. On the *Home* tab, in the *Font* group, click the arrow next to the *Text Highlight Color* button.
3. Click the color you want to use.

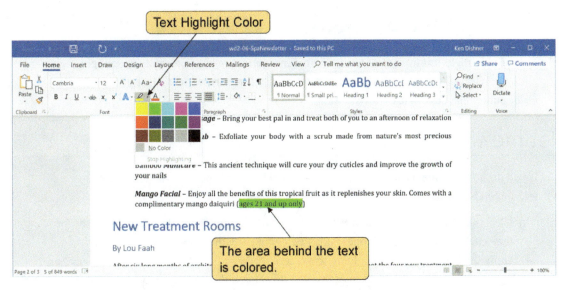

FIGURE WD 2.7

tips & tricks

> Be careful when selecting colors to use for highlighting. If both the color of the text and the highlight color are dark, the text will be hard to read. If the highlight color is too light, it may not give the text enough emphasis.

> To remove highlighting from text, select the highlighted text and then select the **No Color** option at the bottom of the *Text Highlight Color* palette.

tell me more

Rather than applying highlighting to text you have already selected, you can use the highlighter to apply highlighting to text throughout your document. Click the **Text Highlight Color** button without selecting any text first. Your cursor changes to a highlighter shape. Click and drag across text with the highlighter cursor to highlight text. To change your cursor back, click the **Text Highlight Color** button again.

another method

You can highlight text from the Mini toolbar. First, select the text you want to highlight; right-click the selected text to display the Mini toolbar. Click the arrow next to the *Text Highlight Color* button and select the color you want.

let me try Live!

If you do not have the data file from the previous skill open, open the student data file **wd2-06-SpaNewsletter** 📥 and try this skill on your own:

1. Select the text **ages 21 and up** in the *Mango Facial* description on the second page of the newsletter. Do not select the opening and closing parentheses.
2. Apply the **Bright Green** highlighting to the text.
3. If you will be moving on to the next skill in this chapter, leave the document open to continue working. If not, save the file as directed by your instructor and close it.

Skill **2.7** Using Format Painter

When you want to copy text from one part of your document to another, you use the *Copy* and *Paste* commands. What if you don't want to copy the text but instead copy all the formatting from text in one part of your document to text in another part of your document? The **Format Painter** tool allows you to copy formatting styles that have been applied to text. You can then "paste" the formatting, applying it to text anywhere in the document.

To use *Format Painter*:

1. Select the text that has the formatting you want to copy.
2. On the *Home* tab, in the *Clipboard* group, click the **Format Painter** button.
3. Select the text that you want to apply the formatting to.
4. The formats are automatically applied to the selected text.

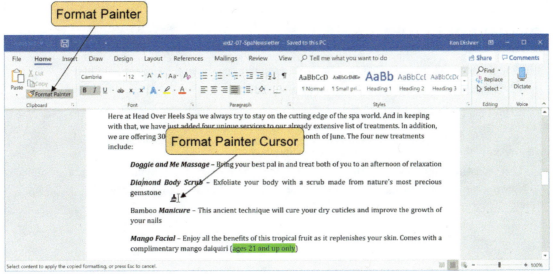

FIGURE WD 2.8

tips & tricks

> ❯ If you want to apply the formats more than once, double-click the **Format Painter** button when you select it. It will stay on until you click the **Format Painter** button again or press **Esc** to deselect it.
>
> ❯ If the text you are copying the formatting from is formatted using a paragraph style, then you don't need to select the entire paragraph. Just place the cursor anywhere in the paragraph and click the **Format Painter** button. To apply the same paragraph style formatting to another paragraph, click anywhere in the paragraph to which you want to apply the formatting.

another method

To activate *Format Painter*, you can right-click the text with formatting you want to copy and click the **Format Painter** button on the Mini toolbar.

let me try Live!

If you do not have the data file from the previous skill open, open the student data file **wd2-07-SpaNewsletter** 📥 and try this skill on your own:

1. Use the **Format Painter** to copy the formatting of the text **Diamond Body Scrub** in the *Four New Services* article.
2. Apply the copied formatting to the word **Bamboo**.
3. If you will be moving on to the next skill in this chapter, leave the document open to continue working. If not, save the file as directed by your instructor and close it.

Skill 2.8 Clearing Formatting

After you have applied a number of character formats and effects to text, you may find that you want to return your text to its original formatting. You could perform multiple undo commands on the text, or you could use the **Clear All Formatting** command. The *Clear All Formatting* command removes any formatting that has been applied to text, including character formatting, text effects, and styles, and leaves only plain text.

To remove formatting from text:

1. Select the text you want to remove the formatting from.
2. On the *Home* tab, in the *Font* group, click the **Clear All Formatting** button.

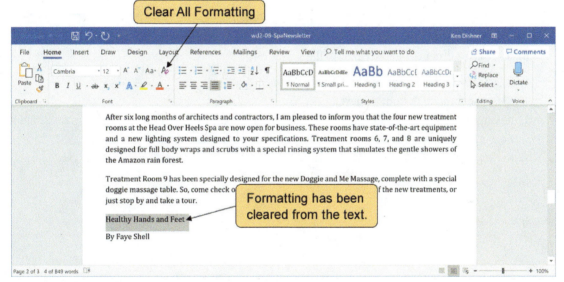

FIGURE WD 2.9

tips & tricks

If you clear the formatting from text and then decide that you want to keep the formatting that was removed, you can use the **Undo** command to apply the previous formatting to the text.

tell me more

The *Clear All Formatting* command does not remove highlighting that has been applied to text. In order to remove highlighting from text, you must click the **Text Highlighting Color** button and select **No Color**.

another method

To clear the formatting from text, you can also:

1. On the *Home* tab, in the *Styles* group, click the **More** button.
2. Click **Clear Formatting**.

let me try Live!

If you do not have the data file from the previous skill open, open the student data file **wd2-08-SpaNewsletter** and try this skill on your own:

1. Select the **Healthy Hands and Feet** article title.
2. Clear the formatting from the text.
3. If you will be moving on to the next skill in this chapter, leave the document open to continue working. If not, save the file as directed by your instructor and close it.

Skill 2.9 Creating Numbered Lists

Some lists, such as directions to complete a task, need to have the items displayed in a specific order. **Numbered lists** display a number next to each list item and display the numbers in order. Numbered lists help you organize your content and display it in a clear, easy-to-understand manner.

To create a numbered list:

1. Select the text you want to change to a numbered list. In order to appear as separate items within a numbered list, each item must be followed by a hard return (press Enter).
2. On the *Home* tab, in the *Paragraph* group, click the **Numbering** button arrow and select an option.
3. Click outside the list to deselect it.

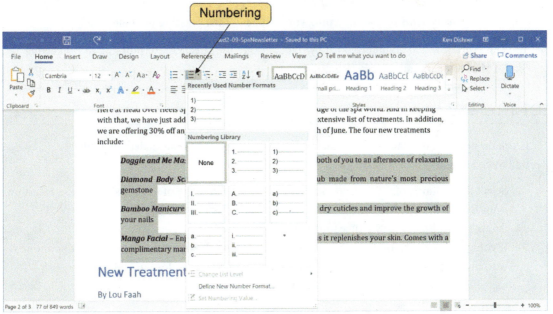

FIGURE WD 2.10

tips & tricks

> Sometimes you will want to add more items to an existing list. To add another item to the list, place your cursor at the end of an item and press Enter to start a new line. The list will renumber itself to accommodate the new item.
> You can turn off the numbering feature by pressing Enter twice.
> You can create new numbered list styles by selecting **Define New Number Format...** at the bottom of the *Numbering* menu.

another method

You can start a numbered list by:

> Typing **1.**, a space, and your list item, then pressing the **Enter** key.
> Clicking the **Numbering** button, typing your list item, then pressing the **Enter** key.

You can convert text to a numbered list by right-clicking the selected text, pointing to **Numbering** on the Mini toolbar, and selecting an option.

let me try Live!

If you do not have the data file from the previous skill open, open the student data file **wd2-09-SpaNewsletter** and try this skill on your own:

1. Select descriptions of the four new services on the second page of the newsletter. Select starting from **Doggie and Me Massage** and ending at **(ages 21 and up only)**.
2. Apply the **a), b), c)** number style to the text.
3. If you will be moving on to the next skill in this chapter, leave the document open to continue working. If not, save the file as directed by your instructor and close it.

Skill 2.10 Creating Bulleted Lists

When typing a document you may want to include information that is best displayed in list format rather than paragraph format. If your list does not include items that need to be displayed in a specific order, use a **bulleted list** to help information stand out from surrounding text. A **bullet** is a symbol that is displayed before each item in a list. When a bullet appears before a list item, it indicates that the items in the list do not have a particular order to them.

To create a bulleted list:

1. Select the text you want to change to a bulleted list. As with numbered lists, in order to appear as separate items within a bulleted list, each item must be followed by a hard return (press Enter).
2. On the *Home* tab, in the *Paragraph* group, click the **Bullets** button.
3. Click outside the list to deselect it.

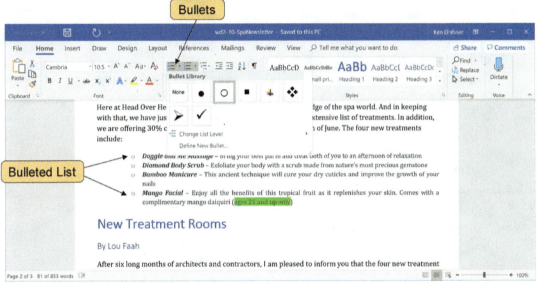

FIGURE WD 2.11

tips & tricks

> Sometimes you will want to add more items to an existing list. Place your cursor at the end of a list item and press Enter to start a new line. A bullet will automatically appear before the list item.

> You can turn off the **Bullets** formatting feature by pressing Enter twice.

tell me **more**

To change the bullet type, click the **Bullets** button arrow and select an option from the *Bullet Library*. You can create new bullets by selecting **Define New Bullet...**

another method

> You can start a bulleted list by typing an asterisk, a space, and your list item, then pressing the [Enter] key.
> You can convert text to a bulleted list by right-clicking the selected text, pointing to **Bullets**, and selecting an option.

let me **try Live!**

If you do not have the data file from the previous skill open, open the student data file **wd2-10-SpaNewsletter** ⬇ and try this skill on your own:

1. Select the numbered list on the second page of the newsletter.
2. Apply the **open circle** bullet style to the text.
3. If you will be moving on to the next skill in this chapter, leave the document open to continue working. If not, save the file as directed by your instructor and close it.

Skill **2.11** Using Styles

A **style** is a group of formatting, including character and paragraph formatting, that you can easily apply to text in your document. Styles can be applied to body text, headings, quotes, or just about any type of text you may have in your document.

It is a good idea to use styles to format text in your documents. When you use styles to format text, you can quickly change the look of that style across your document by changing the document's theme. Certain styles, such as headings, are also used by other features in Word, such as creating a table of contents and the Navigation task pane.

The *Styles* group on the *Home* tab displays the latest styles you have used. If you want to apply a recently used style, you can click the option directly from the Ribbon without opening the *Styles* gallery.

FIGURE WD 2.12

To apply a style to text:

1. Select the text you want to change.
2. On the *Home* tab, in the *Styles* group, click the **More** button.
3. Select an option from the *Styles* gallery.

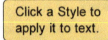

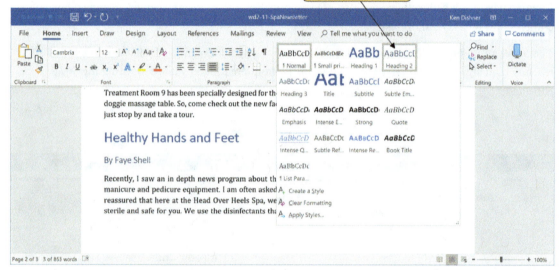

FIGURE WD 2.13

tips & tricks

> ❯ If you modify a style, you can save the style with a new name and then use it throughout your document. To save a new text style, open the *Styles* gallery and select **Create a Style**.
> ❯ Click the **dialog launcher** in the *Styles* group to open the **Styles** pane where you can work with and modify styles.

tell me more

When you select a new style, it replaces the formatting of the text. If you want to clear all the formatting from text, open the *Styles* gallery and select **Clear Formatting**.

let me try Live!

If you do not have the data file from the previous skill open, open the student data file **wd2-11-SpaNewsletter** and try this skill on your own:

1. Select the text **Healthy Hands and Feet** article title on the second page of the newsletter.
2. Apply the **Heading 1** style to the text.
3. Select the text **By Faye Shell** on the next line.
4. Apply the **Heading 2** style to the text.
5. If you will be moving on to the next skill in this chapter, leave the document open to continue working. If not, save the file as directed by your instructor and close it.

from the perspective of . . .

COLLEGE GRADUATE

When creating my résumé to send out to potential employers, I always make sure I use the right combination of fonts and styles to create the most eye-catching and professional document. I use tab stops and indents to align text just the way I want it and add space before and after paragraphs to control the layout on the page. I learned my lesson with the first résumé I sent out. Apparently, using a different color font for each section and using pink highlighting on my achievements was not the way to land an interview at the firm I applied to.

Skill 2.12 Changing Paragraph Alignment

Paragraph alignment refers to how text is aligned with regard to the left and right margins.

Left alignment aligns the text on the left side, leaving the right side ragged.

Center alignment centers each line of text relative to the margins.

Right alignment aligns the text on the right side, leaving the left side ragged.

Justified alignment evenly spaces the words, aligning the text on the right and left sides of the printed page.

It is important to understand common uses of different alignments. Paragraph text and headers are typically left aligned, but titles are often centered. Newspaper columns are often justified, and columns of numbers are typically right aligned.

To change the alignment of text:

1. Click in the paragraph you want to change.
2. On the *Home* tab, in the *Paragraph* group, click an alignment button— **Align Left**, **Center**, **Align Right**, or **Justify**.

FIGURE WD 2.14

another method

The following keyboard shortcuts can be used to apply horizontal alignment:

> Align Left = [Ctrl] + [L]
> Center = [Ctrl] + [E]
> Align Right = [Ctrl] + [R]
> Justify = [Ctrl] + [J]

let me try Live!

If you do not have the data file from the previous skill open, open the student data file **wd2-12-SpaNewsletter** 📥 and try this skill on your own:

1. Select the **Four New Services** article title.
2. Change the text so it is **left aligned.**
3. Select the **first paragraph** of text in the *Four New Services* article.
4. Change the paragraph text so it is **justified**.
5. If you will be moving on to the next skill in this chapter, leave the document open to continue working. If not, save the file as directed by your instructor and close it.

Skill 2.13 Changing Line Spacing

Line spacing is the white space between lines of text. The default line spacing in Word is 1.08 spacing. This gives each line the height of single spacing with a little extra space at the top and bottom. This line spacing is a good choice to use for the body of a document. Other commonly used spacing options include single spacing, double spacing, and 1.5 spacing.

To change line spacing:

1. Select the text you want to change.
2. On the *Home* tab, in the *Paragraph* group, click the **Line Spacing** button.
3. Select the number of the spacing you want.

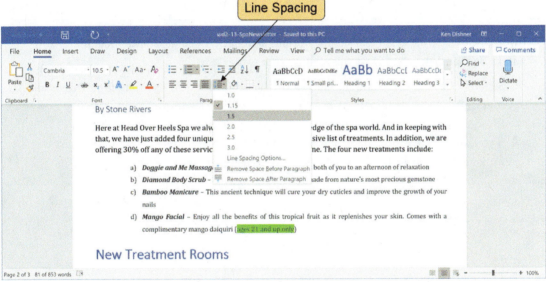

FIGURE WD 2.15

tips & tricks

To change the line and paragraph spacing for the entire document, you can select an option from the **Paragraph Spacing** gallery in the *Document Formatting* group on the *Design* tab.

tell me **more**

In Word 2007, Microsoft changed the default line spacing from single space to 1.15 lines. This option is still available from the *Line Spacing* menu. However, in Word 2013, the default was changed to 1.08 lines. The new default line spacing is designed to help with readability of online documents on a number of devices, including traditional desktop and laptop computers, tablets, and smart phones.

another method

> To apply single spacing, you can also press `Ctrl` + `1` on the keyboard.
> To apply double spacing, you can also press `Ctrl` + `2` on the keyboard.

let me **try** Live!

If you do not have the data file from the previous skill open, open the student data file **wd2-13-SpaNewsletter** and try this skill on your own:

1. Select the bulleted list on the second page of the newsletter. Select starting from **Doggie and Me Massage** and ending at **(ages 21 and up only)**.
2. Change the line spacing from double spaced to **1.5 spacing**.
3. If you will be moving on to the next skill in this chapter, leave the document open to continue working. If not, save the file as directed by your instructor and close it.

Skill 2.14 Revealing Formatting Marks

When creating a document it is important to use consistent formatting, such as a single space after the period at the end of a sentence. As you create a document, Word adds **formatting marks** that are hidden from view. For example, a paragraph mark, ¶ , is created every time the Enter key is pressed.

When creating professional documents, it is considered bad practice to use extra line breaks to add space between paragraphs in a document. By displaying formatting marks, you can quickly see where these extra line breaks occur in your documents and then easily delete them. Formatting marks appear on-screen only. They do not appear in the printed document.

To display formatting marks in a document:

1. On the *Home* tab, in the *Paragraph* group, click the **Show/Hide** button.
2. The formatting marks are displayed in the document.
3. Review the document for extra ¶ symbols between paragraphs or for more than one dot between words or after punctuation.
4. Use the **Delete** key to remove extra paragraph marks or spaces.
5. Click the **Show/Hide** button again to hide the formatting marks.

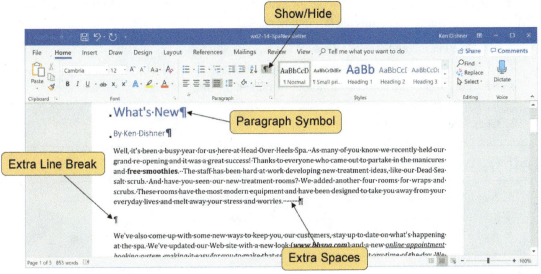

FIGURE WD 2.16

Formatting marks include symbols that represent spaces, nonbreaking spaces, tabs, paragraphs, and page breaks. The following table shows examples of formatting marks and the keyboard commands used to create them:

Character	Formatting Mark	Keystroke/Command
Space	·	Spacebar
Paragraph	¶	Enter
Tab	→	Tab
Line Break	↵	Shift + Enter
Nonbreaking Space	°	Ctrl + Shift + Enter
Page Break	--------------- Page Break --------------- ¶	Ctrl + Enter

tips & tricks

You can choose to always show specific formatting marks on-screen even when the Show/Hide button is inactive. To show specific formatting marks:

1. Click the **File** tab and select **Options**.
2. In the *Word Options* dialog, click the **Display** category.
3. Select the formatting marks you want to display in the *Always show these formatting marks on the screen* section.
4. Click **OK**.

tell me more

> A nonbreaking space is a space between two words that keeps the words together and prevents the words from being split across two lines.
> A line break forces the text on to a new line, but does not treat the text as a separate paragraph.

another method

To show formatting marks, you can press Ctrl + Shift + 8.

let me try Live!

If you do not have the data file from the previous skill open, open the student data file **wd2-14-SpaNewsletter** ⬇ and try this skill on your own:

1. Show the formatting marks in the document.
2. On the first page, there is an extra blank line. Remove the extra blank line from the document.
3. In the *I'm So Gelish* article, there should be no spaces after punctuation at the end of a paragraph. Remove the extra spaces from the article.
4. Hide the formatting marks.
5. If you will be moving on to the next skill in this chapter, leave the document open to continue working. If not, close the file.

Skill 2.15 Adding Borders and Shading to Paragraphs

If you have an important paragraph of information in a document and want it to stand out from the rest of the text, you can format it using **borders** and **shading**. Shading refers to color that appears behind the text of the paragraph. Borders are lines that appear along the top, bottom, left side, and right side of the paragraph. You can quickly apply borders and shading to paragraphs directly from the Ribbon.

To apply shading:

1. Place the cursor in the paragraph you want to format.
2. On the *Home* tab, in the *Paragraph* group, click the **Shading** button.
3. Click a color in the color palette to apply the shading.

To apply borders:

1. Place the cursor in the paragraph you want to format.
2. On the *Home* tab, in the *Paragraph* group, click the **Borders** button.
3. Select a border option on the menu to apply it to the paragraph.

FIGURE WD 2.17

You can also apply borders and shading to paragraphs through the *Borders and Shading* dialog. To apply a simple border from the *Borders and Shading* dialog:

1. Place the cursor in the paragraph you want to add the border to.
2. On the *Home* tab, in the *Paragraph* group, click the **Borders** button, and select **Borders and Shading...**
3. Select **Box** under *Setting*.
4. A preview of the border appears in the *Preview* area. Click the **Top Border**, **Bottom Border**, **Left Border**, or **Right Border** buttons to turn that part of the border on and off. The *Preview* area will display the changes as you make them.
5. Click **OK** to apply your changes.

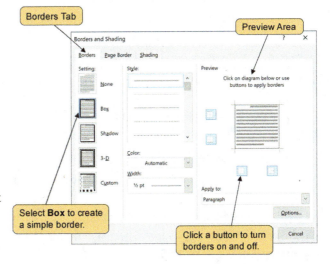

FIGURE WD 2.18

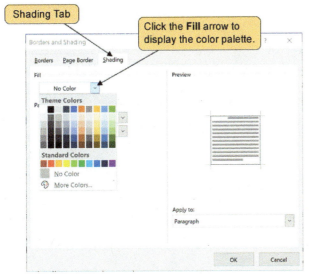

FIGURE WD 2.19

To apply shading from the *Borders and Shading* dialog:

1. Open the *Borders and Shading* dialog and click the **Shading** tab.
2. Click the **Fill** arrow and select a color from the palette.
3. Click **OK** to apply your changes.

tips & tricks

Notice that when you apply shading and borders from the buttons on the Ribbon, each button updates to reflect the most recently used option. To apply the same option again, just click the button on the Ribbon rather than opening the menu and making a selection.

let me try Live!

If you do not have the data file from the previous skill open, open the student data file **wd2-15-SpaNewsletter** and try this skill on your own:

1. Place the cursor in the title of the newsletter.
2. Change the paragraph shading to **Gold, Accent 4, Lighter 80%**. It is the third to last option in the second row under *Theme Colors*.
3. Add an **outside border** to the paragraph using the default settings.
4. If you will be moving on to the next skill in this chapter, leave the document open to continue working. If not, save the file as directed by your instructor and close it.

Skill 2.16 Adjusting Spacing Before and After Paragraphs

The default spacing after paragraphs in Word is 8 pt. This creates an evenly spaced document with some spacing between paragraphs to make it easier to tell when one paragraph ends and another begins. Sometimes you will want to increase the amount of space after paragraphs or add space above the paragraph in addition to below the paragraph.

To adjust the amount of white space that appears above and below paragraphs:

1. Place the cursor in the paragraph you want to change.
2. Click the **Layout** tab.
3. In the *Paragraph* group, click the up and down arrows next to the *Before* box to adjust the spacing above the paragraph.
4. Click the up and down arrows next to the *After* box to adjust the spacing below the paragraph.

FIGURE WD 2.20

You can also adjust the spacing around paragraphs from the *Line Spacing* menu:

1. On the *Home* tab, in the *Paragraph* group, click the **Line Spacing** button.
2. Select **Add Space Before Paragraph** to add space above the paragraph.
3. Select **Remove Space After Paragraph** to remove space below the paragraph.

While this is a quick way to adjust spacing before and after paragraphs, be aware that with this method you cannot customize the amount of space added before or after the paragraph.

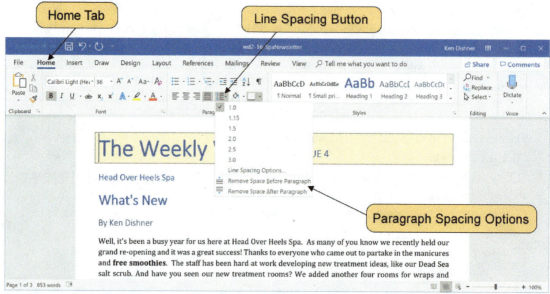

FIGURE WD 2.21

tips & tricks

> When you click the up and down arrows, the value for the spacing adjusts by 6 pts. You can also type a value in the box to apply more precise spacing.

> If you want to adjust how paragraphs appear on the page, add space before or after the text rather than pressing Enter to add space. Pressing Enter adds unnecessary line breaks and can cause issues with the page layout if future edits are made to the document.

another method

To adjust spacing before and after paragraphs, you can also open the *Paragraph* dialog and change the spacing in the *Before* and *After* boxes in the *Spacing* section.

let me try Live!

If you do not have the data file from the previous skill open, open the student data file **wd2-16-SpaNewsletter** and try this skill on your own:

1. Place the cursor in the first line of the document (beginning with **The Weekly Wrap**).
2. Change the spacing before the paragraph to **12 pt.** and the spacing after the paragraph to **12 pt.**
3. If you will be moving on to the next skill in this chapter, leave the document open to continue working. If not, save the file as directed by your instructor and close it.

Skill 2.17 Applying Indents

When you create a document, the margins control how close the text comes to the edge of a page. But what if you don't want all your paragraphs to line up? Indenting paragraphs increases the left margin for a paragraph, helping it stand out from the rest of your document.

To change the indentation of a paragraph:

1. Place the cursor anywhere in the paragraph you want to change.
2. To increase the indent of the paragraph by one level, on the *Home* tab, in the *Paragraph* group, click the **Increase Indent** button.
3. To reduce the indent of the paragraph and bring it closer to the edge of the page by one level, click the **Decrease Indent** button.

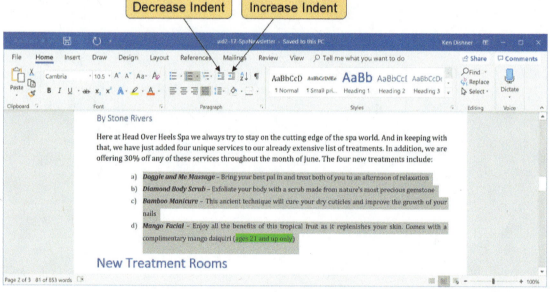

FIGURE WD 2.22

Using the *Decrease Indent* and *Increase Indent* commands allows you to indent only from the left side of the paragraph and only in set amounts. You can adjust both the right and left indents, each by one-tenth of an inch, from the *Layout* tab, giving you more control over the layout of your document.

To increase and decrease the left and right indentation for a paragraph:

1. Click the **Layout** tab.
2. In the *Paragraph* group, click the up arrow next to *Left* and *Right* to increase the indentation by one-tenth of an inch at a time.
3. Click the down arrow next to *Left* and *Right* to decrease the indentation by one-tenth of an inch at a time.

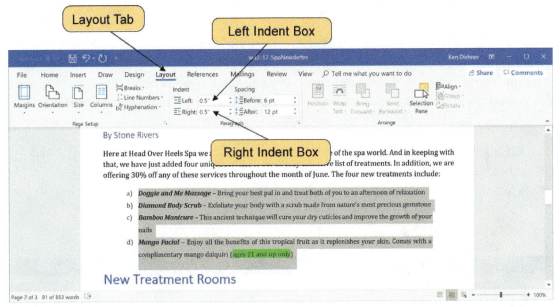

tell me **more**

The *Indent* commands indent all lines in a paragraph the same amount. If you want only the first line of a paragraph to be indented and the remainder of the paragraph to be left-aligned, use a **First Line Indent**. If you want the first line of a paragraph to be left-aligned and the remainder of the paragraph to be indented, use a **Hanging Indent**.

In the *Format Paragraph* dialog, you can precisely set options for first line indents and hanging indents. To open the *Format Paragraph* dialog, click the **Dialog Launcher** in the *Paragraph* group on the *Home* tab or in the *Paragraph* group on the *Layout* tab.

let me **try** **Live!**

If you do not have the data file from the previous skill open, open the student data file **wd2-17-SpaNewsletter** and try this skill on your own:

1. Select the four bullet points on the second page of the newsletter.
2. Increase the indent for the text by one level.
3. Decrease the indent for the text by one level.
4. Change the right indent to be the same as the left indent.
5. If you will be moving on to the next skill in this chapter, leave the document open to continue working. If not, close the file.

Skill 2.18 Displaying the Ruler

When working with documents, it is helpful to display the **ruler**. The ruler displays horizontally across the top of the window just below the Ribbon and vertically along the left side of the window. The ruler gives you a quick view of the margins and position of elements in your document. From the ruler you can also control other document layout controls such as tabs, first line indents, and hanging indents.

To display the ruler:

1. Click the **View** tab.
2. In the *Show* group, click the check box next to **Ruler** so a checkmark appears.
3. To hide the ruler, click the check box again so the checkmark disappears.

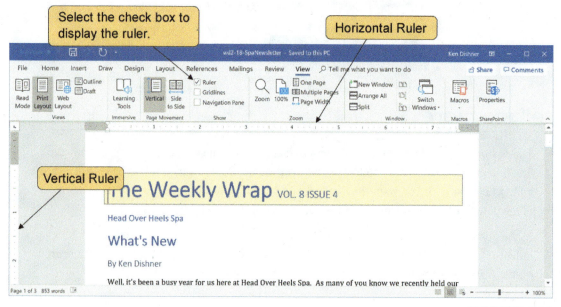

FIGURE WD 2.24

tips & tricks

Double-click the ruler to open the *Page Setup* dialog where you can control page layout elements such as margins and page orientation.

tell me more

Gridlines are a series of vertical and horizontal lines that divide the page into small boxes, giving you visual markers for aligning graphics, tables, and other elements on the page. Click the *Gridlines* check box on the *View* tab to show and hide the gridlines on the screen.

let me try Live!

If you do not have the data file from the previous skill open, open the student data file **wd2-18-SpaNewsletter** and try this skill on your own:

1. Practice showing and hiding the ruler from the *View* tab.
2. If you will be moving on to the next skill in this chapter, leave the document open to continue working. If not, close the file.

Skill 2.19 Using Tab Stops

A **tab stop** is a location along the horizontal ruler that indicates how far to indent text when the Tab key is pressed. There are five types of tab stops:

> **Left Tab**—displays text to the right of the tab stop

> **Center Tab**—displays text centered over the tab stop

> **Right Tab**—displays the text to the left of the tab stop

> **Decimal Tab**—aligns the text along the decimal point

> **Bar Tab**—displays a vertical line through the text at the tab stop

To set a tab stop:

1. Select the text in which you want to set a tab stop.
2. Click the **tab selector** at the far left of the horizontal ruler until it changes to the type of tab you want.
3. Click the horizontal ruler where you want to set a tab stop.

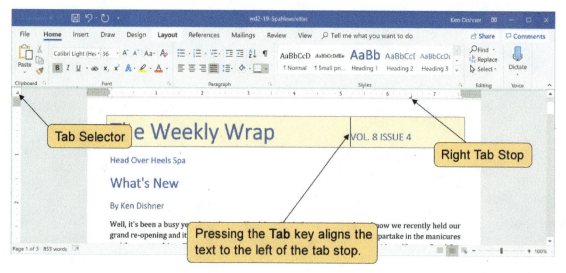

FIGURE WD 2.25

tips & tricks

> To clear a tab stop, drag the tab marker down from the horizontal ruler to remove it.
> To move a tab stop, drag the tab marker to the right or left along the horizontal ruler to its new position.

tell me more

The tab selector also includes two options for adding indents to your document:

> ▽ **First Line Indent**—Controls where the first line of a paragraph begins.
> △ **Hanging Indent**—Controls where the remainder of the paragraph is indented.

let me try Live!

If you do not have the data file from the previous skill open, open the student data file **wd2-19-SpaNewsletter** and try this skill on your own:

1. Place the cursor before the text **Vol. 8 Issue 4** in the first line of the document.
2. Click the **tab selector** two times so the right tab icon appears.
3. Click the ruler at the **6.5"** mark.
4. Use the Tab key to indent the **Vol. 8 Issue 4** text and align it along the right side of the tab stop.
5. If you will be moving on to the next skill in this chapter, leave the document open to continue working. If not, save the file as directed by your instructor and close it.

Skill 2.20 Using the Tabs Dialog

You can quickly add tabs to a document by selecting a tab stop type and clicking the ruler where you want the tab to appear. Another way to set tabs in your document is through the *Tabs* dialog. From the *Tabs* dialog, you can add new tabs or modify or clear existing tabs.

To set tabs in the *Tabs* dialog:

1. Select the text in which you want to set a tab.
2. On the *Home* tab, in the *Paragraph* group, click the **dialog launcher**.
3. In the *Paragraph* dialog, click the **Tabs...** button.
4. The *Tabs* dialog opens.
5. In the *Tab stop position* box, type the number of where you want the tab stop to appear.
6. Click a radio button in the *Alignment* section.
7. Click **OK**.

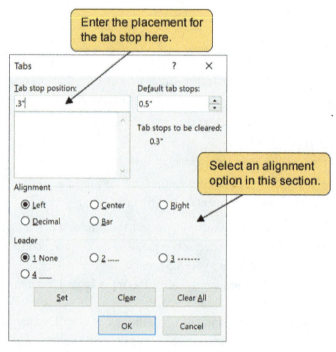

FIGURE WD 2.26

tips & tricks

> Click the **Clear All** button to clear all the tabs displayed in the *Tabs* dialog.
> To add the tab stop and continue working in the *Tabs* dialog, click the **Set** button instead of **OK**.

tell me more

A tab leader fills the tabbed space with dotted, dashed, or solid lines. Tab leaders are helpful if there is a long distance in the tabbed space in a list of items, like in a table of contents or an index.

another method

To open the *Tabs* dialog, you can double-click a tab stop on the ruler.

let me try Live!

If you do not have the data file from the previous skill open, open the student data file **wd2-20-SpaNewsletter** and try this skill on your own:

1. Press `Ctrl` + `A` on the keyboard to select the entire document.
2. Open the **Paragraph** dialog.
3. Open the **Tabs** dialog.
4. Add a **left tab stop** at **.3"**.
5. Place the cursor before the text **By Ken Dishner** under the *What's New* article title. Press the `Tab` key. Notice the text is indented **.3"** inches.
6. Use the `Tab` key to increase the remaining bylines in the newsletter. There are an additional four lines of text that will be indented.
7. Save the file as directed by your instructor and close it.

key terms

Character effects	Right alignment
Bold	Justified alignment
Italic	Line spacing
Underline	Formatting marks
Font	Borders
Serif fonts	Shading
Sans serif fonts	Increase Indent
Points	Decrease Indent
Change Case	First Line Indent
Highlighting	Hanging Indent
Format Painter	Ruler
Clear All Formatting	Gridlines
Numbered list	Tab stop
Bulleted list	Left Tab
Bullet	Center Tab
Style	Right Tab
Paragraph alignment	Decimal Tab
Left alignment	Bar Tab
Center alignment	

concept review

1. Which type of font has an embellishment at the end of each stroke to lead the eye from one character to the next?
   a. heading
   b. theme
   c. serif
   d. sans serif

2. Which command would you use to change the text from uppercase to having each word capitalized?
   a. Shrink Font
   b. Change Case
   c. Change Font
   d. Grow Font

3. Which command would you use to call attention to text by coloring the background behind the text?
   a. Text Highlight Color
   b. Text Effects
   c. Font Color
   d. Format Painter

4. Which command is used to copy the styles from one word to another?
   a. Format Painter
   b. Text Effects
   c. Styles
   d. Text Highlight Color

5. Styles ensure parts of your document, such as headings, all use the same formatting.
   a. true
   b. false

6. Which kind of list would you use for instructions that do not need to be performed in a certain order?
   a. bulleted list
   b. numbered list
   c. multilevel list
   d. justified list

7. To evenly space words, aligning the text on the right and left sides of the printed page, use the _____ command.
   a. Align Left
   b. Center
   c. Align Right
   d. Justify

8. Which command displays hidden formatting marks in a document, including paragraph and spacing marks?
   a. Formatting dialog
   b. Show/Hide
   c. Clear All Formatting
   d. Styles

9. You can adjust the amount of space that appears before and after paragraphs from the *Design* tab on the Ribbon.
   a. true
   b. false

10. Which tab stop displays the text to the left of the tab stop?
    a. Center Tab
    b. Decimal Tab
    c. Left Tab
    d. Right Tab

projects
skill review **2.1**

In this project you will be adding basic formatting to a brochure for the Suarez Agency. First, you will remove unwanted formatting from a line of text. Next, you will change the font and line spacing for the entire document. You will remove extra lines and spaces in the document. You will apply styles to text as well as use the *Format Painter* tool to copy and paste formatting from one selection to another. You will also convert text into a numbered list and a bulleted list.

Skills needed to complete this project:

- Clearing Formatting (Skill 2.8)
- Changing Fonts (Skill 2.2)
- Changing Font Sizes (Skill 2.3)
- Changing Line Spacing (Skill 2.13)
- Revealing Formatting Marks (Skill 2.14)
- Using Styles (Skill 2.11)
- Adjusting Spacing Before and After Paragraphs (Skill 2.16)
- Using Bold, Italic, and Underline (Skill 2.1)
- Changing Font Colors (Skill 2.5)
- Using Format Painter (Skill 2.7)
- Creating Numbered Lists (Skill 2.9)
- Applying Indents (Skill 2.17)
- Creating Bulleted Lists (Skill 2.10)
- Changing Paragraph Alignment (Skill 2.12)
- Adding Borders and Shading to Paragraphs (Skill 2.15)

1. Open the start file **WD2019-SkillReview-2-1** and resave the file as: `[your initials] WD-SkillReview-2-1`
2. If the document opens in Protected view, click the **Enable Editing** button in the Message Bar at the top of the document so you can modify it.
3. Clear the formatting on text.
    a. Select the third line in the document. The one beginning with *Phone:*.
    b. On the *Home* tab, in the *Font* group, click the **Clear All Formatting** button.
4. Change the font and size on all the text in the document.
    a. Press `Ctrl` + `A` to select all text in the document.
    b. On the *Home* tab, in the *Font* group, click the arrow next to the **Font** box and choose **Calibri Light**.
    c. In the *Font* group, click the arrow next to the **Font Size** box and choose **12**.

5. Change the line spacing on all the text in the document.

   a. Verify the entire document is still selected.

   b. On the *Home* tab, in the *Paragraph* group, click the **Line and Paragraph Spacing** button and select **1.5** to change the line spacing.

6. Show formatting marks and remove extra spaces and blank lines.

   a. On the *Home* tab, in the *Paragraph* group, click the **Show/Hide** button to reveal formatting marks in the document.

   b. Delete the extra spaces at the end of the first line of the document.

   c. Delete all the extra blank lines between paragraphs in the document. *Hint*: There are four blank lines that need to be deleted.

   d. Click the **Show/Hide** button again to hide the formatting marks.

7. Use styles to apply a heading format to a section heading in the document.

   a. Select the **Our Goal** heading on the first page.

   b. On the *Home* tab, in the *Styles* group, click the **Heading 1** style to apply it to the text.

   c. Apply the *Heading 1* style to the following lines of text:

      - **Experience**
      - **Why Suarez?**
      - **The Suarez Marketing Belief System**
      - **Client Quotes**
      - **Professional Credentials**

8. Change the spacing before the paragraph on the selected heading.

   a. Select the **Our Goal** heading on the first page.

   b. Click the **Layout** tab.

   c. In the *Paragraph* group, click the **Before** down arrow three times to change the spacing before the text to **6 pt**.

   d. Use this method to change the spacing before all the headings in the brochure.

9. Change the character formatting, font, and color of text.

   a. Select the text **The Suarez Agency** at the top of the document.

   b. Click the **Home** tab.

   c. In the *Font* group, click the **Bold** button.

   d. In the *Font* group, click the arrow next to the **Font** box and select **Verdana**.

   e. In the *Font* group, click the arrow next to the **Font Size** box and select **22**.

   f. In the *Font* group, click the **Font Color** button and select **Orange, Accent 2**. (it is the sixth color in the first row under *Theme Colors*).

10. Use the Format Painter to change the format of text.
    a. With the text *The Suarez Agency* still selected, on the *Home* tab, in the *Clipboard* group, click the **Format Painter** button.
    b. Select the text **"Putting Your Needs First"** to apply the copied formatting.
    c. On the *Home* tab, in the *Font* group, click the arrow next to the **Font Size** box and select **12** to change the size of the text.

11. Add a numbered list to and decrease the indent on a section of the brochure.
    a. In the *Why Suarez?* section, select all of the text below the heading.
    b. On the *Home* tab, in the *Paragraph* group, click the **Numbering** button arrow and select the **1), 2), 3)** option to apply the numbering style to the selected text.
    c. Click the **Decrease Indent** button once to change the left indent to **0"**.

12. Add a bulleted list to sections of the brochure.
    a. In the *The Suarez Marketing Belief System* section, select all of the text below the heading.
    b. On the *Home* tab, in the *Paragraph* group, click the **Bullets** button arrow and select the **open circle bullet** option to apply the bullet style.
    c. In the *Professional Credentials* section, select all of the text below the heading.
    d. Apply **open circle bullet** style to the text.

13. Apply a style to text.
    a. In the *Client Quotes* section, select the first quote and include the quotation marks.
    b. On the *Home* tab, in the *Styles* group, apply the **Quote** style. You might have to click the **More** button to locate this style.
    c. Select the second quote in the section and apply the same style.

14. Change the paragraph alignment and apply a style on selected text.
    a. Select **–Jason Brown, Chesterfield, MO**.
    b. On the *Home* tab, in the *Paragraph* group, click the **Align Right** button.
    c. On the *Home* tab, in the *Paragraph* group, apply the **Subtle Emphasis** style. You might have to click the **More** button to locate this style.
    d. Select the text **–Scott Morris and Associates, St. Louis, MO** and apply the same formatting.

15. Add shading and borders to paragraphs of text.
    a. In the *Client Quotes* section, place the cursor in the first quote.
    b. On the *Home* tab, in the *Paragraph* group, click the **Shading** button, and select **Blue, Accent 1, Lighter 80%**. It is the fifth option in the second row under *Theme Colors*.
    c. In the *Paragraph* group, click the **Borders** button, and select **Top Border**.
    d. Apply the same formatting to the second quote in the section.

16. Save and close the document.

projects
Data files for projects can be found by logging into your SIMnet account and going to the Library section.

skill review 2.2

In this project you will be adding text and paragraph formatting to the Tri-State Book Festival agenda. First, you will clear the formatting from the entire document. You will then apply change the font, font size, and line spacing for the document. You will use the *Show/Hide* command to display formatting marks and remove extra line breaks and spaces in the document. You will apply styles, adjust font formatting, and then copy and paste text formatting using the *Format Painter* tool. Finally, you will set tabs both from the ruler and the *Tabs* dialog, and then apply those tabs to text.

Skills needed to complete this project:

- Clearing Formatting (Skill 2.8)
- Changing Fonts (Skill 2.2)
- Changing Font Sizes (Skill 2.3)
- Changing Line Spacing (Skill 2.13)
- Revealing Formatting Marks (Skill 2.14)
- Changing Text Case (Skill 2.4)
- Using Styles (Skill 2.11)
- Adjusting Spacing Before and After Paragraphs (Skill 2.16)
- Changing Paragraph Alignment (Skill 2.12)
- Changing Font Colors (Skill 2.5)
- Adding Borders and Shading to Paragraphs (Skill 2.15)
- Using Format Painter (Skill 2.7)
- Applying Highlights (Skill 2.6)
- Using Bold, Italic, and Underline (Skill 2.1)
- Displaying the Ruler (Skill 2.18)
- Using Tab Stops (Skill 2.19)
- Using the Tabs Dialog (Skill 2.20)

1. Open the start file **WD2019-SkillReview-2-2** and resave the file as:
   `[your initials] WD-SkillReview-2-2`
2. If the document opens in Protected View, click the **Enable Editing** button in the Message Bar at the top of the document so you can modify the document.
3. Clear formatting from the entire document.
   a. Press `Ctrl` + `A` to select the entire document.
   b. On the *Home* tab, in the *Font* group, click the **Clear All Formatting** button.

4. Change font and font size for the entire document.

    a. Verify the entire document is still selected.

    b. On the *Home* tab, in the *Font* group, click the arrow next to the **Font** box and choose **Century Gothic**.

    c. In the *Font* group, click the arrow next to the **Font Size** box and choose **11**.

5. Change the line spacing for the entire document.

    a. Verify the entire document is still selected.

    b. On the *Home* tab, in the *Paragraph* group, change the line spacing to **1.15**.

6. Reveal formatting marks and remove extra line breaks in the document.

    a. On the *Home* tab, in the *Paragraph* group, click the **Show/Hide** button to reveal formatting marks in the document.

    b. Delete the extra spaces at the end of the first paragraph.

    c. Delete the extra spaces before *Agenda* and before *Authors.*

    d. Delete all the extra blank lines between paragraphs in the document. *Hint:* There are five blank lines to delete.

    e. Click the **Show/Hide** button again to hide the formatting marks.

7. Change the text case for the title of the document.

    a. Select the first line of text in the document.

    b. On the *Home* tab, in the *Font* group, click the **Change Case** button, and select **Capitalize Each Word**.

8. Apply styles.

    a. Verify the first line of text is still selected.

    b. On the *Home* tab, in the *Styles* group, click the **Title** style to apply it to the text.

    c. Place the cursor in the **Agenda** heading. It appears after the first two introductory paragraphs of the document.

    d. On the *Home* tab, in the *Styles* group, click the **Heading 1** style to apply it to the text.

9. Adjust the space that appears before and after the paragraph.

    a. Verify the cursor still appears in the **Agenda** heading.

    b. Click the **Layout** tab.

    c. In the *Paragraph* group, click the **Before up arrow** once so **18 pt** appears in the box.

    d. Click the **After up arrow** four times so **24 pt** appears in the box.

10. Change the alignment of text.

    a. Click the **Home** tab.

    b. In the *Paragraph* group, click the **Align Right** button.

11. Change the color of text.

    a. On the *Home* tab, in the *Font* group, click the **Font Color** arrow.

    b. Select **Orange, Accent 4**. It is the third option from the right in the first row under *Theme Colors.*

12. Add a border to a paragraph.

    a. On the *Home* tab, in the *Paragraph* group, click the **Borders** button.

    b. Click **Bottom Border**.

13. Copy and paste formatting using the *Format Painter* tool.

    a. With the cursor in the *Agenda* heading, on the *Home* tab, in the *Clipboard* group, click the **Format Painter** button.

    b. Apply the copied formatting to the **Authors** heading by clicking on the heading.

14. Apply another style to text.

    a. Place the cursor in the **Fiction** heading.

    b. On the *Home* tab, in the *Styles* group, click the **Heading 3** style to apply it to the text.

    c. Place the cursor in the **Nonfiction** heading.

    d. Apply the **Heading 3** style to the text.

15. Add space before paragraphs of text.

    a. Select the first two paragraphs of text (from *The Tri-State Book festival will take place* to *additional $25.00 per attendee.*).

    b. Click the **Layout** tab.

    c. In the *Paragraph* group, click **After up arrow** two times so **18 pt** appears in the box.

16. Bring attention to text using the highlighter tool.

    a. In the first sentence of the first paragraph, select the text **September 6-9**.

    b. Click the **Home** tab.

    c. In the Font group, click the **Text Highlight Color** button. Select the **Bright Green** option.

17. Apply character formatting.

    a. Scroll down to the *Fiction* section.

    b. Under the name *Max Wallace*, select the text **Showcased work:**.

    c. On the *Home* tab, in the *Font* group, click the **Italic** button.

    d. Apply the italics character formatting to the text **Showcased work:** under each author's name in the *Fiction* and *Nonfiction* sections.

18. Display the ruler and set a tab stop.

    a. Select the text in the *Fiction* and *Nonfiction* sections (be sure to select the headings as well).

    b. Click the **View** tab. In the *Show* group, click the **Ruler** check box to select it.

    c. Verify the tab at the left side of the ruler is the *Left Tab*.

    d. Add a tab stop at the **1"** mark.

19. Set tab stops using the *Tabs* dialog.

    a. Click the **Home** tab.

    b. In the *Paragraph* group, click the **dialog launcher**.

    c. In the *Paragraph* dialog, click the **Tabs...** button.

    d. In the *Tabs* dialog, type **.75** in the *Tab stop position* box.

    e. Verify the tab will be a left tab and click **OK**.

20. Apply the tabs you set.

    a. Place the cursor before the author name **Max Wallace**. Press the Tab key one time.

    b. Repeat this for all the author names in the *Fiction* and *Nonfiction* sections.

    c. Place the cursor at the beginning of the line below **Max Wallace** (before the **Showcased work:**). Press the Tab key two times.

    d. Repeat this for all the lines beginning with **Showcased work:**.

21. Save and close the document.

projects

Data files for projects can be found by logging into your SIMnet account and going to the Library section.

challenge yourself **2.3**

In this project, you will be formatting a safety report from the Winter Springs Community. You will be updating the font, font size, and line spacing for the entire document. You will remove unnecessary line breaks and apply styles. You will modify paragraphs by changing alignment, applying shading, and adjusting the space that appears before and after the paragraphs. You will then copy that formatting and paste it to other text using the Format Painter tool. You will apply character formatting and change the case of text. Finally, you will convert text to both a bulleted list and a numbered list.

Skills needed to complete this project:

- Changing Fonts (Skill 2.2)
- Changing Font Sizes (Skill 2.3)
- Changing Line Spacing (Skill 2.13)
- Revealing Formatting Marks (Skill 2.14)
- Using Styles (Skill 2.11)
- Changing Paragraph Alignment (Skill 2.12)
- Adding Borders and Shading to Paragraphs (Skill 2.15)
- Adjusting Spacing Before and After Paragraphs (Skill 2.16)
- Using Format Painter (Skill 2.7)
- Changing Text Case (Skill 2.4)
- Using Bold, Italic, and Underline (Skill 2.1)
- Creating Bulleted Lists (Skill 2.10)
- Applying Indents (Skill 2.17)
- Creating Numbered Lists (Skill 2.9)

1. Open the start file **WD2019-ChallengeYourself-2-3** and resave the file as:
   `[your initials] WD-ChallengeYourself-2-3`
2. If the document opens in Protected View, enable editing so you can make changes to the document.
3. Change font on the entire document to **Times New Roman** and the size to **14 pt.**
4. Change the line spacing on the entire document to **1.15** line spacing.
5. Display the formatting marks for the document and delete all the extra blank lines between paragraphs in the document including the extra blank line at the end of the document. When you are finished, hide the formatting marks.
6. Apply the **Title** style to the first line of text in the document.
7. Change the font size to **26 pt**.
8. **Center** the title.

9. Apply the **Heading 1** style to the text **INTRODUCTION**.

10. Apply the **Gray, Accent 6, Lighter 80%** shading to the section heading. It is the last option in the second row of the gallery.

11. Change the spacing before the paragraph to **18 pt.** and the spacing after to **6 pt.**

12. Use the *Format Painter* to apply the formatting of the first section heading to the other two section headings in the document (*Most Targeted Electronic Devices* and *Guidelines For Staying Safe*).

13. Use the **Change Case** tool to change the title text to **Uppercase**.

14. Select the text **basic safety procedures** in the first paragraph and **underline** the text.

15. Select the text **Winter Springs** in the first paragraph and **italicize** the text.

16. Select the text **most targeted** in the second paragraph and **bold** the text.

17. Select all the five targeted electronic items in the *Most Targeted Electronic Devices* section (from *Smartphones* to *Laptop computers*). Apply the **1), 2), 3)** number format to the text.

18. Select all the lines in the *Guidelines For Staying Safe* section (from *Avoid walking* to *reflective clothing*). Apply the **black square** bullet style.

19. Select the items in the numbered list and increase the indent of the list by one level.

20. Select the items in the bulleted list and increase the indent of the list by two levels.

21. Place the cursor at the beginning of the numbered list (before the word *Smartphone*). Change the spacing before the text to **18 pt.**

22. Place the cursor at the beginning of the numbered list (before the word *Avoid*). Change the spacing before the text to **18 pt.**

23. Save and close the document.

projects

Data files for projects can be found by logging into your SIMnet account and going to the Library section.

challenge yourself 2.4

In this project, you will be adding text and paragraph formatting to a section of a research paper on alternative assessments for students. You will change the font, font size, and line spacing for the entire document. You will then show formatting marks and remove unnecessary line breaks and spaces. You will apply a style, and then add additional formatting to the text and apply that formatting to other text using the *Format Painter* tool. You will convert text to a bulleted list and add emphasis to text by adding bold and italics character formatting.

Skills needed to complete this project:

- Changing Fonts (Skill 2.2)
- Changing Font Sizes (Skill 2.3)
- Changing Line Spacing (Skill 2.13)
- Revealing Formatting Marks (Skill 2.14)
- Using Styles (Skill 2.11)
- Using Bold, Italic, and Underline (Skill 2.1)
- Adding Borders and Shading to Paragraphs (Skill 2.15)
- Adjusting Spacing Before and After Paragraphs (Skill 2.16)
- Using Format Painter (Skill 2.7)
- Creating Bulleted Lists (Skill 2.10)
- Applying Indents (Skill 2.17)
- Changing Text Case (Skill 2.4)

1. Open the start file **WD2019-ChallengeYourself-2-4** and resave the file as:
   `[your initials] WD-ChallengeYourself-2-4`
2. If the document opens in Protected view, click the **Enable Editing** button in the Message Bar at the top of the document so you can modify the document.
3. Change the font on the entire document to **Calibri** and **11 pt**.
4. Change the line spacing for the entire document to **single** line spacing.
5. Display the formatting marks for the document.
6. Delete all the extra blank lines between paragraphs in the document.
7. Text has been indented by adding spaces. Delete the extra spaces before each line of text.
8. When you are finished, hide the formatting marks.
9. Apply the **Heading 1** style to the **Introduction** heading at the beginning of the document.
10. Bold the **Introduction** heading.
11. Apply a top border and a bottom border to the **Introduction** heading.

12. Change the spacing before the **Introduction** heading to **24 pt**. and the spacing after the heading to **12 pt**.

13. Use the *Format Painter* to copy the formatting from the **Introduction** heading and copy it to the following lines of text:
    - Alternate Assessment
    - No Child Left Behind (NCLB)
    - Modified Achievement Standards
    - Which Students Will Benefit
    - Who is Eligible
    - Conclusion

14. Select the four learning tasks in the *Introduction* section (beginning with *Taking a test*) and convert the text to a bulleted list using the closed circle bullet style.

15. Increase the indent on the bulleted list by two levels.

16. Bold the text **basic educational tasks** in the last paragraph of the introduction section.

17. In the first paragraph in the *Alternate Assessment* section, italicize the word **learning** and italicize the phrase **ability to show what they know and can do**.

18. Find the text **(iep)** in the document. Use the *Change Case* command to change the text to uppercase letters.

19. Find both instances of **C-Baas** in the document and use the *Change Case* command to change the text to uppercase letters.

20. Save and close the document.

projects

on your own **2.5**

In this project, you will be formatting a service document from Greenscapes, a landscaping company. First, you will remove all formatting from the document and then show formatting marks and remove all extra line breaks and spaces. You will change the font, font size, and line spacing on the entire document. You will then apply a style, modify the formatting, and copy and paste the formatting using the *Format Painter* tool. Finally, you will create a list and add and apply tabs where appropriate.

Skills needed to complete this project:

- Clearing Formatting (Skill 2.8)
- Revealing Formatting Marks (Skill 2.14)
- Changing Fonts (Skill 2.2)
- Changing Font Sizes (Skill 2.3)
- Changing Line Spacing (Skill 2.13)
- Using Styles (Skill 2.11)
- Changing Font Colors (Skill 2.5)
- Adding Borders and Shading to Paragraphs (Skill 2.15)
- Using Format Painter (Skill 2.7)
- Creating Bulleted Lists (Skill 2.10)
- Applying Indents (Skill 2.17)
- Displaying the Ruler (Skill 2.18)
- Using Tab Stops (Skill 2.19)
- Using Bold, Italic, and Underline (Skill 2.1)
- Changing Text Case (Skill 2.4)

1. Open the start file **WD2019-OnYourOwn-2-5** and resave the file as:
   `[your initials] WD-OnYourOwn-2-5`
2. If the document opens in Protected View, click the **Enable Editing** button in the Message Bar at the top of the document so you can modify the document.
3. Select the entire document and clear all formatting from the text.
4. Show formatting marks and delete extra spaces from the beginning and end of paragraphs.
5. Delete the extra line breaks between paragraphs.
6. Change the font, font size, and line spacing for the entire document to selections of your choice.
7. Apply the **Title** style to the first line of the document.
8. Change the font color for the title to a color of your choice.
9. Apply the **Subtitle** style to the second line of the document.
10. Change the font color for the subtitle to a color of your choice.

11. Adjust the font size of the subtitle to a size of your choice.
12. Apply the **Heading 1** style to the three main headings (*Our Way of Life*, *What We Provide*, and *Costs and Pricing*).
13. Apply the **Heading 2** style to the first subheading under the *What We Provide* heading (*Lawn Care Plans*).
14. Change the font color for the **Lawn Care Plans** heading to a color of your choice.
15. Add shading and a border of your choice to the **Lawn Care Plans** heading.
16. Copy the formatting from the **Lawn Care Plans** heading and paste it to the remaining three subheadings in the *Services* section (*Lawn Maintenance*, *Leaf and Debris Removal*, and *Unique Services*).
17. Convert the four items under **Lawn Maintenance** into a bulleted list using a style of your choice.
18. Adjust the indentation on the bulleted list to an appropriate level.
19. In the *Unique Services* section, indent the five services by setting a tab stop on the ruler and pressing Tab to indent the text.
20. In the *Unique Services* section, bold each of the service names.
21. In the *Unique Services* section, use the *Change Case* command so all five service names have the same capitalization as **Nature paths**.
22. Save and close the document.

projects

fix it 2.6

Data files for projects can be found by logging into your SIMnet account and going to the Library section.

In this project, you will be fixing the formatting for the résumé of an applicant for a marketing manager position. There are a number of issues with the document that need correcting. First, you will clear all formatting from the document. You will then show formatting marks and remove unnecessary line breaks and extra spaces. You will adjust the font and font size for text as well as apply appropriate styles. You will format paragraphs and copy and paste formatting using the *Format Painter* tool. You will display the ruler and apply tabs. You will create a bulleted list and adjust the indentation of text. Finally, you will adjust the line spacing to ensure the document fits on a single page.

Skills needed to complete this project:

- Clearing Formatting (Skill 2.8)
- Revealing Formatting Marks (Skill 2.14)
- Changing Fonts (Skill 2.2)
- Changing Font Sizes (Skill 2.3)
- Using Styles (Skill 2.11)
- Adjusting Space Before and After Paragraphs (Skill 2.16)
- Changing Paragraph Alignment (Skill 2.12)
- Changing Font Colors (Skill 2.5)
- Using Format Painter (Skill 2.7)
- Displaying the Ruler (Skill 2.18)
- Using Tab Stops (Skill 2.19)
- Using Bold, Italic, and Underline (Skill 2.1)
- Creating Bulleted Lists (Skill 2.10)
- Applying Indents (Skill 2.17)
- Changing Text Case (Skill 2.4)
- Changing Line Spacing (Skill 2.13)

1. Open the start file **WD2019-FixIt-2-6** and resave the file as: `[your initials] WD-FixIt-2-6`
2. If the document opens in Protected View, click the **Enable Editing** button in the Message Bar at the top of the document so you can modify the document.
3. Clear the formatting from all the text in the document.
4. Reveal the formatting marks in the document and remove any extra blank lines and spaces.
5. Change the font and font size for the text in the document. Select all the text in the document and change the font to **Verdana**. Change the font size to **10 pt**.
6. Select the **name at the top of the document** and apply **Heading 1** style.

7. Change the font color of the name to **Blue-Gray, Text 2** (it is the fourth option in the first row under *Theme Colors*).

8. Place your cursor in the first line of the address. Change the spacing after the paragraph to **0 pt**.

9. Select the name and address at the top of the document (from *James Houseman* to *44333*). **Center** align the text.

10. Select the first section heading (**Summary**) and apply the **Heading 1** style.

11. Change the font color of the section heading to **Blue-Gray, Text 2, Darker 25%** (it is the fourth option in the fifth row under *Theme Colors*).

12. Change the spacing after the heading to be **6 pt.**

13. Use the **Format Painter** to copy and paste the formatting from the first section heading to the other section headings (*Skills and Capabilities*, *Experience*, and *Education*).

14. Select the text **Computer** and apply the **Heading 2** style.

15. Change the font color of the heading text to **Blue-Gray, Text 2** (it is the fourth option in the first row under *Theme Colors*).

16. Place the cursor in the first paragraph in the **Summary** section. Display the ruler and set the left tab stop at the **.5"** mark. Use the *Tab* key to indent the paragraph to the tab stop you just set.

17. In the *Experience* section, bold the **dates** and italicize the **position titles** and the **company name**.

18. Select the four lines under *Skills and Capabilities* (from *Marketing* to *Social Media Marketing*) and change the text into a bulleted list using the round open circle bullet style.

19. Decrease the indent on the bulleted items by one level.

20. Apply the same bulleted list style to the items under *Computer*.

21. Apply the same bulleted list style to items listed under each job experience.

22. Increase the indent on the lines under each degree by one level (the **school name** and the **GPA**).

23. Use the *Change Case* command to change the text case on the text BUSINESS ADMINISTRATION so only the first letter of each word is capitalized.

24. Change the line spacing for the entire document to **1.5**.

25. Save and close the document.

chapter 3

Formatting Documents

In this chapter, you will learn the following skills:

> Add consistency to document fonts and colors by using themes

> Use headers and footers to display page numbering and the date/time

> Control document layout by adjusting margins, using page breaks, and adding columns

> Enhance document formatting by using page borders, watermarks, and hyperlinks

> Use building blocks and property controls to save time and provide consistency

> Print multiple copies of a document and specific pages within a document

introduction

This chapter provides you with the skills needed to format and print documents. The first step is to apply and work with document themes. Once you have applied themes, you will add document elements, including headers, footers, page numbers, and automatic dates. Next, you will add building blocks and property controls as well as hyperlinks. You'll learn how to modify the layout of a document by adding breaks, adjusting the margins, and displaying text in columns. You will add a cover page and page borders to add graphic elements to the document. Finally, you will preview and print the document, including printing multiple copies and specific page ranges.

Skill 3.1 Applying Document Themes

A **theme** is a group of formatting options that you apply to an entire document. Themes include font, color, and effect styles that are applied to specific elements of a document. Theme colors control the colors available from the color palette for fonts, borders, and backgrounds. Theme fonts change the fonts used for built-in styles—such as *Normal* style and headings. Theme effects control the way graphic elements in your document appear. Applying a theme to your document is a quick way to take a simple piece of text and change it into a polished, professional-looking document.

To apply a theme to a document:

1. Click the **Design** tab.
2. In the *Document Formatting* group, click the **Themes** button.
3. Click a theme option in the gallery to apply it to your document.

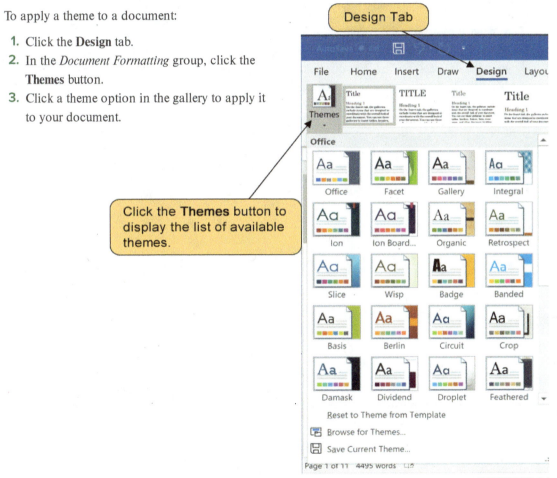

Design Tab

Click the **Themes** button to display the list of available themes.

FIGURE WD 3.1

tips & tricks

To reset the theme to the original theme that came with the document's template, click the **Themes** button and select **Reset to Theme from Template**.

tell me more

You can modify any of the existing themes and save this as your own custom theme. The file will be saved with the *thmx* file extension. The theme will be saved in the *Document Themes* folder and will be available from Excel, PowerPoint, and Outlook as well as Word.

let me try Live!

Open the student data file **wd3-01-SpaProductReport** and try this skill on your own:

1. Change the theme of the document to the **Office** theme.
2. If you will be moving on to the next skill in this chapter, leave the document open to continue working. If not, save the file as directed by your instructor and close it.

Skill 3.2 Applying Style Sets

Each theme comes with a number of style sets you can choose from. A **style set** changes the font and paragraph formatting for an entire document. Style sets apply formatting based on styles. So, in order to see your changes, the text in your document must be formatted using styles. To learn more about applying styles to text, see the skill *Using Styles*. The *Style Set* gallery displays thumbnails of how the text will appear when the style set is applied.

To change the style set:

1. Click the **Design** tab.
2. In the *Document Formatting* group, click the **More** button to open the *Style Set* gallery.
3. Click a style set from the gallery to apply it to the document.

FIGURE WD 3.2

tell me more

The first thumbnail in the *Style Set* gallery displays the style set that is currently in use for the document.

let me try Live!

If you do not have the data file from the previous skill open, open the student data file **wd3-02-SpaProductReport** and try this skill on your own:

1. Apply the **Lines (Simple)** style set to the document.
2. If you will be moving on to the next skill in this chapter, leave the document open to continue working. If not, save the file as directed by your instructor and close it.

Skill 3.3 Using Color Themes

When creating a document, it can sometimes be difficult to choose colors that work well together. Documents can end up monochromatic or with too many colors that don't work well together. A **color theme** is a set of colors that are designed to work well together in a document. A color theme will change the color of text, tables, and drawing objects in a document. When you apply a theme to a document it includes a color theme, which has default theme colors for document elements. You can change the color theme without affecting the other components of the theme.

To apply a color theme to a document:

1. Click the **Design** tab.
2. In the *Document Formatting* group, click the **Colors** button.
3. Click a color theme option to apply it to your document.

FIGURE WD 3.3

tell me **more**

When you change the color theme for a document, the color options for document elements will change. The theme colors will appear in the *Font Color* menu, as well as in the *Table Styles* and *Shape Styles* galleries. Choose your colors from these preset theme colors to ensure your document has a consistent color design.

let me try Live!

If you do not have the data file from the previous skill open, open the student data file **wd3-03-SpaProductReport** ⬇ and try this skill on your own:

1. Change the color theme to **Grayscale**.
2. Notice that the color change is too monochromatic. Click the **Undo** button on the Quick Access Toolbar to reverse the change.
3. If you will be moving on to the next skill in this chapter, leave the document open to continue working. If not, save the file as directed by your instructor and close it.

Skill 3.4 Using Font Themes

There are thousands of fonts for you to choose from to use in your documents. Some fonts are designed to work well as header text, such as Calibri Light and Cambria, and others are designed to work well as body text, such as Calibri. When you apply a theme to a document, this includes a **font theme**, which includes default fonts for body text and header text. As with color themes, you can change the font theme without affecting the other components of the theme.

To apply a font theme to a document:

1. Click the **Design** tab.
2. In the *Document Formatting* group, click the **Fonts** button.
3. Click a font theme option to apply it to your document.

FIGURE WD 3.4

tell me **more**

> The font theme menu displays a preview of the header font (on top) and the body font (on bottom). Notice that some themes include two different fonts, but others include the same font, only in different sizes. The default font theme for Word is the *Office Calibri Light/Calibri* font theme.

let me try Live!

If you do not have the data file from the previous skill open, open the student data file **wd3-04-SpaProductReport** ⤓ and try this skill on your own:

1. Change the font theme to **Candara**.
2. Change the font theme back to the **Office font theme** by clicking the **Undo** button on the Quick Access Toolbar.
3. If you will be moving on to the next skill in this chapter, leave the document open to continue working. If not, save the file as directed by your instructor and close it.

Skill 3.5 Creating Watermarks

A **watermark** is a graphic or text that appears as part of the page background. Watermarks appear faded so the text that appears on top of the watermark is legible when the document is viewed or printed.

There are three categories of watermarks:

> **Confidential**–Includes the text "Confidential" or "Do Not Copy" in different layouts.
> **Disclaimers**–Includes the text "Draft" or "Sample" in different layouts.
> **Urgent**–Includes the text "ASAP" or "Urgent" in different layouts.

To add a watermark to a document:

1. Click the **Design** tab.
2. In the *Page Background* group, click the **Watermark** button and select an option from the gallery.

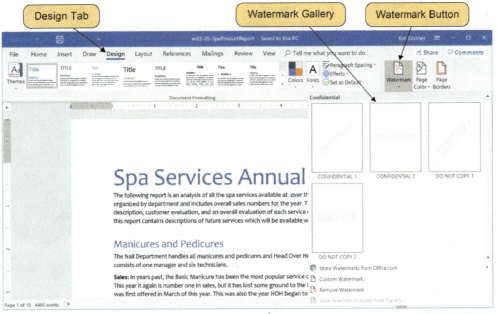

FIGURE WD 3.5

tips & tricks

You do not have to use one of the built-in watermarks from the *Watermark* gallery. You can create your own custom watermark, displaying whatever text or image you like. Click the **Custom Watermark...** command to open the *Printed Watermark* dialog and choose different options for the text watermark. You can add pictures as watermarks from this dialog. When you add a picture as a watermark, it appears faded so any text on top of it is still legible.

let me try Live!

If you do not have the data file from the previous skill open, open the student data file **wd3-05-SpaProductReport** and try this skill on your own:

1. Apply the **CONFIDENTIAL 1** watermark to the document.
2. If you will be moving on to the next skill in this chapter, leave the document open to continue working. If not, save the file as directed by your instructor and close it.

Skill 3.6 Inserting Page Breaks

When text or graphics have filled a page, Word inserts a soft page break and goes on to a new page. However, at times you may want to manually insert a **hard page break**—forcing the text to a new page no matter how much content is on the present page. Typically hard page breaks are used to keep certain information together.

To insert a hard page break:

1. Click the **Layout** tab.
2. In the *Page Setup* group, click the **Breaks** button, and select **Page**.

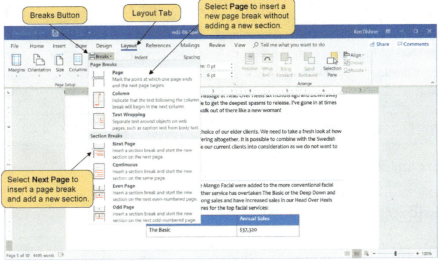

FIGURE WD 3.6

Another type of page break is a **section page break**. A section page break inserts a hard page break and starts a new section in the document. A **section** is a designated part of a document that can be formatted separately from the rest of the document. For example, if you have a large table that needs more horizontal space than the rest of your document, you can add the table in its own section and set the margins for the section to the narrow margin settings while keeping the remaining document with the normal margin settings.

To add a section to a document:

1. Click the **Layout** tab.
2. In the *Page Setup* group, click the **Breaks** button.
3. In the *Section Breaks* section, click **Next Page** to insert a new section and a hard page break.

tips & tricks

> To delete a page break, switch to Draft view. Here all the page breaks are displayed. Select a page break and press the Delete key on the keyboard to delete the break. When you delete a section break, the content from the section takes on the formatting from the preceding section.

> If you want to add a new section, but do not want to add a page break, select **Continuous** in the *Section Breaks* area of the *Breaks* menu.

tell me more

There are two basic types of breaks you can add to a document:

> **Page Breaks**—These breaks create visual breaks in your document but keep the content in the same section. Page breaks include *Page*, *Column*, and *Text Wrapping*.

> **Section Breaks**—These breaks create new sections in your document. Section breaks include *Next Page*, *Continuous*, *Even Page*, and *Odd Page*.

another method

To insert a hard page break:

> On the *Insert* tab, in the *Pages* group, click the **Page Break** button.

> Press Ctrl + Enter on the keyboard.

let me try Live!

If you do not have the data file from the previous skill open, open the student data file **wd3-06-SpaProductReport** 🖱 and try this skill on your own:

1. Place the cursor at the end of the paragraph before the **Facials** heading. It is located near the bottom of page 5.
2. Insert a **page break**.
3. A blank line appears at the top of the new page. Delete the blank line.
4. Place the cursor at the end of the paragraph before the **Future Products** heading. It is located near the bottom of page 10.
5. Insert a **next page section break**.
6. A blank line appears at the top of the new page. Delete the blank line.
7. If you will be moving on to the next skill in this chapter, leave the document open to continue working. If not, save the file as directed by your instructor and close it.

Skill 3.7 Adding Headers

A **header** is text that appears at the top of every page, just below the top margin. Typically, headers display dates, page numbers, document titles, or authors' names. Word comes with several predesigned headers that you can add to your document and then modify to suit your needs. When you add one of Word's predesigned headers, the header will include fields for you to add content to. Some of these fields, such as author name and title, will auto-populate from the document's properties. For others, simply click the field you want to add content to and begin typing.

To add a header to a document:

1. Click the **Insert** tab.
2. In the *Header & Footer* group, click the **Header** button and select a header format from the gallery.
3. Word displays the *Header & Footer Tools Design* tab and inserts a header with content controls for you to enter your own information. Click a content control and enter the information for your header.
4. To close the header and return to your document, click the **Close Header and Footer** button on the contextual tab.

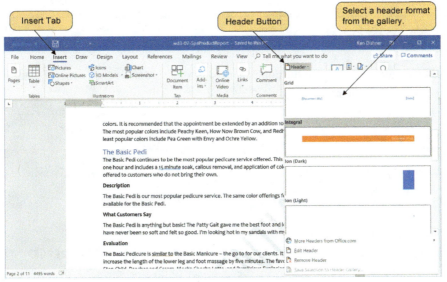

FIGURE WD 3.7

If the first page of your document is a title page, you won't want the header text to display on the page. To display a header on the first page of the document that is different from the header in the rest of the document, display the *Header & Footer Tools* tab. In the *Options* group, select the **Different First Page** check box.

FIGURE WD 3.8

tips & tricks

Headers appear faded out in Print Layout view. If you want to edit a header, double-click it and make your changes. Click the **Close Header and Footer** button to return to the document.

another method

To close the header and return to the document, you can also double-click on the main document area below the header.

let me try Live!

If you do not have the data file from the previous skill open, open the student data file **wd3-07-SpaProductReport** and try this skill on your own:

1. Navigate to **page 2** of the document.
2. Add a header to the document using the **Integral** style.
3. Click the **[Document title]** control and type HEAD OVER HEELS ANNUAL REPORT
4. Have the header display differently on the first page of the document.
5. Close the header and footer.
6. If you will be moving on to the next skill in this chapter, leave the document open to continue working. If not, save the file as directed by your instructor and close it.

Skill 3.8 Adding Footers

A **footer** is text that appears at the bottom of every page, just below the bottom margin. Typically, footers display dates, page numbers, author names, or disclaimers. Word comes with a number of predesigned footers that you can add to your document and then modify to suit your needs. When you add one of Word's predesigned footers, the footer will include fields for you to add content to. Just as with headers, some of these fields will auto-populate from the document's properties. For others, click the field you want to add content to and begin typing.

To add a footer to a document:

1. Click the **Insert** tab.
2. In the *Header & Footer* group, click the **Footer** button and select a footer format from the gallery.
3. Word displays the *Header & Footer Tools Design* tab and inserts a footer with fields for you to enter you own information.
4. Click a field and enter the information for your footer.
5. To close the header and return to your document, click the **Close Header and Footer** button on the contextual tab.

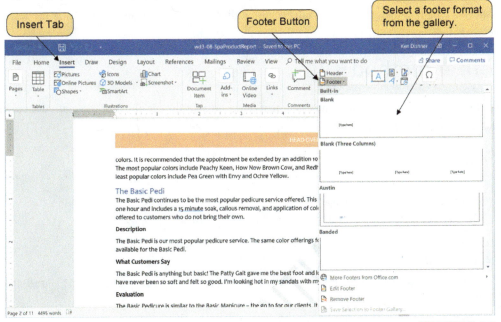

FIGURE WD 3.9

FIGURE WD 3.10

tips & tricks

When you add a header or footer to your document, the *Design* tab under *Header & Footer Tools* displays. This is called a contextual tab because it displays when a header or footer is the active element.

another method

To close the footer and return to the document, you can also double-click on the main document area above the footer.

let me try Live!

If you do not have the data file from the previous skill open, open the student data file **wd3-08-SpaProductReport** and try this skill on your own:

1. Place the cursor anywhere on the second page of the document.
2. Add a footer to the document using the **Blank** style.
3. Click the **[Type Here]** control and type `Not for distribution outside of Head Over Heels Spa`.
4. Close the header and footer.
5. If you will be moving on to the next skill in this chapter, leave the document open to continue working. If not, save the file as directed by your instructor and close it.

Skill 3.9 Adding an Automatic Date Stamp

In addition to information such as the company name and page numbers, headers and footers typically include the current date. You could manually type the date in the header or footer and then update the date every time you work on the document, or you could add an **automatic date stamp**. This pulls the current date from the computer's system clock and displays the date in the document. The date is then automatically updated when the computer's date changes.

To add an automatic date stamp to the header of a document:

1. Double-click the header to switch to header view. Place the cursor where you want the date to appear.
2. Under the *Header & Footer Tools Design Tab* in the *Insert* group, click the **Date & Time** button.
3. In the *Date and Time* dialog, select a date format in the *Available formats* list.
4. Select the **Update automatically** check box.
5. Click **OK**.
6. To close the header and return to your document, click the **Close Header and Footer** button on the contextual tab.

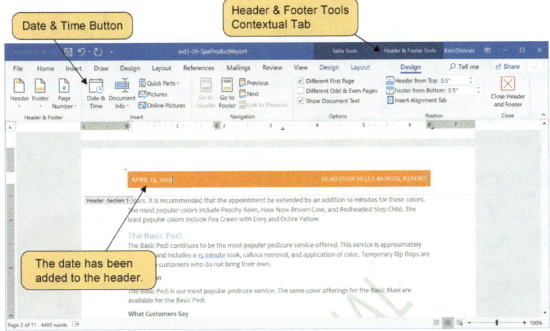

FIGURE WD 3.11

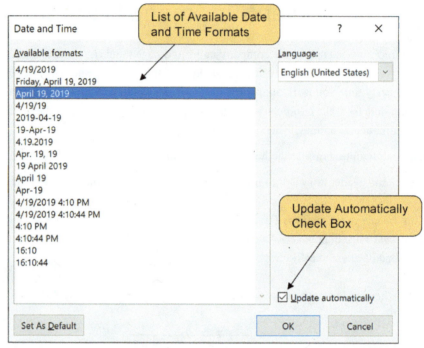

FIGURE WD 3.12

tips & tricks

If all your documents use a date format other than Word's default MM/DD/YYYY format, you can change the date and time format that is preselected in the *Date and Time* dialog. First, select the format you want to set as the default and then click the **Set As Default** button. When you open the dialog, the format you selected and set will be automatically selected for you.

another method

You can also use *Quick Parts* to add the date and time to the header or footer of your document:

1. Double-click the header to make it active.
2. Under the *Header & Footer Tools Design* tab, in the *Insert* group, click the **Quick Parts** button and select **Field...**
3. In the *Field* dialog, click the **CreateDate** or the **Date** field.
4. Select a format for the date.
5. Click **OK**.

let me try Live!

If you do not have the data file from the previous skill open, open the student data file **wd3-09-SpaProductReport** and try this skill on your own:

1. Double-click the header area on page 2 of the document to switch to header view.
2. Open the **Date and Time** dialog.
3. Add a date that will update automatically and use the format **Month Day, Year**. For example, January 1, 2020.
4. Close the header and footer.
5. If you will be moving on to the next skill in this chapter, leave the document open to continue working. If not, save the file as directed by your instructor and close it.

Skill 3.10 Inserting Page Numbers

Headers and footers often include page numbers, but they also include other information, such as author name, date, and document title. If all you want to do is add page numbers to a document, you don't need to use the header and footer feature. Instead, you can insert simple page numbers to a document through the *Page Number* gallery. The *Page Number* gallery includes everything from simple numbers to complex designs to add to your document. You can choose to display page numbers in the page's margin or the cursor's location, in addition to the traditional header or footer of the document.

To add page numbers to the bottom of pages of a document:

1. Click the **Insert** tab.
2. In the *Header & Footer* group, click the **Page Number** button. Point to **Bottom of Page**.
3. Click a page number format from the gallery.

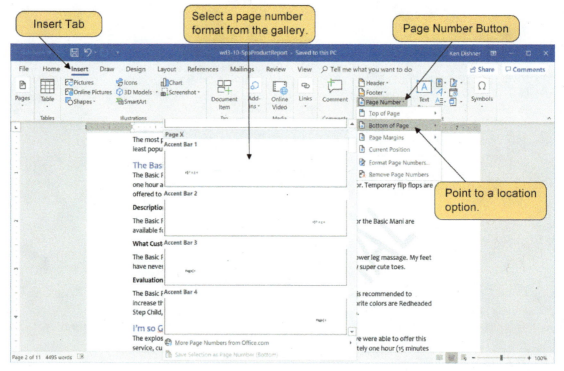

FIGURE WD 3.13

To remove a page number:

1. On the *Header & Footer Tools Design* tab, in the *Header & Footer* group, click the **Page Number** button.

2. Select **Remove Page Numbers**.

FIGURE WD 3.14

tips & tricks

> When adding page numbers to a document, you should always use Word's built-in page numbers. If you type page numbers into your document manually, they will not update when you add or remove pages.

> When choosing a page numbering option, be sure to choose a design that fits with your document. For example, if you are writing a research paper, you will want to use simple page numbering in the header or footer of the document. On the other hand, if you are designing a brochure, you can try using one of Word's more elaborate page numbering options and place the page number in the margin rather than the traditional header or footer.

let me try Live!

If you do not have the data file from the previous skill open, open the student data file **wd3-10-SpaProductReport** and try this skill on your own:

1. Place the cursor anywhere on the second page of the document.
2. Add a page number to the bottom of the page using the **Accent Bar 2** format.
3. Remove the **page number**.
4. Close the header and footer.
5. If you will be moving on to the next skill in this chapter, leave the document open to continue working. If not, save the file as directed by your instructor and close it.

Skill 3.11 Inserting Building Blocks

A **building block** is a piece of content that is reusable in any document. Building blocks can be text, such as page numbers, or they can include graphics, such as a cover page. You can insert building blocks from specific commands on the Ribbon or from the **Building Blocks Organizer**.

The *Building Blocks Organizer* lists the building blocks in alphabetical order by which gallery they appear in and includes *Bibliographies, Cover Pages, Equations, Footers, Headers, Page Numbers, Table of Contents, Tables, Text Boxes,* and *Watermarks.*

To insert a building block from the *Building Blocks Organizer:*

1. Click the **Insert** tab.
2. In the *Text* group, click the **Quick Parts** button and click **Building Blocks Organizer...**
3. Select a building block in the list.
4. A preview of the selected building block displays on the right.
5. Click the **Insert** button to add the building block to the document.

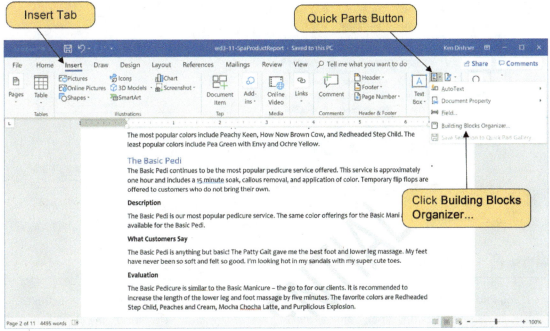

FIGURE WD 3.15

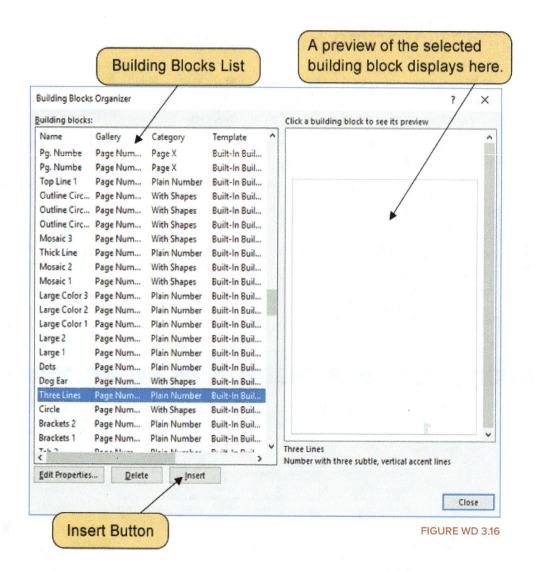

Building Blocks List

A preview of the selected building block displays here.

Insert Button

tips & tricks

If you find that the list of building blocks is too long, you can remove building blocks you don't use. To remove a building block from the *Building Blocks Organizer*, select a building block and click the **Delete** button. Be aware that the *Building Blocks Organizer* is used across all of Word. If you delete a building block from the *Building Blocks Organizer*, it will no longer be available when you are working on other documents.

tell me **more**

You can sort the list of building blocks by clicking the **Name**, **Gallery**, **Category**, or **Template** button at the top of the *Building Blocks Organizer*. You can also modify the properties of a building block, changing properties such as the name or which gallery the building block appears in.

let me **try** Live!

If you do not have the data file from the previous skill open, open the student data file **wd3-11-SpaProductReport** 🔽 and try this skill on your own:

1. Place the cursor anywhere on the second page of the document.
2. Open the *Building Blocks Organizer* dialog.
3. Insert page numbers using the **Three Lines** building block.
4. Close the header and footer.
5. If you will be moving on to the next skill in this chapter, leave the document open to continue working. If not, save the file as directed by your instructor and close it.

Skill 3.12 Inserting Property Controls

A **property control** is an element you can add to your document to save time entering the same information over and over again. Property controls can be used as shortcuts for entering long strings of text that are difficult to type. For example, instead of typing the company name *Head Over Heels Spa*, you can insert the *Company* property control. Many of the built-in property controls, such as company name and author, pull their information from the document's properties.

Before adding a property control, first add the information in the document's *Properties* panel:

1. Click the **File** tab.
2. A brief list of the document's properties is displayed on the left side of the *Info* page.
3. Click the **Show All Properties** link at the bottom of the properties to expand the list and show all the properties for the document.
4. Click the text box next to a property and either type the new text or edit the existing text for a property.

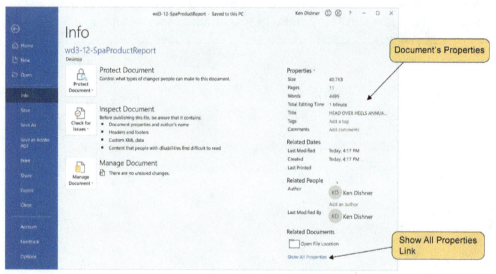

FIGURE WD 3.17

When you add a property control, Word will add the text to the document and update the text automatically if any changes are made to the property control. By using property controls, you can be assured that all the information throughout the document is consistent.

To add a property control to a document:

1. Click the **Insert** tab.
2. In the *Text* group, click the **Quick Parts** button, point to **Document Property**, and select a control.

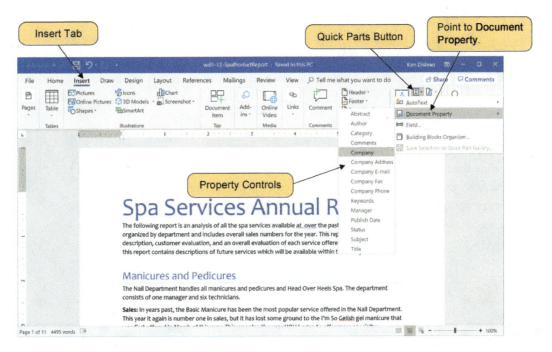

FIGURE WD 3.18

tips & tricks

If you need to update a property control, you only need to either update the control on the *Info* page or type the change once in any property control in the document. As you update any property control, all the other controls created from the same property control as well as the document's properties will update.

let me try Live!

If you do not have the data file from the previous skill open, open the student data file **wd3-12-SpaProductReport** and try this skill on your own:

1. Display the **Info** tab in Backstage view.
2. Type `Head Over Heels Day Spa` in the *Company* property control.
3. Click between the words **at** and **over** in the first sentence of the first paragraph of the document.
4. Insert a **Company** property control.
5. Add a space between property control and the surrounding text to fix any spacing issue.
6. If you will be moving on to the next skill in this chapter, leave the document open to continue working. If not, save the file as directed by your instructor and close it.

Skill 3.13 Inserting Hyperlinks

A **hyperlink** is text or a graphic that, when clicked, opens another page or file. You can use hyperlinks to link to a section in the same document, to a new document, or to an existing document, such as a Web page.

To insert a hyperlink:

1. Select the text or graphic you want to use as the link.
2. Click the **Insert** tab.
3. In the *Links* group, click the **Link** button to open the *Insert Hyperlink* dialog.
4. Select an option under *Link to* and select the file to which you want to link.
5. Type the text of the link in the *Text to display* box.
6. Click **OK** to insert the hyperlink into your document.

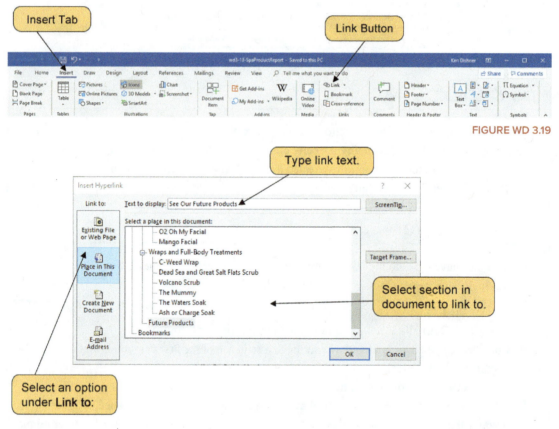

FIGURE WD 3.19

FIGURE WD 3.20

After you have added a hyperlink to your document, you can modify the hyperlink:

> To edit a hyperlink, right-click the link and select **Edit Hyperlink...** from the menu. Make any changes in the *Edit Hyperlink* dialog.

> To remove a hyperlink, right-click the link and select **Remove Hyperlink** from the menu.

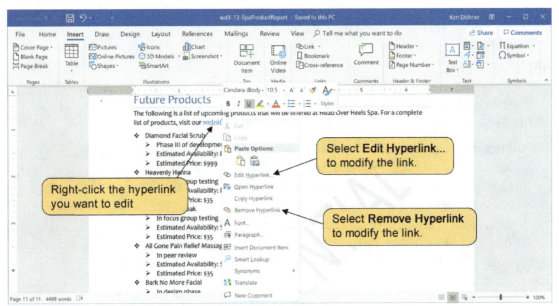

FIGURE WD 3.21

tips & tricks

If you do not have your window size at full screen, the *Links* group may be collapsed on the Ribbon. Click the **Links** button on the *Insert* tab to display the commands in the group, including the *Hyperlink* button. If you are using the SIMnet program along with this textbook, the *Links* button may appear in its collapsed state.

tell me more

Some hyperlinks include ScreenTips. A **ScreenTip** is a bubble that appears when the mouse is placed over the link. Add a ScreenTip to include a more meaningful description of the hyperlink.

another method

To open the *Insert Hyperlink* dialog, you can:

> Right-click the text or object you want as the link and select **Hyperlink...** from the shortcut menu.
> Press `Ctrl` + `K` on the keyboard.

let me try Live!

If you do not have the data file from the previous skill open, open the student data file **wd3-13-SpaProductReport** and try this skill on your own:

1. Place the cursor at the end of the first paragraph and press the spacebar one time.
2. Add a link to the **Future Products** section of the document.
3. Change the link text to read `Our Future Products` and add the link.
4. Navigate to the *Future Products* section.
5. Remove the hyperlink from the word **website** in the first paragraph.
6. If you will be moving on to the next skill in this chapter, leave the document open to continue working. If not, save the file as directed by your instructor and close it.

Skill 3.14 Adjusting Margins

Margins are the blank spaces at the top, bottom, left, and right of a page. Word's default margins are typically 1 inch for the top and bottom and 1 inch for the left and right. Word comes with several predefined margin layout options for you to choose from, including normal, narrow, wide, and mirrored.

To adjust the margins for a document:

1. Click the **Layout** tab.
2. In the *Page Setup* group, click the **Margins** button, and select an option for the page layout.

FIGURE WD 3.22

If you don't want to use one of Word's preset margins, you can set your own margin specifications in the *Page Setup* dialog.

To set custom margins:

1. On the *Layout* tab, in the *Page Setup* group, click the **dialog launcher**.
2. The *Page Setup* dialog opens.
3. Click the up and down arrows next to each margin (*Top*, *Bottom*, *Left*, and *Right*) to adjust the width and height of the margins.
4. Click **OK** to close the dialog.

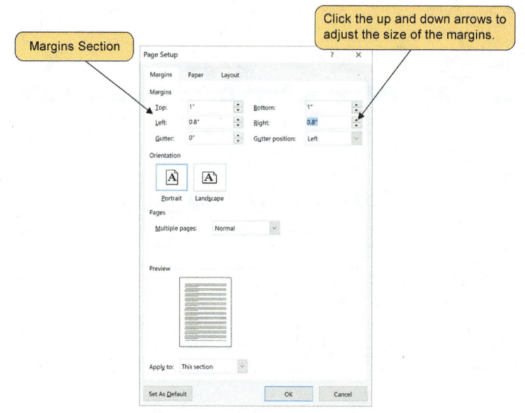

FIGURE WD 3.23

tips & tricks

While most documents you create will use the *Normal* or *Moderate* settings for margins, some documents will require either less or more space around the text. If you have a large exhibit or table, you may want to make the margins narrow so the content will still fit in portrait orientation. On the other hand, if you are writing a letter, you may want to increase your margins to accommodate preprinted stationery.

tell me more

A gutter is additional space you can add to one side of the document when you plan to have the document bound. You can enter the amount of extra space you need for binding in the *Gutter* box in the *Page Setup* dialog. You can then choose how your document will be bound—along the left side or along the top.

another method

> To open the *Page Setup* dialog, you can also click the **Margins** button and select **Custom Margins...**
> To adjust margins in the *Page Setup* dialog, you can also type the number in the box.

let me try Live!

If you do not have the data file from the previous skill open, open the student data file **wd3-14-SpaProductReport** and try this skill on your own:

1. Verify you are on **page 1** of the document.
2. Change the margins for the document to use the **Moderate** margin settings.
3. Open the **Page Setup** dialog.
4. Change the left margin to **0.8"**. Change the right margin to **0.8"**.
5. If you will be moving on to the next skill in this chapter, leave the document open to continue working. If not, save the file as directed by your instructor and close it.

Skill 3.15 Applying Columns

Newsletter pages are often laid out in **columns**. The text of these pages continues from the bottom of one column to the top of the next column. Word comes with a number of preset column options, making it easy to create columns of text in a document.

To apply columns to text:

1. Click the **Layout** tab.
2. In the *Page Setup* group, click the **Columns** button and select an option.
3. Selecting *One*, *Two*, or *Three* will create evenly spaced columns. Choosing *Left* or *Right* will create a two-column layout with one column narrower than the other.

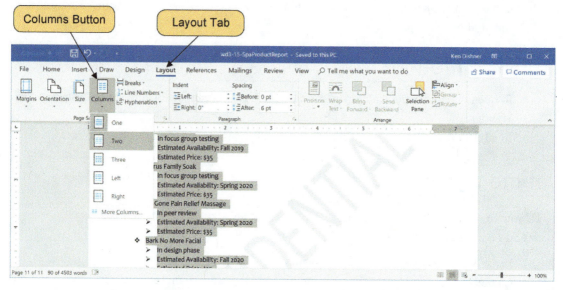

FIGURE WD 3.24

tips & tricks

If you know you want your document to appear in column format, set the columns before you enter the document text. When you type the text for your document, it will automatically be formatted in columns.

tell me more

The *Columns* dialog gives you more control over the display of the columns in your document, including changing the width of columns and adjusting the space that appears between columns. To open the *Columns* dialog, click **More Columns...** at the bottom of the *Columns* gallery .

let me try Live!

If you do not have the data file from the previous skill open, open the student data file **wd3-15-SpaProductReport** and try this skill on your own:

1. Navigate to the **Future Products** section of the document and verify the ruler is displayed.
2. Select the list of future products (from *Diamond Facial Scrub* through *Estimated Price: $25*).
3. Apply the two-column layout to the text.
4. You may not see a visual change in the selected text, but notice on the ruler that two columsn have been applied.
5. If you have an empty bullet item in the list, place the cursor next to the item and press the Delete key to remove it.
6. If you will be moving on to the next skill in this chapter, leave the document open to continue working. If not, save the file as directed by your instructor and close it.

Skill 3.16 Inserting a Column Break

After you have added columns to your document, you may find that the text does not break across the columns exactly as you would like. In this case, you can add a column break where you want the bottom of the column to be. A **column break** marks where one column ends and moves the following text to the top of the next column.

To insert a column break:

1. Place the cursor before the text you want to appear at the top of the next column.
2. Click the **Layout** tab.
3. In the *Page Setup* group, click the **Breaks** button and select **Column**.

A column break is added. The text following the break now appears at the top of the next column.

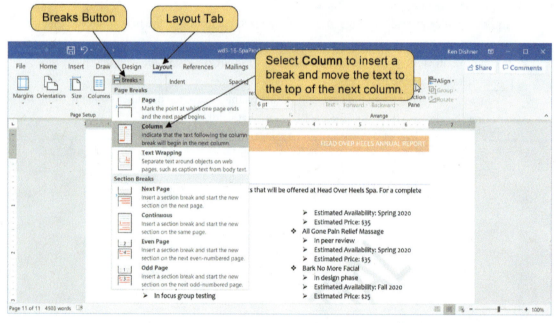

FIGURE WD 3.25

tips & tricks

> To view column breaks in a document, click the **Show/Hide** button in the *Paragraph* group on the *Home* tab.

> If you are displaying a list of items across multiple columns, use column breaks to create columns that contain the same number of items.

another method

To insert a column break, you can also press Ctrl + Shift + Enter.

let me try Live!

If you do not have the data file from the previous skill open, open the student data file **wd3-16-SpaProductReport** ⬇ and try this skill on your own:

1. In the *Future Products* section, place the cursor before the text **Citrus Family Soak**.
2. Insert a column break.
3. If you will be moving on to the next skill in this chapter, leave the document open to continue working. If not, save the file as directed by your instructor and close it.

Skill 3.17 Adding Page Borders

Page borders are graphic elements that can give your document a more polished look. **Page borders** draw a decorative graphic element along the top, right, bottom, and left edges of the page. Borders can be simple lines or 3-D effects and shadows. You can modify borders by changing the style and color. You can apply a border to the entire document or parts of a section.

To add a border to a document:

FIGURE WD 3.26

1. Click the **Design** tab.
2. In the *Page Background* group, click the **Page Borders** button.
3. The *Borders and Shading* dialog opens with the *Page Border* tab displayed.
4. Click a setting for the border.
5. Select a style, color, and width for the page border.
6. The *Preview* area shows how the border will look.
7. Click **OK** to accept your changes and add the page border to the document.

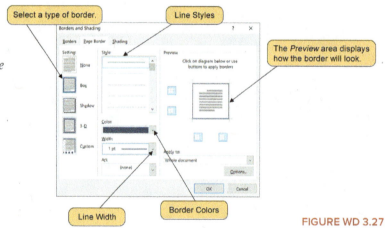

FIGURE WD 3.27

tips & tricks

You can further adjust the look of page borders from the *Borders and Shading* dialog:

> Click on the **Preview** area diagram to add or remove parts of the border.
> Click the **Art** drop-down menu to select graphic elements for the border.

another method

You can also open the *Borders and Shading* dialog from the *Home* tab. In the *Paragraph* group, click the arrow next to the *Borders* button and select **Borders and Shading...** Click the **Page Border** tab in the dialog to add a page border.

let me try Live!

If you do not have the data file from the previous skill open, open the student data file **wd3-17-SpaProductReport** and try this skill on your own:

1. Navigate to **page 1** of the document.
2. Open the **Borders and Shading** dialog with the **Page Border** tab displayed.
3. Change the border to use the **Box** style.
4. Apply the **Blue-Gray, Text 2** color. It is the fourth option in the first row under *Theme Colors*.
5. Change the width of the border to **1 pt**.
6. If you will be moving on to the next skill in this chapter, leave the document open to continue working. If not, save the file as directed by your instructor and close it.

from the perspective of . . .

MARKETING MANAGER

When writing a report, I use Word's built-in themes and style sets to create a cohesive document. A cover page and page borders add visual zing to my report that really grabs the attention of my readers. Before I send it out for review, I always add a footer and watermark to the report to let others know not to share the information outside our organization. Using the *Company* property control has been invaluable, especially when I realized I misspelled our company name in the report! And when it comes to printing, I am often printing at least 10 copies to hand out, but then can easily reprint an individual page when minor edits come in from my boss —which they always do.

Skill 3.18 Adding a Cover Page

When creating documents such as reports, proposals, or business plans, it is a good idea to include a **cover page** that contains the title of the document and the date. You can also add other information such as a subtitle, a short description of the document, and company information. Word comes with a number of prebuilt cover pages that you can quickly and easily add to your documents.

To add a cover page:

1. Click the **Insert** tab.
2. In the *Pages* group, click the **Cover Page** button and select an option.
3. Word inserts a cover page with content controls for you to enter your own information.
4. Click a content control and type the information for your document.

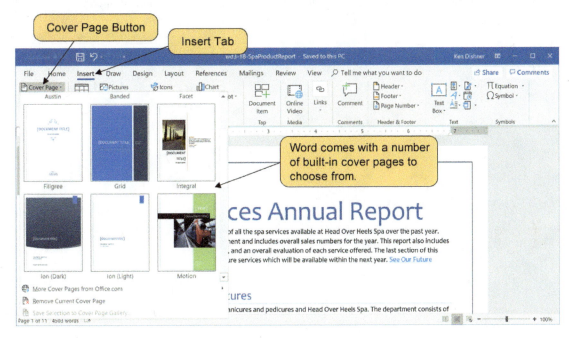

FIGURE WD 3.28

tips & tricks

Most content controls include instructions for adding text to the cover page. However, some content controls, such as the author, do not include text and are hidden from view. One way to see all the fields available in a cover page is to use the *Select All* command by pressing Ctrl + A on the keyboard.

tell me more

When you click a date content control, you will notice a calendar icon next to the text area. Click the icon to display the calendar to select a date to add to the cover page.

let me try Live!

If you do not have the data file from the previous skill open, open the student data file **wd3-18-SpaProductReport** and try this skill on your own:

1. Insert a cover page using the **Ion (Light)** style.
2. In the *Year* content control, type **2020** as the year.
3. In the *Subtitle* control, type **SERVICE BY SERVICE REVIEW**
4. If you will be moving on to the next skill in this chapter, leave the document open to continue working. If not, save the file as directed by your instructor and close it.

Skill 3.19 Printing Multiple Copies of a Document

When creating documents, sometimes you will need only one printed copy, but other times you will need to print more than a single copy. From the *Print* page in Backstage view, you can print multiple copies of a document.

To print multiple copies of a document:

1. Click the **File** tab to open Backstage view.
2. Click **Print**.
3. Type the number of copies you want to print in the **Copies** box.
4. Click the **Print** button to print.

FIGURE WD 3.29

another method

You can also change the number of copies to print by clicking the up and down arrows next to the *Copies* box.

let me try Live!

If you do not have the data file from the previous skill open, open the student data file **wd3-19-SpaProductReport** and try this skill on your own:

1. Display the **Print** page in Backstage view.
2. Print **two copies** of the document. **NOTE:** If you are using this in class or in your school's computer lab, check with your instructor about printing permissions before completing this step.
3. If you will be moving on to the next skill in this chapter, leave this document open to continue working. If not, save the file as directed by your instructor and close it.

Skill 3.20 Printing Page Ranges

When designating which pages to print, you can print a range of pages or individual pages. To print sequential pages type the number of the first page you want to print, followed by a hyphen, followed by the last page you want to print. For example, if you want to print pages 3 through 8 in your document, type **3-8** in the *Pages* box. To print individual pages, type each page number you want to print separated by a comma or semicolon. For example, if you want to print page 3, page 5, page 8, and page 10, type **3,5,8,10** in the *Pages* box.

To print specific pages in a document:

1. Click the **File** tab to open Backstage view.

2. Click **Print**.

3. In the *Settings* section, click in the **Pages** box and type the range of pages you want to print.

4. Click the **Print** button to print.

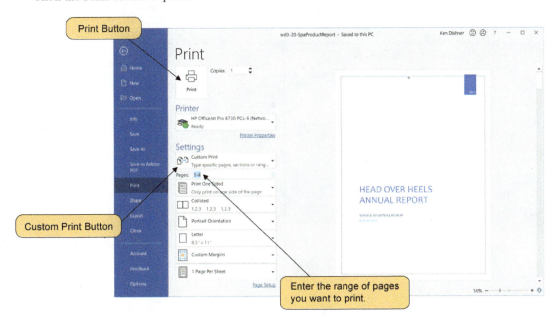

FIGURE WD 3.30

tips & tricks

If you want to print only part of a page, you can choose to print selected content. First, select the content you want to print. On the *Print* page, click the first button under *Settings* and select **Print Selection**. Click the **Print** button to print the selected content only.

tell me **more**

When you enter a range of pages in the *Pages* box, the first button under *Settings* automatically changes to *Custom Print*.

let me **try** Live!

If you do not have the data file from the previous skill open, open the student data file **wd3-20-SpaProductReport** ⬇ and try this skill on your own:

1. Display the **Print** page in Backstage view.
2. Print the **first four pages** of the document. **NOTE:** If you are using this in class or in your school's computer lab, check with your instructor about printing permissions before completing this step and step 3.
3. Now print **pages 2 and 5**.
4. Close the file.

key terms

Theme	Building block
Style set	Building Blocks Organizer
Color theme	Property control
Font theme	Hyperlink
Watermark	ScreenTip
Hard page break	Margins
Section page break	Columns
Section	Column break
Header	Page borders
Footer	Cover page
Automatic date stamp	

concept review

1. Which of the following is a group of formatting elements you apply to a document?
   a. theme
   b. style
   c. building block
   d. property control

2. A(n) _____ changes the font and paragraph formatting for an entire document based on styles.
   a. font theme
   b. color theme
   c. effects theme
   d. style set

3. A _____ is a graphic or text that appears as part of the page background and is usually faded in appearance.
   a. cover page
   b. watermark
   c. margin
   d. property control

4. The text that appears at the top of every page, just below the top margin is known as what?
   a. header
   b. footer
   c. title
   d. cover page

5. A piece of content that is reusable in any document, such as a cover page or a watermark, is known as a _____.
   a. building block
   b. property control
   c. field
   d. style set

6. Which of the following would you use to add your company's name over and over again in a document without typing it every time?
   a. style set
   b. theme
   c. building block
   d. property control

7. What are the blank spaces at the top, bottom, left, and right of a page known as?
    a. borders
    b. margins
    c. page breaks
    d. columns

8. Which of the following will add text that when clicked will take you to another place in the document?
    a. hyperlink
    b. building block
    c. field
    d. property control

9. What would you use to force text on to a new page that will have its own settings separate from the rest of the document?
    a. page break
    b. section break
    c. column break
    d. none of these

10. What would you type in the *Pages* box on the *Print* page to print only the fourth and seventh page in a document?
    a. 4-7
    b. 4,7
    c. 4:7
    d. 47

projects

Data files for projects can be found by logging into your SIMnet account and going to the Library section.

skill review 3.1

In this project you will be formatting and printing a brochure for Suarez Marketing. First, you will apply a document theme and then adjust the look of the document by changing the style set, color theme, and font theme. You will change the layout of the document by adjusting the margins and adding a page break. You will add a page border as a visual element, as well as add a header and footer. You will mark the document as a draft copy by adding a watermark.

Skills needed to complete this project:

- Applying Document Themes (Skill 3.1)
- Applying Style Sets (Skill 3.2)
- Using Color Themes (Skill 3.3)
- Using Font Themes (Skill 3.4)
- Inserting Property Controls (Skill 3.12)
- Adjusting Margins (Skill 3.14)
- Inserting Page Breaks (Skill 3.6)
- Adding Page Borders (Skill 3.17)
- Adding Headers (Skill 3.7)
- Adding Footers (Skill 3.8)
- Creating Watermarks (Skill 3.5)
- Printing Multiple Copies of a Document (Skill 3.19)

1. Open the start file **WD2019-SkillReview-3-1** document and resave the file as:
   `[your initials] WD-SkillReview-3-1`
2. If the document opens in Protected View, click the **Enable Editing** button in the Message Bar at the top of the document so you can modify it.
3. Apply a theme to a document.
   a. Click the **Design** tab.
   b. In the *Document Formatting* group, click the **Themes** button and select **Metropolitan**.
4. Change the style set for the document.
   a. Verify you are still on the **Design** tab.
   b. In the *Style Set* gallery, click the **Lines (Distinctive)** option.
5. Change the color theme.
   a. On the *Design* tab, in the *Document Formatting* group, click the **Colors** button.
   b. Select the **Median** color theme.

6. Change the font theme.

   a. On the *Design* tab, in the *Document Formatting* group, click the **Fonts** button.

   b. Select the **Candara** font theme.

7. Add a company property control.

   a. Place the cursor after *Phone:* and press the Spacebar one time.

   b. Click the **Insert** tab.

   c. In the *Text* group, click the **Quick Parts** button. Point to *Document Property* and select **Company Phone**.

   d. Type **314.555.0144** in the control. Click outside the control to deselect it.

8. Change the margins for the document.

   a. Click the **Layout** tab. In the *Page Setup* group, click the **dialog launcher** to open the *Page Setup* dialog.

   b. Type **1.3″** in the *Left* box. Type **1.3″** in the *Right* box. Click **OK**.

9. Add a page break.

   a. Click before the heading *Client Quotes*.

   b. On the *Layout* tab, in the *Page Setup* group, click the **Breaks** button and select **Page**.

10. Add a page border to the document.

    a. Navigate to the top of the document.

    b. Click the **Design** tab. In the *Page Background* group, click the **Page Borders** button.

    c. Under *Setting*, change the option to **Box**. Click the **Color** arrow and select **Blue-Gray, Accent 6** (it is the last option in the first row under *Theme Colors*). Click the **Width** arrow and select **1 pt**. Click **OK**.

11. Add a header to the document.

    a. Click the **Insert** tab.

    b. In the *Header & Footer* group, click the **Header** button and select the **Banded** header option.

    c. Edit the text in the *Title* property control to read **PUTTING YOUR NEEDS FIRST**

    d. On the *Header & Footer Tools Design* tab, click the **Close Header and Footer** button.

12. Add a footer to the document.

    a. Click the **Insert** tab.

    b. In the *Header & Footer* group, click the **Footer** button and select the **Blank** footer option.

13. Add an automatic date stamp.

    a. In the footer area, click the **Type here** control to select it and press the ⌷Delete⌷ key.

    b. On the *Header & Footer Tools Design* tab, click the **Date & Time** button.

    c. In the *Date and Time* dialog, click the **Month DD, YYYY** option (the third option in the list).

    d. Verify the **Update automatically** checkbox is selected.

    e. Click **OK**.

14. Set a different first page header and footer.
    a. On the *Header & Footer Tools Design* tab, in the *Options* group, click the **Different first page** check box so it appears with a checkmark in it.
    b. Click the **Close Header and Footer** button.
15. Add a watermark to the document.
    a. Navigate to the beginning of the document.
    b. Click the **Design** tab.
    c. In the *Page Background* group, click the **Watermark** button and select the **DRAFT 2** option.
16. Print multiple copies of the document.
    a. Click the **File** tab and click **Print**.
    b. Click the **Copies** up arrow two times, so **3** appears in the box.
    c. Click the **Print** button. **NOTE:** If you are using this in class or in your school's computer lab, check with your instructor about printing permissions before completing this step.
17. Save and close the document.

projects
skill review **3.2**

Data files for projects can be found by logging into your SIMnet account and going to the Library section.

In this project you will be formatting and editing a paper on alternate assessments for students. You will apply a theme and then alter the theme by changing the style set and color theme. You will adjust the margins for the document. You will add information to the footer of the document and a page number and date to the header of the document. You will link to a section in the document. You will add a cover page and then edit the information displayed. Finally, you will print a range of the pages in the document.

Skills needed to complete this project:

- Applying Document Themes (Skill 3.1)
- Applying Style Sets (Skill 3.2)
- Changing Color Themes (Skill 3.3)
- Changing Margins (Skill 3.14)
- Adding Footers (Skill 3.8)
- Inserting Page Numbers (Skill 3.10)
- Adding an Automatic Date Stamp (Skill 3.9)
- Inserting Hyperlinks (Skill 3.13)
- Creating Watermarks (Skill 3.5)
- Inserting Page Breaks (Skill 3.6)
- Adding a Cover Page (Skill 3.18)
- Printing Page Ranges (Skill 3.20)

1. Open the start file **WD2019-SkillReview-3-2** document and resave this document as: [your initials] WD-SkillReview-3-2
2. If the document opens in Protected View, click the **Enable Editing** button in the Message Bar at the top of the document so you can modify it.
3. Apply a theme to a document.
   a. Click the **Design** tab.
   b. In the *Document Formatting* group, click the **Themes** button and select **Facet.**
4. Change the style set for the document.
   a. Verify you are still on the **Design** tab.
   b. In the *Style Set* gallery, click the **Basic (Elegant)** option.
5. Change the color theme.
   a. On the *Design* tab, in *Document Formatting* group, click the **Colors** button.
   b. Select the **Blue Green** color theme.

6. Adjust the margins for the document.

    a. Click the **Layout** tab.

    b. In the *Page Setup* group, click the **Margins** button and select **Moderate**.

7. Add footer text.

    a. Click the **Insert** tab.

    b. In the *Header & Footer* group, click the **Footer** button and select **Ion (Light)**.

    c. Click the **[Title]** control at the far left side of the footer.

    d. Type `ALTERNATE ASSESSMENT`

    e. Click the **[Author]** control in at the far right side of the footer.

    f. Type `ALEXANDER MIRANDA`

    g. Click the **Header & Footer Tools Design** tab.

    h. Click the **Close Header and Footer** button.

8. Insert page numbers and display a different first page for the header.

    a. Click the **Insert** tab.

    b. In the *Header & Footer* group, click the **Page Number** button, point to **Top of Page**, and select **Accent Bar 1**.

    c. On the *Header & Footer Tools Design* tab, in the *Options* group, select the **Different First Page** check box.

    d. Click the **Close Header and Footer** button.

9. Add an automatic date stamp.

    a. Navigate to **page 2** and double-click the header area to activate it.

    b. Place the cursor after the word *Page* and press the `Tab` key two times.

    c. On the *Header & Footer Tools Design* tab, click the **Date & Time** button.

    d. Add a date to the header using the **MM/DD/YY** format (for example, 01/01/19). Have the date update automatically.

    e. Click the **Close Header and Footer** button.

10. Add a hyperlink to another place in the document.

    a. Navigate to the **Modified Achievement Requirements** section.

    b. Place the cursor after the third sentence (ending in to *receive an alternate assessment.*) and press the spacebar one time.

    c. Click the **Insert** tab.

    d. In the *Links* group, click the **Link** button.

    e. Under *Link* to select **Place in This Document**.

    f. Select **Who is Eligible**.

    g. In the **Text to display** box, type `(See the Who is Eligible section)`

    h. Click **OK**.

11. Add a watermark to the document.

    a. Click the **Design** tab.

    b. In the *Page Background* section, click the **Watermark** button and select **DRAFT 1**.

12. Insert a page break.

   a. Navigate to the **Summary** heading and place the cursor at the beginning of the line.

   b. Click the **Layout tab**.

   c. In the *Page Setup* group, click the **Breaks** button and select **Page**.

13. Add a cover page.

   a. Click the **Insert** tab.

   b. In the *Pages* group, click the **Cover Page** button and select **Facet**.

   c. Select the **[Abstract]** control and press **Delete**.

   d. Select the **[Document Subtitle]** control and type `MAKING SURE NO CHILD IS LEFT BEHIND`

14. Preview and print a specific page range.

   a. Click the **File** tab, then click **Print**.

   b. In the *Pages* box, type `2-5`.

   c. Verify the name of your printer appears under **Printer**.

   d. Click the **Print** button. **NOTE:** If you are using this in class or in your school's computer lab, check with your instructor about printing permissions before completing this step.

15. Save and close the document.

projects

Data files for projects can be found by logging into your SIMnet account and going to the Library section.

challenge yourself 3.3

In this project you will be formatting and editing a document for the Tri-State Book Festival. First, you will adjust the look of the document by changing the theme, style set, color theme, and font theme. You will add header and footer information and insert a property control. You will adjust the margins on the document and add a page break. You will display text in columns and adjust how the text is displayed by inserting a column break. Finally, you will add a page border and then print multiple copies of the document.

Skills needed to complete this project:

- Applying Document Themes (Skill 3.1)
- Applying Style Sets (Skill 3.2)
- Using Color Themes (Skill 3.3)
- Using Font Themes (Skill 3.4)
- Adding Headers (Skill 3.7)
- Adding an Automatic Date Stamp (Skill 3.9)
- Adding Footers (Skill 3.8)
- Inserting Property Controls (Skill 3.12)
- Adjusting Margins (Skill 3.14)
- Inserting Page Breaks (Skill 3.6)
- Applying Columns (Skill 3.15)
- Inserting a Column Break (Skill 3.16)
- Adding Page Borders (Skill 3.17)
- Printing Multiple Copies of a Document (Skill 3.19)

1. Open the start file **WD2019-ChallengeYourself-3-3** document and resave this document as:
   `[your initials] WD-ChallengeYourself-3-3`
2. If the document opens in Protected View, click the **Enable Editing** button in the Message Bar at the top of the document so you can modify it.
3. Apply the **Integral** theme to the document.
4. Change the style set to **Lines (Simple)**.
5. Change the color theme to **Green**.
6. Change the font theme to **Century Gothic**.
7. Add a header using the **Sideline** format.
8. Add a footer using the **Retrospect** theme.
9. Delete the **Author** property control and insert a date stamp that will update automatically. Use the **MM/DD/YYYY** format (for example 1/1/2019).

10. Change the header and footer so the first page is different from the rest of the document.

11. Change the margins for the document to the following:
    - *Top*: **1.2"**
    - *Bottom*: **1.2"**
    - *Left*: **1.1"**
    - *Right*:**1.1"**

12. Place the cursor at the beginning of the *Friday September 7* heading in the *Agenda* section. Add a page break.

13. Place the cursor at the beginning of the *Authors* heading at the bottom of page 2. Add a page break.

14. In the *Authors* section, select the text from the heading **Fiction** through **Showcased work: The PM Handbook**. Display text in **two columns**.

15. Add a page border to the document with the following settings:
    - *Setting*: **Box**
    - *Style*: **Solid line (default option)**
    - *Color*: **Green, Accent 1** (it is the fifth option in the first row under *Theme Colors*)
    - *Width*: **1 ½ pt**

16. Print three copies of the document. **NOTE:** If you are using this in class or in your school's computer lab, check with your instructor about printing permissions before completing this step.

17. Save and close the document.

Data files for projects can be found by logging into your SIMnet account and going to the Library section.

projects

challenge yourself 3.4

In this project you will be editing the text of a safety memo from the Winter Springs. You will change the theme for the document and then adjust the theme by changing the style set and color theme. You will add content to the footer and the header of the document. You will link to another place in the document. You will adjust the layout of the document by adding a page break and displaying text in columns. Finally, you will add a watermark and then print multiple copies of a specific page range.

Skills needed to complete this project:

- Applying Document Themes (Skill 3.1)
- Applying Style Sets (Skill 3.2)
- Using Color Themes (Skill 3.3)
- Using Font Themes (Skill 3.4)
- Adding Footers (Skill 3.8)
- Adding Headers (Skill 3.7)
- Adding an Automatic Date Stamp (Skill 3.9)
- Inserting Hyperlinks (Skill 3.13)
- Adjusting Margins (Skill 3.14)
- Applying Columns (Skill 3.15)
- Inserting a Column Break (Skill 3.16)
- Inserting Page Breaks (Skill 3.6)
- Adding a Cover Page (Skill 3.18)
- Creating Watermarks (Skill 3.5)
- Printing Multiple Copies of a Document (Skill 3.19)
- Printing Page Ranges (Skill 3.20)

1. Open the start file **WD2019-ChallengeYourself-3-4** document and resave this document as: `[your initials] WD-ChallengeYourself-3-4`
2. If the document opens in Protected View, click the **Enable Editing** button in the Message Bar at the top of the document so you can modify it.
3. Apply the **Retrospect** theme to the document.
4. Change the style set to **Lines (Simple)**.
5. Change the color theme to **Blue Warm**.
6. Change the font theme to **Candara**.
7. Add a footer using the **Sideline** format.
8. Add a header using the **Grid** format.

9. On page 2, delete the **Date** control and add an automatic date stamp in its place using the **MM/DD/YYYY** format. Be sure the date will update automatically.

10. Add a hyperlink to another place in the document.

    a. Navigate to the **Our Safety Vision** section.

    b. Place the cursor after the second sentence (ending in *overlapping shifts.*) and press the spacebar one time.

    c. Add a hyperlink to the **Round the Clock Officers** section of the document. Have text for the link read `(See the list of officers)`

11. Change the margins for the document to the following:

- *Top*: **1.1"**
- *Bottom*: **1.1"**
- *Left*: **1.2"**
- *Right*: **1.2"**

12. Navigate to the beginning of the document and change the font size of the text *Winter Springs Safety News* to **36 pt**.

13. In the *Round the Clock Officers* section, select the text from the heading **Amy Stephens (12 years)** through **Jeannie Smith (4 years)**. Display the text in **two columns**.

14. In the *Day Shift Officers* section, select the text from the heading **Harriet Hollow (7 years)** through **Gordan Beagle (2 years)**. Display the text in **two columns**.

15. Insert a page break before the **Upcoming Safety Improvements** section.

16. Add a cover page.

    a. Insert a cover page using the **Whisp** design.

    b. Change the *Document subtitle* to read `The latest safety news for you`

    c. Delete the **Date** control on the cover page.

17. Navigate to the *Introduction* section and add a watermark using the **SAMPLE 1** option.

18. Print two copies of all the pages except the cover page. **NOTE:** If you are using this in class or in your school's computer lab, check with your instructor about printing permissions before completing this step.

19. Save and close the document.

projects

on your own **3.5**

In this project you will be formatting and printing a marketing sheet for a landscape company. You will apply a theme of your choice and adjust the theme by changing the style set, color theme, and font theme. You will add a property control to ensure consistent spelling of the company name. You will add content to the header and footer of the document. You will change the layout by adjusting margins and adding a page break. You will add a page border and a cover page. Finally, you will practice printing multiple copies and page ranges.

Skills needed to complete this project:

- Applying Document Themes (Skill 3.1)
- Applying Style Sets (Skill 3.2)
- Using Color Themes (Skill 3.3)
- Using Font Themes (Skill 3.4)
- Inserting Property Controls (Skill 3.12)
- Inserting Page Numbers (Skill 3.10)
- Adding an Automatic Date Stamp (Skill 3.9)
- Adding Headers (Skill 3.7)
- Adjusting Margins (Skill 3.14)
- Inserting Page Breaks (Skill 3.6)
- Adding Page Borders (Skill 3.17)
- Adding a Cover Page (Skill 3.18)
- Printing Multiple Copies of a Document (Skill 3.19)
- Printing Page Ranges (Skill 3.20)

1. Open the start file **WD2019-OnYourOwn-3-5** document and resave this document as: `[your initials] WD-OnYourOwn-3-5`
2. If the document opens in Protected View, click the **Enable Editing** button in the Message Bar at the top of the document so you can modify it.
3. Apply a theme of your choice to the document.
4. Change the style set to one of your choice.
5. Choose a new color theme.
6. Choose a new font theme.
7. Insert a **Company** property control at the beginning of the first paragraph. Be sure a space appears between the property control and the next word.

8. There are four instances where the company name is spelled **GreenScapes**. Find each instance, delete the text, and replace the text with a **Company** property control. Be sure a space appears between the property control and the next word.

9. Add a page number to the bottom of the document. Use a format of your choice.

10. Add an automatic date stamp to the footer of the document. Use a format of your choice.

11. Add a header that will display the **document title**. If there are other property controls in the header, delete them.

12. Change the header and footer so they do not appear on the first page of the document.

13. Adjust the margins for optimal layout.

14. If necessary, insert a page break before any *Heading 1* so the section starts on a new page and does not break across two pages. Be sure to delete any extra lines. **NOTE:** Depending on the margin settings you used, you may not need to insert a page break.

15. Add a page border of your choice. Modify the color and width of the border.

16. Print three copies of the document. **NOTE:** If you are using this in class or in your school's computer lab, check with your instructor about printing permissions before completing this step.

17. Save and close the document.

projects

fix it 3.6

Data files for projects can be found by logging into your SIMnet account and going to the Library section.

In this project you will fix a report on classroom behavior. First, will fix the margins and apply a new theme and style set. You will then apply styles to text and adjust the color and font themes. You will replace manually entered page numbers and add an author property control to the header of the document. You will add information to the footer including an automatic date stamp. You will add a section break and cover page. Finally, you will add a watermark and print multiple copies of the document.

Skills needed to complete this project:

- Adjusting Margins (Skill 3.14)
- Applying Document Themes (Skill 3.1)
- Applying Style Sets (Skill 3.2)
- Using Color Themes (Skill 3.3)
- Using Font Themes (Skill 3.4)
- Adding Headers (Skill 3.7)
- Inserting Property Controls (Skill 3.12)
- Adding Footers (Skill 3.8)
- Adding an Automatic Date Stamp (Skill 3.9)
- Inserting Page Breaks (Skill 3.6)
- Adding a Cover Page (Skill 3.18)
- Creating Watermarks (Skill 3.5)
- Printing Multiple Copies of a Document (Skill 3.19)

1. Open the start file **WD2019-FixIt-3-6** document and resave this document as:
   `[your initials] WD-FixIt-3-6`
2. If the document opens in Protected View, click the **Enable Editing** button in the Message Bar at the top of the document so you can modify it.
3. Change the margins to use the **Normal** preset.
4. Change the document theme to **Ion**.
5. Change the style set to **Basic (Simple)**.
6. On page 1, apply the **Title** style to the text **Behavior Modification Project**.
7. Apply the **Heading 1** style to section titles beginning with a roman numeral:
   - I. Identify the Target Behavior
   - II. Define the target behavior in measurable terms
   - III. Collect and chart baseline data
   - IV. Implement the behavior change program
   - V. Evaluate the result
   - VI. Evaluation and conclusion

8. Change the color theme to **Blue**.

9. Change the font theme to **Office**.

10. The author Joseph Marquez typed his name and a page number at the top of each page. Delete this line from the top of each page. There are four instances of this mistake. **NOTE:** After you have deleted the first instance of this mistake, the remaining instances will no longer appear at the top of the following pages.

11. Review the document and remove any extra line breaks.

12. Add the **Ion (Light)** header to the document.

13. Adjust the header so it does not appear on the first page of the document.

14. In the *Document Properties*, add the name **Joseph Marquez** as the author.

15. In the header area on page 2, add an **Author** property control to the left side of the page.

16. Add a footer to the document using the **Blank (Three Columns)** design. Replace the first instance of **[Type here]** with the text `Not for Distribution`

17. Delete the second instance of **[Type here]**.

18. In the footer, replace the third instance of **[Type here]** with an automatic date and time field using the **MM/DD/YY** format.

19. Insert a next page section break before the *V. Evaluate the result* section.

20. Add a cover page.

    a. Insert a cover page using the **Banded** design.

    b. Change the *Document Title* to read `Behavior Modification Project`

    c. Delete the **COMPANY NAME and Company address** controls on the cover page.

21. Navigate to the next page and add a watermark using the **CONFIDENTIAL 2** format.

22. Print two copies of the document. **NOTE:** If you are using this in class or in your school's computer lab, check with your instructor about printing permissions before completing this step.

23. Save and close the document.

Working with Pictures, Tables, and Charts

chapter 4

introduction

This chapter provides you with the skills to add and modify pictures, graphic elements, tables, and charts. You will learn to insert pictures from an online source as well as from your own computer and add alt text to images. Once you have added pictures to a document, you will manipulate them by resizing, positioning, and changing the text wrapping. You will then stylize pictures using Quick Styles. You will learn about other graphic objects you can add to documents including icons, shapes, WordArt, and SmartArt diagrams. You will create and enter data in a table and then modify the table by adding and deleting rows and columns. You will change the display of data in a table by merging and splitting cells and sorting the data within a table. You will modify the look of a table by applying a table Quick Style and then changing the display of table borders. Finally, you will add a chart to a document and then modify the look of that chart.

Skill **4.1** Inserting a Picture

You can insert pictures that you created in another program into your document. There are a number of graphic formats you can insert into a Word document. Some of the more common file types include JPEG, PNG, BMP, and GIF. By default, Word inserts pictures as embedded objects, meaning they become part of the new document. Changing the source file will not change or affect the newly inserted picture.

FIGURE WD 4.1

To insert a picture from a file:

1. Click the **Insert** tab.
2. In the *Illustrations* group, click the **Pictures** button.
3. The *Insert Picture* dialog opens.
4. Navigate to the file location, select the file, and click **Insert**.

To delete a picture, select it and press the **Delete** key on the keyboard.

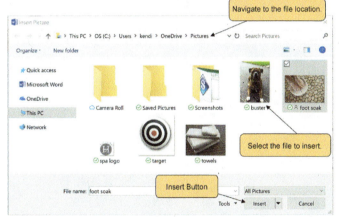

FIGURE WD 4.2

tell me **more**

When you insert a picture to a document, the *Format* tab under *Picture Tools* displays. This tab is called a contextual tab because it displays only when a picture is the active element. The *Format* tab contains tools to change the look of the picture, such as picture style, brightness and contrast, cropping, and placement on the page.

another method

To insert the file from the *Insert Picture* dialog, you can also click the **Insert** button arrow and select **Insert.**

let me try Live!

Open the student data file **wd4-01-SpaProductReport** and try this skill on your own:

1. Place the cursor on the blank line after the first paragraph in the document.
2. Open the dialog where you can insert a picture from your computer.
3. Navigate to the location where you saved the data files for this book.
4. Insert the **foot soak** picture.
5. If you will be moving on to the next skill in this chapter, leave the document open to continue working. If not, save the file as directed by your instructor and close it.

Skill 4.2 Positioning Pictures

When you first add a picture to your document, Word inserts the picture at the insertion point and displays the picture in line with the text. More often than not, you will want to place the picture somewhere else on the page. Word comes with a number of preset picture positions that place the picture at a specific location on the page with text wrapping applied.

To position a picture on a page with text wrapping:

1. Click the **Picture Tools Format** tab.
2. In the *Arrange* group, click the **Position Object** button.
3. In the *With Text Wrapping* section, select an option. The picture is placed on the page according to the option you chose.

FIGURE WD 4.3

tips & tricks

When you position a picture, the location you choose is for the page the picture is on. If you want the picture to appear on another page, move the picture to that page and then use the **Position Object** command to place it.

another method

You can also position pictures on the page from the *Layout* tab. In the *Arrange* group, click the **Position Object** button and select an option.

let me try Live!

If you do not have the data file from the previous skill open, open the student data file
wd4-02-SpaProductReport and try this skill on your own:

1. Select the picture on the first page of the document.
2. Use the **Position Object** command that will place the picture in the upper left corner of the page with square wrapping applied.
3. If you will be moving on to the next skill in this chapter, leave the document open to continue working. If not, save the file as directed by your instructor and close it.

Skill 4.3 Adding Alt Text to Pictures

Adding alt text to pictures in your documents makes your documents accessible to a wider audience, including those that are blind. **Alt text** is a description of a picture, chart, or other object that can be read by screen readers. When creating alt text, write a description that is thorough and to the point. Do not include any unnecessary words. A good rule of thumb is to think of how you would describe the picture to someone who cannot see it.

To add alt text to a picture:

1. Right-click the picture and select **Edit Alt Text...**

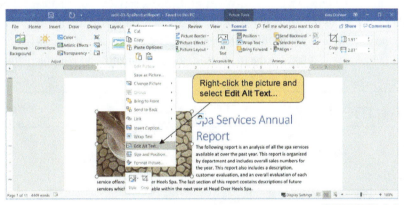

FIGURE WD 4.4

2. In the *Alt Text* task pane, type a detailed description of the picture in the text box.

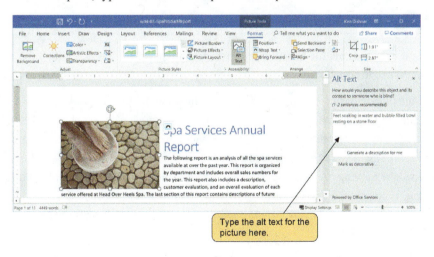

FIGURE WD 4.5

tips & tricks

Word's *Accessibility Checker* feature reviews your document looking for anything that does not meet accessibility standards. To run the *Accessibility Checker*, click the **Review** tab. In the *Accessibility* group, click the **Check Accessibility** button. Issues that might interfere with a screen reader's ability to read the document appear in the *Warnings* section, including any figures that do not include an alt text description.

tell me more

If you have an Office 365 subscription, Word's intelligent services automatically analyzes any picture that is added to the document and creates an alt text description for the picture. However, the description that Word's intelligent services creates is not always accurate. It is important to check the alt text for the pictures in your documents and edit the pictures as necessary.

another method

To add alt text to images, you can also:

1. Select the picture to which you want to add the description.
2. Click the **Picture Tools Format** tab.
3. In the *Accessibility* group, click the **Alt Text** button.

let me try Live!

If you do not have the data file from the previous skill open, open the student data file **wd4-03-SpaProductReport** and try this skill on your own:

1. Select the picture of the feet on the first page of the document.
2. Open the **Alt Text** task pane.
3. Add the following description as alt text and then close the task pane when you are done:
   `Feet soaking in water and bubble filled bowl resting on a stone floor`
4. If you will be moving on to the next skill in this chapter, leave the document open to continue working. If not, save the file as directed by your instructor and close it.

Skill 4.4 Inserting Online Pictures

In addition to adding pictures from your computer, you can also search for **online pictures** to add to documents. You can search for pictures from different online sources, including Bing search or from your OneDrive. When searching for online pictures, you are responsible for understanding copyright issues and obtaining permission from the copyright owner if necessary.

To insert a picture from an online source:

1. Click the **Insert** tab.
2. In the *Illustrations* group, click the **Online Pictures** button.

FIGURE WD 4.6

3. The *Online Pictures* dialog opens.
4. Type a word describing the picture you want to search for in the *Search* box and click the **Search** button.

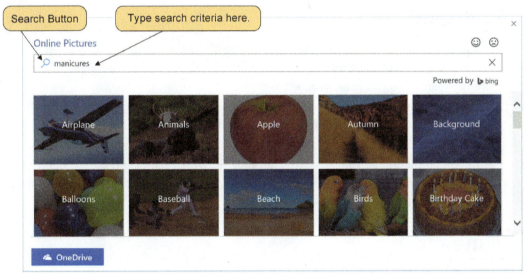

FIGURE WD 4.7

5. Word displays thumbnail results that match the search criteria.
6. Click a thumbnail to select it and click the **Insert** button to add the picture to your document.

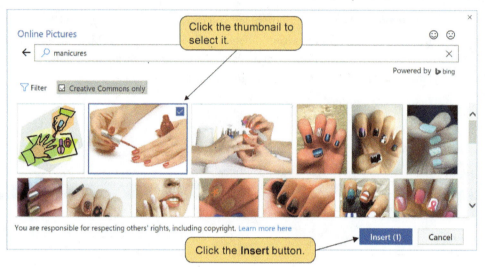

FIGURE WD 4.8

Depending on your version of Office 365, the *Online Pictures* dialog may look different than the one here, but the general steps for searching for online images still apply.

tips & tricks

> When you insert a picture from Creative Commons, Word will automatically insert the source information along with the picture. Be sure to select both the source and the picture when you move or resize the picture.

> You can add more than one image at a time in the *Online Pictures* dialog. As you select images, a checkmark appears next to the selected image and the number on the *Insert* button updates to reflect the number of images that will be added to the document.

> To insert pictures from your OneDrive, click the **OneDrive** button at the bottom of the *Online Pictures* dialog. Navigate to the folder where you have saved the picture you want to insert, select the picture, and click the **Insert** button.

tell me more

If you use Bing search, you will be searching for pictures from across the Internet and Word will return pictures that have the **Creative Commons** licensing tag. However, the results you see may include pictures that are not royalty free. Always check the source of the picture to be sure you only use pictures in your documents that you know you have the proper rights to use.

let me try Live!

If you do not have the data file from the previous skill open, open the student data file **wd4-04-SpaProductReport** ⬇ and try this skill on your own:

1. Place your cursor in the empty line under the first paragraph of the document.
2. Open the dialog where you can insert a picture from an online source.
3. Use *Bing* to search for pictures of `manicures`.
4. Insert the picture that is selected in Figure 4.8. If you do not see this picture in your results, insert a picture of your choice.
5. If you will be moving on to the next skill in this chapter, leave the document open to continue working. If not, save the file as directed by your instructor and close it.

Skill 4.5 Resizing Pictures

When you first add a picture to a document, you may find it is not the right size. The picture may be too large for the page, or it may be too small for the page layout. You can resize pictures in a document by either manually entering the values for the size of the picture or by dragging a **resize handle** on the picture to resize it.

To resize a picture by manually entering values:

1. Select the picture you want to resize.
2. Click the **Picture Tools Format** tab.
3. In the *Size* group, type a value in the *Width* or *Height* box to resize the picture.
4. Press Enter to resize the picture.

To resize a picture by dragging:

1. Select the picture you want to change.
2. To resize a picture, click a **resize handle** and drag toward the center of the picture to make it smaller or away from the center of the picture to make it larger.

FIGURE WD 4.9

tips & tricks

When resizing by dragging, be sure to use one of the resize handles on the four corners of the picture to maintain the aspect ratio of the picture. This means that as the width is increased or decreased, the height of the picture is increased or decreased proportionally. To maintain the aspect ratio when entering values, click the dialog launcher in the *Size* group and verify the **Lock aspect ratio** checkbox is selected in the *Layout* dialog.

let me try Live!

If you do not have the data file from the previous skill open, open the student data file
wd4-05-SpaProductReport ⬇ and try this skill on your own:

1. Select the picture of the manicure on the first page of the document.
2. Resize the picture so it is **2″** in height and **2.68″** in width.
3. If you will be moving on to the next skill in this chapter, leave the document open to continue working. If not, save the file as directed by your instructor and close it.

Skill 4.6 Changing Picture Layouts

When you first add a picture to your document, Word inserts the picture at the insertion point and displays the picture in line with the text. This causes the picture to be treated as its own paragraph. But what if you want the text in your document to wrap around the picture? Word comes with a number of layout options for you to choose from. When a picture is selected, you will see the **Layout Options** button. This button gives you one-click access to text layout options for the picture.

To adjust the layout of a picture:

1. Click the picture to select it.
2. Click the **Layout Options** button.
3. Select a wrapping option.

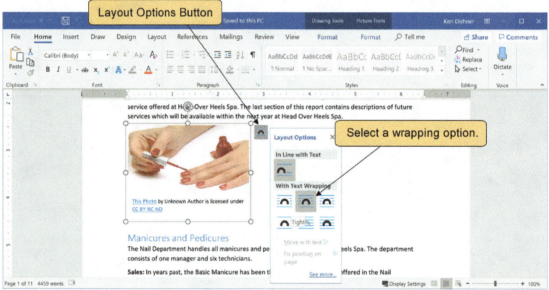

FIGURE WD 4.10

tips & tricks

As you roll the mouse over each layout option, Live Preview will display how the document will look with the text wrapping applied.

another method

To change the layout of pictures, you can also click the **Layout** tab or the **Picture Tools Format** tab. In the *Arrange* group, click the **Wrap Text** button and select an option.

let me try Live!

If you do not have the data file from the previous skill open, open the student data file **wd4-06-SpaProductReport** and try this skill on your own:

1. Select the picture of the manicure on the first page of the document.
2. Change the text wrap option of the picture to the **Tight** layout option.
3. If you will be moving on to the next skill in this chapter, leave the document open to continue working. If not, save the file as directed by your instructor and close it.

Skill 4.7 Moving Pictures

When you first add a picture to a document, you may find it is not positioned where you want it. You can change the position of pictures by dragging and dropping the picture where you want it on the page. When you drag a picture, you will see horizontal and vertical green lines called the **alignment guides**. They appear when the picture's edge is aligned with another element on the page.

To move pictures in a document:

1. Select the picture you want to move.
2. Rest your mouse over the picture.
3. When the cursor changes to the **move cursor**, click and drag the picture to the new location.
4. When an alignment guide appears aligning it with the desired element on the page, release the mouse button to snap the picture in place and align it on the page.

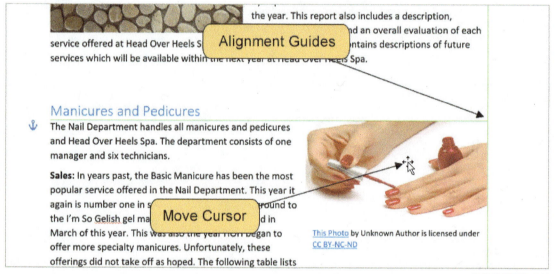

FIGURE WD 4.11

tips & tricks

If you don't see alignment guides when you move a picture, they may be turned off. To turn on alignment guides, click the **Picture Tools Format** tab. In the *Arrange* group, click the **Align** button and select **Use Alignment Guides** so a checkmark appears next to the menu item. Click **Use Alignment Guides** again to turn off the feature.

let me try Live!

If you do not have the data file from the previous skill open, open the student data file **wd4-07-SpaProductReport** ⬇ and try this skill on your own:

1. Select the picture of the manicure on the first page of the document.
2. Move the picture to the right of the first paragraph so the top of the picture aligns with the top of the first paragraph in the *Manicures and Pedicures* section and the right side of the picture aligns with the right margin of the page. You will see horizontal and vertical alignment guides as shown in Figure WD 4.11.
3. If you will be moving on to the next skill in this chapter, leave the document open to continue working. If not, save the file as directed by your instructor and close it.

Skill 4.8 Applying Quick Styles to Pictures

Quick Styles are combinations of formatting that give elements of your document a more polished, professional look without a lot of work. Quick Styles for pictures include a combination of borders, shadows, reflections, and picture shapes, such as rounded corners or skewed perspective. Instead of applying each of these formatting elements one at a time, you can apply a combination of elements at one time using a preset Quick Style.

To apply a Quick Style to a picture:

1. Select the picture you want to apply the Quick Style to.
2. Click the **Picture Tools Format** tab.
3. In the *Picture Styles* group, click the **More** button.
4. In the *Picture Quick Styles* gallery, click an option to apply it to the picture.

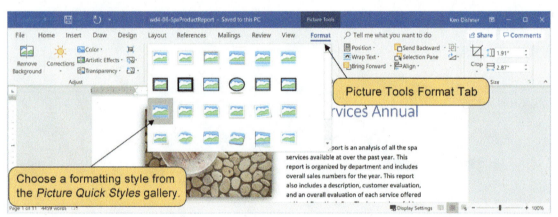

FIGURE WD 4.12

tell me **more**

The same steps for applying Quick Styles to pictures can be used to apply Quick Styles to other drawing objects, such as shapes.

another method

To apply a Quick Style to a picture, you can also right-click the picture, click the **Picture** button, and select a Quick Style from the gallery.

let me try Live!

If you do not have the data file from the previous skill open, open the student data file **wd4-08-SpaProductReport** ⬇️ and try this skill on your own:

1. Select the picture of the **foot soak** on the first page of the document.
2. Apply the **Center Shadow Rectangle** Quick Style to the picture.
3. If you will be moving on to the next skill in this chapter, leave the document open to continue working. If not, save the file as directed by your instructor and close it.

Skill 4.9 Adding Icons

Icons are SVG (Scalable Vector Graphics) images you can add to your documents. They are simple drawings and because they use the SVG format, they can be enlarged, colored, and roatated without losing image quality.

To insert an icon:

1. Navigate to the location where you want to add the icon.
2. Click the **Insert** tab.
3. In the *Illustrations* group, click the **Icons** button.

FIGURE WD 4.13

4. The *Insert Icons* dialog appears. Click a category on the left to navigate to that section.
5. Click an icon to select it.
6. Click the **Insert** button.

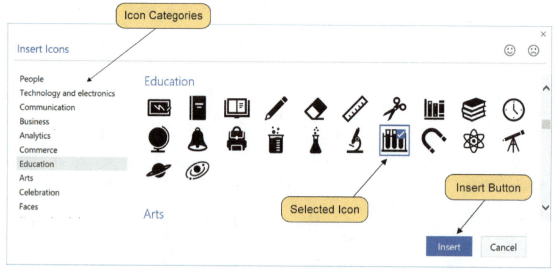

FIGURE WD 4.14

All icons are inserted with a black fill color, but you can modify icons from the *Graphics Tools Format* tab. This tab contains commands for changing the look of the icon, including applying a preset graphics style. Preset graphic styles are a combination of fill and outline settings that can be applied to a graphic at the same time.

To apply a preset graphics style to an icon:

1. With the icon selected, on the *Graphics Tools Format* tab, click the **Graphics Styles More** button.
2. The *Graphics Styles* gallery displays. Click a style in the gallery to apply it to the icon.

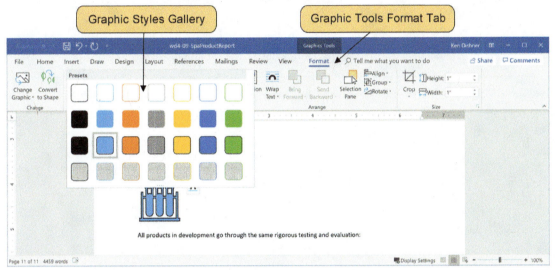

FIGURE WD 4.15

tell me **more**

You can select more than one icon to insert. Selected icons appear with a box around the icon and a checkmark in the upper right corner.

another method

> You can also scroll the icons in the *Insert Icons* dialog rather than using the category list to jump to a section.

> To apply a preset graphics style, you can also click an option in the gallery on the Ribbon.

let me try Live!

If you do not have the data file from the previous skill open, open the student data file **wd4-09-SpaProductReport** ⬇ and try this skill on your own:

1. Navigate to the end of the document and place the cursor on the blank line above the last line of text.
2. Add the icon of the **three test tubes**. It is in the *Education* category.
3. Apply the **Colored Fill – Accent 1, Dark 1 Outline** graphics style to the icon. It is the second icon in the third row of the gallery.
4. If you will be moving on to the next skill in this chapter, leave the document open to continue working. If not, save the file as directed by your instructor and close it.

Skill 4.10 Inserting SmartArt

SmartArt is a way to make your ideas visual. Where documents used to have plain bulleted and ordered lists, now they can have SmartArt, which are visual diagrams containing graphic elements with text boxes in which you can enter your information. Using SmartArt not only makes your document look better, but also helps convey the information in a more meaningful way.

To add SmartArt to a document:

1. Click the **Insert** tab.
2. In the *Illustrations* group, click the **SmartArt** button.

FIGURE WD 4.16

3. In the *Choose a SmartArt Graphic* dialog, click a **SmartArt** option and click **OK**.
4. The SmartArt is added to your document.
5. If necessary, click the arrow tab on the left side of the diagram to display the *SmartArt Text* pane.
6. Click in the first item of the *SmartArt Text* pane and type your first item.
7. Enter the text for each item.
8. Click outside the SmartArt graphic to hide the *Text* pane.

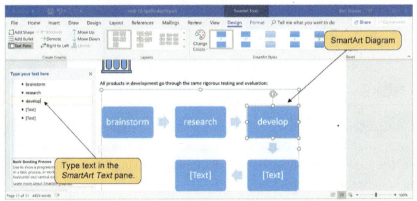

FIGURE WD 4.17

There are eight categories of SmartArt for you to choose from:

List—Use to list items that do not need to be in a particular order.

Process—Use to list items that do need to be in a particular order.

Cycle—Use for a process that repeats over and over again.

Hierarchy—Use to show branching, in either a decision tree or an organization chart.

Relationship—Use to show relationships between items.

Matrix—Use to show how an item fits into the whole.

Pyramid—Use to illustrate how things relate to each other with the largest item on the bottom and the smallest item on the top.

Picture—Use to show a series of pictures along with text in the diagram.

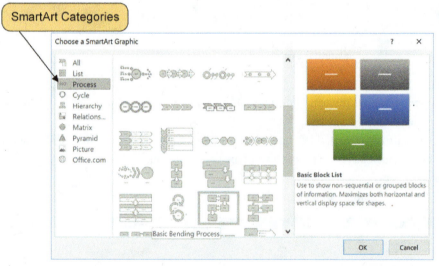

FIGURE WD 4.18

tips & tricks

When choosing a SmartArt diagram, it is important that the diagram type suits your content. In the *Choose a SmartArt Graphic* dialog, click a SmartArt type to display a preview of the SmartArt to the right. The preview not only displays what the diagram will look like, but also includes a description of the best uses for the diagram type.

another method

To enter text in SmartArt, you can click in a text box on the SmartArt diagram and type your text.

let me try Live!

If you do not have the data file from the previous skill open, open the student data file
wd4-10-SpaProductReport 📥 and try this skill on your own:

1. Navigate to the end of the document and place the cursor at the end of the last line of text and press Enter.
2. Insert a **Basic Bending Process** SmartArt diagram. See Figure WD 4.18.
3. Enter the following information in the diagram:
   - `brainstorm`
   - `research`
   - `develop`
   - `focus test`
   - `produce`
4. If you will be moving on to the next skill in this chapter, leave the document open to continue working. If not, save the file as directed by your instructor and close it.

Skill 4.11 Inserting a Shape

A **shape** is a drawing object that you can quickly add to your document. Word comes with a number of shapes for you to choose from, including lines, block arrows, callouts, and basic shapes such as smiley faces, rectangles, and circles.

To add a shape to a document:

1. Click the **Insert** tab.
2. In the *Illustrations* group, click the **Shapes** button and select an option from the *Shapes* gallery.
3. The cursor changes to a crosshair.
4. Click on the document to add the shape with default sizing. If you want to control the size of the shape, click and drag on the document. As you are dragging, you will see an outline of the shape. When the shape is the size you want, release the mouse button.

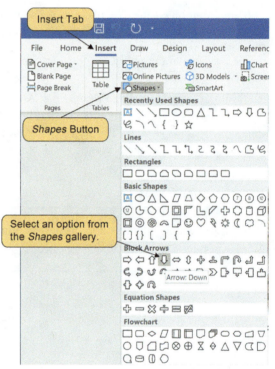

FIGURE WD 4.19

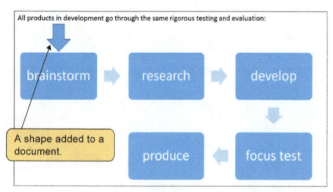

FIGURE WD 4.20

tell me **more**

When you insert a shape into a document, the *Drawing Tools Format* tab displays. This is called a contextual tab because it displays only when a drawing object is the active element. The *Format* tab contains tools to change the look of the shape, such as shape styles, effects, and placement on the page. You can apply Quick Styles to shapes by selecting an option in the *Shape Quick Styles* gallery in the *Shape Styles* group. Click the **More** button for the gallery to expand it and view all the Quick Style options you can apply to shapes.

let me **try** Live!

If you do not have the data file from the previous skill open, open the student data file **wd4-11-SpaProductReport** ⬇ and try this skill on your own:

1. On the last page of the document, add an **Arrow: Down** shape above the *Brainstorm* box in the SmartArt diagram.
2. If necessary, move the shape so it is centered above the *Brainstorm* box. See Figure WD 4.20.
3. If you will be moving on to the next skill in this chapter, leave the document open to continue working. If not, save the file as directed by your instructor and close it.

Skill 4.12 Adding WordArt to Documents

Sometimes you'll want to call attention to text you have added to your document. You could format the text by using character effects, or if you want the text to really stand out, use **WordArt**. WordArt styles are predefined graphic styles you can apply to text. These styles include a combination of color, fills, outlines, and effects.

To add WordArt to a document:

1. Click the **Insert** tab.
2. In the *Text* group, click the **Insert WordArt** button and select a style from the gallery.
3. Replace the text *Your text here* with the text for your document.

After you have added WordArt to your document, you can modify it just as you would any other text. Use the *Font* box and *Font Size* box on the *Home* tab to change the font or font size of WordArt.

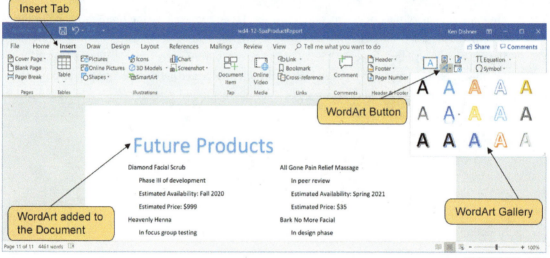

FIGURE WD 4.21

tips & tricks

When you insert WordArt into a document, the *Drawing Tools Format* tab displays. You can modify the look of the WordArt from commands in the *WordArt Styles* and *Text* groups on this tab, including adjusting fill and outline colors and changing the alignment and direction of the text.

let me try Live!

If you do not have the data file from the previous skill open, open the student data file **wd4-12-SpaProductReport** ⬇ and try this skill on your own:

1. Place the cursor at the top of the last page in the document.
2. Add WordArt to the document using the second option of the first row of the WordArt gallery.
3. Replace the text *Your text here* with: `Future Products`
4. Move the WordArt object so it appears above the list aligned with the left side of the left column of text. See Figure WD 4.21.
5. If you will be moving on to the next skill in this chapter, leave the document open to continue working. If not, save the file as directed by your instructor and close it.

Skill 4.13 Creating a Table

A **table** helps you organize information for effective display. Tables are organized by **rows**, which display horizontally, and **columns**, which display vertically. The intersection of a row and column is referred to as a **cell**. Tables can be used to display everything from dates in a calendar to sales numbers to product inventory.

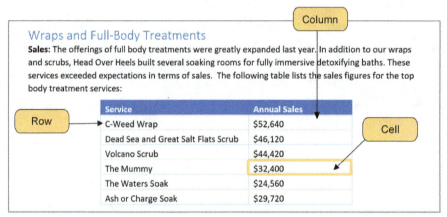

FIGURE WD 4.22

To create a simple table:

1. Click the **Insert** tab.
2. In the *Tables* group, click the **Table** button.
3. Select the number of cells you want by moving the cursor across and down the squares.
4. When the description at the top of the menu displays the number of rows and columns you want, click the mouse.
5. The table is inserted into your document.

FIGURE WD 4.23

tips & tricks

Rather than inserting a table and then adding data, you can convert existing text into a table. After selecting the text to be converted, click the **Table** button and click **Insert Table...** The number of rows and columns will automatically be determined by the tabs and paragraphs in the selection.

tell me **more**

Word comes with a number of **Quick Tables** building blocks. These templates are preformatted for you and include sample data. To insert a Quick Table, click the **Tables** button, point to **Quick Tables**, and select a building block option from the gallery. After you insert a Quick Table, just replace the sample data with your own.

another method

To insert a table, you can also:

1. Click the **Table** button and select **Insert Table...**
2. In the *Insert Table* dialog, enter the number of rows and columns for your table.
3. Click **OK**.

let me **try** Live!

If you do not have the data file from the previous skill open, open the student data file **wd4-13-SpaProductReport** and try this skill on your own:

1. Navigate to the *Facials* section of the document (it is located on page 6 of the document). and place the cursor on the blank line under the first paragraph of the section.
2. Insert a table that has **two columns** and **five rows**.
3. If you will be moving on to the next skill in this chapter, leave the document open to continue working. If not, save the file as directed by your instructor and close it.

from the perspective of . . .

A COMMUNITY NEWSPAPER INTERN

When I first started working for the newspaper, articles were text with all the photographs arranged either above or below the text of the article. The text was well formatted, but didn't convey the information in an exciting, visual manner. We do the layout in Word for delivery either in print or online. So, one of the things I did was jazz up the photographs by adding text wrapping and Quick Styles. I also changed our boring lists into vibrant SmartArt diagrams. I finally convinced my editor to format tables in the newspaper using Quick Styles. No more boring black and white! Now our newspaper has the visual punch that really grabs our readers' attention.

Skill 4.14 Working with Tables

Once you have inserted a blank table, you will need to enter data. When entering data in a table, it is a good idea to use the first row as a heading row by typing a short description of the content for the column in each cell. After you have labeled each column, continue entering the data into your table.

To enter data in a table:

1. Place the cursor in the cell where you want to enter the data.
2. Type the data just as you would in normal text.
3. Press Tab to move to the next cell and enter more data.
4. When you reach the last cell in the last row of a table, pressing Tab on the keyboard will create a new row in the table.
5. Continue pressing Tab until all data are entered.

Table Move Handle

Facials

Sales: Last year the O2 Oh My Facial and the Mango Facial were added to the more conventional facial offerings at Head Over Heels Spa. While neither service has overtaken The Basic or the Deep Down and Clean facial, both new services have had strong sales and have increased sales in our Head Over Heels shop. The following table lists the sales figures for the top facial services:

Service	Annual Sales
Mango Facial	$19,845
Deep Down and Clean Facial	$36,540
O2 Oh My Facial	$21,420
The Basic	

Press the **Tab** key to move to the next cell in the table.

FIGURE WD 4.24

After you have entered data in a table, you will most likely want to manipulate all or part of the table. You can select individual rows, columns, or the entire table:

> To select a row, point to the left side of the row you want to select. When the cursor changes to a white arrow icon , press the mouse button. The selected row will appear highlighted.

> To select a column, point to the top of the column you want to select. When the cursor changes to a black, down-pointing arrow icon ↓, press the mouse button. The selected column will appear highlighted.

> To select the entire table, click the **table move handle** that appears at the upper left corner of the table when it is active.

tips & tricks

When working with tables be sure you have the correct part of the table selected. If you want to change the formatting on a row or column, you must select the row or column first. If you place the cursor in a cell or select a cell, the formatting will apply only to that cell.

tell me more

When working with tables, the conventional way to identify a cell is by column and row. Columns are typically referred to by letters and rows by numbers. Thus, the first cell in the third row would be identified as "cell A3" and the third cell in the first row would be identified as "C1."

another method

> To enter data in another cell in a table, you can also click in the cell and begin typing.
> To select parts of a table, you can also click the **Table Tools Layout** tab. In the *Table* group, click the **Select** button and select an option.

let me try Live!

If you do not have the data file from the previous skill open, open the student data file **wd4-14-SpaProductReport** and try this skill on your own:

1. Navigate to the table in the *Facials* section.
2. Practice selecting a row, a column, and the entire table.
3. Enter the following information in the table. Press Tab to move between cells in the table.

Service	Annual Sales
Mango Facial	$19,845
Deep Down and Clean Facial	$36,540
02 Oh My Facial	$21,420
The Basic	$37,320

4. If you will be moving on to the next skill in this chapter, leave the document open to continue working. If not, save the file as directed by your instructor and close it.

Skill 4.15 Inserting Rows and Columns

Once you have created a table, you often find you need more rows or columns. In Word, you can quickly add rows and columns to tables with **insert controls**. Insert Controls appear when you roll your mouse over the left edge of a row or the top edge of a column.

To add a new row using an insert control:

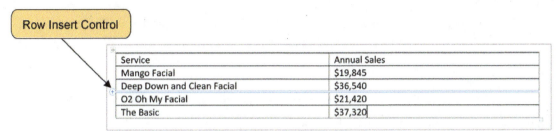

FIGURE WD 4.25

1. Roll your mouse along the left side of the table.
2. When the **insert control** appears where you want to add the new row, click the **control**.

To add a new column using an insert control:

FIGURE WD 4.26

1. Roll your mouse along the top of the table.
2. When the **insert control** appears where you want to add the new column, click the **control**.

tips & tricks

A quick way to insert a new row at the end of a table is to place the cursor in the last cell in the last row and then press ⟨Tab⟩. A new row is automatically added to the table, with your cursor in its first cell.

another method

> To insert an additional row and column, you can also click the **Table Tools Layout** tab. In the *Rows & Columns* group, click the **Insert Above** or **Insert Below** buttons to insert a new row. Click the **Insert Left** or **Insert Right** buttons to insert a new column.
>
> You can also insert rows and columns by right-clicking in a cell, pointing to **Insert**, and selecting **Insert Rows Above**, **Insert Rows Below**, **Insert Columns to the Left**, or **Insert Columns to the Right**.
>
> You can also insert rows and columns by right-clicking in a cell, clicking the **Insert** button on the Mini toolbar, and selecting an option.

let me try Live!

If you do not have the data file from the previous skill open, open the student data file **wd4-15-SpaProductReport** and try this skill on your own:

1. Navigate to the table in the *Facials* section.
2. Insert a new row between the third and fourth row in the table.
3. Insert a new column between the two columns in the table.
4. If you will be moving on to the next skill in this chapter, leave the document open to continue working. If not, save the file as directed by your instructor and close it.

Skill 4.16 Deleting Columns, Rows, and Cells

After you have added information to your table, you may find that you no longer want to include everything you added. Even if you delete the text in a table row or column, the empty row or column still remains. To remove the row or column from the table, you must delete the row or column, not just the text. When you delete a row or column from a table, the content along with the table element is removed.

To delete a row or column:

1. Select the row or column you want to delete.
2. The Mini toolbar displays.
3. Click the **Delete** button and select an option.

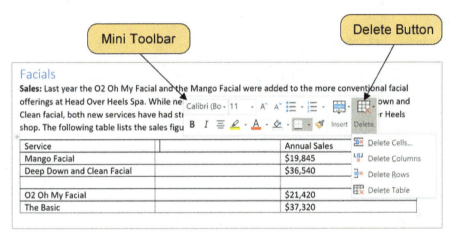

FIGURE WD 4.27

tips & tricks

You can also delete individual cells from a table. When you delete a cell, the *Delete Cells* dialog appears. Here you can choose to shift the cells to the left or up. You can also choose to delete the entire row or column the cell belongs to.

another method

To delete rows and columns you can also:

> Select the row or column you want to delete. Right-click in the row or column and select **Delete Row** or **Delete Column**.
> Click in the row or column you want to delete. Click the **Table Tools Layout** tab. In the *Rows & Columns* group, click the **Delete** button and select an option.

let me try Live!

If you do not have the data file from the previous skill open, open the student data file **wd4-16-SpaProductReport** and try this skill on your own:

1. Navigate to the table in the *Facials* section.
2. Delete the **fourth row** in the table.
3. Delete the **second column** in the table.
4. If you will be moving on to the next skill in this chapter, leave the document open to continue working. If not, save the file as directed by your instructor and close it.

Skill 4.17 Sizing Tables, Columns, and Rows

When you insert a table, it covers the full width of the page and the columns and rows are evenly spaced. Once you have entered your data, you will probably find the table is larger than it needs to be and the columns and rows need adjusting. You can resize your table using Word's AutoFit commands.

To adjust the width and height of cells using the AutoFit command:

1. Click in the table you want to resize.
2. Click the **Table Tools Layout** tab.
3. In the *Cell Size* group, click the **AutoFit** button.
4. Select **AutoFit Contents** to resize the cell to fit the text of the table. Select **AutoFit Window** to resize the table to the size of the page.

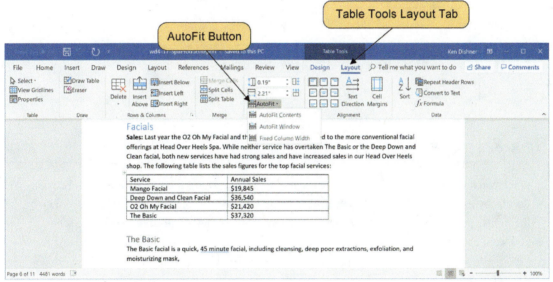

FIGURE WD 4.28

Rather than using the *AutoFit* command, you can specify a width and height for table cells from the Ribbon.

To adjust the width and height of cells:

1. Click in the row or column you want to resize.
2. On the *Table Tools Layout* tab, in the *Cell Size* group, adjust the numbers for the **Table Row Height** and **Table Column Width** by clicking the up and down arrows in the control box.

To resize all the rows in a table so they have the same height, in the *Cell Size* group click the **Distribute Rows** button. Click the **Distribute Columns** to resize all the columns in a table so they have the same width.

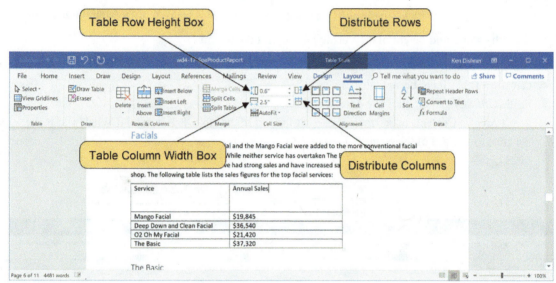

FIGURE WD 4.29

tips & tricks

Once you have resized a table, you will probably want to position it better on the page. You can do this by using the **table move handle** tool that appears at the top-left corner of the table when the mouse pointer is placed over the table. Click the move handle and drag the table to where you want it.

tell me more

Each cell is set up as one line, but if you type more data than will fit in one line, Word will automatically wrap and create another line within the cell, making the row taller. If this happens, all the cells in that row will be affected.

another method

To resize a table, you can also:

1. Select the table you want to resize.
2. When the **resize handle** appears at the bottom right corner of the table, click and drag it until you achieve the desired size. This method can also be used to resize columns and rows.

let me try Live!

If you do not have the data file from the previous skill open, open the student data file **wd4-17-SpaProductReport** and try this skill on your own:

1. Navigate to the table in the *Facials* section.
2. Place the cursor in the *Annual Sales* column. Use the **AutoFit** command to resize the table so it fits the content in the column.
3. Change the **column width** of the *Annual Sales* column to: **2.5"**
4. Change the height of the first row to: **.6"**
5. Use the distribute command to change all the rows to the same height.
6. Use the distribute command to change all the columns to the same width.
7. If you will be moving on to the next skill in this chapter, leave the document open to continue working. If not, save the file as directed by your instructor and close it.

Skill 4.18 Merging and Splitting Cells

When you first create a table, it is a grid of rows and columns. But what if you want to display your content across columns or across rows? For instance, if the first row of your table includes the title for the table, then you will probably want to display the title in a single cell that spans all the columns of the table. In this case, you will want to *merge* the cells in the first row into one cell. On the other hand, if you have a cell that contains multiple values, you may want to *split* the cell so it can display each value in a separate row or column. Use the **merge cells** and **split cells** commands to customize the layout of tables. Merging cells entails combining multiple cells into one; splitting a cell divides the cell into multiple cells.

To merge cells in a table:

1. Select the cells you want to merge into one.
2. Click the **Table Tools Layout** tab.
3. In the *Merge* group, click the **Merge Cells** button.

To split a cell in a table:

1. Select the cell you want to split.
2. In the *Merge* group, click the **Split Cells** button.
3. In the *Split Cells* dialog, enter the number of columns and rows.
4. Click **OK** to split the cell.

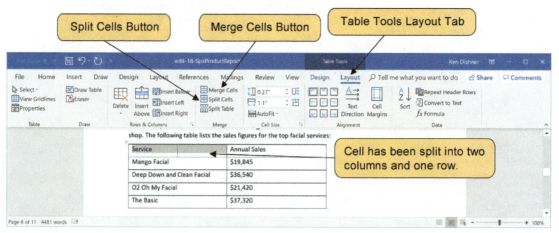

FIGURE WD 4.30

tips & tricks

In addition to splitting cells, you can also split a table, creating two tables from one. To split a table into two tables:

1. Place the cursor in the row where you want to split the table.
2. In the *Merge* group, click the **Split Table** button.

another method

> To merge cells, you can right-click the selected cells and select **Merge Cells** from the menu.
> To split cells, you can right-click a cell and select **Split Cells...** from the menu.

let me try Live!

If you do not have the data file from the previous skill open, open the student data file **wd4-18-SpaProductReport** and try this skill on your own:

1. Navigate to the table in the *Facials* section.
2. Split the first cell of the table into two columns and one row.
3. Merge the two cells back into a single cell.
4. If you will be moving on to the next skill in this chapter, leave the document open to continue working. If not, save the file as directed by your instructor and close it.

Skill 4.19 Sorting Data in Tables

After you have entered data in a table, you may decide they need to be displayed in a different order. **Sorting** rearranges the rows in your table by the text in a column or columns. Word allows you to sort data based on the first character of each entry. You can sort in alphabetical or numeric order, in either ascending (A-Z) or descending (Z-A) order.

To sort a column:

1. Click the **Table Tools Layout** tab.
2. In the *Data* group, click the **Sort** button.

FIGURE WD 4.31

3. The *Sort* dialog opens.
4. Click the **Sort by** arrow and select a field to sort by.
5. The *Ascending* radio button is selected by default. If you want to sort the text in reverse order, from Z to A, click the **Descending** radio button.
6. Click the **Type** arrow and select what to sort by: *Text*, *Number*, or *Date*.
7. If your table has a header row that you do not want to include in the sort, select the **Header row** radio button.
8. Click **OK** to sort the text in the table.

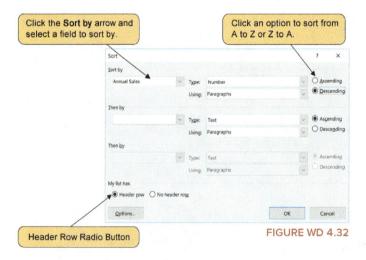

FIGURE WD 4.32

tips & tricks

Word can sort uppercase and lowercase letters differently. Click the **Options...** button in the *Sort* dialog and then click the **Case sensitive** check box in the *Sort Options* dialog.

another method

To open the *Sort* dialog, from the *Home* tab, in the *Paragraph* group, click the **Sort** button.

let me try Live!

If you do not have the data file from the previous skill open, open the student data file **wd4-19-SpaProductReport** and try this skill on your own:

1. Navigate to the table in the *Facials* section and place the cursor in the first row of the table.
2. Open the **Sort** dialog and sort the table in **descending** order based on the number values in the **annual sales** column.
3. If you will be moving on to the next skill in this chapter, leave the document open to continue working. If not, save the file as directed by your instructor and close it.

Skill 4.20 Applying Table Quick Styles

Just as you can apply complex formatting to paragraphs using styles for text, you can apply complex formatting to tables using Quick Styles for tables. Using Quick Styles for tables, you can change the text color along with the borders and shading for a table, giving it a professional, sophisticated look without a lot of work.

To apply a Quick Style to a table:

1. Click the **Table Tools Design** tab.
2. In the *Table Styles* group, click the **More** button.
3. Select a style from the *Quick Styles* gallery.

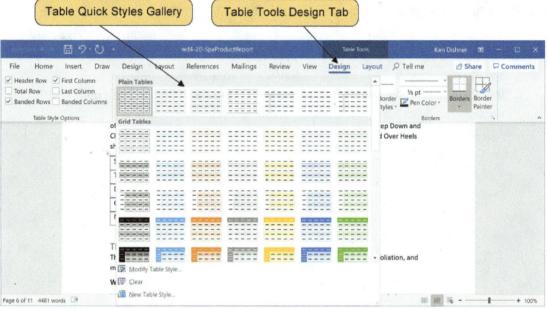

FIGURE WD 4.33

By default, the Word *Table Styles* gallery displays styles that include header rows, banded rows, and first column layouts. Depending on the information in your table, you may not want to format your table using all these options.

To change the options that display in the *Table Styles* gallery:

1. Click the **Table Tools Design** tab.
2. In the *Table Style Options* group, select an option so it appears with a checkmark in the box to include that option in the *Table Styles* gallery.

3. Click an option again to remove the checkmark and remove the option from the *Table Styles* gallery.

4. As you check and uncheck options, open the *Table Styles* gallery to see how the changes affect the available table styles.

FIGURE WD 4.34

tips & tricks

To create your own table style, click the **More** button and select **New Table Style...** In the *Create New Style from Formatting* dialog, you can create a new table style based on an existing table style, changing options such as gridlines and shading to suit your needs. When you save the style, it will appear in the *Table Styles* gallery.

tell me more

In addition to applying a Quick Style to a table, you can change the shading, or background color, applied to the table. Adding shading to a table helps it stand out on a page. To apply shading to a table, click the **Shading** button in the *Table Styles* group. A palette of colors displays. Select a color to change the background color for the table.

another method

The *Table Styles* group on the Ribbon displays the latest Quick Styles you have used. If you want to apply a recently used Quick Style, you can click the option directly from the Ribbon without opening the *Quick Styles* gallery.

let me try Live!

If you do not have the data file from the previous skill open, open the student data file **wd4-20-SpaProductReport** and try this skill on your own:

1. Navigate to the table in the *Facials* section.
2. Change the *Quick Style* gallery display so formats with **first column** and **banded row** formatting do not display. Only *Header row* should be selected.
3. Apply the **List Table 3-Accent 1** Quick Style to the table. It is in the *List Tables* section of the gallery (see Figure WD 4.34).
4. If you will be moving on to the next skill in this chapter, leave the document open to continue working. If not, save the file as directed by your instructor and close it.

Skill 4.21 Adding Borders to a Table

When you first create a table, it uses the simple grid style. You can apply a Quick Style to your table to quickly add formatting, but what if you want to further adjust the look of a table after applying the Quick Style? You can add and remove borders to change the look of the entire table or just parts of the table. The *Border Styles* gallery provides a number of predesigned **border styles** from which to choose.

To change the border style for a table:

1. Click the **Table Tools Design** tab.
2. In the *Borders* group, click the **Border Styles** button.
3. Select an option from the gallery.

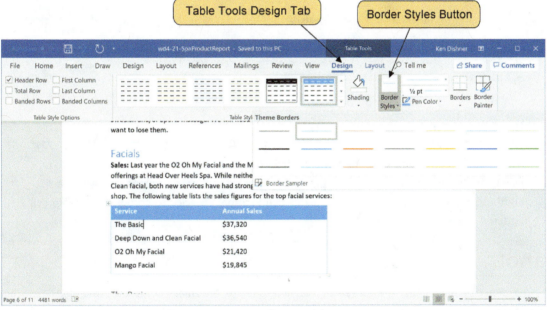

FIGURE WD 4.35

To change the borders for a table:

1. Select the table you want to change.
2. Click the **Table Tools Design** tab.
3. In the *Borders* group, click the **Borders** button arrow.
4. Click a border option to apply it to the table.

If your table does not show borders, you can display **gridlines** to give you a visual guide. The gridlines appear as a dotted line onscreen but do not print as part of the final document. To display gridlines, click the **Borders** button and select **View Gridlines**.

FIGURE WD 4.36

tell me more

When you select a border style, the **Border Painter** becomes active. This feature allows you to quickly apply borders to tables. When the *Border Painter* is active, the cursor changes to a paintbrush. Click a border along the edge of a cell to apply the selected border style to that cell's border.

another method

> You can also change the borders of a table by clicking the **Home** tab. In the *Paragraph* group, click the arrow next to the **Borders** button and select an option.

> You can change borders and shading through the *Borders and Shading* dialog. To open the *Borders and Shading* dialog:
>   • From the *Home* tab or from the *Design* tab, click the arrow next to the *Borders* button and select **Borders and Shading...**
>   • Right-click on the table and select **Borders and Shading...** from the menu.

let me try Live!

If you do not have the data file from the previous skill open, open the student data file **wd4-21-SpaProductReport** and try this skill on your own:

1. Navigate to the table in the *Facials* section and select the table.
2. Display **gridlines** in the table.
3. Change the *Border Style* to **Single solid line, 1/2 point, Accent 1**.
4. Apply the **all borders** option to the table.
5. If you will be moving on to the next skill in this chapter, leave the document open to continue working. If not, save the file as directed by your instructor and close it.

Skill 4.22 Creating a Chart

Charts allow you to take raw data and display them in a visual way. A **chart** takes the values you have entered in a spreadsheet and converts them to graphic representation. In Word, you can create a wide variety of charts, including bar charts, pie charts, column charts, and line charts.

To add a chart to a document:

1. Click the **Insert** tab.
2. In the *Illustrations* group, click the **Chart** button.

FIGURE WD 4.37

3. In the *Insert Chart* dialog, click a chart type category to display that category in the right pane.
4. Click a chart type in the right pane to select it.
5. Click **OK** to add the chart to the document.

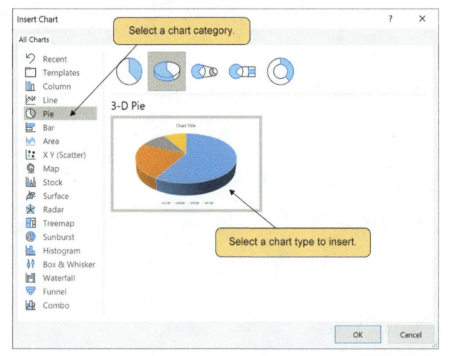

FIGURE WD 4.38

Word automatically opens the *Chart in Microsoft Word* dialog. Think of this dialog as a simplified spreadsheet where you can enter the data for your chart. The dialog opens with sample data entered for you.

1. Replace the sample data with your own data.
2. Click the **Close** button to return to Word to see your finished chart.

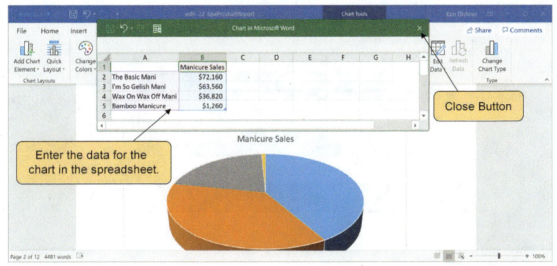

FIGURE WD 4.39

tell me more

As you enter data in the *Chart in Microsoft Word* dialog, Word will update the chart as you enter data and move from cell to cell in the spreadsheet.

let me try Live!

If you do not have the data file from the previous skill open, open the student data file **wd4-22-SpaProductReport** ⬇ and try this skill on your own:

1. Navigate to the *Manicures and Pedicures* section and place the cursor in the blank line below the table.
2. Insert a **3-D pie chart** into the document.
3. Enter the following information for the chart:

	Manicure Sales
The Basic Mani.	$72,160
I'm so Gelish Mani	$63,560
Wax On Wax Off Mani	$36,820
Bamboo Manicure	$1,260

4. If you will be moving on to the next skill in this chapter, leave the document open to continue working. If not, save the file as directed by your instructor and close it.

Skill **4.23** Modifying a Chart

When you insert a chart, Word displays the chart based on the chart type and the document's theme. But what if you want to change the look of your chart? Word includes a number of **chart styles** for you to choose from. These styles are a combination of chart layout styles and formatting options.

To change the style of a chart:

1. Select the chart you want to change.
2. Click the **Chart Styles** button on the right side of the chart.
3. Scroll the list of styles. Click a style to apply it to the chart.

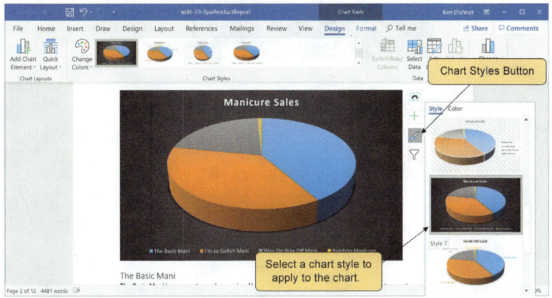

FIGURE WD 4.40

Showing and hiding chart elements, such as the chart title, legend, and data labels, can make a chart easier to read. The **chart title** is a text box that overlays the chart and is typically located above the chart. The **chart legend** tells you which color represents the categories in the chart. **Chart data labels** display the values that go with the categories in the chart.

To show and hide chart elements:

1. Select the chart you want to change.
2. Click the **Chart Elements** button on the right side of the chart.
3. Click the check boxes to show or hide chart elements.

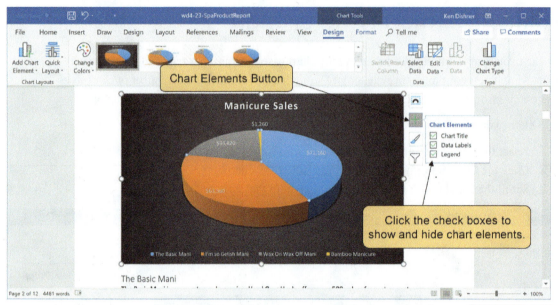

tips & tricks

To change the color of the chart, click the **Color** button in the *Chart Styles* pane. Word displays a number of color sets for you to choose from. These color sets are based on the color theme applied to the document. Select a color set to apply to the chart.

tell me more

The available chart elements will change depending on the type of chart in your document. For example, bar charts include *axes*, *axis title*, and *gridlines* as chart elements you can turn on and off.

another method

> To change the chart style, you can also click the **Chart Tools Design** tab. In the *Chart Styles* group, click the style you want to use, or click the **More** button to see all of the chart styles available.

> To show and hide chart elements, you can also click the **Chart Tools Design** tab. In the *Chart Layouts* group, click the **Add Chart Elements** button, point to the chart element you want, and click an option.

let me try Live!

If you do not have the data file from the previous skill open, open the student data file **wd4-23-SpaProductReport** and try this skill on your own:

1. Select the chart in the *Manicures and Pedicures* section.
2. Apply the **Style 6** chart style to the chart.
3. Show the **data labels** on the chart.
4. Save the file as directed by your instructor and close it.

key terms

Alt text

Online pictures

Creative Commons

Resize handle

Layout Options

Alignment guides

Move cursor

Quick Styles

Icons

SmartArt

Shape

WordArt

Table

Rows

Columns

Cell

Quick Table

Table move handle

Insert Controls

AutoFit

Distribute Rows

Distribute Columns

Merge cells

Split cells

Sorting

Border styles

Gridlines

Border Painter

Chart

Chart styles

Chart title

Chart legend

Chart data labels

concept review

1. Which of the following is a description of a picture, chart, or other object that can be read by screen readers?
    a. ToolTip
    b. *text box*
    c. alt text
    d. AutoText

2. Which button would you click to add a picture you have saved to your OneDrive account?
    a. *Picture*
    b. *Online Picture*
    c. *Icons*
    d. *Shapes*

3. Which button would you click to wrap text around a picture?
    a. *Layout Options*
    b. *Group*
    c. *Align*
    d. *Rotate*

4. Alignment guides are lines that are always visible onscreen and help you align pictures with other elements in the document.
    a. true
    b. false

5. Which of the following is a combination of formatting, including color, shadows, and reflections, that you apply to pictures?
    a. Quick Style
    b. Style Set
    c. Picture Effect
    d. Artistic Effect

6. Which of the following are added to a document as an SVG image?
    a. pictures
    b. shapes
    c. icons
    d. 3-D Models

7. Visual diagrams containing graphic elements with text boxes for you to enter your information in are called SmartArt.
    a. true
    b. false

8. Which of the following are preset drawing objects, such as block arrows and callouts, that you can quickly add to your document?
   a. charts
   b. SmartArt
   c. pictures
   d. shapes

9. Which key would you press to move to the next cells in a table?
   a. Enter
   b. Tab
   c. Shift
   d. Alt

10. The Distribute Columns command resizes all the columns in a table so they are the same width.
    a. true
    b. false

projects
skill review **4.1**

Data files for projects can be found by logging into your SIMnet account and going to the Library section.

In this project you will be editing a marketing brochure for Suarez Marketing. You will add graphic elements to the brochure such as an icon, pictures, and SmartArt. You will then modify the pictures by applying a style and changing the layout, size, and placement. You will organize information in a table and then modify the table.

Skills needed to complete this project:

- Adding Icons (Skill 4.9)
- Inserting Online Pictures (Skill 4.4)
- Resizing Pictures (Skill 4.5)
- Changing Picture Layouts (Skill 4.6)
- Moving Pictures (Skill 4.7)
- Inserting SmartArt (Skill 4.10)
- Creating a Table (Skill 4.13)
- Working with Tables (Skill 4.14)
- Inserting Rows and Columns (Skill 4.15)
- Merging and Splitting Cells (Skill 4.17)
- Sizing Tables, Columns, and Rows (Skill 4.17)
- Applying Table Quick Styles (Skill 4.20)
- Adding Borders to a Table (Skill 4.21)
- Inserting a Picture (Skill 4.1)
- Positioning Pictures (Skill 4.2)
- Adding Alt Text to Pictures (Skill 4.3)

1. Open the start file **WD2019-SkillReview-4-1** and resave the file as:
   `[your initials]WD-SkillReview-4-1`
2. If the document opens in Protected View, click the **Enable Editing** button in the Message Bar at the top of the document so you can modify the document.
3. Insert an icon.
   - a. Place the cursor at the beginning of the heading *Our Goal.*
   - b. Click the **Insert** tab.
   - c. In the *Illustrations* group, click the **Icons** button.
   - d. Navigate to the **Analytics** category and click the icon of the **target with an arrow**.
   - e. Click the **Insert** button.

4. Modify an icon.

    a. With the icon selected, on the *Graphics Tools Format* tab, in the *Size* group, type **.5"** in the *Height* box and **.5"** in the *Width* box.

    b. On the *Graphics Tools Format* tab, in the *Graphics Styles* group, click the **More** button and select the **Colored Fill – Accent 6, No Outline** It is the last option in the second row of the gallery.

5. Insert an online picture.

    a. Place the cursor in the blank line above the *Client Quotes* heading.

    b. Click the **Insert** tab.

    c. In the *Illustrations* group, click the **Online Pictures** button.

    d. In the *Bing Search* box, type **company communication** and click the **Search** button.

    e. Select a photograph of your choice and click the **Insert** button.

6. Resize a picture.

    a. Verify the picture and credit that were inserted are selected.

    b. Click and drag a corner resize handle until the height of the object is approximately **1.5"** tall.

7. Change the layout on a picture.

    a. With the picture and credit still selected, click the **Layout Options** button.

    b. Select the **Tight** wrapping option.

    c. Click outside the *Layout Options* box to hide it.

8. Move a picture.

    a. Click and drag the picture and credit to the right.

    b. Using the alignment guides, place the object so the top of it is aligned with the top of the first quote in the *Client Quotes* section and the left side of it is aligned with the left side of the quote text. See Figure WD 4.42.

FIGURE WD 4.42

9. Insert a *SmartArt* diagram.

   a. Place the cursor in the empty line in the *Our Process* section.

   b. Click the **Insert** tab.

   c. In the *Illustrations* group, click the **SmartArt** button.

   d. Click the **Cycle** category and click the **Circle Arrow Process** option. Click **OK**.

   e. In the upper left segment, type: `Analyze Needs`

   f. In the upper right segment, type: `Design Project`

   g. In the lower segment, type: `Implement Campaign`

   h. Click outside the diagram to deselect it.

10. Add a table to the document and enter text into the table.

   a. Place the cursor in the empty line under the heading *THE SUAREZ MARKETING BELIEF SYSTEM.*

   b. Click the **Insert** tab.

   c. In the *Tables* group, click the **Table** button and select a **2 x 1 (two columns and one row)** table.

   d. Type the information below into the table. Press `Tab` to move forward from cell to cell. Press `Tab` at the end of a row to insert a new row.

Commitment	Putting the needs of the client first
Communication	Seek first to listen
Trust	Begins with open communication
Integrity	Doing the right thing
Customers	Always come first
Teamwork	Working together for success
Creativity	Ideas and know-how
Win-Win	Is always the goal
Success	Results with integrity

11. Insert a row.

    a. Place the cursor in the first row of the table.

    b. Click the **Table Tools Layout** tab.

    c. In the *Rows & Columns* group, click the **Insert Above** button.

    d. Type: `Suarez Marketing Beliefs`

    e. Apply the following formatting to the text:

        i. Font: **Calibri**

        ii. Size: **14 pt**

        iii. Color: **Ice Blue, Accent 1, Darker 50%**. It is the fifth option in the last row under *Theme Colors* in the color palette.

12. Merge cells in a table.

    a. Select the first row in the table.

    b. Click the **Table Tools Layout** tab.

    c. In the *Merge* group, click the **Merge Cells** button.

13. Change the height of rows in a table.

    a. Select the table.

    b. On the *Table Tools Layout* tab, in the *Cell Size* group, type **.25"** in the *Height* box.

14. Apply a Quick Style to the table.

    a. Click the **Table Tools Design** tab.

    b. In *Table Style Options* group, click the **First Column** check box so it is deselected.

    c. In the *Table Styles* group, click the **More** button.

    d. In the *List Tables* section, select the **Grid Table Light 1** Quick Style. It is the first option in the *Grid* section of the gallery.

15. Select a border style.

    a. On the *Table Tools Design* tab, in the *Borders* group, click the **Border Styles** button.

    b. Select the **Single solid line, 1/2 point** border style (it is the first option in the second row of the gallery).

16. Apply a border to the table.

    a. Verify the table is selected.

    b. In the *Borders* group, click the **Borders** button.

    c. Select **Outside Border**.

17. Insert a logo from a location on your computer.

    a. Navigate to the beginning of the document and place the cursor in the blank line above the *Experience* heading.

    b. Click the **Insert** tab.

    c. In the *Illustrations* group, click the **Pictures** button.

    d. In the *Insert Picture* dialog, browse to your student data file location, select the **Suarez logo** file, and click the **Insert** button.

18. Position the logo on the page.

    a. On the *Picture Tools Format* tab, in the *Arrange* group, click the **Position** button.

    b. Select the **Position in Top Left with Square Text Wrapping** option (it is the first option under *With Text Wrapping*).

    c. Delete the blank line above the *Experience* heading.

19. Add alt text to the picture.

    a. Right-click the image of the logo and select **Edit Alt Text...**

    b. In the *Alt Text* task pane, type **Suarez Marketing logo**.

    c. Click the **X** in the upper right corner of the task pane to close it.

20. Save and close the document.

projects

Data files for projects can be found by logging into your SIMnet account and going to the Library section.

skill review **4.2**

In this project you will be editing a document for the Tri-State Book Festival. You will add graphic elements to the document including WordArt, an icon, a shape, and pictures. You will add alt text to a picture. You will adjust the look of images by adding Quick Styles and resizing them. You will organize data in a table and create and modify a chart of information.

Skills needed to complete this project:

- Adding WordArt to Documents (Skill 4.12)
- Changing Picture Layouts (Skill 4.6)
- Adding Icons (Skill 4.9)
- Moving Pictures (Skill 4.7)
- Adding Alt Text to Pictures (Skill 4.3)
- Inserting a Shape (Skill 4.11)
- Resizing Pictures (Skill 4.5)
- Applying Quick Styles to Pictures (Skill 4.8)
- Creating a Chart (Skill 4.22)
- Modifying a Chart (Skill 4.23)
- Working with Tables (Skill 4.14)
- Deleting Columns, Rows, and Cells (Skill 4.16)
- Merging and Splitting Cells (Skill 4.18)
- Inserting Rows and Columns (Skill 4.15)
- Sorting Data in Tables (Skill 4.19)
- Applying Table Quick Styles (Skill 4.20)

1. Open the start file **WD2019-SkillReview-4-2** and resave the file as:
   `[your initials]WD-SkillReview-4-2`
2. If the document opens in Protected View, click the **Enable Editing** button in the Message Bar at the top of the document so you can modify the document.
3. Add WordArt to a document.
   a. Place the cursor at the top of the document.
   b. Click the **Insert** tab.
   c. In the *Text* group, click the **WordArt** button.
   d. Select the **Fill: Green, Accent color 1, Shadow** WordArt style (the second option in the first row of the gallery).
   e. Type: `The Tri-State Book Festival`
   f. Select the text you typed.
   g. Click the **Home** tab. In the *Font* group, click the **Font Size** arrow and select **26**.

4. Change the layout of the WordArt.

    a. Click the **Layout Options** button. If you don't see the *Layout Options* button, select the WordArt object to display it.

    b. Select the **In Line with Text** option.

    c. Click outside the *Layout Options* box to hide it.

5. Insert an icon.

    a. Click the **Insert** tab.

    b. In the *Illustrations* group, click the **Icons** button.

    c. Navigate to the *Education* section and select **3 stacked books** option.

    d. Click the **Insert** button.

6. Modify the icon.

    a. On the *Graphics Tools Format* tab, apply **Colored Fill – Accent 1, Dark 1 Outline** style to the icon. It is the second option in the third row of the gallery.

    b. Click the **Layout Options** button and select the **Square** option.

7. Move the icon using alignment guides.

    a. If necessary, select the icon you inserted.

    b. Click and drag the icon so it is aligned vertically with the WordArt text and the right side of the icon is aligned with the right side of the paragraph text. See Figure WD 4.43.

FIGURE WD 4.43

8. Add alt text to an image.

    a. Right-click the icon and select **Edit Alt Text...**

    b. In the *Alt Text* task pane, if there is a text description, delete it. Type `line drawing of three stacked books` as the alt text for the icon.

9. Insert a shape.

    a. Navigate to the *Authors* section of the document.

    b. In the *Illustrations* group, click the **Shapes** button and select **Star: 5 Points** option in the *Stars and Banners* section.

    c. The cursor changes to a crosshair cursor.

    d. Click to the right of the text **Authors** to add the star shape.

10. Apply a Quick Style to a shape.

    a. Verify the star shape is selected.

    b. On the *Drawing Tools Format* tab, in the *Shape Styles* group, click the **More** button.

    c. In the *Shape Quick Styles* gallery, select **Subtle Effect - Green, Accent 1** (it is the second option in the fourth row under *Theme Styles*).

11. Change the size. layout options, and location of the shape.

   a. Verify the star shape is selected.

   b. On the *Drawing Tools Format* tab, click in the *Height* box and type **.7"**. Click in the *Width* box and type **.7"** and press **Enter.**

   c. Click the **Layout Options** button and select the **Square** option.

   d. Click and drag the icon so it is aligned vertically with the heading text and the left side of the shape is aligned with the left side of the *Fiction* list. See Figure WD 4.44.

FIGURE WD 4.44

12. Add a chart to the document.

   a. Place the cursor in the empty line below the line *The following chart shows the breakdown of authors by genre:*.

   b. Click the **Insert** tab.

   c. In the *Illustrations* group, click the **Chart** button.

   d. In the *Insert Chart* dialog, click the **Pie** category on the left.

   e. Click the **3-D Pie** option (the second option) is selected.

   f. Click **OK**.

   g. In the *Chart in Microsoft Word* dialog, change the data in the chart to match the table below:

	Authors
Fiction General	4
Crime Fiction	2
Non-Fiction General	2
Lifestyle	3

   h. Click the **Close** button in the *Chart in Microsoft Word* dialog.

13. Modify the look of the chart.

   a. Click the **Chart Styles** button.

   b. Scroll the list of chart styles and rest your mouse over each style to see the name of the style. Select the **Style 8** option.

   c. Click outside the chart to deselect it.

14. Delete rows from tables.

    a. Navigate to the *Agenda* section.

    b. In the first table, select the row with the text **Thursday September 6**.

    c. Click the **Table Tools Layout** tab.

    d. In the *Rows & Columns* group, click the **Delete** button.

    e. Click **Delete Rows**.

    f. Repeat these steps to delete the first row of the other two tables in this section.

15. Merge cells in a table.

    a. In the *Thursday September 6* table, select the **Book signing and dinner cell** and the **two empty cells** to the right.

    b. On the *Table Tools Layout* tab, in the *Merge* group, click the **Merge Cells** button.

16. Insert a row to a table.

    a. In the *Thursday September 6* table, place the cursor in the **3:00-4:00 cell**.

    b. Move the cursor to the left until you see the **Insert Row** button above the cell.

    c. Click the **Insert Row** button to add a new blank row.

    d. In the blank cell under *Time*, type: `1:30-3:00`

    e. In the blank cell under *The Washington Theater*, type: `Welcome and Keynote`.

17. Sort data in a table.

    a. In the *Friday September 7* table, select all the rows except the first row.

    b. On the *Table Tools Layout* tab, in the *Data* group, click the **Sort** button.

    c. Verify the column will sort in ascending order, by **Column 1**, using the text in the paragraphs.

    d. Click **OK**.

18. Apply Quick Styles to tables.

    a. Select the **Thursday September 6** table.

    b. Click the **Table Tools Design** tab.

    c. In the *Table Style Options* group, uncheck the **Banded Rows** option. *Header Row* and *First Column* should be the only options selected.

    d. In the *Table Styles* group, click the **More** button.

    e. In the *Grid Tables* section, click the **Grid Table 1 Light - Accent 1** It is the second option in the *Grid* section of the gallery.

    f. Apply this table **Quick Style** to the other two tables in the *Agenda* section. Be sure to uncheck the **Banded Row** option in the *Table Style Options* group before applying the Quick Style.

19. Save and close the document.

projects

Data files for projects can be found by logging into your SIMnet account and going to the Library section.

challenge yourself **4.3**

In this project you will be editing a document from Greenscapes landscaping company. You will add an icon and resize and position the icon in the document. You will add a SmartArt diagram and a picture from your computer to the document. Finally, you will organize information in a table and then format the table by applying Quick Styles and borders.

Skills needed to complete this project:

- Adding Icons (Skill 4.9)
- Resizing Pictures (Skill 4.5)
- Changing Picture Layouts (Skill 4.6)
- Moving Pictures (Skill 4.7)
- Inserting SmartArt (Skill 4.10)
- Inserting a Picture (Skill 4.1)
- Positioning Pictures (Skill 4.2)
- Creating a Table (Skill 4.13)
- Working with Tables (Skill 4.14)
- Sorting Data in Tables (Skill 4.19)
- Inserting Rows and Columns (Skill 4.15)
- Merging and Splitting Cells (Skill 4.18)
- Sizing Tables, Columns, and Rows (Skill 4.17)
- Applying Table Quick Styles (Skill 4.20)
- Adding Borders to a Table (Skill 4.21)

1. Open the start file **WD2019-ChallengeYourself-4-3** and resave the file as:
   `[your initials]WD-ChallengeYourself-4-3`
2. If the document opens in Protected View, click the **Enable Editing** button in the Message Bar at the top of the document so you can modify the document.
3. Place the cursor before the *Our Way of Life* heading and insert an icon of a **watering can**. *Hint:* It is in the *Home* section of the dialog.
4. Change the height of the icon to be **.75"** and the width of the icon to be **.75"**.
5. Apply the **Colored Fill – Accent 1, Dark 1 Outline** style option to the icon. It is the second option in the third row of the gallery.
6. Apply the **Tight** layout option to the icon.

7. Move the icon so it is aligned under the *Our Way of Life* heading with the paragraph text displayed to the right. Use the guides so the top of the icon is aligned with the top of the paragraph text and the left side of the icon is aligned with the left side of the heading text. See Figure WD 4.45.

FIGURE WD 4.45

8. Insert a *SmartArt* diagram.
   a. Place the cursor in the empty line after the first paragraph in the *Leaf and Debris Removal* section.
   b. Insert a **Chevron Accent Process** SmartArt diagram.
   c. Enter `Blow and Rake` in the first box.
   d. Enter `Gather and Haul Away` in the second box.
   e. Enter `Compost` in the third box.
9. Navigate to the *What We Provide* section of the document. Place the cursor before the *Lawn Care Plans* heading. Insert the **greenscapes_logo** picture from your student data file location.
10. Change the position of the logo so it appears **centered at the of the page with square wrapping**.
11. Resize the logo to be **.6"** tall and **55"** wide.
12. Place the cursor at the end of the document. Insert a table with the following information:

Lawn Maintenance	Fertilization, Insect, and Disease Control	$150.00 per treatment
Shrub and Tree Maintenance	Pruning, Fertilization, Insect and Disease Control	$75.00 per hour
Leaf Removal	Composting Included	$25.00 per hour
Lawn Care	Mowing, Edging, Weed-eating	$20.00 per service (weekly) $30.00 per service (bi-weekly)
All Four Services	10% Customer Discount	
Specialty Services	As Requested	Call for a quote

13. Select the first four rows of the table. Sort the text in the selected row in ascending order based on the first column.

14. Insert a new row above the first row in the table. Type **Our Services and Pricing** in the first cell.

15. Change the font of the text to be **Candara, 14 pt**.

16. Merge the three cells in the first row of the table.

17. Change the height of the first row in the table to be **4"** tall.

18. Change the table Quick Styles to show styles without the first column formatted. Apply the **Grid Table 4 Dark - Accent 1** Quick Style to the table. It is in the *Grid Styles* section of the gallery.

19. Change the border style to **Single Solid Line, 1 1/2 pt, Accent 1** It is the second option in the second row of the gallery.

20. Apply **all borders** to the entire table.

21. Save and close the document.

projects

Data files for projects can be found by logging into your SIMnet account and going to the Library section.

challenge yourself **4.4**

In this project you will be editing a document from the Winter Springs community. You will add WordArt and pictures to the document. You will add alt text to a picture. You will modify the size and position of pictures and apply a Quick Style to a picture. Finally, you will create a table and add data to the table and then display the data as a chart.

Skills needed to complete this project:

- Adding WordArt to Documents (Skill 4.12)
- Changing Picture Layouts (Skill 4.6)
- Creating a Chart (Skill 4.22)
- Modifying a Chart (Skill 4.23)
- Working with Tables (Skill 4.14)
- Inserting Rows and Columns (Skill 4.15)
- Deleting Columns, Rows, and Cells (Skill 4.16)
- Sorting Data in Tables (Skill 4.19)
- Applying Table Quick Styles (Skill 4.20)
- Inserting a Picture (Skill 4.7)
- Adding Alt Text to Pictures (Skill 4.3)
- Resizing Pictures (Skill 4.5)
- Positioning Pictures (Skill 4.2)
- Applying Quick Styles to Pictures (Skill 4.8)

1. Open the start file **WD2019-ChallengeYourself-4-4** and resave the file as:
   `[your initials]WD-ChallengeYourself-4-4`
2. If the document opens in Protected View, click the **Enable Editing** button in the Message Bar at the top of the document so you can modify the document.
3. Add WordArt to a document.
   a. Place the cursor at the top of the document (not in the header).
   b. Insert WordArt using the **Fill: Black, Text color 1; Shadow** style.
   c. Change the WordArt text to: `Winter Springs Community News`
4. Change the layout of the WordArt to be in line with the text.

5. Add a chart to the document.

    a. Place the cursor on the blank line after the first paragraph in the *Most Targeted Electronic Devices* section.

    b. Insert a **Clustered Bar** chart.

    c. Change the data in the chart to match the table below.

	Month 1	**Month 2**	**Month 3**
GPS Devices	7	10	9
Laptop Computers	12	14	13
Smartphones	18	21	19
Tablet Computers	13	15	12

6. Modify the look of the chart.

    a. Apply the **Style 6** Quick Style to the chart.

    b. Hide the chart title on the chart.

7. Add a column and a row to a table.

    a. Place the cursor in the first cell in the table under the *Upcoming Safety Improvements* section.

    b. Add a column to the right of the existing column.

    c. Place the cursor in the first cell again and insert a row above the first row in the table.

8. Enter data in a table.

    a. In the first cell of the new row, type: `Improvement`

    b. In the second cell of the new row, type: `Approval Status`

    c. Add the status for each modification as shown in the table below.

Improvement	**Approval Status**
New security gates	`Approved`
Motion sensing security cameras	`Waiting for Approval`
App for reporting incidents	`Denied`
Electric security vehicles	`Approved`
Smartphone entrance for all garages	`Finished`
Reinforcements to perimeter fence	`Approved`
Weekly security meetings with staff	`Approved`

9. Delete the fourth row in the table (the row with the *Denied* status).

10. Apply a Quick Style to the table.

    a. Change the table *Quick Styles* to show styles without the first column formatted.

    b. Apply the **Grid Table 4 – Accent 2** style to the table. It is in the *Grid Styles* section of the gallery.

    c. Apply the same table style to the table in the *Security Meeting Schedule* section. Be sure to deselect the *First Column* option.

11. Sort data in a table.

    a. Select the table in the *Security Meeting Schedule* section.

    b. Sort the table in ascending order based on the **date** in the first column.

12. Insert a picture from a location on your computer.

    a. Place the cursor at the end of the first paragraph in the *Security Staff* section.

    b. Insert the **security-badge** picture from your student data file location.

13. Add the following description as alt text for the picture of the badge: `Security Enforcement Officer badge`

14. Resize the picture so the height is **1.75"** and the width is **1.99"**.

15. Position the picture using the **Position in Bottom Right with Square Text Wrapping** option.

16. Apply the **Drop Shadow Rectangle** Quick Style to the picture. It is the fourth option in the gallery.

17. Save and close the document.

projects

Data files for projects can be found by logging into your SIMnet account and going to the Library section.

on your own 4.5

In this project you will be editing a paper on a behavior change project. You will add and modify pictures in the document. You will display information in a table and then display that information in a chart.

Skills needed to complete this project:

- Inserting Online Pictures (Skill 4.4)
- Add Alt Text to Pictures (Skill 4.3)
- Resizing Pictures (Skill 4.5)
- Changing Picture Layouts (Skill 4.6)
- Moving Pictures (Skill 4.7)
- Applying Quick Styles to Pictures (Skill 4.8)
- Creating a Table (Skill 4.13)
- Working with Tables (Skill 4.14)
- Inserting Rows and Columns (Skill 4.15)
- Merging and Splitting Cells (Skill 4.17)
- Sorting Data in Tables (Skill 4.19)
- Applying Table Quick Styles (Skill 4.20)
- Creating a Chart (Skill 4.22)
- Modifying a Chart (Skill 4.23)

1. Open the start file **WD2019-OnYourOwn-4-5** and resave the file as:
   `[your initials]WD-OnYourOwn-4-5`
2. If the document opens in Protected View, click the **Enable Editing** button in the Message Bar at the top of the document so you can modify the document.
3. From the *Online Pictures* dialog, use *Bing* to search for pictures of students raising their hands. Insert a picture of your choice.
4. Add an appropriate alt text description to the picture.
5. Resize the picture so it fits well in the document.
6. Change the layout options on the picture to wrap with the text.
7. Move the picture so it appears to the right of the first paragraph of the document.
8. Apply a Quick Style of your choice to the picture.
9. Place the cursor in the blank line above the *Totals* line in the *Observation Phase* section. Insert a table for the four columns of data in the section and move the text from the section into the table. When you are finished, delete any extra blank lines.

10. Place the cursor in the blank line above the *Totals* line in the *Implementation Phase* section. Insert a table for the four columns of data in the section and move the text from the section into the table. When you are finished, delete any extra blank lines.

11. Sort the data in the *Implementation Phase* table so the dates appear in ascending order.

12. Insert a new row to the top of the *Implementation Phase* table. In the first cell of the new row, type `Date`. In the second cell of the new row, type `Raises Hand`. In the third cell of the new row, type `Does Not Raise Hand`. In the fourth cell of the new row, type `Percentage`

13. Format the information in the *Implementation Phase* table so it matches the formatting in the *Observation Phase* table.

14. Insert a new row to the top of the *Observation Phase* table. Cut the text **Observation Phase** and paste it into the first cell of the new table. Merge the cells in the new row.

15. Insert a new row to the top of the *Implementation Phase* table. Cut the text **Implementation Phase** and paste it into the first cell of the new table. Merge the cells in the new row.

16. Apply a Quick Style of your choice to the **Observation Phase** table.

17. Apply the same Quick Style to the **Implementation Phase** table.

18. Place the cursor in the blank line below the *Totals* line in the *Observation Phase* section. Add a **pie chart** of your choice using the information in the *Totals* rows.

19. Place the cursor in the blank line below the *Totals* line in the *Implementation Phase* section. Add the same **pie chart** type as the previous step using the information in the *Totals* rows.

20. Change the style of each of the charts to one of your choice.

21. Modify the charts so the titles do not appear on the chart.

22. Save and close the document.

projects
fix it 4.6

Data files for projects can be found by logging into your SIMnet account and going to the Library section.

In this project you will be correcting a marketing brochure from Suarez Marketing. You will fix problems with pictures, including resizing and positioning pictures for a better layout and editing the alt text of a picture. You will replace a shape with an icon and then format that icon. You will display information in a SmartArt diagram and modify the structure and appearance of a table.

Skills needed to complete this project:

- Positioning Pictures (Skill 4.2)
- Adding Alt Text to Pictures (Skill 4.3)
- Adding Icons (Skill 4.9)
- Inserting SmartArt (Skill 4.10)
- Resizing Pictures (Skill 4.5)
- Changing Picture Layouts (Skill 4.6)
- Moving Pictures (Skill 4.7)
- Applying Quick Styles to Pictures (Skill 4.8)
- Working with Tables (Skill 4.14)
- Inserting Rows and Columns (Skill 4.15)
- Deleting Columns, Rows, and Cells (Skill 4.16)
- Sizing Tables, Columns, and Rows (Skill 4.17)
- Merging and Splitting Cells (Skill 4.18)
- Sorting Data in Tables (Skill 4.19)
- Applying Table Quick Styles (Skill 4.20)
- Adding Borders to a Table (Skill 4.21)

1. Open the start file **WD2019-FixIt-4-6** and resave the file as:
   `[your initials]WD-FixIt-4-6`
2. If the document opens in Protected View, click the **Enable Editing** button in the Message Bar at the top of the document so you can modify the document.
3. Select the **Suarez Marketing** logo in the middle of the first page. Position the picture to be in the upper left corner of the page with square wrapping.
4. Edit the alt text of the logo to read **Suarez Marketing logo**.
5. Delete the explosion shape next the *Our Goal* heading.
6. Insert an icon of a **target with an arrow**. *Hint:* It is in the *Analytics* section of the dialog.
7. Change the height of the icon to be **.6"** and the width of the icon to be **.6"**.
8. Apply the **Colored Fill – Accent 6, No Outline** style option to the icon. It is the last option in the second row of the gallery.

9. Navigate to *Our Process* section and place the cursor in the blank line above the bulleted list. Insert a **Closed Chevron Process** diagram.

10. Cut and paste the items from the bulleted list into the segments of the diagram. Remove any extra blank lines.

11. Select the large picture of the people with the talking bubbles. Change the size of the picture to be **1.5"** tall and **2.94"** wide.

12. Change the layout option of the picture to use the **Tight** text wrapping option.

13. Move the picture to the left side of the document using guides to align the picture with the left edge of the text. Have the top of the picture align with the top of the first quote in the *Client Quotes* section. See Figure WD 4.46.

FIGURE WD 4.46

14. Apply the **Drop Shadow Rectangle** Quick Style to the picture. It is the fourth option in the gallery.

15. Navigate to the table on the first page of the document. Insert a new row at the bottom of the table.

16. Cut and paste the **Success** text into the first cell of the new row. Cut and paste the **Results with Integrity** text into the second cell of the new row. Delete any extra blank lines under the table.

17. This table includes a duplicate row of information. Find the duplicated information and delete the second duplicate row.

18. Use the **AutoFit** command to resize the table columns to fit the window.

19. **Merge** the two cells in the first row of the table.

20. Apply the **Grid Table 1 Light** Quick Style to the table (it is the first option in the *Grid Tables* section). Be sure the **First Column Table Style Option** is not part of the design.

21. Apply an **outside border** to the table using the **Double solid lines, 1/2 pt** border style.

22. Save and close the document.

Working with Reports and Collaborating with Others

chapter 5

In this chapter, you will learn the following skills:

> Create a new document from a template
> Use AutoCorrect
> Replace words using the Thesaurus
> Insert and update a table of contents, footnotes, and endnotes
> Use a report reference style, add citations, and create a bibliography
> Mark words in a document to create an index
> Use Track Changes
> Work with Comments
> Change how documents are viewed

introduction

In this chapter you will learn the skills to create reports and collaborate with others. First you will learn to create a new document from a template and to use some of Word's valuable tools for writing documents, including AutoCorrect and the Thesaurus. You will add a number of reference elements to a report, including a table of contents, footnotes, and captions. You will learn about the *Researcher* feature, reference styles, and citations. You will then create a bibliography from citations you have added. You will mark entries and create an index for a document from those entries. You will learn how to turn on track changes and work with changes you have received, including adding comments.

Skill **5.1** Creating a New Document Using a Template

A **template** is a document with predefined settings that you can use as a pattern to create a new file of your own. Using a template makes creating a fully formatted and designed new file easy, saving you time and effort. There are templates available for letters, memos, résumés, newsletters, and almost any other type of document you can imagine.

To create a new document from a template:

1. Click the **File** tab to open Backstage view.
2. Click **New**. Word displays your recently used templates in addition to a set of default templates, so your screen may look different from the one in Figure WD 5.1.
3. Click each template preview picture for a brief description of the template.
4. When you find the template you want to use, click the **Create** button.
5. A new document opens, prepopulated with all of the template elements.

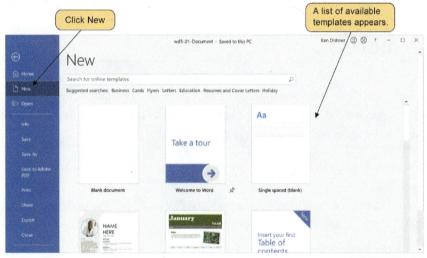

FIGURE WD 5.1

You can search for more document templates online. (You must have an active Internet connection.)

1. Near the top of the *New* page, in the *Search for online templates* box, type a keyword or phrase that describes the template you want.
2. Click the **Start searching** button (the magnifying glass image at the end of the *Search for online templates* box).
3. The search results display previews of the templates that match the keyword or phrase you entered. To further narrow the results, click one of the categories listed in the *Filter by pane* at the right side

of the window. Notice that each category lists the number of templates available.

4. When you find the template you want, click it to display the larger preview with detailed information about the template, and then click **Create**.

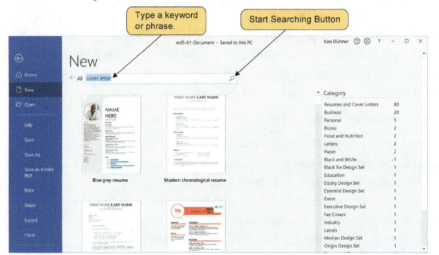

FIGURE WD 5.2

tell me more

Some templates include fully formed documents with sample text for you to replace with your own information. Other templates are empty shells based on a certain design. The template includes the proper styles applied to document elements to help you get started in creating well formatted documents using proper desktop publishing rules.

let me try Live!

If you do not have the data file from the previous skill open, open the student data file **wd5-01-Document** and try this skill on your own:

1. Display the **New** page in Backstage view.
2. Search for a template of a **cover letter**.
3. Create a new document based on the **Cover letter (blue)**.
4. Save the file as directed by your instructor and close it. Close the original file you opened but do not save it.

Skill **5.2** Using the Thesaurus

When writing documents, you may find you are reusing a certain word over and over again and would like to use a different word that has the same meaning. Microsoft Word's **Thesaurus** tool provides you with a list of synonyms (words with the same meaning) and antonyms (words with the opposite meaning).

To replace a word using the Thesaurus:

1. Place the cursor in the word you want to replace.
2. Click the **Review**
3. In the *Proofing* group, click the **Thesaurus** button.
4. The selected word appears in the *Search for* box of the *Thesaurus* task pane with a list of possible meanings below it. Each possible meaning has a list of synonyms (and, in some cases, antonyms).
5. Point to a synonym (or antonym) and click the arrow that appears to display a menu of options.
6. Click **Insert** on the menu to replace the original word with the one you selected.

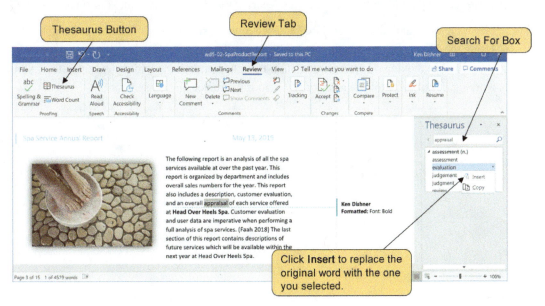

FIGURE WD 5.3

tips & tricks

You can look up and replace words with synonyms without opening the *Thesaurus* task pane. Right-click the word you want to replace and point to **Synonyms**. Word lists a number of possible synonyms on the submenu. Click a synonym to replace the original word with the synonym.

another method

To look up a word using the Thesaurus, you can also:

> Right-click the word, point to *Synonyms*, and select **Thesaurus...**
> With the cursor in the word you want to look up, press Shift + F7 on the keyboard.

let me try Live!

Open the student data file **wd5-02-SpaProductReport** and try this skill on your own:

1. Select the word **appraisal** in the third sentence of the first paragraph of the document.
2. Using the Thesaurus, replace the word with the synonym **evaluation**.
3. If you will be moving on to the next skill in this chapter, leave the document open to continue working. If not, save the file as directed by your instructor and close it.

Skill 5.3 Using AutoCorrect

While you are typing, Word's **AutoCorrect** feature analyzes each word as it is entered. Each word you type is compared to a list of common misspellings, symbols, and abbreviations. If a match is found, AutoCorrect automatically replaces the text in your document with the matching replacement entry. For example, if you type "teh," AutoCorrect will replace the text with "the."

You can create your own AutoCorrect entries, as well as modify pre-existing ones. AutoCorrect also allows you to check for common capitalization errors. If you find yourself making spelling errors that AutoCorrect does not recognize, you can add your own entries to the AutoCorrect replacement list.

To add a new entry to the AutoCorrect list:

1. Click the **File** tab.
2. Click the **Options** button.
3. In the *Word Options* dialog, click the **Proofing** button.
4. Click the **AutoCorrect Options...** button.

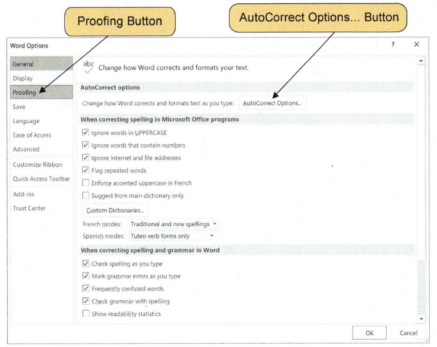

FIGURE WD 5.4

5. Type your commonly made mistake in the *Replace* box.
6. Type the correct spelling in the *With* box.
7. Click **OK** in the *AutoCorrect* dialog.
8. Click **OK** in the *Word Options* dialog.

The next time you type the error, Word will automatically correct it for you.

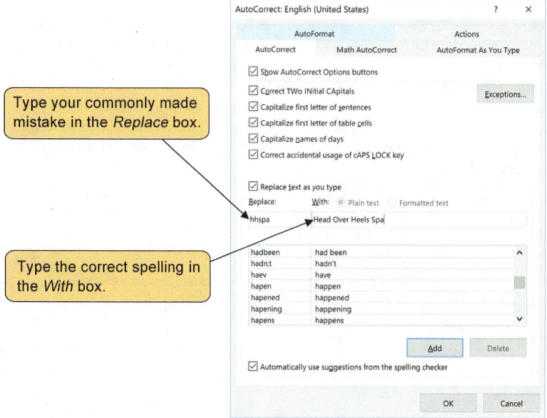

Type your commonly made mistake in the *Replace* box.

Type the correct spelling in the *With* box.

FIGURE WD 5.5

tips & tricks

If you find yourself typing certain long phrases over and over again, you can use the AutoCorrect feature to replace short abbreviations with long strings of text that you don't want to type. For example, you could replace the text *hhspa* with *Head Over Heels Spa*. This will not only save you time when typing, but more important, it will ensure accuracy in your documents.

tell me more

AutoCorrect does more than just fix spelling errors. From the *AutoCorrect* dialog you can set options to:

> Correct accidental use of the Caps Lock key.
> Automatically capitalize the first letter in a sentence or the names of days.
> Automatically apply character formatting such as bold and italic, and format lists and tables.

let me try Live!

If you do not have the data file from the previous skill open, open the student data file **wd5-03-SpaProductReport** and try this skill on your own:

1. Open the **Word Options**
2. Open the **AutoCorrect**
3. Create an AutoCorrect entry to change **hhspa** to **Head Over Heels Spa** when typed.
4. Return to the document and navigate to the first paragraph in the document. Place the cursor before the word **over** in the first sentence of the first paragraph on the page.
5. Type hhspa and press the spacebar. Notice Word replaces the text with the entry you created.
6. If you will be moving on to the next skill in this chapter, leave the document open to continue working. If not, save the file as directed by your instructor and close it.

Skill 5.4 Inserting a Table of Contents

If you have a long document with many sections and headings, it is a good idea to include a table of contents at the beginning of the document. A **table of contents** lists the topics and associated page numbers, so your reader can easily locate information. The table of contents is created from heading styles in the document. If you want your document's section titles to display in the table of contents, be sure to apply heading styles to that text.

To insert a table of contents:

1. Verify the insertion point is at the beginning of the document.
2. Click the **References** tab.
3. In the *Table of Contents* group, click the **Table of Contents** button and select an option from the gallery.
4. The table of contents is added to the beginning of the document.

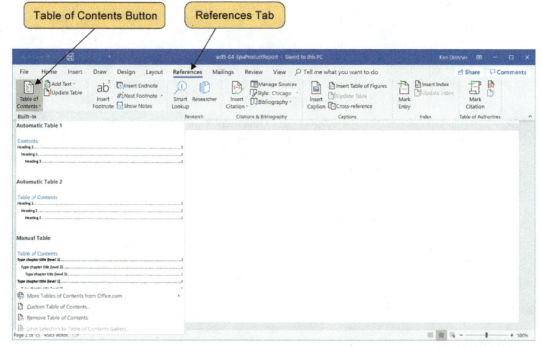

FIGURE WD 5.6

If you make changes to your document after you have inserted a table of contents, you should be sure to update the table of contents to keep the information accurate. To update the table of contents, click the **Update Table** button in the *Table of Contents* group. You can also update the table of contents by clicking on the table of contents and clicking the **Update Table...** button at the top of the control.

To remove a table of contents, click the **Table of Contents** button and select **Remove Table of Contents** at the bottom of the gallery.

FIGURE WD 5.7

tips & tricks

If you want to add your own customized table of contents, click **Custom Table of Contents...** at the bottom of the gallery. The *Table of Contents* dialog opens. Here you can choose different options for the table of contents, including tab leaders, formats, and page number formatting.

tell me more

> A table of contents is typically based on heading styles, but you can create a table of contents based on custom styles or from marked entries.
> A table of contents is a building block that is added to the document. When you select the building block, extra controls appear at the top, including the *Table of Contents* and the *Update Table...*

let me try Live!

If you do not have the data file from the previous skill open, open the student data file **wd5-04-SpaProductReport** and try this skill on your own:

1. Place the cursor on the blank page between the cover page and the beginning of the document.
2. Insert a table of contents based on the **Automatic Table 2** format.
3. If you will be moving on to the next skill in this chapter, leave the document open to continue working. If not, save the file as directed by your instructor and close it.

Skill 5.5 Adding Tab Leaders

Adding **tab leaders** can make data even easier to read. Tab leaders fill in the space between tabs with solid, dotted, or dashed lines. Using tab leaders helps associate columns of text by leading the reader's eye from left to right.

To add tab leaders:

1. Select the text to which you want to add the leader.
2. On the *Home* tab, in the *Paragraph* group, click the **dialog launcher**.
3. In the *Paragraph* dialog, click the **Tabs...** button.
4. In the *Tab stop position* section, select the tab you want to add the leader to, or create a new tab.
5. In the *Leader* section, select the leader option you want.
6. Click **OK**.

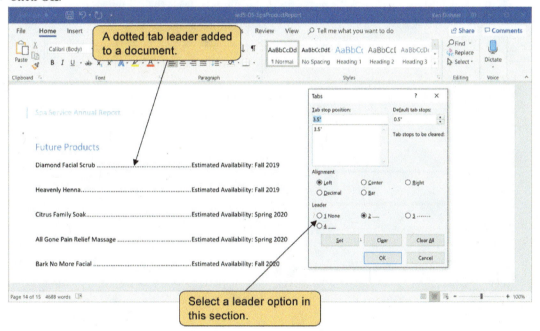

FIGURE WD 5.8

tips & tricks

When creating a table of contents for your document, use tab leaders to visually link section headings with page numbers.

another method

To open the *Tabs* dialog, you can double-click a tab stop on the ruler.

let me try Live!

If you do not have the data file from the previous skill open, open the student data file **wd5-05-SpaProductReport** and try this skill on your own:

1. Select the list of services and dates in the *Future Products* section on the second to last page of the document.
2. Open the **Tabs** dialog.
3. Add a **dotted tab leader** to the text (option **2** in the *Leader* section of the *Tabs* dialog).
4. If you will be moving on to the next skill in this chapter, leave the document open to continue working. If not, save the file as directed by your instructor and close it.

Skill 5.6 Adding a Caption

A **caption** is a brief description of an illustration, chart, equation, or table. Captions can appear above or below the image, and typically begin with a label followed by a number and the description of the image. Captions are helpful when referring to images and tables within paragraphs of text (for example, see Table 1: Manicure and Pedicure Annual Sales).

To add a caption to a figure or table:

1. Select the figure or table you want to add the caption to.
2. Click the **References** tab.
3. In the *Captions* group, click the **Insert Caption** button.
4. The *Caption* dialog opens.
5. Click the **Label** arrow and select a figure type.
6. Click the **Position** arrow and select where you want the caption to appear.
7. Type any additional text, such as a description of the figure, in the *Caption* box.
8. Click **OK** to close the dialog and add the caption.

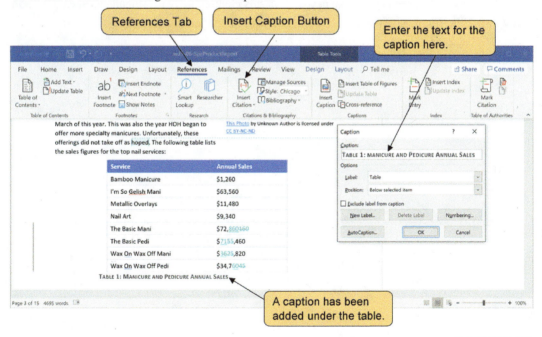

FIGURE WD 5.9

tips & tricks

Word automatically numbers the figures and tables in your document based on the label type. For example, if you have several tables that use the "table" label, those captions will be numbered sequentially. If you have other figures labeled as "figures," those images will be numbered sequentially. If you go back and add a new caption or change the label of an existing caption, Word will renumber the existing captions for you.

let me try Live!

If you do not have the data file from the previous skill open, open the student data file **wd5-06-SpaProductReport** and try this skill on your own:

1. Place the cursor in the **sales figures table** in the *Manicures and Pedicures* section.
2. Add a caption to display below the table. The caption should read:

   `Table 1: Manicure and Pedicure Annual Sales`
3. If you will be moving on to the next skill in this chapter, leave the document open to continue working. If not, save the file as directed by your instructor and close it.

Skill 5.7 Inserting Footnotes and Endnotes

Footnotes and **endnotes** provide your reader with further information on a topic in a document. They are often used for source references. Footnotes and endnotes are composed of two parts: a **reference mark** (a superscript character placed next to the text) and the associated text. Footnotes appear at the bottom of a page, whereas endnotes are placed at the end of the document.

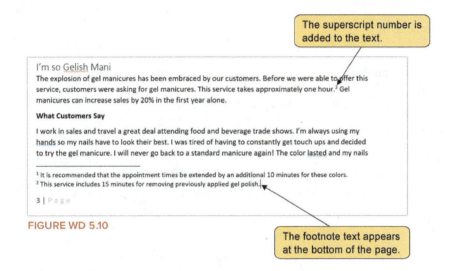

FIGURE WD 5.10

To insert a footnote:

1. Place your cursor where you want the footnote to appear.
2. Click the **References** tab.
3. In the *Footnotes* group, click the **Insert Footnote** button.
4. The superscript number is added next to the text, and the cursor is moved to the footnote area at the bottom of the page.
5. Type the text for your footnote. When you are finished, return to your document by clicking anywhere in the main document area.

FIGURE WD 5.11

To insert an endnote:

1. Place your cursor where you want the endnote to appear.
2. Click the **References** tab.
3. In the *Footnotes* group, click the **Insert Endnote** button.
4. The superscript number is added next to the text, and the cursor is moved to the endnote area at the end of the document.
5. Type the text for your endnote.

To convert footnotes to endnotes or vice versa:

1. Click the **dialog launcher** in the *Footnotes* group.
2. In the *Footnote and Endnote* dialog, click the **Convert...** button and choose an option.
3. Click **OK**.

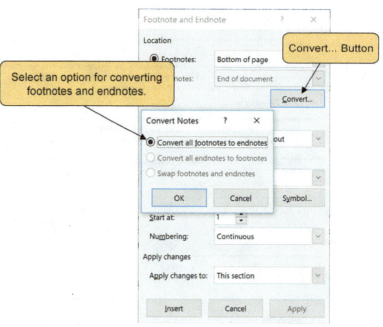

FIGURE WD 5.12

tips & tricks

> Click the **Next Footnote** button to navigate to the next footnote in the document. Click the arrow next to the *Next Footnote* button to display a menu allowing you to navigate to previous footnotes and between endnotes in the document.

> To delete a footnote, you must first select the reference mark in the document and press **Delete** on the keyboard. If you select and delete the text of the footnote, the reference mark will remain and the footnote will not be removed from the document.

tell me **more**

Once you have inserted and formatted your first footnote or endnote, Word automatically numbers all subsequent notes in your document for you. If you add a new footnote between two existing footnotes, Word will renumber all the footnotes in the document, keeping them in sequential order.

another method

To insert a footnote, you can also click the **dialog launcher** in the *Footnotes* group. In the *Footnote and Endnote* dialog, verify that the **Footnote** radio button is selected and click **Insert**.

let me **try** Live!

If you do not have the data file from the previous skill open, open the student data file **wd5-07-SpaProductReport** ⬇ and try this skill on your own:

1. Place the cursor at the end third sentence in the first paragraph in the *I'm So Gelish Mani* section (the sentence ending *approximately one hour*).
2. Add a footnote that reads: `This service includes 15 minutes for removing previously applied gel polish.`
3. Convert the footnotes in the document into endnotes.
4. Convert the endnotes back to footnotes.
5. If you will be moving on to the next skill in this chapter, leave the document open to continue working. If not, save the file as directed by your instructor and close it.

Skill 5.8 Using Researcher

If you are writing a research paper, a quick way to add sources to your document is to use Word's **Researcher** feature. The *Researcher* uses Microsoft's Bing search to find topics on the Internet and then allows you to quickly add a citation for any source you use.

To use *Researcher* to look up information and add a citation:

1. Click the **References** tab.
2. In the *Research* group, click the **Researcher** button.

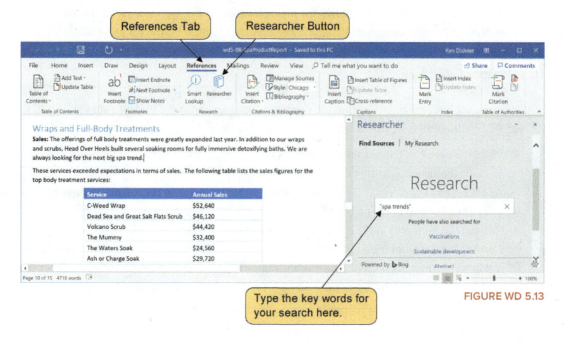

FIGURE WD 5.13

3. The *Researcher* task pane opens.
4. Type the key words for your search in the text box.
5. Click the **Search** button.
6. A list of results appears.
7. When you have added text from a source, click the **Add this source as a citation** button in the upper right corner of the source in the task pane.

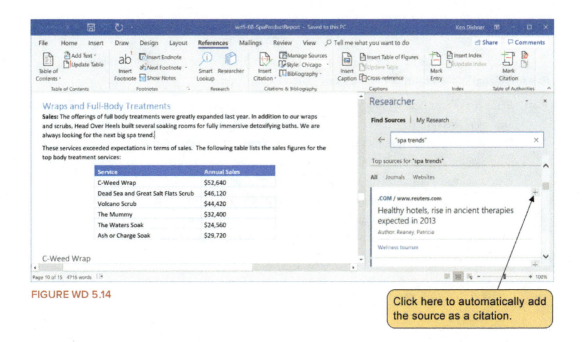

FIGURE WD 5.14

Click here to automatically add the source as a citation.

tips & tricks

When you add a citation from the *Researcher* task pane, Word automatically inserts a properly formatted citation based on the reference style for the document. Word also adds the source information in the source manager, allowing you to quickly add citations to the source later within in the same document or in other documents.

tell me more

The *Researcher* feature is only available in the Office 365 version of Microsoft Office. If you have the 2019 on-premises version, you will not see the Researcher button on the *Reference* tab.

let me try Live!

If you do not have the data file from the previous skill open, open the student data file **wd5-08-SpaProductReport** ⬇ and try this skill on your own:

1. Place the cursor before the period at the end of the first paragraph in the *Wraps and Full-Body Treatments* section (the sentence ending *next big spa trend*).
2. Open the *Researcher* task pane and type **"spa trends"** in the search box. *NOTE:* If you do not have the *Researcher* feature in your version of Microsoft Word, skip to step 5.
3. Type a sentence based on the research you completed.
4. From the *Researcher* task pane, add a citation to the source you used.
5. If you will be moving on to the next skill in this chapter, leave the document open to continue working. If not, save the file as directed by your instructor and close it.

from the perspective of . . .

GRADUATE STUDENT

When I wrote my first term paper, my professor rejected it informing me that it wasn't formatted correctly and I was using the wrong reference style. I didn't understand. I had typed everything very carefully, but apparently I was supposed to use the APA style and not the Chicago style. After that, I started using the reference tools built into Word. Now I can generate a table of contents from headings in my paper, mark entries for my index as I write, and auto-generate the index. Most important, I can set my reference style to use the APA style, add my sources, and create a bibliography in the correct style. When I resubmitted my paper, my professor was impressed with how well it was formatted. I got an A!

Skill 5.9 Selecting a Reference Style

A **reference style** is a set of rules used to display references in a bibliography. These rules include the order of information, when and how punctuation is used, and the use of character formatting, such as italic and bold. The three most common reference styles in use today are *APA*, *MLA*, and *Chicago*; however, there are a number of other reference styles you can choose from. It is important that you use the correct reference style for the subject of your document.

When creating a bibliography, it is important to use a consistent reference style for your citations. Word makes this easy by allowing you to set the reference style for the entire document at once.

To change the reference style for a document:

1. Click the **References** tab.
2. In the *Citations & Bibliography* group, click the arrow next to *Style* and select a style from the list.

FIGURE WD 5.15

The following table lists the available styles in Word and when they are most commonly used.

STYLE ABBREVIATION	FULL NAME	PURPOSE
APA Sixth Edition	American Psychological Association	Education, psychology, and social sciences
Chicago Sixteenth Edition	The Chicago Manual of Style	Books, magazines, and newspapers
GB7714 2005	NA	Used in China
GOST—Name Sort	Russian State Standard	Used in Russia
GOST—Title Sort	Russian State Standard	Used in Russia
Harvard—Anglia 2008	Harvard reference style	For the specification at Anglia Ruskin University
IEEE 2006	IEEE Citation Reference	Research papers in technical fields
ISO 690—First Element and Date	International Standards Organization	Patents and industry (both print and nonprint works)
ISO 690—Numerical Reference	International Standards Organization	Patents and industry (both print and nonprint works)
MLA Seventh Edition	Modern Language Association	Arts and humanities
SIST02	NA	Used in Asia
Turabian Sixth Edition	Turabian	All subjects (designed for college students)

tips & tricks

When you change the reference style for a document, all citations are automatically updated to use the new style.

tell me more

To see a preview of the source style, click the **Manage Sources** button in the *Citations & Bibliography* group. The preview box at the bottom of the *Manage Sources* dialog shows how the selected reference will appear as a citation and in the bibliography.

let me try Live!

If you do not have the data file from the previous skill open, open the student data file **wd5-09-SpaProductReport** and try this skill on your own:

1. Navigate to the first paragraph of the document. Notice the format of the reference *(Faah 2018)* in the first sentence.
2. Change the reference style for the document to use the **APA Sixth Edition** style.
3. Notice how the reference has changed to *(Faah, 2018)*.
4. If you will be moving on to the next skill in this chapter, leave the document open to continue working. If not, save the file as directed by your instructor and close it.

Skill 5.10 Adding Citations to Documents

When you use materials in a document from other sources, such as a book or a journal article, you need to give credit to the original source material. A **citation** is a reference to such source material. Citations include information such as the author, title, publisher, and the publication date.

To add a citation to a document, you must first create the source:

1. Place the cursor where you want to add the citation.
2. Click the **References** tab.
3. In the *Citations & Bibliography* group, click the **Insert Citation** button and select **Add New Source...**

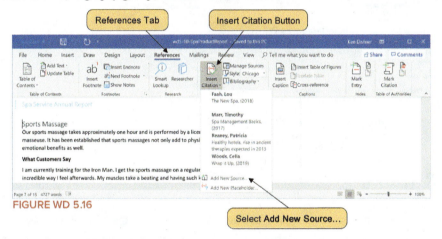

FIGURE WD 5.16

4. In the *Create Source* dialog, click the arrow next to *Type of Source* and select an option.
5. In the *Author* box, type the name of the author.
6. In the *Title* box, type the title of the book or article.
7. In the *Year* box, type the year the book or article was published.
8. Add other information about the source to the appropriate fields.
9. When you are finished, click **OK** to add the citation to the document.

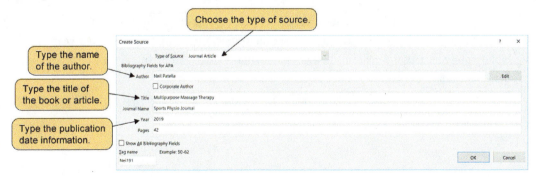

FIGURE WD 5.17

After you have added a new source, it appears on the *Insert Citation* menu. To add the same source to another part of the document, click the **Insert Citation** button and select the source for the citation.

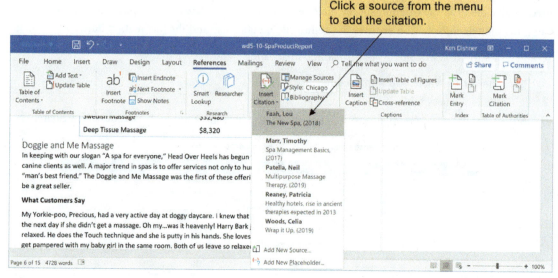

Click a source from the menu to add the citation.

tips & tricks

Citations appear in the document as a control. When you click the control, you will see an arrow on the right side. Click the arrow to display a menu for editing the source and the citation. In the *Edit Source* dialog, you can change the information you added when you created the source. In the *Edit Citation* dialog, you can change information specific to the citation, such as page numbers.

tell me more

When you add a citation, the citation appears inside parentheses at the place where you inserted it. A citation includes basic information from the source, including the author and year. A bibliography lists all the citations in a document and includes more of the source information than the citation does.

let me try Live!

If you do not have the data file from the previous skill open, open the student data file **wd5-10-SpaProductReport** and try this skill on your own:

1. Navigate to the *Sports Massage* section and place the cursor before the period at the end of the first paragraph.
2. Add a new source with the following information:

Type of Source	`Journal Article`
Author	`Neil Patella`
Title	`Multipurpose Massage Therapy`
Journal Name	`Sports Physio Journal`
Year	`2019`
Pages	`42`

3. Navigate to the *Doggie and Me Massage* section and place the cursor before the period at the end of the first paragraph (after *a great seller*).
4. Add a citation that references the **Lou Faah** source.
5. If you will be moving on to the next skill in this chapter, leave the document open to continue working. If not, save the file as directed by your instructor and close it.

Skill 5.11 Using the Source Manager

When you add a new source to a document, it is available to add throughout that document. But what if you want to add a source to multiple documents? The **Source Manager** allows you to save source information to a master list. When you open or create new documents, you can add the sources in the master list to the document, so there is no need to re-enter the same source information.

To add and save sources using the Source Manager:

1. Click the **References** tab.
2. In the *Citations & Bibliography* group, click the **Manage Sources** button.

FIGURE WD 5.19

3. The box on the left displays the sources that have been saved to the master list. Select a source and click the

    Copy → button to add the source for use in the current document.

4. The box on the right displays the sources that are part of the current document. Select a source and click the

    ← **Copy** button to add the source to the master list.

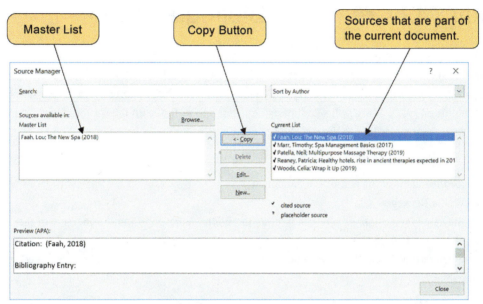

FIGURE WD 5.20

tips & tricks

To delete a source, click the source you want to delete and click the **Delete** button. To edit a source, select the source and click the **Edit...** button. Make the changes in the *Edit Source* dialog and click **OK**. To add a new source, click the **New...** button. Make the changes in the *Create Source* dialog and click **OK**.

let me try Live!

If you do not have the data file from the previous skill open, open the student data file **wd5-11-SpaProductReport** and try this skill on your own:

1. Open the **Source Manager**.
2. Add a source from the master list to the document. If you do not have any sources in the master list, you may skip this step.
3. Add the **Lou Faah** source to the master list of sources.
4. If you will be moving on to the next skill in this chapter, leave the document open to continue working. If not, save the file as directed by your instructor and close it.

Skill 5.12 Creating a Bibliography

A **bibliography** is a compiled list of sources you referenced in your document. Typically, bibliographies appear at the end of a document and list all the sources you marked throughout the document. Word comes with a number of prebuilt bibliography building blocks for you to use. When you select one of these building blocks, Word will search the document and compile all the sources from your document and format them according to the style you chose.

To add a bibliography to a document:

1. Place the cursor at the end of the document.
2. Click the **References** tab.
3. In the *Citations & Bibliography* group, click the **Bibliography** button and select one of the bibliography building blocks.
4. The bibliography is added to the end of the document, listing all the sources referenced in the document.

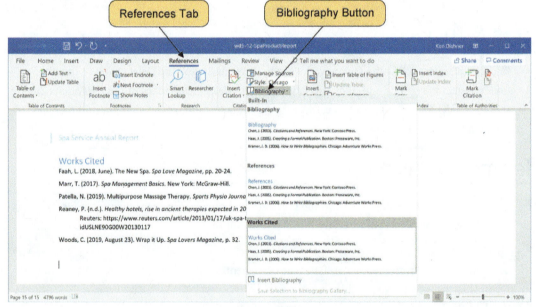

FIGURE WD 5.21

another method

To add a simple bibliography, click the **Insert Bibliography** command at the bottom of the *Bibliography* gallery.

let me try Live!

If you do not have the data file from the previous skill open, open the student data file **wd5-12-SpaProductReport** and try this skill on your own:

1. Navigate to the end of the document. Place the cursor at the top of the blank page.
2. Add a bibliography using the **Works Cited** style.
3. If you will be moving on to the next skill in this chapter, leave the document open to continue working. If not, save the file as directed by your instructor and close it.

Skill 5.13 Marking Entries

When creating long documents, you may want to add an index to the document to help your readers quickly locate specific information. To create an index, you must first mark the topics you want to include, and then create the index. When formatting marks are hidden, marked entries look no different from other text in the document. However, when the index is created, Word finds all the marked entries and adds them to the index.

To mark entries:

1. Select the word or phrase you want to add to the index.
2. Click the **References** tab.
3. In the *Index* group, click the **Mark Entry** button.
4. The word or phrase appears in the *Main entry* Click the **Mark** button to mark the entry.
5. Click the **Close** button to close the *Mark Index Entry* dialog.

After you mark an entry, Word adds the *XE (Index Entry)* formatting mark to the word and displays all formatting marks in the document, so you can double-check your page layout. Click the **Show/Hide** button on the *Home* tab to hide the formatting marks.

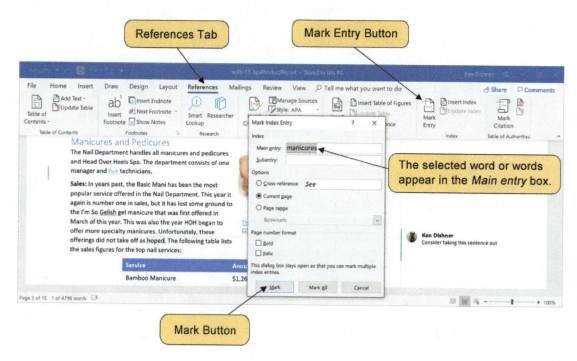

FIGURE WD 5.22

tips & tricks

To add a reference to every instance of a word to the index, click the **Mark All** button in the *Mark Index Entry* dialog.

another method

To open the *Mark Index Entry* dialog, you can also click the **Insert Index** button in the *Index* group. In the *Index* dialog, click the **Mark Entry** button.

let me try Live!

If you do not have the data file from the previous skill open, open the student data file **wd5-13-SpaProductReport** and try this skill on your own:

1. Select the text **manicures** in the first sentence of the *Manicures and Pedicures* section.
2. Mark the text as an entry to use in the index.
3. Close the *Mark Index Entry* dialog and hide the formatting marks in the document.
4. If you will be moving on to the next skill in this chapter, leave the document open to continue working. If not, save the file as directed by your instructor and close it.

Skill 5.14 Creating an Index

An **index** is a list of topics and associated page numbers that typically appears at the end of a document. Adding an index to your document can help your readers find information quickly. An index entry can reference a single word, a phrase, or a topic spanning several pages.

To add an index to a document:

1. Place the cursor at the end of the document.
2. Click the **References** button. In the *Index* group, click the **Insert Index** button.
3. The *Index* dialog opens. Click the **Formats** arrow and select a format.
4. Modify the other options until the preview looks the way you want.
5. Click **OK** to insert the index into your document.

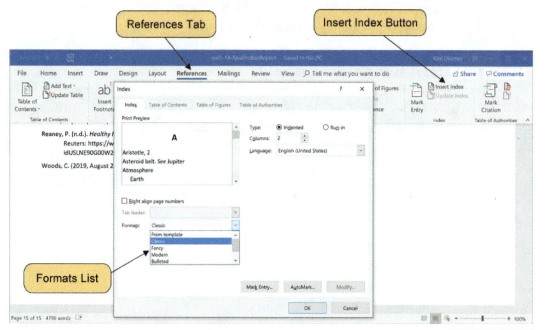

FIGURE WD 5.23

tips & tricks

To add new entries to an index, do not type directly in the index. Instead, mark the entries and then update the index. Any entries typed directly into the index will be deleted when the index is updated. To update an index, first select the index and then click the **Update Index** button in the *Index* group.

tell me more

A cross-reference is an index entry that refers to another entry in the index rather than to a page in the document. Cross-references are often used to direct readers from an uncommon entry to a more frequently used one.

let me try Live!

If you do not have the data file from the previous skill open, open the student data file **wd5-14-SpaProductReport** and try this skill on your own:

1. Navigate to the end of the document. Place the cursor below the bibliography.
2. Insert an index based on the **Classic** format. The entries should display in two columns.
3. If you will be moving on to the next skill in this chapter, leave the document open to continue working. If not, save the file as directed by your instructor and close it.

Skill 5.15 Using Track Changes

The **Track Changes** feature in Word marks any changes made to a document by reviewers. Such changes include any deletions, insertions, or formatting. Word displays some changes directly in the document and other changes in balloons displayed in the margin. When the *Track Changes* feature is active, the *Track Changes* button appears in its active state.

To track changes to a document:

1. Click the **Review** tab.
2. In the *Tracking* group, click the **Track Changes** button.
3. When changes are made to the document, they display either in-line (for insertions and deletions) or in the margin (for comments and formatting changes).
4. Click the **Track Changes** button again to turn off the feature.

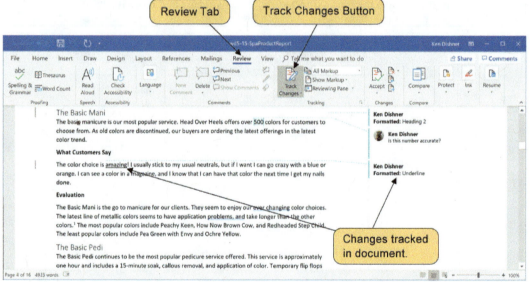

FIGURE WD 5.24

tell me more

> The **Reviewing pane** displays all the changes in a document. It shows a summary of the revisions in a document, including the number of insertions, deletions, moves, formatting changes, and comments. To display the *Reviewing* pane, click the **Reviewing Pane** button in the *Tracking* group on the *Review* tab.

another method

To turn on the *Track Changes* feature, you can also click the bottom half of the **Track Changes** button and select *Track Changes* from the menu.

let me try Live!

If you do not have the data file from the previous skill open, open the student data file **wd5-15-SpaProductReport** ⬇ and try this skill on your own:

1. Turn on the **Track Changes** feature.
2. Select the text **basic manicure** in the first sentence of the first paragraph in *The Basic Mani* section at the top of page 3.
3. Change the selected text to **Basic Mani**.
4. Turn off the **Track Changes** feature.
5. If you will be moving on to the next skill in this chapter, leave the document open to continue working. If not, save the file as directed by your instructor and close it.

Skill 5.16 Working with Comments

A **comment** is a note you add to a document that is not meant to be part of the document. When you add a comment, it appears in the margin of the document. Comments are useful when you are reviewing a document and want to add messages about changes or errors.

FIGURE WD 5.25

To insert a comment:

1. Place the cursor where you want to add the comment.
2. Click the **Review** tab.
3. In the *Comments* group, click the **New Comment** button.
4. The comment balloon appears in the margin of the document. The cursor appears in the comment.
5. Type your comment.
6. Click outside the balloon to deselect the comment and continue working.

There are a number of ways you can work with comments. If your document has multiple comments, click the **Next Comment** and **Previous Comment** buttons to move between comments in a document.

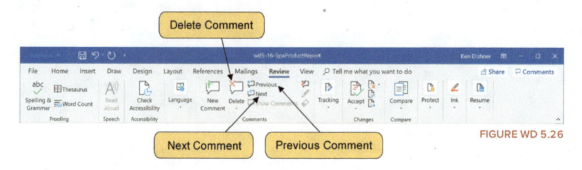

FIGURE WD 5.26

Replying to a comment allows you to directly respond to comments in a document. The comments appear within the same bubble, so it is obvious the comments are related.

To reply to a comment:

1. Roll your mouse over the comment balloon and click the **Reply** button at the bottom of the balloon.
2. Another comment appears inside the original comment. Type your reply and click outside.

If you are done with a comment, you can resolve it or delete the comment. Resolving a comment changes the comment so it appears faded. It can still be read but you can no longer interact with it. If you no longer need to see or interact with the comment, you can delete the comment.

> To resolve a comment, roll your mouse over the comment balloon and click the **Resolve** button.
> To delete a comment, select the comment you want to delete. In the *Comments* group on the *Review* tab, click the **Delete Comment** button.

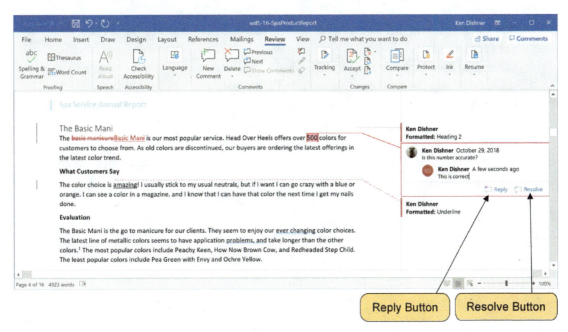

FIGURE WD 5.27

tips & tricks

> After you have resolved a comment, the button changes to **Reopen**. Click **Reopen** to make the comment active again.
> To delete all comments in the document, on the *Review* tab, in the *Comments* group, click the **Delete** button arrow and select **Delete All Comments in Document**.

another method

> > To add a comment, you can also right-click the area you want to add a comment to and select **New Comment** from the shortcut menu.
>
> > To work with comments, you can also right-click the comment and select a command –
> > **Reply to Comment, Delete Comment**, or **Resolve Comment**.

let me try Live!

If you do not have the data file from the previous skill open, open the student data file
wd5-16-SpaProductReport and try this skill on your own:

1. Place the cursor after the text **Annual Sales** in the first row of the table in the *Manicures and Pedicures*

2. Add a new comment that reads: `This table needs to be sorted by sales not services`

3. Navigate to the next comment in the document.

4. Reply to the comment with the following: `This is correct`

5. Resolve the comment.

6. Navigate back to the first comment in the document.

7. Delete the comment.

8. If you will be moving on to the next skill in this chapter, leave the document open to continue working. If not, save the file as directed by your instructor and close it.

from the perspective of . . .

MEDIA ASSISTANT

In my job, I am often working with long scripts that I have to proofread with several other employees. When I work through a script, I like to use the Side to Side view to be able to flip through the pages. Thanks to *Track Changes*, I can share a file with several colleagues, review their input, and decide which changes I want to accept or reject. I can even add a password preventing others from accidentally turning off the feature. The result is a document worth reading!

Skill 5.17 Hiding and Showing Changes in a Document

When you activate the *Track Changes* feature in Word, all changes are displayed by default. This includes any comments, deletions, insertions, or formatting changes. Word displays some changes directly in the document and other changes in balloons displayed in the margin. If your document has gone through some major revisions, it may be difficult to differentiate between all the tracked changes. You can show and hide the various changes from the *Tracking* group on the *Review* tab.

To show and hide the different types of tracked changes in a document:

1. Click the **Review** tab.
2. In the *Tracking* group, click the **Show Markup** button.
3. If a change type appears with a checkmark next to it, it is currently displayed in the document. If a change type appears without a checkmark next to it, it is currently hidden in the document.
4. Click an option on the menu to hide that type of change in the document.
5. Click the same option again to display the hidden changes.

From the *Show Markup* button, you can show or hide comments, ink notations, insertions and deletions, and formatting changes.

FIGURE WD 5.28

You can choose to have all revisions display in balloons or all revisions display in-line. By default, revisions are displayed in-line and comments and formatting changes are displayed in balloons.

To change what displays in balloons:

1. On the *Review* tab, in the *Tracking* group, click the **Show Markup** button.
2. Point to **Balloons** and select an option.

The *Display for Review* menu allows you to display the document in a number of states, including the final version with simplified markup for changes, the final version with all markup for the changes, the final version with no markup for changes, and the original document without any markup.

To change the display of tracked changes in a document:

1. On the *Review* tab, in the *Tracking* group, click the **Display for Review** drop-down arrow.
2. Select a display option.

FIGURE WD 5.29

tips & tricks

You can choose to review all changes by all reviewers or specify the type of changes you want to review and by which reviewer. To modify which reviewer's comments are displayed, click the **Show Markup** button in the *Tracking* group, point to **Specific People**, and select the reviewer(s) you want.

let me try Live!

If you do not have the data file from the previous skill open, open the student data file **wd5-17-SpaProductReport** and try this skill on your own:

1. Navigate to the *Manicures and Pedicures* section where you can see the tracked changes.
2. Hide **insertions and deletions** in the document.
3. Show **insertions and deletions** again.
4. Change the formatting so revisions are shown in balloons in the margin.
5. Change the formatting so only comments and formatting are displayed in balloons in the margin.
6. Change the track changes option to show **no markup** in the document.
7. Change the track changes option to show **all markup** in the document.
8. If you will be moving on to the next skill in this chapter, leave the document open to continue working. If not, save the file as directed by your instructor and close it.

Skill 5.18 Accepting and Rejecting Changes in a Document

When you send a document for review with *Track Changes* on, the document you receive will show all the changes made by reviewers. To finalize the document, you need to accept or reject each change suggested.

There are a number of ways you can accept and reject changes:

Accept or Reject Change and Move to Next—Accepts or rejects the change and automatically moves to the next change in the document.

Accept or Reject Change—Accepts or rejects the change and does not move to the next change in the document.

Accept or Reject All Changes Shown—Accepts or rejects only the currently displayed changes.

Accept or Reject All Changes in Document—Accepts or rejects both visible and hidden changes in the document.

To accept or reject changes in a document:

1. Click the **Review** tab.
2. In the *Changes* group, click the **Next Change** button to navigate to the first change in the document.
3. To accept the selected change and move to the next change, click the **Accept and Move to Next** button.
4. To reject the selected change and move on to the next change, click the **Reject and Move to Next** button.

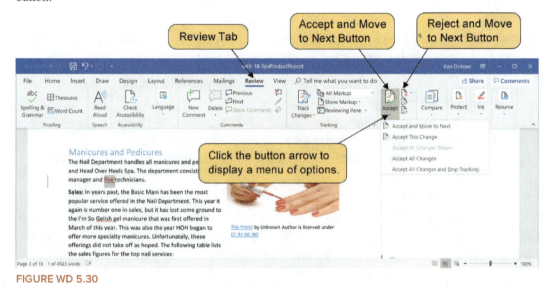

FIGURE WD 5.30

tips & tricks

To navigate between changes in a document, click the **Previous Change** and **Next Change** buttons.

tell me more

If you have sent the document to multiple reviewers, each reviewer's comments and changes will be displayed in a specific color. To see which reviewer is represented by which color, in the *Tracking* group, click the **Show Markup** button and point to **Reviewers**. Each reviewer is listed in the menu by color. If a checkmark appears next to the reviewer's name, that reviewer's comments and changes are visible. If there is no checkmark next to the reviewer's name, that reviewer's comments and changes have been hidden. Click a reviewer's name on the menu to hide or show comments and changes from that reviewer.

another method

> To accept a change and automatically move to the next change, you can click the **Accept and Move to Next** button arrow and select the **Accept and Move to Next** command from the menu.

> To reject a change and automatically move to the next change, you can click the **Reject and Move to Next** button arrow and select the **Reject and Move to Next** command from the menu.

let me try Live!

If you do not have the data file from the previous skill open, open the student data file **wd5-18-SpaProductReport** ⬇ and try this skill on your own:

1. Place the cursor at the beginning of the document.
2. Move to the first change in the document.
3. The first change found is the formatting of **Head Over Heels Spa**. Reject the formatting change and move to the next change.
4. The next change found is the insertion of the word **five**. Accept this change and move to the next change.
5. The next change found is a comment. Move to the next change.
6. The next changes found are the deletion of **160** and the insertion of **860**. Reject both these changes and move to the next change.
7. At this point, all remaining changes are correct. With one command, accept all the remaining changes in the document.
8. If you will be moving on to the next skill in this chapter, leave the document open to continue working. If not, save the file as directed by your instructor and close it.

Skill **5.19** Locking Track Changes

When you send out your documents for review with *Track Changes* on, you may want to prevent your reviewers from turning off the feature. This will ensure that any changes made by reviewers will be marked and gives you the ability to review and then accept or reject all changes made to the document. Use the **Lock Tracking** feature to add a password to a document that will be required to be entered in order to disable *Track Changes*.

To lock Track Changes:

1. Click the **Review** tab.
2. In the Tracking group, click the bottom half of the **Track Changes** button.
3. Select **Lock Tracking**.

FIGURE WD 5.31

4. In the *Lock Tracking* dialog, type a password that will be required to be entered to unlock *Track Changes* in the **Enter Password (optional)** box.
5. Retype the password in the **Reenter to confirm** box.
6. Click **OK**.

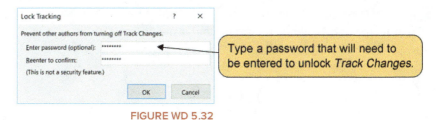

FIGURE WD 5.32

To unlock Track Changes:

1. In the Tracking group, click the bottom half of the **Track Changes** button again and select **Lock Tracking**.
2. In the Unlock Tracking dialog, type the password in the **Password** box.
3. Click **OK**.

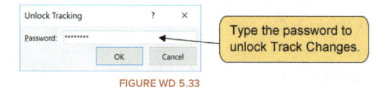

FIGURE WD 5.33

tips & tricks

You do not have to require a password to unlock *Track Changes*. In the *Lock Tracking* dialog, click **OK** without entering a password. *Track Changes* will still be locked, but in order to unlock *Track Changes*, reviewers will only need to select the option from the *Track Changes* menu.

tell me more

Adding a password for locking *Track Changes* is not a security feature. It only unlocks the ability to accept and reject changes and turn off the *Track Changes* feature. It does not require a password for your users to open and modify the document. However, any changes made to the document will be tracked.

let me try Live!

If you do not have the data file from the previous skill open, open the student data file **wd5-19-SpaProductReport** and try this skill on your own:

1. Lock tracking in the document so readers will not be able to turn off *Track Changes*.
2. Add the password: **hhspa789**
3. Unlock the tracking in the document using the password: **hhspa789**
4. Turn off the **Track Changes** feature.
5. If you will be moving on to the next skill in this chapter, leave the document open to continue working. If not, save the file as directed by your instructor and close it.

Back Button

Next Button

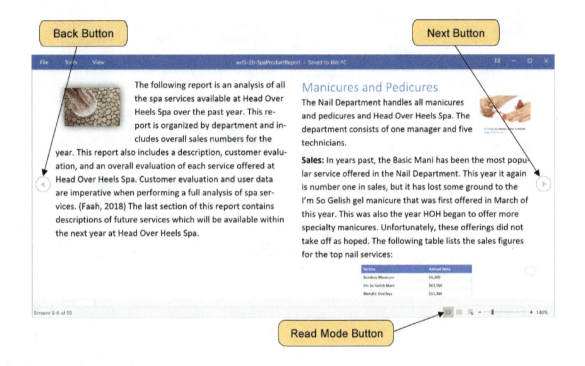

Read Mode Button

> ❯
> ❯
> ❯

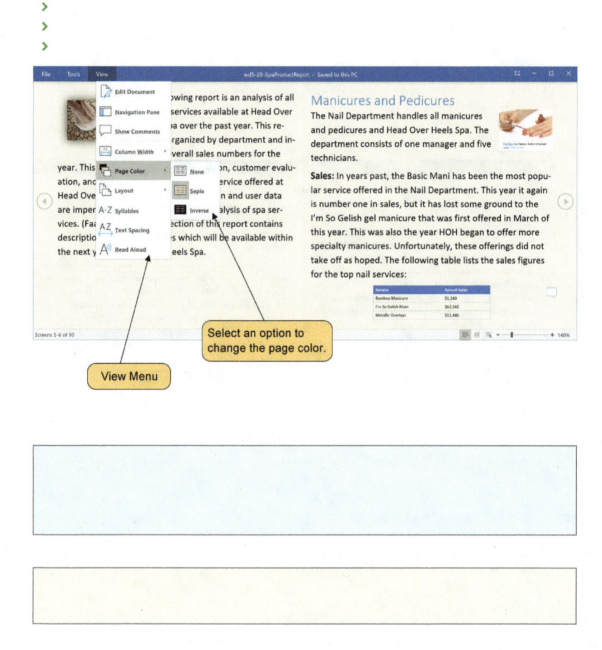

View Menu

Select an option to change the page color.

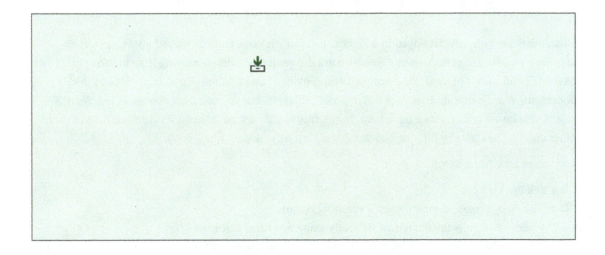

Skill 5.21 Changing How Pages Scroll

Documents are typically displayed in a vertical fashion with one page displayed above or below another page. To navigate between pages, you use the vertical scrollbar, moving it up to move to navigate to an earlier place in the document and moving it down to move to a later place in the document. Word's default display is still this **vertical layout**, but you can also choose to use Word's **side to side layout** to navigate a document. In the side to side layout, pages are displayed next to each other and you navigate by flipping between pages, just as you would in a book.

To change how pages scroll:

1. Click the **View** tab.
2. In the *Page Movement* group, click a scrolling option:
   - **Vertical**—scrolls the document vertically using a vertical scrollbar
   - **Side to Side**—scrolls the document horizontally, one page at a time, using a horizontal scrollbar

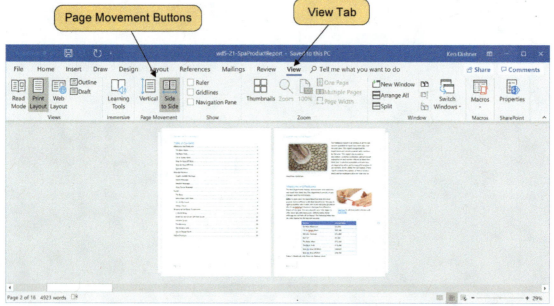

FIGURE WD 5.36

tips & tricks

When you are scrolling a document using the *Side to Side* option, the *Thumbnails* button appears in the *Zoom* group and the other *Zoom* options are no longer available. Click the **Thumbnails** button to display each page in the document as a large thumbnail that provides a quick overview of the page structure of the document and allows you to navigate quickly to the page you want.

tell me more

Side to side layout is helpful when using a touch screen or tablet. Swiping left or right with your finger will flip between the pages.

let me try Live!

If you do not have the data file from the previous skill open, open the student data file **wd5-21-SpaProductReport** ⬇ and try this skill on your own:

1. Change the scrolling of the document to **Side to Side**.
2. Change the scrolling of the document back to **Vertical**.
3. Save the file as directed by your instructor and close it.

key terms

Template

Thesaurus

AutoCorrect

Table of contents

Tab leaders

Caption

Footnotes

Endnotes

Reference mark

Researcher

Reference style

Citation

Source Manager

Bibliography

Index

Track Changes

Reviewing pane

Comment

Lock Tracking

Read Mode

Vertical layout

Side to side layout

concept review

1. What would you use to look up a synonym for a word?
   a. grammar check
   b. Thesaurus
   c. Dictionary
   d. translate tool

2. If you often mistype a word, use Word's _____ to automatically replace the misspelling with the correct spelling as you type.
   a. *Find* and *Replace* commands
   b. spelling checker
   c. grammar checker
   d. AutoCorrect

3. When you add a table of contents to a document, the entries created are based on _____.
   a. marked entries
   b. headings
   c. custom styles
   d. all of the above

4. Which of the following fills in the space between tabs with solid, dotted, or dashed lines?
   a. border
   b. tab leader
   c. tab marker
   d. none of the above

5. You can add a caption for both figures and tables.
   a. true
   b. false

6. Which of the following appears at the bottom of a page and is composed of two parts: a reference mark (a superscript character placed next to the text) and the associated text?
   a. footnote
   b. endnote
   c. index
   d. citation

7. What is the set of rules used to display references in a bibliography known as?
   a. source
   b. reference style
   c. template
   d. citation

8. When *Track Changes* is active, all insertions, deletions, and formatting changes are marked.
   a. true
   b. false

9. Which of the following are notes you add to a document that are not intended to be part of the final document?
   a. tracked changes
   b. balloons
   c. ink notations
   d. comments

10. Which view should you use to view documents optimally on an electronic device, such as a tablet?
    a. Read Mode
    b. Print Layout view
    c. Web Layout view
    d. Draft view

projects
skill review **5.1**

Data files for projects can be found by logging into your SIMnet account and going to the Library section.

In this project you will be working on a research paper about alternate assessments for students. First you will work with track changes by accepting and rejecting changes that have been made. You will also add and reply to comments. You will find a synonym for a word using the Thesaurus. You will add a table of contents. You will add an endnote and then convert the endnote to a footnote. You will change the reference style for the paper to APA, add a new source, and add a citation to the document. You will mark an entry for the index and then add the index along with a bibliography.

Skills needed to complete this project:

- Using Track Changes (Skill 5.15)
- Working with Comments (Skill 5.16)
- Accepting and Rejecting Changes in a Document (Skill 5.18)
- Using the Thesaurus (Skill 5.2)
- Using AutoCorrect (Skill 5.3)
- Inserting a Table of Contents Skill 5.4)
- Inserting Footnotes and Endnotes (Skill 5.7)
- Selecting a Reference Style (Skill 5.9)
- Adding Citations to Documents (Skill 5.10)
- Creating a Bibliography (Skill 5.12)
- Marking Entries (Skill 5.13)
- Creating an Index (Skill 5.14)

1. Open the start file **WD2019-SkillReview-5-1** and resave the file as: `[your initials]WD-SkillReview-5-1`
2. If the document opens in Protected View, click the **Enable Editing** button in the Message Bar at the top of the document so you can modify the document.
3. Use *Track Changes*.
    a. Click the **Review** tab.
    b. In the *Tracking* group, click the **Track Changes** button.
4. Select the first sentence in the first paragraph of *What is an Alternate Assessment* section (the sentence beginning with *All of this brings us to*). Press the **Delete** key to delete the sentence.

5. Accept and reject changes in a document.

   a. Press **Ctrl + Home** to navigate to the beginning of the document.

   b. On the *Review* tab, in the *Changes* group, click the **Next Change** button.

   c. In the Changes group, click the **Accept and Move to Next** button to accept the deletion of the text *particular tasks.*

   d. Click the **Accept and Move to Next** button to accept the insertion of the word *tasks.*

   e. Click the **Accept and Move to Next** button to accept the formatting change.

   f. Click the **Accept and Move to Next** button to accept the deletion you just made.

   g. Click the **Reject and Move to Next** button to reject the formatting change.

   h. Click the **Reject and Move to Next** button to reject the deletion.

   i. Click the **Reject and Move to Next** button to reject the insertion.

   j. Click the **Accept** button arrow and select **Accept All Changes** to accept the remaining changes in the document.

   k. Turn *Track Changes* off by clicking the **Track Changes** button.

6. Reply to a comment and resolve the comment.

   b. Click the **Reply** button in the first comment.

   c. Type the following reply: `This has been fixed`

   d. Click the **Resolve** comment button to resolve the comment.

7. Add a comment to a document.

   a. Place the cursor at the end of the *Introduction* heading at the beginning of the document.

   b. On the *Review* tab, in the *Comments* group, click the **New Comment** button.

   c. Type the following comment: `Review one more time looking for mistakes`

8. Use the Thesaurus to look up synonyms of a word.

   a. In the first paragraph under *Introduction,* select the word **pick** in the second sentence.

   b. On the *Review* tab, in the *Proofing* group, click the **Thesaurus** button.

   c. Scroll the list of synonyms, in the *select (v.)* section, point to the first option **select** and click the **arrow**.

   d. Click **Insert** on the menu.

   e. Close the *Thesaurus* task pane.

9. Add an AutoCorrect entry and type the text to see the correction.

    a. Click the **File** tab.

    b. Click **Options**.

    c. In the *Word Options* dialog, click **Proofing**.

    d. Click the **AutoCorrect Options...** button.

    e. In the *Replace* box, type `acomodations`. In the *With* box, type: `accommodations`

    f. Click the **Add** button.

    g. Click **OK** in the *AutoCorrect* Click **OK** in the *Word Options* dialog.

    h. Place the cursor between the words *of* and *that* in the first sentence of the first paragraph of the document.

    i. Type `acomodations` then press the spacebar. Notice Word replaces the misspelled word with the correct spelling you added.

10. Insert a table of contents.

    a. Place the cursor before the **Introduction** heading.

    b. Click the **Layout** tab.

    c. In the *Page Setup* group, click the **Breaks** button and select **Page**.

    d. Place the cursor at the beginning of the empty line on the newly inserted page.

    e. Click the **References** tab.

    f. In the *Table of Contents* group, click the **Table of Contents** button and select **Automatic Table 2**.

11. Insert a footnote.

    a. Navigate to the *No Child Left Behind* section of the document. Place the cursor after the word *state* in the first sentence.

    b. On the *References* tab, in the *Footnotes* group, click the **Insert Footnote** button.

    c. Type the following text for the footnote: `The Ohio state standards have been used in this project.`

12. Add a new source.

    a. In the *Modified Achievement Standards* section, place the cursor before the period in the second sentence of the last paragraph of the section. This is the sentence ending with *scheduling, presentation format or response format.*

    b. On the *References* tab, in the *Citations & Bibliography* group, click the **Insert Citation** button.

    c. Select **Add New Source...**

    d. In the *Create Source* dialog, select **Journal Article** as the type of source. Enter `Pamela Johnson` as the author. Enter `The Benefits of Administration of Alternate Assessments` as the title. Enter `New Horizons` as the journal name.

    e. Enter `2016` for the year.

    f. Enter `32-33` for the pages.

    g. Click **OK** to create the source.

13. Insert a citation.

  a. Navigate to the *Who Will Benefit* section. Place the cursor before the last period at the end of the second paragraph in the section. This is the sentence ending with *validity of the alternate assessment.*

  b. On the *References* tab, in the *Citations & Bibliography* group, click the **Insert Citation** button and select the **Johnson, Pamela** citation.

14. Change the reference style for the document.

  a. On the *References* tab, in the *Citations & Bibliography* group, click the **Style** arrow.

  b. Select **APA Sixth Edition**.

15. Mark an entry for the index.

  a. Navigate to the *No Child Left Behind* section. Select **No Child Left Behind Act (NCLB)** in the first sentence of the first paragraph.

  b. On the *References* tab, in the *Index* group, click the **Mark Entry** button.

  c. In the *Mark Index Entry* dialog, click the **Mark** button.

  d. Click the **Close** button.

16. Hide the formatting marks in the document.

  a. Click the **Home** tab.

  b. In the *Paragraph* group, click the **Show/Hide** button to hide formatting marks in the document.

17. Add a bibliography to the document.

  a. Place the cursor at the end of the document.

  b. Click the **Layout** tab.

  c. In the *Page Setup* group, click the **Breaks** button and select **Page**.

  d. Click the **References** tab.

  e. In the *Citations & Bibliography* group, click the **Bibliography** button and select **Bibliography**.

18. Create an index for the document.

  a. Verify the cursor is on the empty line under the *Bibliography* section.

  b. Click the **Layout** tab.

  c. In the *Page Setup* group, click the **Breaks** button and select **Page**.

  d. Click the **References** tab.

  e. In the *Index* group, click the **Insert Index** button.

  f. Click the **Formats** arrow and select **Modern**.

  g. Click **OK** to add the index.

19. Save and close the document.

projects
skill review **5.2**

Data files for projects can be found by logging into your SIMnet account and going to the Library section.

In this project, you will be reviewing the document for the Tri-State Book Festival. You will be making changes, accepting and rejecting other changes, and working with comments. You will also use the Thesaurus to replace a word with a synonym. Finally, you will add a footnote and tab leaders to text in the document and a caption to a chart.

Skills needed to complete this project:

- Using Track Changes (Skill 5.15)
- Accepting and Rejecting Changes in a Document (Skill 5.18)
- Working with Comments (Skill 5.16)
- Hiding and Showing Changes in a Document (Skill 5.17)
- Using AutoCorrect (Skill 5.3)
- Using the Thesaurus (Skill 5.2)
- Adding a Caption (Skill 5.6)
- Adding Tab Leaders (Skill 5.5)
- Inserting Footnotes and Endnotes (Skill 5.7)

1. Open the start file **WD2019-SkillReview-5-2** and resave the file as:
   `[your initials]WD-SkillReview-5-2`
2. If the document opens in Protected View, click the **Enable Editing** button in the Message Bar at the top of the document so you can modify the document.
3. Use *Track Changes*.
   a. Click the **Review** tab.
   b. In the *Tracking* group, click the **Track Changes** button to turn the feature on.
   c. In the first sentence of the first paragraph select the text **October 10-12**. Press the **Delete** key to delete the sentence.
   d. Type `September 6-8`
4. Change the display of tracked changes in a document.
   a. On the *Review* tab, in the *Tracking* group, click the **Show Markup** button.
   b. Point to **Balloons** and select **Show Revisions in Balloons**.

5. Accept and reject changes in a document.

   a. Place the cursor at the beginning of the first paragraph of the document.

   b. On the *Review* tab, in the *Changes* group, click the **Next Change** button.

   c. The first item found is a comment. Click **Next Change** again to move to the first change in the document.

   d. Click the **Accept and Move to Next** button to accept the deletion you just made.

   e. Click the **Accept and Move to Next** button to accept the insertion you just made.

   f. In the Changes group, click the **Accept and Move to Next** button to accept the deletion of the text *95.*

   g. Click the **Accept and Move to Next** button to accept the insertion of the text *75.*

   h. Click the **Accept and Move to Next** button to accept the formatting change.

   i. Click the **Accept and Move to Next** button to accept the formatting change.

   j. Click the **Reject and Move to Next** button to reject the formatting change.

   k. Click the **Reject and Move to Next** button to reject the deletion.

6. Accept all changes in the document.

   a. In the *Tracking* group, click the **Accept** button arrow.

   b. Select **Accept All Changes** to accept the remaining changes in the document.

7. Turn *Track Changes* off by clicking the **Track Changes** button.

8. Reply to a comment.

   a. Click the **Reply** button in the comment on page 1.

   b. Type the following reply: `This has been updated`

9. Click the **Resolve** button in the comment balloon to resolve the comment.

10. Add a comment to a document.

    a. Place the cursor at the end of the *Book signing and dinner* text in the last row of the table in the *September 6* section.

    b. On the *Review* tab, in the *Comments* group, click the **New Comment** button.

    c. Type the following comment: `Be sure to confirm with authors`

11. Change the review display of the document.

    a. On the *Review* tab, in the *Tracking* group, click the **Display for Review** drop-down arrow.

    b. Select **No Markup**.

12. Use the Thesaurus.

    a. In the second sentence of the first paragraph, select the word **kinds**.

    b. On the *Review* tab, in the *Proofing* group, click the **Thesaurus** button.

    c. Point to genres in the list of synonyms, click the arrow, and click **Insert**.

13. Insert a footnote.

   a. Place the cursor after the period in the second to last sentence in the second paragraph (after *written by one of our authors.*).

   b. Click the **References** tab.

   c. In the *Footnotes* group, click the **Insert Footnote** button.

   d. Type the following text for the footnote: `Prizes will be awarded to the attendees who solve the crime the fastest`

14. Adding tab leaders.

   a. Navigate to the *Authors* section and select the list of authors (both *Fiction* and *Nonfiction*).

   b. Click the **Home** tab.

   c. In the *Paragraph* group, click the **dialog launcher**.

   d. In the *Paragraph* dialog, click the **Tabs...** button.

   e. In the *Tab stop position* box, type `2.5"`

   f. In the *Leader* section, select the **second option**.

   g. Click **OK**.

   h. Delete the space between **Max Wallace** and **Featured Work** and press the `Tab` key.

   i. Repeat this step for all the authors in the *Fiction* and *Nonfiction*

15. Add a caption.

   a. Navigate to the end of the document and select the chart.

   b. Click the **References** tab.

   c. In the *Captions* group, click the **Insert Caption** button.

   d. Change the text in the *Caption* text box to read: `Figure 1: Authors by Genre`

   e. Click **OK**.

16. Save and close the document.

projects

Data files for projects can be found by logging into your SIMnet account and going to the Library section.

challenge yourself 5.3

In this project you will be working on a safety report from the Winter Springs Community. First, you will work with track changes by accepting and rejecting changes that have been made. You will also add and reply to comments. You will create an AutoCorrect entry and then use the Thesaurus to find synonyms of words. You will add a caption to a chart. You will add tab leaders to text, a table of contents, and a footnote. You will then mark an entry for the index, and add an index to the document.

Skills needed to complete this project:

- Using Track Changes (Skill 5.15)
- Accepting and Rejecting Changes in a Document (Skill 5.18)
- Working with Comments (Skill 5.16)
- Using AutoCorrect (Skill 5.3)
- Using the Thesaurus (Skill 5.2)
- Adding a Caption (Skill 5.6)
- Adding Tab Leaders (Skill 5.5)
- Inserting a Table of Contents (Skill 5.4)
- Inserting Footnotes and Endnotes (Skill 5.7)
- Marking Entries (Skill 5.13)
- Creating an Index (Skill 5.14)

1. Open the start file WD2019-ChallengeYourself-5-3 and resave the file as:
   `[your initials]WD-ChallengeYourself-5-3`
2. If the document opens in Protected View, enable editing so you can make changes to the document.
3. Review the document from the beginning and make the following changes:
   a. Accept the formatting on the title of the document.
   b. Reject the deletion of the word **neighborhood**.
   c. Accept the insertion of the word **electronic**.
   d. Reject the deletion of the word **Never** and reject the insertion of the word **Rarely**.
   e. Accept all the remaining tracked changes in the document.
4. Add a comment to the *Most Targeted Electronic Devices* heading that reads: `Be sure to check these numbers`
5. Navigate to the comment in the *Security Staff* section and type `This took effect 3 months ago` as a reply to the comment.
6. Resolve the comment.
7. Change the display of the document to show no markup.

8. Navigate to the beginning of the document and place the cursor at the beginning of the *Introduction* heading.

9. Create an AutoCorrect entry that will change the letters **wsc** to **Winter Springs Community** when typed.

10. Place the cursor between the words *The* and *currently* in the first sentence of the *Security Staff* section. Type **wsc** and press the spacebar. Notice Word changes the text to the entry you just created.

11. Select the word **neighborhood** in the first sentence of the first paragraph of the document (*secure, gated neighborhood*). Use the Thesaurus to replace the word **neighborhood** with the synonym **community**.

12. Select the word **robberies** in the second sentence of the first paragraph. Use the Thesaurus to replace the word **robberies** with the synonym **thefts**.

13. Select the chart in the document. Add a caption that reads `Figure 1: Most Targeted Electronics`. Have the figure appear below the chart.

14. Select the list of round the clock officers in the *Security Staff* section. Open the *Tabs* dialog, add a **right tab** at the **5"** mark. Include a **dotted tab leader (option 2)**.

15. For each item in the bulleted list, place the cursor between the name and the number of years. Remove the space and press **Tab**.

16. Repeat steps 14-15 for the list of day shift officers.

17. Place the cursor at the end of the document title *Winter Springs Community News* (at the beginning of the document) and press **Enter**. Add a table of contents based on the **Automatic Table 2** style. Delete the extra blank line.

18. Place the cursor at the end of the heading *Guidelines for Staying Safe*. Insert a footnote that reads: `Adapted from Sylvester Bryant's safety presentation`.

19. Select the text *monthly security meetings* in the first sentence of the first paragraph in the *Security Meeting Schedule* section. Mark the text for use in an index. Close the *Mark Index Entry* dialog.

20. Place the cursor in the blank line below the table at the end of the document and add a page break. Insert an index based on the **Classic** format. Have the index display in one column.

21. Hide the formatting marks in the document when you are done.

22. Save and close the document.

projects

Data files for projects can be found by logging into your SIMnet account and going to the Library section.

challenge yourself 5.4

In this project, you will be reviewing a paper on behavioral change. You will be replacing words by looking up synonyms in the Thesaurus. You will add a footnote to the document. Next, you will be working with tracked changes. You will be accepting and rejecting changes, changing the markup display, and locking track changes. Next, you will add captions to charts. Finally, you will work with comments including adding a comment, replying to a comment, and resolving a comment.

Skills needed to complete this project:

- Using the Thesaurus (Skill 5.2)
- Inserting a Footnote (Skill 5.7)
- Hiding and Showing Changes in a Document (Skill 5.17)
- Using Track Changes (Skill 5.15)
- Accepting and Rejecting Changes in a Document (Skill 5.18)
- Adding a Caption (Skill 5.6)
- Working with Comments (Skill 5.16)
- Locking Track Changes (Skill 5.19)
- Changing How Pages Scroll (Skill 5.21)

1. Open the start file **WD2019-ChallengeYourself-5-4** and resave the file as:
   `[your initials]WD-ChallengeYourself-5-4`
2. If the document opens in Protected View, enable editing so you can make changes to the document.
3. Use the Thesaurus to change the word **pupil** to **student** in the last sentence of the first paragraph of the document.
4. Add a footnote at the end of the second sentence of the first paragraph (the sentence ending with *time period*). The footnote should read `Observed the student over five days in both phases`
5. Change the display of the tracked changes to show all revisions in balloons.
6. Review the document from the beginning and make the following changes:
   a. Reject the insertion of the word **absolutely**.
   b. Reject the formatting of **Language Arts**.
   c. Accept the deletion of **observation** and the insertion of **implementation**.
7. Accept all the remaining tracked changes in the document.
8. Select the first chart in the document and add a caption that appears below the chart. Have the caption read `Figure 1: Observation Phase`

9. Select the second chart in the document and add a caption that appears below the chart. Have the caption read `Figure 2: Implementation Phase`

10. Reply to the first comment in the document with: `This has been completed`

11. Resolve the comment.

12. Add a comment to the Techniques heading that reads: `Can this section be deleted?`

13. Change the display of the document to show no markup.

14. Lock tracking on the document.

15. Switch to the **Side to Side** page movement view.

16. Switch back to the **Vertical** page movement view.

17. Save and close the document.

projects

Data files for projects can be found by logging into your
SIMnet account and going to the Library section.

on your own 5.5

In this project, you will be reviewing a memo from the Trade Winds Food company. You will finish out the document by adding a caption, replacing a word using the Thesaurus, and adding tab leaders to the document. You will work with tracked changes and comments, including locking tracking. Finally, you will create an AutoCorrect entry and view the document using Read Mode.

Skills needed to complete this project:

- Adding a Caption (Skill 5.6)
- Using the Thesaurus (Skill 5.2)
- Adding Tab Leaders (Skill 5.5)
- Using Track Changes (Skill 5.15)
- Hiding and Showing Changes in a Document (Skill 5.17)
- Accepting and Rejecting Changes in a Document (Skill 5.18)
- Working with Comments (Skill 5.16)
- Locking Track Changes (Skill 5.19)
- Using AutoCorrect (Skill 5.3)
- Using Read Mode (Skill 5.20)

1. Open the start file **WD2019-OnYourOwn-5-5** and resave the file as:
   `[your initials]WD-OnYourOwn-5-5`
2. If the document opens in Protected View, click the **Enable Editing** button in the Message Bar at the top of the document so you can modify the document.
3. Add a caption to the chart on the second page of the document.
4. Use the Thesaurus to replace the word **rival** in the second paragraph with a word of your choice.
5. Add a tab stop at the **4.5"** mark with a tab leader of your choice to the last line of the document. Insert a tab between **Marketing Strategies** and **Trade Wind Foods**.
6. Turn on **Track Changes**.
7. Change the display of the markup in the document.
8. Change the color of the **Trade Winds Food Committee Memo** text to a color of your choice.
9. Accept the formatting change you made.
10. Review the document and accept and reject the tracked changes as you see fit.
11. Add a comment directing others to review a specific part of the document.
12. Reply to and resolve the comments in the document.
13. Lock tracking in the document.
14. Add an AutoCorrect entry to be able to quickly enter the company name **Trade Wind Foods**.
15. Change the display of the document so comments will be hidden.

16. Switch to **Read Mode** and then back to **Print Layout** view.
17. Save and close the document.

projects

fix it 5.6

Data files for projects can be found by logging into your SIMnet account and going to the Library section.

In this project you will be working on a research paper about alternate assessments for students. You will be fixing a number of errors in the paper. First you will work with track changes by accepting and rejecting changes that have been made. You will also reply to and resolve a comment. You will find a synonym for a word using the Thesaurus. You will change the reference style for the paper to APA and then correct a citation error. You will add a bibliography. You will replace the hand typed table of contents with one that is autogenerated. You will remove a manually entered note and replace it with a footnote. You will mark an entry for the index and then replace the hand typed index with an autogenerated one.

Skills needed to complete this project:

- Using Track Changes (Skill 5.15)
- Accepting and Rejecting Changes in a Document (Skill 5.18)
- Using the Thesaurus (Skill 5.2)
- Selecting a Reference Style (Skill 5.9)
- Adding Citations to Documents (Skill 5.10)
- Creating a Bibliography (Skill 5.12)
- Inserting Footnotes and Endnotes (Skill 5.7)
- Marking Entries (Skill 5.13)
- Creating an Index (Skill 5.14)
- Inserting a Table of Contents (Skill 5.4)
- Working with Comments (Skill 5.16)

1. Open the start file **WD2019-FixIt-5-6** and resave the file as:
   `[your initials]WD-FixIt-5-6`
2. If the document opens in Protected View, click the Enable Editing button in the Message Bar at the top of the document so you can modify the document.
3. Navigate to the first heading in the document (*Introduction*), and review the tracked changes in the document, making the following changes:
   a. Accept the first change of **accommodations** to **modifications**.
   b. Accept the second change of **accommodations** to **modifications**.
   c. Reject the deletion of the word **fundamental**.
   d. Reject the deletion of the word **educational**.
   e. The remaining changes are formatting changes to headings. Accept the remaining changes in the document.

4. In the second sentence in the first paragraph under *What is an Alternate Assessment*, use the *Thesaurus* to replace the word **duties** with **responsibilities**.

5. Change the reference style for the document to **APA Sixth Edition**.

6. Place the cursor before the period in the second to last sentence of the first paragraph in the *Modified Achievement Standards* section (the sentence ending with *demonstrate adequate proficiency.*) Insert a citation to the **Pamela Johnson** source.

7. In the first paragraph of the *No Child Left Behind* section, the citations have been manually entered. Create a new source based on the following information:
   a. Type of Source: **Journal Article**
   b. Author: **Elliot, Stephen; Kettler, Ryan**
   c. Title: **Assessments Based on Modified Standards**
   d. Journal Name: **Exceptional Children**
   e. Year: **2017**
   f. Pages: **44-46**

8. Replace the three manually entered citations in the first paragraph of the *No Child Left Behind* section with the source you just created.

9. The bibliography at the end of the document has been entered in manually. Delete the existing bibliography.

10. Replace the bibliography you deleted with one generated by Word based on the **Bibliography** style.

11. In the *No Child Left Behind* section of the document, a note has been added manually. Delete the superscript number next to the word **state** and the note at the end of the *No Child Left Behind* section (the line beginning with [1] *In this project, the*).

12. Place the cursor after the word **state** in the first sentence of the first paragraph in the *No Child Left Behind* section and add a footnote that reads: `In this project, the Ohio state standards were applied.`

13. Navigate to the *Who Will Benefit* section. In the first sentence of the second paragraph mark the words **determining eligibility** for use in the index.

14. Hide the formatting marks in the document.

15. Navigate to the end of the document and delete the index that was entered in manually.

16. Replace the index you deleted with one generated by Word using the **Classic** format in a two column layout.

17. The table of contents at the beginning of the document has been manually entered. Delete the table of contents.

18. Replace the table of contents you deleted with one generated by Word using the **Automatic Table 1** option.

19. Click the **Reply** button in the comment on the title page and type the following reply: `These have been corrected`

20. Click the **Resolve** comment button to resolve the comment.

21. Save and close the document.

Mailings

introduction

In this addendum chapter, you will learn how to perform a mail merge, including selecting recipients and adding fields. You will also learn how to create and print envelopes and labels based on preformatted templates.

Skill A.1 Starting a Mail Merge

Suppose you have a letter you want to send out to 20 recipients, but you want each person's name to appear on the letter, giving it a more personal touch. You could write the letter and save 20 versions one for each recipient but this is time-consuming and cumbersome. In Word, you can take a list of names and addresses and merge them with a standard document, creating a personalized document for each name on your list. This process is called a **mail merge**.

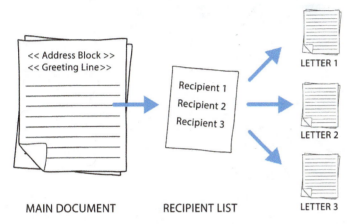

There are six basic steps to creating a mail merge:

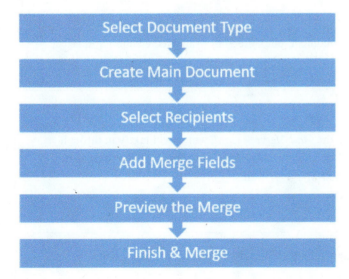

There are a number of document types you can create using mail merge. The most common types are letters, envelopes, and labels. The first step in creating a mail merge is to select the main document type.

To set up the main document for a mail merge using a letter:

1. Start with the document you want to use for the merge open (either a prewritten letter or blank document).
2. Click the **Mailings** tab.
3. In the *Start Mail Merge* group, click the **Start Mail Merge** button and select **Letters**.

FIGURE WD A.1

tips & tricks

To remove merge information from a document, click the **Start Mail Merge** button and select **Normal Word Document**.

tell me more

You can also create a mail merge using the *Mail Merge Wizard*, which will take you through creating the mail merge step by step. To display the *Mail Merge Wizard*, click the **Start Mail Merge** button and select **Step by Step Mail Merge Wizard...**

let me try Live!

Open the student data file **wdA-01-CustomerLetter** and try this skill on your own:

1. Start a new mail merge for a **letter**.
2. If you will be moving on to the next skill in this chapter, leave the document open to continue working. If not, save the file as directed by your instructor.

Skill A.2 Selecting Recipients

The **recipients list** for the mail merge is a table of names and address for the people you want to include in the merge. You can import recipients from an existing Access database or Excel workbook, or you can enter the recipients' information manually.

To select recipients for the mail merge:

1. Click the **Mailings** tab.
2. In the *Start Mail Merge* group, click the **Select Recipients** button.
3. Select **Use an Existing List...**
4. In the *Select Data Source* dialog, select a data source and click **Open**.

FIGURE WD A.2

To enter recipients for the mail merge manually:

1. In the *Start Mail Merge* group, click the **Select Recipients** button and select **Type a New List...**
2. In the *New Address List* dialog, enter the information for the recipient in the appropriate boxes.
3. Click the **New Entry** button to add another recipient.
4. Continue adding all the recipients for the mail merge. When you are done, click **OK** to create the list of recipients.

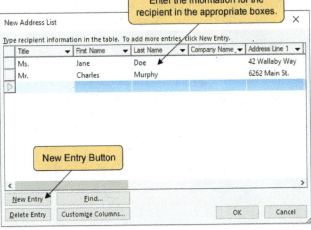

FIGURE WD A.3

Once you have added a list of recipients, you can then edit the recipients list, making any changes to information that may be incorrect.

To edit the recipients list:

1. On the *Mailings* tab, in the *Start Mail Merge* group, click the **Edit Recipient List** button.
2. Click in any field to change the information for the recipients.
3. Click the checkmark next to a name to deselect it and exclude the recipient from the mail merge.
4. Click **OK** to close the dialog and accept the changes.

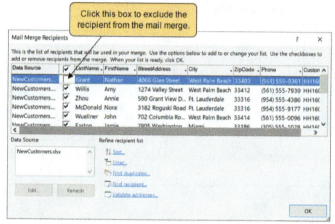

FIGURE WD A.4

tips & tricks

When manually entering recipients, you can make a correction at any time before you close the *New Address List* dialog by selecting the field and entering the modification. After closing the dialog, you can change the data by clicking the **Edit Recipients List** button.

tell me more

When you enter contacts manually, Word creates an Access database from the information you entered. The database is then stored on your hard drive in the *My Data Sources* folder in the *My Documents* folder for your user account.

let me try Live!

If you do not have the data file from the previous skill open, open the student data file **wdA-02-CustomerLetter** ⬇ and try this skill on your own:

1. Navigate to the location where you downloaded your student data files for this book.
2. Add a list of recipients to the mail merge based on the **newCustomers** Excel workbook.
3. Change the list of recipients so **Nathan Grant** will not be part of the merge.
4. If you will be moving on to the next skill in this chapter, leave the document open to continue working. If not, save the file as directed by your instructor.

Skill A.3 Adding an Address Block

The main document of a mail merge contains the text and merge fields, which appear on every version of the merged document. **Merge fields** are placeholders that insert specific data from the recipients list you created. If you are writing business letters, you can add an **address block** merge field where the address for the recipient should appear. An address block will display the name and address of the recipient in the standard business letter format.

To add an address block merge field:

1. Click in the document where you want the merge field to appear.
2. On the *Mailings* tab, in the *Write & Insert Fields* group, click the **Address Block** button.
3. In the **Insert Address Block** dialog, make any changes to the display and click **OK**.
4. When you have inserted the address block you will see <<*AddressBlock*>> where the data will be inserted.

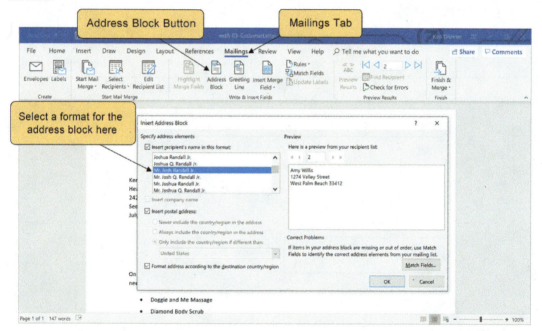

FIGURE WD A.5

tips & tricks

The *Insert Address Block* dialog includes a preview of how the merge fields will display in the document. Click the **Next** and **Previous** buttons to navigate through the list of recipients to see how each one will display before finalizing your choices.

tell me more

The three basic types of merge fields are:

Address Block—Inserts a merge field with the name and address of the recipient.

Greeting Line—Inserts a field with a greeting and the recipient's name.

Merge Fields—Allows you to insert merge fields based on your data source, such as first names, last names, addresses, phone numbers, and e-mail addresses.

let me try Live!

If you do not have the data file from the previous skill open, open the student data file **wdA-03-CustomerLetter** 📥 and try this skill on your own:

1. Place the cursor on the first blank line under the date.
2. Insert an address block using the following format: **Mr. Josh Randall Jr.**
3. If you will be moving on to the next skill in this chapter, leave the document open to continue working. If not, save the file as directed by your instructor.

Skill A.4 Adding a Greeting Line

When writing a letter, you should always open with a **greeting line** personally addressing the reader by name. This is where creating a mail merge can save you a lot of time and effort. When you add a greeting line to a mail merge, you choose the format for the greeting line. Then, Word inserts each name in the recipients list into the greeting line, creating personalized letters without having to create each one individually.

To add a greeting line merge field:

1. Click in the document where you want the merge field to appear.
2. On the *Mailings* tab, in the *Write & Insert Fields* group, click the **Greeting Line** button.
3. In the *Insert Greeting Line* dialog, make any changes to the display and click **OK**.
4. When you have inserted the greeting line you will see <<*GreetingLine*>> where the data will be inserted.

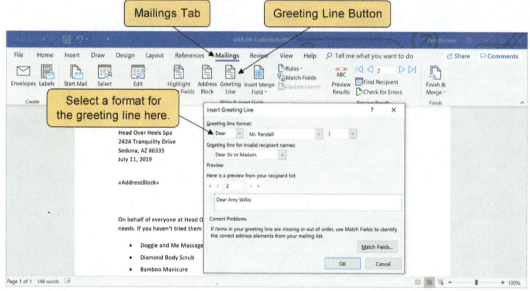

FIGURE WD A.6

tips & tricks

The *Insert Greeting Line* dialog includes a preview of how the merge fields will display in the document. Click the **Next** and **Previous** buttons to navigate through the list of recipients to see how each one will display before finalizing your choices.

tell me more

To add individual merge fields:

1. Click in the document where you want the merge field to appear.
2. Click the **Insert Merge Field** button and select an option to insert.

let me try Live!

If you do not have the data file from the previous skill open, open the student data file **wdA-04-CustomerLetter** and try this skill on your own:

1. Place the cursor on the blank line under the address block.
2. Insert a greeting line based on the following format: **Dear Mr. Randall:**
3. If you will be moving on to the next skill in this chapter, leave the document open to continue working. If not, save the file as directed by your instructor.

Skill A.5 Previewing and Finishing the Merge

Before you complete the mail merge and print your documents, it is a good idea to review each document created in the merge.

To preview the mail merge:

1. On the *Mailings* tab, in the *Preview Results* group, click the **Preview Results** button.
2. Click the **Next Record** and **Previous Record** buttons to navigate among different documents.

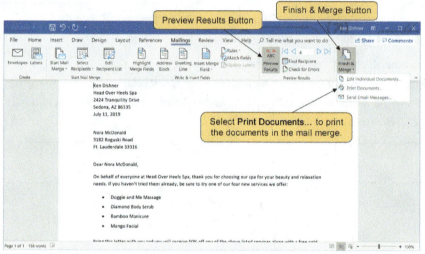

FIGURE WD A.7

After you have previewed the mail merge, the last step is to finish the merge by printing the documents.

To print the documents in the mail merge:

1. On the *Mailings* tab, in the *Finish* group, click the **Finish & Merge** button and select **Print Documents...**
2. In the *Merge to Printer* dialog, verify the **All** radio button is selected to print all the documents in the merge.
3. Click **OK**.
4. The *Print* dialog opens. Verify the correct printer information is displayed in the dialog and click **OK**.

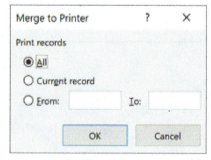

FIGURE A.8

tips & tricks

Before you finish the merge, click the **Check for Errors** button to review your documents for errors.

tell me more

> If you want to modify letters individually, click **Edit individual letters...** Then, in the *Merge to New Document* dialog, select the records you want to change and click **OK**. Word opens a new document based on the selected records. Make any changes you want, and then print or save the document just as you would any other file.

> If you want to send the document via e-mail, click **Send E-mail Messages...** Enter the subject line and mail format. Select the recipients you want to send the document to and click **OK**.

let me try Live!

If you do not have the data file from the previous skill open, open the student data file **wdA-05-CustomerLetter** and try this skill on your own:

1. Preview the mail merge.
2. Navigate through each letter to see how it will display.
3. Print all the letters in the mail merge. **NOTE:** If you are using this in class or in your school's computer lab, check with your instructor about printing permissions before completing this step.
4. Save the file as directed by your instructor and close it.

from the perspective of . . .

PAROLE OFFICER

I have several form letters that I use to send to my clients when they have a parole violation or have missed a court-mandated appointment. Oftentimes I am sending out several letters to clients at the same time, so I use mail merge to make the process go faster. I keep all my clients' information in an Access database that I use to create the recipients list. I can select which clients to add to the merge and then add the address block and greeting line to the form letter. I print all the letters at once, send them out, and I am done until the next violation occurs.

Skill A.6 Creating Envelopes

With Word you can create an envelope and print it without leaving the document you are working on. Word's preset formats take care of the measuring and layout for you.

To create and print an envelope:

1. Click the **Mailings** tab.
2. In the *Create* group, click the **Envelopes** button.
3. Type the address of the person you are sending the document to in the *Delivery address* text box.
4. Type your address in the *Return address* text box.
5. Click the **Print** button in the *Envelopes and Labels* dialog.

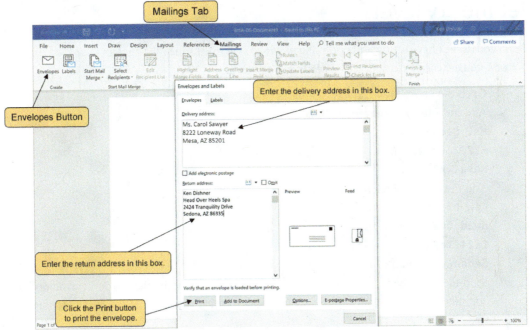

FIGURE WD A.9

tips & tricks

By default, Word selects a standard envelope size. If your envelope is a different size, you can change the size of the envelope through the *Envelope Options* dialog. In the *Envelopes and Labels* dialog, click the **Options...** button. The *Envelope Options* dialog opens. Click the **Envelope size** arrow and select an envelope size. Click **OK** in the *Envelope Options* dialog.

tell me more

When you open the *Envelopes and Labels* dialog, Word searches your document for an address. If it finds what looks like an address, it will copy it directly into the dialog for you. Of course, you can always change this if it's not what you need.

another method

To open the *Envelopes and Labels* dialog, you can also click the **Labels** button, and then click the **Envelopes** tab to create an envelope.

let me try Live!

If you do not have the data file from the previous skill open, open the student data file **wdA-06-Document1** and try this skill on your own:

1. Open the *Envelopes and Labels* dialog.
2. Add the following delivery address:

   Ms. Carol Sawyer
   8222 Loneway Road
   Mesa, AZ 85201

3. Add the following return address:

   Ken Dishner
   Head Over Heels Spa
   2424 Tranquility Drive
   Sedona, AZ 86335

4. Send the envelope to the printer. **NOTE:** If you are using this in class or in your school's computer lab, check with your instructor about printing permissions before completing this step.
5. Save the file as directed by your instructor and close it.

Skill A.7 Creating Labels

Rather than trying to create a document of **labels** with the correct margin and label size, you can use Word's preset label formats. Before creating your labels, first check the packaging for the manufacturer name and the product name or number.

To create labels:

1. Click the **Mailings** tab.
2. In the *Create* group, click the **Labels** button.

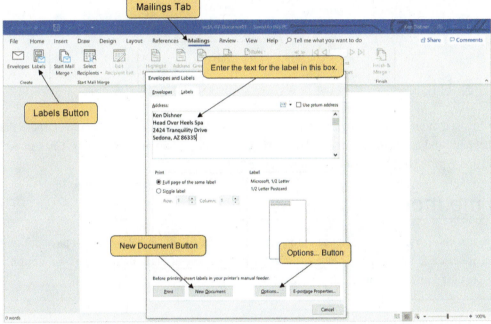

FIGURE WD A.10

3. Type the text for the label in the *Address* box.
4. Click the **Options...** button.
5. Click the **Label vendors** arrow and find the name of the company that made the labels you want to use.
6. Scroll the list of product numbers until you find the one that matches your labels.
7. Click **OK** in the *Label Options* dialog.
8. Click the **New Document** button.

Word creates the document as a table with the proper margins and spacing between cells. The cells in the table are prepopulated with the text you entered in the *Address* box in the *Envelopes and Labels* dialog.

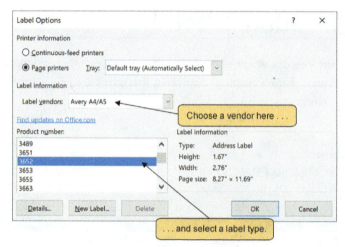

tips & tricks

If you need to create a page of labels with different text, leave the *Address* box empty, choose the label type, and create the document. Word will create a document of empty labels. Click in each cell and type the text for the labels you want to create.

tell me more

You can choose to print a full page of the same label or a single label. Use the full page option if you are printing return address labels that you will need several of. Use the single label option for creating individual labels, such as labels for file folders.

another method

To open the *Envelopes and Labels* dialog, you can also click the **Envelopes** button, and then click the **Labels** tab to create a label.

let me try Live!

If you do not have the data file from the previous skill open, open the student data file **wdA-07-Document1** and try this skill on your own:

1. Open the *Envelopes and Labels* dialog.
2. Add the following return address:

   ```
   Ken Dishner
   Head Over Heels Spa
   2424 Tranquility Drive
   Sedona, AZ 86335
   ```
3. Open the *Label Options* dialog and select the vendor **Avery A4/A5** and the product number **3652**.
4. Create a new document of labels.
5. Save the file as directed by your instructor and close it. Close the original file you opened but do not save it.

key terms

Mail merge

Recipients list

Merge fields

Address block

Greeting line

Labels

projects
skill review **A.1**

Data files for projects can be found by logging into your SIMnet account and going to the Library section.

In this project you will be creating a mail merge for Suarez Marketing. First, you will then create a mail merge by importing a list of recipients from an Excel workbook. Next, you will add fields and then preview and print the mail merge.

Skills needed to complete this project:

- Starting a Mail Merge (Skill A.1)
- Selecting Recipients (Skill A.2)
- Adding an Address Block (Skill A.3)
- Adding a Greeting Line (Skill A.4)
- Previewing and Finishing the Merge (Skill A.5)

1. Open the start file **WD2019-SkillReview-A-1** and resave the file as:
   `[your initials] WD-SkillReview-A-1`
2. If the document opens in Protected View, click the **Enable Editing** button in the Message Bar at the top of the document so you can modify it.
3. Start a new mail merge.
   a. Click the **Mailings** tab.
   b. Click the **Start Mail Merge** button and select **Letters**.
4. Add recipients to the mail merge.
   a. On the *Mailings* tab, in the *Start Mail Merge* group, click the **Select Recipients** button and select **Use an Existing List...**
   b. Browse to your student data file location, select the **Clients** workbook file, and click the **Open** button.
   c. In the *Select Table* dialog, select the **Clients** table and click **OK**.
5. Edit the recipients list.
   a. In the *Start Mail Merge* group, click the **Edit Recipient List** button.
   b. In the *Mail Merge Recipients* dialog, click the check boxes next to **Bruce Garber** and **Gerald Price** so a checkmark no longer displays next to each name and they are no longer included in the mail merge.
   c. Click **OK**.

6. Add an address block to the document.

    a. Place the cursor after the zip code in the company address block and press **Enter**.

    b. Place the cursor after the zip code in the company address block. Click the **Layout** tab. In the *Paragraph* group, click the up arrow in the **Spacing After** box two times.

    c. Place the cursor in the empty line after the zip code in the company address block.

    d. Click the **Mailings** tab. In the *Write & Insert Fields* group, click the **Address Block** button.

    e. In the *Insert recipient's name in this format* box, select the **Joshua Randall Jr.** format. Click **OK**.

7. Add a greeting line to the document.

    a. Place the cursor on the empty line above the first paragraph.

    b. On the *Mailings* tab, in the *Write & Insert Fields* group, click the **Greeting Line** button.

    c. In the *Insert Greeting Line* dialog, click the arrow next to the punctuation under *Greeting line format* and select the **colon (:)**. Click **OK**.

8. Preview the merged documents.

    a. On the *Mailings* tab, in the *Preview Results* group, click the **Preview Results** button.

    b. In the *Preview Results* group, click the **Next Record** button to advance through the letters in the mail merge.

9. Print the merged documents.

    a. On the *Mailings* tab, in the *Finish* group, click the **Finish & Merge** button and select **Print Documents...**

    b. Verify the **All** radio button is selected. Click **OK**.

    c. The *Print* dialog opens. Click **OK** to print all the letters in the merge. If you do not want to print the merge, click **Cancel**. **NOTE:** If you are using this in class or in your school's computer lab, check with your instructor about printing permissions before completing this step.

10. Save and close the document.

projects

challenge yourself **A.2**

Data files for projects can be found by logging into your SIMnet account and going to the Library section.

In this project you will create a mail merge letter and a sheet of address labels for the Greenscapes landscaping company.

Skills needed to complete this project:

- Starting a Mail Merge (Skill A.1)
- Selecting Recipients (Skill A.2)
- Adding an Address Block (Skill A.3)
- Adding a Greeting Line (Skill A.4)
- Previewing and Finishing the Merge (Skill A.5)
- Creating Labels (Skill 5.7)

1. Open the start file **WD2019-ChallengeYourself-A-2** and resave the file as:
   `[your initials] WD-ChallengeYourself-A-2`
2. If the document opens in Protected View, click the **Enable Editing** button in the Message Bar at the top of the document so you can modify it.
3. Start a new mail merge for creating letters.
4. Add recipients to the mail merge.
   a. Add recipients to the mail merge based on an existing list.
   b. Browse to your student data file location, and open the **Customers** workbook file as the recipients source.
   c. In the *Select Table* dialog, select the **Customers** table from the database.
5. Edit the recipients list so **Jamie Easton** and **Ronald Rayner** are not included in the mail merge.
6. Add an address block to the document.
   a. Place the cursor on the first empty line under the date.
   b. Add an address block to the letter based on the **Mr. Josh Randall Jr.** format.
7. Add a greeting line to the document.
   a. Place the cursor on the empty line under the address block.
   b. Add a greeting line to the letter. Have the field follow this format: **Dear Mr. Randall:**
8. Preview the merged documents reviewing how each will appear when printed.
9. Print the merged documents. **NOTE:** If you are using this in class or in your school's computer lab, check with your instructor about printing permissions before completing this step.
10. Save and close the document, but do not exit Word.

11. Create a new document of labels based on the **Avery A4/A5 3652**. Include the following address on the labels:

    ```
    Greenscapes Landscaping
    4583 Ridgewood Rd.
    Copley, OH 44321
    ```

12. Save the sheet of labels with the name `[your initials] WD-ChallengeYourself-A-2-labels` and close the file.

Excel 365

chapter **1**

Getting Started with Excel

In this chapter, you will learn the following skills:

> Identify the elements of a Microsoft Excel workbook

> Navigate a workbook

> Enter and format text, numbers, and dates in cells

> Understand the concept of charts

> Use the Recommended Charts feature

> Enter simple formulas

> Understand relative and absolute cell references

> Understand the concept of a function

> Use AutoSum and the Quick Analysis tool to add totals

> Use the status bar to display totals and other values

> Change the zoom level to view more or less of the worksheet

> Create a new workbook from a template

> Arrange multiple workbook windows

> Spell check a worksheet

> Preview and print a worksheet

introduction

This chapter provides you with the basic skills necessary to start working with Excel. The first step is to become familiar with the Excel interface and learn how to navigate a workbook. Next, you'll learn how to enter data and apply simple number and date formats. You will learn about charts and to use the Recommended Charts feature to add a chart quickly. This chapter introduces the concepts of formulas, functions, and absolute and relative references. Pay close attention to the skill *Understanding Absolute and Relative References.* These concepts are used throughout Excel. You will add totals to worksheet data using the SUM function with a variety of methods including AutoSum and the Quick Analysis tool. To help you start using Excel for your own purposes, you will learn how to create a new workbook from a template and how to manage multiple workbooks at the same time. Finally, the chapter covers how to check a worksheet for spelling errors and how to preview and print.

Skill **1.1** Introduction to Excel

Microsoft Excel is a spreadsheet program in which you enter, manipulate, calculate, and chart numerical and text data. An Excel file is referred to as a **workbook**, which is a collection of worksheets. Each worksheet (also called a "sheet") is made up of rows and columns of data on which you can perform calculations. It's these calculations that make Excel such a powerful tool. Some of the basic elements of a Microsoft Excel workbook include:

> - **Worksheet**—an electronic ledger in which you enter data. The worksheet appears as a grid where you can enter and then manipulate data using functions, formulas, and formatting. Excel workbooks have one worksheet by default named *Sheet1*. You can rename, add, and delete worksheets as necessary.
> - **Row**—a horizontal group of cells. Rows are identified by numbers. For example, the third row is labeled with the number *3*.
> - **Column**—a vertical group of cells. Columns are identified by letters. For example, the fourth column is labeled with the letter *D*.
> - **Cell**—the intersection of a column and a row. A **cell** is identified by the **cell address**—its column and row position. For example, the cell at the intersection of column D and row 3 has a cell address of *D3*.
> - **Cell range**—a contiguous group of cells. A cell range is identified by the address of the cell in the upper left corner of the range, followed by a colon, and then the address of the cell in the lower right corner of the range. The cell range *B3:B5* includes cells B3, B4, and B5. A cell range can incorporate multiple columns and rows as long as the cells are all contiguous. The range *B3:D5* includes cells B3, B4, B5, C3, C4, C5, D3, D4, and D5.
> - **Formula bar**—data entry area directly below the Ribbon and above the worksheet grid. Although you can type any data in the formula bar, the *Insert Function* button at the left side of the formula bar was designed to make it easier to create complex formulas.
> - **Name box**—appears at the left side of the formula bar and displays the address of the selected cell. If a group of cells is selected, the *Name* box displays the address of the first cell in the group.
> - **Status bar**—appears at the bottom of the worksheet grid and can display information about the selected data, including the number of cells selected that contain data (count) and the average and sum (total) of the selected values.

You can use Excel for a wide variety of purposes, from calculating payments for a personal loan, to creating a budget, to tracking cash flow for your business. Excel is not limited to numerical calculations.

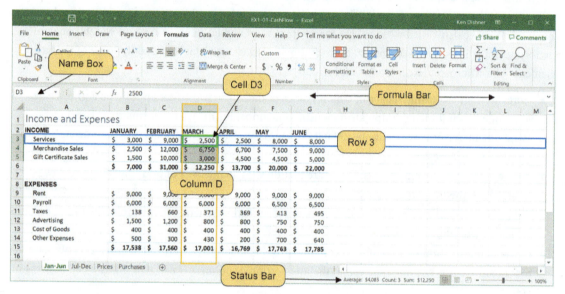

FIGURE EX 1.1

let me try Live!

Open the student data file **EX1-01-CashFlow** ⬇ and explore the Excel workbook on your own:

1. If necessary, click the **Jan-Jun** worksheet tab at the bottom of the workbook.
2. Click anywhere in **column D**.
3. Click anywhere in **row 3**.
4. Click cell **D3**.
5. Click the **formula bar**.
6. Click the **Name box**.
7. Click the **status bar**.
8. If you will be moving on to the next skill in this chapter, leave the workbook open to continue working. If not, save the file as directed by your instructor and close it.

Skill 1.2 Navigating a Workbook

An Excel worksheet can include more than one million rows and more than sixteen thousand columns. That's a lot of potential data to navigate! Luckily, most spreadsheets are not quite that large. However, you may encounter workbooks with multiple worksheets and hundreds of rows and columns of data.

The Excel window includes both a **vertical scroll bar** (at the right side of the window) and a **horizontal scroll bar** (at the bottom of the window). Click the arrows at the ends of the scroll bars to move up and down or left and right to see more cells in an individual worksheet. You can also click and drag the scroll box to reposition your view of the spreadsheet. Notice that when you use the scroll bars, the selected cell does not change. Using the scroll bars changes only your view of the worksheet.

The most obvious way to select a cell in a worksheet is to click it with the mouse. Notice that Excel highlights the appropriate column letter and row number to identify the selected cell. When you select a single cell, the cell address appears in the *Name* box in the upper left corner of the spreadsheet, and the cell content appears in the formula bar (immediately below the Ribbon).

To navigate to another worksheet in the workbook, click the appropriate tab at the bottom of the worksheet grid. If the worksheet tab is not visible, use the navigation arrows located at the left side of the first sheet tab to show one worksheet at a time to the left or the right. These arrows are active only when there are worksheets not visible in your current view.

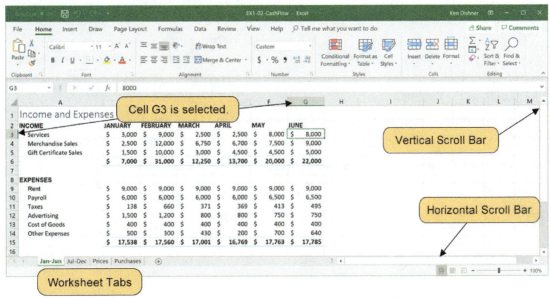

FIGURE EX 1.2

To navigate from cell to cell, use the mouse to click the cell you want to go to. You can also use keyboard shortcuts to navigate around or between worksheets.

↑	Move up one cell
↓	Move down one cell
→	Move one cell to the right
←	Move one cell to the left
Home	Move to the first cell in the row
Ctrl + Home	Go to cell A1
Ctrl + PgDn	Move one worksheet to the right
Ctrl + PgUp	Move one worksheet to the left

To select a range of cells, click the first cell in the range and drag the mouse until the cells you want are selected. Release the mouse button. You can also click the first cell in the range, press Shift, and then click the last cell in the range.

To select an entire row, point to the **row selector** (the box with the row number at the left side of the worksheet grid). When the mouse pointer changes to an arrow, click the left mouse button.

To select an entire column, point to the **column selector** (the box with the column letter at the top of the worksheet grid). When the mouse pointer changes to an arrow, click the left mouse button.

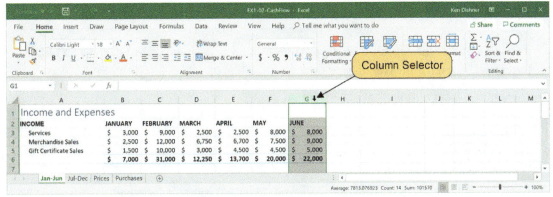

FIGURE EX 1.3

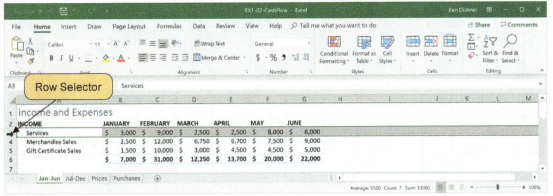

FIGURE EX 1.4

tips & tricks

To make more worksheets visible at one time, adjust the size of the horizontal scroll bar by clicking the dotted line that appears immediately to the left of the scroll bar. Notice that the cursor shape changes to a double-sided arrow. Click and drag to the right to make the horizontal scroll bar shorter and reveal more worksheet tabs.

tell me more

Another way to navigate to a specific cell location is to type the cell address in the *Name* box, and then press **Enter**.

Use the *Go To* dialog to navigate to a specific cell. On the *Home* tab, in the *Editing* group, click the **Find & Select** button and select **Go To** from the menu. In the *Reference* box, type the cell address and then click **OK**.

let me try Live!

> If you do not have the data file from the previous skill open, open the student data file **EX1-02-CashFlow** ⬇ and try this skill on your own:
>
> 1. On the *Jan-Jun* worksheet, select cell **G3**.
> 2. Select column **G**.
> 3. Select row **3**.
> 4. Navigate to the **Jul-Dec** worksheet.
> 5. Select cells **B3:G5**.
> 6. If you will be moving on to the next skill in this chapter, leave the workbook open to continue working. If not, save the file as directed by your instructor and close it.

from the perspective of . . .

SPORTS CLINIC OFFICE MANAGER

I couldn't do my job without Microsoft Excel. All the clinic financial data are kept in Excel spreadsheets, and I use Excel's analysis and formatting tools to visualize our cash flow. Any problem areas are easy to find. We sell rehab equipment directly to our patients, and I also use Excel to track the progress of our orders and sales.

Skill 1.3 Working in Protected View

When you download a workbook from a location that Excel considers potentially unsafe, it opens automatically in Protected View. **Protected View** provides a read-only format that protects your computer from becoming infected by a virus or other malware. Potentially unsafe locations include the Internet, e-mail messages, or a network location. Files that are opened in Protected View display a warning in the **Message Bar** at the top of the window, below the Ribbon.

To disable Protected View, click the **Enable Editing** button in the Message Bar.

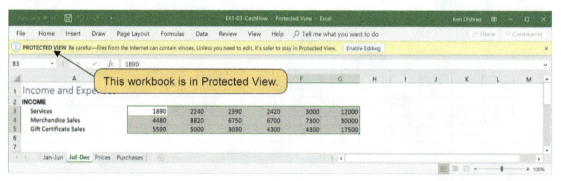

FIGURE EX 1.5

You can also enable editing from the Info page in Backstage view.

1. Click the **File** tab to open Backstage view.
2. If necessary, click **Info**.
3. The *Info* page provides more information about the file. If you are sure you want to remove it from Protected View, click the **Enable Editing** button.

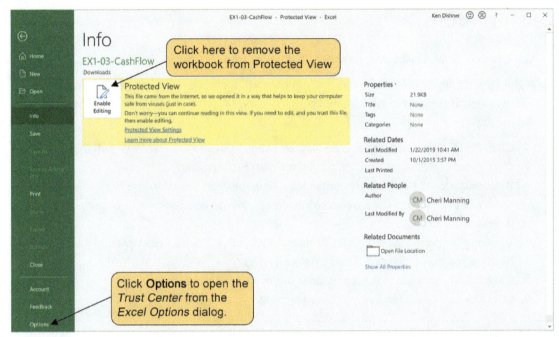

FIGURE EX 1.6

Once you enable editing for a file, it is added to the Trusted Documents list and will not appear in Protected View again unless you clear the *Trusted Documents* list.

To remove all files from the *Trusted Documents* list:

1. Click the **File** tab, and then click the **Options** button to open the *Excel Options* dialog.
2. Click **Trust Center**, and then click the **Trust Center Settings...** button to open the *Trust Center* dialog.
3. If necessary, click **Trusted Documents** at the left side of the *Trust Center* dialog.
4. Click the **Clear** button to clear all Trusted Documents so that they are no longer trusted.
5. Click **Yes**.
6. Click **OK** to close the *Trusted Locations* dialog.
7. Click **OK** again to close the *Excel Options* dialog.
8. The next time you open a file that was trusted previously, it will once again appear in Protected View.

tell me more

You can modify the Trust Center settings to control which files open in Protected View.

If you are currently in Protected View, the Info page will include a link to go to the Protected View settings. If you are not currently in Protected View, open the Trust Center from the *Excel Options* dialog.

1. Click the **File** tab, and then click the **Options** button to open the *Excel Options* dialog.
2. Click **Trust Center**, and then click the **Trust Center Settings...** button.
3. If necessary, click **Protected View** at the left side of the *Trust Center* dialog. Notice that all the options for Protected View are checked by default. We do not recommend changing any of these default settings.
4. To exempt a specific location from Protected View, click **Trusted Locations**, and add the location you trust (such as a secure network folder).
5. Click **OK** to save your changes and close the *Trusted Locations* dialog.
6. Click **OK** again to close the *Excel Options* dialog.

let me try Live!

If you do not have the data file from the previous skill open, open the student data file **EX1-03-CashFlow** 📥 and try this skill on your own:

1. This workbook came from a trusted source. If the workbook opens in Protected View, disable Protected View and allow editing.
2. Open the *Trust Center* dialog and review the settings.
3. Close the *Trust Center* and *Excel Options* dialogs without making any changes.
4. If you will be moving on to the next skill in this chapter, leave the workbook open to continue working. If not, save the file as directed by your instructor and close it.

Skill **1.4** Entering and Editing Text and Numbers in Cells

The most basic task in Excel is entering data in your workbook. Entering numerical data is as easy as typing a number in a cell. Numbers can be displayed as dates, currency values, percentages, or other formats. (Later skills discuss number formatting and using functions and formulas to automate numerical calculations.)

Excel is not just about numbers, though. Without text headers, descriptions, and instructions, your workbook would consist of numbers and formulas without any structure. Adding text headers to your rows and columns creates the structure for you to enter data into your workbook.

To enter data in a cell:

1. Click the cell where you want the data to appear.
2. Type the number or text.
3. Press [Enter] or [Tab].
   Pressing [Enter] after entering text will move the cursor down one cell.
   Pressing [Tab] will move the cursor to the right one cell.

Excel gives you different ways to edit the data in your worksheet. If you want to change the contents of the entire cell, use **Ready mode**. If you want to change only part of the cell data, use **Edit mode**. The status bar, located at the lower left corner of the Excel window, displays which mode you are in—Ready or Edit.

To use Ready mode to change text:

1. Click the cell you want to change.
2. Type the new contents for the cell.
3. Press [Enter] or [Tab] when you are finished.
4. The old contents are completely removed and replaced with what you've typed.

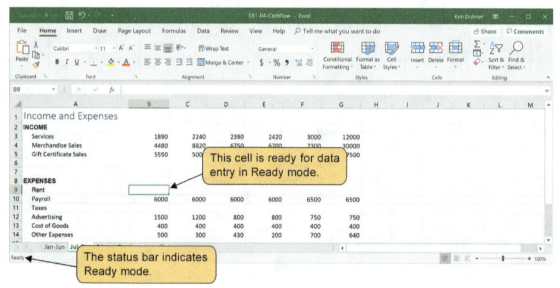

FIGURE EX 1.7

To use Edit mode to change text:

1. Double-click the cell you want to change.
2. You should now see a blinking cursor in the cell.
3. Use → and ← to move the cursor within the cell. Type the changes you want. Use Backspace to delete characters to the left of the cursor. Use Delete to delete characters to the right of the cursor. You can also click and drag your mouse to select a section of text to delete.
4. Press Enter or Tab when you are finished making your changes.

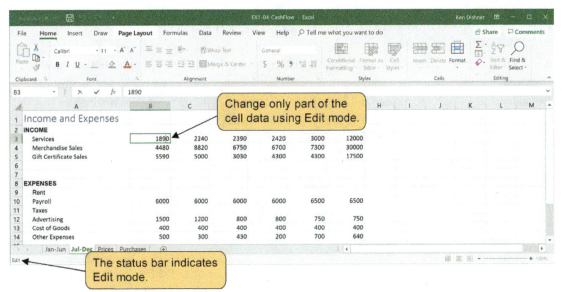

FIGURE EX 1.8

tips & tricks

To add a line break within the cell, press [Alt] while pressing [Enter].

another method

As you type in a cell, the entry is displayed in the formula bar as well as in the active cell. Clicking the **Enter Formula** button ✓ next to the formula bar accepts your entry. Clicking the **Cancel** button ✗ next to the formula bar removes your entry.

let me try Live!

If you do not have the data file from the previous skill open, open the student data file **EX1-04-CashFlow** and try this skill on your own:

1. On the *Jul-Dec* worksheet, add the number **9500** to cell **B9**.
2. Add the word **JULY** to cell **B2**.
3. Change the value in cell **B3** to **1870**. You can use Ready mode or Edit mode.
4. If you will be moving on to the next skill in this chapter, leave the workbook open to continue working. If not, save the file as directed by your instructor and close it.

Skill 1.5 Applying Number Formats

When you first type numbers in a worksheet, Excel applies the **General number format** automatically. The General format right-aligns numbers in the cells but does not maintain a consistent number of decimal places (43.00 will appear as 43, while 42.25 appears as 42.25) and does not display commas (so 1,123,456 appears as 1123456). For consistency, and to make your worksheet easier to read, you should apply the specific number format that is most appropriate for your data. Excel provides several number formats for you to choose from.

Figure EX 1.9 shows common Excel number formats. All numbers in row 2 contain the number 0.567. All numbers in row 3 contain the number 1234. Formatting numbers changes the appearance of the data in your worksheet but doesn't change the numerical values. The formatted number is displayed in the cell, and the actual value is displayed in the formula bar.

> Formula bar displays the full number 0.567 while cell B2 formatted using the Number Style format displays 0.57

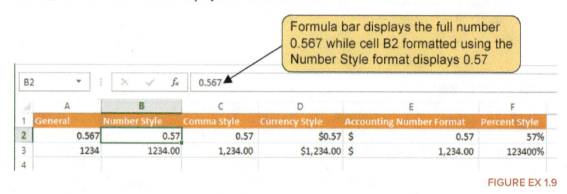

FIGURE EX 1.9

To apply the most common number formats, go to the *Home* tab, *Number* group, and click one of the following buttons:

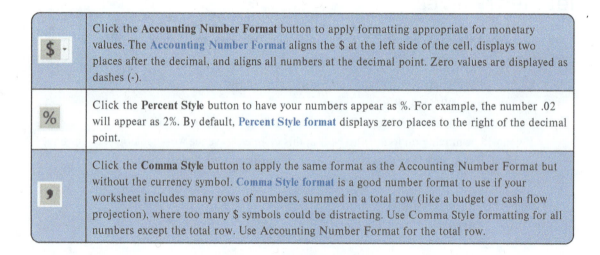

$ ▾	Click the **Accounting Number Format** button to apply formatting appropriate for monetary values. The Accounting Number Format aligns the $ at the left side of the cell, displays two places after the decimal, and aligns all numbers at the decimal point. Zero values are displayed as dashes (-).
%	Click the **Percent Style** button to have your numbers appear as %. For example, the number .02 will appear as 2%. By default, **Percent Style format** displays zero places to the right of the decimal point.
,	Click the **Comma Style** button to apply the same format as the Accounting Number Format but without the currency symbol. Comma Style format is a good number format to use if your worksheet includes many rows of numbers, summed in a total row (like a budget or cash flow projection), where too many $ symbols could be distracting. Use Comma Style formatting for all numbers except the total row. Use Accounting Number Format for the total row.

Use *Increase Decimal* and *Decrease Decimal* to increase or decrease the number of digits that appear to the right of the decimal point. For example, if a cell contains the number 1.234 and you click the **Decrease Decimal** button twice, the cell will display 1.2. The formula bar will still display 1.234 because that is the number stored in the worksheet.

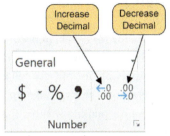

FIGURE EX 1.10

For other common number formats, click the **Number Format** arrow above the buttons in the *Number* group to display the *Number Format* menu.

Number—The default **Number format** shows two decimal places by default so 1,234 displays as 1234.00 but does not include commas.

Currency—With the **Currency format**, columns of numbers do not align at the $ and at the decimal as they do with Accounting Number Format. Instead, the Currency format places the $ immediately to the left of the number.

Percentage—The *Percentage* option on the *Number Format* menu does not apply the same Percent Style format as clicking the *Percent Style* button. The *Percentage* option from the *Number Format* menu displays two digits to the right of the decimal.

More Number Formats...—This option opens the *Format Cells* dialog to the Number tab, where you can select from even more number formats and customize any format, including adding color, specifying the number of decimal places to display, and setting whether or not negative numbers should be enclosed in parentheses.

tips & tricks

If you type $ before a number, Excel automatically applies the Currency number format.

tell me more

On the *Home* tab, in the *Styles* group, click the **Cell Styles** button to expand the *Styles* gallery. At the bottom of the gallery are five number styles. Applying one of these cell styles is the same as applying a number format. However, be aware that applying the Currency cell style actually applies the Accounting Number Format, not the Currency format.

> **Comma**—applies the default Comma Style format, with two digits to the right of the decimal.
> **Comma [0]**—applies the Comma Style format, but with no digits to the right of the decimal.
> **Currency**—applies the default Accounting Number Format, with two digits to the right of the decimal.
> **Currency [0]**—applies the Accounting Number Format, but with no digits to the right of the decimal.
> **Percent**—applies the default Percent Style format.

FIGURE EX 1.11 NUMBER FORMAT MENU

another method

When you right-click a cell, these formats are available from the Mini toolbar: Accounting Number Format, Percent style, and Comma style.

The *Increase Decimal* and *Decrease Decimal* buttons are also available from the Mini toolbar.

To apply the Percent Style, you can use the keyboard shortcut [Ctrl] + [Shift Key] + [5].

let me try Live!

If you do not have the data file from the previous skill open, open the student data file **EX1-05-CashFlow** ⬇ and try this skill on your own:

1. On the *Jul-Dec* worksheet, select cells **B3:G5**.
2. Apply the **Accounting Number Format**.
3. Modify the number format so no decimal places are visible after the decimal point.
4. Go to the **Prices** worksheet and select cells **C2:C10**.
5. Apply the **Currency** number format.
6. If you will be moving on to the next skill in this chapter, leave the workbook open to continue working. If not, save the file as directed by your instructor and close it.

Skill 1.6 Entering Dates and Applying Date Formats

When you enter numbers in a date format such as 6/30/2019 or June 30, 2019, Excel detects that you are entering a date and automatically applies one of the date formats. Excel treats dates as a special type of number, so cells formatted as dates can be used in calculations. There are many types of date formats available, but the underlying number for the date will always be the same.

There are two number formats available from the *Number Format* menu. To apply one of these formats, from the *Home* tab, click the **Number Format** arrow above the buttons in the *Number* group, and then click the format you want:

> **Short Date format**—Applies a simple format displaying the one- or two-digit number representing the month, followed by the one- or two-digit number representing the day, followed by the four-digit year: 6/30/2019.

> **Long Date format**—Applies a longer format displaying the day of the week, and then the name of the month, the two-digit date, and the four-digit year: Sunday, June 30, 2019.

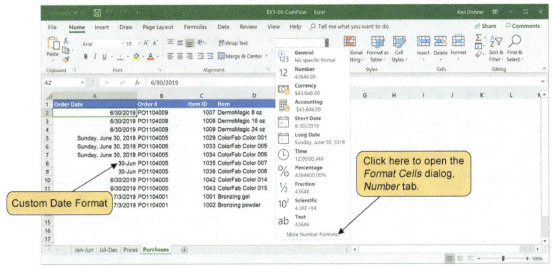

FIGURE EX 1.12

If you would like to use a different date format:

1. Select **More Number Formats...** from the *Number Format*
2. In the *Format Cells* dialog, from the *Number* tab, if necessary, click **Date** in the *Category* Excel offers a variety of prebuilt date formats to choose from.
3. Notice that as you click each format in the *Type* list, the *Sample* box shows how the active cell will display with the selected format.
4. Click the date format you would like and click **OK**.

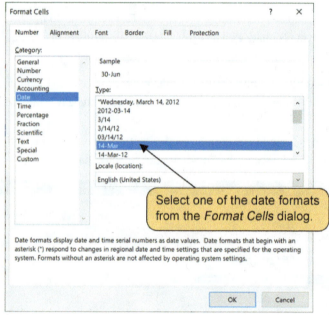

FIGURE EX 1.13

tips & tricks

Only dates from January 1, 1900, through December 31, 9999, are stored as numbers. Dates prior to January 1, 1900 are stored as text and cannot be used in calculations. To see the serial number for a date, change the cell format from Date to *General* or *Number*. The date will be converted to a "regular" number. For example, December 31, 2009, is the number 40178.

tell me more

Every date format can be expressed as a code. The code for the Short Date format is **m/d/yyyy**. The code for the Long Date format is more complicated:

[$ -x-sysdate]dddd, mmmm dd, yyyy. If Excel does not offer the exact date format you want to use, you can modify the date code using the Custom number option.

1. Select **More Number Formats...** from the *Number*
2. In the *Format Cells* dialog, from the *Number* tab, click **Custom** in the *Category*
3. The *Custom* list includes the code for every number format offered. Click the code for the format closest to the format you want, and then make adjustments to the code in the *Type* The *Sample* box shows how the number format will look in your worksheet.
4. Click **OK** to apply your new custom number format.

let me try Live!

If you do not have the data file from the previous skill open, open the student data file **EX1-06-CashFlow** 🔖 and try this skill on your own:

1. On the *Purchases* worksheet, review the date formats used in column A.
2. Select column A, and apply the **Long Date** format.
3. With column A still selected, apply the **Short Date** format.
4. With column A still selected, apply the format to display dates in the format similar to **14-Mar**.

If you will be moving on to the next skill in this chapter, leave the workbook open to continue working. If not, save the file as directed by your instructor and close it.

Skill 1.7 Inserting Data Using AutoFill

Use the **AutoFill** feature to fill a group of cells with the same data or to extend a data series.

With AutoFill, you can copy the same value or formula to a group of cells at once. This is much more efficient than using copy and paste over and over again.

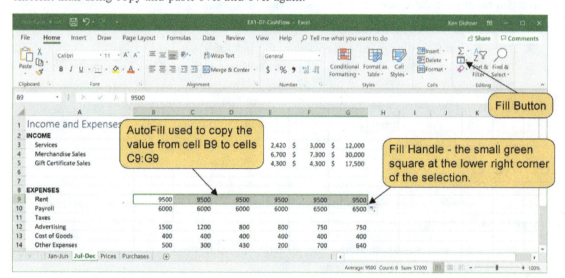

FIGURE EX 1.14

The easiest way to use AutoFill is to use the **Fill Handle** to fill data up or down in a column or to the left or right in a row.

To use the Fill Handle:

1. Select the cell(s) that contain(s) the data you want to use in the AutoFill.
2. Click and drag the **Fill Handle** in the direction you want to fill the data. The Fill Handle is the very small green square at the lower right corner of the cell(s) you selected. As you drag the Fill Handle, a tool tip appears displaying the suggested value for each highlighted cell.
3. Release the mouse button when you have highlighted the last cell you want to fill.

If you have a difficult time using the Fill Handle, use the *Fill* command from the Ribbon instead:

1. Select the entire range you want to fill, beginning with the cell(s) containing the data.
2. On the *Home* tab, in the *Editing* group, click the **Fill** button and select the type of fill you want. The options available will vary depending on the data you selected to use as the source for the fill.

If you have a group of cells with similar data in a series, AutoFill can extend the series automatically. A **data series** is any sequence of cells with a recognizable pattern like those shown in Figure EX 1.15.

	A	B	C	D
1	Numeric Patterns			
2	1	2	3	4
3	3	5	7	9
4	Student 1	Student 2	Student 3	Student 4
5				
6	Date Patterns			
7	January	February	March	April
8	1/1/2020	2/1/2020	3/1/2020	4/1/2020
9	1/1/2020	1/1/2021	1/1/2022	1/1/2023
10				

FIGURE EX 1.15

Excel attempts to detect automatically if the data appear to be a series. Sometimes, however, the series doesn't fill with the data you expect or want. To change the type of data AutoFill inserts, click the **AutoFill Options** button and select a different option. From the *AutoFill Options* button, you can choose to copy the cells or fill the series. By default, Excel includes formatting when copying or filling a series; however, you can choose to copy only the cell formatting or to fill or copy the data series without formatting.

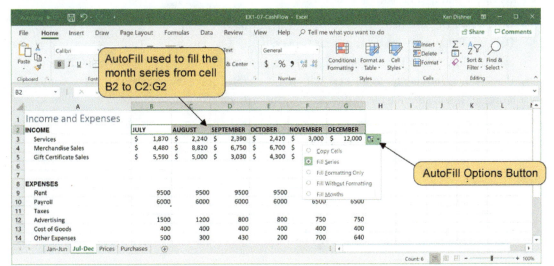

FIGURE EX 1.16

tips & tricks

Use AutoFill to enter repetitive data in your worksheet to avoid errors from entering data manually.

tell me more

The Fill Handle tool can be used to fill a series of dates by month as well as year. For example, if you start the series with Jan-2019 and Feb-2019, the Fill Handle will fill in the next cells with Mar-2019, Apr-2019, May-2019 and so on. When the series reaches Dec-2019, the next cell will be filled in with Jan-2020. If you are filling a series of dates, the *AutoFill Options* button will give you the options to fill by day, weekday, month, or year.

another method

1. Pressing [Ctrl] + [D] will fill the selected cell(s) with the value from the cell above it.
2. Pressing [Ctrl] + [R] will fill the selected cell(s) with the value from the cell to the left of it.

let me try Live!

If you do not have the data file from the previous skill open, open the student data file **EX1-07-CashFlow** ⤓ and try this skill on your own:

1. On the *Jul-Dec* worksheet, select cell **B9** (the rent value for July).
2. Use AutoFill to copy the value of cells **C9:G9**.
3. Select cell **B2** (JULY) and use AutoFill to complete the month series through cell **G2**.
4. If you will be moving on to the next skill in this chapter, leave the workbook open to continue working. If not, save the file as directed by your instructor and close it.

Skill 1.8 Exploring Charts

A **chart** is a graphic that represents numeric data visually. In a chart, the values selected in the worksheet, the **data points**, are transformed into graphic **data markers**. Data markers can be columns, bars, pie pieces, lines, or other visual elements. Related data points, usually in the same row or column, are grouped into a **data series**. Some chart types allow you to plot multiple data series.

Figure EX 1.17 shows a column chart with a single data series—*Services - Individual.* You can tell at a glance that the FEB column is the shortest and, therefore, that February has the fewest sales for individual services.

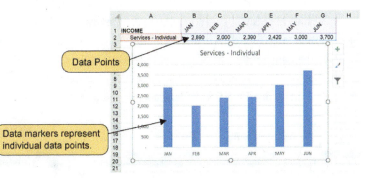

FIGURE EX 1.17

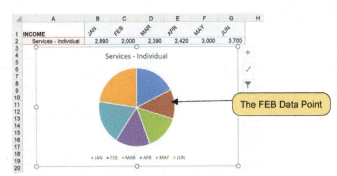

FIGURE EX 1.18

Figure EX 1.18 is a pie chart using the same data as Figure EX 1.17. Each individual data point is represented by a piece of the pie. In this chart, it is not as obvious that FEB is the smallest data point.

Most charts plot data along two axes. The **y axis** goes from bottom to top. It is the vertical axis. The **x axis** goes from left to right. It is the horizontal axis. Typically, but not always, values are plotted against the y axis and categories are listed along the x axis. In Figure EX 1.19, the y axis shows a range of values from 0 to 4,000. The x axis lists the months. For each category (month), the top of the column reaches the appropriate value on the y axis.

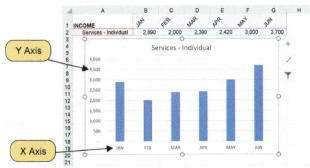

FIGURE EX 1.19

When working with charts, there are a few other common chart elements you should be familiar with:

> The **plot area** is the area where the data series are plotted.
> The **chart area** is the area that encompasses the entire chart including the plot area and optional layout elements, such as title and legend.
> The **chart title** is a text box above or overlaying the chart.
> The **legend** tells you which data point or data series is represented by each color in the chart.

When a chart is selected, two contextual tabs are available: the *Chart Tools Design* tab and the *Chart Tools Format* tab. On the *Chart Tools Format* tab, in the *Current Selection* group, the *Chart Elements* box displays the name of the chart element that is currently selected. This can be helpful if you need to ensure that you have selected the chart area, the plot area, or another chart element. To select a specific chart element, expand the **Chart Elements** list and select the chart element you want to select.

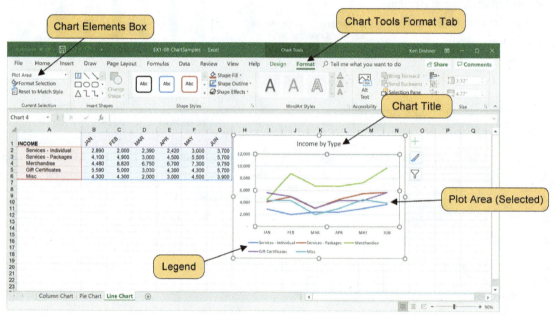

FIGURE EX 1.20

tips & tricks

Because charts make it easier to see trends and relationships, they are an important tool for analyzing data. However, the chart type and formatting can influence how others perceive the data. Be careful that the chart does not present the data in a way that may be misleading.

tell me **more**

If the chart is located on the same worksheet as its data, Excel will highlight that data when you select certain chart elements. For example, select the chart area or the plot area, and Excel highlights the cells containing the data point values in blue, the data series labels in red, and the category labels in purple. If you select a single data series, only those data will be highlighted.

let me **try** Live!

Open the student data file **EX1-08-ChartSamples** ⬇ and try this skill on your own:

1. Begin with the **Column Chart** sheet. Click any of the data markers to select the entire data series. Use the *Chart Elements* box to verify that you have selected the data series. Observe how the worksheet data are represented by the column data markers.
2. Go to the **Pie Chart** sheet. Select the chart legend. Use the legend to match the pie pieces to the data point values.
3. Go to the **Line Chart** sheet. Select the line representing the *Merchandise* data series. Observe that when the *Merchandise* series is selected, cells B4:G4 (the data points) are highlighted in blue.
4. Select the x axis.
5. Select the y axis. Use the *Chart Elements* list if necessary.
6. Close the file without saving any changes you may have made accidentally.

Skill 1.9 Using the Recommended Charts Feature

One trick to working with charts is to select the correct chart type. Excel makes this easier by recommending specific chart types based on the data you have selected in the worksheet. The recommended charts are available from both the Quick Analysis tool and the *Chart Options* dialog.

To add a recommended chart to a worksheet using the Quick Analysis tool:

1. Select the data you want to visualize as a chart.
2. The *Quick Analysis Tool* button appears near the lower right corner of the selected range. Click the **Quick Analysis Tool** button, and then click the **Charts** tab in the Quick Analysis Tool.
3. Hover the mouse cursor over each chart type to see a live preview of the chart. Click the button for the chart type you want. Recommended charts may include multiple versions of the same chart type. Check the live preview carefully to ensure that the data display exactly as you want.

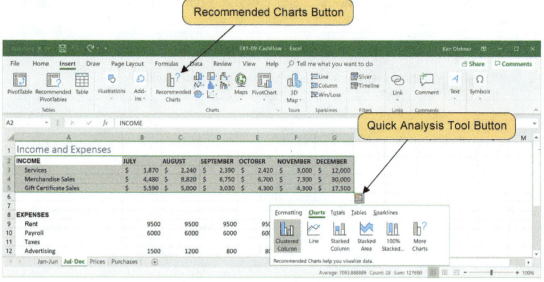

FIGURE EX 1.21

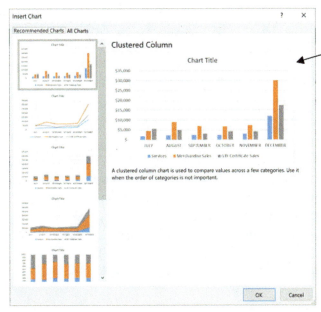

FIGURE EX 1.22

This pane shows a preview of the selected chart type.

If none of the recommended charts presented in the Quick Analysis tool are precisely what you want, use the *Recommended Charts* button to open the *Insert Chart* dialog:

1. Select the data for the chart.
2. On the *Insert* tab, in the *Charts* group, click the **Recommended Charts** button.
3. The first tab in the *Insert Chart* dialog, *Recommended Charts,* displays the same chart options as the *Charts* tab in the Quick Analysis tool, plus a few more. When you select a chart type, a preview of the chart appears in the right pane of the dialog.
4. Click **OK** to insert the selected chart into the worksheet.

When you insert a new chart, there is a title placeholder that displays *Chart Title.* To change the title text, click the *Chart Title* box once to select it and type the new title. The default text is overwritten once you begin typing. You can also type new text in the formula bar and then press Enter.

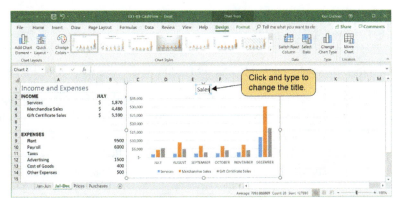

Click and type to change the title.

FIGURE EX 1.23

To edit the chart title, click the *Chart Title* box once to select it and then click it again to enter Edit mode. Edit the text directly in the *Chart Title* box.

To delete a chart, click the chart once to select it, and then press Backspace or Delete.

tips & tricks

The Quick Analysis tool is available only if the data selected for the chart are in contiguous cells —a group of cells that are all next to one another without any cells left out of the group. To create a chart from a noncontiguous group of cells, you must use the *Insert Chart* dialog or one of the insert chart buttons from the *Insert* tab, *Charts* group.

tell me **more**

To create a chart that is not listed as a recommended chart, you can use one of the insert chart buttons from the *Insert* tab, *Charts* group or the *All Charts* tab in the *Insert Chart* dialog. To learn about creating these charts, refer to the skills *Inserting a Column Chart or Bar Chart*, *Inserting a Pie Chart*, and *Inserting a Line Chart*. There are also advanced skills on creating other charts such as hierarchy charts, statistical charts, and waterfall charts.

another method

You can open the *Insert Chart* dialog from the *Quick Analysis Tool* button:

1. Select the data for the chart.
2. Click the **Quick Analysis Tool** button.
3. Click the **Charts** tab, and then click the **More Charts** button to open the *Insert Chart* dialog.

let me **try** Live!

Open the student data file **EX1-09-CashFlow** and try this skill on your own:

1. If necessary, go to the **Jul-Dec** worksheet, and select cells **A2:G5.**
2. Insert a **Clustered Column** chart based on the first recommended chart type.
3. Change the title to: **Sales**
4. If you will be moving on to the next skill in this chapter, leave the workbook open to continue working. If not, save the file as directed by your instructor and close it.

Skill 1.10 Entering Simple Formulas

A **formula** is an equation used to calculate a value. A formula can perform a mathematical calculation, such as displaying the sum of **35 + 47**, or a formula can calculate a value using cell references, such as displaying a value equal to the value of another cell (**=B15**) or calculating an equation based on values in multiple cells (**=B17+B18-B19**).

In Figure EX 1.24, cell B19 contains the formula **=B15**. This formula directs Excel to make the value of cell B19 equal to the value of cell B15. If the value in cell B15 changes, the value displayed in cell B19 will update accordingly.

Notice that when the cell is selected, the result of the formula is displayed in the cell, while the formula is displayed in the formula bar.

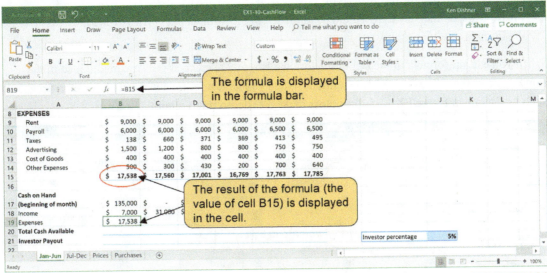

FIGURE EX 1.24

To enter a formula:

1. Click the cell in which you want to enter the formula.
2. Press [=] and begin typing the formula. The [=] tells Excel that you are entering a formula, not standard text or numeric data.
3. Use the following symbols for mathematical operations:

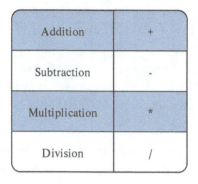

Addition	+
Subtraction	-
Multiplication	*
Division	/

4. To add a cell reference to a formula, you can type the cell address or click the cell. If you are in the middle of typing a formula and you click another cell in the worksheet, Excel knows to add that cell reference to the formula instead of moving to it.

5. Press Enter or click the **Enter** button ✓ to the left of the formula bar when you are finished entering the formula.

When you edit the formula in the cell or the formula bar, any referenced cells are highlighted in the same color as the cell reference in the formula. When you have a formula with multiple cell references, such as the one in Figure EX 1.25, the colors make it easier to troubleshoot any errors.

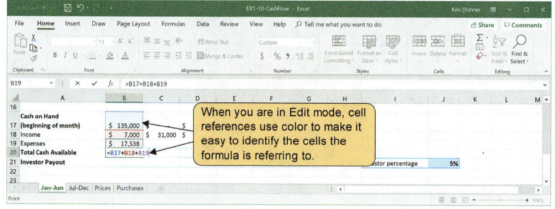

FIGURE EX 1.25

tell me more

When you enter a formula with more than one mathematical operation, the formula is not necessarily calculated from left to right. Excel calculations follow the mathematical rules called the **order of operations** (also called **precedence**).

The rules state that mathematical operations in a formula are calculated in this order:

1. Exponents and roots
2. Multiplication and division
3. Addition and subtraction

Adding parentheses around part of a formula will override the order of operations, forcing Excel to perform the calculation within the parentheses first.

$4 + (5 * 2) = 14$—Excel calculates $5 * 2$ first (10), and then adds 4.

$(4 + 5) * 2 = 18$—Excel calculates $4 + 5$ first (9), and then multiples by 2.

$4 + 5 \wedge 2 = 29$—Excel calculates 5 to the 2nd power first (25), and then adds 4.

$(4 + 5) \wedge 2 = 81$—Excel calculates $4 + 5$ first (9), and then raises that number to the 2nd power.

If you have trouble remembering the order of operations, use the phrase "Please Excuse My Dear Aunt Sally." PEMDAS = Parentheses, Exponents, Multiplication, Division, Addition, Subtraction

let me try Live!

If you do not have the data file from the previous skill open, open the student data file **EX1-10-CashFlow** 📥 and try this skill on your own:

1. On the *Jan-Jun* worksheet, enter a formula in cell **B19** to display the value of cell **B15** (the total expenses for January).
2. In cell B20, enter a formula to calculate the cash balance for the month: the cash available at the beginning of the month (cell **B17**) + income for the month (cell **B18**) - expenses for the month (cell **B19**).
3. On the *Jul-Dec* worksheet, enter a formula in cell **B11** to calculate taxes by multiplying the value of merchandise sales (cell **B4**) by **5%**.
4. If you will be moving on to the next skill in this chapter, leave the workbook open to continue working. If not, save the file as directed by your instructor and close it.

Skill **1.11** Understanding Absolute and Relative References

A cell's address, its position in the workbook, is referred to as a **cell reference** when it is used in a formula. In Excel, the $ character before a letter or number in the cell address means that part of the cell's address is *absolute* (nonchanging). Cell references can be relative, absolute, or mixed.

> A **relative reference** is a cell reference that adjusts to the new location in the worksheet when the formula is copied.
> An **absolute reference** is a cell reference whose location remains constant when the formula is copied.
> A **mixed reference** is a combination cell reference with a row position that stays constant with a changing column position (or vice versa).

Relative reference—A1

Absolute reference—$A$1

Mixed reference with absolute row—A$1

Mixed reference with absolute column—$A1

Here's how relative and absolute references work:

When you type a formula into a cell, it uses *relative* references by default. Excel notes the position of the referenced cell *relative* to the active cell. For example, if cell B19 is the active cell and you type the formula **=B15**, Excel displays the value of the cell that is up four rows from the active cell.

> If you change the structure of the worksheet by adding or removing rows or columns, Excel will automatically update all relative cell references. In this example, Excel will update the formula to reflect the new address of the cell that is up four rows from the cell containing the formula.
> If you copy the formula **=B15** from cell B19 and paste it into cell C19, the pasted formula will update automatically to **=C15** to reflect the cell address that is up four rows from the pasted formula.

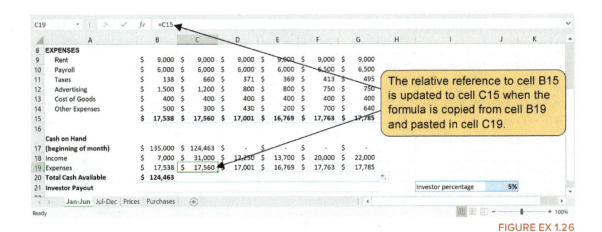

FIGURE EX 1.26

But what if you don't want the cell reference to adjust? For example, in Figure EX 1.27 cell J21 contains a value that you want to use in calculations for multiple cells in a row. If you were to copy the formula **=B20*J21** from cell B21 to cell C21, the formula would update to **=C20*K21** (not what you intended) because both of the cell references are relative. Instead, you want the reference to cell J21 to be *absolute*, so it does not update when you copy it. If you use the formula **=B20*$J$21** instead and copy it from cell B21 to cell C21, the pasted formula will update only the relative reference **B20**. The absolute reference **$J$21** will remain constant. The formula in cell C21 will be **=C20*$J$21**.

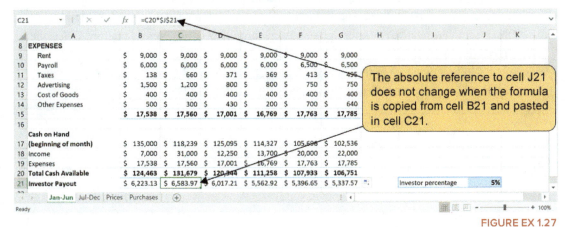

FIGURE EX 1.27

tips & tricks

If you cut and paste a formula, Excel assumes that you want the formula to maintain its previous value and treats the formula as if it had included absolute references, pasting the formula exactly as it was in the original cell.

another method

Another way to change the cell reference type is to select the cell reference in the formula bar, and then press $\boxed{\text{F4}}$ to cycle through the various reference types until you find the one you want (absolute, mixed with absolute row, mixed with absolute column, and then back to relative).

let me try Live!

If you do not have the data file from the previous skill open, open the student data file **EX1-11-CashFlow** ⬇ and try this skill on your own:

1. On the *Jan-Jun* worksheet, use AutoFill to copy the formula from cell **B19** to cells **C19:G19**. Click cell **G19** to observe the updated cell reference. Now copy the formula in cell **B20** to cells **C20:G20**. Note how the relative reference in the formulas update.

2. In cell **B21**, enter a formula to calculate the investor payout for the month: the cash balance (cell **B20**) multiplied by the investor percentage (cell **J21**). Be sure to use an absolute reference for cell J21.

3. Use AutoFill to copy the formula in cell **B21** to cells **C21:G21**. Click cell **G21** to observe the copied formula with the absolute reference to cell *J21*. If you entered the formula in B21 correctly, the cell reference to J21 will remain constant.

4. On the *Jul-Dec* worksheet, use AutoFill to copy the formula in cell **B11** to cells **C11:G11**. Observe that the relative reference updates as the formula is copied across the row. Delete the chart if it is in the way.

5. If you will be moving on to the next skill in this chapter, leave the workbook open to continue working. If not, save the file as directed by your instructor and close it.

Skill 1.12 Using Functions in Formulas

Functions are preprogrammed shortcuts for calculating equations. Functions can simplify a straightforward computation such as figuring the total of a list of values. They can also calculate the answer to a complicated equation such as figuring the monthly payment amount for a loan.

Most functions require you to provide input called the **arguments**. For example, when writing a formula using the SUM function to calculate the total of a list of values, each value or range of values to be included in the calculation is an argument. Multiple arguments are separated by commas $[,]$.

This formula will calculate the total of the values in cells B9 through B14:

SUM(B9, B10, B11, B12, B13, B14)

In this example, each cell reference is an argument.

An easier way to write the arguments for this formula is:

SUM(B9:B14)

In the second example, the function requires only one argument—the cell range containing the values. Both formulas will return the same total value.

The easiest way to enter a formula using a simple function like SUM is to type the formula directly in the cell or the formula bar. Begin the formula by typing $[=]$, and then type the function name. After the function name, type $[(]$ followed by the function arguments, separated by commas, and then $[)]$. Press $[Enter]$ to complete the formula.

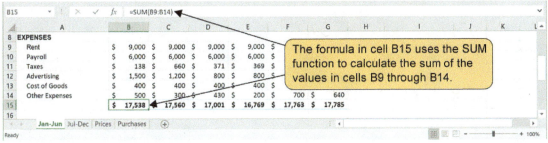

tell me **more**

You can also enter functions in formulas using AutoSum, Formula AutoComplete, and the *Function Arguments* dialog. These methods are covered in later skills.

let me try Live!

If you do not have the data file from the previous skill open, open the student data file **EX1-12-CashFlow** and try this skill on your own:

1. On the *Jan-Jun* worksheet, review the formulas in rows **6** and **15**.
2. On the *Jul-Dec* worksheet, in cell **B6**, enter the formula using the SUM function to calculate the total of cells **B3** through **B5**.
3. If you will be moving on to the next skill in this chapter, leave the workbook open to continue working. If not, save the file as directed by your instructor and close it.

Skill 1.13 Using AutoSum to Insert a SUM Function

If your spreadsheet includes numerical data organized in rows or columns, **AutoSum** can enter totals for you. When you use AutoSum, Excel enters the SUM function arguments using the most likely range of cells based on the structure of your worksheet. For example, if you use AutoSum at the bottom of a column of values, Excel will assume that you want to use the values in the column as the function arguments. If you use AutoSum at the end of a row of values, Excel will use the values in the row. To insert a SUM function using AutoSum:

1. Select the cell in which you want to enter the function.
2. On the *Home* tab, in the *Editing* group, click the **AutoSum** button.
3. Excel automatically inserts a formula with the SUM function, using the range of cells contiguous to (next to) the selected cell as the arguments for the function. You can increase or decrease the range of cells selected by clicking and dragging the corner of the highlighted cell range.
4. Press ⌴Enter⌴ to accept the formula.

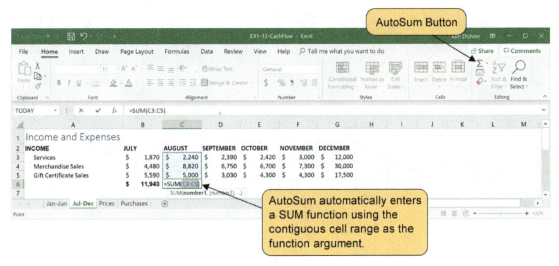

FIGURE EX 1.29

another method

> ❯ AutoSum is also available on the *Formulas* tab, in the *Function Library* group.
> ❯ You can also click the **AutoSum** button arrow and select **SUM** from the list.
> ❯ Another way to use the AutoSum function is to select a range of cells, and then click the **AutoSum** Excel will insert the SUM function in the next available (empty) cell.

let me try Live!

If you do not have the data file from the previous skill open, open the student data file **EX1-13-CashFlow** ⤓ and try this skill on your own:

1. On the *Jul-Dec* worksheet, select cell **C6**.
2. Use AutoSum to enter a formula to calculate the total of cells **C3:C5**.
3. If you will be moving on to the next skill in this chapter, leave the workbook open to continue working. If not, save the file as directed by your instructor and close it.

Skill 1.14 Calculating Totals with the Quick Analysis Tool

When you have a range of cells selected, you can use the **Quick Analysis tool** to calculate totals down entire columns or across entire rows at once. The Quick Analysis tool includes five types of calculations:

> **Sum**—calculates the total of the values in each row or column.

> **Average**—calculates the average of the values in each row or column.

> **Count**—counts the number of cells that contain values in each row or column.

> **% Total**—calculates the percentage of the overall total for the total of each row or column: the sum of values in the row or column divided by the sum of the values in the entire selection.

> **Running Total**—calculates a total for each row or column that includes the values in the row or column plus the values in all the previous rows or columns. Notice that the formula for the running total uses an absolute reference for the first cell in the range and a relative reference for the last cell in the range.

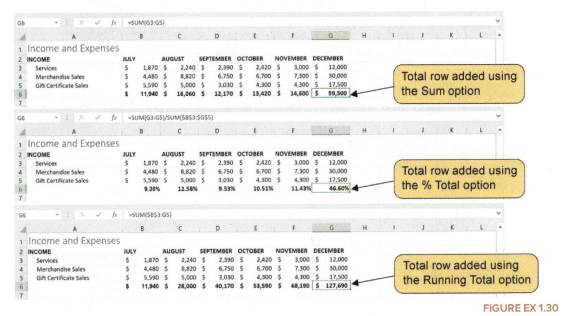

FIGURE EX 1.30

To use the Quick Analysis tool to calculate totals:

1. Select the range of cells. Totals can be inserted below or to the right of the selected cells.

2. The Quick Analysis tool button appears near the lower right corner of the selected range. Click the **Quick Analysis tool** button, and then click the **Totals** tab.

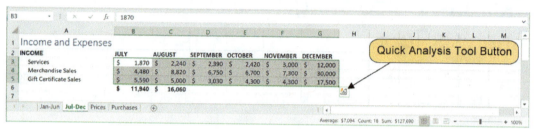

3. Notice that Excel displays a preview of the formulas as you hover the mouse pointer over each option. As shown in Figure EX 1.32, the images in the Quick Analysis tool show where the formulas will be inserted. The first set of buttons shows a blue highlight along the bottom, indicating that the formulas will be inserted below the selected range. The second set of buttons shows a yellow highlight along the right side, indicating that the formulas will be inserted to the right of the selected range.

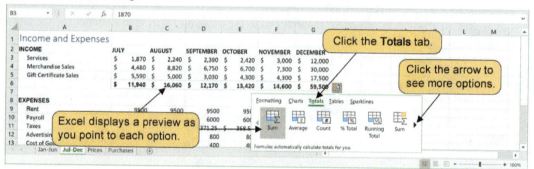

FIGURE EX 1.32

4. Click the button that represents the type of calculation you want to insert.
5. If there are data in any of the cells where the total formulas will be inserted, Excel asks if you want to replace them. Click **OK**.

tips & tricks

If the Quick Analysis tool button is not visible, move your mouse cursor over the selected cell range, without clicking. This action should make the button appear.

let me try Live!

If you do not have the data file from the previous skill open, open the student data file **EX1-14-CashFlow** ⬇ and try this skill on your own:

1. On the *Jul-Dec* worksheet, select the cell range **B3:G5**.
2. Click the **Quick Analysis tool** button, and then click the **Totals** tab.
3. Click the first **Sum** button to insert totals in the row beneath the selected cell range.
4. If Excel asks if you want to replace the existing data, click **OK**.
5. If you will be moving on to the next skill in this chapter, leave the workbook open to continue working. If not, save the file as directed by your instructor and close it.

Skill 1.15 Using the Status Bar

The **status bar** appears at the bottom of the Excel window and displays information about the current worksheet. By default, the status bar displays whether you are in Ready or Edit mode and information about the selected cells (such as the number of cells selected, the sum of the values in the selected cells, or the average of the values in the selected cells). You can customize the status bar to show other information about the worksheet, the minimum or maximum value in the selected cells, and whether Caps Lock is on or off.

To change the information shown on the status bar:

1. Right-click anywhere on the status bar.
2. The *Customize Status Bar* menu appears. Options with checkmarks next to them are currently active. Options without a checkmark are not currently active.
3. Click an item on the menu to add it to or remove it from the status bar display.

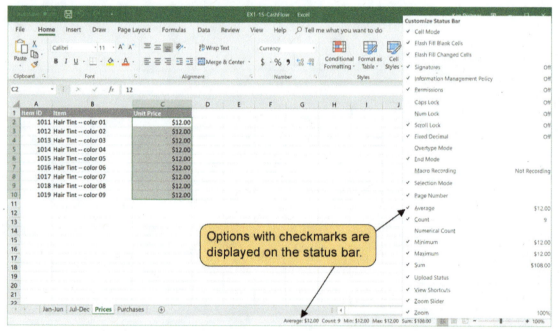

FIGURE EX 1.33

let me try Live!

If you do not have the data file from the previous skill open, open the student data file **EX1-15-CashFlow** and try this skill on your own:

1. On the *Prices* worksheet, select cells **C2:C10** and observe the calculations displayed on the status bar. You should see the average, count, and sum of the selected cells.
2. Add the minimum and maximum values to the status bar.
3. Observe the changes, and then remove the minimum and maximum values from the status bar so it is back to its original state.
4. If you will be moving on to the next skill in this chapter, leave the workbook open to continue working. If not, save the file as directed by your instructor and close it.

Skill 1.16 Changing the Zoom Level

If you are working with a large spreadsheet, you may find that you need to see more of the spreadsheet at one time or that you would like a closer look at a cell or group of cells. You can use the **zoom slider** in the lower right corner of the window to zoom in and out of a worksheet, changing the size of text and images on screen. As you move the slider, the zoom level displays the percentage the worksheet has been zoomed in or zoomed out. Zooming a worksheet affects only how the worksheet appears on-screen. It does not affect how the worksheet will print.

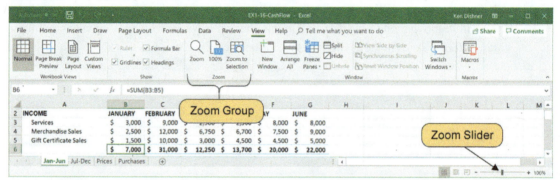

FIGURE EX 1.34

To zoom in on a worksheet, making the text and graphics appear larger:

> Click and drag the zoom slider to the right.
> Click the **Zoom In** button on the slider.

To zoom out of a worksheet, making the text and graphics appear smaller:

> Click and drag the zoom slider to the left.
> Click the **Zoom Out** button on the slider.

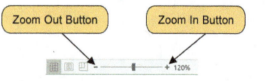

FIGURE EX 1.35

On the *View* tab, the *Zoom* group includes buttons for two of the most common zoom options:

> Click the **Zoom to Selection** button to zoom in as close as possible on the currently selected cell(s).
> Click the **100%** button to return the worksheet back to 100% of the normal size.

You can also change the zoom level through the *Zoom* dialog.

1. On the *View* tab, in the *Zoom* group, click the **Zoom**
2. In the *Zoom* dialog, click the radio button for the zoom option you want, and then click **OK**.

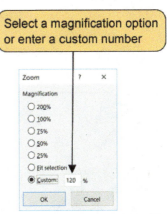

Select a magnification option or enter a custom number

FIGURE EX 1.36

tips & tricks

When you save a workbook, Excel saves the zoom setting. However, if you change the zoom level and then close the workbook without making any other changes, Excel will not warn you about saving your change. The next time you open the workbook, it will be back to the zoom level that was set at the time the workbook was last saved.

another method

You can also open *Zoom* dialog by clicking the zoom level number that appears at the right side of the zoom slider.

let me try Live!

If you do not have the data file from the previous skill open, open the student data file **EX1-16-CashFlow** and try this skill on your own:

1. Change the zoom level to **110%**.
2. Change the zoom level back to **100%**.
3. Change the zoom level to **90%**.
4. If you will be moving on to the next skill in this chapter, leave the workbook open to continue working. If not, save the file as directed by your instructor and close it.

from the perspective of . . .

ACCOUNTING FIRM INTERN

My boss works on two 24" monitors. She always has her files set at 150% or higher because she has the room to spread the worksheet across two large monitors. I work on a laptop with a 15" screen. When I open her files, I can only see part of the worksheet until I set the zoom level back to 100%. It is harder to see details when the zoom level is set lower, but for me, it's more important to see the whole worksheet without having to scroll.

Skill 1.17 Creating a New Workbook Using a Template

A **template** is a file with predefined settings that you can use as a starting point for your workbook. Using an Excel template makes creating a new workbook easy and results in a professional appearance. Many templates use advanced techniques that you may not have learned yet—but you can take advantage of them in a template where someone else has created the workbook framework for you. Templates are available for every imaginable task: from creating budgets to tracking exercise to calculating your grade point average.

To create a new workbook using a template:

1. Click the **File** tab to open Backstage view.
2. Click **New**. Excel includes a variety of templates that are copied to your computer when you install the application. These templates are always available from the *New* page. Additional templates that you download are also displayed on the *New* page, so your screen may look different than the one in Figure EX 1.37.
3. Click a template picture to open the template preview including a brief description of the template.

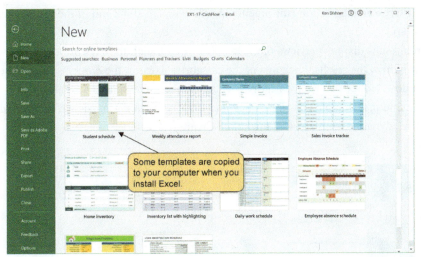

FIGURE EX 1.37

4. You can cycle through the template previews by clicking the arrows that appear on either side of the preview.
5. When you find the template you want to use, click the **Create** button.
6. A new workbook opens, prepopulated with all of the template elements and sample data. Work through the template, replacing the sample data with your own.
7. Don't forget to save the file.

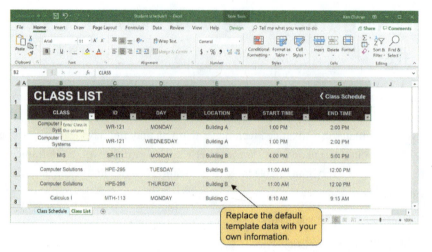

FIGURE EX 1.38

You can search for additional workbook templates online. (You must have an active Internet connection.)

1. Near the top of the *New* page, in the *Search online templates* box, type a keyword or phrase that describes the template you want.

2. Click the **Start searching** button (the magnifying glass image at the end of the *Search online templates* box).

3. The search results display previews of the templates that match the keyword or phrase you entered. To further narrow the results, click one of the categories listed in the *Filter by* pane at the right side of the window. Notice that each category lists the number of templates available.

4. When you find the template you want, click it to display the larger preview with detailed information about the template, and then click **Create**.

FIGURE EX 1.39

tips & tricks

Many Excel templates have a special worksheet labeled Settings, Instructions, or something similar. Be sure to read all of the instructions before entering data.

let me try Live!

If you do not have the data file from the previous skill open, open the student data file **EX1-17-CashFlow** 📥 and try this skill on your own:

1. Create a new file based on the **Student schedule** template. If this template does not appear on your *New* page, search for it using the *Search online templates* feature. You may find more than one template named Student schedule. Select one that appeals to you.

2. Create another new file by searching for a template based on the word **budget**. Use the **Simple monthly budget** template or another budget template that appeals to you.

3. If you will be moving on to the next skill in this chapter, leave the workbooks open to continue working. If not, save the files as directed by your instructor and close them.

from the perspective of . . .

COLLEGE STUDENT

I thought Excel was only for business. It's not! I found some really useful templates—one for tracking my day-to-day expenses and another one to help me budget my expenses for the semester. And even though some of the templates look fancy and complicated, I find that I can use them easily by reading the instructions and taking a little bit of time to personalize the data with my own information.

Skill 1.18 Arranging Workbooks

If you are working with multiple workbooks, you may want to arrange them so you can see them all at the same time. You can arrange workbooks so they are tiled, horizontal, vertical, or cascading windows.

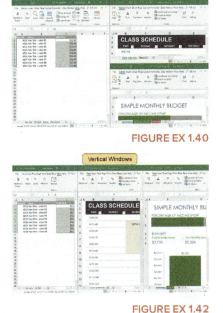

FIGURE EX 1.40

FIGURE EX 1.41

FIGURE EX 1.42

FIGURE EX 1.43

To change the arrangement of workbooks:

1. On the *View* tab, in the *Window* group, click the **Arrange All** button.
2. In the *Arrange Windows* dialog, select an arrangement option:
   - **Tiled**—places the windows in a grid pattern.
   - **Horizontal**—places the windows in a stack one on top of the other.
   - **Vertical**—places the windows in a row next to each other.
   - **Cascade**—places the windows in a staggered, overlapping, diagonal arrangement.
3. Click **OK**.

FIGURE EX 1.44

To switch between workbooks, you can:

> Click anywhere in the workbook you want to make active.
> On the *View* tab, in the *Window* group, click the **Switch Windows** button, then click the name of the workbook you want.

To undo the arrangement and put the workbooks back into separate windows, maximize any of the workbooks by clicking the **Maximize** button on the title bar.

tell me more

If you have two workbooks with similar data, you may want to compare their data row by row. Excel's *Compare Side by Side* feature allows you to compare two workbooks at the same time. When you compare workbooks, the *Synchronous Scrolling* feature is on by default. This feature allows you to scroll both workbooks at once. If you scroll the active workbook, the other workbook will scroll at the same time, allowing you to carefully compare data row by row.

1. Open the workbooks you want to compare.
2. On the *View* tab, in the *Window* group, click the **View Side by Side** button.
3. The two workbooks are displayed one on top of the other.
4. Scroll the active window to scroll both workbooks at once.
5. Click the **View Side by Side** button again to restore the windows to their previous positions.

let me try Live!

If you do not have the data files from the previous skill open, open the student data file **EX1-18-CashFlow** and a few other Excel files to try this skill on your own:

1. Arrange the Excel windows so they are in a staggered arrangement.
2. Arrange the Excel windows so they are in a row next to each other.
3. If you will be moving on to the next skill in this chapter, close all of the workbooks except the *CashFlow* workbook. If not, save the files as directed by your instructor and close them.

Skill 1.19 Checking Spelling

In Excel, the *Spelling* command analyzes the current worksheet for spelling errors. The *Spelling* dialog cycles through each spelling error, allowing you to make decisions about how to handle each one.

To check a worksheet for spelling errors:

1. On the *Review* tab, in the *Proofing* group, click the **Spelling** button or use the keyboard shortcut F7.

2. The first spelling error appears in the *Spelling* dialog.

3. Review the spelling suggestion and then select an action:

- Click **Ignore Once** to make no changes to this instance of the word.
- Click **Ignore All** to make no changes to all instances of the word.
- Click **Add to Dictionary** to make no changes to this instance of the word and add it to the spelling checker dictionary, so future uses of this word will not show up as misspellings.
- Click the correct spelling in the *Suggestions* list, and click **Change** to correct just this instance of the misspelling in your worksheet.
- Click the correct spelling in the *Suggestions* list, and click **Change All** to correct all instances of the misspelling in your worksheet.

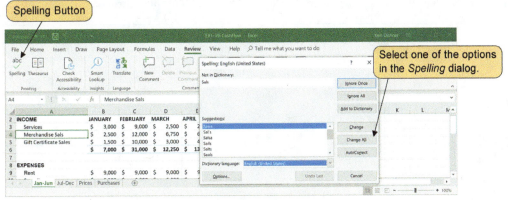

FIGURE EX 1.45

4. After you select an action, the spelling checker automatically advances to the next suspected spelling error.

5. When the spelling checker finds no more errors, it displays a message telling you the check is complete. Click **OK** to close the dialog and return to your worksheet.

tips & tricks

Whether or not you use the Spelling tool, you should always proofread your files. Spelling checkers are not infallible, especially if you misuse a word yet spell it correctly—for instance, writing "bored" instead of "board."

If you misspell a word often, the next time the spelling checker catches the misspelling, use this trick: Click the correct spelling in the *Suggestions* list and then click the **AutoCorrect** button. Now, when you type the misspelled version of the word, it will be corrected automatically as you type.

let me try Live!

If you do not have the data file from the previous skill open, open the student data file **EX1-19-CashFlow** ⬇ and try this skill on your own:

1. Spell check the *Jan-Jun* worksheet and correct any errors you find.
2. If you will be moving on to the next skill in this chapter, leave the workbook open to continue working. If not, save the file as directed by your instructor and close it.

Skill 1.20 Previewing and Printing a Worksheet

In Excel, all the print settings are combined in a single page along with a preview of how the printed file will look. As you change print settings, the preview updates. To preview and print the current worksheet:

1. Click the **File** tab to open Backstage view.
2. Click **Print**.
3. At the right side of the page is a preview of how the printed file will look. Beneath the preview there is a page count. If there are multiple pages, use the *Next* and *Previous* arrows to preview all the pages in the file. You can also use the scroll bar to the right to scroll through the preview pages.
4. Set the number of copies to print by changing the number in the *Copies* box.
5. Click the **Print** button to send the file to your default printer.

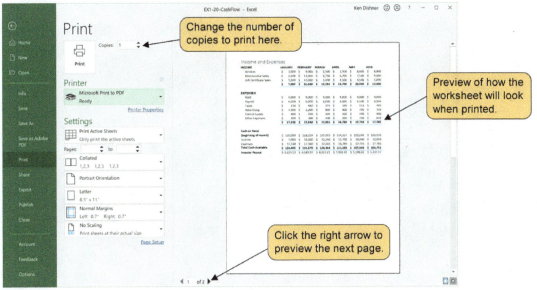

FIGURE EX 1.46

tips & tricks

Add the *Quick Print* command to the Quick Access Toolbar so you can print with a single mouse click. If you do not need to change the default print settings, you can click the *Quick Print* button instead of going through the *Print* tab in Backstage view.

tell me more

To open the *Print* page in Backstage view, you can use the keyboard shortcut [Ctrl] + [P].

let me try Live!

If you do not have the data file from the previous skill open, open the student data file **EX1-20-CashFlow** ⬇ and try this skill on your own:

1. Preview how the worksheet will look when printed.
2. If you can, print the worksheet and compare the printed page to the preview.
3. Save the file as directed by your instructor and close it.

key terms

Workbook

Worksheet

Row

Column

Cell

Cell address

Cell range

Formula bar

Name box

Status bar

Vertical scroll bar

Horizontal scroll bar

Row selector

Column selector

Protected View

Message Bar

Trusted Document

Ready mode

Edit mode

General number format

Accounting Number Format

Percent Style format

Comma Style format

Number format

Currency format

Short Date format

Long Date format

AutoFill

Fill Handle tool

Data series

Chart

Data points

Data markers

Data series (chart)

Y axis

X axis

Plot area

Chart area

Chart title

Legend

Formula

Order of Operations (precedence)

Cell reference

Relative reference

Absolute reference

Mixed reference

Function

Argument

AutoSum

Quick Analysis tool

Status bar

Zoom slider

Template

Tiled window arrangement

Horizontal window arrangement

Vertical window arrangement

Cascade window arrangement

concept review

1. How many worksheets does a new Excel workbook have?

    a. None

    b. one

    c. two

    d. four

2. The cell C4 refers to the cell at _____.

    a. the intersection of row C and column 4

    b. the first cell on the C4 worksheet

    c. the intersection of column C and row 4

    d. none of the above

3. Which of these dates uses the Long Date format?

    a. Saturday, January 1, 2020

    b. 1/1/2020

    c. January 1, 2020

    d. 01/01/2020

4. Data markers are graphic representations of the values of data points in a chart.

    a. true

    b. false

5. Formulas begin with which character?

    a. $

    b. @

    c. ^

    d. =

6. Which of these cell references is an absolute reference?

    a. C9

    b. C$9

    c. $C$9

    d. none of the above

7. AutoSum is located _____.

    a. on the *Home* tab, in the *Formulas* group

    b. on the *Home* tab, in the *Editing* group

    c. on the *Insert* tab, in the *Formulas* group

    d. on the *Insert* tab, in the *Tables* group

8. The zoom slider is located _____.

    a. on the Ribbon

    b. on the *View* tab, in the *Zoom* group

    c. in the *Zoom* dialog

    d. at the lower right corner of the status bar

9. The keyboard shortcut to begin the spelling checker is _____.

    a. F4

    b. F5

    c. F7

    d. F9

10. Which of these tasks can you perform in Backstage view?

    a. Enable Editing when a workbook is in Protected View.

    b. Preview how a workbook will look when printed.

    c. Create a new workbook from a template.

    d. All of the above.

projects

skill review **1.1**

Data files for projects can be found by logging into your SIMnet account and going to the Library section.

The workbook for this project generates client bills from staff hours in multiple worksheets. In this project, you will complete the worksheet for staff member Swinson to calculate the daily bill, the total billable hours per week, and the total weekly bill. The worksheet for staff member Stevens has been completed. You may use it for reference as necessary.

Skills needed to complete this project:

- Working in Protected View (Skill 1.3)
- Navigating a Workbook (Skill 1.2)
- Exploring Charts (Skill 1.8)
- Entering and Editing Text and Numbers in Cells (Skill 1.4)
- Applying Number Formats (Skill 1.5)
- Entering Dates and Applying Date Formats (Skill 1.6)
- Inserting Data Using AutoFill (Skill 1.7)
- Understanding Absolute and Relative References (Skill 1.11)
- Entering Simple Formulas (Skill 1.10)
- Calculating Totals with the Quick Analysis Tool (Skill 1.14)
- Using the Recommended Charts Feature (Skill 1.9)
- Previewing and Printing a Worksheet (Skill 1.20)

1. Open the start file **EX2019-SkillReview-1-1** and resave the file as:
   `[your initials]EX-SkillReview-1-1`
2. If the workbook opens in Protected View, click the **Enable Editing** button in the Message Bar at the top of the workbook so you can modify the workbook.
3. Explore the workbook. If you accidentally make changes while exploring, press Ctrl + Z to undo the change.
   a. Click the worksheet tab labeled *Stevens Hours*.
   b. If necessary, use the vertical scroll bar to scroll down so you can see both weeks of billable hours. (If necessary, use the vertical scroll bar again to return to the top of the worksheet.)
   c. Click cell **B2** (the cell displaying the staff member's last name, Stevens). This is the cell at the intersection of column B and row 2.
      i. Note that the column B and row 2 selector boxes highlight.
      ii. Note that the status bar displays Ready, indicating that you are in Ready mode.
      iii. On the *Home* tab, in the *Number* group, look at the *Number Format* box at the top of the group. Note that the format for this cell is *General*.
      iv. Double-click cell **B2** to switch to Edit mode. Note that the status bar now displays *Edit*, and the blinking cursor appears within the cell. If you needed to, you could edit the text directly in the cell.

d. Press [Esc] to exit Edit mode and return to Ready mode.

e. Press [Enter] twice to move to cell **B4** (the cell displaying the staff member's billable rate). This cell is formatted with the Accounting Number Format number format.

    i. Look in the *Number Format* box and note that the format for this cell is *Accounting*.

    ii. On the *Home* tab, in the *Styles* group, look in the *Cell Styles* gallery, and note that the cell style *Currency* is highlighted. (If the *Cell Styles* gallery is collapsed on your Ribbon, click the **Cell Styles** button to display it.)

f. Click cell **B8** (the cell displaying the number of hours for Monday, August 5). This cell is formatted with the Comma cell style.

    i. Look in the *Number Format* box and note that the format for this cell is also *Accounting*.

    ii. On the *Home* tab, in the *Styles* group, look in the *Cell Styles* gallery, and note that the cell style *Comma* is highlighted for this cell. (If the *Cell Styles* gallery is collapsed on your Ribbon, click the **Cell Styles** button to display it.)

    iii. Note the style differences between cell **B4** (Accounting Number Format, Currency style) and cell **B8** (Accounting Number Format, Comma style).

g. Click cell **B7** (the cell displaying the date 8/5/2019). This cell is formatted using the Short Date format. Note that the *Number Format* box displays *Date*.

h. Double-click cell **B14**.

    i. Note that the status bar now displays *Edit*, indicating that you are in Edit mode.

    ii. This cell contains a formula to calculate the daily bill for Monday, August 5: **=B12*$B$4**

    iii. Note that cells B12 and B4 are highlighted with colors matching the cell references in the formula.

    iv. Note that the reference to cell B4 is an absolute reference ($B$4).

i. Press [Esc] to exit Edit mode.

j. Double-click cell **B12**.

    i. Note that once again the status bar displays *Edit*, indicating that you are in Edit mode.

    ii. This cell contains a formula using the SUM function to calculate the total billable hours for Monday, August 5: **=SUM(B8:B11)**

    iii. In this case, the SUM function uses a single argument **B8:B11** to indicate the range of cells to total.

    iv. Note that the cell range **B8:B11** is highlighted with the color matching the argument in the SUM function formula.

    v. Note that the reference to the cell range **B8:B11** uses relative references.

k. Press [Esc] to exit Edit mode.

l. Press [Tab] to move to cell **C12**. Look in the formula bar and note that this cell contains a similar formula to the one in cell **B12: =SUM(C8:C11)**

m. Press [→] to move through cells **D12 through H12**. Note the formula in the formula bar for each cell.

n. Did you notice that the cell references in the formulas in cells **C12 through H12** all use relative references?

4. The *Stevens Hours* worksheet contains a stacked column chart. Review the chart so you can recreate it on the *Swinson Hours* worksheet.

   a. The stacked column chart to the right of the hours for the week of August 5 represents the hours worked for each client each day.

   b. The column height for each day represents the total hours worked. Each column is divided into segments representing the hours worked for each client.

   c. The number of hours worked is represented on the y axis. The dates are represented along the x axis.

   d. The chart title has been changed to: **Week of 8/5/19**

5. Now you are ready to complete the worksheet for David Swinson. Navigate to the *Swinson Hours* worksheet by clicking the **Swinson Hours** worksheet tab.

6. The staff member's last name is spelled incorrectly. Navigate to cell **B2** and edit the text so the last name is spelled correctly (Swinson – with an *i* instead of an *a*). Use Edit mode.

   a. Double-click cell **B2**.

   b. Edit the text to: `Swinson`

   c. Press [Enter] to accept your changes.

7. The billable rate amount is missing. Navigate to cell **B4** and enter the rate. Use Ready mode.

   a. Click cell **B4**.

   b. Type: `180`

   c. Press [Enter].

8. Modify the billable rate to use the Accounting Number Format.

   a. Press the [↑] to return to cell **B4**.

   b. On the *Home* tab, in the *Number* group, click the **Accounting Number Format** button.

9. The dates are missing from the timesheet. Enter the first date, August 5, 2019.

   a. Click cell **B7**.

   b. Type: `8/5/2019`

   c. Press [Enter].

10. Use Autofill to complete the dates in the timesheet.

    a. Click cell **B7**.

    b. Click the **Fill Handle**, and drag to cell **H7**. Release the mouse button.

11. Change the date format to the 8/5/2019 format.

    a. The cell range **B7:H7** should still be selected. If not, click cell **B7**, press and hold [Shift], click cell **H7**, and then release the [Shift] key.

    b. On the *Home* tab, in the *Number* group, expand the *Number Format* list, and click **Short Date**.

12. Use the Quick Analysis tool to enter total hours for each day.

    a. Select cells **B8:H11**. Click cell **B8**, hold down the left mouse button, and drag the mouse to cell **H11**. Release the mouse button. The cell range B8 through H11 should now appear selected.

    b. The Quick Analysis tool button should appear near the lower right corner of the selected cell range. (If the Quick Analysis tool button is not visible, move your mouse cursor over the selected cell range again, without clicking. This action should make the button appear.)

    c. Click the **Quick Analysis tool** button, and then click **Totals**.

    d. Click **Sum** (the first option).

13. Format the hours billed section to use the Comma Style number format. Be sure to include the total row.
   a. Select cells **B8:H12**. Try another method: Click cell **B8**, press and hold [Shift], click cell **H12**, and release the [Shift] key.
   b. On the *Home* tab, in the *Number* group, click the **Comma Style** button.
14. Enter a formula in cell **B14** to calculate the daily bill for Monday, August 5. The formula should calculate the total billable hours for the day (cell B12) times the billable rate (B4).
   a. Click cell **B14**.
   b. Type: **=**
   c. Click cell **B12**.
   d. Type: *****
   e. Click cell **B4**.
   f. Press [F4] to change the cell reference **B4** to an absolute reference (**$B$4**).
   g. Press [Enter].
   h. The formula should look like this: **=B12*$B$4**
15. Use AutoFill to copy the formula to the remaining days in the timesheet.
   a. Click cell **B14** again.
   b. Click the **AutoFill handle**. Hold down the left mouse button and drag to cell **H14**. Release the mouse button.
   c. The formulas in cells B14 through H14 should look like this.

	B	C	D	E	F	G	H
14	=B12*$B$4	=C12*$B$4	=D12*$B$4	=E12*$B$4	=F12*$B$4	=G12*$B$4	=H12*$B$4

Notice that when the AutoFill copied the formula, it updated the relative reference (B12) to reflect the new column position, but it did not change the relative reference ($B$4).

16. Now you can calculate the bill total for the week by summing the daily bill amounts. Enter a formula using the SUM function with the cell range **B14:H14** as the argument.
   a. Click cell **B15**.
   b. Type: **=SUM(B14:H14)**
   c. Press [Enter].

17. Use the Recommended Charts feature to insert a **stacked column chart** representing hours worked for each day for the week of August 5.

    a. Select cells **A7:H11**. Click cell **A7**, hold down the left mouse button, and drag the mouse to cell **H11**. Release the mouse button. The cell range A7 through H11 should now appear selected.

    b. The Quick Analysis tool button should appear near the lower right corner of the selected cell range. (If the Quick Analysis tool button is not visible, move your mouse cursor over the selected cell range again, without clicking. This action should make the button appear.)

    c. Click the **Quick Analysis tool** button, and then click **Charts**.

    d. Click **Stacked Column** to insert a stacked column chart.

18. Change the chart title.

    a. Click the **Chart Title** placeholder once to select it.

    b. Type: Week of 8/5/2019

    c. Press Enter.

19. Preview how the worksheet will look when printed.

    a. Click cell **A1** to deselect the chart.

    b. Click the **File** tab to open Backstage view.

    c. Click **Print** to display the print preview.

    d. Click the left arrow to close the Backstage view.

20. Save and close the workbook.

projects
skill review **1.2**

Data files for projects can be found by logging into your SIMnet account and going to the Library section.

In this project you will create a new workbook to track the cost of books for your college classes. For each book, you will enter the purchase price, the potential sell-back price, and the cost difference. You will calculate totals using AutoSum. You will then create a new workbook from a template, and practice changing the zoom level and arranging the workbooks.

Skills needed to complete this project:

- Entering and Editing Text and Numbers in Cells (Skill 1.4)
- Navigating a Workbook (Skill 1.2)
- Inserting Data Using AutoFill (Skill 1.7)
- Applying Number Formats (Skill 1.5)
- Using the Status Bar (Skill 1.15)
- Using AutoSum to Insert a SUM Function (Skill 1.13)
- Entering Simple Formulas (Skill 1.10)
- Using the Recommended Charts Feature (Skill 1.9)
- Exploring Charts (Skill 1.8)
- Creating a New Workbook Using a Template (Skill 1.17)
- Checking Spelling (Skill 1.19)
- Arranging Workbooks (Skill 1.18)
- Changing the Zoom Level (Skill 1.16)

1. Start a new blank Excel workbook. Save the file as:
   `[your initials]EX-SkillReview-1-2`
2. The new workbook opens with one sheet (*Sheet1*). Cell *A1* is selected.
3. In cell **A1**, type the title for the worksheet: **Textbooks**

4. Enter data in the worksheet as follows:

	A	B	C	D
1	Textbooks			
2				
3	Book	Cost	Value	Difference
4	Book1	85	45	
5	Book2	100	80	
6	Book3	250	125	
7	Book4	80.95	24.25	

5. Use AutoFill to add two additional books to the list.
    a. Click cell **A4**, hold down the left mouse button and drag the mouse to cell **A7**. Release the mouse button. The cell range A4 through A7 should now appear selected.
    b. Click the **Fill Handle** (located at the lower right corner of the selected cell range).
    c. Drag down to cell **A9**, and release the mouse button.
    d. Excel adds Book 5 and Book 6 to the list.
6. Book 5 cost $125.00 and can be sold for $75.00. Book 6 cost $175.00 and can be sold for $100.00. Add these data to the worksheet.
    a. Click cell **B8** and type: **125**
    b. Press [Tab] and type: **75**
    c. Click cell **B9** and type: **175**
    d. Press [Tab] and type: **100**
    e. Press [Enter].
7. Modify the **status bar** to display the minimum value.
    a. Right-click anywhere on the **status bar**.
    b. Click **Minimum** to add a checkmark.
    c. Click anywhere to dismiss the menu.

8. Use the status bar to check the total value of the books and the minimum value.

    a. Click cell **C4**. Press and hold [Shift] and click cell **C9**. Release the [Shift] key.

    b. Look at the status bar and find the *Sum* value (**449.25**).

    c. Look at the status bar and find the *Min* value (**24.25**).

9. Use AutoSum to calculate total cost and total value. The totals should be placed in cells **B10** and **C10**.

    a. Click cell **A10** and type: `Total`

    b. Press [Tab].

    c. Cell **B10** should be selected. Press and hold [Shift] and click cell **C10**. Release the [Shift] key.

    d. On the *Home* tab, in the *Editing* group, click the **AutoSum** button.

10. Change the number format for the cost and value numbers to the Accounting Number Format.

    a. Click cell **B4**. Press and hold [Shift]. Click cell **C10**. Release [Shift].

    b. On the *Home* tab, in the *Number* group, click the **Accounting Number Format** button.

11. Enter a formula in cell **D4** to calculate the difference between the cost and the value for Book1. The formula will use only relative references because in the next step, you will use AutoFill to copy the formula down the column.

    a. Click cell **D4**.

    b. Type: **=**

    c. Click cell **B4**.

    d. Type: **-**

    e. Click cell **C4**.

    f. Press [Enter].

12. Use AutoFill to copy the formula to calculate the difference for books 2 through 6 and the total.

    a. Click cell **D4**.

    b. Click the **AutoFill handle**. Hold down the left mouse button and drag to cell **D10**. Release the mouse button.

13. Use the Quick Analysis tool to insert a **pie chart** representing the cost of books.

    a. Select cells **A3:B9**. Click cell **A3**, hold down the left mouse button, and drag the mouse to cell **B9**. Release the mouse button. The cell range A3 through B9 should now appear selected.

    b. The Quick Analysis tool button should appear near the lower right corner of the selected cell range. (If the Quick Analysis tool button is not visible, move your mouse cursor over the selected cell range again, without clicking. This action should make the button appear.)

    c. Click the **Quick Analysis tool** button, and then click **Charts**.

    d. Click **Pie** to insert a pie chart.

    e. Observe how each book is assigned a color in the chart legend.

    f. The size of each pie piece represents the cost of each book relative to the total cost of all the books. Book 3 is the most expensive book and is represented by the largest piece of the pie.

14. Change the chart title.

    a. Click the **Cost** chart title once to select it.

    b. Type: `Comparative Cost of Books`

    c. Press `Enter`.

15. Save the workbook. Do not close it or exit Excel.

16. Create a new file from a template called *Personal Monthly Budget*.

    a. Click the **File** tab to open Backstage view.

    b. Click **New**.

    c. Open a new file based on the *Personal Monthly Budget* template. (This step may require an active Internet connection.)

        i. The *Personal Monthly Budget* template may appear in the list of templates automatically. If it does not, you will need to search for it. In the *Search online templates* box, type: `personal monthly budget`

        ii. Click the template preview.

        iii. Click **Create**.

17. The new workbook based on the *Personal Monthly Budget* template opens. This is a complex workbook using many advanced techniques. The good news is that you don't have to understand how this workbook was created in order to use it.

    a. Click the **Personal Monthly Budget** worksheet tab to begin working.

    b. Scroll through the worksheet to review all the budget income and expenses. Edit category names and values to reflect your personal budget.

    c. If you think you might like to come back to this workbook later for your personal use, this is a good point to save it. Be sure not to close the file. Use the file name: `[Your Initials]Personal Monthly Budget`

18. You should still have two workbooks open: the textbooks workbook from the beginning of the project and the *Personal Monthly Budget* workbook based on the template. Arrange the workbooks so you can see both at the same time.

    a. On the *View* tab, in the *Window* group, click the *Arrange All* button.

    b. In the *Arrange Windows* dialog, click the *Vertical* radio button. Click *OK*.

19. The *Personal Monthly Budget* workbook should be active. If not, click the title bar for that window. Review the *Personal Monthly Budget* sheet and change the zoom level to 50% so you can see more of the data at once.

    a. If necessary, click the **Personal Monthly Budget** tab.

    b. On the *View* tab, in the *Zoom* group, click the *Zoom* button.

    c. In the *Zoom* dialog, click the *50%* radio button for the zoom option you want. Click **OK**.

20. Close both workbooks. If you made changes to the *Personal Monthly Budget* workbook and you plan to continue using it, be sure to save the changes.

projects
challenge yourself **1.3**

Data files for projects can be found by logging into your SIMnet account and going to the Library section.

In this project, you will complete a timesheet for David Swinson, similar to the one you worked on in Skill Review 1.1. You will need to enter and format missing dates, correct a data entry mistake, apply number formatting, and enter formulas to calculate the total billable hours per day, the daily total for each day, and the bill total for the week.

Skills needed to complete this project:

- Working in Protected View (Skill 1.3)
- Navigating a Workbook (Skill 1.2)
- Entering and Editing Text and Numbers in Cells (Skill 1.4)
- Inserting Data Using AutoFill (Skill 1.7)
- Entering Dates and Applying Date Formats (Skill 1.6)
- Calculating Totals with the Quick Analysis Tool (Skill 1.14)
- Applying Number Formats (Skill 1.5)
- Understanding Absolute and Relative References (Skill 1.11)
- Entering Simple Formulas (Skill 1.10)
- Using the Recommended Charts Feature (Skill 1.9)
- Exploring Charts (Skill 1.8)
- Previewing and Printing a Worksheet (Skill 1.20)

1. Open the start file **EX2019-ChallengeYourself-1-3** and resave the file as: `[your initials]EX-ChallengeYourself-1-3`
2. If the workbook opens in Protected View, enable editing so you can make changes to the workbook.
3. If necessary, scroll to the bottom of the worksheet so you can see the empty timesheet beginning on row 17.
4. The dates are missing from the timesheet. Enter the date **7/29/2019** in cell **B18**.
5. Use AutoFill to complete the dates in cells **C18:H18**.
6. Change the date format for **B18:H18** to the date format similar to **14-Mar**.
7. The hours reported for the Proctor client on Friday (cell F22) are incorrect. Change the number in cell **F22** to: **4**
8. Use the Quick Analysis tool to enter total hours for each day. Use the cell range **B19:H22**. The daily totals should be inserted into the range **B23:H23**.
9. Format the hours billed section (cells **B19:H23**) to use the Comma Style number format. Be sure to include the total row.

10. Enter a formula in cell **B25** to calculate the daily bill for Monday, July 29. The formula should calculate the total billable hours for the day (cell **B23**) times the billable rate (**B4**). Be sure to use an absolute cell reference for the billable rate.

11. Use AutoFill to copy the formula to the remaining days in the timesheet (cells **C25:H25**).

12. Calculate the bill total for the week by summing the daily bill amounts. In cell **B26**, enter a formula using the SUM function. The function argument should be the range of cells representing the daily bill totals (**B25:H25**).

13. Apply the **Currency** number format to cells **B25:H25** and cell **B26**.

14. Use the Recommended Charts feature to insert a **line chart** representing hours works for each day for the week of July 29. Select cells **A18:H22** for the chart data.

15. Change the chart title to: `Week of July 29`

16. Preview how the worksheet will look when printed. If the print preview shows only the chart, return to the worksheet and click anywhere to deselect the chart. Now the print preview should show the entire worksheet.

17. Save and close the workbook.

projects

challenge yourself **1.4**

Data files for projects can be found by logging into your SIMnet account and going to the Library section.

In this project you will work with a college budget spreadsheet. You will change a few values in the budget, modify number formats, and calculate totals and the difference between expected income and expenses. You will then create a new budget workbook from a template, and practice changing the zoom level and arranging the workbooks.

Skills needed to complete this project:

- Working in Protected View (Skill 1.3)
- Entering and Editing Text and Numbers in Cells (Skill 1.4)
- Navigating a Workbook (Skill 1.2)
- Using AutoSum to Insert a SUM Function (Skill 1.13)
- Calculating Totals with the Quick Analysis Tool (Skill 1.14)
- Using the Status Bar (Skill 1.15)
- Applying Number Formats (Skill 1.5)
- Understanding Absolute and Relative References (Skill 1.11)
- Entering Simple Formulas (Skill 1.10)
- Checking Spelling (Skill 1.19)
- Using the Recommended Charts Feature (Skill 1.9)
- Exploring Charts (Skill 1.8)
- Creating a New Workbook Using a Template (Skill 1.17)
- Arranging Workbooks (Skill 1.18)
- Changing the Zoom Level (Skill 1.16)

1. Open the start file **EX2019-ChallengeYourself-1-4** and resave the file as:
   `[your initials]EX-ChallengeYourself-1-4`
2. If the workbook opens in Protected View, enable editing so you can make changes to the workbook.
3. Make the following changes to the *Budget* worksheet:
   a. Change the *Electric* item to **Utilities** (cell **A12**).
   b. Change the Insurance value from *90* to **125** (cell **B19**).
   c. Update the text in cell **D6** to: **Quarter expenses**
4. The worksheet is missing formulas to calculate totals. Enter formulas using the **SUM** function to calculate the following totals. Use any of the methods you learned in this chapter.
   a. Enter a formula in cell **B7** to calculate the total monthly income.
   b. Enter a formula in cell **B24** to calculate the total monthly expenses.
   c. Enter a formula in cell **E16** to calculate the total quarter expenses.
   d. Use the **status bar** to verify that the formula is calculating the correct total for each cell range.

5. Cell **E18** displays the number of months in the quarter. Change the number format in this cell to the **Number** format with no numbers showing after the decimal (so the number appears as **3** instead of **$3.00**).

6. The number format in the *Quarter Expenses* section does not match the number format in the other sections of the worksheet. Change the number format for cells **E11:E16** to the **Accounting Number Format**.

7. Review the formulas in the *Discretionary Income* section.

   a. Cells **E4:E6** should contain references to the cells where you just entered the formulas to calculate totals. Add the appropriate formula to cell **E6** to reference the value in cell **E16** (the total quarter expenses).

   b. The quarter is three months long, so the formulas in cells **E4** and **E5** should multiply the total monthly income and total monthly expenses by three. Correct the formulas in cells **E4** and **E6**. Use an absolute reference to the value in cell **E18** (the number of months in the quarter).

8. Use spelling checker to find and correct any spelling errors in the *Budget* (*Hint*: There is one spelling error on this worksheet.)

9. Use the Recommended Charts feature to insert a **clustered bar chart** representing the monthly expenses. Select cells **A10:B23** for the chart data.

10. Change the chart title to: `Monthly Expenses`

11. Save the workbook. Do not close it or exit Excel.

12. Create a new file from a template called *Personal Expenses Calculator*. If you do not see this template, search for it using the search phrase *personal expenses*.

13. Explore the worksheets in this workbook.

14. If you think you might like to come back to this workbook later for your personal use, this is a good point to save it. Be sure not to close the file. Use the file name: `[Your Initials]PersonalExpenses`

15. You should still have two workbooks open: the college budget workbook from the beginning of the project and the personal expenses workbook based on the template. Arrange the workbooks so you can see both at the same time.

    a. Try different arrangements until you find the one that works best for you.

    b. Practice moving back and forth between the two workbooks.

16. Make the personal budget workbook active and navigate to the Dashboard worksheet. Modify the zoom to **80%**.

17. Close both workbooks. If you made changes to the personal budget workbook and you plan to continue using it, be sure to save the changes.

projects

on your own 1.5

Data files for projects can be found by logging into your SIMnet account and going to the Library section.

For Spring Break, you've decided to take a seven-day road trip. Use this Excel workbook to calculate the number of miles you will drive each day and the gas cost for each day. Use the techniques you've learned in this chapter to calculate the total miles and the total gas cost. Don't forget to end the trip at the same location you started! You may want to use the Internet to look up mileage, MPG (miles per gallon), and gas price information.

Skills needed to complete this project:

- Navigating a Workbook (Skill 1.2)
- Working in Protected View (Skill 1.3)
- Entering and Editing Text and Numbers in Cells (Skill 1.4)
- Entering Dates and Applying Date Formats (Skill 1.6)
- Inserting Data Using AutoFill (Skill 1.7)
- Understanding Absolute and Relative References (Skill 1.11)
- Entering Simple Formulas (Skill 1.10)
- Calculating Totals with the Quick Analysis Tool (Skill 1.14)
- Using AutoSum to Insert a SUM Function (Skill 1.13)
- Applying Number Formats (Skill 1.5)
- Using the Recommended Charts Feature (Skill 1.9)
- Exploring Charts (Skill 1.8)
- Checking Spelling (Skill 1.19)

1. Open the start file **EX2019-OnYourOwn-1-5** and resave the file as:
   `[your initials]EX-OnYourOwn-1-5`
2. If the workbook opens in Protected View, click the **Enable Editing** button in the Message Bar at the top of the workbook so you can modify the workbook.
3. Complete the *Trip Details* section of the *Spring Break* worksheet:
   a. Enter the dates of your road trip. Use a date format that includes the day of the week.
   b. Enter a start and end location for each day. Remember—the starting location for each day should be the same as the end location for the previous day. If you use a formula with a relative reference rather than retyping the location name for each start location, you can use AutoFill to complete the start location column. Consider using a formula to ensure that the final end location is the same as the first start location.
   c. Look up and enter the miles between each location. Use an appropriate number format for the *Number of Miles* column. (Hint: Use *mapquest.com* or *maps.google.com* to look up the mileage between locations.)

4. Enter your car information including the MPG (miles per gallon). If you don't know your MPG, the government website *www.fueleconomy.gov* has excellent information on average MPG for a variety of car makes, models, and years.

5. Enter the average gas price in your area (or the area of your road trip). Again, the *www.fueleconomy.gov* website has links to this type of information.

6. Enter a formula to calculate the gas cost per mile for your car (gas price per gallon/your car's MPG).

7. Now that you have the gas cost per mile for your car, you can figure the cost of the road trip. Enter a formula to figure the gas cost per day (the number of miles * your gas cost per mile) for the first day of the trip. Be sure to use absolute and relative references as appropriate, so you can use AutoFill to copy the formula to the rest of the cells in the *Gas Cost per Day* column.

8. Apply appropriate number formats to all the cells in the workbook that display costs. *Hint:* The Accounting Number Format is best for costs that appear in a column. For costs that appear on their own, you may want to use the Currency Style format.

9. Use the Recommended Charts feature to insert a chart representing either the number of miles driven per day. Change the chart title.

10. Don't forget to spell check the workbook.

11. Save and close the workbook.

projects
fix it **1.6**

Data files for projects can be found by logging into your SIMnet account and going to the Library section.

The workbook for this project tracks how many miles you walked each day for the week of October 6, 2019, through October 12, 2019. Your goal for each day is to walk at least four miles. Use the skills learned in this chapter to fix the workbook.

Skills needed to complete this project:

- Navigating a Workbook (Skill 1.2)
- Working in Protected View (Skill 1.3)
- Entering and Editing Text and Numbers in Cells (Skill 1.4)
- Entering Dates and Applying Date Formats (Skill 1.6)
- Inserting Data Using AutoFill (Skill 1.7)
- Applying Number Formats (Skill 1.5)
- Understanding Absolute and Relative References (Skill 1.11)
- Entering Simple Formulas (Skill 1.10)
- Calculating Totals with the Quick Analysis Tool (Skill 1.14)
- Using AutoSum to Insert a SUM Function (Skill 1.13)
- Using the Recommended Charts Feature (Skill 1.9)
- Exploring Charts (Skill 1.8)
- Checking Spelling (Skill 1.19)

1. Open the start file **EX2019-FixIt-1-6** and resave the file as:
   `[your initials]EX-FixIt-1-6`
2. If the workbook opens in *Protected View*, click the **Enable Editing** button in the *Message Bar* at the top of the workbook so you can modify the workbook.
3. The worksheet is missing a title. Type this title in cell A1: `My Exercise Log`
4. The daily goal should be 3, not 30. Correct the value in cell **D2**.
5. The dates are missing from cells **A6:A11**. Use AutoFill to complete the dates for the rest of the week.
6. The exercise log would be more useful if the date showed the day of the week in addition to the date. Change the date format for cells **A5:A11** so the date displays in in the **long date** format: **Sunday, October 2, 2016**. If your version of Excel does not include the day of the week in the long date format, use the long date format anyway.
7. The mileage for each day should use the Comma Style number format. Correct the number format in cells **C5:C11**.
8. Use one of the skills you learned in this chapter to enter formulas using the **SUM** function in cells **B12** and **C12** to calculate the weekly total minutes and miles.

9. The formulas in the *Under/Over Goal* column are not quite right. Fix the formula in cell **D5** to use an absolute reference where appropriate, and then use AutoFill to replace the formulas in cells **D6:D11**.

10. The worksheet is missing a chart. Use the Recommended Charts feature to insert a clustered column chart representing how many minutes you walked each day. Title the chart: `Minutes Walked per Day`

11. There may be spelling errors. Be sure to use spelling checker before you finish the project.

12. Preview how the worksheet will look when printed.

13. Save and close the workbook.

chapter **2**

Formatting Cells

In this chapter, you will learn the following skills:

- Move and copy cell contents using cut, copy, and paste
- Insert, delete, and merge cells
- Work with text and font attributes
- Apply borders and shading
- Format cells using cell styles
- Copy formatting using Format Painter
- Format cells using conditional formatting
- Modify cell data using find and replace
- Work with the print area

introduction

This chapter focuses on skills for working with cells and cell ranges. You will learn to move data and to insert, delete, and merge cells to create a worksheet structure that fits your data. This chapter also covers the essential skills for formatting cells, including in-depth coverage of conditional formatting. Formatting not only enhances a workbook's appearance, but when used properly, it can make the data easier to understand.

Skill 2.1 Cutting, Copying, and Pasting Cell Content

While you may be familiar with cut, copy, and paste functionality from other applications, keep in mind that in Excel you are working with the cell contents–not the cells themselves. **Cut** removes the content from the selected cell, **Copy** duplicates the content from the selected cell, and **Paste** replaces the cell content with whatever was cut or copied.

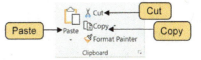

FIGURE EX 2.1

When using *Copy/Paste* or *Cut/Paste* commands in Excel, watch out for cells containing formulas. If you *copy* and paste a cell containing a formula with relative references, Excel will update the references to reflect the new position in the workbook. However, if you *cut* and paste instead, Excel will treat the formula as if it contained absolute references and will not update the cell references in the formula.

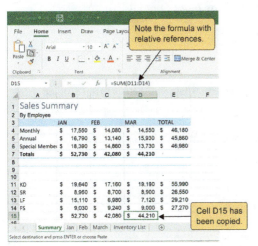

FIGURE EX 2.2

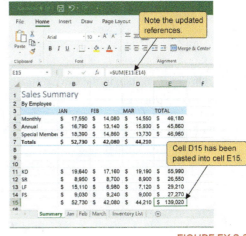

FIGURE EX 2.3

Use the *Cut, Copy,* and *Paste* commands to move or duplicate cell content from one location to another:

1. Select the cell, cell range, row, or column that contains the data you want to move or copy.
2. On the *Home* tab, in the *Clipboard* group, click the **Cut** or **Copy** button.
3. The selection appears with a flashing dotted line around it, and the contents of the cells are stored temporarily in the computer's memory.
4. Click the cell where you want to paste the content. If you selected a range of cells to cut or copy, click the cell in the upper left corner of the area where you want to paste.
5. Click the **Paste** button to paste the cell content and formatting. Notice that if you use the *Cut* command, Excel does not remove the content from its original location until the *Paste* command is used.

tips & tricks

A quick way to move cell content from one location to another is to click and drag with the mouse. Select the cell(s) containing the content you want to move. Place the mouse pointer at the edge of the selection. When the pointer changes to the move pointer, click and drag to the new location, and then release the mouse button.

You can use the same technique to copy cell contents to another location. Press and hold Ctrl to change the move pointer to the copy pointer, drag to the new location, and then release the mouse button.

tell me more

If you paste into a cell that contains data, the original cell data will be overwritten. To paste without overwriting existing cells, use the *Insert Copied Cells* or *Insert Cut Cells* command instead.

1. Copy or cut the cells you want to insert.
2. Select the cell where you want to insert.
3. On the *Home* tab, in the *Cells* group, click the **Insert** button arrow and select **Insert Copied Cells** or **Insert Cut Cells**.

Refer to the skill *Inserting and Deleting Cells* for information about formatting options when using the *Insert* command.

another method

To apply the *Cut*, *Copy*, or *Paste* command, you can also use the following shortcuts:

> **Cut:** Press Ctrl + X, or right-click and select **Cut**.
> **Copy:** Press Ctrl + C, or right-click and select **Copy**.
> **Paste:** Press Ctrl + V, or right-click and select **Paste**.

let me try Live!

Open the student data file **EX2-01-Sales** 📥 and try this skill on your own:

1. On the *Summary* worksheet, copy cell **D15**, and paste to cell **E15**. Note that the formula updated to reflect the new cell range E11:E14.
2. Use the *Cut* and *Paste* commands to move the content in cell **A2** to cell **A10**.
3. If you will be moving on to the next skill in this chapter, leave the workbook open to continue working. If not, save the file as directed by your instructor and close it.

Skill 2.2 Using Paste Options

When you copy and paste data in Excel, you can use the default *Paste* command to paste the copied data (including formulas and formatting) into the selected cell, or you can select from the paste options to control more precisely what is pasted.

	Paste—The default paste command that pastes all of the source content and formatting.
	Formulas—Pastes the formulas but none of the formatting. The pasted content will use the cell and number formatting of the cell into which it was pasted.
	Formulas & Number Formatting—Pastes the formulas and number formatting but none of the cell formatting such as font size, borders, and shading.
	Keep Source Formatting—Pastes the content, including formulas, and all formatting from the source.
	No Borders—Pastes the content, including formulas, and all formatting except borders.
	Keep Source Column Widths—Pastes the copied cell, including formulas and all number and cell formatting. Also adjusts the column width to match the width of the source column.
	Transpose—Pastes the rows from the source into columns, and the columns from the source into rows.

When your source includes formulas, you have the option to paste the calculated cell values without pasting the underlying formulas.

	Values—Pastes only the values, not the underlying formula or cell formatting.
	Values & Number Formatting—Pastes only the values, not the underlying formulas. Includes number formatting but not other cell formatting such as borders and shading.
	Values & Source Formatting—Pastes only the values, not the underlying formulas. Includes all formatting from the source.

The final group of paste options provides alternatives to pasting the actual contents of one cell into another.

	Formatting—Pastes only the cell and number formatting, not the formula or cell value from the source.
	Paste Link—Pastes a formula that references the source cell rather than pasting the contents of the source itself. When the source cell is updated, the linked cell displays the update automatically.
	Picture—Pastes an image of the source cell rather than the actual cell contents. The pasted cell looks like any other cell in the worksheet, except it cannot be edited, and when you select the cell, nothing appears in the formula bar.
	Linked Picture—Pastes an image, like the Picture paste option, but updates when the source cell is updated.

To use paste options from the *Paste* button on the Ribbon:

1. Copy the content you want to paste and then navigate to the location where you want to paste.

2. On the *Home* tab, in the *Clipboard* group, click the bottom part of the **Paste** button (the **Paste** button arrow) to expand the *Paste Options* menu.

3. Move your mouse over the icon for each paste option to see a live preview of how the paste would look, and then click the paste option you want.

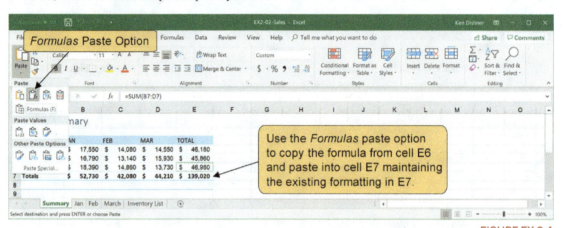

Use the *Formulas* paste option to copy the formula from cell E6 and paste into cell E7 maintaining the existing formatting in E7.

FIGURE EX 2.4

To use the *Paste Options* button:

1. Copy the content you want to paste.

2. Use the standard *Paste* command to paste the content where you want it.

3. The source content is pasted using the default *Paste* option, and the *Paste Options* button appears at the lower right corner of the pasted content.

4. Click the **Paste Options** button or press Ctrl to display the *Paste Options* menu. This is the same menu that is available from the *Paste* button on the Ribbon, but moving your mouse over the icons does not show a preview of how the paste would look.

5. Click the paste option you want.

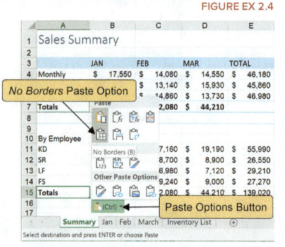

FIGURE EX 2.5

tips & tricks

A useful paste option is *Keep Source Column Widths*. Often, when you paste data into a new worksheet, the default column width is too narrow to display the data. Use the *Keep Source Column Widths* paste option to maintain any column width adjustments you made in the source worksheet.

tell me more

Additional paste options are available from the *Paste Special* dialog. To open the *Paste Special* dialog, select **Paste Special...** from the bottom of the paste options from the *Paste* button on the Ribbon or from the right-click menu.

another method

You can also access the paste options from the right-click menu. Six of the paste options appear on the right-click menu (*Paste, Values, Formulas, Transpose, Formatting,* and *Paste Link*). To select an option from the full *Paste Options* menu, point to **Paste Special...**, and then click the paste option you want.

let me try Live!

If you do not have the data file from the previous skill open, open the student data file **EX2-02-Sales** 📥 and try this skill on your own:

1. On the *Summary* worksheet, copy cell **E6** and paste only the formula to cell **E7**. Do not paste the original cell formatting.
2. Copy cell **A7** and paste the cell value and formatting without borders into cell **A15**.
3. If you will be moving on to the next skill in this chapter, leave the workbook open to continue working. If not, save the file as directed by your instructor and close it.

Skill 2.3 Inserting and Deleting Cells

Use the *Insert* command to insert an empty cell, group of cells, row, or column into your worksheet.

To insert an empty cell range, select the range where you want to insert the new cells.

1. If you have a vertical cell range selected, click the **Insert** button and Excel will automatically shift existing cells to the right to make room for the new cells.
2. If you have a single cell or a horizontal cell range selected, click the **Insert** button and Excel will automatically shift existing cells down to make room for the new cells.

If you want more control over whether cells are shifted to the right or down, use the *Insert* dialog.

1. Select the cell or cell range where you want to insert the new cell(s).
2. On the *Home* tab, in the *Cells* group, click the **Insert** button arrow.
3. Click **Insert Cells...** to open the *Insert* dialog.
4. Select the option you want and then click **OK**.

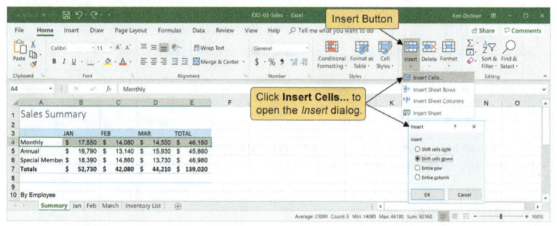

FIGURE EX 2.6

Recall that in Excel, pasting cell content that has been cut or copied will overwrite the content of the cell where it is pasted. If you want to insert the content instead, use the *Insert* command.

1. Cut or copy the cell content and then click the cell where you want to insert the new content.
2. On the *Home* tab, in the *Cells* group, click the **Insert** button arrow.
3. Instead of the *Insert Cells...* option, you now have *Insert Cut Cells* or *Insert Copied Cells*. Select this option to insert new cells with the cut or copied content. These commands are only available immediately after using the *Cut* or *Copy* command.

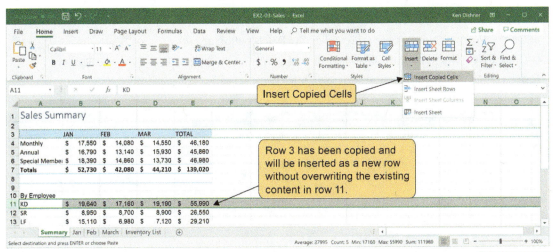

FIGURE EX 2.7

When you insert new cells, the cells will use the same formatting as the cells above (if you shifted cells down) or to the left (if you shifted cells to the right). If you want to use formatting from the cells below or to the right instead, or to insert the cells with no formatting, click the **Insert Options** button that appears at the lower right of the insertion and make a selection from the menu options.

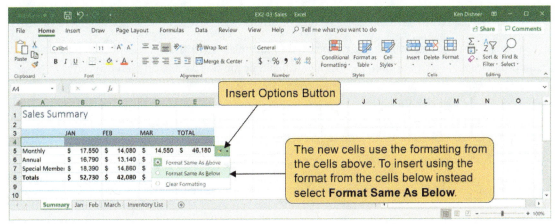

FIGURE EX 2.8

Of course, you can also delete cells. Deleting cells not only deletes the information and formatting in the cell, but also shifts the layout of the worksheet. Even if you delete an empty cell, you shift all the surrounding cells into new positions.

1. If you have a vertical cell range selected, click the **Delete** button and Excel will automatically shift existing cells to the left.
2. If you have a single cell or a horizontal cell range selected, click the **Insert** button and Excel will automatically shift existing cells up.

If you want more control over how the remaining cells are shifted, use the *Delete* dialog.

1. On the *Home* tab, in the *Cells* group, click the **Delete** button arrow.
2. Click **Delete Cells...** to open the *Delete* dialog.
3. Select the option you want and then click **OK**.

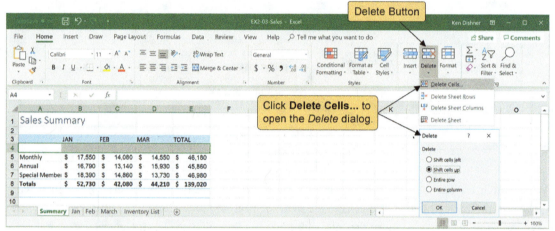

FIGURE EX 2.9

tips & tricks

Be careful not to delete cells that are referenced in formulas. Even though a new value may shift into the original cell's position, the formula will still be looking for the original cell (now deleted), causing an invalid cell reference error.

another method

Both *Insert...* and *Delete...* commands are available from the right-click menu.

Pressing ⌨Delete will delete the contents of the cell but not the cell itself.

let me try Live!

If you do not have the data file from the previous skill open, open the student data file **EX2-03-Sales** and try this skill on your own:

1. On the *Summary* worksheet, select cells **A4:E4**.
2. Insert cells so the remaining cells shift down.
3. Display the *Insert Options* menu and select the option to format the new cells the same as those below.
4. Delete cells **A4:E4**, shifting the remaining cells up.
5. Copy row **3** and insert a copy above row **11**.
6. If you will be moving on to the next skill in this chapter, leave the workbook open to continue working. If not, save the file as directed by your instructor and close it.

Skill 2.4 Wrapping Text in Cells

When you type text in a cell, the text will appear to continue to the right as far as it can until there is another cell that contains data. At that point, the text will appear to be cut off. You could increase the width of the cell to show all the text, but do you really want the entire column to be that wide? If your worksheet includes cells with more text than will comfortably fit in the cell, you should use the wrap text feature. When wrap text is enabled for a cell, the text in the cell will automatically wrap to multiple lines, just as a paragraph would.

To wrap text in a cell:

On the *Home* tab, in the *Alignment* group, click the **Wrap Text** button. Notice the button appears selected when text wrapping is active for the cell.

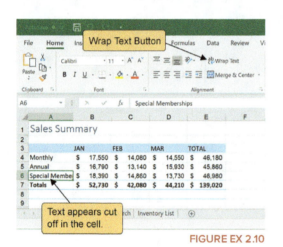

FIGURE EX 2.10

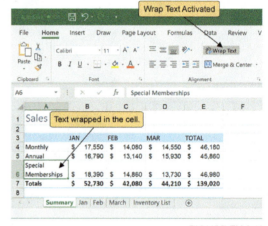

FIGURE EX 2.11

To turn off text wrapping in a cell, click the **Wrap Text** button again to deselect it.

tips & tricks

The text wrapping feature works only for cells that contain text. If a column is too narrow to display its numerical data, Excel will not wrap it. Instead, the cell will show a series of # symbols, indicating that the cell contains numerical data, but the column is too narrow to display it.

another method

You can also turn on the text wrapping feature from the *Format Cells* dialog.

1. On the *Home* tab, in the *Alignment* group, click the **Alignment Settings dialog launcher** to open the *Format Cells* dialog.
2. In the *Text control* section, click the **Wrap text** check box.
3. Click **OK**.

let me try Live!

If you do not have the data file from the previous skill open, open the student data file **EX2-04-Sales** and try this skill on your own:

1. On the *Summary* worksheet, activate text wrapping for cell **A6**.
2. If you will be moving on to the next skill in this chapter, leave the workbook open to continue working. If not, save the file as directed by your instructor and close it.

Skill 2.5 Using Undo and Redo

If you make a mistake when working, the **Undo** command allows you to reverse the last action you performed. The **Redo** command allows you to reverse the *Undo* command and restore the file to its previous state. The Quick Access Toolbar gives you immediate access to both these commands.

To undo the last action taken, click the **Undo** button on the Quick Access Toolbar.

To redo the last action taken, click the **Redo** button on the Quick Access Toolbar.

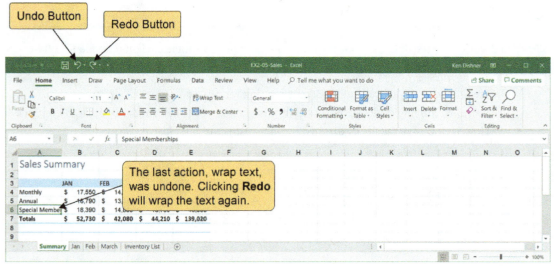

FIGURE EX 2.12

To undo multiple actions at the same time:

1. Click the **Undo** button arrow to expand the list of your most recent actions.
2. Click an action in the list.
3. The action you click will be undone, along with all the actions completed after that. In other words, your workbook will revert to the state it was in before that action.

tips & tricks

Be careful when using the *Undo* and *Redo* commands in Excel. In other Office applications, undo and redo actions are confined to the file you are currently working on–even if you have multiple files open. However, in Excel, the undo-redo list of actions includes all the open workbooks. This means that if you are working on multiple Excel files at the same time, using the *Undo* command can actually undo an action in one of the other open workbooks.

another method

> ❯ To undo an action, you can also press ☐Ctrl☐ + ☐Z☐.
> ❯ To redo an action, you can also press ☐Ctrl☐ + ☐Y☐.

let me try Live!

If you do not have the data file from the previous skill open, open the student data file **EX2-05-Sales** 📥 and try this skill on your own:

1. Undo the last action.
2. Redo the last action.
3. If you will be moving on to the next skill in this chapter, leave the workbook open to continue working. If not, save the file as directed by your instructor and close it.

Skill 2.6 Aligning Cells

Alignment refers to how text and numbers are positioned within the cell both horizontally and vertically. By default, cells use the **General horizontal alignment**. When cells are formatted using the General horizontal alignment, Excel detects the type of content in the cell. Cells that contain text are aligned to the left, and cells that contain numbers are aligned to the right.

To change the horizontal alignment of a cell, click one of the horizontal alignment buttons located on the *Home* tab, in the *Alignment* group: **Align Left**, **Center**, or **Align Right**.

To change the vertical alignment of a cell, click one of the vertical alignment buttons located on the *Home* tab, in the *Alignment* group: **Top Align**, **Middle Align**, or **Bottom Align**.

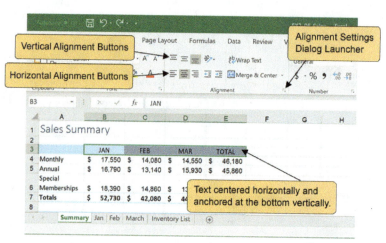

FIGURE EX 2.13

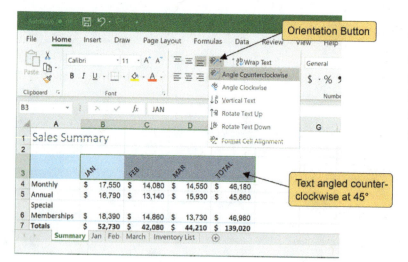

You can also change the angle at which the content displays. On the *Home* tab, in the *Alignment* group, click the **Orientation** button and select one of the options.

FIGURE EX 2.14

The alignment and orientation options are also available from the *Format Cells* dialog, *Alignment* tab. To change alignment using the *Format Cells* dialog:

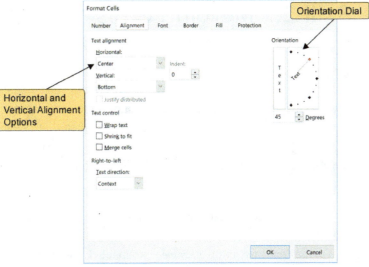

FIGURE EX 2.15

1. Click the **Alignment Settings dialog launcher** at the lower right corner of the *Alignment* group.
2. The *Format Cells* dialog opens to the *Alignment* tab.
3. In the *Text alignment* section, select the options you want from the **Horizontal** and **Vertical** drop-down lists.
4. In the *Orientation* section, change the angle of rotation by clicking one of the dots on the *Orientation* dial, by clicking and dragging the *Orientation* dial to the position you want, or by entering the specific degree of rotation in the *Degrees* box.
5. Click **OK**.

tips & tricks

If you have narrow columns of data with descriptive headers, try using one of the orientation options to angle the cells containing the header text.

let me try Live!

If you do not have the data file from the previous skill open, open the student data file **EX2-06-Sales** and try this skill on your own:

1. On the *Summary* worksheet, select cells **B3:E3**.
2. Center the content in each cell horizontally.
3. Change the angle of rotation for these cells to counterclockwise at 45°.
4. If you will be moving on to the next skill in this chapter, leave the workbook open to continue working. If not, save the file as directed by your instructor and close it.

Skill 2.7 Merging Cells and Splitting Merged Cells

Merging cells is one way to control the appearance of your worksheet. You can merge cells to create a header cell across multiple columns of data or center a title across your worksheet. The *Merge & Center* button automatically merges the selected cells and then centers the data from the first cell across the entire merged area. When you merge cells together, Excel will keep only the data in the uppermost left cell. All other data will be lost.

To merge cells and center their content:

1. Select the cells you want to merge, making sure the text you want to keep is in the uppermost left cell.
2. On the *Home* tab, in the *Alignment* group, click the **Merge & Center** button.

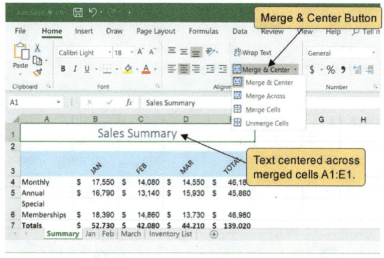

FIGURE EX 2.16

Click the *Merge & Center* button arrow for additional merge commands:

Merge Across—lets you merge cells in multiple rows without merging the rows together. The cells in each row are merged together, keeping the data in the leftmost cell in each row, while still keeping each row separate.

Merge Cells—lets you merge cells together without centering the data. Like the *Merge & Center* command, *Merge Cells* combines all the selected cells into one cell, keeping only the data in the uppermost left cell.

Unmerge Cells—splits a merged cell back into its original cells.

You can also merge and center cells from the *Format Cells* dialog:

1. On the *Home* tab, in the *Alignment* group, click the **Alignment Settings dialog launcher** to open the *Format Cells* dialog.
2. On the *Alignment* tab, in the *Text alignment* section, click the **Horizontal** arrow and select **Center** from the dropdown list. (You can also select **Center Across Selection**. When you merge the cells, it does not matter if the horizontal alignment is *Center* or *Center Across Selection.*)
3. In the *Text control* section, click the **Merge cells** check box.
4. Click **OK**.

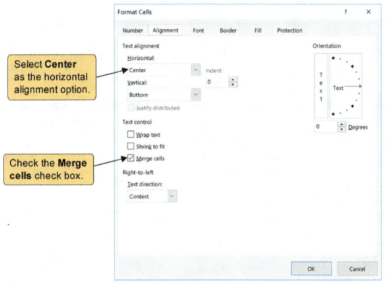

FIGURE EX 2.17

To unmerge a merged cell, use one of these methods:

> On the *Home* tab, in the *Alignment* group, click the **Merge & Center** button. When the selected cell is a merged cell, clicking the *Merge & Center* button will undo the merge and reset the horizontal alignment to *General.*

> On the *Home* tab, in the *Alignment* group, click the **Merge & Center** button arrow and select **Unmerge Cells**.

> In the *Format Cells* dialog, on the *Alignment* tab, in the *Text alignment* section, the *Text control* section, click the **Merge cells** check box to uncheck it.

tips & tricks

You cannot split cells in Excel. You can unmerge a merged cell back into its original cells, but you cannot split a single cell into two new columns or two new rows (like you can with a table in Word or PowerPoint). However, if you have a column of data that you would like to split across multiple cells, you can use the *Text to Columns* command (on the *Data* tab, in the *Data Tools* group).

let me try Live!

If you do not have the data file from the previous skill open, open the student data file **EX2-07-Sales** ⬇ and try this skill on your own:

1. On the *Summary* worksheet, select cells **A1:E1**.
2. Merge the cells so the text appears centered across the merged cells.
3. On the *Jan* worksheet, cells **A1:D1** have been merged and centered. Unmerge them.
4. If you will be moving on to the next skill in this chapter, leave the workbook open to continue working. If not, save the file as instructed by your instructor and close it.

Skill 2.8 Applying Bold, Italic, and Underline

You may be familiar with using bold, italic, and underline formatting to emphasize text in a Word document or a PowerPoint presentation. You can use these same techniques in Excel to emphasize cells in your workbook.

To apply bold, italic, and underline formatting:

1. Select a cell or cell range to apply the formatting to all the content in the cell(s). To apply formatting to only part of the content in a cell, double-click the cell to enter Edit mode, and then select the text you want to apply the formatting to.
2. On the *Home* tab, in the *Font* group, click the appropriate button to apply formatting to the selected cell(s).

FIGURE EX 2.18

When a cell includes bold, italic, or underline formatting, the applicable buttons appear highlighted on the Ribbon. To remove the formatting, click the highlighted button.

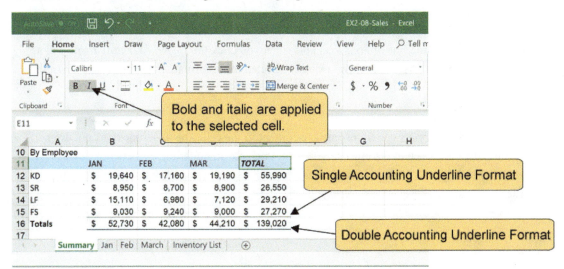

FIGURE EX 2.19

Underline styles used in accounting spreadsheets are slightly different from "regular" underline styles. If you need to apply the accounting style of underline or double underline, do not use the *Underline* button on the Ribbon. Instead, use one of the accounting underline options from the *Format Cells* dialog:

1. On the *Home* tab, in the *Font* group, click the **Font Settings dialog launcher** to open the *Format Cells* dialog.
2. On the *Font* tab, in the *Underline* section, expand the **Underline** list and select **Single Accounting** or **Double Accounting**.
3. Click **OK**.

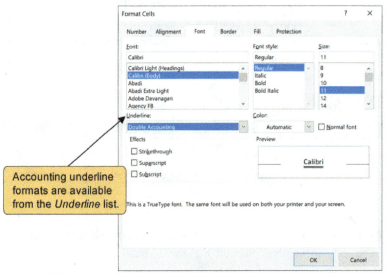

FIGURE EX 2.20

The single and double underline options available when you click the *Underline* button arrow will apply the accounting underline styles only if you recently selected those formats from the *Format Cells* dialog.

tips & tricks

The cell underline formats underline only the content in the cell. The underline does not extend from one edge of the cell to the other. If you want to create an underline that extends across a range of cells without a break in between, use a border instead. (For more information about borders, refer to the skill *Adding Borders*.)

another method

When you right-click a cell, the *Bold* and *Italic* buttons are available on the Mini toolbar.

Bold, italic, and underline font styles are available from the *Format Cells* dialog, *Font* tab. You can also use the keyboard shortcuts:

> Bold: Ctrl + B
> Italic: Ctrl + I
> Underline: Ctrl + U

let me try Live!

If you do not have the data file from the previous skill open, open the student data file **EX2-08-Sales** and try this skill on your own:

1. On the *Summary* worksheet, select cell **E11** and apply **bold** and **italic** formatting.
2. Remove just the **bold** formatting.
3. Select cells **B15:E15** and apply the **Single Accounting** underline format.
4. Select cells **B16:E16** and apply the **Double Accounting** underline format.
5. If you will be moving on to the next skill in this chapter, leave the workbook open to continue working. If not, save the file as directed by your instructor and close it.

Skill 2.9 Changing Fonts, Font Size, and Font Color

A **font**, or typeface, refers to a set of characters of a certain design. The font is the shape of a character or number as it appears on-screen or when printed. Use the commands from the *Home* tab, *Font* group to change font attributes such as font family, font size, and font color.

> To change the font, click the **Font** box arrow to expand the list of available fonts, and then select the font you want.
> To change the font size, click the **Font Size** box arrow and select the size you want.
> To change the font color, click the **Font Color** button arrow to expand the color palette, and then select the color you want.

FIGURE EX 2.21

The font color palette is divided into three parts:

1. The top part shows the *Automatic* color choice (black or white, depending on the color of the background).
2. The middle part shows the *Theme Colors* included in the theme that is applied to the workbook. These colors are designed to work together.
3. The bottom part of the palette shows the *Standard Colors* (dark red, red, orange, etc.). These colors are always available, no matter what theme is in use.

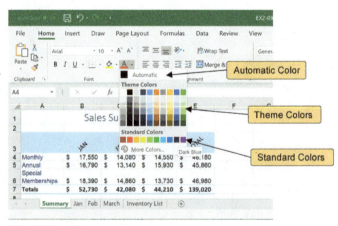

FIGURE EX 2.22

You can also change the font, font size, and font color from the *Format Cells* dialog:

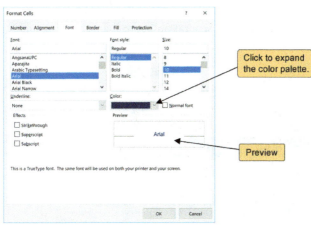

FIGURE EX 2.23

1. On the *Home* tab, in the *Font* group, click the **Font Settings dialog launcher** to open the *Format Cells* dialog.
2. On the *Font* tab, make the font and size selections you want.
3. In the *Color* section, click the arrow to expand the color palette, and then click a color. The color palette from the Ribbon and in the *Format Cells* dialog is the same.
4. Review the sample text in the *Preview* box to see how your choices will look.
5. Click **OK** to apply the changes.

tell me more

You can pick a custom color by clicking **More Colors...** from the bottom of the font color palette.

another method

You can also change the font, font size, or font color by right-clicking and making the font, font size, and font color selections you want from the Mini toolbar.

let me try Live!

If you do not have the data file from the previous skill open, open the student data file **EX2-09-Sales** and try this skill on your own:

1. On the *Summary* worksheet, select cells **A4:A6**.
2. Change the font to **Arial**.
3. Change the font size to **10**.
4. Change the font color to **Dark Blue** (in the row of standard colors, the second color from the right).
5. If you will be moving on to the next skill in this chapter, leave the workbook open to continue working. If not, save the file as directed by your instructor and close it.

Skill 2.10 Adding Borders

Add borders to your workbook to emphasize a cell or group of cells. Use borders to make your workbook look more like a desktop publishing form or to show separation between a column of values and the total row.

FIGURE EX 2.24

To add borders to your workbook:

1. Select the cell(s) you want to add a border to.
2. On the *Home* tab, in the *Font* group, click the **Borders** button arrow and select the border style you want.

To remove borders:

1. Select the cell(s) you want to remove the borders from.
2. On the *Home* tab, in the *Font* group, click the **Borders** button arrow and select **No Border** from the list of border styles.

For more control over the look of cell borders, select **More Borders...** from the *Borders* menu to open the *Format Cells* dialog. From the *Border* tab, you can specify the line style and color for the border.

You can also see a preview of how the border will look.

1. On the *Home* tab, in the *Font* group, click the **Borders** button arrow and select **More Borders...** from the list of border styles.
2. Select a line style from the *Style* section.
3. Expand the **Color** palette and select a color.
4. To add borders around the outside or inside the selected cells, click the appropriate button(s) in the *Presets* section.
5. In the *Border* section, add a border line by clicking the button representing the location of the border or by clicking directly in the area of the preview image where you want the border to appear.
6. Click **OK**.

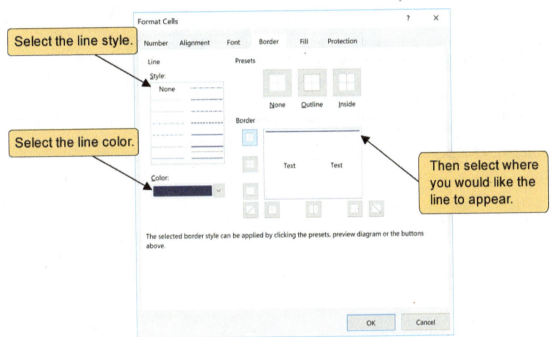

FIGURE EX 2.25

tips & tricks

A properly formatted spreadsheet for accounting purposes should use the cell underline formatting instead of borders on total rows. However, most non-accountant Excel users favor borders above and below total rows instead of using cell underlining.

another method

The *Borders* button displays the most recently used border style. If you want to reuse this style, you can just click the button. You do not need to reselect the border style from the menu again.

The *Borders* button is also available from the Mini toolbar when you right-click a cell.

let me try Live!

If you do not have the data file from the previous skill open, open the student data file **EX2-10-Sales** 📥 and try this skill on your own:

1. On the *Summary* worksheet, select cells **A9:E9** and remove the borders.
2. If necessary, remove the underline formatting from cells **B15:E16**.
3. Apply the **Top and Double Bottom Border** to cells **A16:E16**.
4. Add a **Dark Blue** (in the row of standard colors, the second color from the right) top border to cells **A10:E10**. Use the thickest single line style available.
5. If you will be moving on to the next skill in this chapter, leave the workbook open to continue working. If not, save the file as directed by your instructor and close it.

Skill 2.11 Adding Shading with Fill Color

Another way to emphasize cells in your workbook is to use a **fill color** to change the background color of cells. Fill colors are available in a variety of shades to make it easy to read the cell content. Shading is often used to differentiate alternating rows in a large table or to make the heading row stand out. To add shading to your workbook:

1. Select the cell(s) you want to add shading to.
2. On the *Home* tab, in the *Font* group, click the **Fill Color** button arrow to display the color palette. The color palette includes colors from the workbook theme as well as a row of standard colors along the bottom. Notice that as you hold the mouse over each color in the palette, a tool tip appears displaying the color name.
3. Click the color you want.

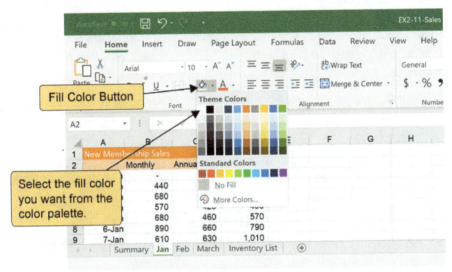

FIGURE EX 2.26

To remove shading:

1. Select the cell(s) you want to remove shading from.
2. On the *Home* tab, in the *Font* group, click the **Fill Color** button arrow to display the color palette.
3. Click **No Fill** to remove the fill color from the selected cells.

tips & tricks

> Avoid overusing shading and using too many colors in your workbook. Shading should be used for emphasis and to make the workbook easier to read, not to make the workbook more colorful.
> If you use a dark color for shading, change the font color to white or another light color.

tell me more

In the *Format Cells* dialog, options for fill effects and pattern styles are available under the *Fill* tab.

another method

Like the *Borders* button, the *Fill Color* button displays the most recently used shading color. If you want to reuse this color, just click the button. You do not need to reselect the color from the Fill Color palette.

The *Fill Color* button is also available from the Mini toolbar when you right-click a cell.

let me try Live!

If you do not have the data file from the previous skill open, open the student data file **EX2-11-Sales** and try this skill on your own:

1. On the *Summary* worksheet, select cells **A11:E11** and remove the fill color.
2. On the *Jan* worksheet, select cells **A2:D2** and apply the **Orange, Accent 2, Lighter 60%** fill color (in the third row of theme colors, the fifth color from the right).
3. If you will be moving on to the next skill in this chapter, leave the workbook open to continue working. If not, save the file as directed by your instructor and close it.

from the perspective of . . .

HEALTH CLUB OFFICE MANAGER

I use Excel to prepare financial reports for the club owners and their accountant. Proper formatting makes it easier for the owners to read the reports. I would never submit a report without checking for text that appears cut off or titles that aren't centered across columns. And I always use the accounting underline formats instead of borders in my financial reports. Our accountant insists on it!

Skill 2.12 Applying Cell Styles

A **cell style** is a combination of effects that can be applied at one time. Styles can include formatting such as borders, fill color, font size, and number formatting.

Excel includes an extensive gallery of prebuilt cell styles. You can use these styles to help visualize your data by consistently applying them to your worksheet. Use text styles such as *Title* for the title of your worksheet and *Calculation* and *Input* to highlight cells used in formulas. The *Total* style applies borders and font formatting appropriate for a total row in a table.

To apply a cell style:

1. Select the cell(s) you want to apply the style to.
2. On the *Home* tab, in the *Styles* group, click the **Cell Styles** button.
3. Click the style you want to apply to your cell(s).

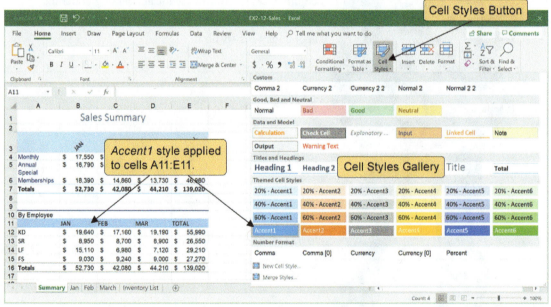

FIGURE EX 2.27

tips & tricks

If you have Live Preview enabled, you can move your mouse over each style in the *Cell Styles* gallery to see a preview of how that style would look applied to your worksheet.

let me try Live!

If you do not have the data file from the previous skill open, open the student data file **EX2-12-Sales** and try this skill on your own:

1. On the *Summary* worksheet, select cells **A11:E11** and apply the **Accent1** cell style.
2. Select cells **A16:E16** and apply the **Total** style.
3. If you will be moving on to the next skill in this chapter, leave the workbook open to continue working. If not, save the file as directed by your instructor and close it.

Skill 2.13 Using Format Painter

A professional, well-organized workbook uses consistent formatting. Use the **Format Painter** tool to copy formatting from one part of your worksheet to another, rather than trying to re-create the exact combination of font color and size, number formatting, borders, and shading to reuse.

To use *Format Painter*:

1. Begin with a cell that has the formatting you want.
2. On the *Home* tab, in the *Clipboard* group, click the **Format Painter** button to copy the cell formatting.
3. Notice that your mouse pointer changes to the Format Painter shape 🖌. Click a cell to apply the formatting or click and drag to apply the formatting to a range of cells.

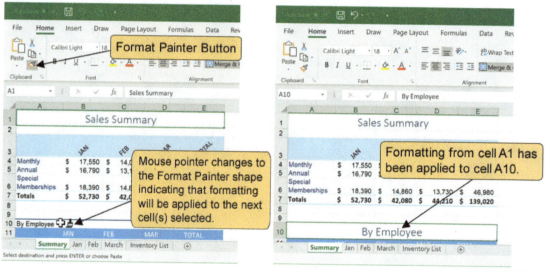

FIGURE EX 2.28

tell me more

If you want to apply the formatting to different parts of a worksheet or workbook, double-click the **Format Painter** button when you select it. It will stay on until you click the **Format Painter** button again or press **Esc** to deselect it.

another method

To activate *Format Painter*, you can also right-click the cell with formatting you want to copy and click the **Format Painter** button on the Mini toolbar.

let me try Live!

If you do not have the data file from the previous skill open, open the student data file **EX2-13-Sales** ⏶ and try this skill on your own:

1. On the *Summary* worksheet, use **Format Painter** to copy the formatting from cell **A1** and apply it to cell **A10**.
2. If you will be moving on to the next skill in this chapter, leave the workbook open to continue working. If not, save the file as directed by your instructor and close it.

Skill 2.14 Applying Conditional Formatting Using the Quick Analysis Tool

Conditional formatting provides a visual analysis of data by applying formatting to cells based on their values. Excel offers a wide variety of conditional formatting options from the *Conditional Formatting* menu (available on the *Home* tab, in the *Styles* group).

> Data bars, color scales, and icon sets display a visual representation comparing all cell values in the selection.

> *Highlight Cells Rules* highlight only cells that meet specific criteria (conditions).

> *Top/Bottom Rules* highlight cells that have the highest or lowest values compared to other cells in the selection.

If you're not sure which conditional formatting option is best for the selected data, use the Quick Analysis tool. The Quick Analysis tool detects whether you've selected numerical or text data and displays only the conditional formatting options appropriate for each type of data. From the Quick Analysis tool, you can also preview conditional formatting before applying it to your data.

To apply conditional formatting with the Quick Analysis tool:

1. Select the cells to which you want to apply conditional formatting.
2. Click the **Quick Analysis** tool button at the lower right corner of the selection.
3. Notice that Live Preview displays the effect of the conditional formatting on your data as you hover the mouse pointer over each of the formatting options. Review each formatting option before making your selection.
4. Click the button for the type of conditional formatting you want to apply.

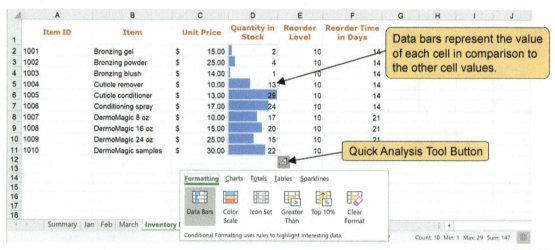

FIGURE EX 2.29

tips & tricks

You should resist the temptation to overuse conditional formatting. Conditional formatting should be used to highlight important data or data trends, not to colorize the entire worksheet.

tell me more

Some types of conditional formatting apply formatting to all the cells in the selection and are applied automatically when you click the button in the Quick Analysis tool. Other types require a comparison value and will open a dialog where you can specify the value for the rule and select formatting options.

another method

You can press Ctrl + Q to open the Quick Analysis tool instead of clicking the *Quick Analysis* tool button.

let me try Live!

If you do not have the data file from the previous skill open, open the student data file **EX2-14-Sales** and try this skill on your own:

1. On the *Inventory List* worksheet, select cells **D2:D11** and apply the **Data Bars** conditional formatting option from the Quick Analysis tool.
2. If you will be moving on to the next skill in this chapter, leave the workbook open to continue working. If not, save the file as directed by your instructor and close it.

from the perspective of . . .

HELP DESK COORDINATOR

I love conditional formatting! Every week, each department sends me a spreadsheet of all the help desk calls for each software package we support. I use color scales to identify the software packages with the highest volume of calls. In my spreadsheet that combines the weekly data, I use icon sets to indicate whether the number of calls went up or down for each software package on a week-by-week basis.

Skill 2.15 Applying Conditional Formatting with Data Bars, Color Scales, and Icon Sets

Data bars, colors scales, and icon sets can be used to visually represent the value of each cell relative to the other cells in the data selection. These types of conditional formatting apply formatting to all the selected cells.

Data Bars—Display a color bar (gradient or solid) representing the cell value in comparison to other values (cells with higher values have longer data bars).

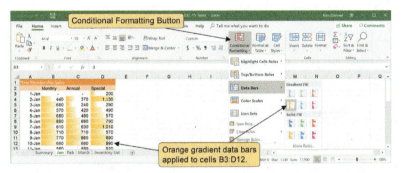

FIGURE EX 2.30

Color Scales—Color the cells according to one of the color scales (e.g., red to green [bad/low to good/high] or blue to red [cold/low to hot/high]).

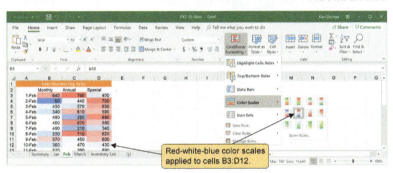

FIGURE EX 2.31

Icon Sets—Display a graphic in the cell representing the cell value in relation to other values.

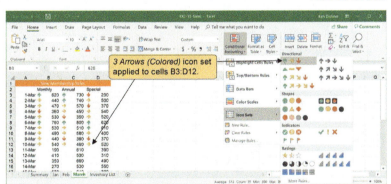

FIGURE EX 2.32

To apply conditional formatting using data bars, color scales, or icon sets:

1. Select the data you want to apply conditional formatting to.
2. On the *Home* tab, in the *Styles* group, click the **Conditional Formatting** button.
3. From the menu, point to **Data Bars**, **Colors Scales**, or **Icon Sets**, and then click the specific style of formatting you want. Notice that Live Preview displays the effect of the conditional formatting on your data as you hover the mouse pointer over each of the formatting options.

let me try Live!

If you do not have the data file from the previous skill open, open the student data file **EX2-15-Sales** and try this skill on your own:

1. On the *Jan* worksheet, select cells **B3:D12** and apply conditional formatting using the **orange gradient fill data bar**.
2. On the *Feb* worksheet, select cells **B3:D12** and apply conditional formatting using the **Red-White-Blue color scale**.
3. On the *March* worksheet, select cells **B3:D12** and apply conditional formatting using the **3 Arrows (Colored)** icon set (the first icon set in the *Directional* section).
4. If you will be moving on to the next skill in this chapter, leave the workbook open to continue working. If not, save the file as directed by your instructor and close it.

Skill 2.16 Applying Conditional Formatting with Highlight Cells Rules

Conditional formatting with **Highlight Cells Rules** allows you to define formatting for cells that meet specific numerical or text criteria (e.g., greater than a specific value or containing a specific text string). Use this type of conditional formatting when you want to highlight cells based on criteria you define.

To apply *Highlight Cells Rules*:

1. Select the data you want to apply conditional formatting to.
2. On the *Home* tab, in the *Styles* group, click the **Conditional Formatting** button.
3. From the menu, point to **Highlight Cells Rules**, and click the option you want.
4. Each option opens a dialog where you can enter a value or date to which the value of each cell will be compared. The default formatting is light red fill with dark red text. To change the formatting, expand the dropdown list in the dialog and select another option.
5. Click **OK** to apply the conditional formatting.

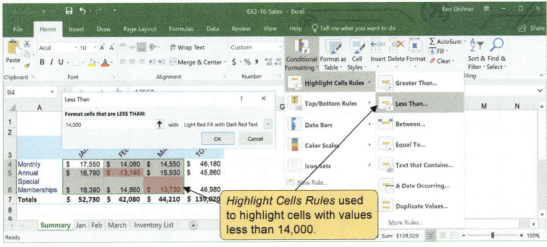

FIGURE EX 2.33

tips & tricks

The *Highlight Cells Rules* menu includes an option to highlight duplicate values. This option can be especially helpful when you are trying to find a potential data entry error in a long list of values.

let me try Live!

If you do not have the data file from the previous skill open, open the student data file **EX2-16-Sales** ⬇ and try this skill on your own:

1. On the *Summary* worksheet, select cells **B4:D6** and apply conditional formatting so cells with a value **less than 14,000** are formatted using a light red fill with dark red text.
2. If you will be moving on to the next skill in this chapter, leave the workbook open to continue working. If not, save the file as directed by your instructor and close it.

Skill 2.17 Applying Conditional Formatting with Top/Bottom Rules

One way to analyze worksheet data is to compare cell values to other cell values. When analyzing a worksheet, you may want to highlight the highest or lowest values or values that are above or below the average. In these cases, use conditional formatting **Top/Bottom Rules**. When you use *Top/Bottom Rules*, Excel automatically finds the highest, lowest, and average values to compare values to, rather than asking you to enter criteria (as you do when using *Highlight Cells Rules*).

To highlight cells with conditional formatting *Top/Bottom Rules*:

1. Select the data you want to apply conditional formatting to.
2. On the *Home* tab, in the *Styles* group, click the **Conditional Formatting** button.
3. From the menu, point to **Top/Bottom Rules**, and click the option you want.
4. Each option opens a dialog where you can select the formatting to apply when cells meet the condition. The top and bottom options allow you to modify the threshold to a value other than 10 (top/bottom 10 items and top/bottom 10%).
5. Click **OK** to apply the conditional formatting.

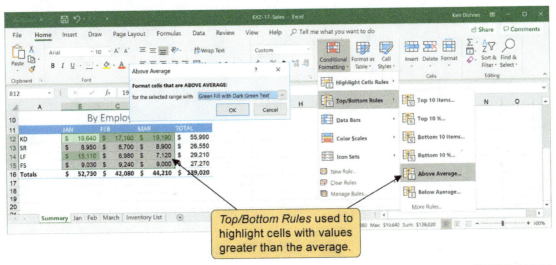

Top/Bottom Rules used to highlight cells with values greater than the average.

FIGURE EX 2.34

let me try Live!

If you do not have the data file from the previous skill open, open the student data file **EX2-17-Sales** and try this skill on your own:

1. On the *Summary* worksheet, select cells **B12:D15** and apply conditional formatting so cells with a value **greater than the average** are formatted using a green fill with dark green text.
2. If you will be moving on to the next skill in this chapter, leave the workbook open to continue working. If not, save the file as directed by your instructor and close it.

Skill 2.18 Removing Conditional Formatting

You cannot remove conditional formatting from cells by clearing the data or pressing $\boxed{\text{Delete}}$ or $\boxed{\text{Backspace}}$. Instead, you must remove the conditional formatting rule from the cells.

To remove conditional formatting:

1. On the *Home* tab, in the *Styles* group, click the **Conditional Formatting** button.
2. Point to **Clear Rules**, and click the option you want from the menu: **Clear Rules from Selected Cells, Clear Rules from Entire Sheet, Clear Rules from This Table** (available if the selected cells are part of a table), or **Clear Rules from This PivotTable** (available if the selected cells are part of a PivotTable).

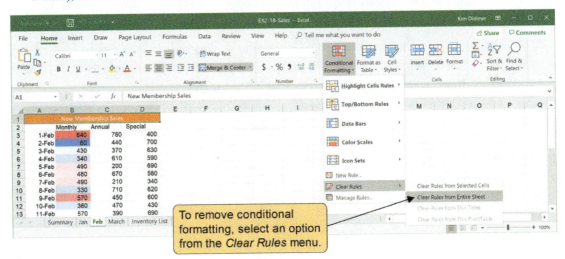

To remove conditional formatting, select an option from the *Clear Rules* menu.

FIGURE EX 2.35

tell me more

Through the Conditional Formatting Rules Manager, you can view all of your conditional formatting rules at one time and add, modify, or delete rules. Open the Conditional Formatting Rules Manager from the *Manage Rules...* option at the bottom of the *Conditional Formatting* menu.

another method

You can also clear conditional formatting from the Quick Analysis tool:

1. Select the cells from which you want to remove conditional formatting.
2. Click the **Quick Analysis** tool button at the lower right corner of the selection, and click the **Clear Format** button.

let me try Live!

If you do not have the data file from the previous skill open, open the student data file **EX2-18-Sales** and try this skill on your own:

1. Go to the *Feb* worksheet and clear the conditional formatting rules from this worksheet.
2. If you will be moving on to the next skill in this chapter, leave the workbook open to continue working. If not, save the file as directed by your instructor and close it.

Skill **2.19** Clearing Cell Content

To remove the contents of a cell without removing the cell from the structure of your workbook, on the *Home* tab, in the *Editing* group, click the **Clear** button and select one of the *Clear* menu options. You can remove everything from the cell—contents, formats, comments, and hyperlinks, or remove contents or formatting only.

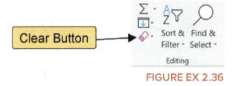

FIGURE EX 2.36

Figure EX 2.37 shows the original content and formatting in cells A3:E3.

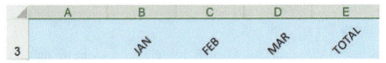

FIGURE EX 2.37

Clear All—clears all cell contents and formatting and deletes any comments or hyperlinks attached to the cell.

	A	B	C	D	E
3					
4	Monthly	$ 17,550	$ 14,080	$ 14,550	$ 46,180
5	Annual	$ 16,790	$ 13,140	$ 15,930	$ 45,860

FIGURE EX 2.38

Clear Formats—clears only the cell formatting and leaves the cell contents, comments, and hyperlinks. The *Clear Formats command* does not remove conditional formatting.

	A	B	C	D	E
3		JAN	FEB	MAR	TOTAL
4	Monthly	$ 17,550	$ 14,080	$ 14,550	$ 46,180
5	Annual	$ 16,790	$ 13,140	$ 15,930	$ 45,860

FIGURE EX 2.39

Clear Contents—clears only the contents (including hyperlinks) and leaves the cell formatting and comments. Figure EX 2.40 has sample text added to cell B3 to illustrate the cell formatting.

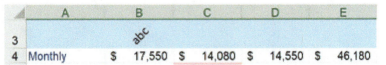

FIGURE EX 2.40

tell me **more**

There are two additional options available from the Clear menu:

Clear Comments—deletes any comments attached to the cell while leaving the cell contents, formatting, and hyperlinks intact.

Clear Hyperlinks—removes the hyperlink action from the cell without removing the content or the hyperlink style of formatting.

another method

To clear the contents of a cell, you can:

> Right-click the cell and select **Clear Contents** from the menu. Using the right-click method, there are no options to clear formats or comments.

> Select the cell and then press Delete or Backspace to clear the cell contents but not the cell formatting.

NOTE: These methods leave the cell formatting intact.

let me **try** Live!

If you do not have the data file from the previous skill open, open the student data file **EX2-19-Sales** and try this skill on your own:

1. On the *Summary* worksheet, select cells **A3:E3** and clear the formatting only (leaving the content).
2. Select cells **A11:D11** and clear only the content (leaving the formatting).
3. Select cell **A10** and use a single command to clear everything (content and formatting).
4. If you will be moving on to the next skill in this chapter, leave the workbook open to continue working. If not, save the file as directed by your instructor and close it.

Skill 2.20 Using Find and Replace

All of the Microsoft Office applications include **Find** and **Replace** commands that allow you to search for and replace data in your file. In Excel, these commands can be used to find and replace not only text but also numbers in values and formulas in a single worksheet or across an entire workbook.

Before using the *Replace* command, you should use *Find* to make sure the data you are about to replace are what you expect:

1. On the *Home* tab, in the *Editing* group at the far right side of the Ribbon, click the **Find & Select** button.
2. From the *Find & Select* menu, click **Find...**

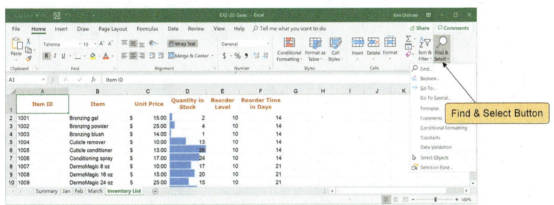

FIGURE EX 2.41

3. The *Find and Replace* dialog opens, with the *Find* tab selected.
4. Type the word, phrase, or number you want to find in the *Find what* box.
   1. To go to just the first instance, click the **Find Next** button.
   2. To find all instances, click the **Find All** button. When you click *Find All*, Excel displays a list detailing every instance of the data—workbook file name, worksheet name, cell name, cell address, the value of the cell, and the formula (if there is one).

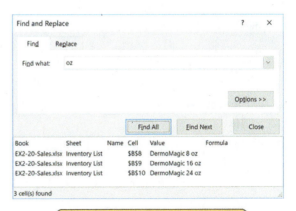

Find All **results show details about every cell that matches.**

FIGURE EX 2.42

Once you have verified the data you want to replace, switch to the *Replace* tab in the *Find and Replace* dialog:

1. Click the **Replace** tab.
2. Excel keeps the data you typed in the *Find what* box.
3. Now type the replacement text or values in the *Replace with* box.
    1. Click the **Replace** button to replace one instance of the data at a time.
    2. Click the **Replace All** button to replace all instances at once.
4. If you select *Replace All*, Excel displays a message telling you how many replacements were made. Click **OK** to dismiss the message. The results now display details about every cell that was updated with the *Replace* command.
5. Click **Close** to close the *Find and Replace* dialog.

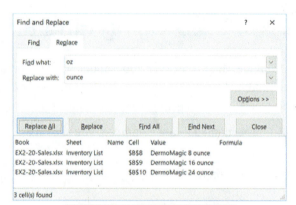

After *Replace All*, results show all updated cell data.

FIGURE EX 2.43

tell me more

By default, Excel searches for the data both in cell values and within formulas. If you want to limit the search to only cell values, first click the **Options>>** button in the *Find and Replace* dialog to display the find and replace optional settings. Next, expand the *Look in* list by clicking the arrow, and select **Values**.

another method

Use the keyboard shortcut Ctrl + F to open the *Find and Replace* dialog with the *Find* tab selected.

Use the keyboard shortcut Ctrl + H to open the *Find and Replace* dialog with the *Replace* tab selected.

let me try Live!

If you do not have the data file from the previous skill open, open the student data file **EX2-20-Sales** ⬇ and try this skill on your own:

1. On the *Inventory* worksheet, find all instances of the word **oz**.
2. Replace all instances of the word **oz** with **ounce**.
3. If you will be moving on to the next skill in this chapter, leave the workbook open to continue working. If not, save the file as directed by your instructor and close it.

Skill 2.21 Replacing Formatting

The *Find and Replace* commands allow you to find and replace formatting as well as data. This feature is especially helpful when replacing number formats throughout a workbook.

To find and replace formatting:

1. On the *Home* tab, in the *Editing* group, click the **Find & Select** button and select .. to open the *Find and Replace* dialog.

2. If necessary, click the **Options >>** button to display the find and replace optional settings. Notice that next to the *Find what* and *Replace with* boxes, the *Preview* box displays *No Format Set*.

FIGURE EX 2.44

3. If you want to find specific data, enter it in the *Find what* If the *Find what* box is empty, Excel will find all cells with the formatting defined in the next step.

4. Click the **Format...** button next to the *Find what* box to open the *Find Format* dialog where you can define the formatting you want to find. The *Find Format* dialog includes all the tabs and formatting options available in the *Format Cells* dialog. Set the formatting to find just as you would set formatting to apply to cells.

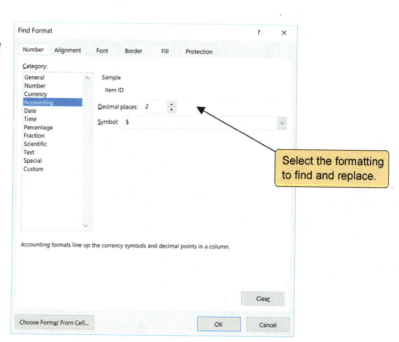

FIGURE EX 2.45

5. The *Preview* box next to the *Find what* box displays the word *Preview* using the formatting you defined. If you included number formatting, *Preview* will appear with an * after it (because the word *Preview* cannot display number formatting).

6. Now repeat the same steps to define the replacement formatting.

7. If you want to replace data as well as formatting, enter the replacement data in the *Replace with* box. If you do not enter anything, Excel will modify the formatting and leave the data in each cell unchanged.

FIGURE EX 2.46

8. Click the **Format...** button next to the *Replace with* box and repeat the same process to define the new format you want to use.

9. The *Preview* box next to the *Replace with* box displays the word *Preview* using the formatting you defined. If you included number formatting, *Preview* will appear with an * after it (because the word *Preview* cannot display number formatting).

10. Click **Replace All**.

11. Click **OK** in the message that appears.

12. Click **Close** to close the *Find and Replace* dialog.

another method

You can also define the formatting styles to find and replace by picking cells that are already formatted with those attributes.

1. In the *Find and Replace* dialog, click the **Format** button arrow next to the *Find what* box and select **Choose Format from Cell...**

2. The cursor changes to a picker shape ⊕🖊 .

3. Click a cell with the formatting attributes you want to find.

4. Click the **Format** button arrow next to the *Replace with* box and select **Choose Format from Cell...**

5. Click a cell with the formatting attributes you want to apply.

6. Click **Replace All.**

7. Click **OK**.

8. Click **Close** to close the *Find & Replace* dialog.

let me try Live!

If you do not have the data file from the previous skill open, open the student data file **EX2-21-Sales** ⬇ and try this skill on your own:

1. On the *Inventory List* worksheet, using the *Replace* command, find and replace all cells formatted with the **Accounting Number Format** with the **Currency** format.
2. If you will be moving on to the next skill in this chapter, leave the workbook open to continue working. If not, save the file as directed by your instructor and close it.

Skill **2.22** Setting and Clearing the Print Area

By default, Excel will print the entire active worksheet as shown in Figure EX 2.47.

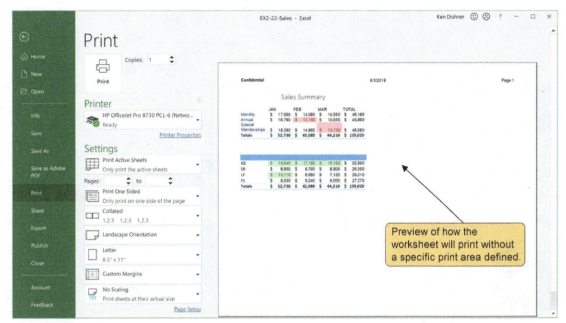

FIGURE EX 2.47

If you do not want to print your entire worksheet, you can set a print area. The **print area** is a range of cells that you designate as the default print selection. If you have defined a print area for your worksheet, it will be the only part of the worksheet that prints.

To set a print area:

1. Select the area you want to print.
2. On the *Page Layout* tab, in the *Page Setup* group, click the **Print Area** button.
3. Click **Set Print Area.**

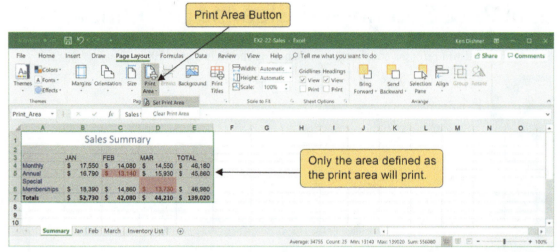

FIGURE EX 2.48

Now only the defined print area will print.

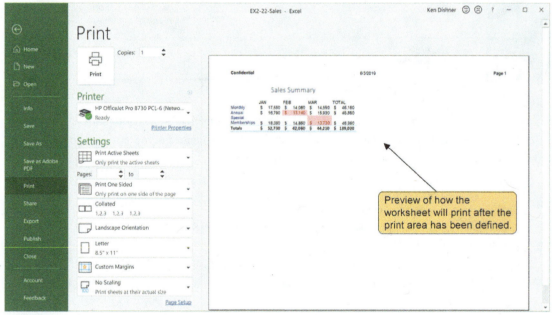

FIGURE EX 2.49

When you save the worksheet, the print area is saved as well. To clear a print area:

1. On the *Page Layout* tab, in the *Page Setup* group, click the **Print Area** button.
2. Click **Clear Print Area**.

tips & tricks

Notice that when the print area is selected, the *Name* box to the left of the address bar displays *Print_Area*. When you define a print area, Excel automatically creates a named range called *Print_Area*.

tell me more

You can define more than one print area per worksheet. Select the cells you want in the first print area, and then press Ctrl and drag the mouse to select the range of cells for the second print area. Each print area will print on a separate page.

let me try Live!

If you do not have the data file from the previous skill open, open the student data file **EX2-22-Sales** and try this skill on your own:

1. Go to the *Summary* worksheet and preview how the worksheet will look when printed.
2. Set the print area so only cells **A1:E7** will print.
3. Preview how the worksheet will look when printed after the new print area has been set.
4. Save the file as directed by your instructor and close it.

key terms

Cut	Format Painter
Copy	Conditional formatting
Paste	Data bars
Undo	Color scales
Redo	Icon sets
Alignment	Highlight Cells Rules
General horizontal alignment	Top/Bottom Rules
Font	Find
Fill color	Replace
Cell style	Print area

concept review

1. When you cut and paste a cell containing a formula with relative references, Excel _____.
    a. updates the cell references to the new location
    b. does not update the cell references to the new location
    c. treats the formulas as if it contained absolute references
    d. b and c

2. Which paste option pastes formulas and number formatting but none of the cell formatting?
    a. Keep Source Formatting
    b. Values
    c. Formulas
    d. Formulas & Number Formatting

3. To split a cell into two cells _____.
    a. in the *Format Cells* dialog, on the *Alignment* tab, in the *Text Control* section, click the **Merge cells** box to uncheck it
    b. on the *Home* tab, in the *Alignment* group, click the **Merge & Center** button and select **Unmerge Cells**
    c. on the *Data* tab, in the *Data Tools* group, click the **Text to Columns** button
    d. you cannot split a cell into two cells; you can only unmerge merged cells

4. To apply the Double Accounting underline format _____.
    a. Press [Ctrl] + [U]
    b. in the *Font* dialog, on the *Font* tab, expand the **Underline** list and select **Double Accounting**
    c. on the *Home* tab, in the *Font* group, click the **Underline** button
    d. on the *Home* tab, in the *Font* group, click the **Underline** button arrow and select **Double Underline**

5. Clicking the **Borders** button on the Ribbon applies which border style?
    a. none
    b. outline
    c. bottom border only
    d. the most recently used border style

6. The keyboard shortcut to open the Quick Analysis tool is _____.
    a. [Ctrl] + [A]
    b. [Ctrl] + [Q]
    c. [F7]
    d. [F10]

7. To highlight cells with values in the top 10% of the select range, use _____ conditional formatting.
   a. *Highlight Cells Rules*
   b. *Top/Bottom Rules*
   c. data bars
   d. icon sets

8. You can remove conditional formatting using the _____.
   a. *Clear All* command
   b. Ctrl + X keyboard shortcut
   c. Delete keyboard shortcut
   d. *Clear Rules from Selected Cells* command

9. Selecting a cell and pressing Delete clears _____.
   a. cell content only
   b. cell content and formatting
   c. cell content, formatting, and formulas
   d. cell formatting only

10. Where is the *Set Print Area* command located?
    a. on the *Page Layout* tab, in the *Page Setup* group
    b. in the *Page Layout* dialog
    c. in the *Print* dialog
    d. on the *Home* tab, in the *Print* group

projects
skill review **2.1**

Data files for projects can be found by logging into your SIMnet account and going to the Library section.

In this project you will add formatting to a daily vitamin and supplement plan to make the spreadsheet more attractive and easier to read.

Throughout the project, use the *Undo* command (Ctrl + Z) if you make a mistake.

Skills needed to complete this project:

- Using Undo and Redo (Skill 2.5)
- Merging Cells and Splitting Merged Cells (Skill 2.7)
- Applying Cell Styles (Skill 2.12)
- Inserting and Deleting Cells (Skill 2.3)
- Aligning Cells (Skill 2.6)
- Changing Fonts, Font Size, and Font Color (Skill 2.9)
- Using Format Painter (Skill 2.13)
- Adding Borders (Skill 2.10)
- Cutting, Copying, and Pasting Cell Content (Skill 2.1)
- Wrapping Text in Cells (Skill 2.4)
- Applying Conditional Formatting Using the Quick Analysis Tool (Skill 2.14)
- Applying Conditional Formatting with Data Bars, Color Scales, and Icon Sets (Skill 2.15)
- Applying Conditional Formatting with Highlight Cells Rules (Skill 2.16)
- Removing Conditional Formatting (Skill 2.18)
- Applying Conditional Formatting with Top/Bottom Rules (Skill 2.17)
- Replacing Formatting (Skill 2.21)

1. Open the start file **EX2019-SkillReview-2-1** and resave the file as: `[your initials]EX-SkillReview-2-1`
2. If the workbook opens in Protected View, click the **Enable Editing** button in the Message Bar at the top of the workbook so you can modify the workbook.
3. Merge and center the worksheet title across cells A1:H1 and cells A2:H2.
   a. Select cells **A1:H1**.
   b. On the *Home* tab, in the *Alignment* group, click the **Merge & Center** button.
   c. Select cells **A2:H2**.
   d. On the *Home* tab, in the *Alignment* group, click the **Merge & Center** button.
4. Apply the Title style to the main worksheet title.
   a. Select the merged cells **A1:H1**.
   b. On the *Home* tab, in the *Styles* group, click the **Cell Styles** button.
   c. Click the **Title** style.

5. Apply the Accent5 style to the worksheet subtitle.

    a. Select the merged cells **A2:H2**.

    b. On the *Home* tab, in the *Styles* group, click the **Cell Styles** button.

    c. Click the **Accent5**

6. There are extra cells to the left of the patient name and daily cost. Delete them.

    a. Select cells **B3:B4**.

    b. On the *Home* tab, in the *Cells* group, click the **Delete** button.

7. The patient name would look better aligned at the right side of the cell.

    a. Select cell **B3**.

    b. On the *Home* tab, in the *Alignment* group, click the **Align Right** button.

8. Format the *Patient Name* and *Daily Cost* labels with bolding and the Blue, Accent 5 font color.

    a. Select cells A3:A4.

    b. On the *Home* tab, in the *Font* group, click the **Bold** button.

    c. On the *Home* tab, in the *Font* group, click the **Font Color** button arrow, and select the **Blue, Accent 5** color. It is the second to last color in the first row under *Theme Colors*.

9. Use *Format Painter* to apply the label formatting to the data table header row (cells A6:H6).

    a. If necessary, click cell **A3** or **A4**.

    b. On the *Home* tab, in the *Clipboard* group, click the **Format Painter** button.

    c. Click cell **A6** and drag to cell **H6** to apply the formatting.

10. Add a border beneath the data table header row to separate the titles from the data. The border should be the same color as the font.

    a. If necessary, select cells **A6:H6**.

    b. On the *Home* tab, in the *Font* group, click the **Borders** button arrow, and select **More Borders...**

    c. In the *Format Cells* dialog, on the *Border* tab, expand the **Color** palette, and select the **Blue, Accent 5** color from the first row of the theme colors.

    d. Click the bottom border area of the preview diagram to add the border.

    e. Click **OK**.

11. The data in row 14 are misplaced and belong in the data table. Cut it and insert the cut cells above row 9.

    a. Select cells **A14:H14**.

    b. On the *Home* tab, in the *Clipboard* group, click the **Cut** button.

    c. Click cell **A9**.

    d. On the *Home* tab, in the *Cells* group, click the **Insert** button arrow, and select **Insert Cut Cells**.

IMPORTANT: You must complete step 11 correctly in order to receive points for completing the next steps. Check your work carefully.

12. Apply the Note cell style to the note in cell A13.

    a. Select cell **A13**.

    b. On the *Home* tab, in the *Styles* group, click the **Cell Styles** button.

    c. Click the **Note** style.

13. The note text is much longer than the width of cell A13, and it looks odd with the cell style applied. Apply text wrapping so all the text is visible within the cell formatted with the *Note* style.

    a. If necessary, select cell **A13**.

    b. On the *Home* tab, in the *Alignment* group, click the **Wrap Text** button.

14. Apply conditional formatting using solid blue data bars to cells H7:H11 to represent the relative daily cost of each supplement.

    a. Select cells **H7:H11**.

    b. Click the **Quick Analysis** tool button.

    c. Click the **Data Bars** button.

15. Apply conditional formatting using Highlight Cells Rules to the cost per bottle data (cells F7:F11) to format cells with a value greater than 20 with yellow fill with dark yellow text.

    a. Select cells **F7:F11**.

    b. On the *Home* tab, in the *Styles* group, click the **Conditional Formatting** button.

    c. Point to **Highlight Cells Rules**, and select **Greater Than...**

    d. In the *Greater Than* dialog, type **20** in the **Format cells that are GREATER THAN** box.

    e. Click the *with* drop-down arrow and select **Yellow Fill with Dark Yellow Text**.

    f. Click **OK**.

16. There might be too much conditional formatting in this worksheet. Remove the conditional formatting from cells G7:G11.

    a. Select cells **G7:G11**.

    b. On the *Home* tab, in the *Styles* group, click the **Conditional Formatting** button.

    c. Point to *Clear Rules*, and select **Clear Rules from Selected Cells**.

17. You would still like to highlight the least expensive cost per pill. Apply conditional formatting to cells **G7:G11** using **Top/Bottom Rules** to format only the lowest value with green fill with dark green text.

    a. Select cells **G7:G11**.

    b. On the *Home* tab, in the *Styles* group, click the **Conditional Formatting** button.

    c. Point to **Top/Bottom Rules**, and select **Bottom 10 Items...**

    d. In the *Bottom 10 Items* dialog, type **1** in the **Format cells that rank in the BOTTOM** box.

    e. Expand the formatting list and select **Green Fill with Dark Green Text**.

    f. Click **OK**.

18. Click cell **G12** so the cost per pill data is no longer selected.

19. Find all of the values that use the *Accounting Number Format* with four digits after the decimal and change the formatting to the *Accounting Number Format* with two digits after the decimal.
    a. On the *Home* tab, in the *Editing* group, click the **Find & Select** button, and select **Replace....**
    b. In the *Find and Replace* dialog, ensure that there are no values in the Find what and Replace with boxes..
    c. If necessary, click the **Options>>** button to display the *Find and Replace* options.
    d. Click the **Format...** button next to the *Find What* box.
    e. In the *Find Format* dialog, on the *Number* tab, click **Accounting** in the *Category* list. If necessary, change the *Decimal* places value to **4**. Verify that the *Symbol* value is **$**.
    f. Click **OK.**
    g. Click the **Format...** button next to the *Replace* with box.
    h. In the *Replace Format* dialog, on the *Number* tab, click **Accounting** in the *Category* list. If necessary, change the *Decimal* places value to **2**. Verify that the *Symbol* value is **$**.
    i. Click **OK**.
    j. Click **Replace All**.
    k. Excel should make nine replacements. Click **OK**.
    l. Click **Close**.
20. Save and close the workbook.

projects
skill review **2.2**

Data files for projects can be found by logging into your SIMnet account and going to the Library section.

You want to share your recipe for Greek yogurt with friends, but the spreadsheet is a little rough. Use the formatting skills you learned in this chapter to make the recipe look as good as it tastes.

Throughout the project, use the *Undo* command ($\boxed{\text{Ctrl}}$ + $\boxed{\text{Z}}$) if you make a mistake.

Skills needed to complete this project:

- Using Undo and Redo (Skill 2.5)
- Merging Cells and Splitting Merged Cells (Skill 2.7)
- Applying Cell Styles (Skill 2.12)
- Inserting and Deleting Cells (Skill 2.3)
- Using Format Painter (Skill 2.13)
- Changing Fonts, Font Size, and Font Color (Skill 2.9)
- Applying Bold, Italic, and Underline (Skill 2.8)
- Adding Borders (Skill 2.10)
- Using Find and Replace (Skill 2.20)
- Cutting, Copying, and Pasting Cell Content (Skill 2.1)
- Using Paste Options (Skill 2.2)
- Setting and Clearing the Print Area (Skill 2.22)
- Replacing Formatting (Skill 2.21)

1. Open the start file **EX2019-SkillReview-2-2** and resave the file as: `[your initials]EX-SkillReview-2-2`

2. If the workbook opens in Protected View, click the **Enable Editing** button in the Message Bar at the top of the workbook so you can modify it.

3. Center and merge the recipe title across cells **A1:D1**.
   a. Select cells **A1:D1**.
   b. On the *Home* tab, in the *Alignment* group, click the **Merge & Center** button.

4. Format the title using the *Accent 2* themed cell style.
   a. If necessary, select the merged cells **A1:D1**.
   b. On the *Home* tab, in the *Styles* group, click the **Cell Styles** button.
   c. In the *Themed Cell Styles* section of the gallery, click the **Accent 2** style.

5. Delete cell **B2**, shifting other cells to the left.
   a. Select cell **B2**.
   b. On the *Home* tab, in the *Cells* group, click the **Delete** button arrow and select **Delete Cells...**
   c. Click the **Shift cells left** radio button.
   d. Click **OK**.

6. Use *Format Painter* to copy formatting from the title and apply it to the Ingredients (**A5**) and Directions (**A10**) headers.
   a. Select the merged cells **A1:D1**.
   b. On the *Home* tab, in the *Clipboard* group, double-click the **Format Painter** button.
   c. Click cell **A5**. Notice that *Format Painter* merged cells **A5:D5** and centered the text across the merged cells.
   d. Click cell **A10**. Notice that *Format Painter* merged cells **A10:D10** and centered the text across the merged cells.
   e. On the *Home* tab, in the *Clipboard* group, click the **Format Painter** button again to disable it.
7. The worksheet title should be more prominent than the section headers. Increase the font size to 14 and bold the text.
   a. Select the merged cells **A1:D1**.
   b. On the *Home* tab, in the *Font* group, click the **Font Size** button arrow, and select **16**.
   c. On the *Home* tab, in the *Font* group, click the **Bold** button.
8. Add a bottom border to cells **B6:D6** to separate the headings from the data.
   a. Select cells **B6:D6**.
   b. On the *Home* tab, in the *Font* group, click the **Borders** button arrow and select **Thick Bottom Border**.
9. This recipe is better using whole milk. Find and replace all instances of *non fat* with *whole*.
   a. On the *Home* tab, in the *Editing* group, click the **Find & Select** button and select **Replace...**
   b. If necessary, display the find and replace options and clear any formats.
      i. Click the **Options >>** button.
      ii. If the button next to the *Find what* box does not display *No Format Set*, click the **Format** button arrow and select **Clear Find Format**.
      iii. If the button next to the *Replace with* box does not display *Not Format Set*, click the **Format** button arrow and select **Clear Replace Format**.
      iv. Click the **Options <<** button to hide the find and replace options.
   c. Type **non fat** in the *Find what* box.
   d. Type **whole** in the *Replace with* box.
   e. Click the **Replace All** button.
   f. Excel should make three replacements. Click **OK**.
   g. Click **Close**.
10. Apply thick outside borders around the entire recipe (cells **A1:D20**).
    a. Select cells **A1:D20**.
    b. On the *Home* tab, in the *Font* group, click the **Borders** button arrow and select **Thick Outside Borders**.

11. Now that your recipe is formatted, make a copy of it and change the number of servings to **5**. Be sure to retain formulas and column widths.

    a. If necessary, select cells **A1:D20**.

    b. On the *Home* tab, in the *Clipboard* group, click the **Copy** button.

    c. Click cell **F1**.

    d. On the *Home* tab, in the *Clipboard* group, click the **Paste** button arrow.

    e. Select **Keep Source Column Widths**.

12. Change the value in cell **G2** to **5**.

13. Set the print area so only the original version of the recipe will print. Be sure to preview the printed worksheet.

    a. Select cells **A1:D20**.

    b. On the *Page Layout* tab, it the *Page Setup* group, click the **Print Area** button and select **Set Print Area**.

    c. Click the **File** tab.

    d. Click **Print**.

14. Save and close the workbook.

projects

Data files for projects can be found by logging into your SIMnet account and going to the Library section.

challenge yourself 2.3

In this project, you will format a blood pressure report to make it look less like a spreadsheet and more like a form. You will use conditional formatting to highlight important data.

Skills needed to complete this project:

- Using Undo and Redo (Skill 2.5)
- Adding Shading with Fill Color (Skill 2.11)
- Merging Cells and Splitting Merged Cells (Skill 2.7)
- Applying Cell Styles (Skill 2.12)
- Changing Fonts, Font Size, and Font Color (Skill 2.9)
- Aligning Cells (Skill 2.6)
- Adding Borders (Skill 2.10)
- Using Format Painter (Skill 2.13)
- Applying Bold, Italic, and Underline (Skill 2.8)
- Applying Conditional Formatting with Data Bars, Color Scales, and Icon Sets (Skill 2.15)
- Applying Conditional Formatting with Top/Bottom Rules (Skill 2.17)
- Setting and Clearing the Print Area (Skill 2.22)

1. Open the start file **EX2019-ChallengeYourself-2-3** and resave the file as: **[your initials]EX-ChallengeYourself-2-3**
2. If the workbook opens in Protected View, click the **Enable Editing** button in the Message Bar at the top of the workbook so you can modify it.
3. Select cells **A1:F26** and apply the **White, Background 1** fill color. It is the first option in the first row under *Theme Colors*.
4. Merge and center the title across cells **A1:F1**.
5. Apply the **Title** cell style to the merged cells.
6. Apply the **Tan, Accent 6, Lighter 80%** fill color to the merged cells. It is the last option in the second row under *Theme Colors*.
7. Change the font color to **Dark Purple, Accent 5**. It is the second to last color in the first row under *Theme Colors*.
8. Merge cells **C2:D2** and right-align the content in the cell.
9. Apply the default **Outside Borders** border style to the merged cells **C2:D2**.
10. Apply the **40% - Accent5** cell style to cells **C4:D4**.
11. Apply the same formatting to cells **C7:D7**.
12. Apply the default **Outside Borders** border style to cells **C4:D5** and cells **C7:D8**.
13. Bold cells **B2**, **B5**, **B8**, and **B10**.

14. Merge cells **C10:D10** and right-align the content in the cell.

15. Apply the default **Outside Borders** border style to the merged cells.

16. Apply the **Dark Green, Accent 4, Lighter 60%** fill color to cells **A12:F12**. It is the eighth color in the third row under *Theme Colors*.

17. Left-align the content in cells **A13:A26**.

18. Apply the default **All Borders** border style to cells **A13:F26**.

19. Add conditional formatting to cells **E13:E26** using the **Red to Black** icon set.

20. Add conditional formatting to cells **C13:C26** to format values **greater than 136** with **light red fill with dark red text.**

21. Add conditional formatting to cells **C13:C26** to format values **between 120 and 136** with **yellow fill with dark yellow text.**

22. Add conditional formatting to cells **D13:D26** to format values **greater than 82** with **light red fill with dark red text.**

23. Add conditional formatting to cells **D13:D26** to format values **between 80 and 82** with **yellow fill with dark yellow text.**

24. Add conditional formatting to cells **D13:D26** to format values **less than 80** with **green fill with dark green text.**

25. Apply the default **Thick Outside Borders** border style around cells **A1:F26**.

26. Set cells **A1:F26** as the print area.

27. Preview how the worksheet will look when printed.

28. Save and close the workbook.

projects

Data files for projects can be found by logging into your SIMnet account and going to the Library section.

challenge yourself 2.4

In this project you will add formatting to a college budget spreadsheet and rearrange items that are in the wrong categories.

Skills needed to complete this project:

- Using Undo and Redo (Skill 2.5)
- Merging Cells and Splitting Merged Cells (Skill 2.7)
- Applying Cell Styles (Skill 2.12)
- Adding Shading with Fill Color (Skill 2.11)
- Applying Bold, Italic, and Underline (Skill 2.8)
- Cutting, Copying, and Pasting Cell Content (Skill 2.1)
- Using Paste Options (Skill 2.2)
- Inserting and Deleting Cells (Skill 2.3)
- Using Format Painter (Skill 2.13)
- Applying Conditional Formatting with Data Bars, Color Scales, and Icon Sets (Skill 2.15)
- Wrapping Text in Cells (Skill 2.4)
- Adding Borders (Skill 2.10)

1. Open the start file **EX2019-ChallengeYourself-2-4** and resave the file as: `[your initials]EX-ChallengeYourself-2-4`
2. If the workbook opens in Protected View, click the **Enable Editing** button in the *Message Bar* at the top of the workbook so you can modify it.
3. Center and merge the title across cells **A1:E1**.
4. Apply the **Heading 1** cell style to the merged cells.
5. Merge and center the four section titles across the appropriate cells (**Monthly Income**, **Available Income**, **Monthly Expenses**, and **Semester Expenses**).
6. Apply cell styles to the section titles as follows:
   a. Monthly Income—**Accent5**
   b. Available Income—**Accent2**
   c. Monthly Expenses—**Accent6**
   d. Semester Expenses—**Accent1**
7. Add the **Gray, Accent 6, Lighter 80%** fill color to cells **A3:B3**. It is the last color in the second row under *Theme Colors*.
8. Bold cells **A3:B3**.
9. Copy only the formatting of cells **A3:B3** to the headers in the other sections (cells **A10:B10**, **D3:E3**, and **D10:E10**).

10. The line item for lab fees (cells **A21:B21**) is in the wrong category. Cut the cells and insert them into cells **D13:E13**, shifting the other cells down. Do not overwrite the existing data.

11. Delete the empty cells **A21:B21**, shifting the other cells up.

12. Cell **E6** has the wrong number format applied. Copy the formatting from cell **E5** and apply it to cell **E6**.

13. Apply conditional formatting to cells **B11:B23** to display a red gradient data bar in each cell.

14. The text in cell **A21** appears cutoff. Apply text wrapping to the cell.

15. Apply the default **All Borders** border style to the following cell ranges: **A3:B7**, **D3:E7**, **A10:B24**, and **D10:E16**.

16. Save and close the workbook.

projects

on your own **2.5**

Data files for projects can be found by logging into your SIMnet account and going to the Library section.

In this project, you will add your own data to a worksheet that tracks the original cost and current resell value for textbooks. As you format the worksheet, keep in mind that you want the worksheet to be visually appealing, but you don't want it to look like a circus! Try a variety of formatting options and keep using the Undo command until you find the formats you like best.

Skills needed to complete this project:

- Using Undo and Redo (Skill 2.5)
- Adding Shading with Fill Color (Skill 2.11)
- Merging Cells and Splitting Merged Cells (Skill 2.7)
- Applying Cell Styles (Skill 2.12)
- Inserting and Deleting Cells (Skill 2.3)
- Aligning Cells (Skill 2.6)
- Changing Fonts, Font Size, and Font Color (Skill 2.9)
- Using Format Painter (Skill 2.13)
- Adding Borders (Skill 2.10)
- Cutting, Copying, and Pasting Cell Content (Skill 2.1)
- Applying Conditional Formatting Using the Quick Analysis Tool (Skill 2.14)
- Applying Conditional Formatting with Data Bars, Color Scales, and Icon Sets (Skill 2.15)
- Replacing Formatting (Skill 2.21)
- Wrapping Text in Cells (Skill 2.4)
- Applying Bold, Italic, and Underline (Skill 2.8)
- Applying Conditional Formatting with Highlight Cells Rules (Skill 2.16)
- Applying Conditional Formatting with Top/Bottom Rules (Skill 2.17)

1. Open the start file **EX2019-OnYourOwn-2-5** and resave the file as: `[your initials]EX-OnYourOwn-2-5`
2. If the workbook opens in Protected View, click the **Enable Editing** button in the Message Bar at the top of the workbook so you can modify it.
3. Update the data in the workbook with an inventory of textbooks you own. Include the purchase price and estimated resell value for each title.
4. Add and delete cells as necessary.
5. Wrap text if any of your book titles are too long to fit in the cell.
6. Format the worksheet title and data table using cell styles, borders, and fill color. Change fonts, font color, and font size as appropriate.
7. Remember to use *Format Painter* to copy formatting from one part of the worksheet to another.

8. You can also use the *Replace* command if you want to change formatting from one style to another in multiple cells at the same time.

9. Apply conditional formatting to identify the most expensive books and the ones with the highest resell values. Use any type of conditional formatting you'd like.

10. Apply conditional formatting to identify the book with the best resell value and the book with the worst resell value.

11. When you are satisfied with the appearance of the worksheet, save and close the workbook.

projects

fix it **2.6**

Data files for projects can be found by logging into your SIMnet account and going to the Library section.

In this project, you will fix a rather unattractive worksheet that was intended for recording walking/running miles and times.

Skills needed to complete this project:

- Using Undo and Redo (Skill 2.5)
- Adding Shading with Fill Color (Skill 2.11)
- Merging Cells and Splitting Merged Cells (Skill 2.7)
- Applying Cell Styles (Skill 2.12)
- Inserting and Deleting Cells (Skill 2.3)
- Changing Fonts, Font Size, and Font Color (Skill 2.9)
- Using Format Painter (Skill 2.13)
- Adding Borders (Skill 2.10)
- Wrapping Text in Cells (Skill 2.4)
- Applying Conditional Formatting Using the Quick Analysis Tool (Skill 2.14)
- Applying Conditional Formatting with Data Bars, Color Scales, and Icon Sets (Skill 2.15)
- Using Find and Replace (Skill 2.20)
- Applying Bold, Italic, and Underline (Skill 2.8)

1. Open the start file **EX2019-FixIt-2-6** and resave the file as: `[your initials]EX-FixIt-2-6`
2. If the workbook opens in Protected View, click the **Enable Editing** button in the Message Bar at the top of the workbook so you can modify it.
3. Begin by removing all the fill color, font colors, and borders from the worksheet. This worksheet has so many different formats, it is probably easier to start from a clean slate.

Hint: Do not use the *Clear Formats* command. Using this command will remove all numbering formats to the General number format.

4. All fonts in the worksheet should be set to **Calibri, 12** point size.
5. Merge cells **A1:D1** and center the title across the merged cells.
6. Apply appropriate formatting for the title. Use the **Title** cell style.
7. Apply the **Blue, Accent 1, lighter 80%** fill color to cells **B4:D9** to make the data table stand out. It is the fifth color in the second row under *Theme Colors*.
8. Apply a dotted border to the inside of cells **A4:D10**. *Hint:* Use the *Format Cells* dialog, and select the second border style in the list after *None*. In the *Presets* section, apply the **Inside** option.
9. Apply a border around cells **A3:D9** using the **Thick Outside Borders** (or **Thick Box Border**) option.
10. Apply a border to cells **A3:D3** using the **Bottom Double Border** option.
11. Apply bold to cells **B3:D3** and **A4:A9** to make row and column headers stand out from the data.

12. Apply text wrapping in cell **D3**.

13. An entry for October 9 is missing. You walked for 45 minutes that day and went 3.7 miles. Insert the data in the appropriate place. (You can copy the formula to calculate miles per hour from one of the other cells).

14. Apply conditional formatting using data bars to visually compare the distance jogged each day.

15. Ensure that all entries for miles and miles per hour display using the Number format with two digits after the decimal.

16. Ensure that all average calculations display using the Number format with two digits after the decimal.

17. Find all instances of *walk* and replace with *jog*.

18. Save and close the workbook.

chapter **3**

Using Formulas and Functions

In this chapter, you will learn the following skills:

- Use a variety of methods to enter functions
- Use statistical functions
- Use date and time functions
- Use text functions
- Work with named ranges
- Use the IF logical function
- Use the PMT financial function
- Use lookup functions
- Troubleshoot formulas
- Display and print formulas

Skill 3.1 Using the Function Arguments Dialog to Enter Functions

Skill 3.2 Using Formula AutoComplete to Enter Functions

Skill 3.3 Calculating Averages

Skill 3.4 Finding Minimum and Maximum Values

Skill 3.5 Using Date and Time Functions

Skill 3.6 Creating Formulas Using Counting Functions

Skill 3.7 Formatting Text Using Functions

Skill 3.8 Using CONCAT to Combine Text

Skill 3.9 Using TEXTJOIN to Combine Text

Skill 3.10 Creating Formulas Referencing Data from Other Worksheets

Skill 3.11 Naming Ranges of Cells

Skill 3.12 Working with Named Ranges

Skill 3.13 Updating Named Ranges with the Name Manager

Skill 3.14 Editing and Deleting Names with the Name Manager

Skill 3.15 Using the Logical Function IF

Skill 3.16 Calculating Loan Payments Using the PMT Function

Skill 3.17 Finding Data Using the VLOOKUP Function

Skill 3.18 Checking Formulas for Errors

Skill 3.19 Finding Errors Using Trace Precedents and Trace Dependents

Skill 3.20 Displaying and Printing Formulas

introduction

It is time to go beyond simple formulas. In this chapter you will learn to use the functions built into Excel to compute statistics, insert dates, modify text, work with logical expressions, compute loan payments, and perform table lookups. Also, you will create formulas that reference named ranges and other worksheets for fast replication. Finally, you will learn skills necessary for troubleshooting formulas.

Skill 3.1 Using the Function Arguments Dialog to Enter Functions

Previously, you learned to enter functions three ways:

1. **Typing the formula directly in the cell or the formula bar.** This method is easiest for simple functions.
2. **Using the *AutoSum* button.** This method works well when your spreadsheet includes numerical data organized in rows or columns. Functions available via AutoSum are limited to simple math and statistical functions (SUM, AVERAGE, COUNT, MIN, and MAX).
3. **Using the Quick Analysis tool.** This method is the easiest way to enter totals for multiple rows or columns of data at once. Like AutoSum, the Quick Analysis tool offers a limited number of functions (SUM, AVERAGE, and COUNT). It has the advantage of including options not available from AutoSum (calculating running totals and calculating the percentage of the overall total for each row or column) and showing a live preview of the totals before you make a selection.

Every function can be entered using its *Function Arguments* dialog. This dialog is different for each function. There are two primary methods for opening the *Function Arguments* dialog.

1. **Select the function from the *Formulas* tab, *Function Library* group.** Each button in this Ribbon group represents a category of functions. Clicking a button displays a menu of functions in that category. Selecting a function opens its *Insert Function* dialog.

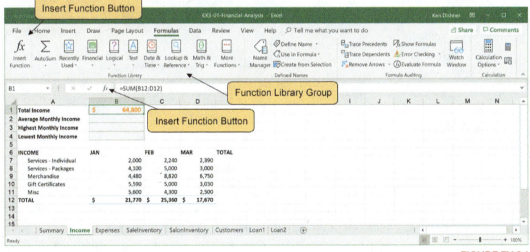

FIGURE EX 3.1

2. **Select the function from the *Insert Function* dialog.** To open the *Insert Function* dialog, on the *Formulas* tab, in the *Function Library* group, click the **Insert Function** button. You can also click the **Insert Function** button to the left of the formula bar.

To use the *Insert Function* dialog:

1. Functions in the *Insert Function* dialog are organized in the same categories as the *Function Library* group. By default, the category list will default to the category you last used or it will show the *Most Recently Used* list. To select another category, expand the **Or select a category** list and select the function category you want.

2. Click a function in the *Select a function* box to see a brief description of what it does and the arguments it takes.

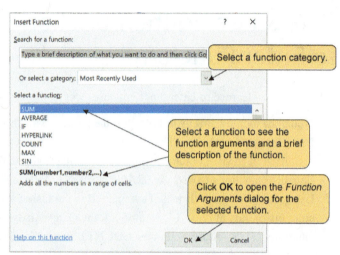

FIGURE EX 3.2

3. Click **OK** to open the *Function Arguments* dialog for the selected function.

To use the *Function Arguments* dialog:

1. Enter values or cell references in each of the argument boxes as needed by typing or by clicking the cell or cell range in the worksheet. As you click each argument box, a brief description of the argument appears near

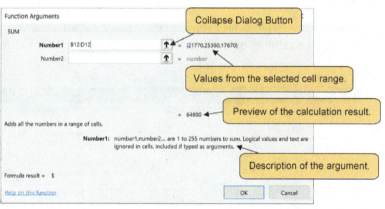

FIGURE EX 3.3

the bottom of the dialog. The *Function Arguments* dialog also displays a preview of the result of the calculation. This value updates as you add arguments.

2. If the position of the *Function Arguments* dialog makes it difficult to click the cell you want, click the **Collapse Dialog** button next to the argument box. As shown in Figure EX 3.4, the *Function Arguments* dialog collapses to show only the function argument box you are working with. Click the cell(s) to add the reference to the dialog.

3. Click the **Expand Dialog** button to return the *Function Arguments* dialog to its full size.

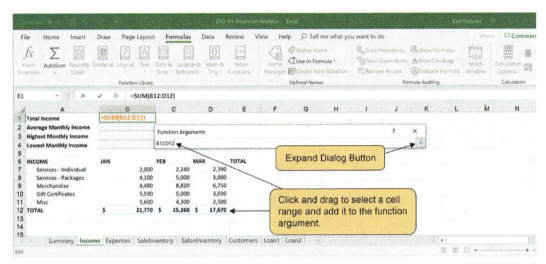

FIGURE EX 3.4

4. When you are finished entering arguments, click **OK**.

tips & tricks

The *SUM Function Arguments* dialog shown in Figure EX 3.3 includes an extra argument box. For functions that calculate a value based on a series of cells, Excel adds a blank argument box each time you enter an argument (up to 256 arguments). Enter values or cell references only in the argument boxes you need.

tell me more

If you're not sure of the name of the function you want, open the *Insert Function* dialog and type keywords describing the function in the *Search for a function* box, and then click the **Go** button. The *Or select a category* box changes to *Recommended*, and the *Select a function* box now displays a list of functions that match the keywords you typed.

let me try Live!

Open the student data file **EX3-01-Financial-Analysis** ⤓ and try this skill on your own:

1. On the **Income** worksheet, enter a SUM function in cell **B1** to calculate the total of cells **B12:D12.** Open the *Function Arguments* dialog from the *Formulas* tab, *Function Library* group, **Math & Trig** button. You will have to scroll down the list to find SUM.

2. Enter a SUM function in cell **E7** to calculate the total of cells **B7:D7.** Use the *Insert Function* dialog. If the SUM function is not listed in the *Select a Function* box, expand the **Or select a category list,** and select either **Math & Trig** or **Most Recently Used.** Again, Excel enters the adjacent cell range as the function arguments for you.

3. If you will be moving on to the next skill in this chapter, leave the workbook open to continue working. If not, save the file as directed by your instructor and close it.

Skill 3.2 Using Formula AutoComplete to Enter Functions

Formula AutoComplete is a shortcut for entering functions. When you type = and then a letter, Formula AutoComplete displays a list of potential matches (functions and other valid reference names). This is a good method to use if you prefer typing the function arguments, but you need a reminder of what the arguments are or the order in which they should be entered.

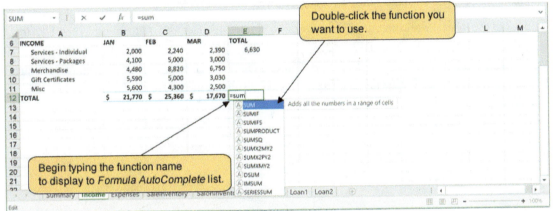

FIGURE EX 3.5

1. Type = in the cell or the formula bar to begin the formula. Formula AutoComplete displays the list of potential matches.
2. Type more letters to shorten the Formula AutoComplete list.
3. Double-click a function name to enter it in your formula.
4. Enter the expected arguments by typing values or selecting a cell or cell range.
5. Press Enter to complete the formula. Excel enters the closing) for you.

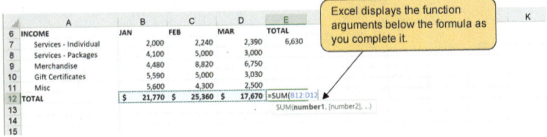

FIGURE EX 3.6

tips & tricks

When you use Formula AutoComplete, you can click the function name in the ScreenTip to open the Excel help topic for that function.

let me try Live!

If you do not have the data file from the previous skill open, open the student data file **EX3-02-Financial-Analysis** ⬇ and try this skill on your own:

1. On the **Income** worksheet, use Formula AutoComplete to enter a SUM function in cell **E12** to calculate the total of cells **B12:D12.**
2. If you will be moving on to the next skill in this chapter, leave the workbook open to continue working. If not, save the file as directed by your instructor and close it.

Skill 3.3 Calculating Averages

The **AVERAGE** statistical function is used to calculate the average value of a group of values. Average is calculated by adding the values, and then dividing the sum by the number of values.

A formula using the AVERAGE function looks like this: **=AVERAGE(B12:D12)**

The result of this formula is the sum of the values in cells B12:D12 divided by the number of values in that cell range.

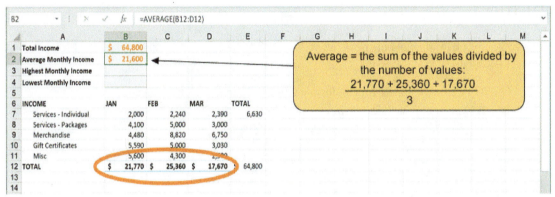

FIGURE EX 3.7

To create a formula with the AVERAGE function, use any of these methods:

> If you prefer typing in the cell or the formula bar, try using Formula AutoComplete.
> If the data are organized in rows or columns, you can use AutoSum. On the *Home* tab, *Editing* group or on the *Formula* tab, *Function Library* group, click the **AutoSum** button arrow and select
> If you want to calculate the average for multiple rows or columns at once, use one of the average options in the Quick Analysis tool, *Totals* tab.
> If you prefer using the *Function Arguments* dialog, on the *Formulas* tab, in the *Function Library* group, click the **More Functions** button, point to **Statistical,** and click **AVERAGE.**

tips & tricks

When calculating an average, Excel will ignore empty cells. If you want to include those cells in your average calculations, make sure they have a value of zero.

tell me **more**

What you might think of as the "average" is actually the statistical mean. *Average* is a general term in statistics that includes **mean** (the sum of a group of values divided by the number of values in the group), **median** (the middle value of a set of values) and **mode** (the value that appears most often in a group of values). In Excel, the AVERAGE function calculates the mean value. Most people say *average* when they really want to calculate the mean value.

let me **try** Live!

If you do not have the data file from the previous skill open, open the student data file **EX3-03-Financial-Analysis** and try this skill on your own:

1. On the **Income** worksheet, enter a formula in cell **B2** to calculate the average value of cells **B12:D12.** Use any method you like.
2. If you will be moving on to the next skill in this chapter, leave the workbook open to continue working. If not, save the file as directed by your instructor and close it.

Skill 3.4 Finding Minimum and Maximum Values

In addition to AVERAGE, there are a few other statistical functions you may find useful in working with day-to-day spreadsheets.

The **MAX** (maximum) statistical function will give you the largest value in a range of values. A formula using the MAX function looks like this: **=MAX(A3:A6)**

The **MIN** (minimum) statistical function will give you the smallest value in a range of values. A formula using the MIN function looks like this: **=MIN(A3:A6)**

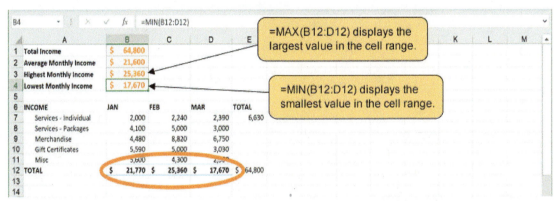

FIGURE EX 3.8

To create a formula with the MAX or MIN function, use any of these methods:

> If you prefer typing in the cell or the formula bar, try using Formula AutoComplete.
> If the data are organized in rows or columns, you can use AutoSum. On the *Home* tab, *Editing* group or on the *Formula* tab, *Function Library* group, click the **AutoSum** button arrow and select **Max** or **Min**.
> If you prefer using the *Function Arguments* dialog, on the *Formulas* tab, in the *Function Library* group, click the **More Functions** button, point to **Statistical,** and click **MAX** or **MIN**.

let me try Live!

If you do not have the data file from the previous skill open, open the student data file **EX3-04-Financial-Analysis** and try this skill on your own:

1. On the **Income** worksheet, in cell **B3,** enter a formula to find the highest (maximum) monthly income total (cells **B12:D12**).

2. On the **Income** worksheet, in cell **B4,** enter a formula to find the lowest (minimum) monthly income total (cells **B12:D12**).

3. If you will be moving on to the next skill in this chapter, leave the workbook open to continue working. If not, save the file as directed by your instructor and close it.

Skill 3.5 Using Date and Time Functions

Excel includes two functions that insert the current date or date and time. The **NOW** function inserts the current date and time. The **TODAY** function inserts only the current date. Both of these functions are **volatile**—that is, they are not constant. They update with the current date or date and time each time the workbook is opened.

A formula using the NOW function looks like this: **=NOW()**

A formula using the TODAY function looks like this: **=TODAY()**

Notice that both of these functions include parentheses, but there are no arguments inside them. These functions do not require arguments.

To create a formula with NOW or TODAY, use either of these methods:

> If you prefer typing in the cell or the formula bar, try using Formula AutoComplete.
> If you prefer using the *Function Arguments* dialog, on the *Formulas* tab, in the *Function Library* group, click the **Date & Time** button and click **NOW** or **TODAY**.

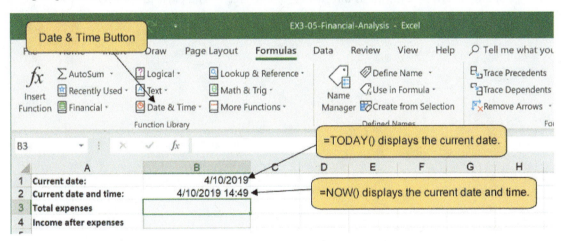

FIGURE EX 3.9

tips & tricks

Both NOW and TODAY use the date and time from your computer's clock. If your computer's clock is wrong, the date and time displayed in your workbook will be wrong as well.

tell me more

If the cell is formatted to use a date format that does not display the time, the result of the NOW and TODAY functions will appear the same. However, the underlying value will be different. If you change the formatting of the cell to display the time, a cell using the TODAY function will always display a time of 12:00 AM, whereas a cell using the NOW function will display the correct time.

let me try Live!

If you do not have the data file from the previous skill open, open the student data file **EX3-05-Financial-Analysis** ⬇️ and try this skill on your own:

1. On the **Summary** worksheet, enter a formula in cell **B1** to display only the current date.
2. On the **Summary** worksheet, enter a formula in cell **B2** to display the current date and time.
3. If you will be moving on to the next skill in this chapter, leave the workbook open to continue working. If not, save the file as directed by your instructor and close it.

Skill 3.6 Creating Formulas Using Counting Functions

The counting functions are useful when you need to know how many numbers or items are in a list or how many rows are missing data for a particular column.

COUNT—Counts the number of cells that contain numbers within a specified range of cells. A formula using the COUNT function looks like this: **=COUNT(A7:A20)**

The result of this formula is the number of cells in **A7** through **A20** that contain numerical values. If you want to include cells that contain text, use COUNTA instead.

To count numbers, you have two additional options:

> If the data are organized in rows or columns, you can use AutoSum to enter the COUNT function. On the *Home* tab, *Editing* group or on the *Formula* tab, *Function Library* group, click the **AutoSum** button arrow and select **Count Numbers.**

> If you want to count the numbers in multiple rows or columns at once, use one of the *Count* options from the Quick Analysis tool, *Totals* tab.

COUNTA—Counts the number of cells that are not blank within a specified range of cells. Use COUNTA if your cell range includes text data or a mix of text and numbers. A formula using the COUNTA function looks like this: **=COUNTA(B7:B20)**

The result of this formula is the number of cells in **B7** through **B20** that contain any data (numerical or text).

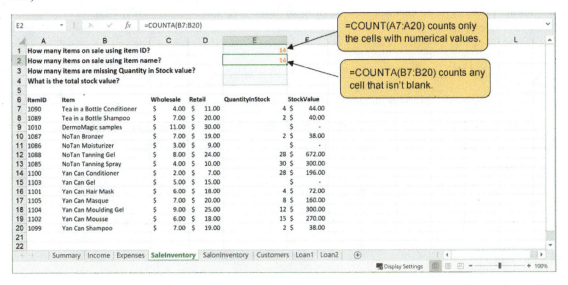

FIGURE EX 3.10

COUNTBLANK—Counts the number of empty (blank) cells within a specified range of cells. Cells that contain a zero (0) or a formula that results in zero are not considered blank. Use COUNTBLANK to find the number of rows missing values in a column. A formula using the COUNTBLANK function looks like this: **=COUNTBLANK(E7:E20)**

The result of this formula is the number of cells in **E7** through **E20** that are empty.

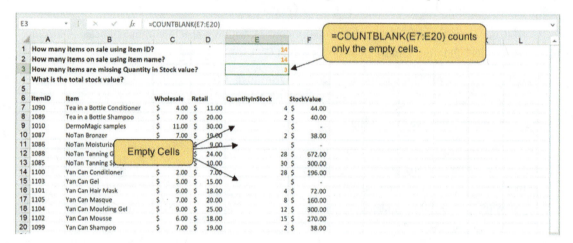

To create a formula with COUNT, COUNTA, or COUNTBLANK, use either of these methods:

> If you prefer typing in the cell or the formula bar, try using Formula AutoComplete.

> If you prefer using the *Function Arguments* dialog, on the *Formulas* tab, in the *Function Library* group, click the **More Functions** button, point to **Statistical,** and click **COUNT, COUNTA,** or **COUNTBLANK**.

tips & tricks

The COUNT and COUNTA functions can take multiple arguments.

COUNTBLANK accepts only a single argument. If you want to count blanks across a non-contiguous range of cells, you will need to create a formula adding together the results of multiple functions.

   =COUNTBLANK(A1:C1)+COUNTBLANK(B10:C15)

let me try Live!

If you do not have the data file from the previous skill open, open the student data file **EX3-06-Financial-Analysis** 📥 and try this skill on your own:

1. On the **SaleInventory** worksheet, in cell **E1,** enter a formula using a counting function to count the number of items on sale. Count the numerical values in the *ItemID* column (cells **A7:A20**).

2. On the **SaleInventory** worksheet, in cell **E2,** enter a formula using a counting function to count the number of items on sale. Count the values in the *Item* column (cells **B7:B20**).

3. In cell **E3,** enter a formula using a counting function to count the number of blank cells in the *QuantityInStock* column (cells **E7:E20**).

4. If you will be moving on to the next skill in this chapter, leave the workbook open to continue working. If not, save the file as directed by your instructor and close it.

Skill 3.7 Formatting Text Using Functions

Functions can do more than perform calculations. Excel includes a special group of functions to modify text. These text functions are useful for ensuring that text data have a consistent appearance. In functions, text is referred to as a **string** or **text string**.

Commonly used text functions are:

PROPER—Converts the text string to proper case (the first letter in each word is capitalized). A formula using the PROPER function looks like this: **=PROPER(D2)**

UPPER—Converts the text string to all uppercase letters. A formula using the UPPER function looks like this: **=UPPER(F2)**

LOWER—Converts the text string to all lowercase letters. A formula using the LOWER function looks like this: **=LOWER(H2)**

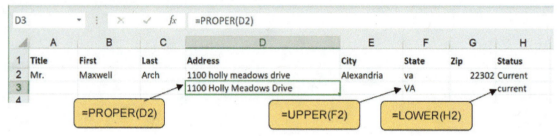

FIGURE EX 3.12

To create a formula with PROPER, UPPER, or LOWER, use either of these methods:

> If you prefer typing in the cell or the formula bar, try using Formula AutoComplete.
> If you prefer using the *Function Arguments* dialog, on the *Formulas* tab, in the *Function Library* group, click the **Text** button and click **PROPER, UPPER,** or **LOWER**.

tips & tricks

Typically, when you use one of the text functions, you are left with two groups of cells containing the same data: One group has the original incorrectly formatted text; the second group contains the formulas and displays correctly formatted text. There are two options for managing this:

> Hide the columns or rows that contain the original text. For information on hiding rows and columns, refer to the skill *Hiding and Unhiding Rows and Columns.*
> Copy the cells containing the text formulas; use one of the *Paste Values* options to paste just the values of the text formulas over the original cells, then delete the cells containing the text formulas. For information on using the *Paste Values* commands, refer to the skill *Using Paste Options.*

let me try Live!

If you do not have the data file from the previous skill open, open the student data file **EX3-07-Financial-Analysis** ⬇ and try this skill on your own:

1. On the **Customers** worksheet, enter a formula in cell **D3** to display the text from cell **D2** so the first letter in each word is capitalized.
2. On the **Customers** worksheet, enter a formula in cell **F3** to display the text from cell **F2** so all the letters display in uppercase.
3. On the **Customers** worksheet, enter a formula in cell **H3** to display the text from cell **H2** so all the letters display in lowercase.
4. If you will be moving on to the next skill in this chapter, leave the workbook open to continue working. If not, save the file as directed by your instructor and close it.

Skill 3.8 Using CONCAT to Combine Text

To **concatenate** means to link items together. You can use the **CONCAT** function to combine the text values of cells or cell ranges. CONCAT replaces the old CONCATENATE function. In Figure EX 3.13, the customer name in cell B3 is created by concatenating the values in column B (first name) and column C (last name). The formula looks like this:

   =CONCAT(B2 ," ", C2)

The argument in the middle (" ") places a one-space text string between the values of cells B2 and C2.

If you are building a long string from multiple cells, you may want to use the *Function Arguments* dialog until you become familiar with this function. Of course, you can always type directly in the cell or formula bar and use Formula AutoComplete.

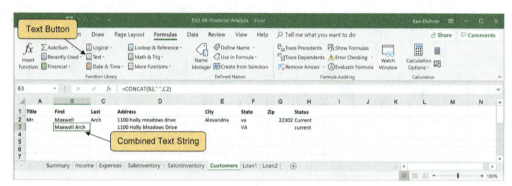

FIGURE EX 3.13

1. On the *Formulas* tab, in the *Function Library* group, click the **Text** button.

2. Click **CONCAT**.

3. In the *Function Arguments* dialog, enter each cell reference or text string you want to combine in its own argument. If one of the arguments is a blank space, enter **"
 "** in the argument box.

4. Click **OK**.

FIGURE EX 3.14

tips & tricks

For sorting purposes, you may want to keep the cells that you concatenate. If you do not want them to display in your worksheet, hide the columns or rows that contain the original text. For information on hiding rows and columns, refer to the skill *Hiding and Unhiding Rows and Columns.*

let me try Live!

If you do not have the data file from the previous skill open, open the student data file **EX3-08-Financial-Analysis** and try this skill on your own:

1. On the **Customers** worksheet, enter a formula in cell **B3** to combine the text from cells **B2** and **C2** to display the customer name in the format *Maxwell Arch.* Don't forget the argument for the space.
2. If you will be moving on to the next skill in this chapter, leave the workbook open to continue working. If not, save the file as directed by your instructor and close it.

Skill 3.9 Using TEXTJOIN to Combine Text

Another way to combine text is to use the **TEXTJOIN** function. TEXTJOIN concatenates cells using a **delimiter** character to separate values in the new text string. In Figure EX 3.15, the customer name in cell B4 is created by combining the values in A2 (title), B2 (first name), and C2 (last name) and separating each text value with a space. The formula looks like this:

=TEXTJOIN(" ", TRUE,A2:C2)

To combine text using TEXTJOIN:

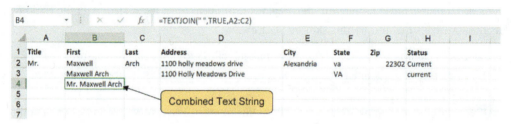

FIGURE EX 3.15

1. On the *Formulas* tab, in the *Function Library* group, click the **Text** button.
2. Click **TEXTJOIN**.
3. Enter the **Delimiter** argument. This argument defines the character to use between each text item.
4. Enter the **Ignore_empty** argument. If set to TRUE, the function will skip blank cells. If set to FALSE, the function will include the blank cells, resulting in two of the delimiter characters together.

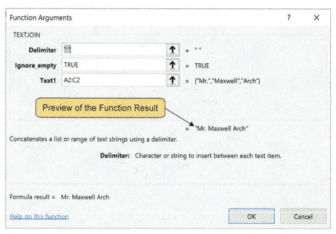

FIGURE EX 3.16

5. Enter the **Text1** argument. This argument is first text string, cell, or cell range to combine. If you use a cell range, the delimiter character will be added between the values from each cell in the range.
6. Continue adding **Text** arguments as necessary.
7. Click **OK**.

tips & tricks

When using a space as the delimiter in a TEXTJOIN formula, if you type the formula directly in the cell or address bar, you must enclose the space in quotation marks. If you use the *Function Arguments* dialog, you can just type the space in the *Delimiter* argument box. Excel will add the quotation marks for you.

let me try Live!

If you do not have the data file from the previous skill open, open the student data file **EX3-09-Financial-Analysis** and try this skill on your own:

1. On the **Customers** worksheet, enter a formula in cell **B4** to combine the text from cells **A2:C2** to display the customer name in the format *Maxwell Arch*. Use a space as the delimiter. Ignore blank cells. Use a cell range as the *Text1* argument.
2. If you will be moving on to the next skill in this chapter, leave the workbook open to continue working. If not, save the file as directed by your instructor and close it.

Skill 3.10 Creating Formulas Referencing Data from Other Worksheets

Cell references are not limited to cells within the same worksheet. To specify a cell location in another worksheet, begin the reference with the name of the worksheet followed by an exclamation point ! and then the cell reference. This feature is useful when you want to create summary sheets or perform analysis on data from multiple sheets at once.

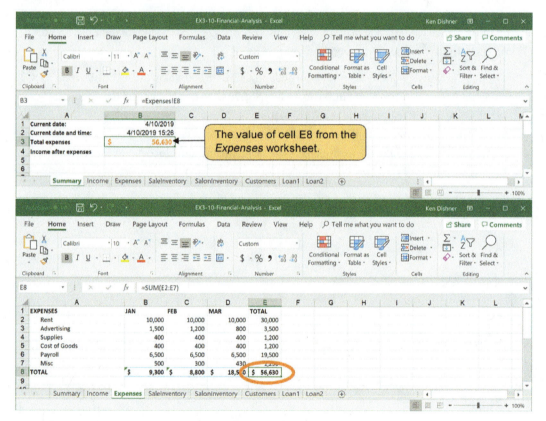

FIGURE EX 3.17

The formula shown in Figure EX 3.17 displays the value of cell E8 from the *Expenses* worksheet:

= Expenses!E8

To include a reference to a cell from another sheet in your workbook:

1. Click the cell where you want the formula.
2. Type: =

3. Navigate to the cell you want to reference by clicking the sheet tab and then clicking the cell. Notice Excel adds the worksheet name to the cell reference for you.

4. Press Enter to complete the formula.

You can also refer to cells in other worksheets within formulas as shown in Figure EX 3.18.

=Income!B1-Expenses!E8

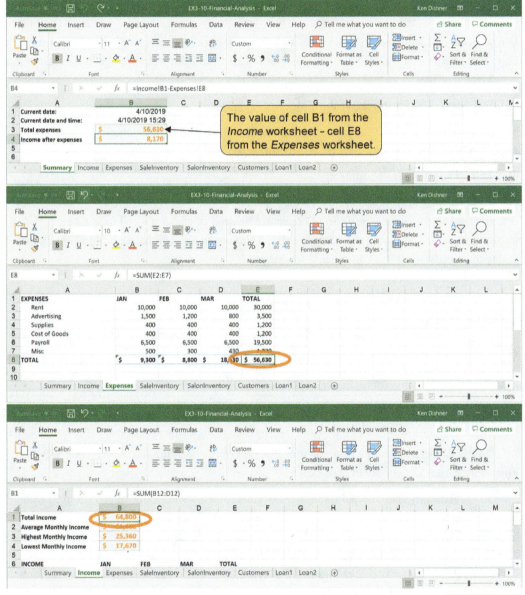

FIGURE EX 3.18

3.10 | Creating Formulas Referencing Data from Other Worksheets   **EX3-25**

To include a reference to another worksheet in a formula:

1. Begin entering the formula as normal.
2. When you want to add a reference to a cell in another sheet, click the sheet tab, then click the cell(s) you want to add to the formula or click and drag to select a cell range.
3. When you are finished with the formula, Press [Enter].

tips & tricks

If your workbook includes multiple sheets with the same data structure, you can create a formula that references the same cell(s) on multiple sheets. This is called a **3-D reference**. A formula with a 3-D reference looks like this:

=SUM(ExpensesQ1:ExpensesQ4!A4:A7)

The result of this formula is the sum of the values in cells A4 through A7 on all worksheets from *ExpensesQ1* through the worksheet named *ExpensesQ4*.

To add a 3-D reference to a formula:

1. Begin entering the formula as you would normally.
2. Then, when you want to add the 3-D reference, instead of clicking a cell on a single worksheet, first select the sheet tabs for all the sheets you want included, and then click the specific cell(s) you want on the first worksheet.
3. Press [Enter].

tell me more

You can use the same techniques taught in this skill to reference cells in other workbooks. When you reference a cell in another workbook, you create a link between the two workbooks.

let me try Live!

If you do not have the data file from the previous skill open, open the student data file **EX3-10-Financial-Analysis** ⬇ and try this skill on your own:

1. On the **Summary** sheet, in cell **B3,** enter a formula to display the value of cell **E8** from the **Expenses** worksheet.
2. On the **Summary** sheet, in cell **B4,** enter a formula to calculate the value of cell **B1** from the **Income** worksheet **minus** cell **E8** from the **Expenses** worksheet.
3. If you will be moving on to the next skill in this chapter, leave the workbook open to continue working. If not, save the file as directed by your instructor and close it.

Skill 3.11 Naming Ranges of Cells

Cell references like A4 and F7:F20 do not provide much information about what data the cells contain —they just tell you where the cells are located in the worksheet. However, you can assign names to cells or ranges of cells to give your cell references names that are more user-friendly. These **names** (also called **range names** or **named ranges**) act as a list of shortcuts to the cell locations.

To create a named range:

1. Select the cell or range of cells to which you want to assign a name.
2. Type the name in the *Name* box to the left of the formula bar.
3. Press Enter to apply the name to the cell(s).

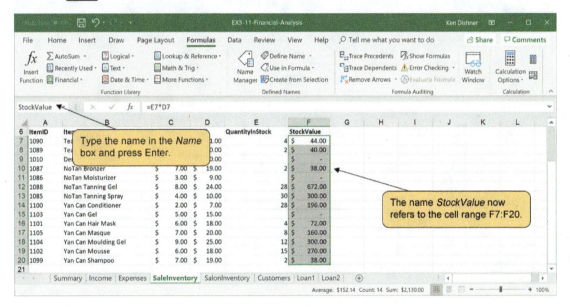

FIGURE EX 3.19

If your worksheet is organized in a table format, with column or row labels, you can automatically create named ranges for each column or row using the labels as names:

1. Select the range of cells you want to name including the labels.
2. On the *Formulas* tab, in the *Defined Names* group, click the **Create from Selection** button.
3. In the *Create Names from Selection* dialog, click the check box to indicate where the names are (*Top row, Left column, Bottom row,* or *Right column*).
4. Click **OK**.

Excel automatically creates named ranges for the cell range associated with each label. The named ranges will not include the labels. The *Create Names from Selection* command in Figure EX 3.20 will create the following named ranges:

Name:	ItemID	Item	Wholesale	QuantityInStock	ReorderLevel
Refers to cell range:	A5:A20	B5:B20	C5:C20	D5:D20	E5:E20

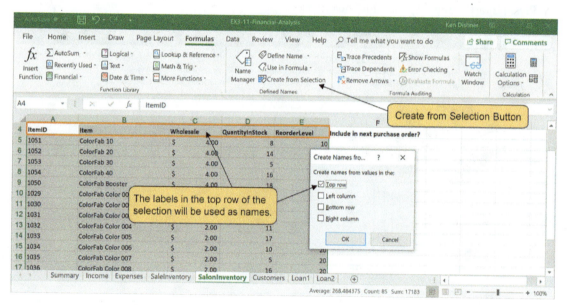

FIGURE EX 3.20

tips & tricks

Remember, names may not include spaces. If you use the *Create Names from Selection* command and the values for your names include spaces, Excel will replace the spaces with underscore _ characters.

Also, you cannot use numbers as names. When using *Create Names from Selection*, be sure to check that the text in the row or column containing labels is valid for names.

another method

You can also create new names through the *New Name* dialog.

1. On the *Formulas* tab, in the *Defined Names* group, click the **Define Name** button.
2. The selected cell(s) is (are) entered in the *Refers to* box.
3. Type the name you want in the *Name* box. If the cell to the immediate left or immediately above the selected cell appears to include a label, Excel will prepopulate the *Name* box with that text.
4. Click **OK**

let me try Live!

If you do not have the data file from the previous skill open, open the student data file **EX3-11-Financial-Analysis** 📥 and try this skill on your own:

1. On the *SaleInventory* worksheet, select cells **F7:F20,** and name them as follows: **StockValue**
2. Go to the **SalonInventory** worksheet, select cells **A4:E20** and use the *Create from Selection* command to create named ranges for the data table **A5:E20** using the labels in row **4** as the basis for the names.
3. If you will be moving on to the next skill in this chapter, leave the workbook open to continue working. If not, save the file as directed by your instructor and close it.

Skill 3.12 Working with Named Ranges

Rather than using a range of cells in your formulas, you can use a named range. The name will always refer to the cells, even if their position in the worksheet changes. Using named ranges in your formulas also makes it easier for others to use your workbook. Which formula is easier to understand: **=SUM(F7:F20)** or **=SUM(StockValue)**?

Formula AutoComplete lists named ranges as well as functions. Named ranges are identified by the label icon next to the name 🏷. Using the AutoComplete list is a good way to avoid typographical errors and ensure that you enter the name correctly.

To use a named range in a formula:

1. Click the cell where you want to enter the new formula.
2. Type the formula, substituting the range name for the cell references.
3. As you type alphabetical characters, Formula AutoComplete will offer name suggestions. If you see the name you want, double-click it and Excel will insert the name into the formula.
4. Press Enter to accept the formula.

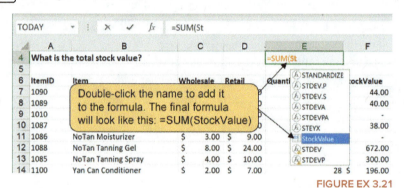

FIGURE EX 3.21

tips & tricks

> When you copy and paste a formula containing a named range, the name does not change with the new position in the workbook (similar to using an absolute reference).
> If you move a named cell, the name updates with the new cell location automatically.

another method

> - On the *Formulas* tab, in the *Defined Names* group, click the **Use in Formula** button to display a list of names in your workbook, and then click one of the names to insert it into your formula.
> - You can also click **Paste Names...** from the bottom of the *Use in Formula* The *Paste Names* dialog opens and lists all of the names in your workbook. Click a name and then click **OK** to add it to your formula.

let me try Live!

If you do not have the data file from the previous skill open, open the student data file **EX3-12-Financial-Analysis** and try this skill on your own:

1. On the *SaleInventory* worksheet, in cell **E4**, enter a formula to calculate the total stock value. Use the **SUM** function and use the range name **StockValue** as the function argument.
2. If you will be moving on to the next skill in this chapter, leave the workbook open to continue working. If not, save the file as directed by your instructor and close it.

Skill 3.13 Updating Named Ranges with the Name Manager

The **Name Manager** lists all the named ranges used in your workbook, the current value for each, the cells to which the name refers (including the sheet name), the scope of the name (whether it is limited to a specific worksheet or applies to the entire workbook), and comments (if there are any).

To open the Name Manager, on the *Formulas* tab, in the *Defined Names* group, click the **Name Manager** button.

FIGURE EX 3.22

To change the cell or range of cells to which a name refers:

1. Open the Name Manager and select the name you want to modify.

2. Edit the cell references in the *Refers to* You can also click the **Collapse Dialog** button to hide the Name Manager, and then click and drag to select the new cell range. When you are finished, click the **Expand Dialog** button to display the Name Manager again.

3. Click the checkmark icon to the left of the *Refers to* box to accept the change.

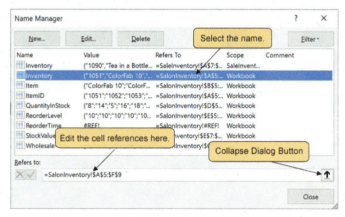

FIGURE EX 3.23

4. Click **Close** to close the Name Manager. If you forgot to save your change, Excel will ask if you want to save the change you made to the cell reference. Click **Yes**.

let me try Live!

If you do not have the data file from the previous skill open, open the student data file **EX3-13-Financial-Analysis** and try this skill on your own:

1. Open the Name Manager.
2. Edit the workbook **Inventory** name so it refers to cells **A5:F20** on the **SalonInventory** worksheet. Be sure to modify the second Inventory name, not the one that is limited in scope to just the **SaleInventory** worksheet.
3. Close the Name Manager.
4. If you will be moving on to the next skill in this chapter, leave the workbook open to continue working. If not, save the file as directed by your instructor and close it.

Skill 3.14 Editing and Deleting Names with the Name Manager

When you copy data, you may find that some of the names in your workbook are repeated. Remember that names must be unique—but only within their scopes. You can have more than one named range with the same name, but only one can belong to the entire workbook. The others are specific to the worksheet in which they are defined.

In Figure EX 3.24, there are two *Inventory* names. The first is limited in scope to the *SaleInventory* worksheet. If you refer to the name *Inventory* in a formula in any other sheet in the workbook, it will refer to the second *Inventory* named range.

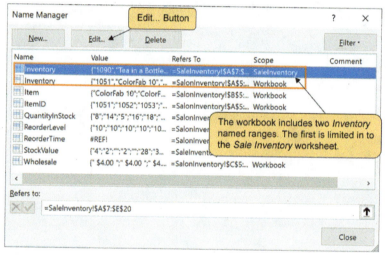

FIGURE EX 3.24

Duplicate names can be confusing. A good practice is to rename duplicates to make them easier to identify and use.

To change a name:

1. Open the Name Manager.
2. Click the name you want to modify, and then click the **Edit...** button.
3. The *Edit Name* dialog opens.
4. Type the new name in the *Name* box.
5. Click **OK** to save your changes.
6. Click the **Close** button to close the Name Manager.

FIGURE EX 3.25

When you change a name, Excel updates the name in any formulas that reference that name.

If your workbook includes names you no longer need, you should delete them.

To delete a name:

1. On the *Formulas* tab, in the *Defined Names* group, click the **Name Manager** button.

2. Click the name you want to delete, and then click the **Delete** button.

3. Excel displays a message asking if you are sure you want to delete the name. Click **OK**.

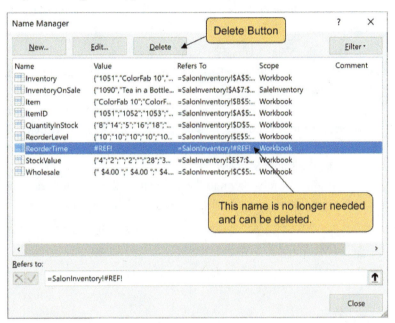

FIGURE EX 3.26

tips & tricks

> There are two types of names identified in the Name Manager. **Defined names** are the names you created and names that Excel creates automatically when you define a print area or print titles. Table names are names created automatically when you define a data range as a table. By default, tables are named Table1, Table2, Table3, and so on. To make table names easier to use, consider renaming them through the Name Manager.

> If your workbook includes many named ranges, you may find it useful to filter the list of names in the Name Manager. Click the **Filter** button in the upper right corner of the Name Manager and filter the list to show only names with errors or only names limited in scope to a worksheet.

let me try Live!

If you do not have the data file from the previous skill open, open the student data file **EX3-14-Financial-Analysis** ⬇ and try this skill on your own:

1. Open the Name Manager.
2. There are two *Inventory* Rename the one that is limited in scope to the *SaleInventory* worksheet to: **InventoryOnSale**
3. In the Name Manager, review the information about the *ReorderTime* The name results in an error—probably because the data to which it referred were deleted. Delete the **ReorderTime** name.
4. Close the Name Manager.
5. If you will be moving on to the next skill in this chapter, leave the workbook open to continue working. If not, save the file as directed by your instructor and close it.

Skill 3.15 Using the Logical Function IF

The **IF** logical function returns one value if a condition is true and another value if the condition is false. The IF function can return a numerical value or display a text string.

The formula in Figure 3.27 uses the IF function to determine whether or not an item should be ordered. If the value of cell D2 (the quantity in stock) is greater than the value of cell E2 (the reorder level), the formula will return "do not order". If the value of cell D2 is not greater than the value of cell E2, the formula will return "order". The formula looks like this:

=IF(D5>E5,"do not order","order")

In Figure EX 3.27, the value of cell D5 is *not* greater than the value of cell E5, so the IF function returns the *Value_if_false* argument displaying the word *order*. In the next row in the worksheet, the value of cell D6 *is* greater than the value of cell E6, so the IF function returns the *Value_if_true* argument displaying the phrase *do not order*.

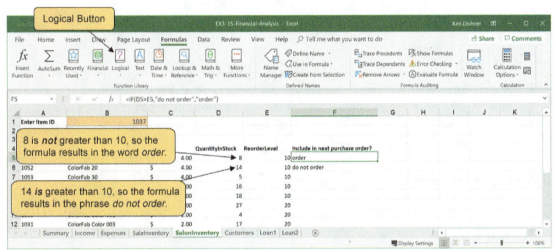

FIGURE EX 3.27

To create a formula using the IF function:

1. Select the cell where you want to enter the formula.
2. On the *Formulas* tab, in the *Function Library* group, click the **Logical** button.
3. Select **IF** to open the *Function Arguments* dialog. IF functions take three arguments as shown in the *Function Arguments* dialog in Figure EX 3.28.
4. Enter the **Logical_test** argument. This argument states the condition you want to test for. The *Logical_test* always includes a comparison operator (=, >, <, etc.).
5. Enter the **Value_if_true** argument. This argument is the text string or value that will be displayed or the formula that will be calculated if the *Logical_test* argument is true.

6. Enter the **Value_if_false** argument. This argument is the text string or value that will be displayed or the formula that will be calculated if the *Logical_test* argument is false.

7. Click **OK.**

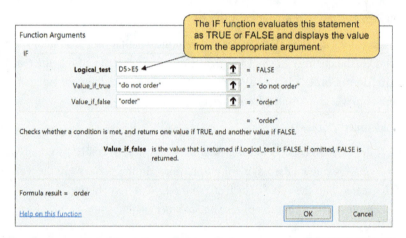

FIGURE EX 3.28

tips & tricks

If you use the *Function Arguments* dialog to enter text as the *Value_if_true* or the *Value_if_false* argument, you do not need to include the quotation marks. Excel will add them for you. However, if you type the formula directly in the cell or the formula bar, you must include quotation marks around the text.

let me try Live!

If you do not have the data file from the previous skill open, open the student data file **EX3-15-Financial-Analysis** and try this skill on your own:

1. On the **SalonInventory** worksheet, enter a formula in cell **F5** using the logical function IF to display **do not order** if the quantity in stock (cell **D5**) is greater than the reorder level (cell **E5**) and **order** if it is not.

2. Copy the formula to cells **F6:F20** and review the results for each row.

3. If you will be moving on to the next skill in this chapter, leave the workbook open to continue working. If not, save the file as directed by your instructor and close it.

from the perspective of . . .

INSTRUCTOR

I use a spreadsheet to keep a grid of class attendance by student and by day. Using formulas and functions for grading gives me the flexibility to add scores, calculate averages, and provide feedback to my students.

Skill 3.16 Calculating Loan Payments Using the PMT Function

One of the most useful financial functions in Excel is **PMT** (payment), which you can use to calculate loan payments. The PMT function is based on constant payments and a constant interest rate. To calculate a payment using PMT, you need three pieces of information: the interest rate (the *Rate* argument), the number of payments (the *Nper* argument), and the amount of the loan (the *Pv* argument).

> **=PMT(Rate,Nper,Pv)**

Because the result of the formula is a payment (money going out), it is expressed as a negative number. If you want the result expressed as a positive number instead, add a negative symbol before the loan amount (the *Pv* argument).

When working with complex functions like PMT, use cell references as arguments rather than entering values directly. This way you can change values in your spreadsheet and see the results instantly without opening the *Function Arguments* dialog again.

> Using cell references, the PMT function in Figure EX 3.29 looks like this:
> **=PMT(B4/12,B5,-B3)**

In this example, the ***annual*** interest rate in cell B4 is 4%. To calculate ***monthly*** payments, the interest rate must be divided by the number of payments per year (12).

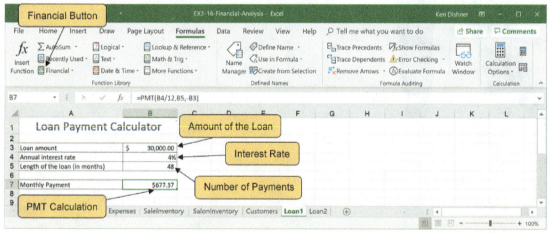

FIGURE EX 3.29

To use the PMT function:

1. Select the cell where you want to enter the formula.

2. On the *Formulas* tab, in the *Function Library* group, click the **Financial** button.

3. Select **PMT** from the list to open the *Function Arguments* dialog. PMT takes three required arguments and two optional arguments as shown in Figure EX 3.30.

4. Enter the **Rate** argument. This argument is the interest rate. Usually, interest rate is expressed as an annual rate. If the loan requires a monthly payment, the annual percentage rate (APR) should be divided by 12.

5. Enter the **Nper** argument. This argument is the total number of payments over the life of the loan.

6. Enter the **Pv** argument. This argument is the present value of the loan—how much you owe now (the loan principal).

7. (Optional) The **Fv** argument is future value of the loan. Excel assumes a value of 0 unless you include the argument and specify a different value. If you will make payments on the loan until it is completely paid off, you can leave this argument blank or enter 0.

8. (Optional) The **Type** argument represents when payments will be made during each loan period. Enter 1 if the payment is at the beginning of the period. If you omit this argument, Excel assumes a value of 0 (meaning each payment is at the end of the period).

9. Click **OK**.

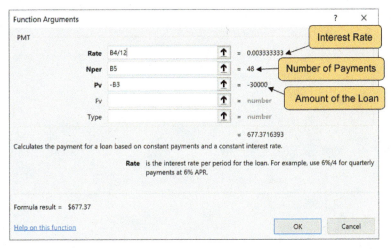

FIGURE EX 3.30

tips & tricks

It can be helpful to name the cells containing data for the function arguments with the same name as the argument. For example, name the cell with the interest rate **Rate**. Then when you build the PMT function, the cell names match the argument names. It makes creating the function easy.

let me try Live!

If you do not have the data file from the previous skill open, open the student data file
EX3-16-Financial-Analysis ⬇ and try this skill on your own:

1. On the **Loan1** worksheet, enter a formula in cell **B7** using the PMT function to calculate the monthly loan payment. Use cell references as the function arguments. Remember, payments will be monthly, so divide the annual interest rate by 12. Use a negative number for the **Pv** argument. Do not include the optional arguments.

2. If you will be moving on to the next skill in this chapter, leave the workbook open to continue working. If not, save the file as directed by your instructor and close it.

Skill 3.17 Finding Data Using the VLOOKUP Function

Excel includes a group of functions that can be used to look up matching values in a cell range. The **VLOOKUP** function finds a value or cell reference in a cell range and returns another value from the same row. VLOOKUP requires you to specify the value you want to find, the cell range that contains the data, and the column that contains the value you want the function to return.

$$=VLOOKUP(Lookup\_value, Table\_array, Col\_index\_num, Range\_lookup)$$

The formula in Figure 3.31 finds the value from cell **B2** in the cell range named **Inventory** and then returns the value from the second column of the range. In other words, VLOOKUP finds the item ID and returns the item name.

$$=VLOOKUP(B2, Inventory, 2, FALSE)$$

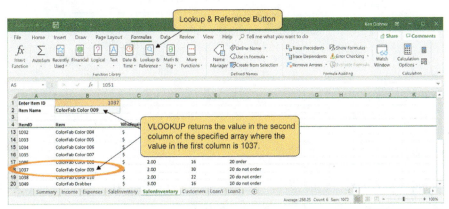

FIGURE EX 3.31

To use the VLOOKUP function:

1. Select the cell where you want to enter the formula.
2. On the *Formulas* tab, in the *Function Library* group, click the **Lookup & Reference** button.
3. Select **VLOOKUP** from the list to open the *Function Arguments* dialog. VLOOKUP takes three required arguments and one optional argument as shown in Figure EX 3.32.
4. Enter the **Lookup_value** argument. Enter the cell reference for which you want to find a corresponding value, in other words, the value you want to look up. The *Lookup_value* must be located in the first column of the cell range defined in the *Table_array* argument.
5. Enter the **Table_array** argument. Enter the range of cells (or the range name) that contains the lookup data. If your data include a header row, do not include it in the range used for the *Table_array* argument.

6. Enter the **Col_index_num** argument. This argument is the position of the column in the *Table_array* from which the function should return a matching value. Enter the column number, not the letter or the column heading.

7. (optional) Enter the **Range_lookup** argument. Type FALSE if you want to find only an exact match for the value entered in the *Lookup_value* box. If you omit this argument, Excel assumes a value of **TRUE** and will return the value for the closest match in the first column.

8. Click **OK.**

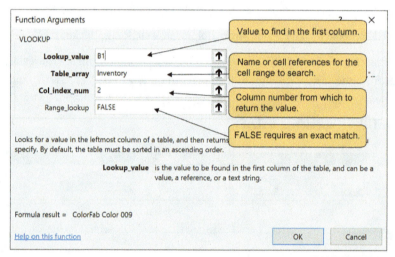

FIGURE EX 3.32

tips & tricks

If you do not specify *False* for the *Range_lookup* argument, be aware that the formula will return the first close match it finds. You may see unexpected results.

tell me more

The examples here all use the VLOOKUP function to find corresponding values in different columns within the same row (a *vertical* lookup). The **HLOOKUP** function works similarly, except you use it to find corresponding values in different rows within the same column (a *horizontal* lookup).

    Use HLOOKUP when your worksheet uses a horizontal layout—few rows with many columns.

    Use VLOOKUP when your worksheet uses a vertical layout—few columns with many rows.

let me try Live!

If you do not have the data file from the previous skill open, open the student data file **EX3-17-Financial-Analysis** ⬇ and try this skill on your own:

1. On the **SalonInventory** worksheet, enter a formula in cell **B2** using the VLOOKUP function to find the item name for the item number listed in cell **B1**. Use the name **Inventory** for the lookup table. The item names are located in column **2** of the lookup table. Require an exact match.

2. If you will be moving on to the next skill in this chapter, leave the workbook open to continue working. If not, save the file as directed by your instructor and close it.

Skill 3.18 Checking Formulas for Errors

Some worksheet errors are easily identifiable—such as divide by zero errors, which look like this in your worksheet: **#DIV/0!** (because Excel cannot calculate a value to display). Other potential errors, like formulas that leave out part of a cell range, are harder to find yourself. You can use Excel's error checking features to review your worksheet for errors.

Cells that include potential errors are marked with a green triangle in the upper-left corner of the cell. When you click the cell, Excel displays a **Smart Tag** to help you resolve the error.

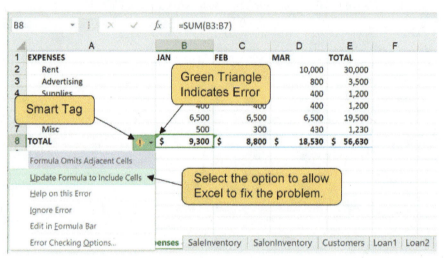

FIGURE EX 3.33

To use Smart Tags to resolve errors in formulas:

1. When a Smart Tag appears, move your mouse over the icon to display a tool tip describing the possible error.
2. Click the **Smart Tag** to display the possible error resolutions.
3. If you want to keep the formula as it is, select **Ignore Error.**
4. If you want to resolve the error, select one of the options:
   - The first option is usually a suggestion of how to resolve the error. Click it to accept Excel's suggestion.
   - Select **Help on this error** to open Microsoft Office Help.
   - Select **Ignore Error** to leave the cell unchanged.
   - Select **Edit in Formula Bar** to manually edit the formula.
   - Select **Error Checking Options...** to open the *Options* dialog and modify the way that Excel checks for errors.
5. Once you have made a selection from the Smart Tag options, the Smart Tag is dismissed.

Error checking is also available from the *Formulas* tab, *Formula Auditing* group. The *Error Checking* dialog displays each error it finds, allowing you to resolve or ignore each error in turn.

To use error checking to find errors in your worksheet:

1. On the *Formulas* tab in the *Formula Auditing* group, click the **Error Checking** button.
2. The *Error Checking* dialog displays information about the first error. The buttons available in the dialog will differ, depending on the type of error found.
   - If Excel is able to offer a solution to the error, the dialog will include a button to accept the suggested fix.
   - Click the **Help on this error** button to open Microsoft Office Help.
   - Click **Ignore Error** to dismiss the error. Excel will ignore this error until you manually reset ignored errors through Excel *Options.*
   - Click **Edit in Formula Bar** to fix the error manually.
3. Click the **Next** button to see the next error in your worksheet.
4. When you have reviewed all errors, Excel displays a message that the error check is complete. Click **OK** to dismiss the message box.

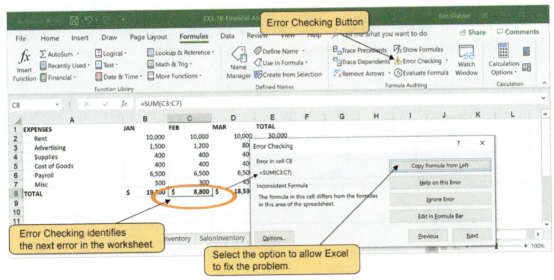

FIGURE EX 3.34

tips & tricks

You can make changes to your worksheet without closing the *Error Checking* dialog. When you click away from the dialog, one of the buttons changes to a *Resume* button and none of the other buttons in the dialog are available. When you are ready to return to error checking, click the **Resume** button.

another method

You can also start the Error Checking feature by clicking the **Error Checking** button arrow and selecting **Error Checking...**

let me try Live!

If you do not have the data file from the previous skill open, open the student data file **EX3-18-Financial-Analysis** ⬇ and try this skill on your own:

1. On the **Expenses** worksheet, cell **B8** has an error. Display the **Smart Tag** and accept Excel's suggestion for fixing the error.
2. On the *Formulas* tab, in the *Formula Auditing* group, open the *Error Checking* dialog and check the rest of the worksheet for errors.
3. Review the information about the next error and select the option to edit the error in the formula bar.
4. Correct the error and resume error checking until Excel reports that the error check is complete.
5. If you will be moving on to the next skill in this chapter, leave the workbook open to continue working. If not, save the file as directed by your instructor and close it.

Skill 3.19 Finding Errors Using Trace Precedents and Trace Dependents

In a complex worksheet where formulas often reference each other, an error in one formula can cause a ripple effect of errors throughout the entire workbook. However, finding and fixing the formula that is the root cause of the errors can be difficult. One way to review your workbook for errors is to display the dependencies between formulas.

There are two types of dependencies: precedents and dependents. A **precedent** is the cell containing the formula or value the selected cell refers to. A **dependent** is the cell containing a formula that references the value or formula in the selected cell. On the *Formulas* tab, the *Formula Auditing* group includes commands for displaying and hiding arrows tracing dependencies.

Tracer arrows normally appear blue. If the tracer arrow points to a cell that contains an error, the tracer arrow will appear red. If the tracer arrow points to a cell that references a cell in another worksheet or workbook, the arrow will appear black and include a small worksheet icon. Double-click the tracer arrow to open the *Go To* dialog to navigate to the worksheet or workbook that contains the referenced cell.

Figure EX 3.35 shows both precedent tracer arrows for cell B8. You can see that the precedent arrow changes from blue to red at cell B6. The formula in that cell is the first error. (However, the error itself is not necessarily in that cell. It could be in another cell that B6 refers to.)

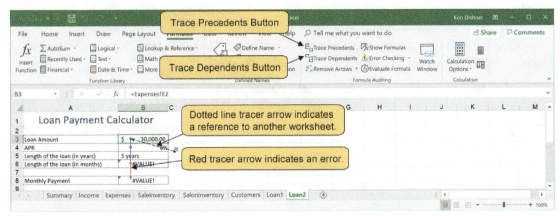

FIGURE EX 3.35

To trace precedents:

1. Select the cell containing the formula for which you want to trace precedents.
2. On the *Formulas* tab, in the *Formula Auditing* group, click the **Trace Precedents** button.
3. Tracer arrows appear pointing to the selected cell from precedent cells.

To trace dependents:

1. Select the cell containing the formula for which you want to trace dependents.
2. On the *Formulas* tab, in the *Formula Auditing* group, click the **Trace Dependents** button.
3. Tracer arrows appear pointing from the selected cell to dependent cells.

To remove the tracer arrows from your worksheet, on the *Formulas* tab, in the *Formula Auditing* group, click the **Remove Arrows** button arrow and select the option you want:

> To remove the precedent tracer arrows, select **Remove Precedent Arrows.**
> To remove the dependent tracer arrows, select **Remove Dependent Arrows.**
> To remove all tracer arrows at once, select **Remove Arrows.** Clicking the *Remove Arrows* button instead of the button arrow will also remove all the tracer arrows.

tips & tricks

Tracer arrows cannot identify cells with incorrect values or values of the wrong type (for example, a text value where a number is expected). However, using the tracer arrows may help you find those errors yourself.

tell me more

There may be multiple layers of dependencies in your workbook. Clicking the **Trace Precedents** button or the **Trace Dependents** button once only displays the immediate dependencies. To display tracer arrows from the precedent and dependent cells to their precedents and dependents, click the appropriate button again. Continue clicking the **Trace Precedents** button or the **Trace Dependents** button until you reach the end of the trail.

Selecting **Remove Precedent Arrows** and **Remove Dependent Arrows** removes the tracer arrows one level at a time.

another method

If the selected cell contains an error, you can display tracer arrows by clicking the **Error Checking** button arrow and selecting **Trace Error.**

let me try Live!

If you do not have the data file from the previous skill open, open the student data file **EX3-19-Financial-Analysis** and try this skill on your own:

1. On the **Loan2** worksheet, show the dependent arrows for cell **B6.**
2. Show the precedent arrows for cell **B8.**
3. Show the next level of precedent arrows. Note that cell B3 refers to a cell in another worksheet.
4. Change the value in cell **B5** to: 5. Note that the arrows change color from red to blue.
5. Hide all of the arrows at once.
6. If you will be moving on to the next skill in this chapter, leave the workbook open to continue working. If not, save the file as directed by your instructor and close it.

Skill 3.20 Displaying and Printing Formulas

How do you troubleshoot a worksheet that is displaying unexpected values? When you look at a worksheet, you see only the results of formulas–cells display the values, not the formulas themselves. When you click a cell, the formula is displayed in the formula bar. But what if you want to view all of the formulas in your worksheet at once?

To display the formulas in the current worksheet instead of values:

> On the *Formulas* tab in the *Formula Auditing* group, click the **Show Formulas** button.

To hide the formulas and display calculated values:

> Click the **Show Formulas** button again.

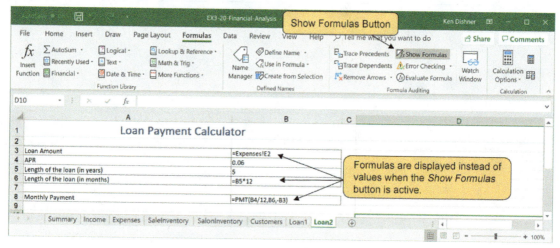

FIGURE EX 3.36

tips & tricks

When you show formulas in your worksheet, Excel automatically adjusts the column sizes so the formulas are visible

another method

The keyboard shortcut to display (or hide) formulas is [Ctrl] + [` ] (the [ `] key is directly to the left of [1] at the top of the keyboard).

let me try Live!

If you do not have the data file from the previous skill open, open the student data file **EX3-20-Financial-Analysis** and try this skill on your own:

1. On the **Loan2** worksheet, display the formulas in this worksheet.
2. Preview how the worksheet will look when printed.
3. Save the file as directed by your instructor and close it.

key terms

Formula AutoComplete	Concatenate
AVERAGE	CONCAT
Mean	TEXTJOIN
Median	Delimiter (TEXTJOIN)
Mode	3-D Reference
MAX	Name
MIN	Range name
NOW	Named range
TODAY	Name Manager
Volatile	Defined name
COUNT	IF
COUNTA	PMT
COUNTBLANK	VLOOKUP
String	HLOOKUP
Text String	Smart Tag
PROPER	Precedent
UPPER	Dependent
LOWER	

concept review

1. Which of these methods can you use to enter a formula using the AVERAGE function?
    a. Formula AutoComplete
    b. AutoSum
    c. Function Arguments dialog
    d. all of the above
2. Which of these functions returns the current date and time?
    a. TIME
    b. DATE
    c. TODAY
    d. NOW
3. To count the number of cells that contain text or numerical values, but not blanks, use which function?
    a. COUNT
    b. COUNTALL
    c. COUNTA
    d. COUNTBLANK
4. What is the definition of *concatenate*?
    a. to convert text to proper case
    b. to link items together
    c. to look up a value
    d. a logical comparison
5. A formula to display the value of cell A5 on the Inventory worksheet looks like this:
    a. =Inventory(A5)
    b. =Inventory!A5
    c. =A5,Inventory!
    d. =Inventory,A5
6. Which of these is *not* an acceptable name for a named range?
    a. CURRENTINVENTORY
    b. Current Inventory
    c. CurrentInventory
    d. Current_Inventory
7. Identify the *Value_if_true* argument in this formula: =IF(A2>100,"high","low")
    a. A2
    b. 100
    c. high
    d. low

8. Identify the *Pv* argument in this formula: =PMT(B1/12,B2,-B3)

    a. B1

    b. B1/12

    c. B2

    d. -B3

9. In a PMT function, what is the *Pv* argument?

    a. the number of payments

    b. the present value of the loan

    c. the interest rate

    d. the value of the loan at the end of the loan period

10. A(n) _____ is the cell containing a formula that references the value or formula in the selected cell.

    a. argument

    b. precedent

    c. dependent

    d. 3-D reference

projects

Data files for projects can be found by logging into your SIMnet account and going to the Library section.

skill review **3.1**

In this project you will complete a staff billing workbook similar to the one you worked on in Chapter 1. This worksheet is more complicated and uses a variety of formulas to calculate information about each staff member's weekly billing and to generate client bills from the staff hours. As you work on the *Marshall Hours* worksheet, you can use the *Lutz Hours* or *Stevens Hours* worksheet as a guide. This is a long project. Be sure to save your work often!

Skills needed to complete this project:

- Naming Ranges of Cells (Skill 3.11)
- Using CONCAT to Combine Text (Skill 3.8)
- Creating Formulas Referencing Data from Other Worksheets (Skill 3.10)
- Finding Data Using the VLOOKUP Function (Skill 3.17)
- Working with Named Ranges (Skill 3.12)
- Using the Function Arguments Dialog to Enter Functions (Skill 3.1)
- Creating Formulas Using Counting Functions (Skill 3.6)
- Using Formula AutoComplete to Enter Functions (Skill 3.2)
- Calculating Averages (Skill 3.3)
- Finding Minimum and Maximum Values (Skill 3.4)
- Using the Logical Function IF (Skill 3.15)
- Displaying and Printing Formulas (Skill 3.20)
- Using Date and Time Functions (Skill 3.5)
- Checking Formulas for Errors (Skill 3.18)
- Finding Errors Using Trace Precedents and Trace Dependents (Skill 3.19)
- Updating Named Ranges with the Name Manager (Skill 3.13)
- Editing and Deleting Names with the Name Manager (Skill 3.14)
- Calculating Loan Payments Using the PMT Function (Skill 3.16)

1. Open the start file **EX2019-SkillReview-3-1** and resave the file as:
   `[your initials]EX-SkillReview-3-1`
2. If the workbook opens in Protected View, click the **Enable Editing** button in the Message Bar at the top of the workbook so you can modify it.
3. The *Lutz Hours* and *Stevens Hours* worksheets are completed, but they contain errors. You'll need to fix the errors before working on the *Marshall Hours* worksheet.
   a. Click the **Lutz Hours** sheet tab.
   b. Click cell **C4.**
   c. Notice the #NAME? error. Move your mouse over the **Smart Tag** icon to display a tool tip describing the possible error—*The formula contains unrecognized text.*

    d. The formula =VLOOKUP(C3,BillableRates,4,FALSE) references the named range BillableRates. That name has not yet been defined. That's what is causing the error.

4. Billable rates are kept in the *Rates* worksheet. Create the name **BillableRates** to use in formulas throughout the workbook.

    a. Click the **Rates** sheet tab.

    b. Select cells **A3:D5.**

    c. Type BillableRates in the *Name* box.

    d. Press [Enter].

    e. Return to the *Lutz Hours* worksheet. Notice all the errors have been fixed. Now you can move on to completing the *Marshall Hours* sheet.

5. Use a formula to display Marshall's full name in the format *Bob Smith.* Staff names are kept in the *Rates* worksheet.

    a. Click the **Marshall Hours** sheet tab, and click cell **C2.**

    b. On the *Formulas* tab, in the *Function Library* group, click the **Text** button, and select **CONCAT.**

    c. Click the **Rates** sheet tab. If necessary, position the *Function Arguments* dialog so you can click the sheet tabs.

    d. Click cell **C4** to enter the cell reference in the *Text1* argument box.

    e. Press [Tab] to move to the *Text2* argument box.

    f. Type " " to place a space between the first and last names.

    g. Press [Tab] to move to the *Text3* argument box.

    h. Click the **Rates** tab again.

    i. Click cell **B4** to enter the text reference in the *Text3* argument box.

    j. Click **OK.** The completed formula should look like this: **=CONCAT(Rates!C4," ",Rates!B4)**

6. Use a formula to look up Marshall's current billable rate. Use the employee number as the lookup value.

    a. Click cell **C4.**

    b. On the *Formulas* tab, in the *Function Library* group, click the **Lookup & Reference** button, and select **VLOOKUP.**

    c. Click cell **C3** to enter it in the *Lookup_value* argument box.

    d. Type `BillableRates` in the *Table_array* argument box.

    e. The rates are located in the fourth column of the lookup table. Type 4 in the *Col_index_num* argument box.

    f. Ensure that the function will return only an exact match. Type `false` in the *Range_lookup* argument box.

    g. Click **OK.** The completed formula should look like this: **=VLOOKUP(C3,BillableRates,4,FALSE)**

7. Enter formulas to calculate the number of clients served each day.

    a. Click cell **B16.**

    b. Type `=COU`

    c. Double-click **COUNT** in the Formula AutoComplete list.

    d. Click cell **B8** and drag to cell **B11.**

    e. Press ⎡Enter⎤. The completed formula should look like this: **=COUNT(B8:B11)**

    f. Copy the formula in cell **B16** to cells **C16:H16.** Use any method you want.

8. Use a formula to calculate the average daily billable hours.

    a. Click cell **H18.**

    b. Type `=AV` and then double-click **AVERAGE** in the Formula AutoComplete list.

    c. Click cell **B12** and drag to cell **H12.**

    d. Press ⎡Enter⎤. The completed formula should look like this: **=AVERAGE(B12:H12)**

9. Use a formula to calculate the total billable hours for the week.

    a. Click cell **H19.**

    b. Type `=SU` and then double-click **SUM** in the Formula AutoComplete list.

    c. Click cell **B12** and drag to cell **H12.**

    d. Press ⎡Enter⎤. The completed formula should look like this: **=SUM(B12:H12)**

10. Use a formula to calculate the lowest daily bill for the week.

    a. Click cell **H21.**

    b. Type `=MIN(` and then click cell **B14** and drag to cell **H14.**

    c. Press ⎡Enter⎤. The completed formula should look like this: **=MIN(B14:H14)**

11. Use a formula to calculate the highest daily bill for the week.

    a. Click cell **H22.**

    b. Type `=MAX(` and then click cell **B14** and drag to cell **H14.**

    c. Press ⎡Enter⎤. The completed formula should look like this: **=MAX(B14:H14)**

12. Each staff member is required to log a minimum number of billable hours per week. Enter a formula using an IF statement to display "yes" if the total billable hours for the week are greater than or equal to the required hours and "no" if they are not.

    a. Click cell **H3.**

    b. On the *Formulas* tab, in the *Function Library* group, click **Logical.**

    c. Click **IF.**

    d. If necessary, move the *Function Arguments* dialog to the side so you can see the worksheet data.

    e. In the *Logical_test* argument box, type: `H19>=H2`

    f. In the *Value_if_true* argument box, type: `yes`

    g. In the *Value_if_false* argument box, type: `no`

    h. Click **OK.** The completed formula should look like this: **=IF(H19>=H2,"yes","no")**

13. Display your formulas temporarily to check for accuracy.

    a. On the *Formulas* tab, in the *Formula Auditing* group, click the **Show Formulas** button.

    b. When you are ready to continue, hide the formulas and display formula values by clicking the **Show Formulas** button again.

14. Now that the worksheet for Marshall is complete, you can generate a bill for the Smith client for the week. All bills are due 60 days from the date the bill was created. Calculate the bill due date using the TODAY function.

    a. Click the **Smith Bill** sheet tab.

    b. Double-click cell **C2.**

    c. Type the formula: **=TODAY()+60**

    d. Press ⌷Enter⌷.

15. Enter formulas to reference the number of hours each staff member billed for Smith.

    a. Click cell **B5** and type = to begin the formula.

    b. Click the **Lutz Hours** sheet, and click cell **J11.**

    c. Press ⌷Enter⌷. The completed formula should look like this: **='Lutz Hours'!J11**

    d. Type **=** to begin the next formula in cell B6.

    e. Click the **Marshall Hours** sheet, and click cell **J11.**

    f. Press ⌷Enter⌷. The completed formula should look like this: **='Marshall Hours'!J11**

    g. Type **=** to begin the next formula in cell B7.

    h. Click the **Stevens Hours** sheet, and click cell **J11.**

    i. Press ⌷Enter⌷. The completed formula should look like this: **='Stevens Hours'!J11**

16. There are errors in the *Rate* and *Bill Amount* columns in the *Smith Bill* worksheet. Use your error checking skills to track down the cause of the error.

    a. On the *Formulas* tab, in the *Formula Auditing* group, click the **Error Checking** button to open the *Error Checking* dialog.

    b. After you've reviewed the first error, click the **Next** button to go to the next error. Continue reviewing each error and clicking **Next** until you receive the message that the error check is complete for the entire sheet. Click **OK.**

17. Did you notice that every error in the worksheet is a "value not available" error? You probably need to dig deeper to find the root cause of the problem.

    a. Click cell **D5** and look at the formula in the formula bar: **=B5*C5**

    b. Display the Trace Precedent and Trace Dependent arrows for this cell. On the *Formulas* tab, in the *Formula Auditing* group, click both the **Trace Precedents** button and the **Trace Dependents** button.

    c. You can see that the problem appears to start in the precedent cell C5. Hide the arrows for cell **D5** by clicking the **Remove Arrows** button, and then click cell **C5** and click the **Trace Precedents** button.

    d. Notice that one of the precedent arrows for cell C5 refers to another worksheet. Double-click the dashed precedent arrow line.

e. In the *Go To* dialog, click the worksheet reference and then click the **OK** button.

18. The link takes you to the *Rates* sheet where cells A2:D5 are selected. Notice that the *Name* box displays the name *ClientRates*. (Depending on your screen resolution, the name may be slightly cut off.) The formula in cell C5 is a lookup formula that uses the named range *ClientRates* as the *Table_array* argument. There are two problems with the definition of the named range: It includes the label row (A2:D2), and it includes the employee number data (A2:A5).

    a. On the *Formulas* tab, in the *Defined Names* group, click the **Name Manager** button.

    b. Click the **ClientRates** name and review the cell range in the *Refers to* box. The range is incorrect. The ClientRates name should refer to cells **B3:D5** on the *Rates* sheet.

    c. Click in the *Refers to* box and then click and drag to select the cell range **B3:D5**. The reference in the *Refers to* box should update to:

    =Rates!$B$3:$D$5

    d. Click the **Close** button to close the Name Manager.

    e. When Excel asks if you want to save the changes to the name reference, click **Yes.**

19. Now that the total bill amount is computing correctly, you can create a formula to give the client the option of a monthly payment plan. You are authorized to offer a 9-month payment plan at a 4% annual percentage rate. Use cell references in the formula.

    a. If necessary, click the **Smith Bill** sheet.

    b. Click cell **D12.**

    c. On the *Formulas* tab, in the *Function Library* group, click the **Financial** button.

    d. Scroll down the list, and click **PMT.**

    e. In the *Function Arguments* dialog, enter the *Rate* argument: **D11/12**

    f. Click in the **Nper** argument box, and then click cell **D10** (the number of payments).

    g. Click in the **Pv** argument box, type - and then click cell **D8** (the present value of the loan). You want to use a negative value for the *Pv* argument so the result of the formula will appear as a positive number.

    h. In the *Function Arguments* dialog, click **OK.** The completed formula should look like this:

    =PMT(D11/12,D10,-D8)

20. Save and close the workbook.

projects

Data files for projects can be found by logging into your SIMnet account and going to the Library section.

skill review **3.2**

In this project you will edit a worksheet to compute student grades and grade statistics. Be sure to save your work often!

Skills needed to complete this project:

- Using Date and Time Functions (Skill 3.5)
- Using CONCAT to Combine Text (Skill 3.8)
- Formatting Text Using Functions (Skill 3.7)
- Creating Formulas Using Counting Functions (Skill 3.6)
- Using Formula AutoComplete to Enter Functions (Skill 3.2)
- Displaying and Printing Formulas (Skill 3.20)
- Naming Ranges of Cells (Skill 3.11)
- Using the Logical Function IF (Skill 3.15)
- Using the Function Arguments Dialog to Enter Functions (Skill 3.1)
- Working with Named Ranges (Skill 3.12)
- Finding Minimum and Maximum Values (Skill 3.4)
- Calculating Averages (Skill 3.3)
- Finding Data Using the VLOOKUP Function (Skill 3.17)
- Checking Formulas for Errors (Skill 3.18)

1. Open the start file **EX2019-SkillReview-3-2** and resave the file as:
   `[your initials]EX-SkillReview-3-2`
2. If the workbook opens in *Protected View*, click the **Enable Editing** button in the *Message Bar* at the top of the workbook so you can modify it.
3. Take a look at the two sheets. The first sheet contains the students' names and their scores. The second sheet will be used to look up the letter grade for each student.
4. On the *Scores* worksheet, enter a function in cell **B3** to display the current date and time.
   a. If necessary, click the **Scores** worksheet tab. Click cell **B3**.
   b. On the *Formulas* tab, in the *Function Library* group, click the **Date & Time** button.
   c. Click **NOW**.
   d. Click **OK**.

5. The first column should display the full student name. Use CONCAT to combine the values from the *First Name* and *Last Name column.*
   a. Click cell **A10.**
   b. On the *Formulas* tab, in the *Function Library* group, click the **Text** button, and select **CONCAT.**
   c. Click cell **C10** to enter the cell reference in the *Text1* argument box.
   d. Press Tab to move to the *Text2* argument box.
   e. Type **" "** to place a space between the first and last names.
   f. Press Tab to move to the *Text3* argument box.
   g. Click cell **B10** to enter the text reference in the *Text3* argument box.
   h. Click **OK.** The completed formula should look like this: **=CONCAT(C10," ",B10)**

6. Add the PROPER function to the formula so student names do not appear in all uppercase.
   a. Double-click cell **A10** to edit the formula.
   b. Create a nested formula by typing **PROPER(** between the = symbol and **CONCAT.**
   c. Type another **)** at the end of the formula.
   d. Press Enter. The completed formula should look like this: **=PROPER(CONCAT(C10," ",B10))**
   e. Copy the formula from cell **A10** to **A11:A26** to fill the list of student names. Use any method you want.

7. Count the number of students to calculate the class size.
   a. Click cell **B2.**
   b. Type **=COU**
   c. Double-click **COUNTA** in the *Formula AutoComplete* list.
   d. Click cell **A10** and drag to cell **A26.**
   e. Press Enter. The completed formula should look like this: **=COUNTA(A10:A26)**

8. Display your formulas to check for accuracy.
   a. On the *Formula* tab, in the *Formula Auditing* group, click the **Show Formulas** button.
   b. When you are ready to continue, hide the formulas and display formula values by clicking the **Show Formulas** button again.

9. Define a named range for the total possible points up to the class drop cut-off point.
   a. Select cells **D7:R7.**
   b. In the **Name** box, type: **PossiblePtsMid**
   c. Press Enter.

10. Find out which students have a grade below C at the cut-off point for dropping the class. Enter an IF function in cell **S10** to check if the student's total points divided by the total possible points through the midterm is less than 70% (the lowest percentage for a C grade). Use SUM functions within the IF function. Be sure to use the range name you just defined for possible points. If the student is below a C grade, display **Warning!** in the cell; otherwise leave the cell blank.

    a. Click cell **S10.**

    b. On the *Formulas* tab, in the *Function Library* group, click **Logical**.

    c. Click **IF**.

    d. If necessary, move the *Function Arguments* dialog so you can see the worksheet data.

    e. In the *Logical_test* argument box, type: `SUM(D10:R10)/SUM(PossiblePtsMid)<70%`

    f. In the *Value_if_true* argument box, type: `Warning!`

    g. In the *Value_if_false* argument box, type: `""`

    h. Click **OK**. The completed formula should look like this:

       =IF(SUM(D10:R10)/SUM(PossiblePtsMid)<70%,"Warning!"," ")

    i. Fill the IF function in cell **S10** down for all students. Use any method you want. There should be three students with **Warning!** in the *Class Drop Cut-Off Point* column.

11. Find the highest score for each assignment.

    a. Click cell **D4**.

    b. Type `=MAX(` and then click cell **D10** and drag to cell **D26**.

    c. Press Enter. The completed formula should look like this: **=MAX(D10:D26)**

    d. Copy the formula across the row to cell **AB4**. Use any method you want. Be sure to leave cell S4 blank.

12. Find the lowest score for each assignment.

    a. Click cell **D5**.

    b. Type `=MIN(` and then click cell **D10** and drag to cell **D26**.

    c. Press Enter. The completed formula should look like this: **=MIN(D10:D26)**

    d. Copy the formula across the row to cell **AB5**. Use any method you want. Be sure to leave cell S5 blank.

13. Calculate the average score for each assignment.

    a. Click cell **D6**.

    b. Type `=AV` and then double-click **AVERAGE** in the *Formula AutoComplete* list.

    c. Click cell **D10** and drag to cell **D26**.

    d. Press Enter. The completed formula should look like this: **=AVERAGE(D10:D26)**

    e. Copy the formula across the row to cell **AB6**. Use any method you want. Be sure to leave cell S6 blank.

14. Compute the students' total points. Enter a SUM function in cell **AC10** to add all the points across for the first student.
    a. Click cell **AC10.**
    b. Type **=SU** and then double-click **SUM** in the Formula AutoComplete list.
    c. Click cell **D10** and drag to cell **AB10.**
    d. Press Enter. The completed formula should look like this: **=SUM(D10:AB10)**
    e. Copy the formula from **AC10** through cell **AC26.** Use any method you want.
15. Enter a formula to compute the percentage for the first student. Divide the student's total points by the total possible points. You will be copying this formula, so make sure the reference to the total possible points uses an absolute reference.
    a. In cell **AD10**, enter the following formula to calculate the percentage: **=AC10/$AC$7**
    b. Copy the formula from **AD10** through **AD26.** Use any method you want.
16. The grade scale is stored in the *Grades* worksheet. Before calculating students' final grades, create a named range to use in the formula.
    a. Click the **Grades** sheet tab.
    b. Select cells **B4:C8.**
    c. Type **GradeScale** in the *Name* box.
    d. Press Enter.
17. Now you are ready to create a lookup formula to display each student's final letter grade.
    a. Return to the **Scores** sheet, and click cell **AE10.**
    b. On the *Formulas* tab, in the *Function Library* group, click the **Lookup & Reference** button, and select **VLOOKUP.**
    c. Click cell **AD10** to enter it in the *Lookup_value* argument box.
    d. Type **GradeScale** in the *Table_array* argument box.
    e. The rates are located in the second column of the lookup table. Type **2** in the *Col_index_num* argument box.
    f. In this case, you do not want to specify an exact match, as the percentage grades do not match the grade scale percentages exactly. An approximate match will return the correct letter grade.
    g. Click **OK.** The completed formula should look like this: **=VLOOKUP(AD10,GradeScale,2)**
    h. Fill down for all students. Use any method you want.
18. Before closing the project, check your workbook for errors.
    a. On the *Formulas* tab, in the *Formula Auditing* group, click the **Error Checking** button.
    b. If errors are found, use the error checking skills learned in this chapter to find and fix the errors.
    c. When Excel displays a message that the error check is complete, click **OK.**
19. Save and close the workbook.

projects

Data files for projects can be found by logging into your SIMnet account and going to the Library section.

challenge yourself 3.3

In this project you will complete a vehicle shopping workbook to compare the purchase of several vehicles. After completing the project, you can make a copy of the file and use it to compare vehicle purchases you are considering for yourself. Be sure to save your work often!

Skills needed to complete this project:

- Naming Ranges of Cells (Skill 3.11)
- Calculating Averages (Skill 3.3)
- Finding Data Using the VLOOKUP Function (Skill 3.17)
- Working with Named Ranges (Skill 3.12)
- Using the Function Arguments Dialog to Enter Functions (Skill 3.1)
- Using the Logical Function IF (Skill 3.15)
- Calculating Loan Payments Using the PMT Function (Skill 3.16)
- Creating Formulas Referencing Data from Other Worksheets (Skill 3.10)
- Displaying and Printing Formulas (Skill 3.20)
- Finding Errors Using Trace Precedents and Trace Dependents (Skill 3.19)
- Finding Minimum and Maximum Values (Skill 3.4)
- Using Formula AutoComplete to Enter Functions (Skill 3.2)
- Updating Named Ranges with the Name Manager (Skill 3.13)
- Editing and Deleting Names with the Name Manager (Skill 3.14)
- Checking Formulas for Errors (Skill 3.18)

1. Open the start file **EX2019-ChallengeYourself-3-3** and resave the file as:
   `[your initials]EX-ChallengeYourself-3-3`
2. If the workbook opens in Protected View, click the **Enable Editing** button in the Message Bar at the top of the workbook so you can modify it.
3. The registration fee information in cells **B11:C17** on the **Data** sheet will be used in lookup formulas later in this project. Name the range `RegistrationFees` to make it easier to use later.
4. Return to the **Purchase** worksheet.

5. Calculate the average MPG for each vehicle.
   a. Enter a formula in cell **C10** using the AVERAGE function to calculate the average value of **C8:C9.** Use only one argument.
   b. Copy the formula to the appropriate cells for the other vehicles.
   c. Excel will detect a possible error with these formulas. Use the **SmartTag** to ignore the error. *Hint:* Use the **SmartTag** while cells **C10:F10** are selected and the error will be ignored for all the selected cells.
6. Calculate the registration fee for each vehicle.
   a. Enter a formula in cell **C13** to look up the registration fee for the first vehicle. Use the vehicle type in cell **C4** as the *Lookup_value argument.* Use the **RegistrationFees** named range as the *Table_array* argument. The registration fees are located in column **2** of the data table. Require an exact match.
   b. Copy the formula to the appropriate cells for the other vehicles.
7. Determine whether or not you will need a loan for each potential purchase.
   a. In cell **C15**, enter a formula using an IF function to determine if you need a loan. Your available cash is located on the *Data* sheet in cell **A3**. If the price of the car is less than or equal to your available cash, display **"no"**. If the price of the car is more than your available, cash, display **"yes"**. Use absolute references where appropriate—you will be copying this formula across the row.
   b. Copy the formula to the appropriate cells for the other vehicles.
8. Calculate how much you would need to borrow for each purchase.
   a. In cell **C16**, enter a formula to calculate the price of the vehicle minus your available cash (from cell **A3** in the **Data** worksheet). Use absolute references where appropriate—you will be copying this formula across the row.
   b. Copy the formula to the appropriate cells for the other vehicles.
9. Calculate the monthly payment amount for each loan.
   a. In cell **C20**, enter a formula using the PMT function to calculate the monthly loan payment for the first vehicle. *Hint:* Divide the interest rate by 12 in the *Rate* argument to reflect monthly payments.
   b. *Hint:* Multiply the number of years by 12 in the *Nper* argument to reflect the number of monthly payments during the life of the loan. *Hint:* Use a negative value for the loan amount in the *Pv* argument so the payment amount is expressed as a positive number.
   c. Copy the formula to the appropriate cells for the other vehicles.

10. Compute the monthly cost of gas.
    a. In cell **C21**, enter a formula to calculate the number of miles you expect to drive each month. Divide the value of number of miles (cell **A5** from the **Data** sheet) by the average MPG for the vehicle multiplied by the price of a gallon of gas (cell **A6** from the **Data** sheet).
    b. Copy the formula to the appropriate cells for the other vehicles.
    c. If cells **D21:F21** display an error or a value of 0, display formulas and check for errors.
    d. If you still can't find the error, try displaying the precedent arrows.
    e. *Hint:* The references to the cells on the *Data* sheet should use absolute references. If they do not, the formula will update incorrectly when you copy it across the row.

11. Compute the monthly cost of maintenance.
    a. In cell **C22**, enter a formula to calculate the monthly maintenance cost: Divide cell **C12** by 12.
    b. Copy the formula to the appropriate cells for the other vehicles.

12. Compute the monthly cost of insurance.
    a. In cell **C23**, enter a formula to calculate the monthly insurance cost: Divide cell **C14** by 12.
    b. Copy the formula to the appropriate cells for the other vehicles.

13. In cells **C24:F24**, compute the total the monthly cost for each vehicle.

14. Determine which vehicles are affordable.
    a. In cell **C26**, enter a formula using the IF function to display **"yes"** if the total monthly cost (cell **C24**) is less than or equal to the total monthly amount available for vehicle expenses (*Data* sheet, cell **A4**). Display **"no"** if the total monthly cost is not less than or equal to the total monthly amount available.
    b. Copy the formula to the appropriate cells for the other vehicles.
    c. Display formulas and use the error checking skills learned in this lesson to track down and fix any errors.

15. Complete the Analysis section using formulas with statistical functions. Use named ranges instead of cell references in the formulas.
    a. *Hint:* Select cells **B7:F24** and use Excel's **Create from Selection** command to create named ranges for each row using the labels at the left side of the range as the names.
    b. *Hint:* Open the **Name Manager** and review the names Excel created. Notice that any spaces or special characters in the label names are converted to _ characters in the names.
    c. *Hint:* To avoid typos as you create each formula, try using Formula AutoComplete to select the correct range name.

16. Before finishing the project, check the worksheet for errors.

17. Save and close the workbook.

projects

challenge yourself 3.4

In this project, you will record data about your completed and planned college courses. You will compute your GPA, college course costs, and various statistics. You will compute your expected college loan payment and count down the days to graduation and paying off the loan. Be sure to save your work often!

Skills needed to complete this project:

- Finding Errors Using Trace Precedents and Trace Dependents (Skill 3.19)
- Finding Data Using the VLOOKUP Function (Skill 3.17)
- Using the Function Arguments Dialog to Enter Functions (Skill 3.1)
- Checking Formulas for Errors (Skill 3.18)
- Creating Formulas Referencing Data from Other Worksheets (Skill 3.10)
- Calculating Loan Payments Using the PMT Function (Skill 3.16)
- Using Date and Time Functions (Skill 3.5)
- Finding Minimum and Maximum Values (Skill 3.4)
- Using Formula AutoComplete to Enter Functions (Skill 3.2)
- Calculating Averages (Skill 3.3)
- Using the Logical Function IF (Skill 3.15)

1. Open the start file **EX2019-ChallengeYourself-3-4** and resave the file as:
   `[your initials]EX-ChallengeYourself-3-4`
2. If the workbook opens in Protected View, click the **Enable Editing** button in the Message Bar at the top of the workbook so you can modify it.
3. There are three sheets. Start with the *GPA* sheet.
4. There is at least one error on this sheet. Click the cell that displays an error and use the precedent arrows to find the cause of the error. If the error is caused by missing values in other cells in the worksheet, you will probably fix the error by the end of this project. Hide the arrows before continuing.
5. Enter the formulas for the GPA worksheet as follows.
   a. In cell **B14** compute the cost for the first course by multiplying the unit cost (cell **C11**) by the number of units for the course (cell **G14**). Use absolute references where appropriate.
   b. Fill and copy to compute the cost for each course, both semesters (cells **B15:B16** and **B19:B22**).

6. Look up the grade points for each letter grade as follows:
   a. In cell **I14,** enter a formula using the VLOOKUP function. Use the cell range **J3:K7** as the *Table_array* argument. The grade points are located in column **2** of this table. Use absolute references where appropriate.
   b. Fill and copy to look up the grade points for each course, both semesters (cells **I15:I16** and **I19:I22**).

7. Multiply the grade points by the units to calculate the quality points for each course, for both semesters.
   a. In cell **J14,** enter a formula to multiply **I14** (the grade points) * cell **G14** (the units).
   b. Copy the formula to cells **J15:J16** and **J19:J22.**

8. Use AutoSum to calculate totals for cost (cells **B17** and **B23**), units (cells **G17** and **G23**), and quality points (cells **J17** and **J23**) for each semester.

9. In cell **K17,** compute the GPA for the first semester by dividing the total quality points by the total units (**J17/G17**).

10. In cell **K23,** compute the GPA for the second semester using the same formula.

11. Check the worksheet for errors. Is the error you found in step 4 fixed now? (It should be!)

12. Next go to the *Loan* worksheet.

13. In cell **B3,** enter a formula to display the total cost shown in cell **B9** on the *GPA* sheet.

14. Enter a formula in cell **B7** to look up the number of years to pay based on the loan amount shown in cell **B3.** Use the data table in cells **G6:H11** as the *Table_array* argument. Do not require an exact match.

15. Now that you have the loan amount and the number of payments, enter a formula using the PMT function in cell **B8** to calculate the payment amount. Allow the payment to display as a negative number.

16. In cell **B10,** enter a formula to display the current date (just the date, not the date and time).

17. Enter a formula in cell **B16** to estimate the date of the last loan payment. Take the number of years to pay (cell **B7**) times **365.3** and add that to the date of the first loan payment (cell **B15**).

18. Enter a formula in cell **B17** to estimate the number of days until the loan is paid off.

19. Complete the *Summary* sheet information.

20. On the *Summary* sheet, in cell **B5,** enter a simple formula to reference the *Cumulative GPA* number from the *GPA* worksheet (*GPA*worksheet, cell **B5**).

21. Do the same for Total Units (cell **B6**), Total Cost (cell **B9**), and Total Debt (cell **B3**). For Total Debt, reference the Amount Owed number from the *Loan* sheet.

22. Compute the Average Cost Per Unit by dividing the Total Cost (cell **B8**) by the Total Units (cell **B6**).

23. Compute Average Debt Per Unit in the same way.

24. In cell **B14,** enter a formula using a statistical function to calculate the most paid for any semester. Reference cells **B17** and **B23** in the *GPA* sheet. *Hint:* You will need two arguments.

25. In cell **B16,** enter a formula to calculate the average semester cost. Reference cells **B17** and **B23** in the *GPA* sheet. *Hint:* You will need two arguments.

26. In cell **F1,** enter a formula using the IF function to determine if the student met her GPA goal. Display **"yes"** if the goal was met and **"no"** if it was not.

27. In cell **F2,** enter a formula using the IF function to determine if the student met her unit goal. Display **"yes"** if the goal was met and **"no"** if it was not.

28. Before finishing the project, check each worksheet for errors.

29. Save and close the workbook.

projects

Data files for projects can be found by logging into your SIMnet account and going to the Library section.

on your own 3.5

In this project you will complete a dental plan workbook. Be sure to save your work often!

Skills needed to complete this project:

- Updating Named Ranges with the Name Manager (Skill 3.13)
- Editing and Deleting Names with the Name Manager (Skill 3.14)
- Naming Ranges of Cells (Skill 3.11)
- Working with Named Ranges (Skill 3.12)
- Finding Data Using the VLOOKUP Function (Skill 3.17)
- Using the Function Arguments Dialog to Enter Functions (Skill 3.1)
- Calculating Averages (Skill 3.3)
- Finding Minimum and Maximum Values (Skill 3.4)
- Using Formula AutoComplete to Enter Functions (Skill 3.2)
- Creating Formulas Using Counting Functions (Skill 3.6)
- Using CONCAT to Combine Text (Skill 3.8)
- Creating Formulas Referencing Data from Other Worksheets (Skill 3.10)
- Formatting Text Using Functions (Skill 3.7)
- Using Date and Time Functions (Skill 3.5)
- Using the Logical Function IF (Skill 3.15)
- Calculating Loan Payments Using the PMT Function (Skill 3.16)
- Checking Formulas for Errors (Skill 3.18)
- Finding Errors Using Trace Precedents and Trace Dependents (Skill 3.19)
- Displaying and Printing Formulas (Skill 3.20)

1. Open the start file **EX2019-OnYourOwn-3-5** and resave the file as:
   `[your initials]EX-OnYourOwn-3-5`
2. If the workbook opens in Protected View, click the **Enable Editing** button in the Message Bar at the top of the workbook so you can modify it.
3. Start with the *Pocket Chart* worksheet. This dental chart is designed to be used to record measurements of the depth of gum pockets around the teeth. Each tooth is identified by number and name. The teeth of the upper and lower jaws are arranged across the worksheet from the patient's right side to the left. Pocket depth measurements have been entered.
4. Enter your name as the patient's name and enter the date of the examination. Do not use a function for the date. (You don't want the value to update every time you open the workbook.)

5. Review the information in the *Look Up* worksheet and assign names as necessary to each of the lookup tables to use in formulas in other worksheets. One of the lookup tables already has a name assigned.

6. Return to the *Pocket Chart* worksheet and complete the patient data.
    a. Use VLOOKUP functions to determine the severity level for each tooth.
    b. Use statistical functions to calculate the smallest pocket depth, the largest pocket depth, and the average pocket depth for the upper and lower teeth sections. Use similar formulas in **O2:O4** to calculate the overall statistical information for the patient (the average, minimum, and maximum pocket depths for both upper and lower teeth).
    c. Count the number of cells missing pocket depth information (blank cells). *Hint:* Remember, the COUNTBLANK function accepts only one argument, so you will need to count the blank cells for the upper teeth and the lower teeth and then add those values together.

7. Now switch to the *Treatment Plan* worksheet and fix any errors. **Hint:** Display formulas and then use the **Name Manager** to review names and create missing names as needed. Delete any duplicate names you may have accidentally created.

8. Create a formula to display the patient name in the format Bob Smith. Reference the patient name cells from the *Pocket Chart* sheet. Be sure to include a space between the first and last names.

9. Modify the formula that displays the patient name so the name appears in all uppercase.

10. Enter a formula to display today's date in cell **I1.**

11. Cells B7:C9 summarize the number of teeth with each severity level. Use this data table to complete the treatment plan. For each treatment, display **"yes"** if the patient meets the requirement below and **"no"** if he does not.
    a. Sonic Toothbrush: Recommend only if the patient has more than five mild pockets.
    b. Scaling & Planing: Recommend only if the patient has more than seven moderate pockets.
    c. Surgery: Recommend only if the patient has more than three severe pockets.

12. Complete the billing information.
    a. Look up the cost of each treatment.
    b. Compute the amount the insurance company will cover for each treatment. Multiply the treatment cost by the insurance company rate. *Hint:* Use the HLOOKUP function to find the insurance company rate.
    c. Compute the billable amount for each treatment. If the treatment is recommended, compute the billable amount by subtracting the amount insurance will cover from the cost of the treatment. If the treatment is not recommended, display **"N/A"** instead.
    d. Enter a formula to calculate the total bill for the patient.

13. Enter a formula to compute the monthly payment for the payment plan option. Be sure to display the number as a positive value.

14. Display your formulas and check for errors. Use the error checking skills you learned in this chapter as needed.

15. Save and close the workbook.

projects
fix it 3.6

Data files for projects can be found by logging into your SIMnet account and going to the Library section.

In this project, you will correct function mistakes and other formula errors in a workbook designed for planning a large party or event. Be sure to save your work often!

Skills needed to complete this project:

- Checking Formulas for Errors (Skill 3.18)
- Finding Errors Using Trace Precedents and Trace Dependents (Skill 3.19)
- Displaying and Printing Formulas (Skill 3.20)
- Creating Formulas Using Counting Functions (Skill 3.6)
- Finding Minimum and Maximum Values (Skill 3.4)
- Formatting Text Using Functions (Skill 3.7)
- Using CONCAT to Combine Text (Skill 3.8)
- Finding Data Using the VLOOKUP Function (Skill 3.17)
- Using the Function Arguments Dialog to Enter Functions (Skill 3.1)
- Using Formula AutoComplete to Enter Functions (Skill 3.2)
- Calculating Averages (Skill 3.3)
- Naming Ranges of Cells (Skill 3.11)
- Working with Named Ranges (Skill 3.12)
- Updating Named Ranges with the Name Manager (Skill 3.13)
- Editing and Deleting Names with the Name Manager (Skill 3.14)
- Using Date and Time Functions (Skill 3.5)
- Using the Logical Function IF (Skill 3.15)
- Creating Formulas Referencing Data from Other Worksheets (Skill 3.10)
- Calculating Loan Payments Using the PMT Function (Skill 3.16)

1. Open the start file **EX2019-FixIt-3-6** and resave the file as:
   `[your initials]EX-FixIt-3-6`
2. If the workbook opens in Protected View, click the **Enable Editing** button in the Message Bar at the top of the workbook so you can modify the workbook.

3. On the *GuestList* sheet, check all the formulas. Cells to check are filled with the light purple color. Most of them need to be corrected. Use error checking as needed and/or display the formulas on-screen for easy viewing.

   a. In the *Name Tag* column, modify the formula to display the guest name in this format: **BILL SMITH** *Hint:* There are multiple errors in this formula. Fix the formula in cell **D10** and then copy it to the other cells in the column.

   b. Correct the function used in cell **A3** to calculate the sum of the values in the *NumAttending* column.

   c. Correct the function used in cell **A4** to count the number of values in the *Street column.*

   d. Correct the function used in cell **A5** to count the number of blank cells in the *NumAttending* column.

   e. Correct the function used in cell **A6** to display the largest value in the *NumAttending* column.

   f. Correct the function used in cell **A7** to display the average value in the *NumAttending* column.

4. On the *Shopping List* sheet, check all the formulas. Cells to check are filled with the light purple color. Most of them need to be corrected. Many of the problems on this worksheet can be solved by creating named ranges or using a name that already exists.

   a. The formula in cell **B2** uses the wrong function.

   b. The formulas in cells **A9:A23** reference a named range that doesn't exist. There is more than one correct way to fix this problem using the cell range **A5:H18** on the *Places to Shop* worksheet. You can create the named range referenced in the formulas, or you can change the function arguments to reference the cell range instead.

   c. The formula in cell **H9** results in the correct value. However, the workbook author copied this formula to the remaining cells in the column and those values are definitely not correct! Fix the formula in cell **H9** and copy it to cells **H10:H23**. *Hint:* Notice that cell **H8** is named *Tax.*

5. If you've fixed the formulas in cells **H9:H23** correctly, the formulas in cells I9:I23 and G5 should calculate properly now. However, the formulas in cells **G2:G4** still have errors that need to be fixed. *Hint:* Use error checking as needed and/or display the formulas on-screen for easy viewing.

   a. Correct the function used in cell **G2** to average value of the *Cost* column.

   b. Correct the function used in cell **G3** to display the largest value in the *Cost* column.

   c. Correct the function used in cell **G4** to display the smallest value in the *Cost* column.

6. On the *Summary* sheet, you will be entering all the formulas. Cells to complete are filled with the light purple color. *Hint:* Use error checking as needed and/or display the formulas on-screen for easy viewing.

    a. Cell **B2** should use a function that will update the date to the current date every time the workbook is opened.

    b. Cell **B4** references a named range that doesn't exist. It should reference cell **A4** on the *Guest List* sheet. You can create the named range or edit the formula to reference the cell instead.

    c. Cell **B5** references a named range that doesn't exist. It should reference cell **A3** on the *Guest List* sheet. You can create the named range or edit the formula to reference the cell instead.

    d. Cell **B8** is missing the formula to calculate whether or not the total *Cost* with tax on the *Shopping List* sheet + the total *Cost* for purchasing and mailing invitations on the *Guest List* sheet is greater than the available cash. The cell should display *yes* or *no*.

    e. Add a formula to cell **B9** to calculate the amount to borrow (total *Cost* with tax on the *Shopping List* sheet + the total *Cost* for purchasing and mailing invitations on the *Guest List* sheet – the cash available) if the value in cell **B8** is *yes*. If the value in cell **B8** is not *yes*, the cell should display 0.

    f. Add a formula to cell **B12** to calculate the monthly loan payment based on the information in cells **B9:B11**. Use a negative number for the *Pv* argument.

7. Save and close the workbook.

Formatting Worksheets and Managing the Workbook

chapter 4

introduction

As Excel projects get bigger and more complicated, more formatting skills are required. In this chapter, you will learn how to manage the organization and appearance of worksheets for the optimal display of data both onscreen and when printed.

Skill 4.1 Inserting Worksheets

When you create a new workbook, it contains a single worksheet named *Sheet1.* If you need more than one worksheet, you can add more. It is a good practice to keep all related information in the same workbook by adding more worksheets, rather than starting a new workbook.

> To add a new worksheet to the right of the active worksheet, click the **New sheet** button to the right of the last worksheet tab ⊕.

> To add a worksheet to the left of the active worksheet, on the *Home* tab, in the *Cells* group, click the **Insert** button arrow, and select **Insert Sheet.**

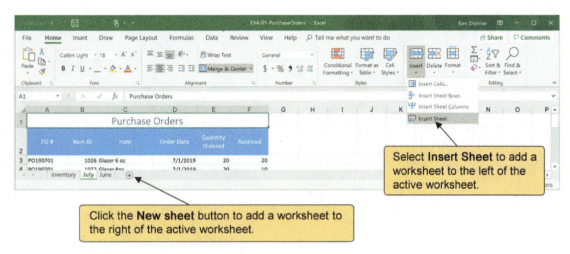

Select **Insert Sheet** to add a worksheet to the left of the active worksheet.

Click the **New sheet** button to add a worksheet to the right of the active worksheet.

FIGURE EX 4.1

The new sheet is given the name Sheet# (where # is the next number available—for example, if your workbook contains *Sheet1* and *Sheet2,* the next sheet inserted will be named *Sheet3*).

another method

To add a worksheet, you can also:

1. Right-click on a sheet tab and select **Insert...** on the shortcut menu.
   - To insert a blank worksheet, click the **Worksheet** icon in the dialog.
   - To insert a formatted worksheet, click the **Spreadsheet Solutions** tab, and click any of the template icons.
2. Click **OK**.

let me try Live!

Open the student data file **EX4-01-PurchaseOrders** and try this skill on your own:

1. Add a new worksheet to the right of the *July* sheet.
2. Add another new worksheet to the left of the worksheet you just added.
3. If you will be moving on to the next skill in this chapter, leave the workbook open to continue working. If not, save the file as directed by your instructor and close it.

Skill 4.2 Naming Worksheets

When you create a new workbook, Excel automatically includes a worksheet named *Sheet1*. Additional worksheets that you insert are automatically named *Sheet2, Sheet3,* and so forth. It is a good idea to rename your worksheets to something more descriptive. Giving your worksheets descriptive names can help organize multiple worksheets, making it easier for you to find and use information.

To rename a worksheet:

1. Double-click the sheet tab or right-click the worksheet tab and select **Rename**.
2. Excel highlights the sheet name, allowing you to replace it as you type.
3. Type the new sheet name, and press Enter.

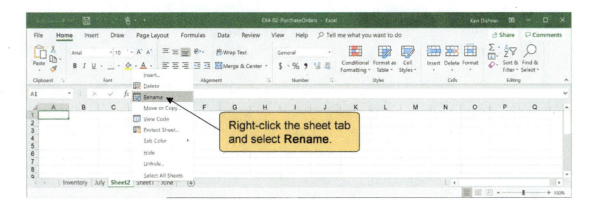

Right-click the sheet tab and select **Rename**.

FIGURE EX 4.2

another method

You can also use the Ribbon to rename a worksheet.

1. Click the sheet tab you want to rename.
2. On the *Home* tab, in the *Cells* group, click the **Format** button.
3. Select **Rename Sheet**.
4. Type the new sheet name, and press Enter.

let me try Live!

If you do not have the data file from the previous skill open, open the student data file **EX4-02-PurchaseOrders** and try this skill on your own:

1. Rename *Sheet1*: **August**
2. Rename *Sheet2*: **Orders**
3. If you will be moving on to the next skill in this chapter, leave the workbook open to continue working. If not, save the file as directed by your instructor and close it.

Skill 4.3 Changing the Color of Sheet Tabs

By default, all the worksheet tabs in Excel are white. If you have many sheets in your workbook, changing the tab colors can help you organize your data.

To change a worksheet tab color:

1. Right-click the sheet tab and point to **Tab Color** to display the color palette.
2. Hover the mouse pointer over each color to preview how the color will look when the worksheet is active.
3. Click the color you want.

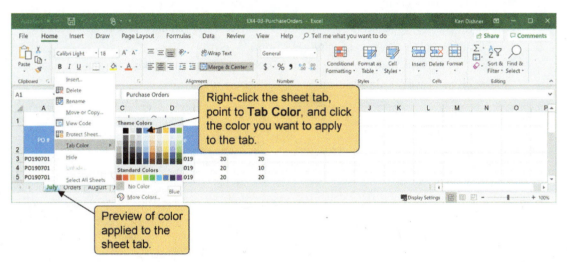

Right-click the sheet tab, point to **Tab Color**, and click the color you want to apply to the tab.

Preview of color applied to the sheet tab.

FIGURE EX 4.3

tips & tricks

> The color palette used for worksheet tab color is the same color palette used for font color, fill color, and border color. The colors available change depending on the theme applied to the workbook.

> If you have sheets that contain related data, color them using different shades of the same color.

another method

1. Click the sheet tab you want to color.
2. On the *Home* tab, in the *Cells* group, click the **Format** button.
3. Point to **Tab Color** to display the color palette.
4. Click the color you want.

let me try Live!

If you do not have the data file from the previous skill open, open the student data file **EX4-03-PurchaseOrders** ⬇ and try this skill on your own:

1. Change the color of the sheet tab for the *July* worksheet to the standard **Blue** color (the third color from the right in the row of standard colors).
2. If you will be moving on to the next skill in this chapter, leave the workbook open to continue working. If not, save the file as directed by your instructor and close it.

Skill 4.4 Moving and Copying Worksheets

You can move worksheets around in a workbook, rearranging them into the most logical order.

To move a worksheet within a workbook:

1. Click the worksheet tab and hold down the mouse button.
2. Notice that the mouse pointer changes to the ⬚ shape.
3. Drag the mouse cursor to the position where you want to move the sheet, and release the mouse button. Excel places a small black triangle ▼ to let you know where the sheet will be placed.

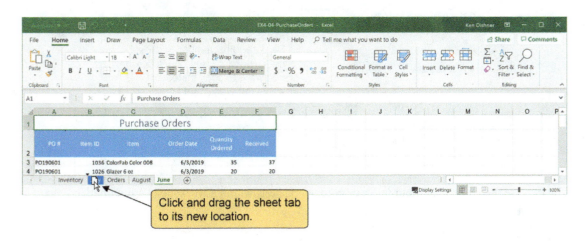

If you want to experiment with worksheet layouts or formulas, you can create a copy of the worksheet in case you want to go back to the original version.

To create a copy of a worksheet:

1. Click the worksheet tab, hold down the mouse button, and press and hold Ctrl.
2. Notice that the mouse pointer changes to the ⬚ shape.
3. Drag the mouse cursor to the position where you want to insert a copy of the selected sheet, and release the mouse button.

To move or copy a worksheet to another workbook or to a new workbook:

1. Right-click the sheet tab, and select **Move or Copy...** to open the *Move or Copy* dialog.
2. In the *Move or Copy* dialog, expand the **To book** list at the top of the dialog. The *To book* list shows all the Excel workbooks you have open. Click the workbook you want. To move or copy the sheet to a new blank workbook, select **(new book)**.

3. The list of sheets in the *Before sheet* box will update to show the sheets available in the workbook you selected. Click the name of the sheet you want to move the selected sheet before. If you want to move the sheet to the end of the workbook, select **(move to end)** in the *Before sheet* box.

4. If you want to create a copy of the selected sheet, instead of moving the original, click the **Create a copy** check box.

5. Click **OK**.

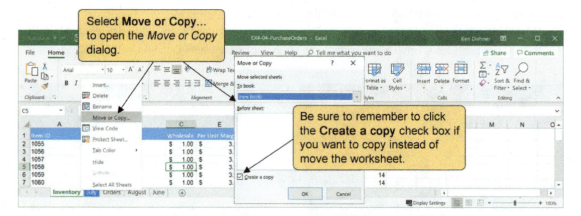

FIGURE EX 4.5

You can use this same method to move or copy worksheets within a workbook by not changing the workbook listed in the *To book* list in the *Move or Copy* dialog.

tips & tricks

Moving a worksheet from one workbook to another deletes the worksheet from the original workbook. Consider copying the worksheet to the second workbook first, and then, once you are confident that formulas work as you intend, delete the worksheet from the original workbook.

tell me more

To move or copy more than one worksheet, press Shift and click the worksheets you want to move or copy. If the worksheets are not consecutive, then press Ctrl instead.

another method

You can also open the *Move or Copy* dialog from the Ribbon. On the *Home* tab, in the *Cells* group, click the **Format** button, and select **Move or Copy Sheet...**

let me try Live!

If you do not have the data file from the previous skill open, open the student data file **EX4-04-PurchaseOrders** ⬇ and try this skill on your own:

1. Move the **June** worksheet so it is positioned before the *July* worksheet.
2. Copy the **Inventory** worksheet to a new workbook.
3. Save the new workbook with the name **InventoryCopy** and close it.
4. If you will be moving on to the next skill in this chapter, leave the *PurchaseOrders* workbook open to continue working. If not, save the file as directed by your instructor and close it.

Skill 4.5 Deleting Worksheets

It is always a good practice to delete any unnecessary worksheets in your workbook.

To delete a worksheet:

1. Select the sheet you want to delete by clicking the worksheet tab.
2. On the *Home* tab, in the *Cells* group, click the **Delete** button arrow, and select **Delete Sheet**.
3. If you try to delete a sheet that contains data, Excel will display a warning that the sheet may contain data and ask if you are sure you want to permanently remove it from your workbook. Click the **Delete** button to continue and delete the worksheet.

Be careful—you cannot undo the *Delete Sheet* command.

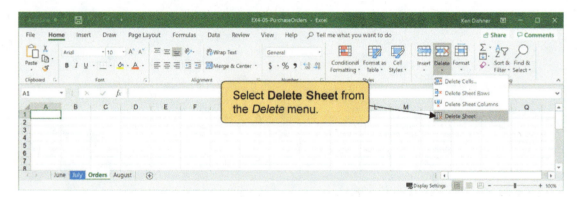

FIGURE EX 4.6

tips & tricks

If you have multiple copies of the same worksheet in a workbook, be sure to delete the versions you no longer need.

tell me more

You can delete multiple worksheets at the same time. First, select all the sheet tabs you want to remove, and then invoke the *Delete Sheet* command.

another method

To delete a worksheet, right-click on a sheet tab and then select **Delete** from the shortcut menu.

let me try Live!

If you do not have the data file from the previous skill open, open the student data file **EX4-05-PurchaseOrders** ⬇ and try this skill on your own:

1. Delete the **Orders** worksheet.
2. If you will be moving on to the next skill in this chapter, leave the workbook open to continue working. If not, save the file as directed by your instructor and close it.

Skill 4.6 Grouping Worksheets

If you have multiple worksheets with the same structure, you can make changes to all of the worksheets at the same time by **grouping** them. This is convenient when you are setting up a series of worksheets with the same row or column headings. When sheets are grouped together, you can also change column widths and formatting, add formulas such as totals, or add headers and footers. Using grouping saves time and ensures that the sheets share a consistent format.

To group worksheets:

1. Click the first worksheet tab.
2. Hold down ⌈Shift⌉ and click the tab for the last worksheet you want included in the group. If you want to select noncontiguous worksheets (sheets that are not next to each other), press ⌈Ctrl⌉ instead, and then click each sheet tab.
3. Notice that the title bar now includes *Group* after the file name.
4. Make the change you want to the sheet. The change will be made to all sheets in the group.
5. To ungroup, click any sheet tab that is not part of the group.

FIGURE EX 4.7

tell me **more**

To group together all the sheets in your workbook, right-click any sheet tab and then click **Select All Sheets**.

To ungroup sheets, right-click one of the grouped sheet tabs and then click **Ungroup**. If all of the sheets in your workbook are grouped together, clicking any sheet will ungroup them all.

let me try Live!

If you do not have the data file from the previous skill open, open the student data file **EX4-06-PurchaseOrders** and try this skill on your own:

1. Group sheets **June** and **July**.
2. Change the text in cell **E2** to: `Ordered`
3. Review cell **E2** in sheets *June* and *July* to ensure that the change was made to both sheets. Notice that the sheets remain grouped as you click back and forth between them.
4. Ungroup the worksheets.
5. If you will be moving on to the next skill in this chapter, leave the workbook open to continue working. If not, save the file as directed by your instructor and close it.

Skill 4.7 Inserting and Deleting Rows and Columns

You may find you need to add rows or columns of new information into the middle of your workbook. Adding a new row will shift down other rows; adding a new column will shift other columns to the right.

To insert a column:

1. Place your cursor in a cell in the column to the right of where you want the new column.
2. On the *Home* tab, in the *Cells* group, click the **Insert** button arrow and select **Insert Sheet Columns**.
3. The new column will appear to the left of the selected cell.

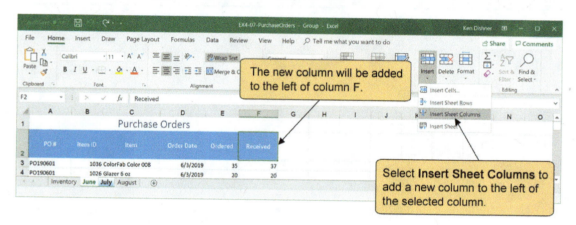

FIGURE EX 4.8

To insert a row:

1. Place your cursor in a cell in the row below where you want the new row.
2. On the *Home* tab, in the *Cells* group, click the **Insert** button arrow and select **Insert Sheet Rows**.
3. The new row will appear above the selected cell.

Of course, you can also delete rows and columns. Deleting a row will shift other rows up; deleting a column will shift the remaining columns to the left.

To delete a row:

1. Place your cursor in a cell in the row you want to delete.
2. On the *Home* tab, in the *Cells* group, click the **Delete** button arrow and select **Delete Sheet Rows**.
3. The row will be deleted and the rows below it will shift up.

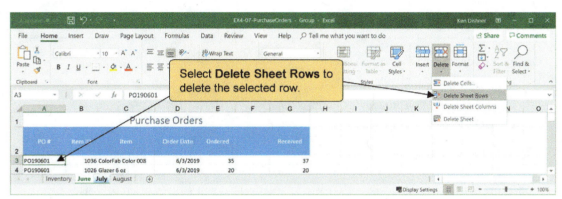

To delete a column:

1. Place your cursor in a cell in the column you want to delete.
2. On the *Home* tab, in the *Cells* group, click the **Delete** button arrow and select **Delete Sheet Columns.**
3. The column will be deleted, and columns to the right of the deleted column will shift left.

tips & tricks

Depending on whether you have a cell, a range of cells, a row, or a column selected, the behavior of the *Insert* and *Delete* commands will change. If you have a single cell selected and click the **Insert** button instead of the button arrow, Excel will insert a single cell, automatically moving cells down. However, if you select the entire column first, and then click the **Insert** button, Excel will automatically insert a column.

tell me more

When you insert a row or column, a Smart Tag will appear. Click the **Smart Tag** to choose formatting options for the new row or column—**Format Same as Above**, **Format Same as Below**, or **Clear Formatting** for rows and **Format Same as Left**, **Format Same as Right**, or **Clear Formatting** for columns. The Smart Tag formatting options are not available if you are inserting a row or column in two or more grouped worksheets.

another method

To insert or delete rows and columns:

1. Right-click in a cell, then select **Insert...** or **Delete...**
2. In the dialog, select **Entire row** or **Entire column**.
3. Click **OK**.

You can also insert or delete an entire row or column by right-clicking the row or column selector and selecting **Insert** or **Delete** from the menu. Because you have already selected an entire row or column, Excel will not ask you to specify what you want to insert or delete.

let me try Live!

If you do not have the data file from the previous skill open, open the student data file **EX4-07-PurchaseOrders** ⬇ and try this skill on your own:

1. On the *June* worksheet, insert a new column to the left of column **F**.
2. Delete row **3**.
3. Verify that the changes were made to both worksheets.
4. If you will be moving on to the next skill in this chapter, leave the workbook open to continue working. If not, save the file as directed by your instructor and close it.

Skill 4.8 Applying Themes

A **theme** is a unified color, font, and effects scheme. When you apply a theme to the workbook, you ensure that all visual elements work well together, giving the workbook a polished, professional look. When you create a new blank workbook in Excel, the Office theme is applied by default.

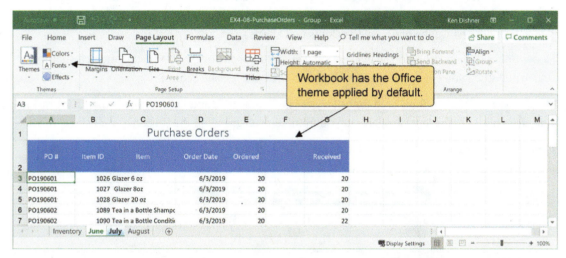

FIGURE EX 4.10

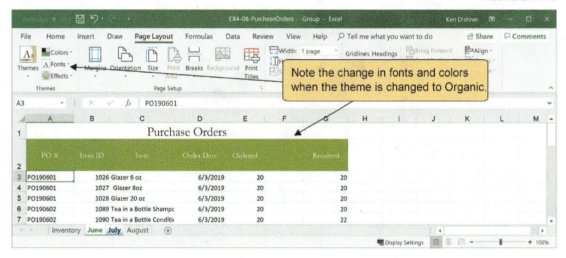

FIGURE EX 4.11

To apply a theme to a workbook:

1. On the *Page Layout* tab, in the *Themes* group, click the **Themes** button to expand the gallery.
2. Roll your mouse over each theme in the gallery to preview the formatting changes.
3. Click one of the themes to apply it to your workbook.

From the *Themes* group, you can apply specific aspects of a theme by making a selection from the *Theme Colors, Theme Fonts,* or *Theme Effects* gallery. Applying one aspect of a theme (for example, colors) will not change the other aspects (fonts and effects).

Theme Colors—Limits the colors available from the color palette for fonts, borders, and cell shading. Notice that when you change themes, the colors in the color palette change.

Theme Fonts—Affects the fonts used for cell styles (including titles and headings). Changing the theme fonts does not limit the fonts available to you from the *Font* group on the Ribbon.

Theme Effects—Controls the way graphic elements in your worksheet appear. Chart styles change according to the theme color and effects.

FIGURE EX 4.12

tips & tricks

Changing the theme affects all the worksheets in the workbook.

When you change the workbook theme, the look of the built-in cell styles changes. Be careful, as the change in style may increase the font size, causing some of your data to be too wide for the columns. If you change themes, you may need to adjust some of your column widths or row heights.

let me try Live!

If you do not have the data file from the previous skill open, open the student data file **EX4-08-PurchaseOrders** 📥 and try this skill on your own:

1. If necessary, click the **June** sheet tab.
2. Expand the *Themes* gallery and preview how each theme would affect the workbook.
3. Apply the **Organic** theme and note the changes to the workbook.
4. Reapply the **Office** theme.
5. If you will be moving on to the next skill in this chapter, leave the workbook open to continue working. If not, save the file as directed by your instructor and close it.

Skill 4.9 Modifying Column Widths and Row Heights

Some columns in your spreadsheet may be too narrow to display the data properly. If a cell contains text data, the text appears cut off. (If the cell to the right is empty, however, the text appears to extend into the empty cell.) If the cell contains numerical data, Excel displays a series of pound signs (#) when the cell is too narrow to display the entire number. You should adjust the column widths so the spreadsheet is easy to read.

Excel offers an easy way to automatically set columns to the width to best fit the data in the column:

To make the column automatically fit the contents:

1. Move your mouse over the right column boundary.
2. The cursor will change to a ✛ shape.
3. Double-click the right column border.

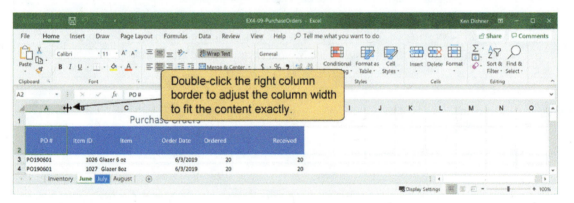

FIGURE EX 4.13

You can also modify column widths manually:

1. Move your mouse over the right column boundary.
2. The cursor will change to a ✛ shape.
3. Click and drag until the column is the size you want, and then release the mouse button.

To specify an exact column width for multiple columns:

1. Select the columns you want to modify. Click the column selector for the first column, press and hold ⎡Shift⎤, and click the column selector for the last column.
2. On the *Home* tab, in the *Cells* group, click the **Format** button.
3. Select **Column Width...**
4. Enter the value you want in the *Column Width* dialog.
5. Click **OK**.

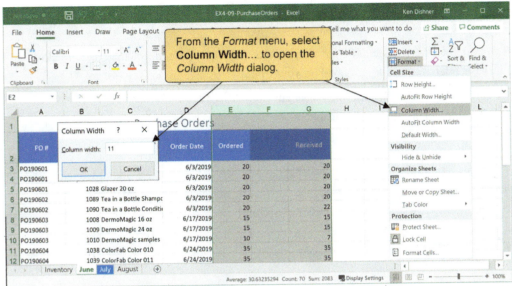

FIGURE EX 4.14

Rows in Excel are automatically sized to fit the font size. However, if you change the font size or apply a new theme, you may need to modify row heights. Use the same techniques you use for resizing columns:

> To make the row automatically fit the contents, double-click the bottom row boundary.
> To modify row heights manually, click and drag until the bottom row boundary up or down.
> Select the row(s) you want to modify and then from the *Format* button menu, select **Row Height...** to enter the row height value in the *Row Height* dialog.

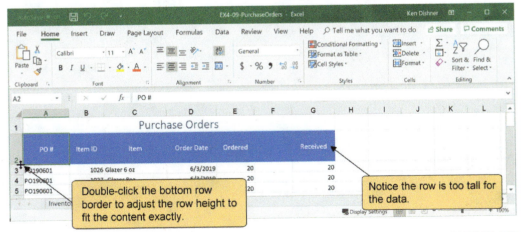

FIGURE EX 4.15

let me try Live!

If you do not have the data file from the previous skill open, open the student data file **EX4-09-PurchaseOrders** 📥 and try this skill on your own:

1. If necessary, click the **June** worksheet tab.
2. Autofit column **A** to best fit the data.
3. Select columns **E:G** and change the column width to **11**.
4. Autofit row **2** to best fit the data.
5. If you will be moving on to the next skill in this chapter, leave the workbook open to continue working. If not, save the file as directed by your instructor and close it.

Skill 4.10 Freezing and Unfreezing Rows and Columns

If you have a large spreadsheet, you may want to **freeze** part of the worksheet so it is always visible. By doing this, you can keep column headings and row labels visible as you scroll through your data.

To freeze part of the worksheet:

1. Arrange the worksheet so the row you want to be visible is the top row or the column you want is the first column visible at the left.
2. On the *View* tab, in the *Window* group, click the **Freeze Panes** button.
   - If you want the first row to always be visible, click **Freeze Top Row.**
   - If you want the first column to always be visible, click **Freeze First Column.**

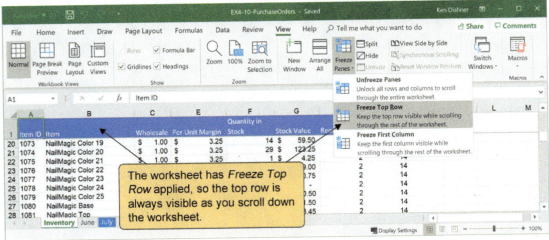

FIGURE EX 4.16

If your worksheet has both a header row and a column of labels in the first column, use the *Freeze Panes* option to freeze the worksheet at the selected cell, so the rows above the cell and the columns to the left of the cell are always visible.

1. Select the cell immediately below the header row and immediately to the right of the label column (usually cell B2).
2. On the *View* tab, in the *Window* group, click the **Freeze Panes** button, and select **Freeze Panes.**

To return your worksheet to normal, click the **Freeze Panes** button and select **Unfreeze Panes.**

let me try Live!

If you do not have the data file from the previous skill open, open the student data file **EX4-10-PurchaseOrders** 🔖 and try this skill on your own:

1. Verify that the *Inventory* sheet is selected and the header row (row 1) is visible at the top of the worksheet.
2. Apply the **Freeze Panes** command so the top row will remain visible as you scroll down the worksheet.
3. If you will be moving on to the next skill in this chapter, leave the workbook open to continue working. If not, save the file as directed by your instructor and close it.

Skill 4.11 Hiding and Unhiding Rows and Columns

When you hide a row or column, the data still remain in your workbook, but they are no longer displayed onscreen and are not part of the printed workbook. Hiding rows can be helpful when you want to print a copy of your workbook for others but do not want to share all the information contained in your workbook.

To hide a row or column:

1. Select any cell in the row or column you want to hide.
2. On the *Home* tab, in the *Cells* group, click the **Format** button.
3. Point to **Hide & Unhide,** and click **Hide Rows** or **Hide Columns**.

To unhide a row or column:

1. Select the rows or columns on either side of the row or column you want to unhide.
2. On the *Home* tab, in the *Cells* group, click the **Format** button.
3. Point to **Hide & Unhide,** and click **Unhide Rows** or **Unhide Columns**.

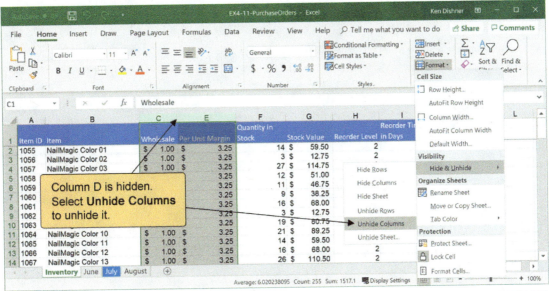

FIGURE EX 4.17

another method

The *Hide* and *Unhide* commands are also available from the right-click menu when columns or rows are selected.

let me try Live!

If you do not have the data file from the previous skill open, open the student data file **EX4-11-PurchaseOrders** ⬇ and try this skill on your own:

1. Verify that the *Inventory* sheet is selected.
2. Unhide column **D**.
3. Hide column **G** (Stock Value).
4. If you will be moving on to the next skill in this chapter, leave the workbook open to continue working. If not, save the file as directed by your instructor and close it.

Skill 4.12 Hiding and Unhiding Worksheets

Just as you can hide rows and columns in a worksheet, you can also hide entire worksheets. When you hide a worksheet, the sheet is hidden from view, but it is not deleted from the workbook. Hiding worksheets can be helpful when you have several worksheets in a large workbook, but only need to be working in a few sheets at once.

To hide a worksheet:

1. On the *Home* tab, in the *Cells* group, click the **Format** button.
2. Point to **Hide & Unhide** and click **Hide Sheet**.

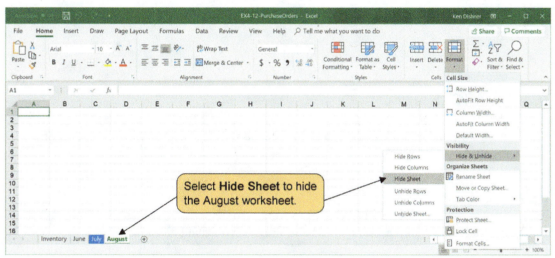

FIGURE EX 4.18

To unhide a worksheet:

1. On the *Home* tab, in the *Cells* group, click the **Format** button.
2. Point to **Hide & Unhide** and click **Unhide Sheet**.
3. In the *Unhide* dialog, if necessary, select the worksheet to unhide, and click **OK**.

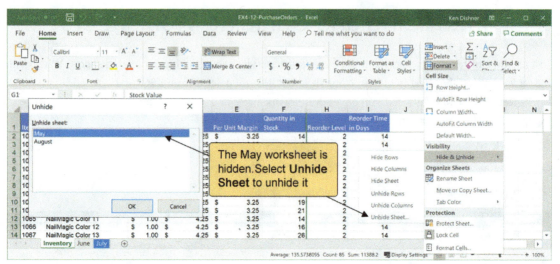

FIGURE EX 4.19

tips & tricks

Be careful when hiding worksheets. Sometimes you may forget that a worksheet is hidden, or other people using the workbook may not know that there are hidden worksheets.

tell me more

If there is only one worksheet in the workbook, the *Hide* command is unavailable.

another method

To hide a worksheet, right-click the sheet tab and select **Hide**.

let me try Live!

If you do not have the data file from the previous skill open, open the student data file **EX4-12-PurchaseOrders** and try this skill on your own:

1. Hide the **August** worksheet.
2. Unhide the **May** worksheet.
3. If you will be moving on to the next skill in this chapter, leave the workbook open to continue working. If not, save the file as directed by your instructor and close it.

from the perspective of . . .

PROJECT MANAGER

I was troubleshooting a budget spreadsheet for another department when I realized some formulas were referencing values in a worksheet that didn't appear to be in the workbook. I couldn't figure out where that worksheet was. Then I realized it was hidden! Now I use the same trick and hide unfinished worksheets or worksheets that contain data used for calculations only.

Skill 4.13 Splitting Workbooks

In Excel, you can split the worksheet view into two or four panes. Each pane scrolls independently of the other(s), so you can see two (or four) different areas of the worksheet at the same time. This can be especially helpful if you want to compare data in multiple parts of the worksheet at the same time.

To split the worksheet view:

1. Click the cell in the worksheet where you would like to split the view. You can select an entire row or column as the split point.
   - If you want to split the worksheet into two horizontal panes, click a cell in column **A**.
   - If you want to split the worksheet into two vertical panes, click a cell in row **1**.
   - If you want to split the worksheet into four panes, click any cell in the worksheet. The cell you selected will be the top left cell in the pane in the lower-right quadrant.
2. On the *View* tab, in the *Window* group, click the **Split** button.

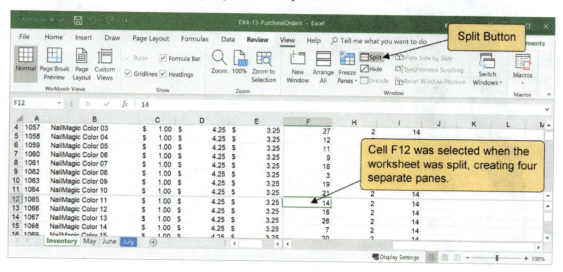

FIGURE EX 4.20

To undo the split and return the worksheet to a single view, click the **Split** button again.

tips & tricks

Splitting your worksheet will undo the *Freeze Panes* command.

tell me more

To adjust the size of a pane, click and drag the pane border.

let me try Live!

If you do not have the data file from the previous skill open, open the student data file **EX4-13-PurchaseOrders** and try this skill on your own:

1. Select the **Inventory** worksheet.
2. Select cell **F12**, and then split the worksheet into four panes. Observe how using the scroll bars affects the view in each of the panes.
3. Remove the split and return the worksheet to a single view. *Hint:* The *Undo* command will not undo the *Split* command.
4. If you will be moving on to the next skill in this chapter, leave the workbook open to continue working. If not, save the file as directed by your instructor and close it.

Skill 4.14 Changing the Worksheet View

Excel offers three ways to view a worksheet.

Just as the name implies, **Normal view** is the typical working view. In Normal view, Excel shows the aspects of the worksheet that are visible only onscreen. Elements that are visible only when printed (like headers and footers) are hidden.

Page Layout view shows all the worksheet elements as they will print, including page margins and headers and footers as shown in Figure EX 4.21. You will work with Page Layout view when you learn about headers and footers.

Page Break Preview view allows you to manipulate where page breaks occur when the worksheet is printed. You will work with Page Break Preview view when you learn about inserting page breaks.

To switch between worksheet views, click the appropriate button in the status bar at the bottom of the Excel window, or on the *View* tab, in the *Workbook Views* group, click the button for the view you want.

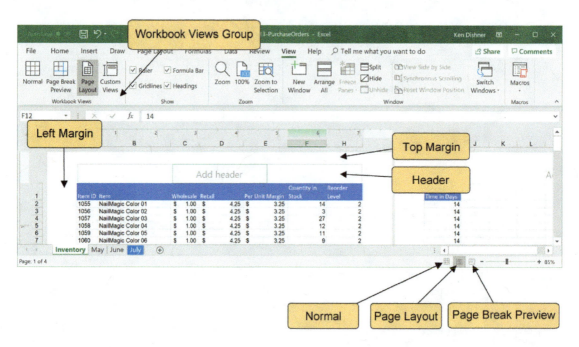

FIGURE EX 4.21

tips & tricks

Page Layout view is not compatible with *Freeze Panes*. If you have *Freeze Panes* applied to your worksheet, Excel will warn you before switching to Page Layout view. Click **OK** in the message box to continue to *Page Layout* view and undo *Freeze Panes*.

let me try Live!

If you do not have the data file from the previous skill open, open the student data file **EX4-14-PurchaseOrders** and try this skill on your own:

1. Select the **Inventory** worksheet.
2. Switch to **Page Break Preview** view.
3. Switch to **Page Layout** view. If Excel warns you that Page Layout view is not compatible with *Freeze Panes*, click **OK**.
4. If you will be moving on to the next skill in this chapter, leave the workbook open in Page Layout view to continue working. If not, save the file as directed by your instructor and close it.

Skill **4.15** Adding Headers and Footers

A **header** is text that appears at the top of every page, just below the top margin; a **footer** is text that appears at the bottom of every page, just above the bottom margin. Typically, headers and footers display information such as dates, page numbers, sheet names, file names, and authors' names.

To add a header or footer to a worksheet from Page Layout view:

1. Switch to Page Layout view by clicking the **Page Layout** button on the status bar.
2. The header area has three sections with the text *Add header* in the center section. If you do not see the *Add header* text, move the mouse pointer to the area just above row 1 to make the header area visible. Click the header section where you want to add information (left, center, or right).
3. The *Header & Footer Tools Design* tab appears.
4. In the *Header & Footer* group, click the **Header** button and select one of the predefined headers, or click a button in the *Header & Footer Elements* group to add a specific header element such as the sheet name or the current date. Excel inserts the code for the header element as show in Figure EX 4.22. Once you click away from the header, you will see the actual header text as shown in Figure EX 4.23.

FIGURE EX 4.22

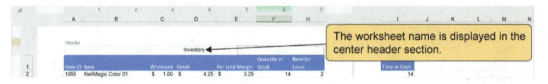

FIGURE EX 4.23

5. To switch to the footer, on the *Header & Footer Tools Design* tab, in the *Navigation* group, click the **Go to Footer** button. Add footer elements the same way you add header elements.

6. Another way to add header or footer is to select an option from the *Header and Footer Tools Design* tab, *Header & Footer* Click the **Header** or **Footer** button, and then select from the list. Be aware that this method will completely replace the entire header or footer, not just add an element to the selected section.

7. When you are finished adding your header and footer elements, click anywhere in the worksheet and then switch back to Normal view to continue working.

Another method for adding headers and footers uses the *Page Setup* dialog. This method will be familiar to users who have worked with older versions of Excel. When the *Header & Footer Tools Design* tab is active, you cannot use this method.

To add a header or footer to a worksheet using the *Page Setup* dialog:

1. On the *Page Layout* tab, in the *Page Setup* group, click the **Page Setup Dialog Launcher** to open the *Page Setup* dialog.

2. Click the **Header/Footer** tab.

3. Click the arrow beneath the *Header* or *Footer* area to expand the list of predefined header/footer options. Click the option you want to use.

4. Click **OK**.

FIGURE EX 4.24

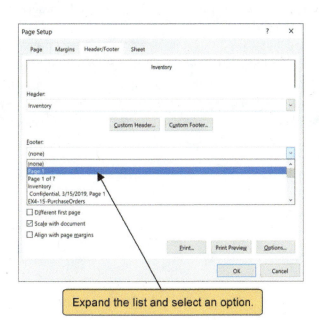

Expand the list and select an option.

FIGURE EX 4.25

tell me more

> If the predefined header/footer options in the *Page Setup* dialog do not meet your needs, you can customize the header or footer by clicking the **Custom Header...** or **Custom Footer...** button and adding elements through the *Header* or *Footer* dialog. In the *Header* or *Footer* dialog, click the section you want, and then click one of the header/footer element buttons.

another method

> Another way to add a header or footer to your worksheet is to click the *Insert* tab. In the *Text* group, click the **Header & Footer** button. The worksheet will automatically switch to Page Layout view when you click the **Header & Footer** button.

let me try Live!

> If you do not have the data file from the previous skill open, open the student data file **EX4-15-PurchaseOrders** and try this skill on your own:
>
> 1. If necessary, select the *Inventory* sheet and switch to Page Layout view.
> 2. From the *Header & Footer Tools Design* tab, add a header that displays the sheet name in the center section.
> 3. Add a footer that displays the word *Page* and then the page number in the center section.
> 4. Click anywhere in the worksheet grid, and then switch back to Normal view.
> 5. Preview how the worksheet will look when printed and note the header and footer.
> 6. If you will be moving on to the next skill in this chapter, leave the workbook open to continue working. If not, save the file as directed by your instructor and close it.

Skill 4.16 Inserting Page Breaks

Excel automatically inserts page breaks so columns and rows are not split across pages when you print. However, you may want to control where page breaks happen so your worksheet prints in a more logical order. When the worksheet is in Normal view, page breaks appear as faint dotted lines. To view the page breaks more clearly, switch to Page Break Preview view.

To manually insert a new page break:

1. From Normal view or Page Break Preview view, begin by selecting the cell below and/or to the right of where you want the new page break.
2. On the *Page Layout* tab, in the *Page Setup* group, click the **Breaks** button.
3. Click **Insert Page Break**.
4. A new page break is inserted to the left of the selected column or above the selected row.

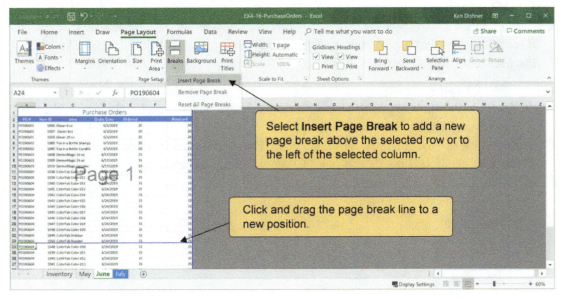

FIGURE EX 4.26

When the worksheet is in Page Break Preview view, automatic page breaks appear as blue dotted lines and manually inserted page breaks appear as solid blue lines. You can manually move a page break by clicking the page break line, and then dragging to the right or left or up or down. Release the mouse button when the line appears where you want the break. Notice that if you move an automatic page break, the line changes from dotted to solid.

To remove a manual page break, select any cell adjacent to (to the right of or below) the break, then on the *Page Layout* tab, in the *Page Setup* group, click the **Breaks** button, and click **Remove Page Break**.

tips & tricks

If you insert a page break but nothing seems to happen, check to see if you have the scaling option set for printing. For example, if you have the worksheet set to print all columns on a single page, inserting a new page break between columns will not appear to have any effect on the worksheet. However, if you remove the scaling option, the new manual page break will appear.

tell me more

To remove all the manual page breaks at once, on the *Page Layout* tab, in the *Page Setup* group, click the **Breaks** button, and click **Reset All Page Breaks**.

let me try Live!

If you do not have the data file from the previous skill open, open the student data file **EX4-16-PurchaseOrders** and try this skill on your own:

1. Select the **June** worksheet.
2. Switch to Page Break Preview view and observe the page breaks.
3. Insert a page break immediately above cell **A23**.
4. If you will be moving on to the next skill in this chapter, leave the workbook open to continue working. If not, save the file as directed by your instructor and close it.

from the perspective of . . .

WAREHOUSE LOGISTICS SUPERVISOR

Part of our company's "green" initiative is to minimize paper usage for printing. Using Excel's page break controls and layout controls like scaling, page orientation, and margins, we make sure that the reports we *have* to print use as little paper as possible.

Skill 4.17 Showing and Hiding Worksheet Elements

Gridlines are the lines that appear on the worksheet defining the rows and columns. Gridlines make it easy to see the individual cells in your worksheet. By default, gridlines are visible onscreen when you are working in Excel, but they do not print.

Headings are the numbers at the left of rows and the letters at the top of columns. By default, Excel displays the row and column headings onscreen to make it easy to identify cell references but they do not print.

To hide gridlines or headings onscreen for the active worksheet:

On the *Page Layout* tab, in the *Sheet Options* group, click the **View** check box under **Gridlines** or **Headings** to remove the checkmark.

To print the gridlines and headings when you print the worksheet:

On the *Page Layout* tab, in the *Sheet Options* group, click the **Print** check box under **Gridlines** or **Headings**.

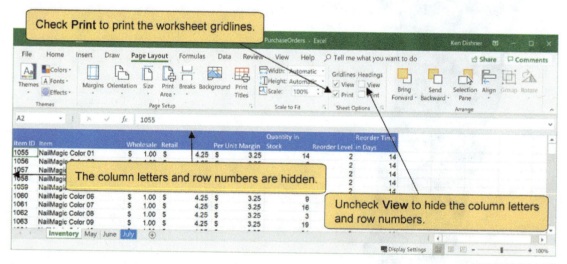

FIGURE EX 4.27

another method

> Set gridlines to print from the *Page Setup* On the *Page Layout* tab, in the *Page Setup* group, click the **Page Setup Dialog Launcher**. In the *Page Setup* dialog, click the **Sheet** tab. In the *Print* section, click the **Gridlines** check box. Click **OK**.

> To show or hide gridlines and headings onscreen, you can also check or uncheck the appropriate boxes on the *View* tab, in the *Show*

let me try Live!

If you do not have the data file from the previous skill open, open the student data file **EX4-17-PurchaseOrders** ⬇ and try this skill on your own:

1. Go to the **Inventory** worksheet and switch to Normal view if necessary.
2. Modify the **Inventory** worksheet so gridlines will print.
3. Modify the **Inventory** worksheet so headings are hidden onscreen.
4. If you will be moving on to the next skill in this chapter, leave the workbook open to continue working. If not, save the file as directed by your instructor and close it.

Skill 4.18 Changing Worksheet Orientation

Orientation refers to the direction the worksheet prints. It doesn't affect the way the worksheet looks on your computer screen. The default print setting is for **portrait orientation**—when the height of the page is greater than the width (like a portrait hanging on a wall). If your workbook is wide, you may want to use **landscape orientation** instead, where the width of the page is greater than the height.

You can set the worksheet orientation from the *Page Layout* tab on the Ribbon:

1. On the *Page Layout* tab, in the *Page Setup* group, click the **Orientation** button.
2. Click the **Portrait** or **Landscape** option.

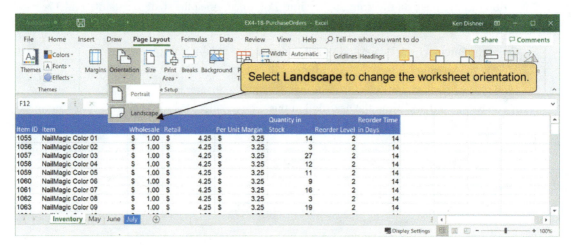

FIGURE EX 4.28

You can also change the worksheet orientation when you print:

1. Click the **File** tab to open Backstage view.
2. Click **Print**.
3. In the *Settings* section, click the button displaying the current orientation setting, and then click the orientation setting you want.

tips & tricks

Changing the *Orientation* setting affects only the active worksheet.

another method

On the *Page Layout* tab, in the *Page Setup* group, click the **Page Setup Dialog Launcher**. In the *Page Setup* dialog, click the **Page** tab. Click the **Portrait** or **Landscape** radio button. Click **OK**.

let me try Live!

If you do not have the data file from the previous skill open, open the student data file **EX4-18-PurchaseOrders** ⤓ and try this skill on your own:

1. Verify that the **Inventory** worksheet is active. Note the page break line between the *Reorder Level* and *Reorder Time in Days* columns.
2. Change the worksheet orientation to **Landscape**.
3. Note that the page is wider now and all the columns fit on one page.
4. If you will be moving on to the next skill in this chapter, switch back to **Portrait** orientation, and leave the workbook open to continue working. If not, save the file as directed by your instructor and close it.

Skill 4.19 Setting Up Margins for Printing

Margins are the blank spaces at the top, bottom, left, and right of a printed page. You may need to adjust the margins individually for each worksheet in your workbook to ensure they print exactly as you intend. Excel provides three margin settings:

> **Normal**—Uses Excel's default margins: 0.75 inch for the top and bottom and 0.7 inch for the left and right.

> **Wide**—Adds more space at the top, bottom, left, and right sides.

> **Narrow**—Reduces the amount of space at the top, bottom, left, and right sides, so more of your worksheet fits on each printed page.

If none of the automatic margins options is exactly what you want, the *Custom Margins...* option opens the *Page Setup* dialog where you can specify exact margins.

To change the margins, on the *Page Layout* tab, in the *Page Setup* group, click the **Margins** button, and click one of the preset margins options: **Normal, Wide,** or **Narrow,** or click **Custom Margins...** to specify your own values.

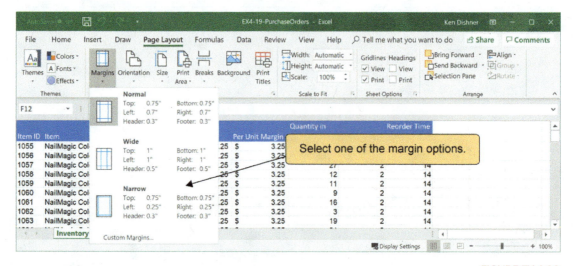

FIGURE EX 4.29

Because you will often want to adjust margins once you are ready to print, Excel allows you to adjust the margins directly from Backstage view.

1. Click the **File** tab to open Backstage view.
2. Click **Print**.
3. In the *Settings* section, click the button displaying the current margins setting, and then select the option you want.

let me try Live!

If you do not have the data file from the previous skill open, open the student data file **EX4-19-PurchaseOrders** and try this skill on your own:

1. Verify that the **Inventory** worksheet is active. If necessary, set the orientation back to **portrait**. Note the page break line between the *Reorder Level* and *Reorder Time in Days* columns.
2. Change the worksheet margins to the **Narrow** option.
3. Note the printable area has become larger and all the columns fit on one page now.
4. If you will be moving on to the next skill in this chapter, switch back to **Normal** margins and leave the workbook open to continue working. If not, save the file as directed by your instructor and close it.

Skill 4.20 Scaling Worksheets for Printing

When printing your worksheet, you can set the **scale** and specify that the worksheet prints at a percentage of the original size or at a maximum number of pages wide and/or tall. Each worksheet in the workbook has its own scale settings.

On the *Page Layout* tab, in the *Scale to Fit* group, select the option(s) you want.

> Click the **Width** arrow and select the maximum number of pages you want the worksheet to print across.

> Click the **Height** arrow and select the maximum number of pages you want the worksheet to print vertically.

> Click the **Scale** box and enter a percentage to grow or shrink the worksheet when printed.

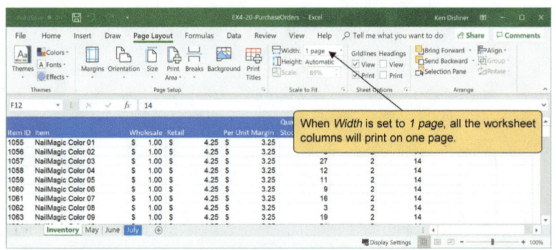

FIGURE EX 4.30

Because you often need to adjust scaling once you are ready to print, Excel has included scaling options on the Print page in Backstage view:

1. Click the **File** tab to open Backstage view.
2. Click **Print**.
3. In the *Settings* section, click the button displaying the current scaling setting and select the setting you want to use.

tips & tricks

When scaling your worksheet, be careful not to make the worksheet too small to read.

let me try Live!

If you do not have the data file from the previous skill open, open the student data file **EX4-20-PurchaseOrders** ⤓ and try this skill on your own:

1. Verify that the **Inventory** worksheet is active. If necessary, switch the orientation back to **portrait** and the margins to **Normal**.
2. Set the scaling options so all the columns will print on one page across.
3. If you will be moving on to the next skill in this chapter, leave the workbook open to continue working. If not, save the file as directed by your instructor and close it.

Skill 4.21 Printing Titles

If your worksheet includes a large table of data that prints on more than one page, you should ensure that the column or row labels print on every page.

To repeat rows and columns on every printed page:

1. On the *Page Layout* tab, in the *Page Setup* group, click the **Print Titles** button.
2. In the *Page Setup* dialog, on the *Sheet* tab, click in the **Rows to repeat at top** box, and then click and drag to select the rows to repeat. You can also type the row reference(s) using the format $1:$1. This example would repeat the first row only.
3. Click in the **Columns to repeat at left** box, and then click and drag to select the columns to repeat. You can also type the column reference(s) using the format $A:$A. This example would repeat the first column only. $A:$B would repeat columns A and B on every printed page.
4. Click **OK**.

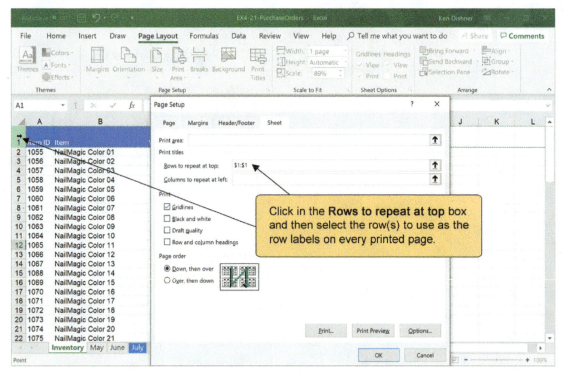

FIGURE EX 4.31

let me try Live!

If you do not have the data file from the previous skill open, open the student data file **EX4-21-PurchaseOrders** ⬇️ and try this skill on your own:

1. Verify that the **Inventory** worksheet is active. If necessary, check the worksheet *Headings* **View** option so the column letters and row numbers are visible. This will make it easier to understand which row is set to print on every page.
2. Set row **1** to print on every page.
3. Go to Backstage view and preview how the worksheet will look when printed. Verify that the titles from row 1 are included at the top of every page.
4. If you will be moving on to the next skill in this chapter, leave the workbook open to continue working. If not, save the file as directed by your instructor and close it.

Skill 4.22 Printing Selections, Worksheets, and Workbooks

By default, Excel will print the current, active worksheet. You can change the printing options, however, to print only part of a worksheet or the entire workbook at once.

1. Click the **File** tab to open Backstage view.
2. Click **Print**.
3. In the *Settings* section, the first button displays which part of the workbook will print. By default, **Print Active Sheets** is selected. To change the print selection, click the button, and then click one of the other options:
   - **Print Entire Workbook**—Prints all the sheets in the workbook.
   - **Print Selection**—Prints only the selected cells in the active worksheet, overriding any print area definitions in the active worksheet.
   - **Print Selected Table**—Prints the table only (available only if the current selection is within a defined table).
4. If you want to ignore the defined print area, click **Ignore Print Area** at the bottom of the list.
5. Click the **Print** button to print.

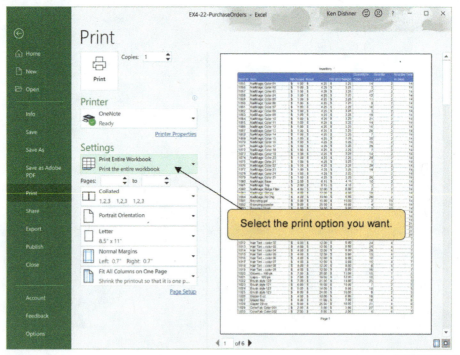

FIGURE EX 4.32

let me try Live!

If you do not have the data file from the previous skill open, open the student data file **EX4-22-PurchaseOrders** and try this skill on your own:

1. Change the print option to print the entire workbook.
2. Verify that all the worksheets in the workbook are included in the print preview.
3. Save the file as directed by your instructor and close it.

key terms

Group	Header
Theme	Footer
Theme Colors	Gridlines
Theme Fonts	Headings
Theme Effects	Orientation
Freeze	Portrait orientation
Normal view	Landscape orientation
Page Layout view	Margins
Page Break Preview view	Scale

concept review

1. If you delete a worksheet, you can undo the action.
    a. true
    b. false

2. To group worksheets that are not next to each other, select the first worksheet and press the key, and then click the other sheet tabs you want included in the group.
    a. Ctrl
    b. Shift
    c. Alt
    d. None of the above

3. A _____ is a unified color, font, and effects scheme you apply to a workbook.
    a. style
    b. conditional format
    c. theme
    d. cell format

4. To keep column headings as you scroll through a large spreadsheet you should use the _____ command.
    a. *Freeze First Column*
    b. *Freeze Top Row*
    c. *Split*
    d. *View Headings*

5. When you hide a row or column, the data remain in your workbook. They are no longer displayed onscreen but will be part of the printed workbook.
    a. true
    b. false

6. To display a worksheet in two or four panes, you should _____ the worksheet.
    a. merge
    b. freeze
    c. group
    d. split

7. A _____ is text that appears at the bottom of every page just above the margin.
    a. title
    b. header
    c. footer
    d. sheet tab

8. _____ are the numbers at the left of rows and the letters at the top of columns.
   a. Headings
   b. Gridlines
   c. Headers
   d. Footers

9. If your worksheet is wide, you may want to use portrait orientation where the height of the page is greater than the width.
   a. true
   b. false

10. If you want more or less white space around your worksheet area when printing, you should adjust the _____.
    a. orientation
    b. scaling
    c. margins
    d. page size

projects
skill review **4.1**

Data files for projects can be found by logging into your SIMnet account and going to the Library section.

In this project, you will work on an attendance log for a 16-week college course. For one section of the course, you will set up the sheet to print as an attendance sign-in sheet. For another section, you will set up the sheet to print as an attendance report for the administration office. This is a long project. Be sure to save often!

Skills needed to complete this project:

- Naming Worksheets (Skill 4.2)
- Changing the Color of Sheet Tabs (Skill 4.3)
- Moving and Copying Worksheets (Skill 4.4)
- Grouping Worksheets (Skill 4.6)
- Modifying Column Widths and Row Heights (Skill 4.9)
- Changing the Worksheet View (Skill 4.15)
- Adding Headers and Footers (Skill 4.15)
- Applying Themes (Skill 4.8)
- Splitting Workbooks (Skill 4.14)
- Inserting and Deleting Rows and Columns (Skill 4.7)
- Hiding and Unhiding Worksheets (Skill 4.12)
- Freezing and Unfreezing Rows and Columns (Skill 4.10)
- Hiding and Unhiding Rows and Columns (Skill 4.11)
- Changing Worksheet Orientation (Skill 4.18)
- Setting Up Margins for Printing (Skill 4.21)
- Scaling Worksheets for Printing (Skill 4.20)
- Showing and Hiding Worksheet Elements (Skill 4.17)
- Printing Selections, Worksheets, and Workbooks (Skill 4.22)
- Printing Titles (Skill 4.21)
- Inserting Page Breaks (Skill 4.16)

1. Open the start file **EX2019-SkillReview-4-1** and resave the file as: `[your initials]EX-SkillReview-4-1`
2. If the workbook opens in Protected View, click the **Enable Editing** button in the Message Bar at the top of the workbook so you can modify the workbook.
3. Rename *Sheet1* and change the color of the sheet tab.
   a. Right-click on the *Sheet1* tab, choose **Rename,** and type: `WF300`
   b. Press Enter.

    c. Right-click the sheet tab again, point to **Tab Color,** and select **Blue, Accent 1** (the fifth color in the first row of theme colors).

4. Make a copy of the *WF300* sheet.

    a. Right-click the sheet tab and select **Move or Copy...** to open the *Move or Copy* dialog.

    b. In the *Before sheet* box, select **Sheet2**.

    c. Check the **Create a copy** check box.

    d. Click **OK**.

5. Name the new sheet `WF301` and change the tab color.

    a. Right-click the new *WF300(2)* sheet tab, choose **Rename,** and type: `WF301`

    b. Press Enter .

    c. Right-click the sheet tab again, point to **Tab Color,** and select **Green, Accent 6** (the last color in the first row of theme colors).

6. Group sheets *WF300* and *WF301* so you can apply formatting changes to both sheets at once.

    a. Click the **WF300** sheet tab, press and hold Ctrl , and click the **WF301** sheet tab. Now any changes made to one of the sheets will be made to both sheets.

    b. Verify that *Group* appears in the title bar, indicating that the selected sheets are grouped.

7. Resize **column A** in both worksheets at once to best fit the data by double-clicking the right border of the column heading.

8. Add a header and footer to both worksheets at once.

    a. Switch to Page Layout view by clicking the **Page Layout** button on the status bar.

    b. Click in the center section of the header.

    c. On the *Header & Footer Tools Design* tab, in the *Header & Footer Elements* group, click the **File Name** button. The code **&[File]** will be entered in the center section of the header. Once you click somewhere else, this will display the name of your file.

    d. Click in the right section of the header and type your own name.

    e. On the *Header & Footer Tools Design* tab, in the *Navigation* group, click the **Go to Footer** button.

    f. Click in the center section of the footer.

    g. On the *Header & Footer Tools Design* tab, in the *Header & Footer Elements* group, click the **Sheet Name** button. The code **&[Tab]** will be entered. Once you click somewhere else, this will display the name of the sheet.

    h. Click in the right section of the footer.

    i. On the *Header & Footer Tools Design* tab, in the *Header & Footer Elements* group, click the **Current Date** button. Once you click somewhere else, this will display the current date.

    j. Click in any cell of the worksheet and click the **Normal** button on the status bar.

9. Ungroup the sheets by clicking *Sheet2*. Verify that the same formatting was applied to both sheets and that they are now ungrouped.

10. Apply the **Gallery** theme to the workbook.

    a. On the *Page Layout* tab, in the *Themes* group, click the **Themes** button to display the *Themes* gallery.

b. Notice that as you hover the mouse pointer over each option in the *Themes* gallery, Excel updates the worksheet to display a live preview of how the theme would affect the worksheet.

c. Click the **Gallery** option.

11. Select the **WF300** sheet. It can be difficult to work with such a wide worksheet. Scroll to the right to see the end of the semester, and you can no longer see the student names. Split the screen into two views of different parts of this worksheet.

a. Click cell **D1**. On the *View* tab, in the *Window* group, click the **Split** button. Now you can scroll each pane separately, but it is all still the same worksheet. You can drag the split bar to the right or left as needed.

b. Scroll to show the student names and the last few weeks of the semester on your screen.

c. Click the **Split** button again to return to normal.

12. Insert a new row to add a new student to the list.

a. Right-click on the row heading for row number **9** and select **Insert**.

b. Click the **Insert Options** button that appears immediately below where you right-clicked, and select **Format Same As Below**.

c. Enter the new student name: `Abrams, Maria`

d. Enter her student ID #: **1350417**

13. Select the **WF301** sheet. Because this sheet was copied from the WF300 class worksheet, the student names and ID numbers are not those of the students in WF301 class. Copy the student data from *Sheet2,* and then hide *Sheet2* when it is no longer needed.

a. On sheet *WF301*, select cells **A9:B29**. Press Delete to delete the content.

b. Go to **Sheet2** and copy the student names and ID numbers from cells **A2:B20**.

c. Paste the copied names and ID numbers to cell **A9** in the *WF301* sheet.

d. Hide *Sheet2* by right-clicking on the sheet name and selecting **Hide**.

14. Mary Wahl has decided to drop the class. Remove her from the WF301 class roster.

a. On worksheet *WF301*, delete the entire row for Mary by right-clicking on the row heading for row number **25** and selecting **Delete**.

15. Use the *Freeze Panes* option to keep rows 1:8 and columns A:B visible at all times.

a. Verify that the *WF301* sheet is selected, and click cell **C9**.

b. On the *View* tab, in the *Window* group, click the **Freeze Panes** button, then click the **Freeze Panes** option.

c. Verify that you selected the correct point at which to freeze panes. Scroll down and to the right. Are rows 1:8 and columns A:B visible regardless of where you scroll?

16. There is an extra blank worksheet in the workbook. Right-click **Sheet3** and select **Delete**.

Modify sheet *WF301* to print as an attendance sign-in sheet.

17. First, hide the student ID numbers by right-clicking on the **column B** heading and selecting **Hide**.

18. Set the page layout options.

a. On the *Page Layout* tab, in the *Page Setup* group, click the **Orientation** button, and select **Landscape**.

b. On the *Page Layout* tab, in the *Page Setup* group, click the **Margins** button, and select **Narrow**.

c. On the *Page Layout* tab, in the *Scale to Fit* group, expand the **Width** list and select **1 page,** and expand the **Height** list and select **1 page**.

d. On the *Page Layout* tab, in the *Sheet Options* group, click the **Print** check box under **Gridlines**.

19. Print only the part of the worksheet to use as the attendance sign-in sheet.

a. Select the appropriate cells to print as an attendance sign-in by selecting cells **A1:C26**.

b. Click the **File** tab to open Backstage view, and then click **Print** to display the Print page.

c. Under *Settings,* click the **Print Active Sheets** button to expand the options, and select **Print Selection**.

d. If your instructor has directed you to print the attendance sign-in list, click the **Print** button.

e. Click the **Back** arrow to exit Backstage view.

At the end of the semester you will need to print all the attendance records to turn in to the administration office. Let's set this up for the *WF300* class worksheet.

20. Select the **WF300** worksheet, and hide the attendance sign-in column by right-clicking the **column C** heading and selecting **Hide**.

21. Modify the worksheet so column A and rows 1 through 8 will print on every page.

a. On the *Page Layout* tab, in the *Page Setup* group, click the **Print Titles** button.

b. Click in the **Rows to repeat at top** box, and then click and drag with the mouse to select rows **1:8**. When you release the mouse button, you should see $1:$8 in the box.

c. Click in the **Columns to repeat at left** box, and then click with the mouse to select column **A**. When you release the mouse button, you should see $A:$A in the box.

d. Click **OK**.

22. Preview how the worksheet will look when printed and make adjustments from the Print page to keep the report to four or fewer pages.

a. Click the **File** tab to open Backstage view, and then click **Print**.

b. If necessary, click the **Print** Selection under *Settings* and select **Print Active Sheets**. Click the **Show Print Preview** button.

c. Note that the current settings will cause the worksheet to print on five pages.

d. Under *Settings,* click the **Portrait Orientation** button and switch to **Landscape Orientation** instead.

e. Under *Settings,* click the **Normal Margins** button, and select **Custom Margins...** to set your own margins.

f. In the *Page Setup* dialog, on the *Margins* tab, change the **Top, Bottom, Left,** and **Right** values to **0.5 inches**. Click **OK**.

g. Under *Settings,* click the **No Scaling** button, and select **Fit All Rows on One Page**.

h. Click the **Back** arrow to exit Backstage.

23. Modify the worksheet page breaks so weeks 1-8 print on the first page and weeks 9-16 print on the second page.

    a. If necessary, scroll to the right so columns T:V are visible. Note that the current page break occurs between columns U and V (after week 9).

    b. Click cell **T1**.

    c. On the *Page Layout* tab, in the *Page Setup* group, click the **Breaks** button, and select **Insert Page Break**. This inserts a page break to the left of the selected cell (after week 8).

    d. Click the **File** tab to open Backstage view, and then click **Print** to preview how the change will affect the printed pages.

    e. If your instructor has directed you to print the worksheet, click the **Print** button.

    f. Click the **Back** arrow to exit Backstage view.

24. Save and close the workbook.

projects
skill review **4.2**

Data files for projects can be found by logging into your SIMnet account and going to the Library section.

In this project, you will be working with a workbook designed to plan employees' or volunteers' work schedules.

Skills needed to complete this project:

- Naming Worksheets (Skill 4.2)
- Changing the Color of Sheet Tabs (Skill 4.3)
- Deleting Worksheets (Skill 4.5)
- Applying Themes (Skill 4.8)
- Grouping Worksheets (Skill 4.6)
- Modifying Column Widths and Row Heights (Skill 4.9)
- Splitting Workbooks (Skill 4.14)
- Freezing and Unfreezing Rows and Columns (Skill 4.10)
- Moving and Copying Worksheets (Skill 4.4)
- Hiding and Unhiding Rows and Columns (Skill 4.11)
- Showing and Hiding Worksheet Elements (Skill 4.18)
- Changing the Worksheet View (Skill 4.15)
- Adding Headers and Footers (Skill 4.16)
- Changing Worksheet Orientation (Skill 4.19)
- Setting Up Margins for Printing (Skill 4.20)
- Scaling Worksheets for Printing (Skill 4.21)
- Inserting Page Breaks (Skill 4.17)
- Printing Titles (Skill 4.22)
- Printing Selections, Worksheets, and Workbooks (Skill 4.23)

1. Open the start file **EX2019-SkillReview-4-2** and resave the file as:
   `[your initials]EX-SkillReview-4-2`
2. If the workbook opens in Protected View, click the **Enable Editing** button in the Message Bar at the top of the workbook so you can modify the workbook.
3. Look at the various worksheets. The monthly schedule worksheets need to be named and color coded.
   a. Double-click the tab for **Sheet 1,** type **January** and press Enter.
   b. Right-click the tab, point to **Tab Color,** and select **Blue, Accent 5** (the second color from the right in the top row of theme colors).
   c. Double-click the tab for **Sheet 2,** type **February** and press Enter.

d. Right-click the tab, point to **Tab Color,** and select **Orange, Accent 2** (the fifth color from the right in the top row of theme colors).

e. Double-click the tab for **Sheet 3,** type `March` and press Enter.

f. Right-click the tab, point to **Tab Color,** and select **Gold, Accent 4** (the third color from the right in the top row of theme colors).

4. The *Sheet 4* worksheet is unnecessary. Delete it.

a. Click the **Sheet 4** tab.

b. On the *Home* tab, in the *Cells* group, click the **Delete** button arrow and select **Delete Sheet**.

c. Click the **Delete** button when prompted.

5. Apply a new theme to the workbook.

a. On the *Page Layout* tab, in the *Themes* group, click the **Themes** button. Slide the mouse over different themes and notice the preview of the theme appearance on the worksheet.

b. Choose the **Ion** theme.

6. The monthly schedule sheets all need formatting. Group them and then format them all at once.

a. Click the **January** sheet tab, hold down Shift, click the **March** sheet tab, and then release Shift. Notice the three sheet tabs' appearance has changed to indicate that the three are selected. The *Regular Schedule* tab is not selected.

b. Verify that the title bar displays *Group*. Any changes you make to the current sheet will be made to all three of the selected sheets, so be very careful.

7. Adjust column widths and row heights to fit the contents and to make the worksheet more readable.

a. Look in column **A**. If you see ########## it means that the cell content is too wide for the column. Double-click the right column border to autofit the column to the data.

b. Select all the time columns (**B:U**). Locate the columns that are too narrow to display both the *From* time and the *To* Double-click the right column border to best fit the column width to the content. All the selected columns will size to match.

c. Select all the rows (**5:35**).

d. On the *Home* tab, in the *Cells* group click the **Format** button, and select **Row Height**. In the *Row Height* dialog, change the height value to **20** to make each row a little roomier.

e. Click **OK**.

8. Ungroup the sheets by clicking the *Regular Schedule* sheet.

a. Look at the *January, February,* and *March* sheets; they should all have been formatted.

b. Verify that the sheets are now ungrouped.

9. Select just the **Regular Schedule** sheet. It is hard to work with such a wide worksheet. Scroll to the right to see the night shift and you can no longer see the dates. Split the screen into two views of different parts of this worksheet.

a. Click cell **G1**. On the *View* tab, in the *Window* group, click the **Split** button. Now you can scroll each pane separately, but it is all still the same worksheet. You can drag the split bar to the right or left as needed.

    b. Scroll to show the morning and night shifts on your screen.

    c. Click the **Split** button again to return to normal.

10. Another way to deal with large worksheets is to freeze panes.

    a. Select any one of the month worksheets.

    b. Select cell **B5**. On the *View* tab, in the *Window* group, click **Freeze Panes,** and select **Freeze Panes**.

    c. Now you can scroll up or down and everything above and to the left of B5 remains visibly frozen on the screen.

    d. Freeze panes must be set on each of the month sheets separately. Grouping does not work for freeze panes. Repeat the freeze panes process for each of the month worksheets.

11. Drag the sheet tab for **Regular Schedule** before the sheet tab for **January** so that *Regular Schedule* is the first worksheet in the workbook.

12. Look closely at the *Regular Schedule* sheet. There are two row numbers missing.

    a. Select the rows before and after the missing rows. Select the entire rows by dragging over the row heading numbers at the far left.

    b. With both rows selected, right-click on the selection, and select **Unhide** to reveal the rows for Tuesdays and Wednesdays.

13. Ensure that the worksheet gridlines will print with the worksheet.

    a. On the *Page Layout* tab, in the *Sheet Options* group, click the **Print** check box under *Gridlines*.

    b. Repeat this process for the *January, February,* and *March* worksheets (If you group the sheets first, be sure to ungroup them when you are finished.)

14. Prepare to print your worksheets by adding headers and footers. You will need to use the *Page Setup* dialog instead of Page Layout view because your worksheets have *Freeze Panes* applied.

    a. Group all the worksheets to save time. This way the headers and footers may be added to all the sheets at once. Verify that all the sheets are selected.

    b. On the *Page Layout* tab, in the *Page Setup* group, click the **Page Setup dialog launcher** button.

    c. In the *Page Setup* dialog, click the **Header/Footer** tab.

    d. Click the **Custom Header**... button.

    e. Click in the **Center section** and then click the **Insert File Name** button.

    f. Click **OK**.

    g. Click the **Custom Footer**... button.

    h. Click in the **Center section** and then click the **Insert Sheet Name** button.

    i. Click **OK**.

    j. Click **OK** again to close the *Page Setup* dialog.

    k. Ungroup the sheets. Right-click on any sheet tab and choose **Ungroup Sheets**.

15. Set up printing options for the *Regular Schedule* sheet.

    a. Select the **Regular Schedule** sheet. Click the **File** tab, and then click **Print**.

    b. Scroll down to see all the pages for your worksheet. Scroll back up to the first page.

    c. Click the **Portrait Orientation** button and select **Landscape**.

    d. Click the **Normal Margins** button and select **Narrow**.

    e. Click the **No Scaling** button, and select **Fit Sheet on One Page**.

16. The monthly schedules would be easier to read if the morning, afternoon, and night shifts each printed on a separate page in a reasonably large font size.

    a. Click the **Back** arrow to return to the worksheet.

    b. Group sheets **January:March**.

    c. On the *Page Layout* tab, in the *Page Setup* group, click the **Orientation** button, and select **Landscape**.

    d. On the *Page Layout* tab, in the *Page Setup* group, click the **Margins** button, and select **Narrow**.

    e. Review the current page break. Switch to Page Break Preview view if you want by clicking the **Page Break Preview** button at the lower right corner of the status bar.

    f. Notice that the schedule just barely requires two pages vertically. On the *Page Layout* tab, in the *Scale to Fit* group, click the **Height** box arrow and select **1 Page**.

    g. Click cell **I1**. On the *Page Layout* tab, in the *Page Setup* group, click the **Breaks** button. Select **Insert Page Break**. (Note that you cannot drag the page break lines when the worksheets are grouped. You must use the Ribbon method to insert manual page breaks.)

    h. Click in cell **N1**. On the *Page Layout* tab, in the *Page Setup* group, click the **Breaks** button. Select **Insert Page Break**.

    i. Click the **Normal** button to return to Normal view.

17. The days will show only on the first sheet, so the second and third sheets will make no sense. Set the worksheets so column A will print on every page. You must ungroup the sheets first.

    a. Click the **Regular Schedule** sheet to ungroup the sheets, and then click the **January** sheet tab again.

    b. On the *Page Layout* tab, in the *Page Setup* group, click **Print Titles** button.

    c. In the *Columns to repeat at left* box enter $A:$A or click in the box and then click anywhere in column **A**.

    d. Click **OK** in the *Page Setup* dialog.

    e. Repeat this process with the **February** and **March** worksheets.

18. Preview how the entire workbook will print. Be sure to verify that column A will print at the left side of the *January, February,* and *March* worksheets.

    a. Click the **File** tab to open Backstage view.

    b. Click **Print**.

    c. Click the **Print Active Sheets** button and select **Print Entire Workbook**.

    d. Use the **Next Page** button below the print preview to review how every printed page will look. There should be 10 pages. Note the worksheet name in the footer area at the bottom of each page.

19. Save and close the workbook.

projects

Data files for projects can be found by logging into your SIMnet account and going to the Library section.

challenge yourself 4.3

In this project, you will be working with a workbook used to analyze loan payments.

Skills needed to complete this project:

- Naming Worksheets (Skill 4.2)
- Applying Themes (Skill 4.8)
- Changing the Color of Sheet Tabs (Skill 4.3)
- Changing the Worksheet View (Skill 4.14)
- Adding Headers and Footers (Skill 4.15)
- Freezing and Unfreezing Rows and Columns (Skill 4.10)
- Moving and Copying Worksheets (Skill 4.4)
- Inserting and Deleting Rows and Columns (Skill 4.7)
- Grouping Worksheets (Skill 4.6)
- Modifying Column Widths and Row Heights (Skill 4.9)
- Hiding and Unhiding Rows and Columns (Skill 4.11)
- Showing and Hiding Worksheet Elements (Skill 4.17)
- Hiding and Unhiding Worksheets (Skill 4.12)
- Deleting Worksheets (Skill 4.5)
- Changing Worksheet Orientation (Skill 4.18)
- Printing Titles (Skill 4.21)
- Scaling Worksheets for Printing (Skill 4.20)
- Printing Selections, Worksheets, and Workbooks (Skill 4.22)

1. Open the start file **EX2019-ChallengeYourself-4-3** and resave the file as:
   `[your initials]EX-ChallengeYourself-4-3`
2. If the workbook opens in Protected View, click the **Enable Editing** button in the Message Bar at the top of the workbook so you can modify the workbook.
3. Change the name of *Sheet1* to: `NewHybrid`
4. Apply the **Retrospect** theme.
5. Change the *NewHybrid* sheet tab color to **Orange, Accent 1** (the fifth color from the left in the top row of theme colors).
6. Add header and footer information to the *NewHybrid* worksheet.
   a. Set the center header section to display the sheet name.
   b. Add the page number to the left footer section.
   c. Set the right footer section to display the current date.

7. Freeze panes so rows **1:8** and columns **A:B** remain in place when you scroll through the worksheets.

8. Make a copy of the *NewHybrid* sheet, placing before the *Working* worksheet.

9. Change the name of the new sheet to: `Option2`

10. Change the *Option2* sheet tab color to **Green, Accent 6** (the first color from the right in the top row of theme colors).

11. Change the values in the *Option2* worksheet.
    a. Change the amount borrowed (cell **B3**) to: `14,000`
    b. Change the APR (cell **B5**) to: `1.9%`

12. Delete any extra rows at the bottom of the worksheet where the payment due is 0 (row **41**).

13. Group the *NewHybrid* and *Option2* worksheets. Make the following changes to both sheets at once.
    a. Change the width of the *Payment Date* column (column **C**) to exactly **19**.
    b. Delete the extra column (column **H**).
    c. Unhide column **G**.
    d. Hide the gridlines so they do not appear onscreen.
    e. Ungroup the worksheets.

14. Hide the *Working* worksheet.

15. Delete the *Sheet2* worksheet.

16. Change the page orientation for the *NewHybrid* sheet to **Landscape**.

17. Modify the *NewHybrid* sheet so row **8** will repeat at the top of every printed page.

18. Scale the *Option2* sheet so all columns will fit on one page and all rows will fit on one page.

19. Print preview the entire workbook.

20. Save and close the workbook.

projects

challenge yourself 4.4

In this project, you will be working with data about automobile emissions and fuel economy. These green car data were downloaded from the website fueleconomy.gov. The SmartWay scores range from 0 to 10, where 10 is best. The vehicles with the best scores on both air pollution and greenhouse gas receive the Elite designation. More information about the SmartWay program can be found at http://www3.epa.gov/greenvehicles/you/smartway.htm.

Skills needed to complete this project:

- Naming Worksheets (Skill 4.2)
- Applying Themes (Skill 4.8)
- Changing the Color of Sheet Tabs (Skill 4.3)
- Changing the Worksheet View (Skill 4.15)
- Adding Headers and Footers (Skill 4.16)
- Moving and Copying Worksheets (Skill 4.4)
- Inserting and Deleting Rows and Columns (Skill 4.7)
- Grouping Worksheets (Skill 4.6)
- Modifying Column Widths and Row Heights (Skill 4.9)
- Hiding and Unhiding Rows and Columns (Skill 4.11)
- Showing and Hiding Worksheet Elements (Skill 4.18)
- Setting Up Margins for Printing (Skill 4.20)
- Changing Worksheet Orientation (Skill 4.19)
- Scaling Worksheets for Printing (Skill 4.21)
- Printing Titles (Skill 4.22)
- Freezing and Unfreezing Rows and Columns (Skill 4.10)
- Inserting Page Breaks (Skill 4.17)
- Printing Selections, Worksheets, and Workbooks (Skill 4.23)

1. Open the start file **EX2019-ChallengeYourself-4-4** and resave the file as: `[your initials]EX-ChallengeYourself-4-4`
2. If the workbook opens in Protected View, click the **Enable Editing** button in the Message Bar at the top of the workbook so you can modify the workbook.
3. Rename the *all_alpha_10* worksheet: `Raw Data`
4. Apply the **Facet** workbook theme.
5. Color the *Raw Data* worksheet tab **Green, Accent 1** (the sixth color from the right in the first row of theme colors).

6. Review the worksheet header and footer.

   a. Delete the text in the left footer section and replace it with: `Source: fueleconomy.gov`

   b. Add the sheet name to the footer center section. *Hint:* Do not type the sheet name in the footer. Insert a code so Excel will display the name of the current worksheet.

7. Copy the *Raw Data* worksheet. Place the new worksheet at the end of the workbook.

8. Rename the new worksheet: `Nissan`

9. Color the *Nissan* worksheet tab **Dark Green, Accent 2** (the fifth color from the right in the first row of theme colors).

10. In the *Nissan* worksheet, delete rows **2:233** and then delete rows **22:92** so only the 20 Nissan models remain.

11. Group the *Raw Data* and *Nissan* worksheets.

    a. Autofit column **K** to best fit the data.

    b. Set the column width for columns **L:Q** to: **6**

    c. Set the row height for row **1** to: **70**

    d. Hide the **Underhood ID** and **Stnd Description** columns.

    e. Set the worksheet gridlines to print.

    f. Set **Wide** margins.

    g. Set the worksheet orientation to **Landscape**.

    h. Scale the worksheets so all columns will print on one page.

    i. Ungroup the sheets.

12. Set the worksheet options so row **1** will print on every page. You will need to do this individually for each worksheet.

13. Review the page breaks in the *Raw Data* worksheet. Move the page break between pages 2 and 3 to after row **53** so the fourth page begins with the first Ford model.

14. Apply **Freeze Panes** to the *Raw Data* worksheet so the first row is always visible as you scroll down the worksheet.

15. Preview how the entire workbook will print.

16. Save and close the workbook.

projects

on your own **4.5**

In this project you will work with data from the United States Census Bureau. The data were downloaded from https://www.census.gov/data/tables/time-series/demo/popest/2010s-state-total.html.

Skills needed to complete this project:

- Moving and Copying Worksheets (Skill 4.4)
- Naming Worksheets (Skill 4.2)
- Applying Themes (Skill 4.8)
- Changing the Color of Sheet Tabs (Skill 4.3)
- Inserting and Deleting Rows and Columns (Skill 4.7)
- Modifying Column Widths and Row Heights (Skill 4.9)
- Changing the Worksheet View (Skill 4.15)
- Adding Headers and Footers (Skill 4.16)
- Freezing and Unfreezing Rows and Columns (Skill 4.10)
- Changing Worksheet Orientation (Skill 4.19)
- Setting Up Margins for Printing (Skill 4.20)
- Scaling Worksheets for Printing (Skill 4.21)
- Showing and Hiding Worksheet Elements (Skill 4.18)
- Inserting Page Breaks (Skill 4.17)
- Printing Selections, Worksheets, and Workbooks (Skill 4.23)

1. Open the start file **EX2019-OnYourOwn-4-5** and resave the file as: `[your initials]EX-OnYourOwn-4-5`
2. If the workbook opens in Protected View, click the **Enable Editing** button in the Message Bar at the top of the workbook so you can modify the workbook.
3. The workbook includes one worksheet with census data for regions and individual states. Create one or more copies of the original worksheet and modify the data in each so each worksheet has a unique set of data.
4. Delete any rows you do not want to include in each worksheet. *Hint:* The Note near the bottom of the original worksheet is very long and will print across multiple pages. You may want to delete it or move it to a cell with *Wrap Text*
5. Rename each worksheet.
6. Apply a theme of your choice to the workbook.
7. Apply a color to the tab of each worksheet.
8. Add header and footer elements of your choice to all the worksheets at once. *Hint:* You may want to move the suggested citation from the last rows in the worksheet into the worksheet footer.

9. Add a row at the top of each sheet and enter an appropriate title.

10. Adjust column widths to best fit the data (all worksheets individually).

11. Apply cell styles and cell formatting to make the data easier to read.

12. As appropriate, apply *Freeze Panes* to make it easier to work with each worksheet.

13. Make an attractive readable printout of each worksheet. Each should fit neatly on one page or have logical page breaks and print titles when more than one page is required. Print the worksheets only if directed to do so by your instructor.

    a. Set the worksheets' orientation appropriately.

    b. Set appropriate margins.

    c. Scale the worksheets appropriately.

    d. Add manual page breaks if necessary.

    e. Set at least one of the sheets to print with gridlines and at least one to print without gridlines.

    f. For worksheets that print on more than one page, ensure that the label row will be included on every page.

    g. For one worksheet, adjust the print settings to print a useful selection of just some cells that will fit all on one page.

14. Save and close the workbook.

projects
fix it **4.6**

Data files for projects can be found by logging into your SIMnet account and going to the Library section.

In this project, you will correct errors in a party planning workbook.

Skills needed to complete this project:

- Changing the Worksheet View (Skill 4.14)
- Applying Themes (Skill 4.8)
- Deleting Worksheets (Skill 4.5)
- Adding Headers and Footers (Skill 4.15)
- Showing and Hiding Worksheet Elements (Skill 4.18)
- Naming Worksheets (Skill 4.2)
- Moving and Copying Worksheets (Skill 4.4)
- Modifying Column Widths and Row Heights (Skill 4.9)
- Inserting and Deleting Rows and Columns (Skill 4.7)
- Hiding and Unhiding Rows and Columns (Skill 4.11)
- Changing Worksheet Orientation (Skill 4.18)
- Setting Up Margins for Printing (Skill 4.19)
- Scaling Worksheets for Printing (Skill 4.20)
- Freezing and Unfreezing Rows and Columns (Skill 4.10)
- Printing Titles (Skill 4.21)
- Inserting Page Breaks (Skill 4.16)

1. Open the start file **EX2019-FixIt-4-6** and resave the file as:
   `[your initials]EX-FixIt-4-6`
2. If the workbook opens in Protected View, click the **Enable Editing** button in the Message Bar at the top of the workbook so you can modify the workbook.
3. The workbook was last saved in Page Break Preview view. Switch it back to **Normal** view.
4. The workbook uses a very unattractive theme. Change the theme to **Office**.
5. The copy of the *Shopping List* worksheet is incomplete. Delete it. Be careful to delete the copy, not the original.
6. Both worksheets should include the sheet name in the header center section.
7. Both worksheets should include the gridlines when printed.
8. Correct the following errors in the *Shopping List* worksheet:
   a. The *Shopping List* worksheet should be first in the workbook.
   b. One of the columns is not wide enough to display the data. Autofit that column.
   c. There is an extra row between the label row and the shopping data. Delete the extra row.

9. Correct the following errors in the *Guest List* worksheet:

   a. The worksheet tab is misspelled. Correct the spelling of *Gest*.

   b. Column **D** should not be visible.

   c. Row **3** is too tall. Autofit the row to fit the content.

   d. Page orientation should be **Portrait**.

   e. Margins should be set to the **Narrow** option.

   f. All columns should fit on one page when printed.

   g. The right footer section should include the page number.

   h. Rows **1:3** should always be visible as you scroll down the worksheet. *Hint:* Select the entire row where you want to apply the *Freeze Panes* command.

   i. Rows **1:3** should also print on every page.

   j. The page break should be between rows **56** and **57** so the guests who have not yet RSVP'd are grouped together on the second page.

   k. If you were working in Page Layout view or Page Break Preview view, be sure to switch back to **Normal** view.

10. Review your work by previewing how each worksheet will print and then save and close the workbook.

Adding Charts and Analyzing Data

chapter 5

In this chapter, you will learn the following skills:

> Create and format charts
> Create and format tables
> Sort and filter data
> Create PivotTables and PivotCharts
> Conduct what-if analysis using Goal Seek and data tables

introduction

This chapter introduces data analysis. You will learn to use charts to visualize data; to use tables and PivotTables to quickly sort, filter, and summarize data; and to conduct what-if analyses using data tables and Goal Seek.

Skill 5.1 Inserting a Column Chart or a Bar Chart

Column charts work best with data that are organized into rows and columns like a table. Data point values are transformed into vertical columns, with the values plotted along the vertical (y) axis. Each row in the table is grouped as a data series. Excel uses the column labels as the categories along the horizontal (x) axis.

In the **clustered column chart** shown in Figure EX 5.1, each column represents a single data point. The data points are grouped (clustered) together by category. Each data series is represented by a single color as shown in the legend below the chart.

To insert a column chart:

1. Select the data you want to include in the column chart.
2. On the *Insert* tab, in the *Charts* group, click the **Insert Column or Bar Chart** button.
3. Click the chart type you want to insert the chart into the worksheet.

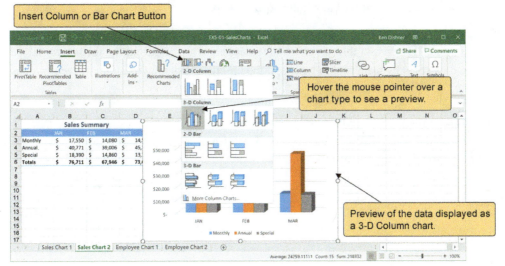

FIGURE EX 5.1

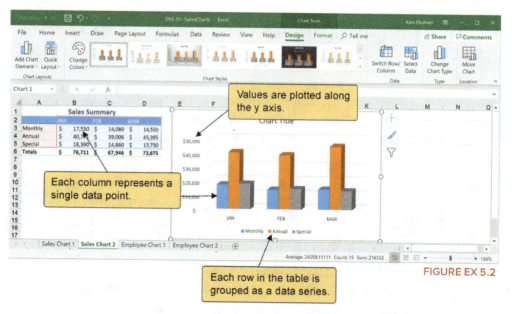

Bar charts are like column charts turned on their side. The categories are displayed on the vertical axis, and the data point values are plotted along the horizontal axis.

The clustered bar chart in Figure EX 5.3 displays the same data as Figure EX 5.2. Each bar represents a single data point. However, in this bar chart, the sales values are plotted along the horizontal axis, grouped into data series by membership type, and the months are displayed along the vertical axis.

To insert a bar chart:

1. Select the data you want to include in the bar chart.
2. On the *Insert* tab, in the *Charts* group, click the **Insert Column or Bar Chart** button.
3. Click the chart type you want to insert the chart into the worksheet.

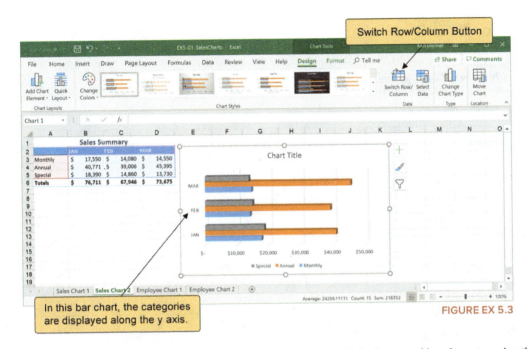

FIGURE EX 5.3

In this bar chart, the categories are displayed along the y axis.

If you don't like the way Excel grouped the data series, you can switch them, making the categories the data series and the data series the categories. On the *Chart Tools Design* tab, in the *Data* group, click the **Switch Row/Column** button. Figure EX 5.4 charts the same data as Figure EX 5.3 with the rows and columns switched, so the data points are organized into data series by column instead of by row.

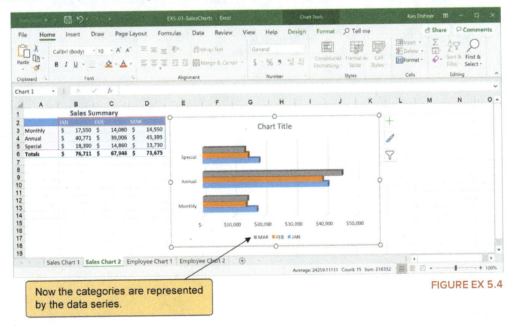

FIGURE EX 5.4

Now the categories are represented by the data series.

tips & tricks

In previous versions of Excel, column charts and bar charts had separate buttons on the *Insert* tab, *Charts* group.

tell me more

A **stacked column chart** displays each data series as a single vertical column divided into sections representing each data point. A **stacked bar chart** is similar—combining the data points of each data series into a single horizontal bar. Stacked charts are useful for comparing parts of a whole or showing how parts of a whole change over time.

another method

You can also insert a column chart or a bar chart from the *Insert Chart* dialog, *All Charts* tab.

let me try Live!

Open the student data file **EX5-01-SalesCharts** and try this skill on your own:

1. If necessary, go to the **Sales Chart 2** worksheet, and select cells **A2:D5.**
2. Insert a **3-D Clustered Bar** chart (the first chart type in the *3-D Bar* section of the *Insert Column or Bar Chart* menu).
3. Switch the rows and columns in the chart, so the data points are grouped into data series by column.
4. If you will be moving on to the next skill in this chapter, leave the workbook open to continue working. If not, save the file as directed by your instructor and close it.

from the perspective of . . .

COLLEGE STUDENT

I use Excel to track my monthly budget. Before I started using charts, the spreadsheets were just numbers. I knew how much money was going out each month, but I didn't really understand how much of my money I was spending on unnecessary expenses. Once I started using charts, it was obvious that I was spending more on lattes than on transportation! I bought a coffee maker, and now I have a little extra cash each month to put away for a rainy day.

Skill 5.2 Inserting a Pie Chart

Pie charts represent data as parts of a whole. They do not have x and y axes like column charts. Instead, each value is a visual "slice" of the pie. Pie charts work best when you want to evaluate values as they relate to a total value—for example, departmental budgets in relation to the entire budget, or each employee's bonus in relation to the entire bonus pool.

In Figure EX 5.5, the total sales for each salesperson is represented by a slice of the pie.

To add a pie chart:

1. Select the data you want to include in the pie chart.
2. On the *Insert* tab, in the *Charts* group, click the **Insert Pie Chart** button.
3. Click the chart type you want to insert the chart into the worksheet.

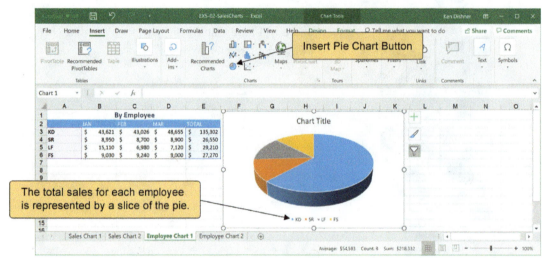

FIGURE EX 5.5

tips & tricks

In an "exploded" pie chart, each slice is slightly separated from the whole. You can explode a single slice by clicking it and dragging it away from the rest of the slices. Exploding a single slice of data gives it emphasis.

tell me more

Doughnut charts are similar to pie charts, but they can display more than one series. Each series is represented by a ring around the doughnut. Each data point in the series is represented by a piece of the ring proportional to the total. Doughnut charts can be confusing and are not commonly used.

another method

You can also insert a pie chart from the *Insert Chart* dialog, *All Charts* tab.

let me try Live!

If you do not have the data file from the previous skill open, open the student data file **EX5-02-SalesCharts** ⤓ and try this skill on your own:

1. If necessary, go to the **Employee Chart 1** worksheet, and select cells **A3:A6** (the row labels) and cells **E3:E6** (the row totals). *Hint:* Remember to press Ctrl to select noncontiguous cells.
2. Insert a **3-D Pie** chart.
3. If you will be moving on to the next skill in this chapter, leave the workbook open to continue working. If not, save the file as directed by your instructor and close it.

Skill 5.3 Inserting a Line Chart

Line charts feature a line connecting each data point—showing the movement of values over time. Line charts work best when data trends over time are important.

The line chart in Figure EX 5.6 shows sales over a three-month period. Each data series represents sales for a specific employee. This type of line chart, called a **line with markers**, includes dots along the line for each data point.

To add a line chart:

1. Select the data you want to include in the line chart. Be sure to include both values and the related cells that represent time segments (dates, calendar quarters, etc.).
2. On the *Insert* tab, in the *Charts* group, click the **Insert Line Chart** button.
3. Click the chart type you want to insert the chart into the worksheet.
4. If Excel does not display the time categories along the x axis, switch the data series and the categories. On the *Chart Tools Design* tab, in the *Data* group, click the **Switch Row/Column** button.

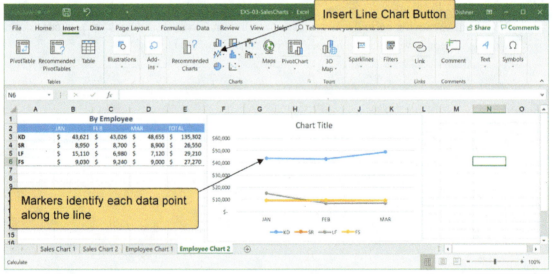

FIGURE EX 5.6

tips & tricks

While line charts are a good choice if the data set has many data points, use a line chart with markers only if there are relatively few data points.

another method

You can also insert a line chart from the *Insert Chart* dialog, *All Charts* tab.

let me try Live!

If you do not have the data file from the previous skill open, open the student data file
EX5-03-SalesCharts and try this skill on your own:

1. If necessary, go to the **Employee Chart 2** worksheet, and select cells **A2:D6.**
2. Insert a **Line with Markers** chart (the fourth chart type in the *Insert Line Chart* menu).
3. If necessary, switch the rows and columns in the chart to list the months along the x axis.
4. If you will be moving on to the next skill in this chapter, leave the workbook open to continue working. If not, save the file as directed by your instructor and close it.

Skill 5.4 Resizing and Moving Charts

When you first create a chart, Excel places the chart in the middle of the worksheet. Often, you will need to resize and move the chart so it doesn't cover the worksheet data.

With the chart selected, resize the chart using the resize handles located at the four corners and the middle of each side of the chart area. Click and drag toward the center of the chart to make it smaller or outward to make it larger.

FIGURE EX 5.7

To move a chart to a new position on the worksheet:

1. Select the chart. Be careful not to click in the plot area or you will move just the plot area instead of the entire chart. Your mouse cursor will change to the move cursor.
2. With your left mouse button depressed, drag the chart to the new location on the worksheet, and then release the mouse button to "drop" the chart at the new location.

If your chart is large or complex, you may want the chart to appear on its own worksheet. To move a chart to a new sheet:

1. If necessary, select the chart. If you just created the chart, it will still be selected.
2. On the *Chart Tools Design* tab, in the *Location* group, click the **Move Chart** button.
3. In the *Move Chart* dialog, click the **New sheet** radio button to move the chart to its own worksheet. If you want to specify a name for the new sheet, type it in the *New sheet* box. To move the chart to an existing worksheet, click the **Object in** radio button, and then select the name of the sheet you want to move the chart to.
4. Click **OK.**

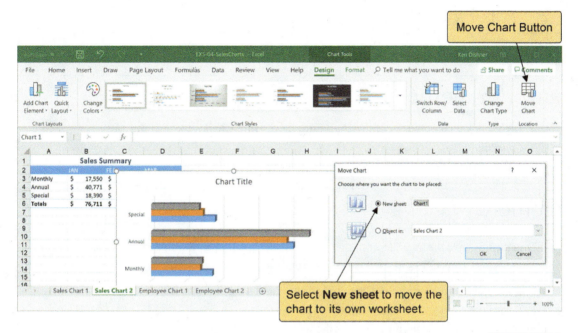

FIGURE EX 5.8

When you use the *Move Chart* dialog to move a chart to its own sheet, Excel creates a special type of worksheet called a **chart sheet**. The chart sheet does not include the columns, rows, and cells you are used to seeing in Excel; it contains only the chart object. The new chart sheet automatically changes the zoom level so the entire chart is visible.

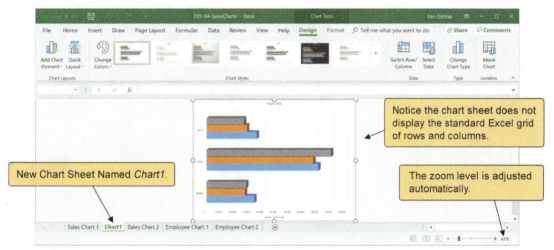

FIGURE EX 5.9

tips & tricks

You cannot resize a chart in a chart sheet.

another method

> Right-click an empty area of the chart and select **Move Chart...** to open the *Move Chart* dialog.
> Use the *Cut, Copy,* and *Paste* commands to move a chart from one sheet to another.

let me try Live!

If you do not have the data file from the previous skill open, open the student data file
EX5-04-SalesCharts and try this skill on your own:

1. If necessary, go to the **Sales Chart 1** worksheet and select the chart.
2. Resize the chart so it is approximately 13 rows tall.
3. Move the chart to the empty area of the worksheet to the right of the data.
4. Go to the **Sales Chart 2** worksheet and move the chart to a new worksheet.
5. If you will be moving on to the next skill in this chapter, leave the workbook open to continue working. If not, save the file as directed by your instructor and close it.

Skill 5.5 Applying Quick Layouts to Charts

When you insert a chart, Excel displays the *Chart Tools Design* contextual tab. From this tab, you can change the chart layout. **Quick Layouts** apply combinations of data labels, titles, and data tables.

Data labels—Display data values for each data marker.

Data table—Displays a table of the data point values below the chart.

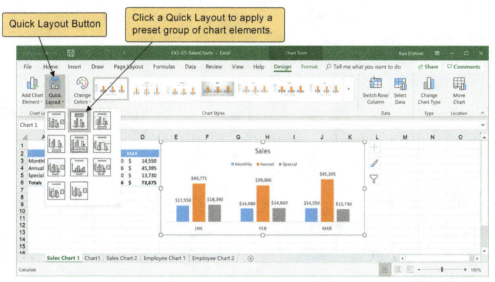

FIGURE EX 5.10

To apply a Quick Layout to a chart:

1. Select the chart.
2. On the *Chart Tools Design* tab, in the *Chart Layouts* group, click the **Quick Layout** button.
3. Notice that as you move over each Quick Layout option, Excel shows a preview of the layout. Click the layout you want to apply it to the chart.

let me try Live!

If you do not have the data file from the previous skill open, open the student data file **EX5-05-SalesCharts** ⬇ and try this skill on your own:

1. Go to the **Sales Chart 1** worksheet and select the chart.
2. Apply the **Layout 2** Quick Layout to the chart.
3. If you will be moving on to the next skill in this chapter, leave the workbook open to continue working. If not, save the file as directed by your instructor and close it.

Skill 5.6 Showing and Hiding Chart Elements

If there is not a Quick Layout with exactly the look you want, you can hide or show chart elements individually. Showing and hiding chart elements such as the chart title, axes, and gridlines can make a chart easier to read.

To hide or show chart elements:

1. Click any empty area of the chart area to select the chart.
2. Click the **Chart Elements** button that appears near the upper right corner of the chart.
3. Click the check boxes to show or hide chart elements.
4. To select a specific option for a chart element, click the arrow that appears at the right side of the element name, and then click an option.

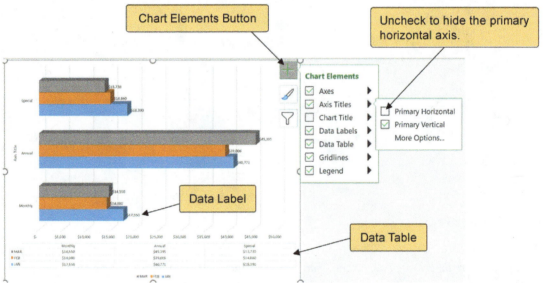

FIGURE EX 5.11

another method

> You can hide or show chart elements and control their appearance and position from the *Chart Tools Design* tab, *Chart Layouts* group. Click the **Add Chart Elements** button, point to the chart element you want, and click an option.

let me try Live!

If you do not have the data file from the previous skill open, open the student data file
EX5-06-SalesCharts and try this skill on your own:

1. If necessary, select the chart on the **Chart1** worksheet.
2. Hide the chart title.
3. Hide the primary horizontal axis.
4. Display the data table, including the legend keys.
5. Display the data labels.
6. If you will be moving on to the next skill in this chapter, leave the workbook open to continue working. If not, save the file as directed by your instructor and close it.

Skill 5.7 Applying Quick Styles and Colors to Charts

You can change the style of a chart using the predefined Quick Styles. Quick Styles apply combinations of fonts, line styles, fills, and shape effects. You can also change the color scheme from a preset list of colors that coordinate with the workbook theme.

To change the chart style:

1. Select the chart.
2. On the *Chart Tools Design* tab, in the *Chart Styles* group, click the style you want to use, or click the **More** button to see all of the Quick Styles available.
3. To change the color scheme, on the *Chart Tools Design* tab, in the *Chart Styles* group, click the **Change Colors** button and select the color scheme you want.

FIGURE EX 5.12

another method

Quick Styles and color schemes are also available from the *Chart Styles* button that appears near the upper right corner of the chart when it is selected.

let me try Live!

If you do not have the data file from the previous skill open, open the student data file
EX5-07-SalesCharts and try this skill on your own:

1. If necessary, select the chart on the **Sales Chart 1** worksheet.
2. Apply the **Style 3** Quick Style.
3. Apply the **Color 3** color scheme from the *Colorful* section.
4. If you will be moving on to the next skill in this chapter, leave the workbook open to continue working. If not, save the file as directed by your instructor and close it.

Skill 5.8 Changing the Chart Type

If you find that your initial chart selection wasn't quite right, you can change the chart type from the *Change Chart Type* dialog without having to delete and recreate the chart.

To change the chart type:

1. On the *Chart Tools Design* tab, in the *Type* group, click the **Change Chart Type** button.

Change Chart Type Button

FIGURE EX 5.13

2. In the *Change Chart Type* dialog, click a chart type category to display that category in the right pane.

3. Click one of the chart types along the top of the right pane to see previews of the options available, and then click the chart type you want.

4. Click **OK**.

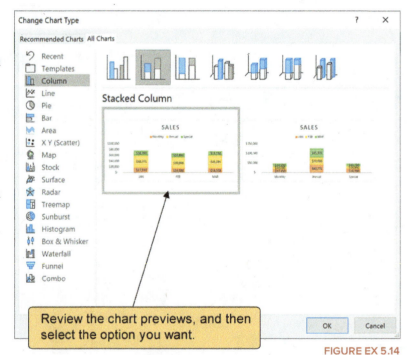

Review the chart previews, and then select the option you want.

FIGURE EX 5.14

The chart type you select affects the story your chart tells. A **clustered column chart** would show a separate column for sales of each membership type per month, but it doesn't depict the total sales for all memberships. By changing the chart type to a **stacked column chart** as shown in the preview in Figure EX 5.14, each column will represent the total sales for the month, and individual sales for each membership type are represented by a piece of that column. Using this chart type makes it easier to compare total sales as well as sales for each individual type of membership.

another method

> To change the chart type, you can also right-click in the chart area and select **Change Chart Type...**

let me try Live!

> If you do not have the data file from the previous skill open, open the student data file **EX5-08-SalesCharts** ⬇ and try this skill on your own:
>
> 1. If necessary, select the chart on the **Sales Chart 1** worksheet.
> 2. Change the chart type to the first stacked column option.
> 3. If you will be moving on to the next skill in this chapter, leave the workbook open to continue working. If not, save the file as directed by your instructor and close it.

Skill 5.9 Filtering Chart Data

Excel includes a feature that allows you to hide and show data in a chart without having to modify the chart data source.

To filter chart data:

1. Select the chart.
2. Click the **Chart Filters** button that appears near the upper right corner of the chart.
3. Notice that when you hover the mouse pointer over the chart filter options, the live preview does not take into account the options that are checked or unchecked. The preview shows only what the chart would look like if the highlighted option were the only one checked. All other series or categories are dimmed in the preview. In Figure EX 5.15, the *Annual* series is highlighted, so the chart preview shows the *Annual* series in full color and the other series faded.
4. Click the check boxes to add or remove data series or categories from the chart. Note that the live preview does not update to reflect these changes.
5. Click the **Apply** button to apply the changes.

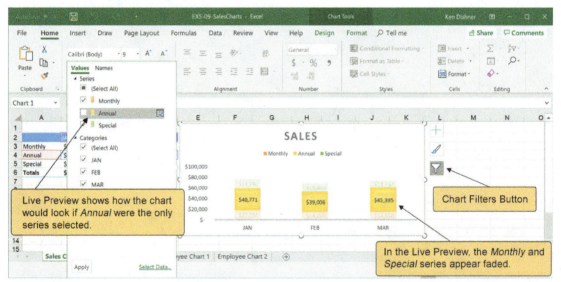

Live Preview shows how the chart would look if *Annual* were the only series selected.

Chart Filters Button

In the Live Preview, the *Monthly* and *Special* series appear faded.

FIGURE EX 5.15

The chart in Figure EX 5.16 shows the chart after the *Annual* series has been hidden. Only the data for the *Monthly* and *Special* series remain. Observe that the chart data still shows the *Annual* row. Filtering the chart affects only the chart display, not the data in the spreadsheet.

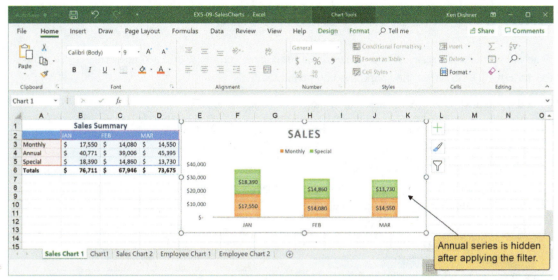

tips & tricks

When a chart is selected, the filter options on the *Data* tab, *Sort & Filter* group are unavailable. If you want to filter the underlying chart data, you must deselect the chart first.

tell me more

If you apply a filter to the underlying chart data, the chart will update automatically to reflect the data change.

let me try Live!

If you do not have the data file from the previous skill open, open the student data file **EX5-09-SalesCharts** 📥 and try this skill on your own:

1. If necessary, select the chart on the **Sales Chart 1** worksheet.
2. Without changing the data source, filter the chart so the **Annual** series is hidden.
3. If you will be moving on to the next skill in this chapter, leave the workbook open to continue working. If not, save the file as directed by your instructor and close it.

Skill 5.10 Inserting Sparklines

Sparklines represent a series of data values as an individual graphic within a single cell. As you update the underlying data series, the Sparklines update immediately.

To add Sparklines to your worksheet using the Quick Analysis tool:

1. Select the data you want to visualize as Sparklines. If you want the Sparklines to appear in empty cells, ensure that there are empty cells to the right of your selection.
2. The Quick Analysis Tool button appears near the lower right corner of the selected range. Click the **Quick Analysis Tool** button, and then click the **Sparklines** tab.
3. Click the button for the Sparkline type you want.

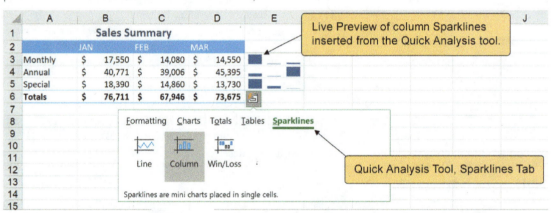

FIGURE EX 5.17

If you do not want Excel to place the Sparklines automatically, or if you are adding Sparklines in a situation where the Quick Analysis tool is not available, use the *Create Sparklines* dialog to specify their location:

1. Select the data range with the data points for the Sparklines.
2. On the *Insert* tab, in the *Sparklines* group, click the button for the type of Sparkline you want to insert: **Line, Column,** or **Win/Loss.**
3. The *Create Sparklines* dialog opens with the selected range added to the *Data Range* box.
4. In the *Location Range* box, enter the cell range where you want the Sparklines to appear. You can type the cell range or click and drag in the worksheet to select the cells.
5. Click **OK** to insert the Sparklines.

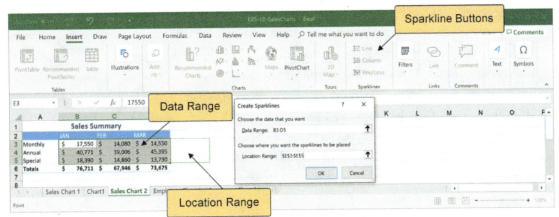

FIGURE EX 5.18

When cells containing Sparklines are selected, the *Sparkline Tools Design* contextual tab becomes active. From this tab you can customize the look of the Sparklines including emphasizing high or low points, changing the type of Sparkline used, and changing colors.

To remove Sparklines, you must select the cells containing the Sparklines, and then on the *Sparkline Tools Design* tab, in the *Group* group, click the **Clear** button.

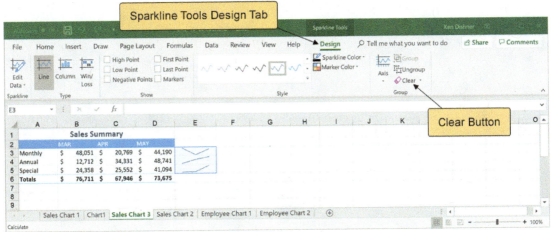

FIGURE EX 5.19

tips & tricks

Sparklines are not actually chart objects—they are charts in the background of the cells. You can add text and other data to the cells that contain Sparklines. You can also extend the Sparklines over multiple cells using the *Merge & Center* commands.

let me try Live!

If you do not have the data file from the previous skill open, open the student data file
EX5-10-SalesCharts ⬇ and try this skill on your own:

1. Go to the **Sales Chart 2** worksheet and select cells **B3:D5** as the data range for the Sparklines.
2. Insert column Sparklines in cells **E3:E5**.
3. Go to the **Sales Chart 3** worksheet and clear the Sparklines.
4. Save the file as directed by your instructor and close it.

Skill 5.11 Converting Data into Tables

In Excel, you can define a series of adjacent cells as a **table**. When you define data as a table, Excel provides a robust tool set for formatting and analyzing the data. In the table, the header row automatically includes filtering and sorting. When you add data to the right of the table, Excel includes the new column in the table automatically.

To define data as a table:

1. Click any cell in the data range. You do not need to select the entire range.
2. On the *Home* tab, in the *Styles* group, click the **Format as Table** button to display the *Table Styles* gallery.
3. Click the style you want to use for your table.

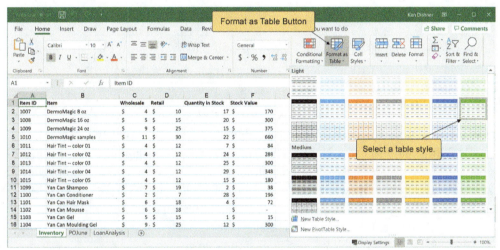

FIGURE EX 5.20

4. Excel will automatically populate the *Format As Table* dialog with the entire data range. If the data range is not correct, you can manually enter the cell range in the dialog.
5. Be sure to check the **My table has headers** check box if appropriate.
6. Click **OK** to create the table.

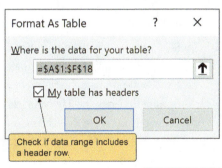

FIGURE EX 5.21

FIGURE EX 5.22

tips & tricks

You cannot create a table in a shared workbook. If your workbook contains a table, you will need to convert the table back to a normal cell range before sharing the workbook.

tell me more

One of the most useful features of tables is the ability to reference table column names in formulas. When you enter a formula in a table, you can reference column names by enclosing the column header text in brackets. For example, to add a new column to the table in Figure EX 5.22 to calculate the cost of each inventory record, you would enter the formula [Wholesale]* [Quantity in Stock] in the first row of the new column. Excel will copy the formula to the remaining cells in the table column automatically.

another method

To insert a table without specifying the table formatting:

1. Select any cell in the data range for the table.
2. On the *Insert* tab, in the *Tables* group, click the **Table** button.
3. Excel will populate the *Insert Table* dialog automatically with the appropriate data range.
4. Be sure to check the **My table has headers** check box if appropriate.
5. Click **OK** to create the table. Excel will format the table with the most recent table style used.

let me try Live!

Open the student data file **EX5-11-PurchaseOrders** ⬇ and try this skill on your own:

1. On the **Inventory** worksheet, click any cell in the range **A1:F18**.
2. Convert the cell range to a table using table style **Green, Table Style Light 14**. The data range contains a header row.
3. If you will be moving on to the next skill in this chapter, leave the workbook open to continue working. If not, save the file as directed by your instructor and close it.

Skill 5.12 Applying Quick Styles to Tables

When you are working with a table, use the *Table Tools Design* tab to apply formatting. This contextual tab is available when you select any cell in the table. From the *Table Styles* gallery, you can select a **Quick Style** to apply a combination of font colors, fill colors, and banding options. **Banding** applies a fill color to alternating rows or columns, making the table easier to read.

To apply a table Quick Style:

1. Click anywhere in the table.
2. On the *Table Tools Design* tab, in the *Table Styles* group, click the **Quick Styles** button to display the full *Table Styles* gallery. Depending on the width of your Excel window, you may see part of the *Quick Styles* gallery displayed in the Ribbon. In this case, click the **More** ⏷ button to expand the entire gallery.
3. Click a style to apply it to the table.

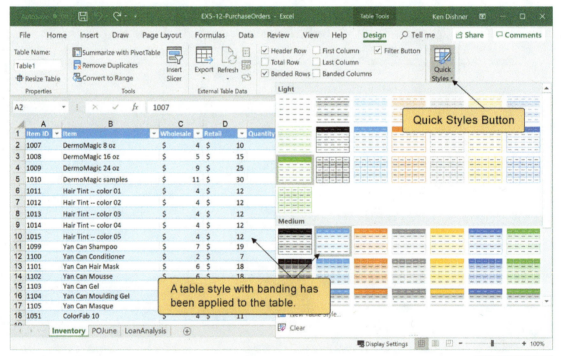

FIGURE EX 5.23

tips & tricks

> If your table includes a header row like the one in Figure EX 5.23, select a style that includes formatting for the first row to help it stand out from the rest of the table.

tell me more

Use the check boxes in the *Table Style Options* group to customize the table formatting by adding or removing banding for rows or columns.

let me try Live!

If you do not have the data file from the previous skill open, open the student data file **EX5-12-PurchaseOrders** ⬇ and try this skill on your own:

1. On the **Inventory** worksheet, if necessary, click any cell in the table.
2. Apply the **Blue, Table Style Medium 2** Quick Style.
3. If you will be moving on to the next skill in this chapter, leave the workbook open to continue working. If not, save the file as directed by your instructor and close it.

Skill 5.13 Adding Total Rows to Tables

If you have data formatted as a table, you can add a **Total row** to quickly calculate an aggregate function such as the sum, average, minimum, or maximum of all the values in the column.

To add a Total row to a table:

1. On the *Table Tools Design* tab, in the *Table Style Options* group, click the **Total Row** check box.
2. In the Total row at the bottom of the table, click the cell where you want to add the calculation.
3. Click the arrow, and select a function. Excel inserts the formula for you.

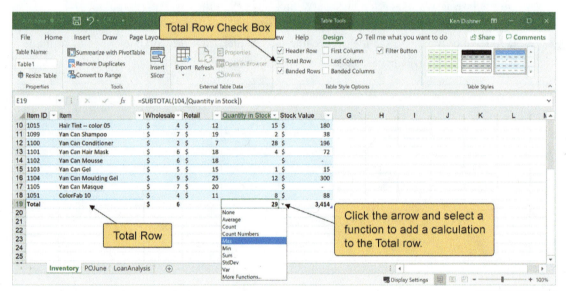

FIGURE EX 5.24

tips & tricks

The **Count** option can be useful when filtering records in a table. Count tells you how many records are included in the filtered table. The Count option from the Total row uses the COUNTA function.

tell me more

When you enable the Total row, the first cell in the Total row displays the word "Total" automatically and the last cell in the Total row calculates the sum of the values in that column (if the column contains numbers).

another method

To add the Total row to the table, right-click any cell in the table, point to **Table**, and click **Total Row**.

let me try Live!

Open the student data file **EX5-13-PurchaseOrders** and try this skill on your own:

1. On the **Inventory** worksheet, if necessary, click any cell in the table.
2. Add a Total row to the table.
3. In the Total row, display the **average** value for the **Wholesale** column.
4. In the Total row, display the **maximum** value for the **Quantity in Stock** column.
5. If you will be moving on to the next skill in this chapter, leave the workbook open to continue working. If not, save the file as directed by your instructor and close it.

Skill 5.14 Removing Duplicate Rows from Tables

If you have a large table, it may be difficult to identify rows with duplicate data. Excel includes a tool to find and remove duplicate rows. A "duplicate" can be an exact match, where every cell in the row contains the same data, or you can specify matching data for certain columns only.

To remove duplicate rows from a table:

1. Select any cell in the table.
2. On *Table Tools Design* tab, in the *Tools* group, click the **Remove Duplicates** button.
3. By default, all the columns are selected in the *Remove Duplicates* dialog and Excel will remove duplicates only where the data in the rows are 100 percent identical. To identify duplicate rows where only some of the columns have duplicate data, click the check boxes to uncheck column names. Now Excel will identify rows as duplicates only when the checked columns have the same data.
4. Click **OK** to remove duplicate rows from the table.
5. Excel displays a message box, telling you how many duplicate rows were found and removed and how many unique values remain in the table. Click **OK** to dismiss the message box.

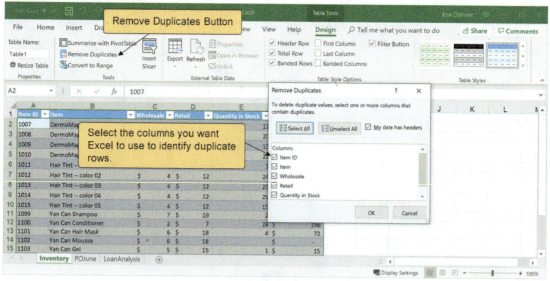

FIGURE EX 5.25

another method

If the data are not formatted as an Excel table, you can access the *Remove Duplicates* command from the *Data* tab, *Data Tools* group.

let me try Live!

If you do not have the data file from the previous skill open, open the student data file **EX5-14-PurchaseOrders** and try this skill on your own:

1. If necessary, click any cell in the table on the **POJune** worksheet.
2. Remove duplicate rows where data in all the columns are identical. Excel should remove one duplicate row, leaving 15 unique values.
3. If you will be moving on to the next skill in this chapter, leave the workbook open to continue working. If not, save the file as directed by your instructor and close it.

Skill 5.15 Sorting Data

Sorting rearranges the rows in your worksheet by the data in a column or columns. You can **sort** alphabetically by text, by date, or by values. Sorting works the same whether or not the data have been formatted as a table.

To sort data:

1. Click any cell in the column you want to sort by.
2. On the *Data* tab, in the *Sort & Filter* group, click the button for the sort order you want:

   > A↓Z sorts text in alphabetical order from A to Z, numbers from smallest to largest, and dates from oldest to newest.

   > Z↓A sorts text in reverse alphabetical order from Z to A, numbers from largest to smallest, and dates from newest to oldest.

If the data are formatted as a table, you can click the arrow at the top of any column and select the sort order you want from the options available.

When a table column has been sorted, the column header displays an arrow indicating which way the column has been sorted. An arrow pointing up indicates an A-Z sort order; an arrow pointing down indicates a Z-A sort order.

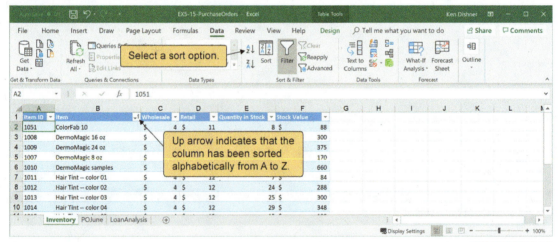

FIGURE EX 5.26

another method

Sort options are also available from the *Home* tab, *Editing* group. Click the **Sort & Filter** button and then select the option you want.

You can also right-click any cell in the column you want to sort by. Point to **Sort**, and select the option you want.

let me try Live!

If you do not have the data file from the previous skill open, open the student data file **EX5-15-PurchaseOrders** ⤓ and try this skill on your own:

1. Verify that the **Inventory** worksheet is active.
2. Sort the **Item** column in alphabetical order from A to Z.
3. Go to the **POJune** worksheet, and sort the **Order Cost** column so the largest numbers are listed first.
4. If you will be moving on to the next skill in this chapter, leave the workbook open to continue working. If not, save the file as directed by your instructor and close it.

Skill 5.16 Filtering Data

If your worksheet has many rows of data, you may want to **filter** the data to show only rows that meet criteria you specify. If your data are formatted as a table, filtering is enabled automatically. If your data are not formatted as a table, you must first enable filtering:

1. On the *Home* tab, in the *Editing* group, click the **Sort & Filter** button.
2. Click the **Filter** button to enable filtering. An arrow will appear in each cell of the heading row just as if the data were formatted as a table.

Once filtering is enabled, it works the same whether or not the data have been formatted as a table.

To filter data:

1. Click the arrow at the top of the column that contains the data you want to filter for.
2. At first, all the filter options are checked. Click the **(Select All)** check box to remove all the checkmarks.
3. Click the check box or check boxes in front of the values you want to filter by.
4. Click **OK.** Excel displays only the rows that include the values you specified.

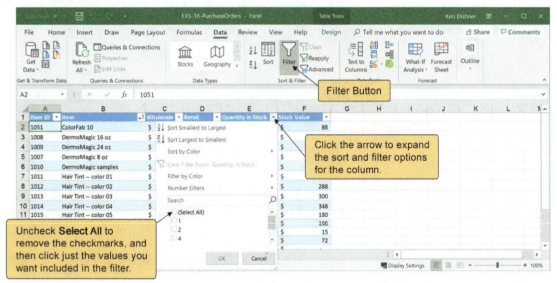

FIGURE EX 5.27

When a filter has been applied to a column, the column header will display a funnel icon.

To clear the filter, on the *Data* tab, in the *Sort & Filter* group, click the **Clear** button. You can also click the funnel icon at the top of the filtered column and select **Clear Filter From "Name of Column"**.

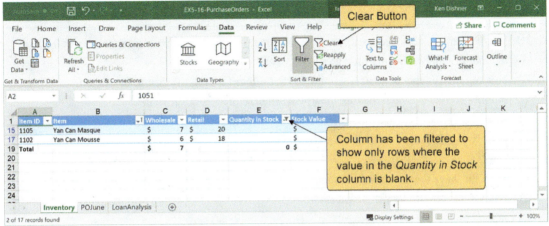

FIGURE EX 5.28

If the column values are dates, Excel will group the dates in the filter list if possible. You can filter for an entire grouping such as a year or month or for a specific date. Use the + and – buttons in front of each date grouping to expand or collapse the group.

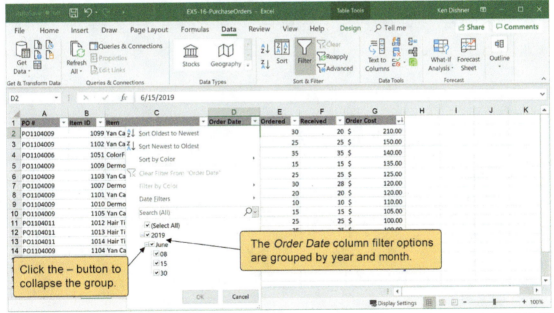

FIGURE EX 5.29

another method

> > When filtering is enabled, you can clear the filter and disable filtering from the *Data* tab, *Sort & Filter* group, by clicking the **Filter** button again.
> > You can also enable or clear filtering from the *Home* tab, *Editing* group, by clicking the **Sort & Filter** button and then making the appropriate choice from the menu.

let me try Live!

If you do not have the data file from the previous skill open, open the student data file **EX5-16-PurchaseOrders** and try this skill on your own:

1. If necessary, go to the **Inventory** worksheet.
2. If necessary, enable filtering.
3. Filter the **Quantity in Stock** column so only rows with the blanks are shown. *Hint:* Scroll to the bottom of the filter list to find the *(Blanks)* option.
4. If you will be moving on to the next skill in this chapter, leave the workbook open to continue working. If not, save the file as directed by your instructor and close it.

Skill 5.17 Filtering Table Data with Slicers

A **slicer** is a visual representation of filtering options. You can display multiple slicers and filter the table by multiple values from each. Slicers are available only when the data have been formatted as a table.

To add a slicer:

1. Click anywhere in the table to activate the *Table Tools Design* tab.
2. On the *Table Tools Design* tab, in the *Tools* group, click the **Insert Slicer** button.
3. In the *Insert Slicers* dialog, click the check boxes for the column(s) you want in the slicers.
4. Click **OK.**

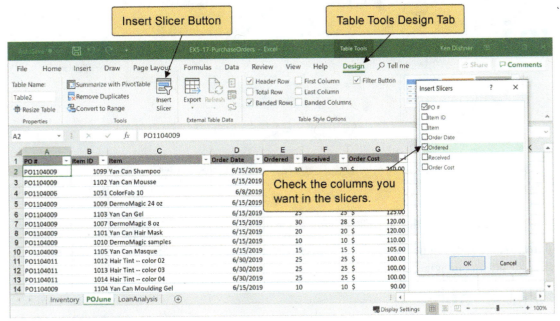

FIGURE EX 5.30

> In the slicer, click the option you want to use as the data filter. If you click another option in the slicer, the first option you selected will toggle off and the new selection will be used as the filter.

> To use more than one filtering option in a slicer, click the **Multi-Select** button at the upper right corner of the slicer box. When you enabled multi-select, all the slicer options remain *on* by default. Click the options you do *not* want included in the filter to turn them off.

> Notice that as you make selections in one slicer, options in the other slicer may become unavailable—indicating that there are no data available for that option under the current filtering conditions.

The table in Figure EX 5.31 has been filtered to show only rows with **PO1104009** in the *PO #* column and **20** and **25** in the *Ordered* column. Notice that the PO1104008 and PO1104011 options in the PO # slicer are disabled—indicating that they do not include rows with 20 or 25 in the *Ordered* column. Also, in the Ordered slicer, the 35 option is disabled—indicating that PO1104009 does not include any rows with the value 35 in the *Ordered* column.

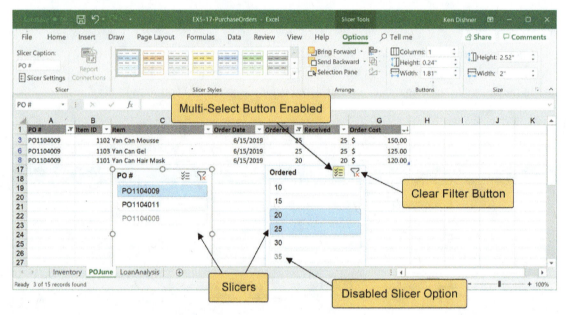

FIGURE EX 5.31

To remove filtering, click the **Clear Filter** button in the upper right corner of the slicer.

To remove a slicer from the table, click the slicer and then press Delete. Removing a slicer does not clear the filtering from the table.

tell me more

> To move a slicer, move your mouse pointer over the slicer. When the cursor changes to the move cursor, click and drag the slicer to a new position on the worksheet.
> When a slicer is selected, the *Slicer Tools Options* tab becomes available. From this tab, you can apply a style to the slicer and control slicer settings.

let me try Live!

If you do not have the data file from the previous skill open, open the student data file **EX5-17-PurchaseOrders** ⤓ and try this skill on your own:

1. If necessary, select the **POJune** sheet and click any cell in the table.
2. Add slicers for **PO #** and **Ordered**.
3. Using the slicers, filter the table to show only rows where the PO # is **PO1104009**.
4. Filter the data further to display only records where the value in the *Ordered* column is **20** or **25**. *Hint:* Enable the **Multi-Select** button to apply more than one filter option in the **Ordered** slicer.
5. If you will be moving on to the next skill in this chapter, leave the workbook open to continue working. If not, save the file as directed by your instructor and close it.

Skill 5.18 Converting Tables to Ranges

Although Excel tables are extremely useful, there are times when you do not want your data formatted as a table. Certain data analysis tools, including creating subtotals and grouping outlines, are not available if data are formatted as a table.

To convert a table to a normal range:

1. On the *Table Tools Design* tab, in the *Tools* group, click the **Convert to Range** button.
2. Excel displays a message box asking if you want to convert the table to a normal range. Click **Yes.**

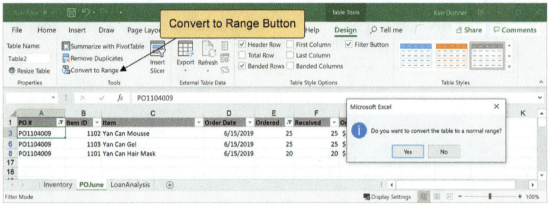

FIGURE EX 5.32

As shown in Figure EX 5.33, when you convert from a table to a normal range, Excel removes any filtering that may have been applied. Any table formatting such as banding and the Total row are still applied to the range.

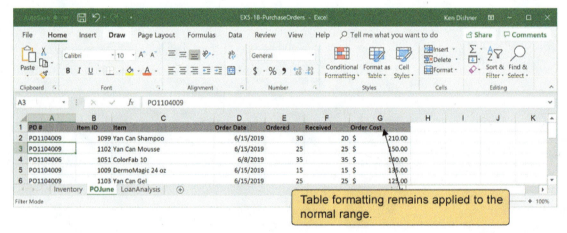

FIGURE EX 5.33

tips & tricks

If you want to use one of the table styles but do not want the data formatted as a table, begin by formatting the range as a table, applying the table style you want, and then convert the table back to a normal range.

another method

You can also right-click anywhere in the table, point to **Table**, and select **Convert to Range.**

let me try Live!

If you do not have the data file from the previous skill open, open the student data file **EX5-18-PurchaseOrders** and try this skill on your own:

1. If necessary, click any cell in the table on the **POJune** sheet.
2. Convert the table to a normal range.
3. If you will be moving on to the next skill in this chapter, leave the workbook open to continue working. If not, save the file as directed by your instructor and close it.

Skill 5.19 Creating PivotTables Using Recommended PivotTables

A **PivotTable** is a special report view that summarizes data and calculates the intersecting totals. PivotTables do not contain any data themselves—they summarize data from a cell range or a table in another part of your workbook.

The easiest way to begin a new PivotTable is to use one of the recommended PivotTables:

1. Select any cell within the table or cell range you want to use for your PivotTable.
2. On the *Insert* tab, in the *Tables* group, click the **Recommended PivotTables** button.
3. Preview each of the options in the *Recommended PivotTables* dialog. Click the one that is closest to how you want your final PivotTable to look.
4. Click **OK** to create the PivotTable in a new worksheet.

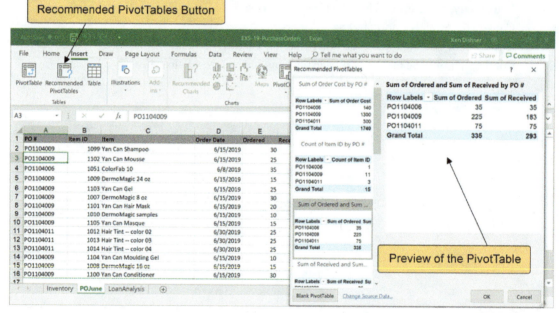

FIGURE EX 5.34

Use the *PivotTable Fields* pane to review and modify the structure of the PivotTable. The top part of the *PivotTable Fields* pane shows you the list of available fields—the columns from the PivotTable's data source. The bottom part of the *PivotTable Fields* pane allows you to build or modify the PivotTable by adding field data to one of four areas: *Filters*, *Columns*, *Rows*, or *Values*. In Figure EX 5.35, the recommended PivotTable added the *PO #* field to the *Rows* section and the *Ordered* and *Received* fields to the *Values* section. The PivotTable summarizes values in the *Ordered* and *Received* fields for each value in the *PO #* field.

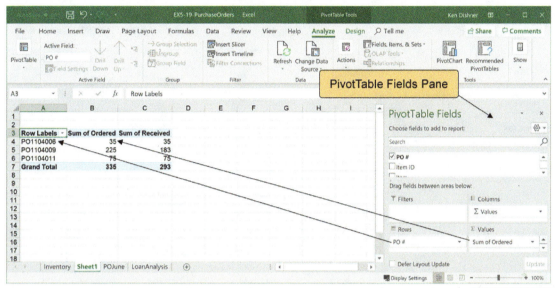

In the *PivotTable Fields* pane, check the boxes in from of each column name to add or remove fields from the PivotTable.

> Fields that contain text or date data are added to the *Rows* section automatically. If there are multiple rows, Excel will attempt to group them in a logical way.

> Fields that contain numeric data are added to the *Values* section automatically. For each row in the PivotTable, Excel summarizes the values in each of the fields listed in the *Values* section. In Figure EX 5.36, adding the *Order Cost* field to the PivotTable adds it to the *Values* section and calculates the total value ordered for each PO #.

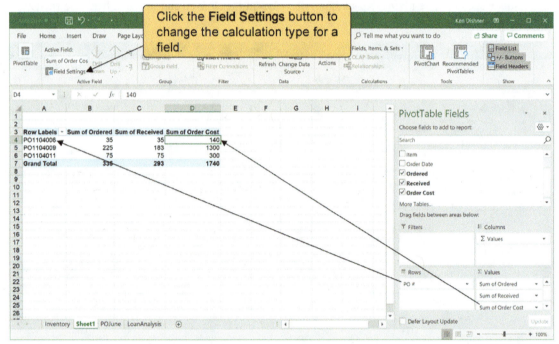

FIGURE EX 5.36

Excel summarizes numerical data in the PivotTable using the SUM function by default. You can choose another calculation type such as count or average.

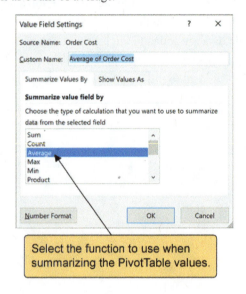

FIGURE EX 5.37

To change the calculation type for a field:

1. Click anywhere in the field you want to change.
2. On the *PivotTable Tools Analyze* tab, in the *Active Field* group, click the **Field Settings** button.
3. In the *Value Field Settings* dialog, *Summarize Values By* tab, select the function for the type of calculation you want.
4. Click **OK.**

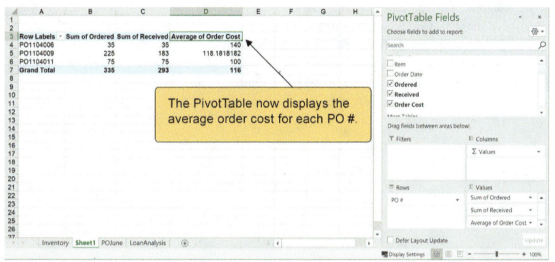

FIGURE EX 5.38

tips & tricks

> Click and drag the field names in the *PivotTable Fields* pane to move them between the *Filters, Columns, Rows,* or *Values* boxes.
> Click and drag fields in the *Rows* and *Values* boxes in the *PivotTable Fields* pane to reorder them in the PivotTable.

another method

> If you have the data range for the PivotTable selected, the recommended PivotTables are also available from the *Tables* tab in the Quick Analysis tool.
> You can also open the *Value Field Settings* dialog by clicking the arrow next to the field name in the *Values* box, and then selecting **Value Field Settings...**

let me try Live!

If you do not have the data file from the previous skill open, open the student data file **EX5-19-PurchaseOrders** ⬇ and try this skill on your own:

1. Verify that the **POJune** sheet is active and one of the cells in the data range is selected.
2. Insert a recommended PivotTable using the **Sum of Ordered and Sum of Received by PO #** option.
3. Add the **Order Cost** field to the PivotTable.
4. Modify the **Order Cost** field to use the **Average** function instead of the Sum function.
5. If you will be moving on to the next skill in this chapter, leave the workbook open to continue working. If not, save the file as directed by your instructor and close it.

Skill 5.20 Creating a PivotChart from a PivotTable

A **PivotChart** is a graphic representation of a PivotTable. In a column chart, the category fields are represented along the x (horizontal) axis while the data values are represented along the y (vertical) axis.

To create a PivotChart from a PivotTable:

1. Select any cell in the PivotTable.
2. On the *PivotTable Tools Analyze* tab, in the *Tools* group, click the **PivotChart** button.

FIGURE EX 5.39

3. Select a chart type from the *Insert Chart*
4. Click **OK.**

The *Insert Chart* dialog used when creating a PivotChart is very similar to the one used when creating regular charts. Click a chart type at the left side of the dialog, and then click an option from the examples along the top of the right hand pane. Excel displays a preview of the chart. There are no recommended charts for PivotCharts.

If you need more room to display the PivotChart, you may want to hide the *PivotTable Fields* pane. On the *PivotChart Tools Analyze* tab, in the *Show/Hide* group, click the **Field List** button to hide or display the *PivotTable Fields* pane.

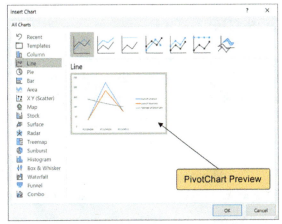

FIGURE EX 5.40

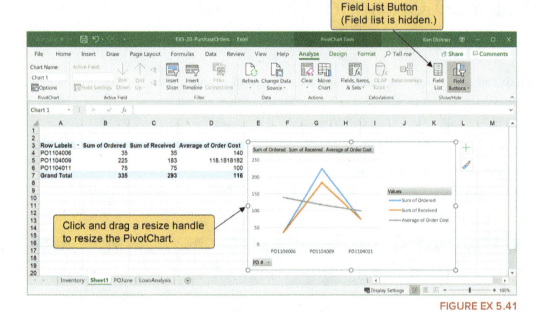

FIGURE EX 5.41

PivotCharts include all the formatting options that regular charts do. You can apply Quick Styles and hide or show chart elements from the *PivotChart Tools Design* tab. You can also resize the PivotChart or move it to its own sheet.

tell me more

To sort or filter the category data in the PivotChart, click the button in the lower left corner of the PivotChart with the name of the field you want to sort or filter. If your PivotTable used multiple row labels, you will see a button for each.

let me try Live!

If you do not have the data file from the previous skill open, open the student data file **EX5-20-PurchaseOrders** and try this skill on your own:

1. If necessary, click anywhere in the PivotTable. If your workbook does not include a PivotTable, complete the Let Me Try exercise from *Creating PivotTables Using Recommended PivotTables* before continuing.
2. Insert a PivotChart using the first line chart type.
3. If you will be moving on to the next skill in this chapter, leave the workbook open to continue working. If not, save the file as directed by your instructor and close it.

Skill 5.21 Analyzing Data with Data Tables

Data tables provide a quick what-if analysis of the effects of changing one or two variables within a formula. The **data table** is organized with a series of values for the variable(s) in a column or a row or both.

To create a one-variable data table with a column input format:

1. In a column, type the series of values you want to substitute for the variable in your formula.
2. In the cell above and to the right of the first value, type the formula that references the cell you want to replace with the new values.
3. Select the cell range for the data table, beginning with the empty cell above the first value you entered.
4. On the *Data* tab, in the *Forecast* group, click the **What-If Analysis** button, and click **Data Table...**
5. In the *Data Table* dialog, the input cell is the cell that contains the original value for which you want to substitute the data table values. In this data table, the output values will be listed in a column, so enter the cell reference in the *Column input cell*
6. Click **OK.**

In the one-variable data table in Figure EX 5.42, the formula in cell **B9** references the loan amount in cell **B2**—the *pv* argument for the PMT function. This is the **column input cell** for the data table. The substitute values for cell B2 are listed in cells **A10:A14.**

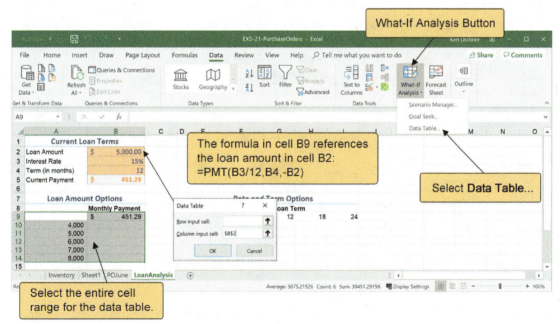

FIGURE EX 5.42

Excel completes the values in the table, using the substitute values in the formula:

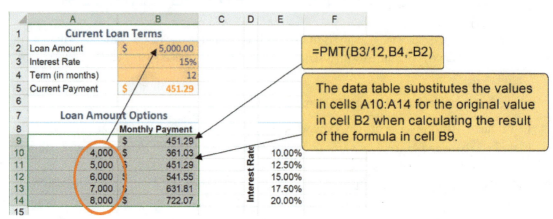

FIGURE EX 5.43

A two-variable data table works the same way as a one-variable data table, using inputs for both a column and a row variable. In a two-variable data table, the formula is located in the cell above the column input values and to the left of the row input values.

In the two-variable data table in Figure EX 5.44, the formula in cell E9 references the loan term in cell **B4**—the *nper* argument for the PMT function. This is the **row input cell** for the data table. The substitute values for cell **B4** are listed in cells **F9:I9.** The formula also references the second variable used in the data table, the interest rate in cell **B3**—the *rate* argument for the PMT function. This is the column input cell for the data table. The substitute values for cell B3 are listed in cells **E10:E14.**

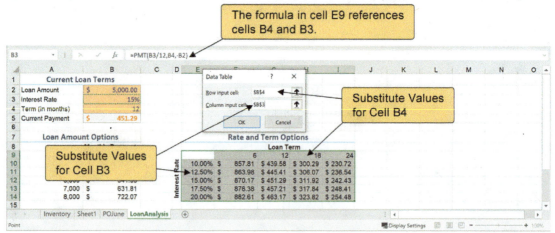

FIGURE 5.44

In a **two-variable data table,** you may want to hide the data table formula by changing the cell font color to match the worksheet background. The data table is easier to follow if the cell in the upper left corner of the data table appears blank as shown in cell E9 in Figure EX 5.44. Of course, you can still see the formula in the formula bar.

tips & tricks

Use Goal Seek if the result you are looking for is a specific value in a single cell. Use data tables when you want to see multiple possible outcomes based on multiple input options.

let me try Live!

If you do not have the data file from the previous skill open, open the student data file **EX5-21-PurchaseOrders** ⬇ and try this skill on your own:

1. Go to the **LoanAnalysis** worksheet.
2. Insert a one-variable data table in cells **A9:B14** to calculate the monthly loan payment for the loan amounts listed in cells A10:A14. The formula has been entered for you in cell B9. It references the original loan amount in cell **B2**.
3. Insert a two-variable data table in cells **E9:I14** to calculate the monthly loan payments for various interest rates and loan terms. The formula in cell E9 has been formatted using the white font color so it appears hidden. It references the original interest rate in cell **B3** and the loan term in cell **B4**.
4. If you will be moving on to the next skill in this chapter, leave the workbook open to continue working. If not, save the file as directed by your instructor and close it.

Skill 5.22 Analyzing Data with Goal Seek

Excel's **Goal Seek** function lets you enter a desired value (outcome) for a formula and specify an input cell that can be modified in order to reach that goal. Goal Seek changes the value of the input cell incrementally until the target outcome is reached. In Figure EX 5.45, the outcome cell is cell **B5,** the loan payment; the desired outcome value is 750; and the input cell is cell **B2,** the loan amount.

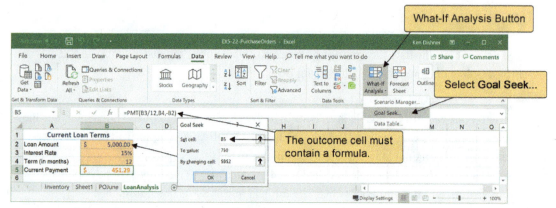

FIGURE EX 5.45

To find a value using Goal Seek:

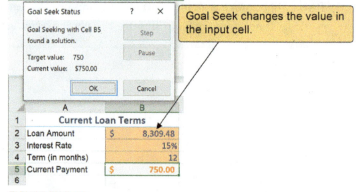

FIGURE EX 5.46

1. On the *Data* tab, in the *Forecast* group, click the **What-If Analysis** button, and then click **Goal Seek...**
2. Enter the outcome cell in the *Set cell* This cell must contain a formula.
3. Enter the outcome value you want in the *To value*
4. Enter the input cell (the cell that contains the value to be changed) in the *By changing cell* box. This cell must be referenced in the formula in the outcome cell either directly or indirectly and must contain a value, not a formula.
5. Click **OK.**
6. The *Goal Seek Status* box appears, letting you know if Goal Seek was able to find a solution. Click **OK** to accept the solution and change the value in the input cell or click **Cancel** to return the input cell to its original value.

tips & tricks

Goal Seek works best in situations where there is only one variable, such as:

> Finding the loan amount to result in a specific loan payment when the loan rate and terms are inflexible.

> Finding the required number of units to sell to reach a sales goal when the price is inflexible.

let me try Live!

If you do not have the data file from the previous skill open, open the student data file **EX5-22-PurchaseOrders** and try this skill on your own:

1. On the *LoanAnalysis* worksheet, use Goal Seek to find the amount of loan you can afford (cell **B2**) that will result in a payment of **750** in cell **B5**.
2. If Goal Seek is able to find a solution, accept it.
3. Save the file as directed by your instructor and close it.

key terms

Column chart	Table
Clustered column chart	Quick Style (table)
Bar chart	Banding
Stacked column chart	Total row
Stacked bar chart	Sort
Pie chart	Filter
Doughnut chart	Slicer
Line chart	PivotTable
Line with markers	PivotChart
Chart sheet	Data table (what-if analysis)
Quick Layout	Column input cell
Data labels	Two-variable data table
Data table (chart)	Row input cell
Quick Style (chart)	Goal Seek
Sparklines	

concept review

1. Data markers are graphic representations of the values of data points in a chart.
   a. true
   b. false

2. _____ charts represent data as parts of a whole.
   a. Column
   b. Bar
   c. Line
   d. Pie

3. _____ apply combinations of fonts, line styles, fills, and shape effects to charts.
   a. Quick Layouts
   b. Quick Styles
   c. Chart Effects
   d. Chart Templates

4. _____ represent each data series as an individual graphic within a single cell.
   a. Charts
   b. Sparklines
   c. Tables
   d. PivotCharts

5. A Total row can be used to quickly calculate the _____ of all the values in a column.
   a. sum
   b. average
   c. both a and b
   d. neither a nor b

6. When you format data as a table, the header row automatically includes filtering and sorting.
   a. true
   b. false

7. _____ rearranges the rows in your worksheet by the data in a column or columns.
   a. Grouping
   b. Filtering
   c. Sorting
   d. Formatting

8. _____ is a special report view that summarizes data and calculates the intersecting totals.
   a. Table
   b. Chart
   c. PivotTable
   d. Scenario

9. The _____ command provides a quick what-if analysis of the effects of changing one or two variables within a formula.

    a. *Scenario*

    b. *Consolidate*

    c. *Data Table*

    d. *Goal Seek*

10. The _____ command lets you enter a designated value for a formula and specify an input cell that can be modified in order to reach that goal.

    a. *Scenario*

    b. *Consolidate*

    c. *Data Table*

    d. *Goal Seek*

projects
skill review **5.1**

In this project, you will analyze data for an event planning company.

Skills needed to complete this project:

- Converting Data into Tables (Skill 5.11)
- Adding Total Rows to Tables (Skill 5.13)
- Sorting Data (Skill 5.15)
- Filtering Data (Skill 5.16)
- Analyzing Data with Data Tables (Skill 5.21)
- Inserting a Column Chart or a Bar Chart (Skill 5.1)
- Changing the Chart Type (Skill 5.8)
- Applying Quick Styles and Colors to Charts (Skill 5.7)
- Showing and Hiding Chart Elements (Skill 5.6)
- Resizing and Moving Charts (Skill 5.4)
- Analyzing Data with Goal Seek (Skill 5.22)
- Inserting a Pie Chart (Skill 5.2)
- Applying Quick Layouts to Charts (Skill 5.5)
- Creating PivotTables Using Recommended PivotTables (Skill 5.19)
- Creating a PivotChart from a PivotTable (Skill 5.20)

1. Open the start file **EX2019-SkillReview-5-1** and resave the file as:
   `[your initials]EX-SkillReview-5-1`
2. If the workbook opens in Protected View, click the **Enable Editing** button in the Message Bar at the top of the workbook so you can modify the workbook.
3. Format the data on the *Table* worksheet into a table using one of the table Quick Styles.
   a. Select all the data including the headings, being careful not to select any blank rows or columns.
   b. On the *Home* tab, in the *Styles* group, click the **Format as Table** button to display the *Table Styles*
   c. Click the **Orange, Table Style Medium 3** Quick Style. It is the third option in the *Medium* section of the gallery.
   d. Verify that the correct cells will be used. Check the **My table has headers** check box. Click **OK**.

4. Add a Total row to the table to count the number of invitations sent.

   a. On the *Table Tools Design* tab, in the *Table Style Options* group, click the **Total Row** check box.

   b. In the Total row at the bottom of the table, note the total count of guests attending.

   c. In the Total row at the bottom of the table, click in the **City** column, click the arrow, and select the **Count** function to count the invitations sent.

5. Sort the table by city in alphabetical order:

   a. Click anywhere in the **City** column.

   b. On the *Data* tab, in the *Sort & Filter* group, click the **A-Z** button.

6. Filter the data in the table to show only guests from the city of Auburn.

   a. Click the arrow in the **City** column header.

   b. Click the **(Select All)** check box to remove all of the checkmarks.

   c. Click the check box in front of **Auburn** to filter for only guests from Auburn.

   d. Click **OK.** Excel displays only the rows for invitations sent to Auburn.

7. Switch to work with the *Data Table* worksheet and use a data table to estimate costs for different numbers of attendees. Cell C18 contains a formula that sums the costs in cells **C3:C15.** The formulas in those cells all refer to the number of guests in cell **C1.**

   a. Select cells **B18:C25** to use as the data table.

   b. On the *Data* tab, in the *Forecast* group, click the **What-If Analysis** button, and click **Data Table...**

   c. In the *Column input cell* box, type **C1** and then click **OK.**

   d. Review the data table results computing the party costs for the various numbers of guests.

8. Create a column chart to compare the cost of various size parties.

   a. Select cells **B17:C25.**

   b. Click the **Insert** tab.

   c. In the *Charts* group, click the **dialog launcher** to open the *Insert Chart* dialog.

   d. Click the **All Charts** tab and, if necessary, select the **Column** chart category.

   e. Click the second option under *Clustered Column.* It is the one with the number of guests displayed on the x axis.

   f. Click **OK.**

9. Change the chart to a line chart.

   a. If necessary, click to select the chart.

   b. On the *Chart Tools Design* tab, in the *Type* group, click the **Change Chart Type** button.

   c. In the *Change Chart Type* dialog, click **Line,** and click the first line chart type.

   d. Click **OK.**

10. Format the chart using a Quick Style. On the *Chart Tools Design* tab, in the *Chart Styles* group, click **Style 3.**

11. Display the chart gridlines and hide the data labels.
    a. Click the **Chart Elements** button that appears near the upper right corner of the chart.
    b. Click the **Gridlines** check box to add a checkmark.
    c. Click the **Data Labels** check box to add a checkmark.

12. Move the chart to its own sheet in the workbook.
    a. On the *Chart Tools Design* tab, in the *Location* group, click the **Move Chart** button.
    b. In the *Move Chart* dialog, click the **New sheet** radio button.
    c. In the *New sheet* box, type: Data Table Chart
    d. Click **OK.**

13. Use Goal Seek to determine the most you can afford for dinner per person on a total $14,000 budget for 130 guests assuming all other per guest costs remain the same.
    a. Switch to the *Goal Seek* sheet.
    b. Select the outcome cell **C18** and review the formula.
    c. On the *Data* tab, in the *Forecast* group, click the **What-If Analysis** button and click **Goal Seek...**
    d. Verify that the outcome cell **C18** is referenced in the *Set cell* box.
    e. Enter the outcome value of 14000 in the *To value* box.
    f. Enter the input cell **A4** in the *By changing cell* box.
    g. Click **OK** to run Goal Seek.
    h. Click **OK** again to accept the Goal Seek solution.

14. Insert a 3-D pie chart to show the breakdown of the per guest costs.
    a. Select cells **B3:C11.**
    b. On the *Insert* tab, in the *Charts* group, click the **Pie** button, and click the **Pie** option.
    c. If necessary, move the chart to the right so it does not cover the worksheet data.
    d. On the *Chart Tools Design* tab, click the **Quick Layout** button and select **Layout 6.**
    e. Change the chart title to: **Per Guest Costs**

15. Create a PivotTable listing the number attending from each city
    a. Return to the *Table* worksheet.
    b. Click anywhere in the table.
    c. On the *Insert* tab, in the *Tables* group, click the **Recommended PivotTables** button.
    d. Select the option **Sum of NumAttending by City.**
    e. Click **OK.**

16. Modify the PivotTable to calculate the average number of attendees per city instead of the total.
    a. Click anywhere in the **Sum of NumAttending** field.
    b. On the *PivotTable Tools Analyze* tab, in the *Active Field* group, click the **Field Settings** button.
    c. In the *Value Field Settings* dialog, *Summarize Values By* tab, select **Average** to change the calculation from SUM to AVERAGE.
    d. Click **OK.**

17. Create a PivotChart from the PivotTable.

    a. Select any cell in the PivotTable.

    b. On the *PivotTable Tools Analyze* tab, in the *Tools* group, click the **PivotChart** button.

    c. Verify that the Clustered Column chart type is selected in the *Insert Chart* dialog.

    d. Click **OK.**

    e. Click the title and change it to read: **Number of Guests Attending from Each City**

    f. Hide the legend by clicking the **Chart Elements** button that appears near the upper right corner of the PivotChart and clicking the **Legend** check box to remove the checkmark.

    g. If necessary, move the PivotChart to the right so it does not cover the PivotTable.

18. Save and close the workbook.

projects
skill review 5.2

Data files for projects can be found by logging into your SIMnet account and going to the Library section.

In this project you will analyze real estate data.

Skills needed to complete this project:

- Converting Data into Tables (Skill 5.11)
- Adding Total Rows to Tables (Skill 5.13)
- Sorting Data (Skill 5.15)
- Filtering Data (Skill 5.16)
- Inserting a Line Chart (Skill 5.3)
- Resizing and Moving Charts (Skill 5.4)
- Showing and Hiding Chart Elements (Skill 5.6)
- Applying Quick Styles and Colors to Charts (Skill 5.7)
- Creating PivotTables Using Recommended PivotTables (Skill 5.19)
- Inserting Sparklines (Skill 5.10)
- Creating a PivotChart from a PivotTable (Skill 5.20)
- Analyzing Data with Data Tables (Skill 5.21)
- Analyzing Data with Goal Seek (Skill 5.22)

1. Open the start file **EX2019-SkillReview-5-2** and resave the file as:
   [your initials]EX-SkillReview-5-2
2. If the workbook opens in Protected View, click the **Enable Editing** button in the Message Bar at the top of the workbook so you can modify the workbook.
3. Format the data on the *Sales Data* worksheet as a table using the **Blue, Table Style Medium 2** table style:
   a. Select any cell in the data.
   b. On the *Home* tab, in the *Styles* group, click the **Format as Table** button to display the *Table Styles* gallery.
   c. Click the **Blue, Table Style Medium 2** Quick Style. It is the second option in the *Medium* section of the gallery.
   d. Verify that the **My table has headers** check box is checked and that the correct data range is selected.
   e. Click **OK**.

4. Add a Total row to the table to display the number of buyers; the average number of bedrooms and bathrooms for each sale; and the average purchase price, interest rate, and mortgage length.

  a. On the *Table Tools Design* tab, in the *Table Style Options* group, click the **Total Row** check box.

  b. In the Total row at the bottom of the table, click in the **Buyers** column, click the arrow, and select the **Count** function.

  c. In the Total row at the bottom of the table, click in the **Bedrooms** column, click the arrow, and select the **Average** function.

  d. In the Total row at the bottom of the table, click in the **Bathrooms** column, click the arrow, and select the **Average** function.

  e. In the Total row at the bottom of the table, click in the **Purchase Price** column, click the arrow, and select the **Average** function.

  f. In the Total row at the bottom of the table, click in the **Rate** column, click the arrow, and select the **Average** function.

  g. In the Total row at the bottom of the table, click in the **Mortgage Years** column, click the arrow, and select the **Average** function.

5. Sort the data so the newest purchases appear at the top.

  a. Click anywhere in the **Date of Purchase** column.

  b. On the *Data* tab, in the *Sort & Filter* group, click the **Z-A** button.

6. Filter the data to show only houses sold by owner with three or four bedrooms.

  a. Click the arrow at the top of the **Agent** column.

  b. Click the **(Select All)** check box to remove all of the checkmarks.

  c. Click the check box in front of **By Owner.**

  d. Click **OK**.

  e. Click the arrow at the top of the **Bedrooms** column.

  f. Click the **(Select All)** check box to remove all of the checkmarks.

  g. Click the check boxes in front of **3** and **4**.

  h. Click **OK**.

7. Create a line chart showing the purchase prices for houses by date.

  a. Select the **Date of Purchase** data cells. Be careful not to include the column heading. Press and hold Ctrl and click and drag to select the **Purchase Price** data cells, again being careful not to include the column heading.

  b. On the *Insert* tab, in the *Charts* group, click the **Insert Line or Area Chart** button.

  c. Select the first line chart type shown.

  d. Click **OK**.

8. Move the chart to its own sheet named *Purchase Prices.*
    a. If necessary, select the chart. On the *Chart Tools Design* tab, in the *Location* group, click the **Move Chart** button.
    b. In the *Move Chart* dialog, click the **New sheet** radio button.
    c. In the box type: Purchase Prices
    d. Click **OK**.
9. Update the chart title and display the data labels as callouts.
    a. Change the chart title to: Homes For Sale By Owner
    b. Click the **Chart Elements** button near the upper right corner of the chart.
    c. Click the **Data Labels** check box to add a checkmark.
    d. Point to **Data Labels,** click the arrow that appears at the right side, and click **Data Callout.**
10. Apply the **Style 2** Quick Style to the chart.
    a. Click the **Chart Styles** button that appears near the upper right corner of the chart.
    b. Click **Style 2**.
11. Create a PivotTable to summarize the average purchase price of different house types for each agent.
    a. Return to the *Sales Data* worksheet and click anywhere in the table.
    b. Click the **Insert** tab. In the *Tables* group, click the **Recommended PivotTables** button.
    c. Verify that the first recommended PivotTable is **Sum of Purchase Price by Agent.**
    d. Click **OK**.
    e. Select any cell in the **Sum of Purchase Price** column.
    f. On the *PivotTable Tools Analyze* tab, in the *Active Field* group, click the **Field Settings** button.
    g. In the *Summarize value field by* box, select **Average**.
    h. Click **OK**.
    i. Add the **House Type** field to the PivotTable by clicking the check box in the *Fields List* Excel automatically places the *House Type* field in the Rows box and displays the house type data as a subgroup of rows below each agent.
    j. To summarize the house type data for each agent, use the *House Type* field as columns in the PivotTable. Click and drag the **House Type** field from the Rows box to the Columns box in the *PivotTable Fields* pane.
12. Add column Sparklines to the right of the PivotTable.
    a. Select cells **B5:E9** to use as the data for the Sparklines. You do not want to include the grand total column or row.
    b. On the *Insert* tab, in the *Sparklines* group, click the **Column** button.
    c. In the *Create Sparklines* dialog, verify that the cell range **B5:E9** is listed in the *Data Range* box.
    d. Add the range **G5:G9** to the *Location Range* box either by typing the cells range or by clicking and dragging to select it in the worksheet.
    e. Click **OK**.

13. Create a PivotChart from the PivotTable.
    a. Select any cell in the PivotTable.
    b. On the *PivotTable Tools Analyze* tab, in the *Tools* group, click the **PivotChart** button.
    c. Select the first bar chart type from the *Insert Chart* Click **OK.**
    d. If necessary, move the PivotChart to another part of the worksheet so it does not cover the PivotTable data.
14. Use the data in the *Loan Worksheet* sheet to run a what-if scenario for a client to show loan payments for a variety of interest rates and loan lengths. This what-if scenario requires a two-variable data table.
    a. Go to the **Loan Worksheet** sheet and familiarize yourself with the formula in cell Pay close attention to the cell references.
    b. Select cells **B5:E25** to use the payment formula in B5 and the various years and rates as the data table.
    c. On the *Data* tab, in the *Forecast* group, click the **What-If Analysis** button, and click **Data Table.**
    d. In the *Row input cell* box, enter the cell reference for the length of the loan—the *nper* argument from the formula in cell B5: C2.
    e. In the *Column input cell* box, enter the cell reference for the loan interest rate—the *interest* argument from the formula in cell B5: A2.
    f. Click **OK.** (Data table values are inserted)
15. Use Goal Seek to determine the most you can afford to borrow, on a $950 per month budget:
    d. On the *Loan Worksheet* sheet, select the outcome formula cell, **H4.**
    e. On the *Data* tab, in the *Forecast* group, click the **What-If Analysis** button and click **Goal Seek...**
    f. Verify that the outcome cell **H4** is referenced in the *Set cell* box.
    g. Enter the outcome value of **950** in the *To value* box.
    h. Enter the input cell **H9** in the *By changing cell* box.
    i. Click **OK.**
    j. Click **OK** again to accept the Goal Seek solution.
    k. Notice the loan payment changed to $950 and the amount to borrow was computed to be $206,395.
16. Save and close the workbook.

projects

challenge yourself **5.3**

Data files for projects can be found by logging into your SIMnet account and going to the Library section.

In this project, you will analyze shoe sales data and use what-if analysis to determine your commission potential and your sales goal.

Skills needed to complete this project:

- Converting Data into Tables (Skill 5.11)
- Adding Total Rows to Tables (Skill 5.13)
- Removing Duplicate Rows from Tables (Skill 5.14)
- Filtering Data (Skill 5.16)
- Sorting Data (Skill 5.15)
- Inserting a Line Chart (Skill 5.3)
- Filtering Chart Data (Skill 5.9)
- Resizing and Moving Charts (Skill 5.4)
- Filtering Table Data with Slicers (Skill 5.17)
- Creating PivotTables Using Recommended PivotTables (Skill 5.19)
- Creating a PivotChart from a PivotTable (Skill 5.20)
- Showing and Hiding Chart Elements (Skill 5.6)
- Inserting Sparklines (Skill 5.10)
- Analyzing Data with Data Tables (Skill 5.21)
- Analyzing Data with Goal Seek (Skill 5.22)

1. Open the start file **EX2019-ChallengeYourself-3-3** and resave the file as:
   `[your initials]EX-ChallengeYourself-3-3`
2. If the workbook opens in Protected View, click the **Enable Editing** button in the Message Bar at the top of the workbook so you can modify the workbook.
3. Convert the shoe sales data in the *Sales* worksheet into a table.
   a. Use the **Orange, Table Style Medium 3** table style. It is the third option in the *Medium* section of the gallery.
   b. Add a Total row to the table to display the total for the *Total Sale* column.
   c. In the Total row, display the average for the *# of Pairs* and the *Price Per Pair* columns.
   d. Delete any rows in the table that have duplicate data in all the columns. There are four.
4. Filter to show just the sales for the **Washington** region.
5. Sort the table by order date with the newest orders first.

6. Insert a line chart to show the total sale amount for each order by order date.
   a. Create the line chart using just the data from the *Order Date* and *Total Sale* columns. Be sure to include the header row when selecting the data for the chart.
   b. There was an ordering glitch on August 31 that caused a spike in sales. Apply a filter to the chart to hide orders from that date. Notice the effect on the chart.
   c. If necessary, move the chart so it does not cover the table data.
7. Add a slicer to the table so you can filter by shoe name. Use the slicer to display data for the **Sperry** shoe only. Notice the effect on the chart.
8. Create a PivotTable from the data in the *Sales* worksheet. Use the **Sum of Price Per Pair** by **Region** recommended PivotTable.
   a. Modify the PivotTable so the *Price Per Pair* data are averaged, not totaled.
   b. Add the **Shoe** field to the *PivotTable*. It should appear in the *Rows* section below the *Region* field.
   c. Format all the values in the *PivotTable* using the **Accounting Number Format.**
9. Create a clustered column PivotChart based on the PivotTable data. Use the first recommended column chart type.
   a. Hide the chart title and legend.
   b. If necessary, move the *PivotChart* on the worksheet so it does not cover the *PivotChart* data.
10. Go to the *By Region* worksheet and add **Column Sparklines** in **F3:F7** for data in columns **B3:E7.**
11. On the *By Region* worksheet, create a pie chart to display the sales by region for the Sperry shoe.
    a. Display the data labels as data callouts.
    b. Hide the chart legend.
    c. If necessary, move the chart so it does not cover the table data.
12. You have been told that you will receive a commission between 5 and 10 percent. On the *Commission* sheet, make a one-variable data table using cells **A4:B14** to determine how much that commission may be based on $17,000 in sales. The column input cell is **A4.**
13. You owe $9,000 in student loans and would like to pay it all off with your commissions. Use Goal Seek to determine the amount you must sell (cell **G5**) in order for cell **G3** (your commission) to equal $9,000 so you can fully pay off your student loans. Accept the Goal Seek solution.
14. Save and close the workbook.

projects

Data files for projects can be found by logging into your SIMnet account and going to the Library section.

challenge yourself **5.4**

In this project, the local library has received a significant collection of DVDs as a donation and has asked you to provide an analysis of the titles. It needs to decide whether it should keep the collection or sell it to raise money for a new computer.

Skills needed to complete this project:

- Converting Data into Tables (Skill 5.11)
- Adding Total Rows to Tables (Skill 5.13)
- Removing Duplicate Rows from Tables (Skill 5.14)
- Applying Quick Styles to Tables (Skill 5.12)
- Sorting Data (Skill 5.15)
- Filtering Data (Skill 5.16)
- Filtering Table Data with Slicers (Skill 5.17)
- Creating PivotTables Using Recommended PivotTables (Skill 5.19)
- Creating a PivotChart from a PivotTable (Skill 5.20)
- Showing and Hiding Chart Elements (Skill 5.6)
- Analyzing Data with Data Tables (Skill 5.21)
- Analyzing Data with Goal Seek (Skill 5.22)

1. Open the start file **EX2019-ChallengeYourself-5-4** and resave the file as:
   [your initials]EX-ChallengeYourself-5-4
2. If the workbook opens in Protected View, click the **Enable Editing** button in the Message Bar at the top of the workbook so you can modify the workbook.
3. Convert the data on the *Videos* sheet into a table using the style **Red, Table Style Medium** 3.It is the third option in the *Medium* section of the gallery.
   a. Add a Total row to the table and count the number of movie titles and the average price.
   b. Delete all the duplicate rows. Be careful, there may be duplicate rows with the same movie title, but different data in the other columns. When you are finished, there should be 294 unique titles in the collection.
   c. Change the table style to use the **Purple, Table Style Medium 5** Quick Style. It is the fifth option in the *Medium* section of the gallery.
4. Sort the data in the table alphabetically by category.
5. Filter the table to show only **Horror** and **Sci Fi** movies that are rated **PG-13**.
6. Create a PivotTable from the table data using the **Sum of Price by Rating** recommended PivotTable.

7. Create a pie PivotChart from the PivotTable.
   a. Display the data labels using the **Inside End** option.
   b. Hide the chart title.
8. On the *Data Table* worksheet, create a one-variable data table to determine the amount of money that would be raised if 150 DVDs were sold at the various prices listed. Review the formula in cell **C7** to identify the appropriate cell to use as the input cell for the data table.
9. How many DVDs would the library need to sell at $1.50 each to raise $500? Use Goal Seek to find a value for cell **F9** that will result in a value of 500 for cell
10. Save and close the workbook.

projects

on your own 5.5

Data files for projects can be found by logging into your SIMnet account and going to the Library section.

In this project, you will be working with data about automobile emissions and fuel economy. These green car data were downloaded from the website fueleconomy.gov. The SmartWay scores range from 0 to 10, where 10 is best. The vehicles with the best scores on both air pollution and greenhouse gas receive the Elite designation. More information about the SmartWay program can be found at http://www3.epa.gov/greenvehicles/you/smartway.htm.

Skills needed to complete this project:

- Converting Data into Tables (Skill 5.11)
- Filtering Data (Skill 5.16)
- Filtering Table Data with Slicers (Skill 5.17)
- Sorting Data (Skill 5.15)
- Inserting a Column Chart or a Bar Chart (Skill 5.1)
- Showing and Hiding Chart Elements (Skill 5.6)
- Applying Quick Styles and Colors to Charts (Skill 5.7)
- Changing the Chart Type (Skill 5.8)
- Creating PivotTables Using Recommended PivotTables (Skill 5.19)
- Creating a PivotChart from a PivotTable (Skill 5.20)
- Analyzing Data with Data Tables (Skill 5.21)
- Analyzing Data with Goal Seek (Skill 5.22)

1. Open the start file **EX2019-OnYourOwn-5-5** and resave the file as:
   [your initials]EX-OnYourOwn-5-5
2. If the workbook opens in Protected View, click the **Enable Editing** button in the Message Bar at the top of the workbook so you can modify the workbook.
3. The *Green Cars* worksheet contains almost 500 rows. That's a lot of data! Use filtering techniques to find the subset of cars that meet the following criteria:
   a. Display only cars with the **Elite** Smartway designation. *Hint:* The *Smartway* column is at the far right side of the data. You may need to scroll to find it.
   b. Include only cars in the **midsize car** class (use the *Veh Class* column).
   c. Include only cars with **Gasoline** as the fuel (use the *Fuel* column).
   d. You should end up with three records visible.
4. Sort the data so the cars with the best combination MPG (*Cmb MPG* column) appear at the top.

5. Create a chart comparing the **City MPG, Hwy MPG,** and **Cmb MPG** for the cars shown.
   a. Add and remove chart elements as necessary to make the chart clear and easy to read.
   b. Apply one of the chart Quick Styles.
   c. Try changing the chart to another chart type. Is there another chart type available that's appropriate for the data?
6. Create a PivotTable from the car data. Use one of the recommended PivotTables or create one from scratch. Add at least two fields to the *Values* Change the function used for at least one of the value fields. Name the worksheet: Pivot
7. Create a PivotChart from the PivotTable data.
8. On the *Commuting Costs* worksheet, create a two-variable data table to calculate the daily cost of gas for a variety of gas prices and a variety of miles driven per day. If you have a daily commute to school or work, use variations on your actual commuting miles in the data table.
   a. The formula to calculate the cost of your daily commute is: Commuting miles/your car's MPG*price of gas per gallon
   b. In the data table formula, you can use the MPG in cell B3 or change the value to your car's estimated MPG.
   c. Find a way to hide the data table formula.
   d. Add formatting as appropriate.
9. You're in the market for a new car, and you'd like to reduce your monthly gas costs to around $30. What's the minimum gas mileage you should look for in your new car? Can you use Goal Seek with the data on this worksheet to find an answer?
10. Save and close the workbook.

Data files for projects can be found by logging into your SIMnet account and going to the Library section.

projects
fix it **5.6**

The staff members of a private college preparatory school have been trying to analyze student data and create what-if scenarios regarding investment decisions. Unfortunately, they've made a mess of this workbook. Can you help them fix it?

Skills needed to complete this project:

- Sorting Data (Skill 5.15)
- Converting Data into Tables (Skill 5.11)
- Filtering Table Data with Slicers (Skill 5.17)
- Removing Duplicate Rows from Tables (Skill 5.14)
- Adding Total Rows to Tables (Skill 5.13)
- Creating PivotTables Using Recommended PivotTables (Skill 5.19)
- Inserting a Pie Chart (Skill 5.2)
- Changing the Chart Type (Skill 5.8)
- Analyzing Data with Data Tables (Skill 5.21)

1. Open the start file EX2019-FixIt-5-6 and resave the file as:
   `[your initials]EX-FixIt-5-6`
2. If the workbook opens in Protected View, click the **Enable Editing** button in the Message Bar at the top of the workbook so you can modify the workbook.
3. The data in the *Student Test Data* worksheet has a couple of problems to fix:
   a. The data should be organized alphabetically by student.
   b. Format the data so the school faculty can use slicers to filter data. Use any style you want.
   c. Display slicers so data can be filtered by month, by subject, or by student or by any combination of the three. Go ahead and display the slicers, but you don't need to apply any filtering.
   d. Find and delete the duplicate records. There should be 90 unique records.
   e. The data should include a Total row to calculate the average score.
4. The PivotTable on the *Student Pivot* sheet should summarize the average scores for each subject for each student by month. However, the *Score* field data have been added to the wrong section of the PivotTable.
   a. Move the *Score* field to the correct section of the PivotTable.
   b. Modify the calculation to display the average score instead of the total score.

5. The PivotChart on the *Faculty Pivot* sheet should show the size of each department as a proportional part of a whole. A line chart was the wrong choice.
   a. Change the chart type to a better choice.
   b. Display Data Labels using the **Data Callout**
6. The school finance committee has determined that a $30,000 facilities upgrade will be needed in 12 years. An alumnus has donated $24,000. If invested, will it grow to be enough? That depends on the rate of return. On the *Data Table* worksheet, an attempt has been made to use Excel's data table feature to determine the value of the investment after 12 years at different rates of return. The formula in cell D6 is correct, but something went wrong with the data table. Delete the zeros in cells **D7:D30** and try again. Even if you're not familiar with the FV formula used in cell D6, you should be able to figure this out.
7. Save and close the workbook.